CorelDRAW™ 9
Bible

CorelDRAW™ 9
Bible

Deborah Miller

IDG Books Worldwide, Inc.
An International Data Group Company

Foster City, CA ✦ Chicago, IL ✦ Indianapolis, IN ✦ New York, NY

CorelDRAW™ 9 Bible

Published by
IDG Books Worldwide, Inc.
An International Data Group Company
919 E. Hillsdale Blvd., Suite 400
Foster City, CA 94404
www.idgbooks.com (IDG Books Worldwide Web site)

ISBN: 0-7645-3315-0

Printed in the United States of America

10 9 8 7 6 5 4 3 2 1

1B/RW/QZ/ZZ/FC

Distributed in the United States by IDG Books Worldwide, Inc.

Distributed by CDG Books Canada Inc. for Canada; by Transworld Publishers Limited in the United Kingdom; by IDG Norge Books for Norway; by IDG Sweden Books for Sweden; by Woodslane Pty. Ltd. for Australia; by Woodslane (NZ) Ltd. for New Zealand; by TransQuest Publishers Pte Ltd. for Singapore, Malaysia, Thailand, Indonesia, and Hong Kong; by ICG Muse, Inc. for Japan; by Intersoft for South Africa; by Eyrolles for France; by International Thomson Publishing for Germany, Austria and Switzerland; by Distribuidora Cuspide for Argentina; by Livraria Cultura for Brazil; by Ediciones ZETA S.C.R. Ltda. for Peru; by WS Computer Publishing Corporation, Inc., for the Philippines; by Contemporanea de Ediciones for Venezuela; by Express Computer Distributors for the Caribbean and West Indies; by Micronesia Media Distributor, Inc. for Micronesia; by Chips Computadoras S.A. de C.V. for Mexico; by Editorial Norma de Panama S.A. for Panama; by American Bookshops for Finland.

For general information on IDG Books Worldwide's books in the U.S., please call our Consumer Customer Service department at 800-762-2974. For reseller information, including discounts and premium sales, please call our Reseller Customer Service department at 800-434-3422.

For information on where to purchase IDG Books Worldwide's books outside the U.S., please contact our International Sales department at 317-596-5530 or fax 317-596-5692.

For consumer information on foreign language translations, please contact our Customer Service department at 800-434-3422, fax 317-596-5692, or e-mail rights@idgbooks.com.

For information on licensing foreign or domestic rights, please phone +1-650-655-3109.

For sales inquiries and special prices for bulk quantities, please contact our Sales department at 650-655-3200 or write to the address above.

For information on using IDG Books Worldwide's books in the classroom or for ordering examination copies, please contact our Educational Sales department at 800-434-2086 or fax 317-596-5499.

For press review copies, author interviews, or other publicity information, please contact our Public Relations department at 650-655-3000 or fax 650-655-3299.

For authorization to photocopy items for corporate, personal, or educational use, please contact Copyright Clearance Center, 222 Rosewood Drive, Danvers, MA 01923, or fax 978-750-4470.

Library of Congress Cataloging-in-Publication Data

Miller, Deborah, [DATE]
   CorelDRAW 9 Bible / Deborah Miller.
      p.   cm.
   ISBN 0-7645-3315-0 (alk. paper)
   1. Computer graphics.   2. CorelDRAW!   I. Title.
T385.M5446   1999
006.6'869 - - dc21   99-32152
                                                 CIP

is a registered trademark under exclusive license to IDG Books Worldwide, Inc., from International Data Group, Inc.

ABOUT IDG BOOKS WORLDWIDE

Welcome to the world of IDG Books Worldwide.

IDG Books Worldwide, Inc., is a subsidiary of International Data Group, the world's largest publisher of computer-related information and the leading global provider of information services on information technology. IDG was founded more than 30 years ago by Patrick J. McGovern and now employs more than 9,000 people worldwide. IDG publishes more than 290 computer publications in over 75 countries. More than 90 million people read one or more IDG publications each month.

Launched in 1990, IDG Books Worldwide is today the #1 publisher of best-selling computer books in the United States. We are proud to have received eight awards from the Computer Press Association in recognition of editorial excellence and three from Computer Currents' First Annual Readers' Choice Awards. Our best-selling *...For Dummies*® series has more than 50 million copies in print with translations in 31 languages. IDG Books Worldwide, through a joint venture with IDG's Hi-Tech Beijing, became the first U.S. publisher to publish a computer book in the People's Republic of China. In record time, IDG Books Worldwide has become the first choice for millions of readers around the world who want to learn how to better manage their businesses.

Our mission is simple: Every one of our books is designed to bring extra value and skill-building instructions to the reader. Our books are written by experts who understand and care about our readers. The knowledge base of our editorial staff comes from years of experience in publishing, education, and journalism — experience we use to produce books to carry us into the new millennium. In short, we care about books, so we attract the best people. We devote special attention to details such as audience, interior design, use of icons, and illustrations. And because we use an efficient process of authoring, editing, and desktop publishing our books electronically, we can spend more time ensuring superior content and less time on the technicalities of making books.

You can count on our commitment to deliver high-quality books at competitive prices on topics you want to read about. At IDG Books Worldwide, we continue in the IDG tradition of delivering quality for more than 30 years. You'll find no better book on a subject than one from IDG Books Worldwide.

John Kilcullen
Chairman and CEO
IDG Books Worldwide, Inc.

Steven Berkowitz
President and Publisher
IDG Books Worldwide, Inc.

WINNER

Eighth Annual
Computer Press
Awards 1992

IX WINNER

Ninth Annual
Computer Press
Awards 1993

Tenth Annual
Computer Press
Awards 1994

X WINNER

XI WINNER

Eleventh Annual
Computer Press
Awards 1995

IDG is the world's leading IT media, research and exposition company. Founded in 1964, IDG had 1997 revenues of $2.05 billion and has more than 9,000 employees worldwide. IDG offers the widest range of media options that reach IT buyers in 75 countries representing 95% of worldwide IT spending. IDG's diverse product and services portfolio spans six key areas including print publishing, online publishing, expositions and conferences, market research, education and training, and global marketing services. More than 90 million people read one or more of IDG's 290 magazines and newspapers, including IDG's leading global brands — Computerworld, PC World, Network World, Macworld and the Channel World family of publications. IDG Books Worldwide is one of the fastest-growing computer book publishers in the world, with more than 700 titles in 36 languages. The "...For Dummies®" series alone has more than 50 million copies in print. IDG offers online users the largest network of technology-specific Web sites around the world through IDG.net (http://www.idg.net), which comprises more than 225 targeted Web sites in 55 countries worldwide. International Data Corporation (IDC) is the world's largest provider of information technology data, analysis and consulting, with research centers in over 41 countries and more than 400 research analysts worldwide. IDG World Expo is a leading producer of more than 168 globally branded conferences and expositions in 35 countries including E3 (Electronic Entertainment Expo), Macworld Expo, ComNet, Windows World Expo, ICE (Internet Commerce Expo), Agenda, DEMO, and Spotlight. IDG's training subsidiary, ExecuTrain, is the world's largest computer training company, with more than 230 locations worldwide and 785 training courses. IDG Marketing Services helps industry-leading IT companies build international brand recognition by developing global integrated marketing programs via IDG's print, online and exposition products worldwide. Further information about the company can be found at www.idg.com.   1/24/99

Credits

Acquisitions Editor
Kathy Yankton

Development Editors
Alex Miloradovich
Steven Anderson
Kenyon Brown

Technical Editor
David Farkas

Copy Editors
Richard H. Adin
Timothy J. Borek
Nancy Rapoport
Marlene Paul

Production
York Graphic Services

Proofreading and Indexing
York Production Services

Cover Design
Murder By Design

About the Author

Drawing and art have been a part of **Deborah Miller's** life since the beginning. Very few surfaces have been sacred or safe. She's drawn on everything from toilet paper (it wasn't cushy soft in those days) and redwood boards to drum skins and virtual paper on the computer. Since her first professional show at age 12, she's been the recipient of numerous art awards in a career that has spanned well over 30 years.

Trained in the traditional tools of drawing boards and airbrushes, she moved to computers several years ago, during the days of programming sprites in basic. Today her tools are far more sophisticated, as she explores the worlds of CorelDRAW, 3D animation, the Web, and multimedia development. Coauthor and author of several books on computer graphics, and illustrator of anything that does not move fast enough, her goal is to make graphics software *understandable*. She believes that users should not have to be techie wizards to create computer graphics.

Having escaped the city, she resides in the hills of Tennessee with her husband, Mike, her family, and an assortment of cats, dogs, and a wolf. When she's not working, she can be found haunting the Internet.

*This book is dedicated to the unwitting participants in my adventures...
who love me anyway.*

Preface

Draw is the best selling illustration program available. A major reason for its popularity is its versatility. This powerful package works equally well for the hobbyist or the professional in a production environment. Draw's interface can be customized to work the way you work. You can change or create new toolbars, menus, and roll-ups. In short, you can design and build your own illustration and layout environment to make your Draw sessions more creative and productive.

Note Throughout this book I refer to CorelDRAW 9 as Draw. The name appears in its complete form, however, when I've referenced version differences. Notes just like this one are scattered throughout the book to illuminate the topic under discussion and to help you stay on track.

I've used these same dynamic and powerful concepts in designing and writing the book you now hold in your hands. To find out more, please read on.

This Book's for You

In writing this book, I addressed the needs of a diverse range of users. If you're a graphics novice, I provide starter tutorial files (located on the Bonus CD-ROM attached to the inside back cover of this book) to help you through some of the exercises.

On the CD-ROM Look for this distinctive icon. These handy notes lead you to the exact file required — on the CD at the back of the book — to complete the tutorial at hand.

I don't assume that anyone is an artist, although I haven't left artists out. After all, I'm an artist. What this means, though, is that you won't find instructions that say, "Draw a chair," which if you are an artist will leave you wondering, what kind of chair? If you're a nonartist, such an instruction would ensure that this book's primary function would be as a paper weight.

✦ **If you're a Draw neophyte** — or a cross-platform user, you're going to find many familiar looking tools and features. You should be aware that most of Draw's features and tools can be customized, which puts a new spin on things. This program is incredibly feature packed, and I introduce you to the variety of ways that you can use the tools and features to achieve some incredible results.

✦ **If you're an intermediate user** — who has upgraded to CorelDRAW 9, you're going to feel like you just wandered into the toy store with a blank, signed check. While the interface is new, you'll find tools and features to which you've become accustomed.

I pay special attention to new features and tools that will let you work more efficiently and creatively. As you use this book, look for an icon like the one to the left of this paragraph for handy references to everything that's new in CorelDRAW 9.

✦ **If you are an old hand with Draw** — you'll notice some new features the first time you start the program. If you are new to Draw, but familiar with other graphics packages, you'll see several tools that have become somewhat standardized in graphics packages. Finally, if you are a computer graphics novice, I show you where to start.

✦ **If your focus is the World Wide Web** — the evolving trend of illustration packages today is toward electronic publishing and the World Wide Web. I address this trend throughout the book by including sections and tips that pertain exclusively to electronic publishing.

For detailed information on using Draw to create documents that you can publish on the World Wide Web, see Chapter 17.

How it works

If you sit down and read this book from cover to cover, you are a rare user. Most of us approach software manuals like cookbooks. We break out a book when we're in trouble, need more information on a specific topic, or want to know *how-to*. This book allows that. Remember, however, that the book is arranged building-block style and is organized in parts. The first part covers the basics. I recommend that you start here. Even seasoned professionals will benefit from a peek at the new interface and features.

The Author's Humble Beginnings

When I first started creating images on a computer, *drawing* was not the operative term. I was using a Commodore and basically had to program every pixel. It took lines of code to describe what could best be called a very clunky looking circle, which left a lot to be desired for this pen and ink artist.

Eventually, I upgraded to a 386 and a copy of CorelDRAW 1.2, based on a rumor that finally there was a computer drawing package that would treat me like an artist, rather that force me to become a math wizard. Several versions later, the CorelDRAW suite still remains one of my graphics creation tools.

Getting organized

In the book, information is organized into these special features, parts, chapters, and appendixes:

♦ **Glossary:** A complete listing of all the special terms and concepts used in this book with definitions in plain English.

♦ **Index:** When you can't find it in the table of contents, and you need a quick reference to the information you need to solve an urgent problem (or just out of plain old curiosity) here's where to look. It's copious and complete!

♦ **Bonus CD-ROM:** You'll find it tucked inside the back cover, and on it are all the files you need to complete the exercises in the book. As an added bonus, there are clip art samples, demo programs, and utilities. Check out the "On the CD-ROM" icons that show you where, and Appendix C that tells you how and what.

Before you begin

In writing this book, I made several basic assumptions about its readers. You must be familiar with the use of a mouse or other pointing device; have a functional grasp of navigating in Windows 95, Windows 98, or Windows NT; and have CorelDRAW 9 installed on your computer. If any of the items above is not true, then you need to stop here. Several books exist that will assist you in becoming familiar with Windows 95 or 98, or Windows NT.

Tip

If you haven't installed elements from the CorelDRAW 9 suite, I recommend you install the program before continuing. The installation of Draw is pretty straightforward, and the program contains an Installation Wizard to assist you.

Using the book's features

This book is designed to be as user/reader friendly as possible. Essentially, instructions are organized in steps, with supporting images, but there are several special features that will make your reading experience smoother and more informative.

♦ **Menu instructions:** The following example basically directs you to choose Options from the Tools menu, and then select an option topic to display the related information:

1. Select Tools ➪ Options and expand the options tree by clicking the plus sign (+) next to General. Choose Edit from the expanded tree to display the Edit property sheet of the Options dialog box.

♦ **Dialog box entries:** If you are directed to enter specific text, it is shown in **bold type**.

♦ **"Enabling" features:** This means to click the box or radio button beside the option. Enabled options appear with a check mark or a black dot in the box.

✦ **Margin icons:** In the margins, you'll find icons — just like those you've encountered in this Preface — that guide and show you how to get the most from Draw:

- *Tip:* Documented or undocumented hints to help you

- *New Feature:* New or enhanced features in Draw

- *Note:* Another way of performing a task or hints to remember

- *On the CD-ROM:* Serves as a guide to the tutorial files located on the companion CD-ROM

- *Caution:* This icon is a warning to use caution, as indicated

- *Cross-Reference:* Guides you to other information about a specific topic

- *Shortcut:* Provides you with common keyboard shortcuts for commands

✦ **Sidebars:** In addition to these aids, periodically there are interesting asides, lengthy tips, hints, and tricks in sidebars (like the one in this Preface entitled "Visit My Web Site!" These provide more information about the topic, or allow you to try something new and different in Draw.

Understanding Draw

Before you move on to Chapter 1, review the following sections to get a quick overview of Draw — from who uses it, how to start it, how to navigate in it, what's new in CorelDRAW 9, to tips on planning things on paper before you begin a project. Read them thoroughly. The information here will enhance your experience immeasurably.

Who uses Draw?

By coupling power, speed, and a wide range of features, Draw meets the needs of users as diverse as designers, artists, multimedia developers, layout artists, educators, Web mavens, desktop publishers, service bureaus, printers, screen printers, engineers, signage designers, specialty media artists, quilters, crafters, students, and doodlers.

Visit My Web Site!

I believe in this book, and invite your comments, suggestions, and questions. I've put up a Web site `http://www.rainwatermedia.com/cd9bible` dedicated to you and this book. I invite you to visit. You'll find tips, tricks, hints, and extra stuff for you to use and view.

The site is designed to be an evolving page, with frequent updates. You can also contact me directly on the site. My thanks to the folks at Esper for providing me the space to maintain it.

Starting Draw

The best way to begin to explore a program is with it open. Draw is not an exception to this concept. When you installed the Draw suite, the installation routine placed startup shortcuts in the Windows Startup Program menu. To start Draw or Photo-Paint, select Startup ⇨ Programs ⇨ CorelDRAW 9 or Corel Photo-Paint 9. If the program seems to take a while to start, don't be alarmed. It is reading the information it requires and initializing several of its elements.

Navigating in Draw

Draw has elements, such as the Title bar and scroll bars, that are common to most Windows applications. Other elements, such as dialog boxes, roll-ups, and dockers, are specific to Corel products. These Corel-specific items include:

✦ The Menu bar

✦ Toolboxes and toolbars

✦ The Status bar

✦ The Onscreen palette

✦ The Property bar

✦ Roll-ups

✦ Dockers

✦ Dialog boxes

✦ Flyout menus

New features in CorelDRAW 9

CorelDRAW 9 is the most streamlined version of Draw ever. That doesn't mean a compromise in power, though. It boasts a variety of new features and enhancements. In some cases, the new features have replaced two or more other features from previous versions of Draw. In many ways, this means that CorelDRAW 9 was rebuilt from the ground up. It was designed to conserve screen real estate while providing more powerful tools. The result is the fastest and most versatile drawing package available. Here's a peek at Draw's new features:

✦ Supports multiple onscreen color palettes, which allows you to keep your favorite palettes in the drawing window for quick access

✦ Sound support allows you to associate sounds with events in Draw

✦ Enhanced docker windows present commands at your fingertips and collapse to provide you with more screen real estate

✦ Web-link update support lets you increase your knowledge of Draw and obtain add-ons

✦ Custom workspaces that work like you do, while maximizing cross-platform support between the PC and Mac

✦ Microsoft Visual Basic for Applications 6, which allows you to build custom business solutions that interface seamlessly with Draw

✦ IXLA Digital Camera Interface, which allows you to acquire images using a variety of popular digital cameras

✦ Publish to PDF support, which increases your publishing capabilities by letting you reach a wider audience while maintaining the look and feel of your Draw documents

✦ Enhanced connector line tool, which allows you to quickly build and modify organizational and other charts linked with lines

✦ Interactive contour tool, which allows you to create and adjust contour effects in the drawing window

✦ Mesh fills, which allow you to create custom fills that provide smooth transitions between objects

✦ Perspective Drop Shadow, which allows you to add depth by controlling the direction of the shadow

✦ Enhanced node reduction with the Shape tool

✦ Round corners of rectangles uniformly or independently

✦ Preset guidelines for many popular documents

✦ Live smoothing that you can adjust to smooth freehand lines quickly

✦ Live positioning and sizing, which allows you to see the location and size of objects as they are being created

✦ Expanded bitmap effects, which provide an even greater variety of effects

✦ Imposition tool, which allows you to quickly create advanced layouts

✦ Mini Print Preview, which allows you to see a thumbnail of how your document will look in the main Print dialog box

✦ ICC Color Management support for error-free printing

✦ Printing Preflight dialog box that warns you in advance of possible printing errors in your document

✦ Redesigned Palette Editor, which makes it easier to create and edit custom color palettes

How Draw Works — When You're not Looking

Draw's illustration capabilities are based on vector graphics. Unlike bitmap programs, such as Corel Photo-Paint, that are pixel-based, vector images can be resized and manipulated easily, with no loss to the quality of the image. Fully OLE compliant, Draw lets you share files and information with other OLE-compliant applications, without using import and export filters.

Internally, Draw uses dynamic linking to enhance its editing capabilities. When you edit a control object of an effect, such as the Blend effect, the power of this dynamic linking becomes apparent. The Blend effect is automatically updated to reflect the changes that you make in the control object. Tedious editing is a thing of the past!

Planning ahead

Output devices and cameras are some of the most unforgiving pieces of equipment on this planet. I'm telling you this, now, because it would be a mistake to tell you at the end of this book. It's extremely tempting to jump right in and start drawing images, and there's nothing wrong with experimentation. It's also very depressing to have an incredible image that does not meet your client's requirements, that won't print correctly, or that looks great on the screen but pathetic when it comes back from the printer. The key to any successful document in Draw is to plan ahead. Backtracking through a drawing is much harder.

+ **Start with pencil and paper:** Computers are wonderful. They let you perform tasks in a fraction of the time that it would take without their assistance. If you are an artist, you also know that computers are cleaner than airbrushes. There is a value, though, in traditional methods of doing things. One example is using paper and a pencil. Drawing rough sketches of your ideas and layout helps you decide how to approach creating an image in Draw. Add notes to your sketches, about budget restrictions, deadlines, and the colors and effects that you want to use. With these sketches and notes in hand, your drawing time is more productive and you can concentrate on being creative.

+ **Save frequently:** This comment should be engraved in stone someplace or used as a mantra. Power hiccups have claimed more than one image and the artist's sanity along with it.

+ **Back up your files:** This comment is related to the previous one. I urge you to back up your files. If you are working with a large and complex file, you might want to consider working with more than one version of the file. Using this method, if things do go wrong, you won't lose hours of work.

Acknowledgments

Draw is a tradition around here, whether I'm creating with it or writing about it. When I write, however, I'm not alone. The words are mine, but I always have a vast number of people who helped participate in the process — if only by tolerating me.

I've been using Draw nearly forever or at least since Version 1.2. Each new version has provided me with a new series of quality tools that make my life as a graphic designer infinitely easier. Without the dedicated people at Corel Corporation, I'd be out of business. It would be great if I could list them all here, but they've grown a bit since Version 1. I'd like to especially acknowledge and thank Dr. Michael Cowpland, Michael BelleFeuille, Michelle Murphy-Croteau, Susan Connerty, and the folks in Quality Assurance and Development.

My special thanks go, as well, to the other corporations, companies, and businesses whose generosity made a profound difference in this book. Your products have made my life easier, more creative, and more productive: Seiko Instruments, USA; MetaTools, Inc.; Ulead Systems; Macromedia, Inc.; McLean Public Relations; Umax Technologies; Nico Mak Computing, Inc.; and Microsoft Corp.

IDG Books Worldwide, Inc. has one of the best editorial staffs with whom I've ever had the pleasure to work. These people put up with me, were patient when life and computers became special, and worked to help make things happen on time: Kathy Yankton — Acquisitions Editor; Alex Miloradovich and Steven Anderson — Development Editors; David Farkas — Technical Editor; Richard H. Adin and Timothy Borek — Copyeditors; everyone in IDG's Production department; and York Graphic Services.

There's one special guy, without whom I'd be totally lost. Mike, my life partner and husband, clears the way for me to write without life intruding too much. He also wears more hats than a hat rack, reads my manuscripts before anyone else (and beats on them), and pitches in to help when I've run out of hands.

Stefanie Rowland graciously contributed her talent and time to create *Vanity* specifically for the color insert of this book. Stefanie went two falls of three with Draw and won, to bring the sensitivity of her rare talent to the image.

Bevin Mallory-Brown and LaRae Mallory lent their photographic talents to create photo images that became part of larger documents. Bevin added her expertise with databases to help me keep the glossary and my life quasi-organized.

Thank you all!

I'm also fortunate to have several wonderful people in my life, who tolerate and love me, despite myself. These folks put up with me, when I'm sure no one else would: Mike, Brenda, Bevin, Chris, LaRae, Matt, and a host of friends. Wa-doo!

Contents at a Glance

Contents

Part II: Draw 9 in the Works   271

Chapter 6: Managing Documents 273

Part IV: Making It Public with Draw — 739

Chapter 15: Using Draw in the Office — 741

Quick Start

Welcome to the versatile world of CorelDRAW 9. This Quick Start gives you a feel for the program and the ease with which you can create documents in Draw. You can create a wide variety of documents in Draw — from fine art to office forms. Throughout this section you use some of Draw's basic tools and commands to create an image map for use on the Web. Although the tutorial is designed around elements that are prepackaged with Draw 9, feel free to exchange your own elements.

Before starting this section, Draw should be installed on your system and you should have your companion CD-ROM for the *CorelDRAW 9 Bible* handy. The tutorial uses images that are stored on the companion CD-ROM in the quickstart folder.

Discovering Image Maps

Web pages use a variety of navigational aids to help viewers move from one page or address to the next. These aids can also move you from one point of a long document page to another point on the same page. All of these aids have something in common. They are all called links or hotspots. They provide the means for the viewer to move around the Web by simply clicking them with their mouse. Some of these navigation aids, which are described in this list, can get pretty exotic:

   ✦ **Buttons:** These can have multiple states. That is, they can appear different in their up and down positions, or they might change when you roll over them with your mouse.

   ✦ **Hypertext links:** These usually appear underlined or highlighted, and they change color if you click on them.

   ✦ **Image maps:** These are a little different than either of the other navigation methods. The following sections tell you why.

In This Chapter

Discovering image maps

Setting up the page

Adding elements

Specifying hotspots

Exporting to HTML format

Cross-Reference More detailed information about using Draw to create Web documents is found in Chapter 17, "Publishing on the Web."

How they work

An image map is a single image that has identified hotspots or places that the viewer can click to move from one location to the next. The hotspots aren't always as obvious as a button and may or may not include text. An image map is also a document and can stand alone—unlike buttons and hypertext links, which must be included in an HTML document.

Note An image map can be included in another HTML document that contains a wide variety of elements, but it is a complete document in and of itself.

Creating image maps in Draw

Draw is ideally suited for creating image maps. You can quickly create and place text, graphics, bitmaps, and effects anywhere on the page without worrying about tables and frames that are common to other types of HTML documents. Once the elements are in place, you can identify the hotspots and add the Internet address links required for navigation. The final document page is exported as a single image in HTML format, ready to be used on the Web. The remainder of this Quick Start guides you through the process.

Caution For the most part, you are free to be as creative as you want with an image map design in Draw. There is one rule, however, that you should observe: never overlap objects identified as hotspots. Overlapping elements that are identified as hotspots can cause cross-linking, which means either the link won't work at all, or that your viewer might not navigate to the correct location.

Starting CorelDRAW

The best way to begin to explore a program is with it open. Draw is not an exception to this concept. When you installed the Draw suite, the installation routine placed startup shortcuts in the Windows Startup Program menu. To start Draw or Photo-Paint, select Startup ➪ Programs ➪ CorelDRAW 9 or Corel Photo-Paint 9. If the program seems to take a while to start, don't be alarmed. It is reading the information it requires and initializing several of its elements.

Setting Up the Page

After starting Draw, the first step to creating any document is to specify the rulers, resolution, page size, and other settings that determine how your page will look when you are done. This also provides a useful boundary guide for placing objects on the page. When creating a page for the Web, you can also set the background and resolution to use for your page at this time. Once you've created the page, you can forget about it and concentrate on adding the elements to your document.

Note

Because all of the page setup occurs in the Options dialog box, leave it open until you've completed the sections that follow.

Ruler and screen resolution settings

Inches don't mean anything on the Web. Everything is measured in pixels. It's a good idea to change the rulers to pixels to reflect the unit of measure that matches your document. This prevents confusion when you are creating your image map.

Caution

Always set the screen resolution on the Rulers property sheet before setting your document's size and resolution, making sure the values are identical. This ensures that your document will appear at the correct size when viewed in a browser, and that you'll avoid the need to reset the size of your document later.

To specify a unit of measurement for the rulers:

   1. From the expanded Document category, choose Rulers to display the Rulers property sheet (see Figure Q-1).

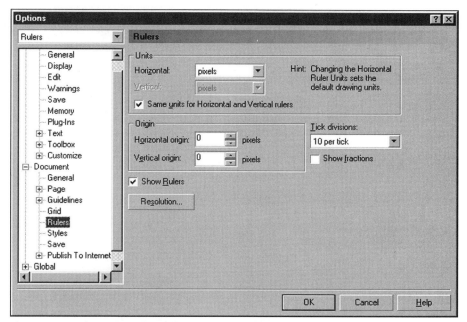

Figure Q-1: Choose pixels as the ruler units for your image map.

2. Select Pixels from the Units drop-down list box.

3. Click the Resolution button and specify 96 dpi (dots per inch) as the screen resolution.

Page size and document resolution

Most Web documents use a page size of either 800×600 pixels or 640×480 pixels at a resolution of 96 dpi. These sizes allow the largest audience of users to view your page as you designed it. If you use another page size, the page may look off balance or the viewer might have to scroll across the width to see the whole page. The resolution of most monitors is 96 dpi. Monitors ignore any setting above that amount, and files created at higher resolutions take a long time to load in a browser. For our purposes, we'll use a page size of 800×600 pixels at a resolution of 96 dpi.

To specify the page size and document resolution:

1. Select Tools ⇨ Options to display the Options dialog box. Click the plus (+) signs beside Document and Page in the left window to expand those categories, and then click Size to display the Size property sheet (see Figure Q-2).

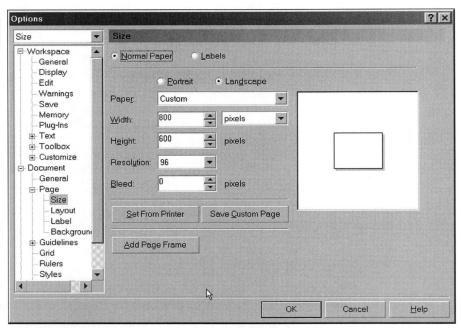

Figure Q2: The Size property sheet lets you specify the page size and resolution for your document.

2. Click Landscape as the orientation and select pixels from the drop-down list box as the unit of measure.

3. Choose 96 from the Resolution drop-down list box.

It's important to select the resolution before you enter values in the Width and Height boxes. Draw changes the page size values to reflect the selected resolution.

4. In the Width box, enter **800** as the value. Similarly, enter **600** as the value in the Height box.

You might want to save the page and resolution settings if you create Web documents on a regular basis. Click Save Custom Page and enter a name for the page size. Draw saves the configuration for future use, so that you can select the name from the drop-down size list and your page settings will be ready to use.

Selecting a background

Selecting the background for your document before you add elements to the page lets you see how objects and text will look against your background. You can change the background later if you want. You can also specify that Draw publish your background with your image map. By default, Draw exports only the elements on the page without the background.

To specify the background for your document:

1. From the expanded Page category of the Options dialog box, select Background to display the Background property sheet (see Figure Q-3).

2. Select Solid and then click the colorswatch box beside it to display the color palette. Scroll down the palette and choose the sand color (first box from the left in the sixth row from the bottom).

3. Click the Print and Export Background box to enable it.

4. Click OK to return to the drawing window.

The appearance of the drawing window and your page are updated to reflect your settings. The rulers in the drawing window have changed to pixels as the unit of measurement. Your Web document is now ready for you to create and place objects and text on the page. This is one of the most critical steps to creating any document because it lets you size objects in your drawing more accurately, saving time and effort.

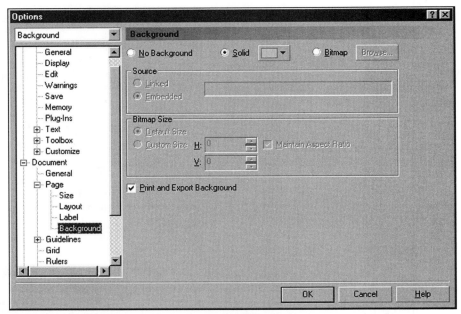

Figure Q-3: Selecting a background lets you view how the objects will look in the final image map.

Adding Elements

Objects are created, modified, and positioned in the drawing window using the tools found in Draw's toolbox (see Figure Q-4). These tools are basic to working in Draw. This section familiarizes you with some of the tools used to add elements to your document.

The companion CD-ROM is the source of the graphic elements for your image map in this tutorial. The design centers on a center graphic. You add a text banner and other smaller graphic symbols. The smaller symbols represent links to other pages on a Web site. Once you understand the principles behind creating an image map, substitute your own graphic elements and text for those shown here.

Adding a main image

When creating an image map, you can use any image or graphic you wish. You might want to import a photoimage or create art in Draw. This example uses a star as the center object in the image map. You won't need to draw anything. The art is complete and ready to use.

— Pick tool
— Shape tool
— Zoom tool
— Freehand tool
— Rectangle tool
— Ellipse tool
— Polygon tool
— Text tool

— Interactive fill tool
— Interactive transparency tool
— Interactive blend tool

— Eyedropper tool
— Outline tool
— Fill tool

Figure Q-4: The tools in Draw's toolbox are used to create, position, and modify objects in the drawing window.

To add the center graphic:

1. Select Tools ⇨ Scrapbook ⇨ Browse to open the Browse view of the Scrapbook docker. Choose your CD-ROM drive and open the quickstart folder. Thumbnails for the images used in this tutorial will appear in the docker window (see Figure Q-5).

2. Scroll through the thumbnails and select star.cdr. Drag it to the center of the drawing page to import it into your document. A blue star and a white star appear in the drawing window.

3. With both stars selected, choose the interactive Blend tool from the Interactive tools flyout menu on the toolbox.

4. Click and drag from the top point of the small star to the top point of the large star. The stars blend to create a star with a 3D appearance (see Figure Q-6).

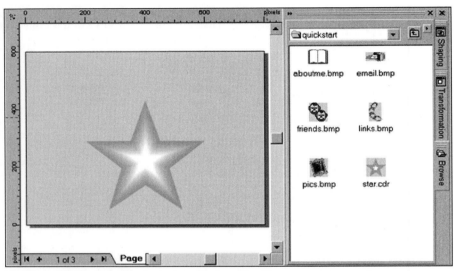

Figure Q-5: The Scrapbook docker displays the files you use to create your image map.

Figure Q-6: The Interactive Blend tool lets you create transitional effects between two objects.

Select File ⇨ Save to display the Save dialog box. Choose a folder on your hard disk in which you want to store your document, and then enter **myimagemap** in the filename box. Click Save to save your drawing. Draw automatically adds its native file format extension of .cdr.

Creating a path

The next step in creating the image map is to create a path along which you add text. Draw lets you enter text directly on a path. Unlike bitmap programs, text in Draw remains editable, so don't worry if you make a mistake or want to change it later. Paths are the outlines of objects. You can add text along any path, regardless of the object type. In this exercise, you use the Ellipse tool to create a 180-degree arc along which you will enter your text.

To create a path for your text:

1. Choose the Ellipse tool from the toolbox. The Property bar at the top of the page has changed to reflect those settings and options available when the Ellipse tool is active (see Figure Q-7).

2. Click the arc on the Property bar to make it active, and then enter 180 degrees in the Ending Angle value box.

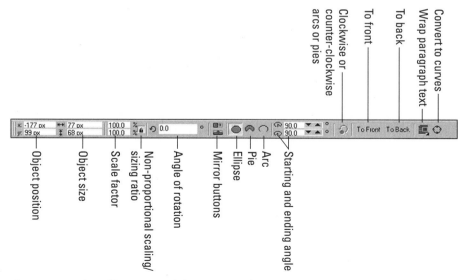

Figure Q-7: The Ellipse view of the Property bar lets you specify the settings for your text path.

3. Moving back to the drawing window, click a point above and to the left of the star. Without releasing the mouse button, drag down and to the right side of the star to create a semicircle and then release the mouse button. Draw displays the arc as you are drawing, making it easy to see the shape you're drawing (see Figure Q-8).

4. Select the Pick tool and drag the arc until it's directly over the star, as shown, if necessary.

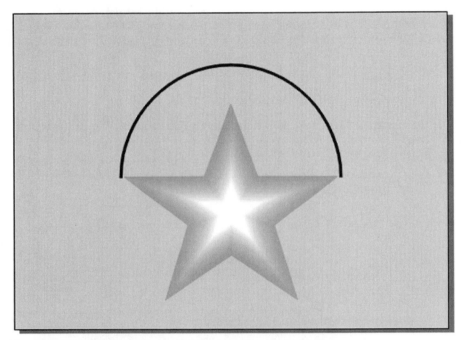

Figure Q-8: Click and drag in the drawing window to create an arc.

Flowing text along a path

Draw's text tool creates two types of text: Paragraph text and Artistic text, which you use in this tutorial. Paragraph text is much like text created with a word processor, which you explore later in the book. Artistic text doesn't have all of the formatting options available for Paragraph text, but it lets you create word art by applying special effects unavailable with Paragraph text. These effects are especially useful for creating banners and headline text for Web pages.

To add Artistic text to the path:

1. Select the Text tool from the toolbox. The Property bar updates to reflect the active text tool (see Figure Q-9).

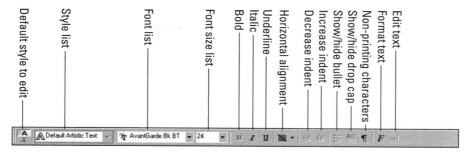

Figure Q-9: The Text view of the property bar lets you choose a font, size, and alignment for your text.

2. On the Property bar, select Arial Black as the font from the Font List and 16 points from the Font Size List.

3. Moving back to the drawing window click the left end of the path to set an insertion point. As you approach the path, the Text tool icon changes to an I-bar.

4. Enter **MY HOME PAGE** on the path. Draw centers the text on the path (see Figure Q-10).

Figure Q-10: Draw centers the text on the path.

5. Select the Pick tool, then click the path to select it. Right-click the X in the color palette. Draw makes the path invisible.

6. Select File ⇨ Save to save your drawing.

Although the path is not visible, it's still there. If you move or edit the path, your text reflows along the new path. You could leave the path visible for emphasis, but it can make a document appear cluttered.

Note   If you enter different text than that shown in this example, you may need to change the font size to ensure that the text flows correctly along the path and isn't truncated.

Adding the link objects

You add the objects that you will use as links to other Web pages in the same manner as you placed the star in the center of the page. Each image identifies the link it represents. For example, the envelope and monitor will be linked to an e-mail address, while the framed picture will be linked to a page of photo images. Using Figure Q-11 as a guide, drag the bitmap images to the drawing page and set them at the points of the star as shown. Save your document.

Figure Q-11: Set the link objects at the points of the star.

Specifying Hotspots

Draw's Internet toolbar makes designating hotspots and addresses easy. For the rest of this tutorial the address for my domain appears in the figures. You'll want to personalize that information by supplying your own Web address and information. The Internet toolbar isn't displayed in Draw by default. To save screen real estate, Draw only displays toolbars that you specify.

Working with the Internet toolbar

To display the Internet toolbar:

1. Select Tools ⇨ Options and expand the Workspace category. Click Customize to display the Customize property sheet (see Figure Q-12).

2. Click the box beside Internet Objects, and then click OK to return to the drawing window.

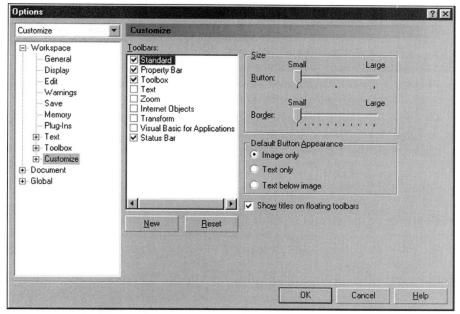

Figure Q-12: The Customize property sheet lets you choose which toolbars are displayed in the drawing window.

The Internet Objects toolbar appears in the drawing window when you select it in the Options dialog box. By default, this is a floating toolbar. You can dock it to the top or side of your drawing window, however, by clicking the title bar and dragging it to the edge where you want it to dock (see Figure Q-13). Docking the toolbar is a good idea. It gets it out of the way so that you don't have to move it around the drawing window as you work.

Identifying your hotspots

Draw has two methods for identifying hotspots: using either the object's shape or the bounding box. When you use the object's shape as the hotspot, the viewer needs to click directly on the object to move to the designated link. This is useful if you have several hotspots close together, but it doesn't lend itself well to small, irregular shapes. It can present a rather difficult target to hit for some viewers. If you identify the object's bounding box as the hotspot, the space the viewer needs to click becomes somewhat larger and rectangular in shape. Use the shape of your object and your layout design to determine which method to use. Each object is identified separately, so you can mix and match these methods.

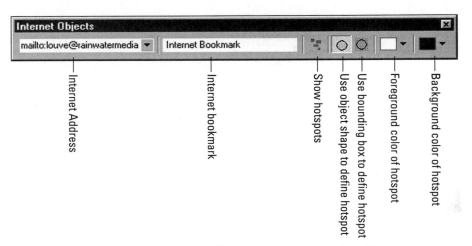

Figure Q-13: The Internet Objects toolbar lets you designate the objects to use as hotspots in your image map.

To specify the hotspots in your image map:

1. Click the Show Hotspots button to enable it. This will allow you to see which objects you've designated as hotspots as you work.

2. Click the color swatches and choose a foreground and background color for your hotspot display. I recommend choosing colors that contrast.

3. Select the book object and click either the Use Object's Shape or the Use Object's Bounding Box as the hotspot button.

4. In the Internet Address box on the toolbar, enter the address: **http://<youraddress>/aboutme.htm**. Remember that you need to change the address to that of your Web site and remove the angle brackets.

5. Repeat steps 3 and 4 for the remaining small icons using this guide:
   - The framed picture: **http://<youraddress>/pictures.htm**
   - The two faces: **http://<youraddress>/friends.htm**
   - The chain: **http://<youraddress>/favlinks.htm**
   - The envelope and monitor: **mailto:<youremailaddress>**

6. Select File ➪ Save As and enter the filename: **index.cdr**.

The envelope is treated a bit differently. Instead of directing the viewer to another Web page, it causes the viewer's default mail client to open with your address in the To: box. For example, if I were creating the link for the envelope, it would say: **mailto:louve@rainwatermedia.com**. The viewer would click this to send me e-mail.

Caution   Your Internet provider probably uses a UNIX- or LINUX-based system for maintaining its Web services. Both of these systems are extremely case sensitive. The address you put in the Internet Address box must match the filename for that page exactly, including case, or the link will not work.

Congratulations! You've just created an image map that you can publish on the Web. All of the hotspots are identified and addresses have been assigned to the links (see Figure Q-14). In the next section, you learn to export your image map document as an HTML document that is readable on the Web.

Figure Q-14: Your image map appears in the drawing window with all of the objects shown as hotspots.

Exporting It to HTML Format

The last step to creating your image map is to export your document in HTML format. This is the format common to the World Wide Web (WWW). Draw provides a Wizard to guide you through the process of exporting your document.

To export your image map for publishing:

1. Select File ⇨ Publish to the Internet to display the Publish To Internet Wizard (see Figure Q-15).

2. Select Single Image with Image Map as the HTML layout method by clicking the down arrow.

3. Select the folder where you want to store your document. For best results, it's a good idea to always store all of the elements of your Web pages in the same location. This helps ensure that all of the necessary files are uploaded to your Internet provider. Click Next.

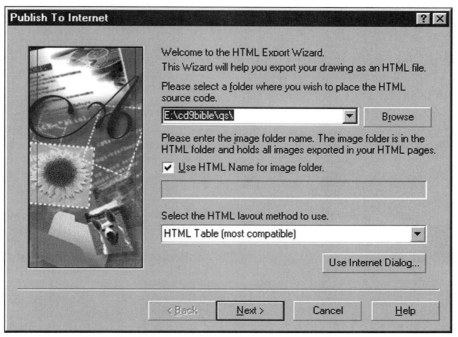

Figure Q-15: The Publish To Internet Wizard guides you through the process of exporting your image map for use on the Web.

4. Select GIF as the output format. GIF is the best choice for graphics with a limited number of colors created in Draw. If your image map contains a photo image, JPEG is a better output format choice.

5. Select the Render All Text as Images box, and then click Next.

6. Check the filename in the window to make sure it's index.htm, and then click Finish. If the filename is not correct, click the filename to highlight it and correct the name.

Naming your home page index.htm is a good idea because that name is the default name for every page on the Web. When a file has this name a viewer can go to the page with just the address. They don't need to specify a filename. You give other pages that you create that are links from your home page other names, such as aboutme.htm, because they are links from a main or index page. Your image map is ready to upload to the WWW. Your Internet provider can give you specific information about uploading image maps and other Web pages.

Note   Image maps are just a tiny part of the nearly limitless types of documents that you can create in Draw. As you explore Draw, let your imagination run free.

✦   ✦   ✦

Essentially CorelDRAW 9

Out of the Box

Draw is about power — not just a little power, but enormous power. I'm talking about the kind of power found in the fastest sports cars or the raw power of a panther. Despite its size, it's sleek and limber enough to enable you to create nearly anything that you can imagine. Moreover, you can manipulate Draw's power to work the way you work. To harness Draw's capabilities to work for you, you need to have a basic understanding of how Draw works.

The best place to start is to look at the drawing window and the various control elements, such as dockers, dialog boxes, toolbars, and menus. These controls are the core tools that imbue Draw with its power. You determine the way they work to create documents in the drawing window.

Once you've taken a look around, you can start working with Draw's basic drawing tools. These tools allow you to create any shape that you can imagine. Each tool has its own properties that determine the way it behaves in the drawing window. You can specify the properties you want to use with each tool.

Getting Started in Draw

When you first start Draw, the drawing window appears with a Welcome Screen (see Figure 1-1). The drawing window is your home base. The results of nearly every action you take in Draw appear in this window. If you are new to Draw, parts of the interface may at first seem confusing. If you are an old hand with Draw, you'll see a few new elements in the drawing window. Regardless of your level of experience, take the time to familiarize yourself with the Drawing window. You'll enjoy your Draw sessions more, and they will be more productive.

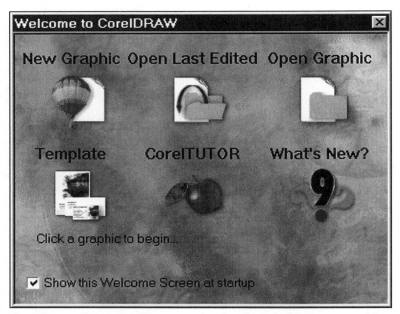

Figure 1-1: When Draw first starts, the drawing window appears with the Welcome Screen.

Starting Draw 9

The Welcome Screen lets you quickly select the files with which you want to work, or start a new drawing. By default, Draw assumes that you want to use the Welcome Screen for quick navigation. You can disable the Welcome Screen if you don't want Draw to display this screen in the future. To disable the Welcome Screen, click the box in the lower left-hand corner of the Welcome Screen marked Show this Welcome Screen at startup. If you decide later that you want to use the Welcome Screen, select Tools ➪ Options to display the Options dialog box. Expand the Workspace category by clicking the plus (+) sign, and then click on General. Near the bottom of the dialog box click the down arrow beside On CorelDRAW! Start-up, and select Welcome Screen from the drop-down list (see Figure 1-2). Click OK to complete the change and to return to the drawing window. The Welcome Screen provides these choices:

✦ **New Graphic:** This option starts a new drawing.

✦ **Open Last Edited:** Opens the last document you edited. When you move your mouse pointer over this icon, the name of the last document you edited appears in the lower left-hand corner of the Welcome Screen.

✦ **Open Graphic:** Select this option to open an existing drawing.

✦ **Template:** This option lets you choose a template to use as the basis for a Drawing.

✦ **CorelTUTOR:** This option starts the CorelTUTOR, which guides you through a series of exercises to assist you with learning to use Draw.

✦ **What's New?:** This option details the new features found in Draw.

Ctrl+J opens the Options dialog box.

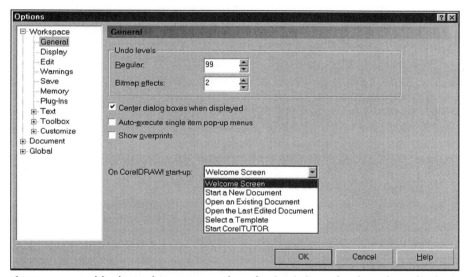

Figure 1-2: Enable the Welcome Screen by selecting it from the drop-down list box in the Options dialog box.

Creating a new drawing

One of the characteristics of Draw is that the program offers you multiple methods for performing most tasks. When you first start Draw, you can start a new document by selecting New Drawing from the Welcome Screen. By default, Draw opens a new document if the Welcome Screen is disabled.

Ctrl+N starts a new Drawing.

If you have been working in Draw and want to open a new drawing, select File ➪ New. When you open a new drawing, a blank virtual page appears on the screen (see Figure 1-3). The new page appears at the size and with the attributes you've saved in the Options dialog box as the default workspace.

Cross-Reference

More information about creating a custom workspace appears in Chapters 6 and 14.

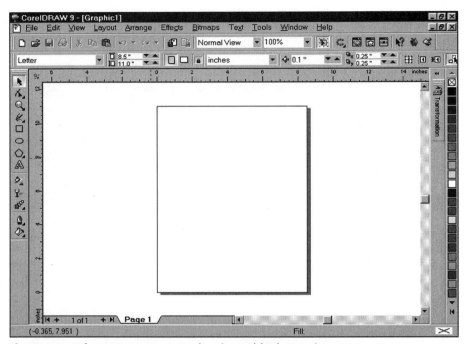

Figure 1-3: When you start a new drawing, a blank Drawing page appears on the screen.

Opening existing drawings

You can open an existing drawing at anytime during a Draw session or from the Welcome Screen when you first start a Draw session. Starting a new drawing does not close any documents that you already have open. If the document you want to open is from a previous version of Draw, such as Draw 6 or Draw 7, the drawing is converted when you open it for editing in the drawing window.

Note

When you select a document in the Open dialog box, Draw displays information about the originating version of Draw in which the document was created. Compression information and the name of the last user who modified the document are also shown below the version number if the file is a version 8 or later.

To open an existing drawing:

1. Click Open Graphic to display the Open Drawing dialog box (see Figure 1-4). If you have been working in Draw, you can select File ⇨ Open to display the Open Drawing dialog box.

Shortcut

Ctrl+O displays the Open Drawing dialog box.

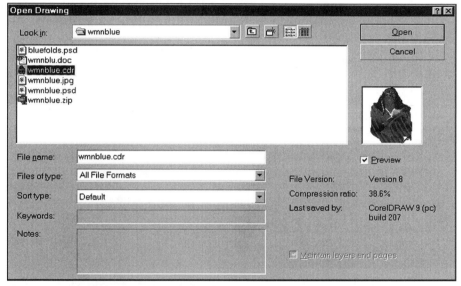

Figure 1-4: The Open Drawing dialog box lets you open an existing image.

2. Click the down arrow beside the Look in drop-down list box, and choose the location where you saved your drawing. A list of files appears in the file window.

3. Select a Drawing by clicking the File name from the list. Enable the Preview window by clicking the checkbox to display a thumbnail of your drawing.

4. Click Open to display the image in the drawing window.

Tip

You can also open files by double-clicking the file name in the Windows Explorer or My Computer folder. In addition, you can drag and drop files from the Scrapbook and Media folders to open existing documents. (More information about using Media folders appears in Chapter 6.)

Opening multiple drawings

Draw lets you open multiple drawings. This feature is useful when you want to move or copy objects from one drawing to another. Open additional documents as shown in the previous sections. Be careful here. Opening multiple documents can be like trying to carry 10 pounds in a 5-pound sack. The number of drawings that you can have open at one time is dependent upon the amount of resources your computer has available. If you have limited resources, performance suffers when you have multiple documents open and could cause an out of memory error.

Like most large programs, Draw requires significant resources for efficient operation. You should exercise caution when opening multiple documents, especially if they contain complex and memory-intensive graphics and effects.

Draw remembers the four most recently edited documents and lists them above the Exit command in the File menu. When you need to work on a series of drawings over multiple sessions, this feature lets you quickly select the drawing with which you want to work. If you have limited resources, it's a good idea to close one document before opening or starting another drawing.

Closing and saving files

To close a drawing, select File ➪ Close. If you close a drawing that hasn't been recently saved, Draw asks if you want to keep any changes, such as additions to your drawing or property changes that have yet to be saved. You have three choices:

+ **Yes:** Saves the latest changes

+ **No:** Loses the changes and closes the drawing

+ **Cancel:** Indicates you've changed your mind and you want to keep working on the drawing

You can quickly close all open documents by selecting File ➪ Close All.

If you try to close a drawing that has no name assigned to it, Draw asks if you want to save it under a new name. If you answer Yes, a dialog box appears where you can enter the name. Draw saves the contents, using the name you specified. The program also saves any settings you made and then closes.

Use Ctrl+S to save a file.

Basic saves

To save files in Draw:

1. Select File ➪ Save (or Save As) and select the folder where you want to save your document (see Figure 1-5).

2. Enter a file name for your document in the File name entry box.

3. Choose any options that you want to use.

See Chapter 6 for more information on Save options.

4. Click Save.

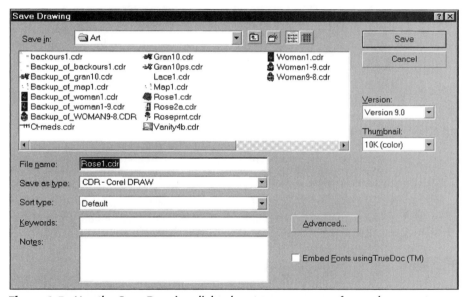

Figure 1-5: Use the Save Drawing dialog box to save a copy of your document.

When you first save a drawing that was previously edited in another version of Draw, the program informs you that your drawing is about to be saved in the new version. If you don't want to save the drawing using the Draw format, click Cancel to abort the operation. You can then use the Save As command (described in the following section) to resave the file in another version.

Using the Save As command

If you are working on a large file and want to try several effects or create a what-if scenario, consider working with a copy of the file, rather than the original image. The Save As command lets you work with a copy, or save a different version of your file, by saving your work with a new name. Saving your Draw document as another version is important when you need to share your documents with users who have a previous version of Draw. Save As is also useful for saving selected objects in your drawing as a separate file if you want to include them in another image.

To use Save As:

1. Select File ⇨ Save As to display the Save Drawing dialog box.
2. Select a location for your document and enter a file name. If you're editing a file, and want to keep the original, or if you want to save the file in a different location, you can make a copy of the file by saving it under a different name in another drive or directory.
3. If you only want to save objects that are selected in your image, enable the Selected Only box.
4. Enter any keywords and notes that you want to add.
5. Click the down arrow to select another version, if desired, and choose a thumbnail file size.

Note

When you choose a thumbnail file size, your selection creates a header that becomes part of the document. The quality of the thumbnail image improves as the size of the thumbnail image increases, although the overall document file size also increases by the value you choose.

6. Click Save to complete the operation. If you change your mind, you can click Cancel at anytime and back out of the Save Drawing dialog box.

Caution

If you edit a drawing and save it in a format for a previous version of Draw, you may lose some of the enhanced changes you made that are Draw 9 specific.

Working with the Save All command

To save all the open documents in Draw, select File ⇨ Save All. If the drawing wasn't previously saved, the Save Drawing dialog box appears, which lets you enter a location and file name for your drawing.

Caution

When you select Save All, Draw automatically presumes that you want to use the existing filename of your documents. It's easy to accidentally overwrite files that you intended to save under another filename. If you create version files where each file is a bit different, be sure to save the file using Save As, instead of Save All, to prevent overwriting your file.

Exiting Draw 9

Probably the hardest part about exiting Draw is deciding to exit. I tend to lose track of time when I'm drawing, and it's hard to tear myself away from an image I'm creating. If you have one computer and multiple users, eventually others will begin to gather like vultures, demanding equal keyboard time. When you are ready to exit Draw, select File ⇨ Exit or click the X in the upper right-hand corner of the application window. If you've made changes to the open documents that haven't yet been saved, Draw prompts you to save the changes.

Exploring the Drawing Window

The appearance of Draw's interface is deceptive. As I mentioned in the previous section, the drawing window is your home base. Every action you perform affects the active document in the drawing window. In some cases, such as the application of special effects, the actions you perform affect the appearance of the drawing. In others, such as object and file management, the actions you perform may not have a visible effect in the drawing window. To work effectively in Draw, you need a grasp of the basic elements of the drawing window. This section is not intended to be exhaustive; instead, it provides a fundamental *map* of the drawing window. Detailed discussions of the various drawing window elements appear throughout this book.

The desktop

If you are a Windows user, I'm sure there have been times when you wished Windows had more than one clipboard to hold information that you wanted to cut, copy, or paste. The desktop area of the drawing window is similar in some respects to the clipboard, except that it can hold more than one image. You can use the desktop as a holding area by dragging objects off the drawing page. The white space that surrounds the drawing page is the desktop space. Objects you place on the desktop are saved with the file, but are not printable. Using the desktop area to hold objects lets you try *what if* situations easily. You can also move objects from one page of a multipage document to another using this method.

 Caution　If you disable the Show Page Border in the Options dialog box, you may have trouble discerning the desktop area of the drawing window. (See Chapter 6 for information about page setup options.)

The Menu bar

Draw is a hefty program in menus alone. Its 12 menus contain nearly all of Draw's commands and options. Related items are grouped on the menus according to use. Rather than get bogged down in a detailed examination of each of these menus, I examine the flavor of each menu. Table 1-1 gives you a brief overview of the commands that are located on each menu.

Table 1-1
Draw's Menus

Menu	Function
Windows Control menu	All Windows 95 applications have a control menu located in the upper left-hand corner of the application. Using this menu you can size, move, minimize, and close application windows.
Draw Control menu	The Draw Control menu lets you perform the same tasks as the Windows Control menu plus swap quickly between open documents. Click the page icon to the left of the File menu to access this menu.
File menu	The File menu is the In and Out basket of Draw. Just as paper shuffling is part of almost any job, document control is part of every Draw session. This menu contains the commands needed to perform a variety of file-related tasks. Managing your document is basic to any application. Draw provides you with the tool to perform the task easily and quickly.
Edit menu	Manipulating the individual objects and actions you perform in Draw determines the appearance of your Drawings. The Edit menu contains the basic commands needed for object control, such as OLE (Object Linking and Embedding) and Windows clipboard functions. In addition, the Edit menu allows you to duplicate and clone selected objects in your Drawing. The controls for Undo and Redo are found on this menu.
View menu	The View menu offers the capability to control the appearance of your display and placement guides in the drawing window. The View menu lets you choose a view quality, as well as select the rollups and Drawing aids that you want displayed in the drawing window.
Layout menu	In a production environment, the organization of a document can be critical to its success. The Layout menu helps you manage the organization by providing commands and options that assist in object placement. The Layout menu lets you add and delete pages, as well as navigate multipage documents.
Arrange menu	The Arrange menu contains the commands and options for basic object manipulation. The Arrange menu lets you access commands that alter the shape of an object and its placement, order, and relationship to other objects in your Drawing.

Menu	Function
Effects menu	The Effects menu contains the commands for applying special effects to objects in your document. Using the Effects menu, you can copy special effects from one object to another, as well as remove effects from objects. Some of the effects can be combined with other effects for spectacular results.
Bitmaps menu	The Bitmaps menu is a new feature in Draw. This menu contains commands for editing and applying effects to imported bitmaps. You can also convert Draw objects to bitmap format on the fly.
Text menu	The Text menu provides access to the dialog boxes and commands for managing text within your document. The Text menu lets you format text, fit text to a path, access writing tools, get information about the text in your document, and export text elements for editing.
Tools menu	The Tools menu provides access to the dialog boxes that allow you to configure Draw. The Tools menu lets you adjust and customize most of Draw's features, create custom fills and arrowheads, access Draw's scrapbook features, apply presets, and add scripts that perform tasks you define.
Window menu	The Window menu lets you control the display when you have multiple documents open in Draw. You can toggle between Drawings or choose an alternate method of display.
Help menu	The Help menu accesses various help assistants. Organized in standard Windows fashion, you can access search functions to assist you in finding the information you need. You can also access one of the Draw-specific help assistants, such as Hints or CorelTUTOR.

The Title bar

The Title bar contains the title of the active document (see Figure 1-6). When you start a new drawing, the name "Graphic1" appears in the Title bar until you save the drawing the first time. The new file name appears after the drawing is saved.

Figure 1-6: The Title bar shows the name of the active document.

The Status bar

The Status bar contains information about the location of your mouse pointer (in pixels) and any selected objects in your document (see Figure 1-7). By viewing the

Status bar, you can see the fill color and outline color, as well as whether a selection is a single object, group, or has effects attributes, such as lens effects.

(15.012, -3.311)   Ellipse on Layer 1   Fill: White
                                                        Outline: Black 3.000 points

Figure 1-7: The Status bar lets you view information about selected objects in your drawing.

Tip   The Status bar displays details of what buttons, controls, and menu commands do as you move the mouse cursor over them.

The scroll bars

The scroll bars help you move around the drawing window (see Figure 1-8). The scroll bars are located at the bottom and right side of the drawing window. By default, Draw displays your entire drawing within the drawing window. If you are using a zoom level that displays only a portion of your drawing, use the scroll bars to move to other parts of your drawing as needed.

To use the scroll bars, click the scroll arrows at either end of the scroll bar to move the view in the desired direction. Alternatively, you can click and drag the scroll thumbs to move in the direction you want. If you use the scroll thumbs, click and drag the thumbs a tiny amount at a time. Why a tiny amount? Now is a good time for me to mention something before you find out for yourself. A drawing-page size of 8 by 11 inches does *not* represent the size of the virtual drawing window. You can create a drawing that is up to 1,800 inches by 1,800 inches. Before you start doing the math, that's approximately half of a football field. The reason it's important to mention those dimensions here is that if you used the scroll thumbs to move around your drawing, your drawing could disappear entirely. It's not really gone, but it is outside the range of the visible drawing window. Should you get overzealous and lose your drawing temporarily, click and drag the scroll thumb back to the approximate center of the scroll bar. If you are using a zoomed view of your drawing, you can also reduce the view to relocate your drawing. You can also select To Page from the Zoom menu on the Property bar, or press Shift+F4, to recenter your drawing.

The Property bar

The Property bar is an interactive feature of Draw that changes according to the selected object and tool. As you change tools or select objects, the Property bar updates to reflect the selection. For example, if the Pick tool is selected, all of the commands on the Property bar refer to the Pick tool and the selected object. If a text object is selected, the transformation and formatting commands appear on the Property bar.

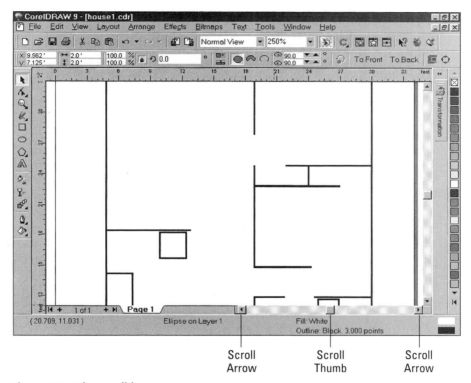

Figure 1-8: The scroll bars.

You can choose to display, hide, resize, or move the Property bar. Hiding or resizing the Property bar is useful if you need more room in the drawing window, or need to get the Property bar out of the way of a portion of your drawing.

Looking at the default view

The Property bar provides an alternate method of manipulating and applying commands to selected objects. Figure 1-9 is a view of the Property bar with no objects selected. This default view contains the page layout information for the document. The settings show that the document is letter size, in portrait orientation, and is using inches as the units of measurement. I have the nudge offset set for $\times^{1}/_{100}$-inch. Duplicate and clone objects are set to be 0-inch offset from the original object. All of the Snap To features are disabled. I also have chosen to display objects while they are being moved, and to treat new objects as filled. (More information and different views of the Property bar appear throughout this book.)

Figure 1-9: The Property bar in default view.

Displaying or hiding the Property bar

To display or hide the Property bar:

1. Select View ➪ Toolbars to display the Toolbars page of the Options dialog box (see Figure 1-10).

2. Click the Property Bar checkbox to display the Property bar or deselect the Property Bar checkbox to hide the Property bar.

3. Click OK to return to the drawing window.

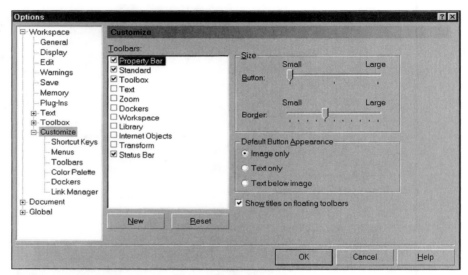

Figure 1-10: Select or deselect the Property Bar checkbox to display or hide it, respectively.

Resizing and moving the Property bar

When the Property bar is undocked, you can resize it by dragging any of its borders. To undock the Property bar, either click and drag in a gray area to the drawing window or double-click a gray area of the Property bar. As your cursor crosses over an edge of the Property bar, it turns into an arrow; click and drag to adjust the size. If you want to move or dock the Property bar, click the Title bar and drag the Property bar to a new location. As you approach either of the sides, the top, or the bottom of the drawing window, it snaps to the edge and becomes a part of the outside perimeter of the drawing window. Double-click the Title bar to dock the Property bar in its last docked position.

Note

When you move the Property bar to an edge to dock it, the Property bar changes shape. It becomes horizontal when placed on the top or bottom side of the application window, or vertical when placed on the left or right side.

The Toolbar

The Toolbar contains shortcuts for several of the most commonly used commands and dialog boxes. Figure 1-11 shows the default Toolbar. By clicking one of these buttons you can perform routine tasks, such as opening Drawings, saving Drawings and applying the Undo command. (More information about each command appears throughout this book.)

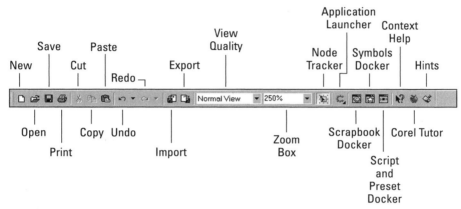

Figure 1-11: The Toolbar in default view.

Note The toolbars are optimized for 800 × 600 resolution. If you are working in a lower resolution, such as 640 × 480, portions of the Property Bar will be too large to display.

Creating Your Workspace

All of Draw's toolbars can be displayed, hidden, resized, and moved in the same manner as the Property bar. The flexibility to organize your workspace is one of Draw's key features that enables you to work more efficiently. In addition, you can customize any of Draw's toolbars to include the tools you use most frequently.

Customizing toolbars lets you work more efficiently and saves time by placing the most frequently used tools at your virtual fingertips. (Information about customizing Draw's toolbars and workspace appears in Chapter 14.)

The Toolbox

The Toolbox contains the tools to create nearly any image or document you can imagine. Figure 1-12 displays the default tools. Other tools are hidden in flyout menus, which keeps the Toolbox tidy and increases the workspace in the drawing window. The tools are grouped by function. Tool buttons with a small triangle in the lower right-hand corner represent flyout menus that allow you to choose from related tools. To display a flyout menu, click one of the tool buttons with a small triangle and hold the mouse button down briefly. The associated flyout menu appears, letting you select from any of the related tools displayed.

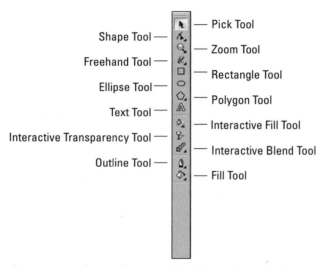

Figure 1-12: The Toolbox contains the tools needed to create a drawing.

The Onscreen Palette

The Onscreen Palette lets you quickly apply solid fills and outline colors to the objects in your drawings (see Figure 1-13). Initially, only one row of the palette is displayed. You can expand the palette and view other colors by clicking the up arrow at the right side of the palette. Alternatively, you can scroll through the colors by clicking the left or right arrows located at the ends of the palette display. If the color palette is docked at the side of the screen, you can expand the palette by clicking the arrow pointing toward the drawing window. Click the arrows at the ends of the palette to scroll through the colors.

Figure 1-13: The Onscreen Palette lets you apply fills and colors to objects.

Tip   If you click a color in the Onscreen Palette and hold the mouse button down briefly, a flyout palette appears that allows you to choose from shades of the selected color.

The Navigator

The Navigator lets you navigate through multipage documents (see Figure 1-14). The center of the Navigator displays the active page and the number of pages in the document. You can go from one page to another by either clicking the arrows or one of the page tabs. If you want to go to the first page in a document, click the left arrow with the barstop in front of it. If you want to go to the last page in a document, click the right arrow with the barstop behind it. Clicking the + (plus) sign lets you add a new page to your document.

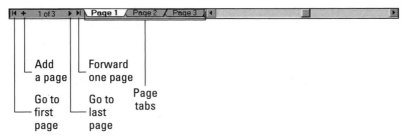

Figure 1-14: The Navigator provides a method for navigating multipage documents.

Using Control Elements in Draw

Control elements enable you to issue instructions for Draw to perform a task in a way that you specify. Control elements include dockers, flyout menus, dialog boxes, and menus. Draw has dozens of control elements. Each serves a different purpose. They share a likeness in that all dockers operate in a similar fashion. The same commonality is true for dialog boxes, flyout menus, and menus. Gaining a basic understanding of how they work makes learning to use Draw easier. Information about specific control elements appears throughout this book.

Understanding dockers

Dockers derive their name from their capability to stick to the edges of the drawing window. Like palettes and toolbars, you can detach, customize, resize, and float them, or you can drag them near an edge of the drawing window to *dock* them in that position. By default, dockers appear docked to the right of the drawing window, but you can also dock them at the top, bottom, or left side. Each docker has unique properties that allow you to control a specific aspect of your document. Draw 9 contains these dockers:

- ✦ Object Manager
- ✦ View Manager
- ✦ Graphic and Text Styles
- ✦ Color Styles
- ✦ Symbols and Special Characters
- ✦ Internet Bookmark Manager
- ✦ HTML Object Conflict
- ✦ Script and Preset Manager
- ✦ Object Data Manager
- ✦ Object Properties

- ✦ Link Manager
- ✦ Scrapbook
- ✦ Bitmap Color Mask
- ✦ Lens
- ✦ Natural Media
- ✦ Transformation
- ✦ Color
- ✦ Color Palette Browser

New Feature

Dockers have replaced rollups in Draw. These control elements snap to the sides of the drawing window. They provide a balance between increased working area and the convenience of keeping commands handy by expanding for use and collapsing when not in use.

All dockers behave similarly and use the same methods to change their location and manage their appearance in the drawing window. When you open more than one docker, they appear stacked (see Figure 1-15). Table 1-2 shows you how to manage dockers in the drawing window.

Table 1-2 Managing Dockers	
To do this:	**Do this:**
Open a docker	Select View ⇨ Dockers and select the docker that you want to use. Alternatively, clicking their respective buttons on the standard toolbar opens the Symbols, Scripts and Presets, and Scrapbook dockers.
Make a docker active	Click the name tab of the docker that you want to be visible in the drawing window.
Resize a docker	Position your cursor over an edge until it turns into a double-headed arrow. Click and drag to resize the docker.
Float a single docker	Make the docker that you want to float the active docker and then click and drag on the name tab toward the drawing window.
Float all open dockers	Click and drag the Title bar toward the drawing window. Alternatively, you can double-click the title bar.
Dock a docker	Click and drag to one of the edges of the drawing window.
Collapse a docker	Click the double arrows at the top left-hand corner of the docker.

Continued

Table 1-2 *(continued)*	
To do this:	**Do this:**
Expand a docker	Click the double arrows at the top right-hand corner of the docker.
Close a single docker	Make the docker that you want to close the active docker and then float the docker in the drawing window. Click the X in the upper right-hand corner to close the docker. Alternatively, you can right-click the name tab of the docker that you want to close, and choose Close from the right mouse button menu.
Close all open dockers	Click the X in the upper right-hand corner of the dockers.

Figure 1-15: When more than one docker is open, they appear stacked in the drawing window.

Working with dialog boxes

Draw's dialog boxes contain parameter options and controls that let you specify the way you want a command to change a selection in your document. Although each of Draw's numerous dialog boxes is unique in the task it performs, dialog boxes share a commonality in the way they operate. Table 1-3 shows the types of controls found in dialog boxes and the way they work.

Tip

Many of the commands and options that are available in dialog boxes are also accessible from the Property bar.

Accessing flyout menus

A flyout menu is a submenu or menu that pops away from the selected area. For example, if you click and hold the mouse button down briefly over the Pen tool, a flyout menu appears, allowing you to select one of the related tools. You can release the mouse button once the menu appears and reposition your cursor over the selection you want and then click to select the item. You don't have to drag your mouse cursor over to the selection as you do with Macintosh-based software.

Draw has two basic types of flyout menus:

✦ **Toolbox:** This flyout menu lets you select tools and options from the Toolbox. The second type of flyout menu lets you access submenus. Flyout menus on the Toolbox are accessed by clicking the small triangle at the bottom right-hand corner of a tool button and then holding the mouse button down momentarily. Once the flyout is displayed, you can select a tool or option from the flyout menu. The tool icon changes to reflect your selection.

✦ **Flyout submenu:** This type of flyout menu is accessed by placing the mouse pointer over the small arrow to the right of menu items. Once the submenu is displayed, click an item to select it. If the selection is a setting, such as snap-to commands, an arrow indicates that the selection is active.

Tip

You can drag a flyout off its host toolbar or the Toolbox by dragging any part outside the button area. This step doesn't actually remove the flyout from the toolbar, but displays it as a separate toolbar. Close the flyout toolbar and return it to its normal position by clicking the X close box in the upper right-hand corner of the toolbar.

Table 1-3
Using Dialog Boxes

Control	Name	Usage
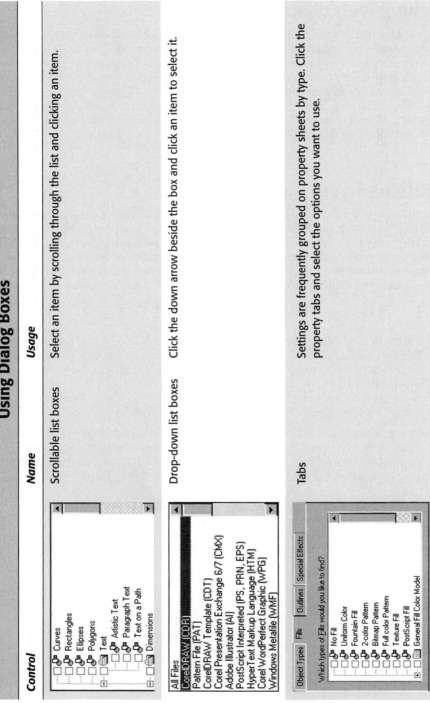	Scrollable list boxes	Select an item by scrolling through the list and clicking an item.
	Drop-down list boxes	Click the down arrow beside the box and click an item to select it.
	Tabs	Settings are frequently grouped on property sheets by type. Click the property tabs and select the options you want to use.

Control	Name	Usage
	Preview boxes	Some dialog boxes have preview boxes that let you preview the results before you click OK.
Apply	Buttons	Perform the specified task or access other dialog boxes that let you specify additional parameters.
Help	Help buttons	Dialog boxes contain context-sensitive help buttons. To get help, click the help button to display information on the contents of the dialog box. Note: You can also get help by pressing F1.
OK	OK buttons	Click the OK button to apply the settings you selected.
Cancel	Cancel buttons	Cancels the operation and returns you to the drawing window without making any changes.
	Check boxes	Click to select options. A selected option appears with a check mark in the box.
	Radio buttons	Click to select options. Selected options appear with a dot in the button.
Grammaphone	Entry boxes	Require you to enter the desired information.
2.0	Value boxes	Either click the up and down arrows to select a value, or highlight the value and enter a new value. If the value you set falls outside the available limits, Draw enters the closest legal value.

Getting Help

Draw supports extensive online help. You can access information and get answers to your questions about Draw by selecting a help assistant from the Help menu. You can get help with performing an operation, using a feature, technical support issues, and understanding terms. Each help assistant operates differently to provide the information you need. To get help, select a type of help assistant from the Help menu.

Help Topics

Selecting Help Topics from the Help menu displays the Help Topics: CorelDRAW Help dialog box. Help topics offer you three methods of getting information: Contents, Index, or Find. To access one of these methods, click the associated property tab.

Ctrl+F1 accesses the Help Topics dialog box.

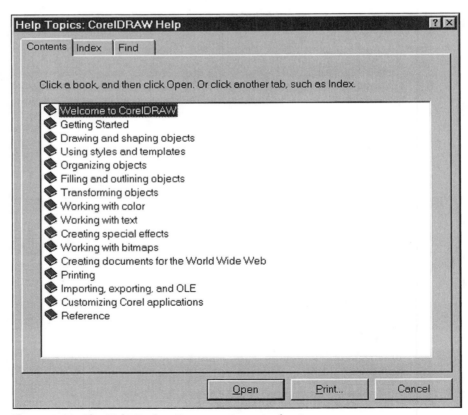

Figure 1-16: The Help Topics: Contents property sheet.

✦ **Contents:** This property sheet contains information arranged by topic (see Figure 1-16). Click one of the books to display the related subtopics. Select a subtopic and click Open to display the information.

✦ **Index:** This property sheet lets you use a search engine to find the topic that you want (see Figure 1-17). Type a word or part of a word in the first entry box. As you enter characters in the entry box, the index box below changes to locate the information. Select a topic from the index and click Display.

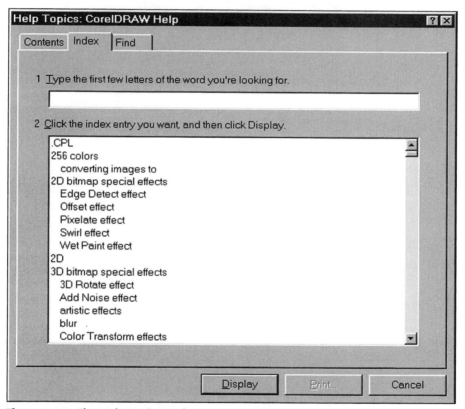

Figure 1-17: The Help Topics: Index property sheet.

✦ **Find:** This property sheet performs a more extensive search by letting you choose words that narrow the search (see Figure 1-18). To start the search, enter a word in the text entry box and then select matching words to narrow the search. The results of the search are listed in the Topic box near the bottom of the property sheet. To select a topic, click the box beside the topic and then click Display.

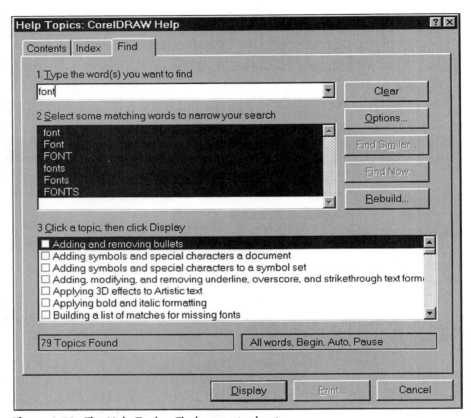

Figure 1-18: The Help Topics: Find property sheet.

Tip

You can get context-sensitive help on any control element in Draw, such as a docker, by right-clicking the element and choosing help from the menu that appears.

What's This?

When you select What's This? from the Help menu, your mouse pointer changes to a question mark superimposed over an arrow. What's This? is a context-sensitive help assistant. To get information, click any element in the application or drawing window.

Shortcut

Shift+F1 accesses the What's This? help assistant.

CorelTUTOR

When you select CorelTUTOR from the Help menu, it launches the Draw tutorial exercises (see Figure 1-19). CorelTUTOR is an interactive set of lessons that are designed to familiarize you with Draw. Select a lesson topic by clicking one of the buttons; follow the prompts to complete the lesson.

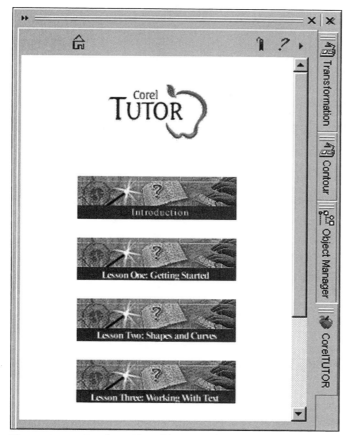

Figure 1-19: CorelTUTOR guides you through a series of interactive tutorial lessons.

Hints

Selecting Hints accesses an interactive dialog box that lets you select information by topic (see Figure 1-20). The dialog box remains on top of Draw, letting you use step-by-step instructions while working with your document.

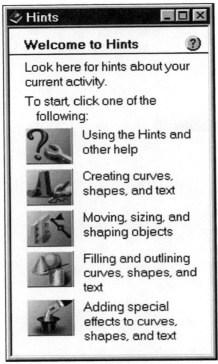

Figure 1-20: The Hints dialog box.

Technical Support

When you choose Technical Support from the Help menu, the dialog box that appears is similar to the Help Topics dialog box. You can choose to search for information using the Contents and Find property sheet as you did with Help Topics.

www.corel.com

If you have an Internet account that supports the WWW (World Wide Web) and a Web browser, this choice lets you connect with Corel Corporation's Web site. Corel's Web site has a wealth of information about new products, technical support, upgrades, frequently asked questions (FAQs), and upcoming technology, as well as other topics.

Getting system information

You want information about Draw, your document, and your system. Perhaps you *need* information. We've all had it happen. Things bog down and a program is running slower than molasses. Or maybe you just have a burning curiosity to know how many objects are in your drawing. Selecting About CorelDRAW from the Help menu can give you the information you want or need (see Figure 1-21). This dialog box lists your serial and pin numbers; contains information about the active drawing; lets you change your serial and pin numbers; and lets you access information about your system.

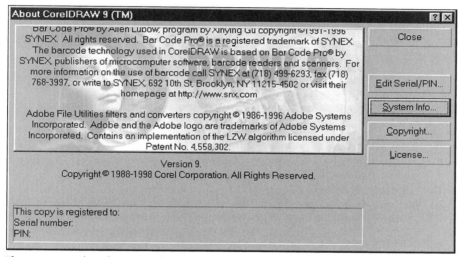

Figure 1-21: The About CorelDRAW 9 dialog box.

If you click the System Info button, you can get information about your computer, operating system, display, printers, CorelDRAW .exe and .DLL files, and your system .DLL files. All of this information is important if you need to call technical support. You can save the information and print it as a text file.

Easter Eggs

Most software companies bury an Easter egg somewhere in their software. Corel is no different. If you double-click either icon at the top of the About CorelDRAW 9 dialog box, your screen will display the Easter egg image. In Draw, the image is animated.

The software industry is a strange business that attracts people who are creative and more than a little unique at times. Easter eggs are born during dreams and 4 a.m. moments when exhaustion has set in, the pizza is cold, the coffee has gone stale, and creativity has become more than a little crazed. It's also notable that authors of technical books undergo a similar experience.

Creating Lines, Shapes, and Curves

A wood sculptor starts with a block of wood and removes the wood that is *not* part of the finished work of art. Removing bits of wood here and there takes time. Similarly, while geometric shapes are good building blocks for creating more complex shapes, editing these shapes to create irregular shapes can be time-consuming. If the shape you want to create does not closely resemble a geometric shape, drawing the shape is a better choice. Draw provides three tools for creating irregular shapes, curves, and lines: the Freehand tool, the Bézier tool, and the Natural Pen tool. Each tool has unique properties that make it suitable for a particular type of task.

Using the Freehand tool

The Freehand tool is simply what the name implies. Using the tool, you draw freehand lines and curves that track the movement of your mouse pointer on the drawing page. Depending on the steadiness of your hand, and to some extent the type of pointing device you use, the results can vary from a smooth flowing curve to one that is rough and requires editing (see Figure 1-22). If you use a digitizer pad instead of a mouse, the results are likely to be better, but getting a smooth curve still requires practice. The Freehand tool's best feature is that it lets you create straight lines while letting you see the position and angle of the line as it is drawn.

Shortcut

Pressing F5 toggles to the active line tool.

Creating straight lines

When you create a straight line with the Freehand tool, you can see the placement and angle of the line as it's drawn. This feedback enables more precise placement of lines and reduces the amount of editing required later.

To create straight lines with the Freehand tool:

1. Select the Freehand tool from the curve flyout menu if it's not the active tool.

2. Click a starting point on the drawing page and release the mouse button.

3. Move to the location where you want to place the end of the line and click again (see Figure 1-23).

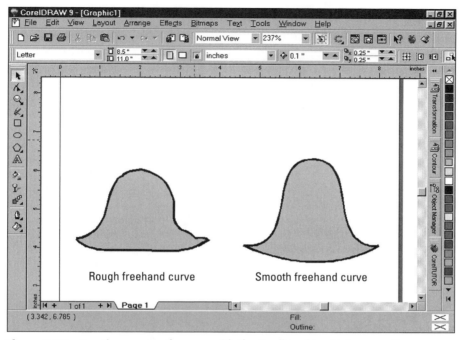

Figure 1-22: Creating a smooth curve with the Freehand tool takes practice. Rough curves usually require editing.

Drawing consecutive line segments

You can draw consecutive line segments using the Freehand tool. The intermediate endpoints of a set of consecutive line segments are known as points of inflection. A point of inflection is any location on a line or curve where the line changes direction. If you press Ctrl while setting points, the line is constrained to increments of the angle that you specified in the Options dialog box under the General tab. The angle is set at 15 degrees by default.

Cross-Reference

For more information on setting line constraints in the Options dialog box and on customizing Draw, see Chapter 14.

To draw consecutive line segments:

1. Select the Freehand tool if it's not already selected.

2. Click a starting point on the drawing page and release the mouse button.

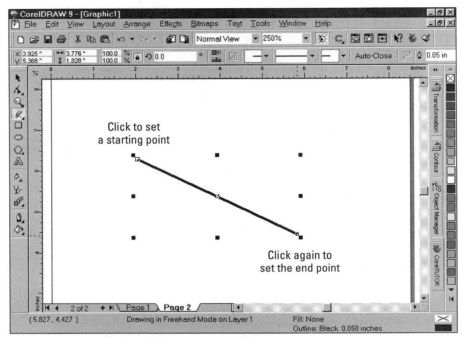

Figure 1-23: Creating a straight line with the Freehand tool.

3. Move to another location and double-click to set the next point. Try pressing Ctrl while moving the endpoint of a line. Note how the line snaps to the specified angle from the previous line segment (see Figure 1-24).

4. Continue double-clicking to set more points until your line looks similar to the one in Figure 1-24. If you make a mistake and want to erase one or more line segments, press Ctrl+Z or Alt+Backspace for each line segment that you want to erase. The number of Undo levels that you have configured Draw to allow limits the number of line segments that you can erase. Double-click the endpoint of the edited line to continue drawing segments.

Cross-
Reference

For more information on configuring Draw (specifically the number of undo levels), see Chapter 2.

Creating freehand curves

You can draw freehand curves using the Freehand tool. These curves are usually rough, however, and require editing if you want a smooth curve.

Curves are edited with the shape tool, as shown later in Chapter 3.

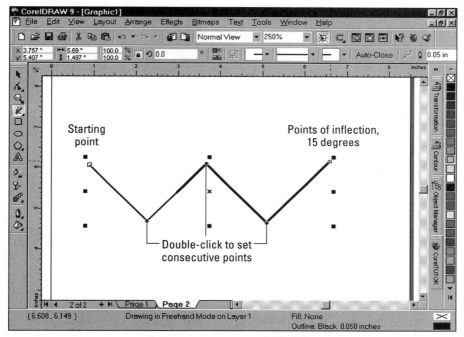

Figure 1-24: Consecutive line segments constrained to 15-degree angles.

To draw a curved line with the Freehand tool:

1. Click a starting point on the drawing page.

2. Without releasing the mouse button, drag the mouse pointer to create the curve you desire (see Figure 1-25). Pressing Ctrl while drawing a freehand curve does not affect the curve.

Connecting two different line types

You can connect straight and curved lines to create a single line while drawing a line. The capability of connecting two different line types together expands the variety of shapes that you can produce.

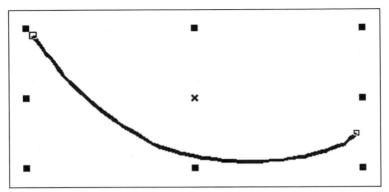

Figure 1-25: Using the Freehand tool, click to set a starting point and then drag to create a curve.

To draw a connected curved or straight line from an existing line:

1. Using the Pick tool, select the line to which you want to connect a new line segment, if it's not already selected.

2. Using the Freehand tool, move to the end of the line segment and click to start the new line segment. Follow the previous instructions to add a straight or curved line.

You must click within five pixels of the endpoint or the two curves will not join. You can adjust this five-pixel threshold by changing the Freehand tool property settings, as shown later in this chapter. If you want to draw a series of unconnected lines that are close together, you may accidentally join the lines. To prevent this from happening, press the Esc key when you complete a line, before drawing the next line.

Caution   The Freehand tool is also used to trace bitmaps. If a bitmap is selected when you select the Freehand tool, Draw automatically toggles to *trace* mode. Be sure no bitmaps are selected if you want to draw lines with the Freehand tool.

Erasing a portion of a line while drawing

Draw lets you erase portions of a freehand curve while drawing. Unlike straight-line segments, which are erased using the keyboard, curves are erased interactively.

To erase a portion of a freehand curve:

1. While drawing the curve, press Shift and drag backward along the curve. Do not release the mouse button while drawing or erasing a portion of a curve. Once the mouse button is released, Draw assumes that you have completed drawing or erasing the curve.

2. When you have finished erasing the portion of the curve that you want removed, you can continue drawing the curve by releasing Shift. Be sure not to release the mouse button until the curve is complete.

When you drag backward along a curve to erase it, you don't have to be exact about following the path. As long as you are close to the original path, the line segment is erased.

Closing an object

A closed object has a common beginning and ending point without gaps. There are two ways to create closed objects, which are described in the following sections.

Using the Freehand tool

To draw a closed shape with the Freehand tool:

1. Select the Freehand tool from the Toolbox.

2. Draw a curve or set of consecutive lines on the drawing page. End the line at the starting point, where you began drawing the line (see Figure 1-26).

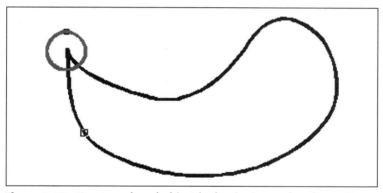

Figure 1-26: Create a closed object by beginning and ending a line at the same point. The circled node in this figure indicates the starting and ending point of the curve.

Using Auto-Close

While the Freehand tool is active, you can also click the Auto-Close button on the Property bar to close any curved object you draw. When you click Auto-Close, Draw calculates the shortest distance between the beginning and ending node and adds a line segment to close the object. You can adjust the distance from the beginning node required to close an object. Depending on the type of connecting nodes, this action can distort an object.

For more information about using Auto-Close and nodes, see Chapter 3.

Filling Closed and Unclosed Objects

Draw lets you apply a fill to any object that you create in the drawing windows. Unlike bitmap programs, filling an object that's not closed doesn't cause the fill to *bleed* to other areas. The fill isn't visible, though, unless the object is closed.

Avoid applying a fill to an open curve or line segment. Doing so can cause errors when printing on PostScript devices.

Using the Bézier curve tool

The Bézier curve tool lets you create smooth curves and straight lines with precision. Curves are created one line segment at a time by setting points and the angle for the next line segment. Draw calculates each line segment mathematically to yield a smooth curve. As with the freehand lines, Bézier curves are described by their points of inflection. You set a new point wherever the line changes direction. Figure 1-27 shows the rough shape of a duck created with the Bézier curve tool. The handles extending away from each point let you adjust the direction of the curve.

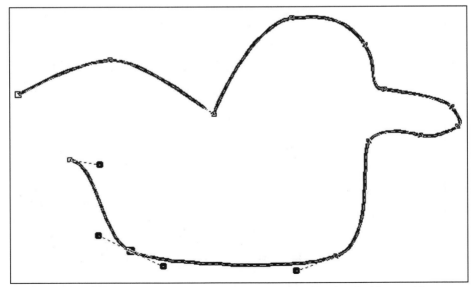

Figure 1-27: The Bézier curve tool lets you create smooth, curved objects with precision.

Bézier Trivia

Named after the French mathematician Pierre Bézier, Bézier curves employ at least three points to define a curve. The two endpoints of the curve are called anchor points. The other points, which define the shape of the curve, are called handles, tangent points, or nodes.

Attached to each handle are two control points. By moving the handles or the control points, you can modify the shape of the curve

Creating straight lines

With the Bézier curve tool, you can create straight lines by setting a series of points. Unlike a Freehand tool line, a straight line created with the Bézier curve tool appears after each successive point is set. When used in conjunction with the onscreen rulers or any of the snap-to features, the Bézier curve tool lets you create lines with a great deal of precision. In the next exercise, you create a simple object using this tool. For this exercise, you need to have the onscreen rulers visible in the drawing window. If the rulers are not visible in the drawing window, select View ➪ Rulers.

Tip   Unlike the Freehand tool, you can't constrain straight lines created with the Bézier tool to specific angles. If you need lines set at a specific angle or increment of an angle setting, I recommend using the Freehand tool to create the line. You can combine Freehand and Bézier lines as you would connect a straight and curved freehand line. Simply select the line to which you want to continue drawing and then change line tools. Continue drawing from the endpoint of the line.

To draw straight lines using the Bézier curve tool:

1. Select the Bézier tool from the curve flyout menu.

2. Using the rulers as a guide, click a starting point at the intersection of 2 inches, 6 inches. (Remember that when referring to coordinates and intersections, the horizontal or x location is listed first; the vertical or y location is listed last.) Draw helps you place the point by displaying dotted lines across the rulers to show the location of your mouse pointer.

3. Click a second point at 2 inches, 4 inches to create the first line segment (see Figure 1-28).

4. Set a third point at 4 inches, 4 inches; a fourth point at 4 inches, 6 inches; and a fifth point at 3 inches, 7 inches.

5. Click the starting point again to set the last point and close the object (see Figure 1-29).

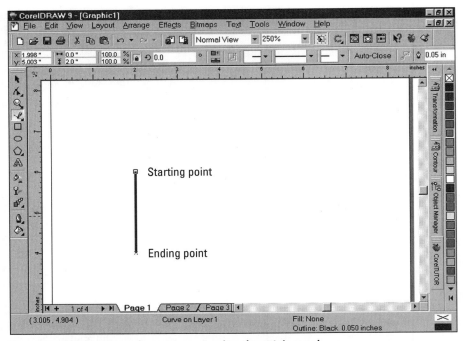

Figure 1-28: Creating a line segment using the Bézier tool.

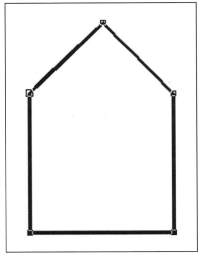

Figure 1-29: A closed object created with straight lines using the Bézier tool.

Displaying the Onscreen Rulers

This is a toggle setting. Rulers are enabled when a check mark appears beside the word in the View menu. To disable the rulers, reselect the option.

The rulers are displayed with inches as the default unit of measurement. Later, you learn to change the units of measurement and work with the rulers.

Creating curves

Earlier in this section, Figure 1-27 showed a curve created with the Bézier tool. The curves shown in this example were created, by clicking and dragging away from each successive point, to set the angle for the next line segment. The next exercise uses the Bézier tool to create a simple curved line. Figure 1-30 follows the steps for creating the line. Compare your results with those illustrated in the figure.

To create Bézier curves:

1. Select the Bézier tool from the curve flyout menu.

2. Click a starting point on the drawing page and drag away from the point. Handles appear as you drag the mouse pointer. Release the mouse button and click a second point below and to the right of the first point (see Figure 1-30, Step 1). If you press Ctrl while dragging, the angle of the handles is constrained by default to increments of 15 degrees.

You can change the degree settings in the Options dialog box under the General ⇨ Edit settings (See Chapter 2).

3. With the mouse button still pressed, drag away from the second point and click to set the third point (see Figure 1-30, Step 2).

4. Drag and click to set the fourth and fifth points as shown in Figure 1-30, Steps 3 and 4.

You can close Bézier curves in the same way that you would close any object drawn with one of the curve tools: click the starting point of the line. Once the object is closed, you can apply fill effects to the object.

Erasing line segments

Drawing curves with the Bézier tool can be tricky. If you make a mistake, however, you don't have to start over. Release the mouse button and press Ctrl+Z or Alt+Backspace to erase the last line segment you drew. Repeat this sequence to erase more than one line segment as needed.

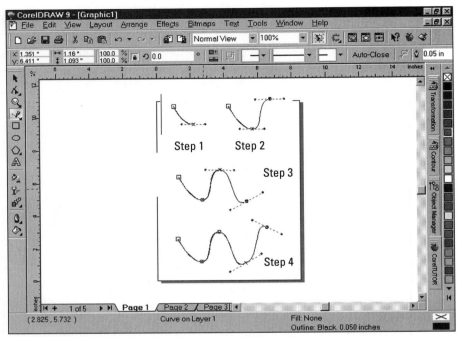

Figure 1-30: Using the Bézier tool, create a simple curve by clicking and dragging to set the points and angles of each successive segment.

Cross-Reference The number of line segments that you can erase is limited by the number of Undo levels that you have specified (see Chapter 2).

Setting Freehand and Bézier tool properties

The Freehand and Bézier tool property settings let you specify the way lines behave as you draw them. To adjust the property settings, select Tools ➪ Options and click the plus (+) to expand the Workspace and Toolbox categories (see Figure 1-31). Select the Freehand and Bézier tool from the tool list and use these guidelines for making adjustments:

Tip Right-click a tool in the Toolbox and then select Properties to display the settings available for that tool in the Options dialog box. You can also double-click a tool to display the property settings for that tool.

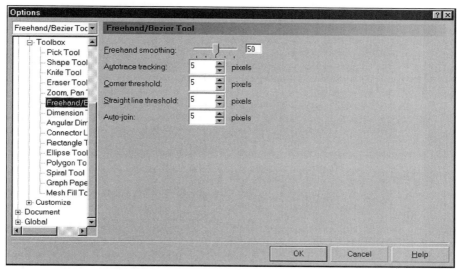

Figure 1-31: Freehand and Bézier property settings.

✦ **Freehand tracking:** The value entered in the Freehand tracking setting should reflect the type of pointing device that you use and the steadiness of your hand. You can enter any value from 1 to 10. Drawing with a mouse is a bit like drawing with a brick. It's difficult to achieve a smooth, flowing movement. If you are using a mouse and the default value of 5 pixels, curves will appear rough. Increasing the value to a maximum of 10 pixels will yield a smoother curve. At the other end of the spectrum, if you are using a digitizer, a value of 3 or 4 pixels may work well for you. I don't recommend that anyone use a value of 1, unless you want a very rough-looking curve.

✦ **Autotrace tracking:** The value you enter in Autotrace tracking determines how closely the Bézier curve follows the edges of a bitmap during onscreen tracing. The default setting is 5 pixels, which provides medium tracking. A curve with a setting of 1 to 3 pixels follows the edges of the bitmap more closely; a curve with a setting of 8 to 10 pixels follows the edges of the bitmap more loosely.

✦ **Corner threshold:** The Corner threshold setting affects the way the Freehand tool and bitmap tracing behave. The default setting is 5 pixels. Lower settings yield tighter corners with more cusps; higher settings create more flowing Bézier curves. If you are using the Freehand tool, consider using a higher setting to create smoother curves.

✦ **Straight line threshold:** When you click and drag with the Freehand tool, it's difficult to make a straight line. Although straight lines are easily created with the tool, if you want to draw a shape with curves and semistraight lines, it can be a challenge to create a line that doesn't look rough. Adjusting the Straight line threshold setting helps solve this problem. The default setting is 5 pixels.

Higher settings create lines that are straighter; lower settings create lines that are more curved.

✦ **Auto-join:** Ends of lines behave like magnets, enabling you to close objects easily. Auto-join settings enable you to adjust how close you have to come to the beginning point of a shape to join the ends and close the object. The default setting is 5 pixels. If you set this value at 10 pixels, line ends that come within a 10-pixel radius are joined. If you set this value at 1 pixel, you have to draw very close to the beginning point of a shape to close the object. Adjust this setting according to your particular drawing style.

Using the Natural Pen tool

Have you ever wanted a tool that behaved like a calligraphic pen, or wanted to apply a fountain or vector fill to a line? The Natural Pen tool lets you create *line* objects of a varying or consistent width. Natural Pen lines are treated as curve objects and are easily edited. What this means to you is that you can apply the same effects and editing to Natural Pen lines that you apply to other objects. You can't apply Natural Pen effects to existing lines. Natural Pen effects are added to your images only as you draw.

Creating lines with variable widths

Technically, you can create a Natural Pen line that is 450 inches wide. That width is worth mentioning just to illustrate the versatility of the tool, though it's doubtful you will ever need a line that is more than 37 feet wide. The Natural Pen tool lets you create calligraphic, variable-width, or pressure-sensitive lines. You can also choose from a series of preset pen shapes to create special effects lines. The Natural Pen tool supports variable line widths, which is extremely useful for cartooning and sketching (see Figure 1-32).

To use the Natural Pen tool:

1. Select the Natural Pen tool from the curve flyout menu.

2. Click and drag to create a line on the drawing page. It doesn't matter what you draw here, just try the pen to get a feel for the way it works. When you release the mouse button, the line becomes a curved object that you can fill and edit as you choose.

Setting Natural Pen properties

The Natural Pen properties let you create the effects shown in the previous illustration, as well as other pen effects. The property settings determine the type of line and the width of the line you draw. Draw offers two methods for setting the Natural Pen properties: the Options dialog box and the property bar. As you work with Draw and the Natural Pen tool, however, you'll find that using the property bar to specify settings is more convenient than altering settings in the Options dialog box.

Figure 1-32: The Natural Pen tool lets you create cartoons and other objects that require variable-width lines.

Using the Options dialog box

To specify Natural Pen tool settings:

1. Select Tools ➪ Options to display the Options dialog box.

2. Expand the General and Toolbox categories by clicking the plus (+) signs beside their names.

3. Choose the Natural Pen tool to display the associated property page (see Figure 1-33). Alternatively, you can right-click the Natural Pen tool in the toolbox and choose Properties from the menu.

4. Choose the Natural Pen tool from the tool list.

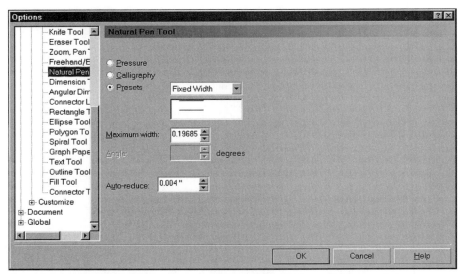

Figure 1-33: The Natural Pen property page of the Options dialog box lets you specify the width, angle, and pen type that you want to use with the Natural Pen.

5. Choose a pen type, using these guidelines:

- **Fixed:** Creates a line object of a consistent width. You can specify the width you desire in the Maximum Width entry box.

- **Pressure:** This option requires that you have a pressure-sensitive digitizer pad. As the pressure of your stylus increases, the width of the line increases. You can specify the maximum width desired. If you use a mouse, settings are ignored, and your lines have a fixed width.

- **Calligraphy:** This option creates a line similar to that used for calligraphic writing. You can specify both the maximum width and the angle of the line.

- **Presets:** Draw provides a variety of pen shapes to add interest to your images. These are variable-width shapes; you can specify the maximum width desired. To select a pen shape, choose a shape from the drop-down list.

6. Specify the maximum width and angle, if applicable to your pen selection. If the angle option is not available, it will be grayed out in the dialog box.

Note

Using the Natural Pen tool requires practice to achieve the effects that you want. The varieties of objects that you can create with this tool are nearly endless. Like many of the pen tools, you will have better success if you use a digitizer instead of a mouse.

Using the Property bar

When the Natural Pen tool is active, you can specify Natural Pen properties on the Property bar. The Property bar lets you quickly change the width and type of Natural Pen.

To specify Natural Pen properties using the Property bar:

1. Select the Natural Pen from the curve flyout menu. The property bar updates to reflect your tool selection (see Figure 1-34).

2. Choose a pen type from the property bar. If you select the preset pen type, choose a pen shape from the Natural Pen presets drop-down menu. A representation of the pen shape lets you choose the shape you want easily.

3. Specify the maximum width and the angle, if applicable.

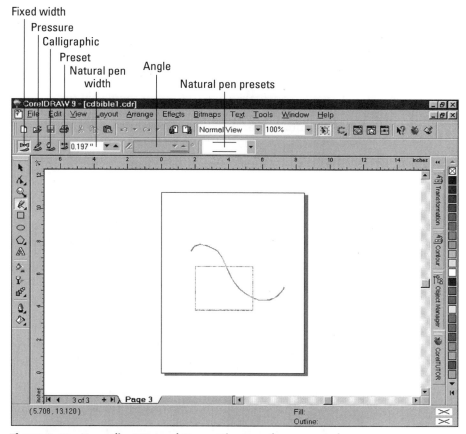

Figure 1-34: You adjust Natural Pen settings on the property bar.

Editing and enhancing Natural Pen objects

I've referred to objects drawn with the Natural Pen as *lines* because the tool itself is used like a line tool. Objects created with the Natural Pen, however, aren't lines. They are objects like any irregular shape you draw, and are edited in the same manner as other objects. You can apply several special-effect fills to Natural Pen objects that you can't apply to lines. This capability is extremely useful when you need to add a special-effect outline around another object.

New Feature

Prior to Draw 8, users could apply variable line widths to existing objects and lines using a feature called Powerlines. Due to popular demand, the feature has been revamped and added to Draw 9. You can now convert outlines to objects that you can edit to add variable line effects. (For more information, see Chapter 12.)

Using Geometric Drawing Tools

Every object in the world is composed of variations on a handful of basic geometric shapes (see Figure 1-35). Rectangles, ellipses, and triangles provide the basis for more complex shapes. From the Parthenon's graceful rectangles and ellipses as reflected in its pillars, to the delicacy of the merging triangles of a starfish, you are surrounded by geometry. These basic shapes, when combined with lines and curves, can help you create lifelike illustrations or indulge in the creations of your mind's eye. Draw provides a wealth of tools for creating and editing shapes and curves. Once you create a shape, you can add a fill that gives the object life.

Figure 1-35: Basic geometric shapes, such as rectangles, ellipses, and triangles, combine to form more complex shapes.

Tip You can now use any of Draw's tools as a temporary selection tool, reducing the need to frequently switch to the Pick tool. When a drawing or the text tool is active and your mouse cursor is over an object, the cursor changes indicating you can use the tool like the Pick tool.

Working with the Ellipse tool

The Ellipse tool lets you create ellipses, circles, arcs, and wedges. Invisible rectangular bounding boxes that define the dimensions of the shape surround ellipses and circles.

Shortcut Press F7 to toggle to the Ellipse tool.

To draw an ellipse:

1. Select the Ellipse tool from the toolbox. When you select the Ellipse tool, the cursor changes to a crosshair with an ellipse to the lower right.

2. Click a starting location on the drawing page and drag the mouse pointer diagonally away from the starting point (see Figure 1-36). Press Ctrl to constrain the ellipse to a circle. Press Shift while dragging to draw the ellipse from the center.

Cross-Reference These shapes can be edited with both the Pick tool and the Shape tool to form other symmetrical shapes (see Chapter 3).

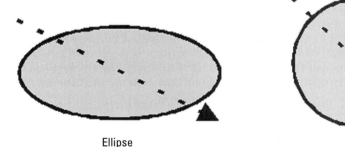

Ellipse   Circle

Figure 1-36: To draw an ellipse, click a starting point and drag diagonally away from the starting point.

Working with the Rectangle tool

The Rectangle tool lets you create rectangles and squares. The Rectangle tool works much like the Ellipse tool. Using the Rectangle tool, you can also create squares and rectangles with rounded corners by specifying rectangle properties.

Press F6 to toggle to the Rectangle tool.

To draw a rectangle:

1. Select the Rectangle tool from the toolbox.

2. Click a starting location on the drawing page and drag the mouse pointer diagonally away from the starting point (see Figure 1-37). Press Shift while dragging to draw the rectangle from the center. Press Ctrl while dragging to constrain the rectangle to a square.

Rectangle   Square

Figure 1-37: To draw a rectangle, click a starting point and drag diagonally away from the starting point.

Creating polygons

Computer graphics programs have evolved significantly over the last several years. Until recently, creating accurate polygons in illustration packages was tedious and challenging. CAD applications, such as AutoCAD, let you create the shapes, but required a level of math wizardry that most of us didn't possess. The Polygon tool first appeared in Draw 6, making the creation of polygons much easier. Using Draw's Polygon tool, you can create a polygon with up to 500 sides. Polygons, like circles, have an invisible rectangular bounding box that defines the dimensions of the shape.

To draw a polygon:

1. Select the Polygon tool from the Toolbox.

2. Click a starting point and drag diagonally away from the starting point to create the shape (see Figure 1-38). If you press Ctrl while dragging, the sides of the polygon are constrained to be the same, or equilateral. If you press Shift while dragging, the polygon is drawn from the center.

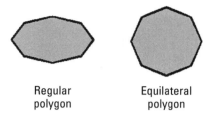

Regular
polygon

Equilateral
polygon

Figure 1-38: The Polygon tool can create both regular and equilateral polygons.

Creating triangles and stars

Using the Polygon tool, you can also create triangles and stars by adjusting the Polygon tool properties. You can only create acute or equilateral triangles with the Polygon tool. Acute triangles have angles that do not exceed 90 degrees. Equilateral triangles have sides whose lengths are equal. Triangles and stars are created the same way as you create a polygon.

To create a triangle or star:

1. Adjust the Polygon tool properties.
2. Select the Polygon tool.
3. Click a starting point and drag diagonally away from the starting point. If you press Ctrl while dragging, the sides of the polygon are constrained to be the same, or equilateral. If you press Shift while dragging, the polygon is drawn from the center.

You cannot create right or obtuse triangles (triangles whose angles are equal to or greater than 90 degrees) using the Polygon tool. You need to use the Pen tool to create obtuse and right triangles.

Drawing spirals

Draw lets you create two kinds of spirals: symmetrical and logarithmic (see Figure 1-39). You can set the number of revolutions for either type of spiral to any value from 1 to 100. Symmetrical spirals appear with lines evenly spaced apart. Logarithmic spirals are based on a more complex math formula in which the spacing is dependent upon the expansion value you set in the Spiral tool properties.

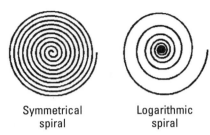

Symmetrical   Logarithmic
spiral   spiral

Figure 1-39: Two spirals, both with
10 revolutions. The logarithmic spiral
has an expansion setting of 50.

To draw a spiral:

1. Click the Polygon tool and hold down the mouse button briefly to display the flyout menu.

2. Select the Spiral tool. The tool icon in the Toolbox changes to that of the Spiral tool.

3. Click a starting point on the drawing page and drag diagonally away from the starting point to create the spiral. If you press Shift while dragging, the spiral is created from the center. If you press Ctrl while dragging, the spiral is constrained to a concentric shape (see Figure 1-40).

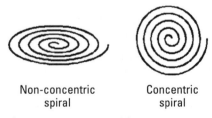

Non-concentric   Concentric
spiral   spiral

Figure 1-40: Concentric versus
nonconcentric spirals. Pressing Ctrl
while dragging creates a concentric
spiral.

Unlike other geometric objects, when drawing a spiral remember that Draw considers it an open path. You can change the outline color. If you apply a fill, the fill won't be visible and could cause printing problems.

Using the Graph Paper tool

Have you ever created a grid background for a graph or other image? Creating, duplicating, and aligning a number of rectangles takes time and can be boring. The Graph Paper tool turns this task into a simple matter of clicking and dragging, like drawing a rectangle. You can specify any number of rows and columns, up to 50, for the grid. Even if you don't draw graphs, don't ignore this tool. Its usefulness doesn't end with graphs. You can use it to create custom calendars or background grids for other images. Or you can place it on the guidelines layer to assist in precision alignment of other objects (see Figure 1-41).

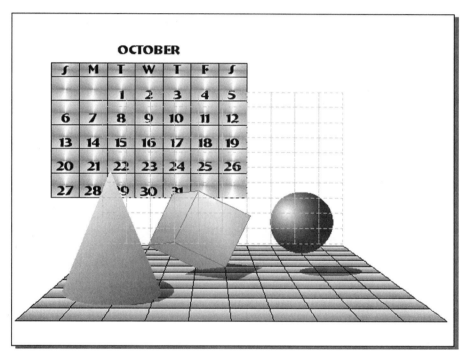

Figure 1-41: Grids are the basis for a number of objects.

To draw with the Graph Paper tool:

1. Select the Graph Paper tool from the toolbox.

2. Click a starting point and drag diagonally away from the starting point to create the grid. Pressing Ctrl while dragging constrains the horizontal and vertical dimensions to identical measurements, resulting in a shape that resembles a square (see Figure 1-42). Pressing Shift while dragging draws the grid from the center.

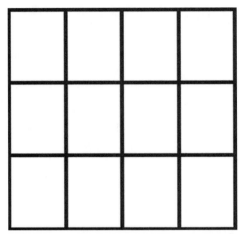

Figure 1-42: Pressing Ctrl while dragging constrains the horizontal and vertical dimensions to identical measurements, resulting in a shape that resembles a square at its perimeter.

Editing Graph Paper Objects

Grids created with the graph paper tool represent a group of objects, as opposed to a single object. They are edited in the same manner as any other group of objects.

However, some of Draw's effects can't be applied to an object group. If you want to edit the individual objects, you need to ungroup them first. (For more information about object groups, see Chapter 2.)

Specifying Geometric tool properties

You specify how you want a geometric drawing tool to behave. By changing the settings of a geometric drawing tool, you can create arcs, set the number of sides for a polygon, and specify settings for each of the tools. While each tool has settings that are unique to that tool, accessing the property settings for the tools are the same. To access the property settings for a tool:

1. Select Tools ➪ Options to display the Options dialog box.

2. Expand the General category by clicking the plus (+) beside the entry, and then expand the Toolbox category.

3. Select the tool whose settings you want to change to display the properties for that tool.

You can also access a tool's property page by right-clicking the tool and choosing Properties from the menu.

Setting ellipse properties

You can create arcs and pie wedges interactively in the drawing window by editing ellipses with the shape tool. Some drawings, however, may require a precision that's not available interactively. Draw enables you to draw these precision objects with the Ellipse tool, without the need to edit the object, by specifying ellipse properties. Tool properties are specified in the Options dialog box. Each tool has properties that are unique to that tool. You can specify starting and ending angle values for pie and wedge shapes.

Using the Ellipse property page

To specify ellipse properties:

1. Use the instruction at the beginning of this section to display the Ellipse property page (see Figure 1-43).

2. On the property page, click the radio button beside the shape you want.

3. Enter the Starting and Ending angles you desire by clicking the arrows beside the values, or by highlighting the value box and entering the angles.

4. Click OK to return to the drawing window.

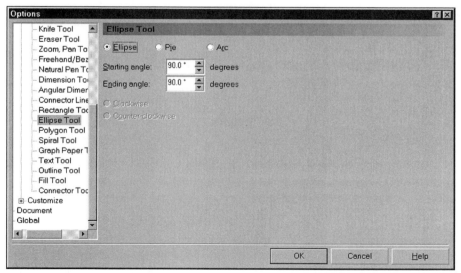

Figure 1-43: The Ellipse property page lets you choose a shape and angle for the object you want to draw.

Once you've specified the properties you want to use, you can use the Ellipse tool to draw the shape in the drawing window. The property settings that you specified in the Options dialog box remain in effect until you change them and are saved with the document.

Using the Property bar

Alternatively, you can set the angles for ellipses on the Property bar in the drawing windows. Figure 1-44 shows the angle settings for an ellipse with a 270-degree angle.

Figure 1-44: You can set the angles for ellipses, pies, and wedges on the Property bar.

Setting rectangle properties

You can create rectangles with rounded corners using two methods. With the first method, you can use the Shape tool to edit a rectangle. The second method lets you specify rounded corners on the rectangle property page. This is especially useful when you need to create a series of rectangles but need to maintain a consistent amount of roundness at the corners. The roundness is the same regardless of the size or shape of the rectangle.

Cross-Reference   For more information on using the Shape tool, see Chapter 3.

Using the Toolbox property page

To specify Rectangle tool properties:

1. Double-click the Rectangle tool to display the Toolbox property page (see Figure 1-45).

2. Click and drag the slider to adjust the roundness.

3. Click OK to return to the drawing window.

Using the Property bar

Alternatively, you can set the amount of roundness of rectangle corners on the Property bar in the drawing windows. Figure 1-46 shows the settings for a rectangle with a corner roundness of 25.

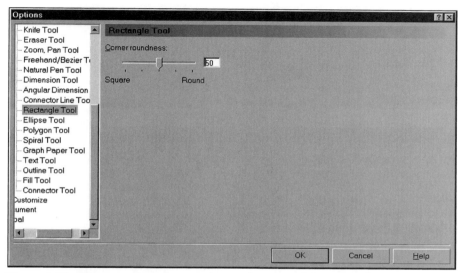

Figure 1-45: You can adjust the roundness of a rectangle's corners by setting the Rectangle tool properties.

Figure 1-46: You can specify the roundness of the corners of a rectangle on the Property bar.

Once you've specified the properties that you want to use, you can use the Rectangle tool to draw the shape in the drawing window. The property settings that you specified in the Options dialog box remain in effect until you change them.

New Feature

Once you've drawn a rectangle, Draw 9 lets you round the individual corners of a rectangle by varying amounts. The lock icon next to the corner value boxes on the Property bar determines whether corners are rounded individually or collectively. If the lock icon is in the depressed position, the corners of a rectangle are all rounded by the same amount by default. If you click the lock icon to disable it, you can choose to round one or all four corners by the same amount, or by differing amounts. This is useful if you only want to round one or two corners of a rectangle.

Setting polygon properties

Using the polygon tool, you can create a variety of multisided shapes, such as hexagons and triangles. Figure 1-47 shows just a few of the types of stars and triangles that you can create using the Polygon tool. You can change the shape and number of sides to meet your needs in the Options dialog box. The variety of shapes that you can create is nearly endless.

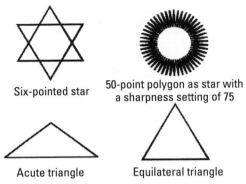

Six-pointed star   50-point polygon as star with
                        a sharpness setting of 75

Acute triangle   Equilateral triangle

Figure 1-47: Using the Polygon tool, you
can create a variety of triangles and stars
by changing the number of sides in the
Options dialog box.

Using the Polygon property page
To specify polygon properties:

1. Display the Polygon property page (see Figure 1-48).

2. Select Polygon, Star, or Polygon as Star, using these guidelines:

   - **Polygon:** Lets you create multisided figures, such as hexagons or octagons.

   - **Star:** Lets you create a star with a variable number of points.

   - **Polygon as Star:** Lets you create a star. Using this choice, you can adjust the sharpness of the angles in the star.

3. If you choose Polygon as Star, adjust the sharpness to the desired amount. As you make adjustments to the polygon property settings, the preview box on the property page changes to reflect the settings.

4. Click OK to accept the settings and to return to the drawing window.

Using the Property bar
Alternatively, you can select the Polygon tool and enter the settings on the Property bar in the drawing window. Figure 1-49 shows the settings for a six-point star with a spread of 25.

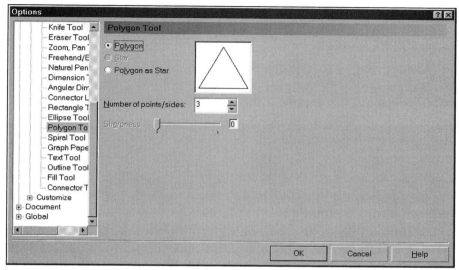

Figure 1-48: The Polygon Tool property page.

Figure 1-49: Setting polygon properties using the Property bar.

Setting spiral properties

The Spiral property page of the Options dialog box lets you choose between symmetrical and logarithmic spirals. You can also specify the number of rotations and the amount of expansion space you want between the lines. When combined with other features and effects, you can add depth to an image and create a variety of symbols.

Using the Spiral property page

1. Display the Spiral property page (see Figure 1-50).

2. Select Symmetrical or Logarithmic for the spiral type. If you choose Logarithmic, use the preview box as a guide to set the expansion to a value from 1 to 100. The lower the setting, the more the spiral will resemble a symmetrical spiral. Higher values make the lines of the spiral appear tighter together in the center.

3. Click OK to accept the settings and to return to the drawing window.

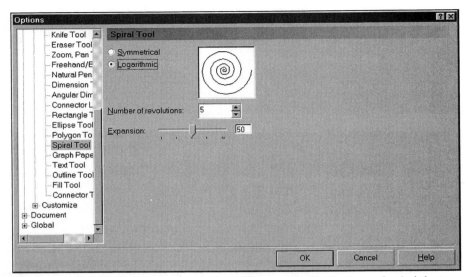

Figure 1-50: The Spiral Tool property page lets you specify the type of spiral that you want to draw.

Note

Note to math wizards: For those of you who want to know, logarithmic spirals are similar to common logarithmic curves in that they normally use a base 10 logarithmic progression to describe the system. The spiral intersects all its radiants at the same angle, and the tangent of the angle is the modulus of the system of logarithms, which the particular spiral represents. In other words, for most of us it's enough to know that Draw knows how to calculate the spiral.

Using the Property bar

Alternatively, you can select the Spiral tool and enter the settings on the Property bar in the drawing window. Figure 1-51 shows the settings for a symmetrical spiral with 10 revolutions.

Figure 1-51: Setting spiral properties using the Property bar.

Setting graph paper properties

The graph paper properties let you specify the number of horizontal and vertical cells you want in a grid. Although you can't specify a grid by measurement, you can specify the number of cells you want horizontally and vertically. The Graph Paper tool setting, like other tool settings, is made in the Options dialog box.

To specify graph paper properties:

1. Display the Graph Paper property page (see Figure 1-52).

2. Click the up or down arrow or enter a value up to 50 in the Number of cells wide box.

2. Repeat the procedure for the Number of cells high box.

3. Click OK to complete the operation and to return to the drawing window.

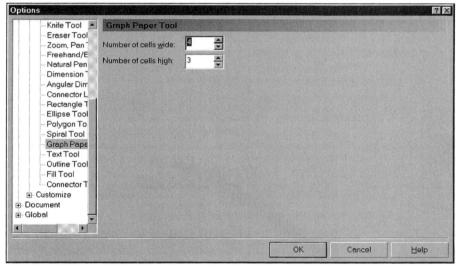

Figure 1-52: Specify the number of horizontal and vertical cells that you want to use on the Graph Paper property page.

When you select the Graph Paper tool, the Property bar in the drawing window updates to display choices available for the tool (see Figure 1-53). You can click the up or down arrows, or enter values to specify the number of horizontal or vertical cells you desire.

Figure 1-53: You can specify the settings for the Graph Paper tool on the Property bar.

Selecting and Viewing Objects

Draw provides tools for selecting objects, navigating your document, and managing the views in which you choose to display them. Selecting objects is basic to most of Draw's operation. Commands can only be applied to selections. A selection can consist of a single object, multiple objects, a group, or a child object of a group. The Pick tool is used to select objects and apply interactive transformations to a selection.

 Cross-Reference For more information about interactively transforming objects with the Pick tool, see Chapter 3.

Draw has grown to proportions that boggle the mind. With all the tools, menus, dockers, and other things that you keep on the screen, it can be hard to see the detail in a drawing. The Panning tool enhances your ability to work at a zoomed level, by letting you move easily around your drawing. Once you create a rough drawing, it's useful to be able to zoom in on parts of the drawing to edit and refine the shape of objects. Draw lets you choose from a preset zoom level or to interactively zoom in on a portion of the drawing using the Zoom tool. The View Manager lets you change the view and save different views of an image or document.

Selecting Objects

In Draw, you can select objects using the Pick tool and one of two methods: clicking the objects or marquee-selecting objects. The method you choose depends upon what you're selecting and personal preference. Clicking objects lets you select with ease individual objects that reside close to one another. Marquee-selecting objects is a good choice if you are selecting several objects that are in close proximity to one another.

 Tip When you select an object, information about that object appears on the Status bar. If you select multiple objects, the Status bar displays the number of objects selected.

By clicking them

To select objects by clicking them:

1. Select the Pick tool from the Toolbox.

2. Click an object to select it. The object appears in the drawing window with square handles around it identifying the object's bounding box (see Figure 1-54).

3. If you want to select more than one object, press Shift while clicking the objects you want to select. Selections containing multiple objects appear with handles identifying the perimeter that surrounds all the objects.

Figure 1-54: Selected objects appear in the drawing window with handles that identify their bounding perimeter.

Note You can only select objects that appear in the active drawing window. If you have a multipage document, you can't select objects from multiple pages at the same time.

Pressing Shift lets you select objects that are distant from one another, or easily select single objects that lie close together in the drawing window. When an object is selected, an X appears on the object to indicate the object's center. If multiple objects are selected, the X indicates the center of the selection.

Tip You can select objects that lie behind the topmost object by pressing Alt while making a selection. With each successive click, you move down through superimposed objects.

By using the marquee

To marquee-select objects:

1. Select the Pick tool from the Toolbox.

2. Click and drag a bounding box around the objects you want to select. As you click and drag, a dotted box appears to show you the selected area (see Figure 1-55).

Caution By default Draw treats all objects as filled, even if you have specified no fill. When marquee-selecting objects, be careful that the starting point of your selection is not over an existing object or you will move the object instead of creating a selection. You can change the way Draw treats unfilled objects in the Options dialog box (see Adding Basic Fills to Objects).

Figure 1-55: A dotted box appears around selected areas when you marquee-select objects.

Marquee selection lets you select multiple objects at once. If you want to select numerous objects in the same area of your drawing with the exception of a few objects, you may find it easier to first marquee-select the portion of the drawing containing the objects. Then you can press Shift and click the objects you don't want to deselect them.

Tip   Marquee-selecting objects can be difficult when objects are close together. Pressing Alt while making a marquee selection includes any object that you touch with the dotted bounding box in the selection.

Using the Panning and Zoom tools

The Panning and Zoom tools are part of a flyout menu of tools located in the toolbox. These tools let you isolate portions of your drawing, or move from one area of a drawing to another.

Working with the Panning tool

To use the Panning tool:

    1. Select the Panning tool from the zoom flyout menu.

    2. Click and drag the cursor in the drawing window to move the view.

The Panning tool is especially useful when you are performing detailed editing at increased zoom levels. If you want to move the view by more incremental amounts, click one of the arrows on the scroll bar to move the view in the direction you desire.

Working with the Zoom tool

To use the Zoom tool:

1. Select the interactive Zoom tool from the Zoom flyout menu.

2. Click and drag on the drawing page to surround the area you want displayed at a zoomed-in level.

If you click an object in the drawing window, Draw doubles the current zoom level. The current zoom level appears in the Toolbar near the top of the screen. When you use the Zoom tool to interactively enlarge a portion of your drawing, you can precisely control what you see in the drawing window.

Shortcut F2 toggles to the interactive Zoom tool; Shift+F2 zooms to make selected objects appear at drawing-window size; F3 returns the screen to the previous zoom level; F4 zooms to include every object on the page.

Choosing zoom levels

You can select a level of zoom, as well as use the Zoom tool interactively, with the Zoom toolbar. To display the Zoom toolbar in the drawing window, select View ➪ Toolbars to display the Toolbar dialog box. Click the box next to Zoom to enable the toolbar, and click OK to return to the drawing window. The Zoom toolbar appears in the drawing window. To hide the Zoom toolbar, deselect it in the Toolbar dialog box, or click the X in the upper right-hand corner of the Zoom toolbar.

The Zoom toolbar lets you choose the zoom level that you want. Click one of the icons to select the associated zoom level. Use Table 1-4 to help you choose a zoom level.

Setting zoom properties

The Zoom property page lets you determine the way the Zoom tool behaves and the way mouse actions affect the zoom level of your image. To specify zoom properties, select Tools ➪ Options and expand the General category. Choose the Zoom tool in the list to display the Zoom property page (see Figure 1-56).

Tip Enabling Zoom Relative to 1:1 increases the accuracy of your display. It helps ensure that objects appear in proportion to their actual shape and size at the 1:1 zoom level. To take full advantage of this option, you should take the time to calibrate the onscreen rulers as shown in the section on calibrating rulers, later in this chapter.

Table 1-4
Choosing a Zoom Level

Zoom command	Action
	Zooms in on the drawing: Choose this option to interactively select a zoom level.
	Zooms out on the drawing: Choose this option to zoom out to the previous zoom level or to a smaller view of the drawing.
	Shows the drawing at the size at which it will print: This option shows objects at their actual size, giving you an idea of what they will look like when you print the document.
	Zooms in on selected objects: Zooms to maximize the view of selected objects. If no objects are selected, the full-page zoom level is displayed.
	Zooms in on all the objects in the drawing: Zooms to include all of the objects in your drawing. If you have placed objects on the desktop, the view could get smaller, as it includes those objects as well.
	Displays the entire printable page: Zooms to maximize the view of objects that fall within the printable page. This page size is determined by the image size supported by your printer.
	Zooms in on the page width: Zooms to maximize the view determined by the width of the drawing page. Objects within your document are ignored in the calculation of this view.
	Zooms in on the page height: Zooms to maximize the view determined by the height of the drawing page. Objects within your document are ignored in the calculation of this view.
	Pans around the drawing and returns to the previous tool: This option is useful when you are working with editing tools at a zoomed-in level. The panning tool reverts to the last tool you used before selecting the panning tool.

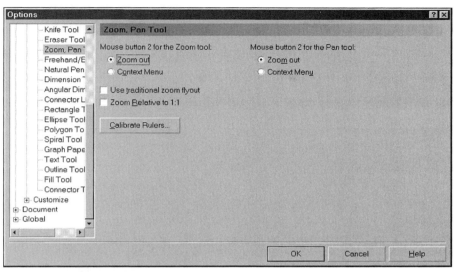

Figure 1-56: The Zoom property page.

The Use traditional zoom flyout option

Despite the increased power of Draw, in many respects the interface is streamlined in its appearance to reduce redundant displays. The Zoom flyout menu is one of the areas in which the appearance has been streamlined. Versions of Draw prior to version 7 displayed all of the zoom options in the Zoom flyout menu. The traditional zoom flyout is redundant in Draw 9. You can keep the Zoom toolbar on the screen for use if you choose, or use the Zoom Property bar to perform the same functions of the Zoom flyout menu. If you want to use the older display, enable the Use traditional zoom flyout option.

Dealing with Two- and Three-Button Mice

Draw lets you program the right button, or button 2, of your mouse. The default setting for this button activates object and document management commands. You can specify that the right mouse button causes Draw to zoom out, for example, by clicking the box next to Zoom out. I don't recommend enabling this option, however. It basically converts your mouse into a one-trick pony. I prefer to have an assortment of commands available for my use when I right-click in the drawing window or on an object. For now, leave the Default action enabled.

Draw ignores the third button, or center button, on three-button mice. Any programming available for the third or middle button is accessed through the configuration software provided by the manufacturer of the mouse, and won't generally affect the way Draw behaves.

Calibrating rulers

One of the ongoing goals of graphics software manufacturers is to achieve WYSIWYG, or What You See Is What You Get. Despite advertising claims to the contrary, no one has achieved this perfection. The number of variables involved, such as the monitor, printer, and software, make this a difficult goal to reach. However, continued efforts have resulted in dramatic improvements. The Zoom property page provides access to the ruler calibration screen. The goal when you calibrate the onscreen rulers is to make one inch onscreen look like one inch in real life. Calibrating the rulers is particularly useful if you are drawing in 1:1 Zoom mode, as it lets you work using actual-world distances as opposed to relative distances that depend on screen resolution.

Note   You need a clear plastic ruler to compare screen measurements with real-life measurements. The ruler should use the same unit of measurement as the rulers in Draw.

To calibrate the rulers:

1. Click the Calibrate Rulers button on the Zoom property page to display the ruler calibration screen (see Figure 1-57).

2. Place your plastic ruler over the onscreen horizontal ruler so that you can view both the screen measurements and the plastic ruler's measurements.

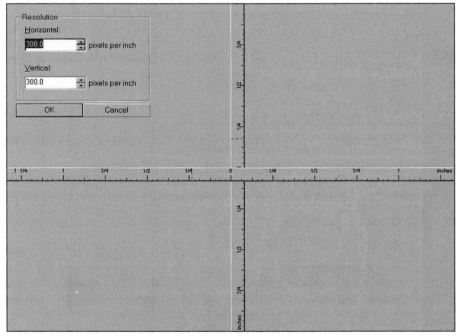

Figure 1-57: The ruler calibration screen.

3. Click the up or down arrow on the Horizontal box until one unit of measurement on the onscreen ruler matches one unit of measurement on the plastic ruler.

4. Repeat for the vertical ruler, making adjustments in the Vertical box.

5. Click OK when you are satisfied with the results.

Using the Zoom Property bar

You can choose various zoom functions using the Zoom Property bar. This is a quick way of toggling between various levels of zoom and other tools without cluttering your screen with extra toolbars. When you select the Zoom tool from the toolbox, the Property bar updates to display zoom choices (see Figure 1-58). Select the zoom function you desire.

Figure 1-58: The Zoom settings on the Property bar allow you to choose the zoom functions you desire.

Using the View Manager

If you work with graphics programs frequently, you know how much time that you spend setting and resetting various functions, such as the zoom level and view. You zoom in on a small portion of the image to edit that area and then zoom out to see how it affects the overall look. If you want to return to the small portion for additional editing, you have to reselect it. What if you want to switch between various parts of the image at a zoomed-in level? Panning works, but if you need to change the zoom level, all the zooming in and out can become tedious and time-consuming. Draw addresses that problem with the View Manager docker.

The View Manager is a great production tool that provides four tools for changing the view and offers the capability to save different views of an image or document (see Figure 1-59). You can switch to different views easily by double-clicking the view that you want. Alternatively, you can select the view you want and then click the right arrow near the top of the View Manager and choose Switch to View from the flyout menu. Draw saves the View Manager information with your document, so it's available for future Draw sessions.

Tip

You can change the way a saved view behaves by enabling or disabling the page and magnifying glass icons in the View Manager. If you disable the page icon beside a saved view, Draw reverts to the magnification level only, not the page. Similarly, if you disable the magnifying glass icon, Draw reverts to the page only, not the magnification level. Disable or enable the icons by selecting them in the View Manager.

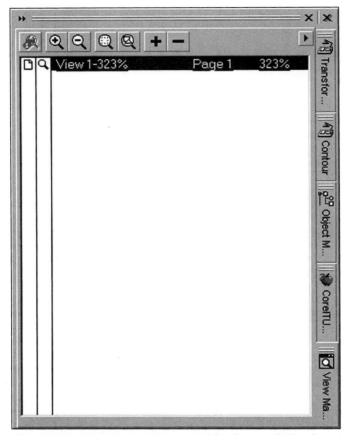

Figure 1-59: The View Manager provides four tools for changing and saving views.

Adding a view

To add a view to the View Manager:

1. Select View ➪ View Manager to display the view manager docker in the drawing window.

2. Use one of the zoom tools in the View Manager to define the view you want.

3. Click the Add Current View (+) button on the View Manager toolbar, or choose New from the flyout menu.

Ctrl+F2 displays the View Manager in the drawing window.

Renaming a view

To rename a view in the View Manager, click the name of the view that you want to rename; this changes the name to highlighted text with a bounding box and blinking cursor. Enter the new name and press the Return key or click off the name. Alternatively, you can select the name and choose Rename from the flyout menu. If you no longer need a specific view, you can easily remove it from the list.

Removing a view

To remove a view from the View Manager:

1. Select View ➪ View Manager to display the View Manager in the drawing window.

2. Click the Delete Current View button on the View Manager toolbar, or choose Delete from the flyout menu.

Using the Onscreen Color Palette

To this point, you haven't applied a fill to any of the objects in a document. Draw provides you with a variety of fills and methods for applying fills. Each of the various fills and application methods has unique properties that recommend it for a specific use. One of Draw's best attributes is that it lets you change your mind. You can change fills until you find the fill you want. If you are creating a document for multiple types of output, you can apply unique fills to different versions of an image to meet the output requirements while retaining the same design. The simplest method of applying a fill is interactively, using the onscreen color palette.

Cross-Reference   More information about fills appears in Chapter 12.

Interactively applying a fill and outline color

When you apply fills interactively using the onscreen color palette, you apply the fills directly to the object on the screen, without using a dialog box. The onscreen color palette allows you to apply uniform fills to your objects. Uniform fills are solid color fills. Uniform fills are ideal for text and other simple objects. By default, the palette displayed is the custom palette. You can change the palette by selecting View ➪ Color Palette and choosing a palette from the flyout menu. They also display well on the Internet.

To apply a uniform fill and outline color:

1. Using the Ellipse tool, draw a circle in the drawing window. The object appears selected in the drawing window.

2. Click a color from the onscreen color palette to apply that color as a fill. Right-click a second color to apply that color as the outline color.

3. Select the Pick tool, and click anywhere away from the circle to deselect the circle.

4. Click and drag another color from the onscreen color palette onto the circle and release the mouse button. The object is filled with the color you selected.

Dragging a color onto an object changes the color swatch. As you pass over an outline, the swatch turns into a hollow border of the color you selected. If you release the mouse button while the swatch has this appearance, the color of the outline changes. If the swatch is solid, the color of the fill changes.

Note   When you first draw an object, the object is selected, even if the active tool is not the Pick tool. You can apply a uniform fill without changing tools. This is useful if you want to draw another object with the same tool.

Manipulating the color palette

If you select the X at the left of the onscreen color palette, the object appears without a fill. Objects that lie below an active object that has no fill are visible. If you don't see the color you want to use displayed in the onscreen color palette, click the right arrow at the right side of the palette to scroll through the colors. Alternatively, you can click the up arrow to expand the palette (see Figure 1-60). Once you select a color from the expanded palette, the color palette collapses to its original position.

Figure 1-60: You can use the onscreen color palette to quickly apply a fill or outline color to objects in your drawing.

On the CD-ROM   Practice tutorials using color palettes are included on the companion CD-ROM to expand your experience using Draw's basic tools.

Summary

This chapter was devoted to providing an overview of Draw's basic elements and tools. While these are not the most exciting topics about Draw, it's important to have a basic grasp of where things are located and how they work. In this chapter, you explored:

✦ Creating new documents and opening existing drawings

✦ Saving your documents

✦ Closing and exiting Draw

✦ Navigating the drawing window

✦ Working with menus, dialog boxes, and toolbars

✦ Accessing tools in the Toolbox and flyout menus

✦ Getting help

✦ Planning ahead

✦ Selecting objects

✦ Using the Zoom and Panning tools

✦ Creating basic lines and shapes

✦ Applying uniform fills and outlines using the onscreen color palette

When you have a program the size of Draw, it's easy to forget where to find features, effects, commands, and options. The Exploring the Menu Bar section of this chapter provided an ongoing quick reference to the contents of the menus. In Chapter 2, you work more with objects to transform and arrange them on the drawing page.

✦   ✦   ✦

Manipulating Objects

One of my hobbies is to create *trash* sculptures out of the
dead computer parts I tend to generate. Regardless of
the odometer reading on the parts or how I organize, arrange,
and manipulate the pieces, you can still recognize the parts
for what they are. Computer parts, and indeed the world, have
a commonality. Very little is an amorphous entity. Beneath
nearly every structure is a framework or skeleton that defines
its fundamental shape. When you transform an object, you
don't actually change the basic shape of the object. A skewed
rectangle, for example, is still a rectangle. By transforming,
modifying, and arranging shapes and text in the drawing
window, you can create documents for any purpose.

Learning What Draw Can Do

Transforming and organizing objects in your documents is
basic to creating any drawing. You determine the position,
orientation, and size of the selected objects by:

- ✦ Positioning objects in the drawing window
- ✦ Rotating objects
- ✦ Skewing objects
- ✦ Mirroring objects
- ✦ Scaling objects
- ✦ Sizing objects

Draw provides three methods of transforming selected objects
in your drawings. You can transform objects interactively in
the drawing window using the Pick and Shape tools. If you
need to apply a precision transformation, you can specify
transformations using the Transform docker or the Property
bar. Transformed objects retain their basic properties. This
means that geometric objects are still considered geometric
objects, which restricts the amount of editing that you can

perform using the Shape tool. If you want to perform more extensive editing to modify the shape of an object, you need to convert it to a curve object first.

Positioning Objects on the Drawing Page

You can move a selection interactively using either the position view of the Transform docker or the Property bar. Each method offers different options and a varying degree of precision. For example, although you can constrain the movement of objects when interactively positioning them, constraining the movement of objects lacks the precision required by some images. The position view of the Transform docker includes this feature as well, but also lets you move objects a precise distance, modify an object's anchor point, and move a copy of the object. The Property bar lets you position a selection relative to the page.

Interactively moving objects

The easiest and least precise method of positioning objects is to select them using the Pick tool and then drag them to a new location. If you want to constrain the movement of an object to a horizontal or vertical movement, press Ctrl while dragging the object. Interactively placing selections on the page is useful for creating quick layout ideas. You can move the objects into their final position later, or perhaps interactive placement is all the precision you need.

 Tip

If you press the plus (+) key while dragging a selection to a new location, a copy of the selection is left behind in the original location. You can also right-click and drag an object in your document. When you release the mouse button, a menu appears. Select Copy from the menu to place a duplicate of the object at the new location.

Pick Tool Tips

The Pick tool has *digger* capabilities, making it easier to select objects that are hidden behind other objects. Pressing Alt while clicking objects lets you *dig* your way to the object that you want to select. When you click a group, this feature doesn't select a child object within the group, but it will select objects that lie below the group. If you want to use the digger feature to select a child object within a group, press Alt+Ctrl while clicking an object within a group. If you press Alt while marquee-selecting objects, Draw selects *all* of the objects the bounding box touches, not just those that it surrounds completely.

You can use any of the drawing tools as a *pick* tool to reposition an object immediately after drawing it. When you move the active drawing tool over the center X of a selected object, the cursor becomes a four-way arrow. When the cursor changes to the arrow, click and drag to move the object.

Moving objects with precision

Draw records the position of objects in your drawing based on their relationship to the 0,0 coordinates in the drawing window. The default location of this position is the bottom-left corner of your drawing page. Using the position view of the Transform docker, you can reposition objects with accuracy. When you select an object with the Pick tool, its relative position appears in the object position boxes on the Transform docker (see Figure 2-1). The position shown represents the center point of the selection. To reposition the selection, click the up and down arrows or enter new coordinates for the object's center point.

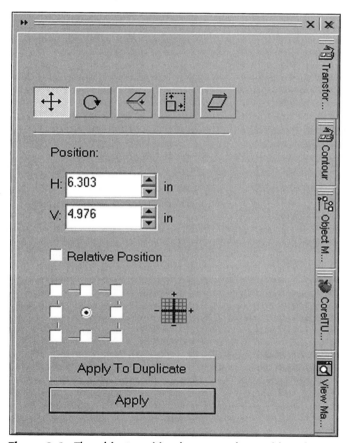

Figure 2-1: The object position boxes on the position view of the Transform docker show the coordinates for the center of a selection.

The position view of the Transform docker lets you move objects relative to the origin coordinates (0,0) of your drawing. You can also move objects relative to their current location and alter the anchor point of an object. The anchor point of an object is the point that remains stationary when you transform an object. The default anchor point of an object is its center of rotation, but you can designate any of the object's handles to serve as the anchor point.

Shortcut

Alt+F7 accesses the position view of the Transform docker.

Positioning objects relative to origin coordinates

To reposition an object relative to origin coordinates:

1. Using the Pick tool, select the object or objects to move.
2. Select View ➪ Dockers ➪ Transform ➪ Position to display the position view of the Transform docker (see Figure 2-1).
3. Disable Relative Position, if it's enabled.
4. Enter new coordinates in the Horizontal and Vertical entry boxes.
5. Click Apply to move the object. You can move a duplicate of the object, rather than the object itself, by clicking Apply To Duplicate.

The selected object moves to the new coordinates that you specified. Note that all movement is relative to the object's anchor point, which by default is the center of the object. If you move the anchor point, the alignment of the object to the coordinates will change accordingly.

Note

Draw's Property bar is interactive. The tool and selection determine the view you see of the Property bar. Controls on the Property bar also let you position a selection with precision by entering new values in the Position boxes.

Positioning objects relative to current location

To move an object relative to its current location:

1. Enable Relative Position in the position view of the Transform docker.
2. Enter the distance you want the object to move in the Horizontal and Vertical entry boxes.
3. Click Apply or Apply To Duplicate to complete the action.

Moving an object's anchor point

You can choose an object's anchor point using the anchor point control on the position view of the Transform docker. The eight checkboxes on this control represent the handles on the object's selection box. The button in the middle represents the object's center of rotation and the default anchor point.

When you change an object's anchor point, it moves in relationship to the new anchor point. For example, in Figure 2-2, the anchor point is changed to the upper-right handle of the object, and Apply to Duplicate is selected. Because Relative Position is enabled, Draw automatically draws the new object directly adjacent to the existing object. If you disable Relative Position, Draw aligns the anchor point with the coordinates you enter.

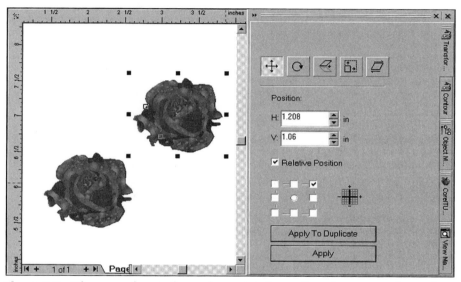

Figure 2-2: When you change the anchor point, Draw aligns the new anchor point at the location that you specify.

Clicking and dragging an object

The quickest way to move an object is to click and drag it to a new location. Remember that objects have an invisible bounding box that defines their shape. The bounding box encloses more than just the selection, however; it also encompasses any handles associated with nodes, which may extend beyond the object itself. This can make it difficult to position an object with accuracy. You can correct this problem by specifying that Draw show the object itself while you are moving it, as described in the following section.

Displaying objects during movement

When you display an object while moving it, the object's outline appears in blue, defining its shape (see Figure 2-3). The capability of displaying the object during movement is invaluable when the object has an irregular shape.

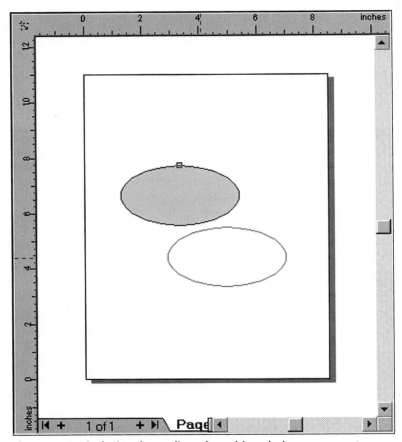

Figure 2-3: Displaying the outline of an object during movement makes it easier to position the object on the page.

To display objects during movement:

1. Select Tools ➪ Options and expand the General and Toolbox categories by clicking the plus (+) sign beside their names.

2. Choose the Pick tool from the list box to display the Pick tool page (see Figure 2-4).

3. Enable Redraw complex objects under the Moving and transforming heading. When Draw displays an object during movement, the object appears as a dotted outline with no fill.

4. The Delay box lets you specify the amount of delay in seconds that you want to apply. The value you specify here is the amount of time Draw waits before

displaying the object. The default value is 0.5 seconds, which is adequate for most purposes.

5. Click OK to return to the drawing window.

Note

Redrawing complex objects stresses video memory. Time lapses greater than 1 second are less resource intensive than lower values.

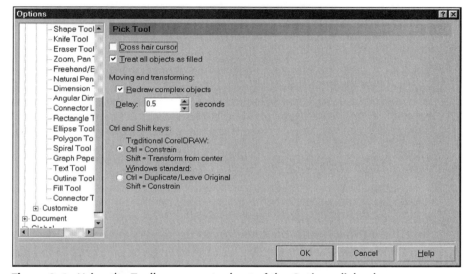

Figure 2-4: Using the Toolbox property sheet of the Options dialog box, you can specify that Draw display objects during interactive movement.

Using the Snap To feature

The Redraw complex objects under the Moving and transforming heading is useful when Draw's Snap To features are enabled. It allows you to view the object in relationship to other Draw elements, such as objects and grids, when you are moving it. Using this option, however, requires extra memory.

Using Nudge and Super Nudge

Nudge and Super nudge let you move objects and nodes in incremental amounts using the cursor (arrow) keys on your keyboard. Settings you specify in the Options dialog box determine the amount of movement (see Figure 2-5). Although you can specify any value between 0.001 inches and 600 inches, the nudge features are most helpful when you are editing an image and need to move an object or node a tiny amount. The nudge features are also useful when you want to quickly move a series of objects a specific distance.

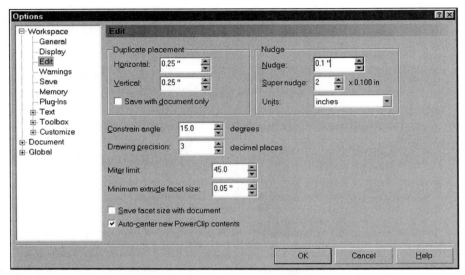

Figure 2-5: You can specify a Nudge and Super nudge value on the Edit property sheet of the Options dialog box.

To specify a Nudge and Super nudge value:

1. Select Tools ➪ Options and expand the Workspace category by clicking the plus (+) sign beside their names. Click Edit to display the Edit page of the Options dialog box.

2. The default value specified in the Nudge box is 0.1 inches. To change the nudge amount, click the up and down arrows, or enter a new value in the Nudge box.

3. The Super nudge amount is determined by the value specified in the Nudge box multiplied by the factor specified in the Super nudge box. The default factor is set at 2. You can specify any factor from 2 to 100.

Once nudge values are set, you can move any selection the specified distance by pressing a cursor (arrow) key on your keyboard. The direction the object moves is determined by the cursor key you press. The object moves one increment each time you press the key. If you want to apply Super nudge to the object, press Ctrl while pressing the cursor key.

Transforming Objects

Precision transformation lets you perform changes that meet exacting requirements. One advantage of precision transformation is that you can quickly apply the same transformation to several objects in your drawing, providing a consistent appearance. A few basics apply to all transformations:

✦ You can apply transformations to the selected object or a duplicate.

✦ Draw uses the anchor point to calculate transformations that affect the orientation of an object.

✦ Transformations, with the exception of positioning, can be reverted to return objects to their original appearance.

Rotating, skewing, and resizing interactively

If not perfect, I'd like to believe that I'm minimally good at what I do, and that I function on an even keel. The reality is that sometimes my life, and my drawings, tend to list a bit to port. Interactive skewing, rotating, and resizing was designed for people like me who need to straighten pictures on walls and transform objects in drawings. The capability of skewing objects can also add depth to the objects in your image. In the following exercises, you interactively rotate, skew, and resize an object. We then discuss rotating and skewing objects with precision.

The file for the following exercise is located on the companion CD-ROM in the exercise\ch02 folder.

Rotating objects interactively

To rotate an object interactively:

1. Open transform1.cdr.

2. Using the Pick tool, double-click the object in the document to display the rotation and skewing handles (see Figure 2-6).

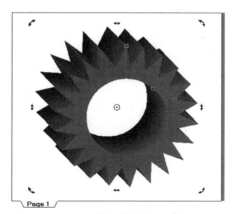

Figure 2-6: Double-click the object to select it and change the handles to the rotation and skew handles.

3. Press Ctrl and click and drag one of the corner handles counterclockwise. Rotate the object till it snaps twice to a 30-degree rotation. As you rotate, the book appears as a blue outline to provide a visual guide making it easier to orient the object (see Figure 2-7).

4. Release the mouse button and then Ctrl to complete the rotation. The object appears at the new angle (see Figure 2-8).

Note   Pressing Ctrl forces the rotation to increments of 15 degrees. This is the default constraint value. For more information about specifying a constraint value see "Setting Constrain Values" in the following sidebar.

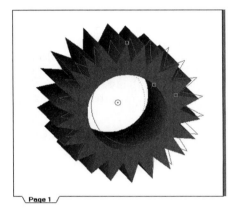

Figure 2-7: As you rotate the object, it appears as a blue outline to assist you in determining the new orientation.

Setting Constrain Values

Many of Draw's tools and functions can be constrained by pressing Ctrl while performing the operation. The default value is 15 degrees. If you want, you can modify that amount on the General property sheet of the Options dialog box.

To change the constrain angle, select Tools ⇨ Options and then expand the Workspace category by clicking the plus (+) sign beside their names. Select Edit to display the Edit options page. Click the up and down arrows or enter a new value in the Constrain Angle box. Click OK to complete the operation and to return to the drawing window.

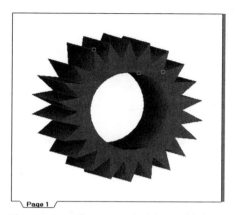

Figure 2-8: The rotated object with its new orientation.

If you interactively rotate an object without pressing Ctrl, you can quickly set the object at any angle you desire. Pressing Ctrl offers a certain amount of precision in the way objects rotate.

Skewing objects interactively

Skewing distorts objects by allowing you to slant a selection horizontally or vertically. The result can make objects appear to recede from the viewer, giving them a feeling of depth. You can also use skewing to slant text that has no italic equivalent or to give objects a feeling of motion or speed.

To skew an object interactively:

1. Using the Pick tool, double-click the object to select it and display the rotation and skewing handles.

2. Click and drag the top handle to the left to skew the object about 10 degrees. As you drag the handle, the object appears as an outline (see Figure 2-9).

3. Release the mouse button to finish skewing the object (see Figure 2-10).

Note   When skewing extruded objects, the objects can appear distorted. You can correct the distortion by resizing the object to appear flatter. Select the extrusion group and then click the down arrow next to VP locked to object on the property bar. Select VP locked to page. Changing the way the viewpoint behaves lets you control the final appearance of the extruded object. (For more information about extruded objects, see Chapter 13.)

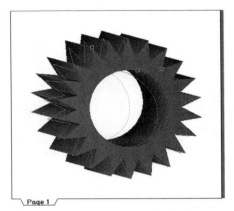

Figure 2-9: As you interactively skew an object, the object is hinted as a blue outline.

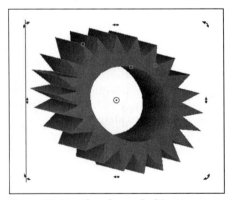

Figure 2-10: The skewed object appears in the drawing window.

Resizing objects interactively

To interactively resize an object:

New Feature Draw 9's new Free Transform tool lets you quickly and interactively transform objects in your drawing. For information about using the Free Transform tool, see Chapter 5.

1. Using the Pick tool, click the object to change the handles to scaling and sizing handles.

2. Click and drag the bottom handle upward to reduce the size of the object to about two-thirds of the original size, and release the mouse button. The object looks better, but probably seems to be a bit thick.

3. Using the Pick tool, drag the object downward slightly while pressing Ctrl. Because the Viewpoint is locked to the page, this action adjusts the thickness of the object (see Figure 2-11).

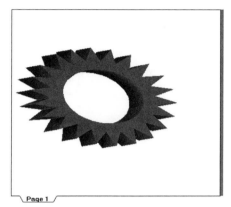

Page 1

Figure 2-11: Resize and move the object to reduce the distortion and adjust the thickness.

Tip

Transforming objects interactively is great if you need to make quick or slight adjustments to an object. If your document requires more precision, use the Transform docker to make the changes to your objects. (See the section later in this chapter on sizing and stretching an object with precision.)

Rotating objects with precision

The rotation view of the Transform docker lets you specify the amount of rotation you want and how you want an object to rotate. By default, Draw rotates objects around the center of rotation. You can also rotate objects around specific ruler coordinates, or around a point relative to the object.

Shortcut

Ctrl+F8 accesses the rotate view of the Transform docker.

Transforming objects around the center of rotation

To rotate objects around the center of rotation or an anchor point:

1. Using the Pick tool, select the object to rotate.

2. Select Arrange ➪ Transform ➪ Rotate, or View ➪ Dockers ➪ Transform ➪ Rotate, to display the rotate view of the Transform docker (see Figure 2-12).

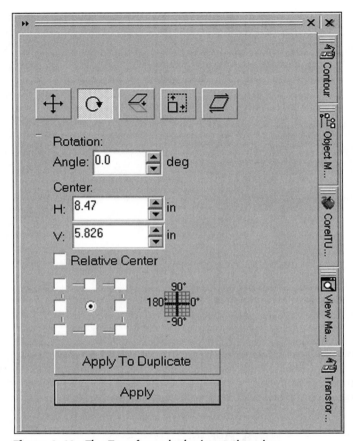

Figure 2-12: The Transform docker's rotation view.

3. Change the anchor point, if desired.

4. Click the up and down arrows to enter the number of degrees you want to rotate the object. Alternatively, you can highlight the value and enter a new value. Positive values rotate the object counterclockwise; negative values rotate the object clockwise.

5. Click Apply or Apply To Duplicate.

You can select multiple objects, if you want, by pressing Shift while making the selection or by marquee-selecting the objects. When you select multiple objects, each object rotates independently around its center of rotation. If you want the selected objects to rotate around a common anchor point, group the objects first (see "Grouping Objects" later in this chapter).

Around ruler coordinates

When you display the rotate view of the Transform docker, it displays the coordinates associated with the center of rotation for that object. If you select multiple objects, Draw locates the center of the selection for you. You can change the coordinates so objects rotate around a specific location in your drawing.

Rotating an object around ruler coordinates:

1. Select the object to rotate and display the rotate view of the Transform docker.

2. Click the up and down arrows to enter new coordinates for the center of rotation associated with your object. Alternatively, highlight the values in the boxes and enter new values.

3. Enter a degree of rotation by clicking the up and down arrows or by highlighting the value and entering a new value. Positive values rotate the object counterclockwise; negative values rotate the object clockwise.

4. Click Apply or Apply To Duplicate.

Transforming objects relative to current location

Relative rotation lets you rotate an object around a specific location relative to the current center of rotation. For example, you could rotate an object around a point 1-inch horizontally and –4-inches vertically distant from the current center of rotation associated with the object (see Figure 2-13).

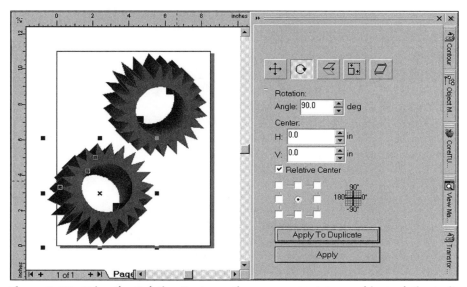

Figure 2-13: Using the Relative Center option, you can rotate an object relative to its current location. The duplicate object was rotated 90 degrees around a point 1-inch horizontally and –4-inches vertically from the original.

To rotate an object relative to its current location:

1. Select the object to rotate and display the rotate view of the Transform docker.

2. Click Relative Center to enable it.

3. Click the up and down arrows in the Horizontal and Vertical boxes to select a center point for the rotation.

4. Enter a degree of rotation by clicking the up and down arrows or by highlighting the value and entering a new value. Positive values rotate the object counterclockwise; negative values rotate the object clockwise.

5. Click Apply or Apply To Duplicate.

Tip
You can also rotate selections with precision by entering values on the Property bar. Select the object and click again to display the interactive rotation handles. The Property bar changes to reflect the selection. Enter a value in the rotation setting box and press Enter. The object rotates the desired amount. Positive values rotate the object clockwise; negative values rotate the object counterclockwise.

Skewing objects with precision

When you skew an object, you apply a slant to the object. Skewing is useful for giving objects a feeling of depth or speed (see Figure 2-14). You can also skew artistic text to give it an italicized appearance, when the typeface doesn't have an italic style. (You cannot skew objects using settings on the Property bar.)

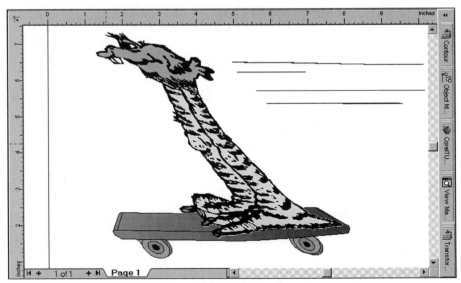

Figure 2-14: Skewing an object can add a feeling of depth or speed.

Shortcut

Alt+F11 accesses the skew view of the Transform docker.

Using the Transform docker

To skew an object using the skew view of the Transform docker:

1. Using the Pick tool, select the object to skew.

2. Select Arrange ⇨ Transform ⇨ Skew, or View ⇨ Dockers ⇨ Transform ⇨ Skew, to display the skew view of the Transform docker (see Figure 2-15).

3. Click the up and down arrows to select the number of degrees that you want to horizontally skew the object. Alternatively, you can highlight the value in the Horizontal box and enter a new value. A positive value skews the object to the left; a negative value skews the object to the right.

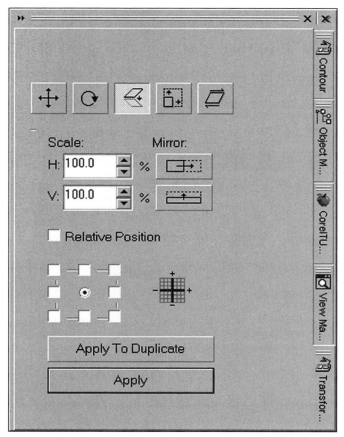

Figure 2-15: The Transform docker's skew view.

4. Click the up and down arrows to select the number of degrees that you want to vertically skew the object. Alternatively, you can highlight the value in the Vertical box and enter a new value. A positive value skews the left side of the object down; a negative value skews the left side of the object up.

5. By default, Draw uses the center of rotation to skew objects. If you want to change the point from which the object is skewed, click an anchor point.

6. Click Apply or Apply To Duplicate.

Changing the anchor point

Changing the anchor point changes the whole appearance of an image when you rotate and skew objects. Figure 2-16 shows the same ellipse rotated and skewed. Note the difference between the position of the ellipse when the anchor is set at the default center anchor versus when it is set at the upper left-hand corner of the object. By adjusting the anchor point of objects, you can create some really great effects, especially when the transformation is applied to a duplicate object.

Tip

If you want to change the anchor point of an object interactively, double-click the object to display the center of rotation. Click and drag the center to a new location. Pressing Ctrl while moving the center of rotation causes it to snap to corner or side handles of the object. If you want to move the center of rotation to another object in your drawing, select Layout ➪ Snap To Objects. Then when you drag the center of rotation to a new location, it will automatically snap to other objects in your drawing.

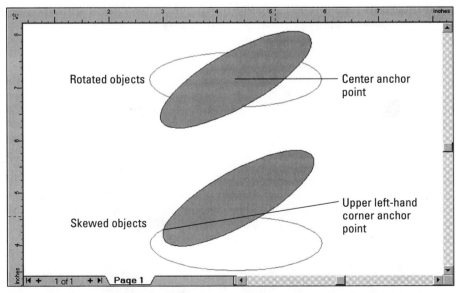

Figure 2-16: By changing the anchor point of objects, you can adjust the position and appearance of the object or effect.

Undoing Transformations

Although you can apply Undo to most actions in Draw, it's useful at times to be able to revert to a different view of an object without reverting the entire document. Draw lets you clear transformations applied to an object, whether the transformations were applied interactively, via the property bar, or using the Transform docker.

When you clear an object's transformations, you clear all of the transformations that have been applied to that object. Position transformations, however, can't be cleared. To clear an object's transformations, select Arrange ⇨ Clear Transformations. The object reverts to its original appearance.

Mirroring objects

Mirroring objects lets you reverse their appearance horizontally, vertically, or both by flipping the object. For example, if you mirror an artistic text string horizontally, the text appears reversed. Similarly, if you mirrored the text vertically, the text appears upside down (see Figure 2-17). Draw lets you apply mirroring effects interactively or by using the mirror view of the Transform docker.

Figure 2-17: Mirrored text appears upside down.

Shortcut   Alt+F9 accesses the scale and mirror view of the Transform docker.

Mirroring interactively

To mirror objects interactively:

1. Using one of the pen tools, draw an object. The type and size of the object doesn't matter, but for the purposes of this exercise, you might want to keep it small.

2. Using the Pick tool, click the right side-handle of the object and drag it to the left of the left handle. The image flips horizontally and moves to a position directly to the left of the original bounding box.

Note Pressing Ctrl while interactively mirroring an object constrains the size of the mirrored object to 100-percent increments of the original size.

Interactive mirroring is a quick way to flip graphics. Using this method you can flip objects horizontally, vertically, or both. Interactively mirroring a duplicate of an object is an easy way to quickly tile symmetrical objects. When you mirror duplicate objects using this method, the position changes to abut the bounding box of the original object.

Tip When transforming an object, pressing the plus (+) before releasing the mouse button automatically applies the transformation to a duplicate of the original object.

Using the Transform docker

To mirror an object using the Transform docker:

1. Using the Pick tool, select the object to mirror.
2. Select Arrange ➪ Transform ➪ Scale and Mirror, or View ➪ Dockers ➪ Transform ➪ Scale and Mirror, to display the scale and mirror view of the Transform docker (see Figure 2-18).
3. Click the Horizontal mirror button if you want to mirror the selected object horizontally.

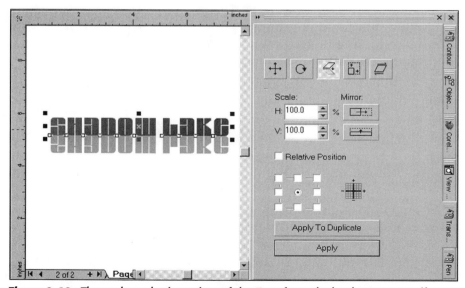

Figure 2-18: The scale and mirror view of the Transform docker lets you specify how your object is to be mirrored.

4. Click the Vertical mirror button if you want to mirror the selected object vertically.

5. If you don't want to use the default anchor point, click a new anchor point. Symmetrical objects don't appear to change or move if the center anchor point is selected.

6. Click Apply or Apply To Duplicate.

While you can change the anchor point of an object, using the scale and mirror view of the Transform Docker lets you retain the position of the object when you apply mirroring. When you interactively mirror an object, the ending position always changes.

Using the Property bar

You can also quickly mirror objects using the mirror controls on the Property bar. Select the objects to mirror with the Pick tool and click one of the mirror buttons. Small blue arrows on the mirror buttons indicate whether the mirroring action is vertical or horizontal.

Scaling objects

Draw's capability to scale graphics lets you create an image at one size and scale the graphic to work with other elements in your drawing. You can choose to scale objects either interactively in the drawing window or by using the scale and mirror view of the Transform docker. Draw lets you choose how you want to scale an object. You can scale it horizontally, vertically, or proportionally.

Scaling interactively

When you interactively stretch or scale objects, the scaling lacks the precision possible with the scale and mirror view of the Transform docker. To stretch or scale objects interactively, simply click and drag any of the selection's handles. If you press Shift while dragging a handle, the object scales toward the center of the selection; if you press Ctrl, the scaling is constrained to increments of 100 percent. For example: If you scaled an object 2×2 inches by dragging a corner handle outward while pressing Ctrl and Shift, the object would snap to an initial size of 4×4 inches.

Scaling with the Transform docker

Using the Transform docker, objects are scaled using a percentage factor of the current size. For example, if you scale an object 200 percent horizontally and vertically, the object doubles in size. Similarly, if you scaled the object 50 percent in both dimensions, the object would become half the original size. If you choose proportional scaling, the aspect ratio of the object is maintained during the scaling operation. By selecting an anchor point, you can specify the direction from which the object is scaled. By default, the anchor point is set at the center of the object and the object is scaled from the center. If you choose another anchor point, Draw uses that as the reference to scale the object.

To scale an object using the scale and mirror view of the Transform docker:

1. Using the Pick tool, select the object to scale.

2. Select Arrange ➪ Transform ➪ Scale and Mirror, or View ➪ Dockers ➪ Transform ➪ Scale and Mirror, to display the scale and mirror view of the Transform docker.

3. Click the up and down arrows to select a percentage in the Horizontal scaling box by which you want to horizontally scale the object. Alternatively, highlight the value in the box and enter a new value.

4. Click the up and down arrows to select a percentage in the Vertical scaling box by which you want to vertically scale the object. Alternatively, highlight the value and enter a new value.

5. Enable Proportional if you want Draw to maintain the aspect ratio. Note that if you select this option, you only need to change the value in either the horizontal or vertical scaling box.

6. If you don't want to use the default anchor point, click a new anchor point. Symmetrical objects don't appear to move if the center anchor point is selected.

7. Click Apply or Apply To Duplicate.

Scaling with the Property bar

The Property bar also contains controls that allow you to scale objects in your drawing with precision. Using the Pick tool, select the objects to scale and enter the scaling percentages that you want to use in the scaling boxes. Press Enter to complete the operation.

Maintaining Outline Proportions When Resizing Objects

Draw doesn't automatically resize the outline width with an object when the object is sized, stretched, or scaled. If you want the outline to be resized in proportion to size changes you apply to a selected object, enable Scale with image in the Outline dialog box.

To access the Outline Pen dialog box, right-click the object and select Properties from the right mouse button menu. Click the property tab and enable Scale with image. Alternatively, you can select the Outline Pen dialog box icon from the Outline tool flyout menu, or press F12 on your keyboard.

Sizing and stretching objects with precision

Sizing objects is similar to the scaling command. Both commands resize the selected object. They differ in that scaling uses a percentage or ratio to resize an object. Sizing uses specific measured values to alter the size of the object. You can size an object horizontally, vertically, or maintain the aspect ratio to resize an object equally. Draw lets you size objects using the size view of the Transform docker. The ability to size objects with precision is useful when creating a technical drawing with specific size requirements.

Shortcut

Alt+F10 accesses the size view of the Transform docker.

For most purposes, resizing objects interactively is sufficient. (See the earlier section in this chapter on interactive resizing.) However, if your drawing requires precision, it's easier to resize objects using the size view of the Transform docker. To size or stretch an object using the size view of the Transform docker:

1. Using the Pick tool, select the object to size or stretch.

2. Select Arrange ⇨ Transform ⇨ Size, or View ⇨ Dockers ⇨ Transform ⇨ Size, to display the size view of the Transform Docker (see Figure 2-19).

3. Click the up and down arrows to select a percentage in the Horizontal size box by which you want to horizontally size or stretch the object. Alternatively, highlight the value in the box and enter a new value.

4. Click the up and down arrows to select a percentage in the Vertical size box by which you want to vertically size or stretch the object. Alternatively, highlight the value and enter a new value.

5. If you are stretching the objects, disable Proportional.

6. Enable Proportional if you are sizing the object and you want Draw to maintain the aspect ratio. Note that if you select this option, you only need to change the value in either the horizontal or vertical size box.

7. If you don't want to use the default anchor point, click a new anchor point. Symmetrical objects don't appear to move if the center anchor point is selected.

8. Click Apply or Apply To Duplicate.

On the
CD-ROM

Practice tutorials are included on the companion CD-ROM to expand your experience transforming objects.

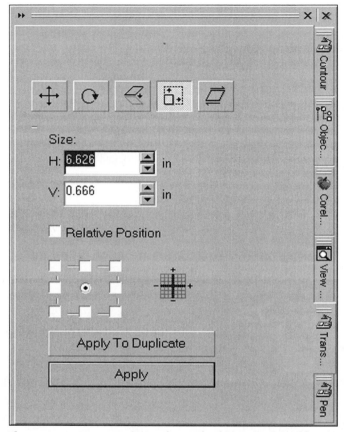

Figure 2-19: You can size and stretch objects by using the size and stretch view of the Transform docker.

When interactively transforming an object, you can use Draw's snap-to features to make sizing proportional to other objects easier.

Cross-Reference For more information on working with objects in layers and using Draw's snap-to features, see Chapter 7.

Using Align and Distribute

A document that has a well-balanced appearance is attractive and helps the viewer to understand the contents more easily. The key to creating a balanced drawing or document is to organize the objects on the drawing page. Draw provides a variety of tools for organizing your document and its contents. Two of these tools, Align and Distribute, enable the precision placement of objects in relation to one another and to the drawing page. The Align feature lets you line up objects based on either their center points or edges, or on the way you want them positioned in your drawing. The Distribute feature lets you specify the spacing between objects and determine their arrangement in relation to the range of the selection or the drawing page. The range of a selection refers to the invisible outside boundaries of the area enclosing all of the selected objects. The range of the page refers to the printable area of the page. The lines and text elements in the employment application shown in Figure 2-20 were aligned and distributed evenly using the Distribute feature.

Draw lets you further refine the position of objects by providing the tools to align and distribute objects in relationship to other objects and the page. The Align and Distribute dialog box is used to align and distribute objects with precision.

Aligning objects to other objects

Aligning objects with one another and with the drawing page is important in any drawing. The settings on the Align property sheet of the Align and Distribute dialog box let you specify how and where you want objects to line up on the drawing page.

Ctrl+A accesses the Align and Distribute dialog box.

Quality Airconditioning

Em ploym ent Application

Plea se Print

Name _____ Social Security # _____

Address _____ Phone _____

_____

Position Desired _____ Sab ry Desired _____

_____

Figure 2-20: The Align and Distribute features let you align objects and distribute them evenly on the drawing page.

To align objects:

1. Using the Pick tool, select the objects to align. How objects align is determined by the order in which the objects are selected. Draw uses the last object selected to determine the alignment. Objects are aligned to the last object selected.

2. Select Arrange ➪ Align and Distribute to display the Align and Distribute dialog box. Alternatively, click the Align button on the Property bar. Click the Align tab to display the Align property sheet.

3. Click Top, Center, or Bottom to specify how you want objects to align horizontally. If you don't want to align objects horizontally, skip this step (see Figure 2-21).

4. Click Left, Center, or Right to specify how you want objects to align vertically. If you don't want to align objects vertically, skip this step.

5. To choose where objects are to align, do one of the following:

   • If you want Draw to use the target object (the last object selected) to determine the alignment, click OK.

   • If you want Draw to use the drawing page as the alignment guide, choose Edge of Page or Center of Page and click OK.

   • If you want Draw to use the grid as the alignment guide, choose Align to Grid.

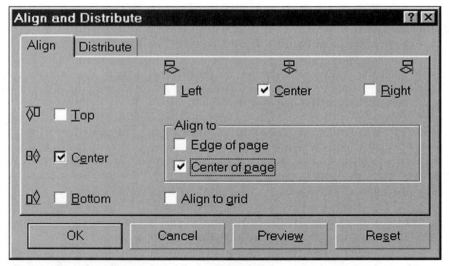

Figure 2-21: The Align and Distribute dialog box lets you determine how objects will appear in relationship to one another and the page.

6. If you want to see how the alignment choices you've made will affect your image, click Preview. You may need to move the dialog box to the side of the drawing window to view the entire drawing page.

7. Click OK to complete the operation and return to the drawing window.

Aligning objects to the center of the page

Sometimes it's useful to align a single object or group of objects to the center of the page. This feature is especially useful as a last step before printing your document, because it lets you check the page and ensure that all the objects are within the printable area of the page.

To align individual objects or a group of objects to the center of the page:

1. If you want to align your entire image to the center of the page, select all the objects in your drawing and group them.

2. With the group or individual object selected, choose Arrange ➪ Align and Distribute. Click the Align tab to display the Align property sheet if it's not already displayed.

3. Choose Center of Page and click OK. Draw automatically chooses the Center options for both the horizontal and vertical alignment. If you only want to align your selection in one direction, disable the other option before clicking OK.

Distributing objects

Draw's distribute feature lets you space objects evenly in your document. Whether the objects are as simple as several strings of artistic text, or as complex as an entire flow chart, the capability to space objects evenly on the drawing page gives your image a balanced appearance. You can choose to distribute objects over the range of the entire drawing page or the range of the selection. If you choose the range of the selection, Draw bases the spacing on the total area of the bounding boxes associated with the selected objects.

To distribute objects:

1. Using the Pick tool, select the objects to distribute.

2. Select Arrange ➪ Align and Distribute to display the Align and Distribute dialog box. Alternatively, click the Align button on the Property bar. Click the Distribute tab to display the Distribute property sheet (see Figure 2-22).

3. Click Left, Center, Spacing, or Right to specify how you want objects to align horizontally. If you don't want to distribute objects horizontally, skip this step. Use the small thumbnails beside the options to help you choose the option to use.

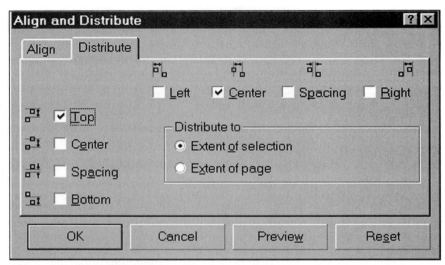

Figure 2-22: Choose distribution options on the Distribute property sheet of the Align and Distribute dialog box.

4. Click Top, Center, Spacing, or Bottom to specify how you want objects to align vertically. If you don't want to distribute objects vertically, skip this step. Use the small thumbnails beside the options to help you choose the option to use.

5. To choose the area over which you want to distribute the objects, click Extent of Selection or Extent of Page.

6. If you want to see how the distribution choices you've made will affect your image, click Preview. You may need to move the dialog box to the side of the drawing window to view the entire drawing page.

7. Click OK to complete the operation and return to the drawing window.

Tip Most of Draw's dialog boxes now include a Preview button. Click this button if you want to see a preview of how the settings you specify will affect your drawing.

Defining the distribution area

The key to distributing objects is to define the area over which you want to distribute the objects before applying the Distribute command. To specify the area, reposition the objects to define the area you want to use. Then apply the Distribute command, using Extent of Selection to define the area. Remember that Draw uses the bounding boxes of the objects, not the objects themselves, to calculate the spacing of your objects.

Editing Elements in Your Document

Draw offers several of the editing commands that are common to many Windows-based programs. These editing commands don't change an object. The commands let you manage the objects themselves. The editing commands can roughly be grouped by function. Undo, Redo, and Repeat affect commands that you have applied to a selection in your document. Duplicate, Clone, and Delete let you create and remove objects from your drawings. Copy, Cut, and Paste let you use the Microsoft Windows clipboard for temporary storage and retrieval of selections in your documents.

Using Undo, Redo, and Repeat

When I was first learning to use Draw, I don't believe there was a single command I used as much as Undo. It was goof insurance. I constantly try out effects, trying to get the perfect look. With Undo and Redo, I can try multistep effects, knowing that I can always back up if the effect is not exactly what I want. In addition to using Undo and Redo for correcting mistakes, you can use these commands to flip through several looks to decide which you like best. Undo causes Draw to restore the appearance of your image to that preceding the most recent command or action. Redo undoes the Undo command, restoring the appearance of the image prior to applying Undo. You can apply Redo as many times as you apply Undo. For example, if you apply the Undo command three times, you can apply the Redo command three times, regardless of the number of levels that you specified for Undo and Redo. Repeat lets you apply the same effect more than once to a selection or several selections.

Shortcut Ctrl+Z or Alt+Backspace applies the Undo command. Ctrl+Shift+Z applies the Redo command.

Applying Undo and Redo

To apply Undo and Redo:

1. To apply Undo, select Edit ⇨ Undo or right-click the object and select Undo from the right mouse button menu.

2. To apply Redo, select Edit ⇨ Redo. Your image returns to the view prior to applying Undo. For Redo to work, it must directly follow the Undo command.

Undoing and redoing multiple actions

You can Undo and Redo multiple actions all at once, using the Undo and Redo list buttons on the standard toolbar (see Figure 2-23). The Undo and Redo lists display the most recent actions you performed in your image. The number of actions displayed is determined by the number of levels of Undo specified in the Options dialog box. Draw lets you select the point at which you want to undo a given action and subsequent actions. You can't undo Open, New, or Save commands. Undo levels are reset when you close Draw. In Draw 9, Undo is now durable. What that means is that you can complete an action, save the file, and still be able to undo actions that occurred prior to saving the file. You can't undo operations performed during a previous Draw session.

Choosing an action from the Undo list undoes not only that action but also all the actions you performed after it. Similarly, choosing an action from the Redo list performs that action and all the actions that preceded it. Depending upon how many actions Draw has to perform, it may take a several minutes to complete the operation.

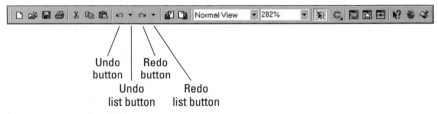

Figure 2-23: The Undo and Redo list buttons display the most recently performed actions.

Setting levels of Undo and Redo

Draw permits up to 99 levels of Undo and Redo. The default setting specifies 99 levels; however, this number should be reduced (see Caution below). You can increase or decrease the number in the Options dialog box. To change the number of levels of Undo and Redo:

1. Select Tools ⇨ Options and expand the Workspace category by clicking the plus (+) sign beside their names. Click General to display the General page view of the Options dialog box (see Figure 2-24).

2. Click the up and down arrows in the Undo box to specify a new value, or highlight the number and enter a new value. You can specify different values for Draw objects and bitmap effects. These values are independent and one does not affect the other.

Caution

It might seem that you'd want to specify the most levels of Undo and Redo that are possible, especially if you are just learning to use Draw. I don't recommend it, though. For each level of Undo and Redo, Draw creates a temporary file of your image. It stores the temporary file in the location you specified for temporary files when you installed the program. If you have limited hard drive space, excess levels of Undo and Redo cause a problem. Set the maximum number of levels to a value with which you are comfortable. If you are new to Draw, I suggest you set the number of levels to 7 or 8 and then reduce them, as you become more proficient with Draw.

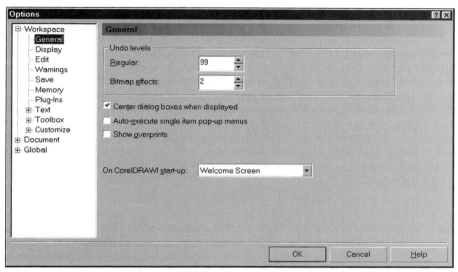

Figure 2-24: The General page of the Options dialog box allows you to specify the number of levels of Undo and Redo.

Using Repeat

Repeat is a useful command if you want to reapply the same effect or action to one or more objects. Suppose you apply a custom fountain fill to an object and then immediately want to apply the same fill to several other objects. You can select the objects and use the Repeat command to apply the fill to the other objects by selecting Edit ➪ Repeat. Repeat cannot be used, however, with certain special effects such as Extrude.

Shortcut

Ctrl+R applies the Repeat command.

To repeat an action:

1. Using the rectangle tool, draw two rectangles in the drawing window.

2. Using the Pick tool, move one of the rectangles.

3. Select the other rectangle with the Pick tool.

4. Select Edit ➪ Repeat. Note that the second rectangle moves the same distance and direction as the first rectangle.

Note

You can only repeat actions when the Pick tool is active. You cannot repeat actions performed on individual nodes in an object.

Working with Duplicate, Clone, and Delete

Duplicate and Clone are similar commands in that they both create a copy of a selection and place it directly in the drawing window without the use of the Windows clipboard. They differ in the way the copy behaves, however. When you duplicate a selection, you create an exact copy of the selected object. The copy is an independent object, so if you edit the original object, the copy is not affected. On the other hand, when you clone an object, you not only create an exact copy of the selected object, but you also establish a relationship between the original object and the copy. The original object becomes the master object, and the copy is referred to as a clone. Most changes that you make to the master object are mirrored in the clone. Delete lets you quickly remove a selection permanently from your document.

Tip   You can quickly create a duplicate of a selection by pressing the plus (+) key on the keypad. This action, unlike the duplicate command, superimposes the copy directly over the original object.

Duplicating objects

When you create a duplicate of an object, Draw places the duplicate on top of the original object. By default, Draw offsets the duplicate 0.25 inches up and to the right of the original object (see Figure 2-25). You can change the amount of the offset in the Options dialog box, as shown later in "Modifying the offset for duplicated and cloned objects."

Shortcut   Ctrl+D applies the Duplicate command.

To duplicate an object:

1. Using the Pick tool, select the object or objects to duplicate.

2. Select Edit ⇨ Duplicate. Draw places the duplicates in your drawing.

Draw's capability to create duplicates of objects provides a *safety* feature by letting you try "what if" effects on the duplicate object without risking your original. If you don't like the effect you're trying, you can simply delete the duplicate instead of waiting for Undo to revert the object. Sometimes I find it convenient to use this method to create several versions of an object for comparison. When I decide which effect I like the best, I delete the other versions of the object.

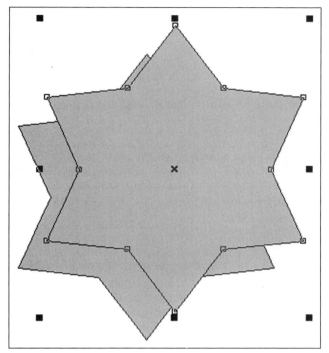

Figure 2-25: By default, Draw places duplicate objects 0.25 inches up and to the right of the original object.

Cloning an object

When creating a clone object, it's important to remember some basics about the way clone objects behave. Cloned objects can be edited independently of the master object if you choose. Once you edit an attribute of a cloned object, the master object no longer controls that attribute. For example, if you changed the fill of a cloned object, any fill changes that you made afterward to the master object would not be mirrored in the cloned object. The master object (see Figure 2-26) would still control other attributes and transformations, such as rotation. If you make changes to a clone and later decide to revert the changes to match the attributes and transformations of the master, right-click on the clone and choose Revert to Master from the right mouse button menu. Select the master attributes and transformations that you want the clone to reassume. The clone's attributes revert to those of the master object.

To clone an object:

1. Select the object to clone.

2. Select Edit ➪ Clone. Draw places the cloned object 0.25 inches up and to the right of the original object.

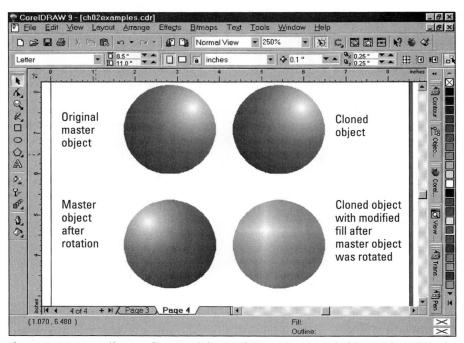

Figure 2-26: Even if you edit one of the attributes of a cloned object, other shared attributes between a master and cloned object remain active and are controlled by the master object.

3. Reselect the master object and change its fill. Note that the fill changes for the cloned object as well.

4. Select the cloned object and change the fill and then reselect the master object and change its fill. The fill of the cloned object no longer changes when you change the fill of the master object.

5. If you move the master object, the cloned object does not move. Click the master object again to display the transformation handles.

6. Click and drag a corner handle to rotate the master object. The cloned object rotates by the same amount.

Locating masters and linked clones

As drawings become more complex and the number of elements increase, it's useful to be able to find specific objects. You can easily locate masters and their linked clones by right-clicking a master or clone. If you right-click a master object and choose Select Clones from the right mouse button menu, clones linked to that master object are selected. Similarly, if you right-click a clone and choose Select Master, the master associated with that clone is selected (see Figure 2-27).

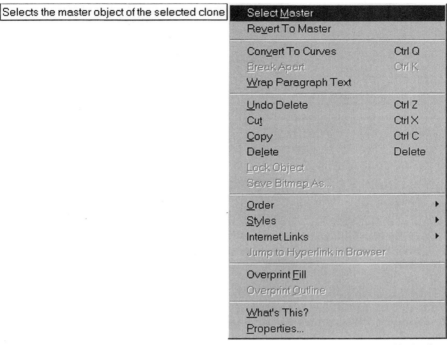

Figure 2-27: Choosing Select Master from the pop-up menu lets you quickly find the master associated with clone objects.

Tip   Some special effects, such as Blend, Extrude, and Contour, aren't mirrored in cloned objects unless they are applied prior to cloning the object. Other special effects, such as Perspective and Envelope, are mirrored in the cloned object, whether they are applied to the master object before or after cloning. (For more information about special effects and cloning, see Chapter 13.)

Modifying the offset for duplicated and cloned objects

Draw lets you specify the placement of duplicated and cloned objects. Using this feature, you can quickly place objects to create repeating patterns or space objects that require specific spacing. For example, if you need to place horizontal lines half an inch apart on a business form, you can specify 0 inches for the horizontal placement and ½ inch for the vertical placement of duplicate objects. After drawing a single line, the Duplicate command places successive duplicates precisely ½ inch apart on the drawing page (see Figure 2-28). The objects are perfectly aligned vertically.

To adjust the placement of duplicates and clones:

1. Select Tools ⇨ Options and then expand the General and Toolbox categories by clicking the plus (+) sign beside their names. Choose Edit to display the Edit page of the Options dialog box.

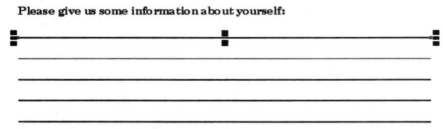

Figure 2-28: By setting the placement of duplicates and clones, you can ensure precise placement of duplicates and clones in your document.

2. Click the up and down arrow on the Horizontal and Vertical placement boxes to adjust the amount of offset. Alternatively, you can highlight the value in the boxes and enter a new value.

3. Click Save with Document Only if you want to use the settings you make with only the current document.

You can also change the horizontal and vertical offset on the Property bar by deselecting all the objects in your drawing and entering new values in the duplicate distance box. You can use the arrows to adjust the value or highlight the value in the Property bar and enter a new value. Either press Enter or click in the drawing window to activate the new settings.

Deleting objects

Most of the images I create are reasonably complex images. I often find it convenient to create or place objects in my drawing either for reference or to use as guides for sizing and positioning other objects. When I'm finished with the objects, I remove them from the drawing. Unlike many paint packages, Draw makes it easy to delete objects without affecting other objects in your image. To delete an object from your drawing, use the Pick tool to select the object. Once you've made the selection, choose Edit ➪ Delete, or press Delete on your keyboard. If you delete an object by accident, you can apply Undo to bring the object back, as long as you specified sufficient levels of Undo.

Working with Cut, Copy, and Paste

Draw offers three methods for creating copies of objects in your documents: the Duplicate command, the Clone command, and using the Windows clipboard. You can use the Windows clipboard to temporarily hold and move information from one Windows application to another. You can also use the clipboard to copy objects between Draw documents and within a single Draw document. When you use the clipboard, you place a copy of an object or objects there for later use. The objects remain on the clipboard until you replace them. If you close Draw with objects still remaining on the clipboard, Draw asks whether you want to leave the objects there for use in another application. If you click Yes, the objects remain there and can be pasted into other Windows-compliant applications. If you choose No, the objects are removed from the clipboard and memory.

Note The Windows clipboard also plays an important role in object linking and embedding (OLE) between documents and applications. (For more information about OLE, see Chapter 8.)

Copying objects to the clipboard

The clipboard is similar to the desktop area of the drawing window. Both serve as containers to hold objects for later use. Unlike the contents of the desktop area, however, the contents of the clipboard aren't saved with your drawing. When you copy an object to the clipboard, the original object remains in your drawing. The clipboard is useful for preserving the appearance of an object so that you can try "what if" actions in your original image. After placing a copy of the object on the clipboard, you can try several effects on the original object; if you don't like the results, you can then delete the original object and paste the copy back into the document. The Windows clipboard isn't controlled by the Undo settings that you specify. You can paste an object from the clipboard at any time, until you replace it with another object.

To copy selections to the clipboard:

1. Using the Pick tool, select the object or objects to copy to the clipboard.

2. Select Edit ⇨ Copy. It may take a few moments to complete the action if you have selected an extremely complex object.

Shortcut Ctrl+C or Ctrl+Insert places copies of a selection on the Windows clipboard.

Using the Cut command

The Cut command is similar to the copy command, except that it removes the object from the drawing as it places it on the clipboard. Cutting objects to the clipboard is useful when you want to remove an object temporarily while you work with other objects in your drawing but you want Draw to remember the object's original location.

To cut selections to the clipboard:

1. Using the Pick tool, select the objects to cut to the clipboard.

2. Select Edit ⇨ Cut. Draw removes the objects from the drawing and places them on the clipboard.

Shortcut Ctrl+X cuts objects to the clipboard.

Pasting objects into your drawing

Once an object is placed on the clipboard, you can paste it into your drawing or into another application. If the object was placed on the clipboard from the current document or another Draw image, Draw remembers the location of the object on the page and pastes it in the same location on the drawing page. If the object was placed on the clipboard in another application, Draw pastes the object in the center of the drawing page. Pasted objects are always placed on top of other objects in the active layer, even if the object was initially lower in the hierarchy. If the object you cut and paste is from the active document, Draw remembers its position in the hierarchy and replaces it there. This is a useful means of temporarily removing an object so that you can see objects that are underneath it.

To paste the contents of the clipboard into your document:

1. If you have a multipage document, go to the page where you want to place the contents of the clipboard.

2. Select Edit ➪ Paste. Draw places the object on the drawing page.

Shortcut

Ctrl+V or Shift+Insert pastes the contents of the clipboard into your document.

Arranging Objects

Arranging objects in relationship to one another is one of the key advantages of using a vector program such as Draw to create drawings and other documents. Draw lets you group objects, which means that they retain their physical location in relationship to other objects in the group. Once objects are grouped, they can be moved and transformed as a unit, or you can select individual objects within the group to edit. Draw also lets you lock objects in your drawings. Locked objects can't be selected or modified.

Locking objects

Have you ever created a portion of an image and wanted to freeze it, making it inaccessible to editing? Draw users have been requesting this feature for a long time. You can now lock objects in your drawing, letting you *freeze* portions of your image. This means that they can't be accidentally moved or modified in any way. The Lock command is located on the Arrange menu. You can lock an object by selecting it and clicking the command. Alternatively, you can right-click the object and choose Lock from the right mouse button menu. You can unlock objects by right-clicking on the object and selecting Unlock, or by choosing Unlock or Unlock All from the Arrange menu.

Note You cannot lock clones or clone master objects.

Using the Group and Ungroup commands

The Group command creates an ordered array of selected objects. The resulting group of objects behaves as a single unit when you move them or when you otherwise apply transformation commands. If you transform a group of objects, each object within the group is transformed, but each maintains its spatial relationship to other objects within the group. Grouped objects behave as a single object in the hierarchy of your drawing; their internal order is frozen. If you move a group of objects to another layer or otherwise change their hierarchy within your drawing, they move as a unit (see Figure 2-29). For example, single objects can be placed above or below a group of objects, but can't be placed between objects within a group, unless they are part of that group.

Each object in the group retains its individual attributes, although you can apply new attributes to the group as a whole. The Group command is useful when you want to apply formatting or other properties and actions, such as resizing, to all the objects in the group. Draw also lets you edit the individual objects within a group without ungrouping the objects. You can have as many objects in a group as you wish. You can also create a nest of groups, or groups within groups.

Grouping objects

Groups are composed of a selection of two or more objects of any type. For example, you could have a draw object, a bitmap, and text in a single group. When you select a group, the status bar displays information about the group, such as the number of objects it includes. If the group is a nested group, the status bar displays the number of subgroups within the group. The order in which objects appear in a group is determined by their order in your drawing. More information about grouping and layers appears later in this section.

Caution Grouping objects can cause some unexpected results. Draw changes the order of grouped objects so that they appear sequentially, from back to front. This can cause some objects to appear in a different order than they held previously, so that they hide other objects or are hidden themselves. The objects in the group assume the order of the last object selected in the hierarchy of your drawing. In other words, if you select an object that appears near the back of a drawing, and then an object in the front, the back object will move to the front behind the last object you selected. The back object may hide any other objects. To avoid layering problems, try to group objects that appear sequentially according to the hierarchy of your drawing. The Object Manager serves as a visual guide to the hierarchy of your drawing and can help you select objects for grouping. (More information about the Object Manager appears in Chapter 7.)

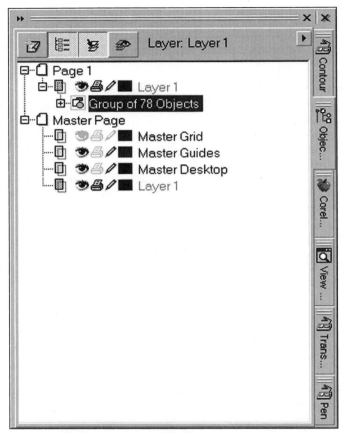

Figure 2-29: The Object Manager displays the hierarchy of grouped objects and their relationship to the rest of your drawing.

To group objects:

1. Using the Pick tool, select the objects to group. If you are selecting a large number of objects, consider marquee-selecting an entire area and then pressing Shift and clicking to deselect the objects that you don't want to include in the group.

2. Select Arrange ⇨ Group. The selected objects form a single unit and appear sequentially in your drawing. The status bar and Object Manager display the results of the action. Alternatively, you can click the Group button on the Property bar.

Ctrl+G groups selected objects.

Locking grouped objects in place

Grouping objects is one way to mentally declare them *complete*, because it locks the physical relationship between objects in the group. If this isn't sufficient, you can apply the lock command to a group of objects, as you would a single object. In addition to maintaining the physical relationship between objects, grouping lets you perform actions on the group as a whole. Sometimes it's convenient to group a selection of objects and then apply a transformation such as rotation to the group as a whole. Transformation commands use the center of the group as the default center point or anchor. This guarantees that the objects maintain their relationship after the transformation is applied.

Creating a nested group

Only your resources limit the number of nested groups that you can create. Nested groups require more memory than individual objects do to refresh and display them, but for most purposes you should not experience memory difficulties with any nest of groups. Complexity issues can, however, affect printing.

For more information about image complexity and printing, see Chapter 16.

To create a nested group:

1. Using the Pick tool, select the groups to include in the nested group. You can also include individual objects in a nested group.

2. Select Arrange ➪ Group. Alternatively, you can click the Group button on the Property bar. The status bar and the Object Manager reflect the group structure.

Nested groups are similar in hierarchy to the neighborhood in which you live. Your house is one of a group of homes in the neighborhood. The neighborhood is a subgroup of the city, county, state, and so forth. Nesting groups can help you keep the elements of your image organized, and makes replacing an element easier. For example, if you are creating a document such as a catalogue, you might want to create subgroups that identify the details of each product in a product line. If a single product changes, you can simply replace the subgroup representing that product without disturbing the rest of your document. In addition, using this method to group objects lets you ensure that all of the related elements are changed at the same time, without leaving stray objects behind.

Ungrouping objects

The Ungroup command separates selected groups into their individual objects. If you apply Ungroup to a nested group, the command separates the nested group into its subsets of groups and objects. You can apply Ungroup repeatedly to the subsets to break the groups down further, until you are left with the individual objects. If you want to ungroup all the individual objects in a nested group, Draw lets you perform the action in a single step by using the Ungroup All command.

Shortcut   Ctrl+U ungroups a group of objects.

To ungroup objects:

1. Using the Pick tool, select the group or nested group to separate into its individual elements.

2. Select Arrange ⇨ Ungroup to separate a group into its individual objects.

3. Select Arrange ⇨ Ungroup All to completely break a nested group into its individual objects.

Alternatively, you can click the Ungroup or Ungroup All button on the Property bar to ungroup single or nested groups.

Grouping and Layers

When objects are grouped, the selected objects are ordered in relationship to the last object that was selected. In other words, they assume the order of the last object selected so that they behave as a single element in the hierarchy of your drawing. Objects that appeared between the selected objects before the selected objects were grouped are then placed behind or in front of the group, depending on the hierarchy of the last object selected. You can change the hierarchy of grouped objects in your drawing using either the Order command or the Object Manager. You can't change the hierarchy of individual objects within a group unless you first ungroup the objects.

Editing child objects

Individual objects within a group are referred to as child objects. Draw lets you edit child objects within a group. This is useful if you want to change attributes such as the fill or the outline of a grouped object. To change a child object, you must first select it to make it temporarily independent from the group.

To select and edit a child object:

1. Using the Pick tool, click the object to edit while pressing Ctrl. When you release Ctrl and the mouse button, Draw displays round handles around the child object, indicating that the object is selected. If you inadvertently select more than one object, or if you select a subset of a nested group, press Ctrl again and click the desired object until only that object is selected.

2. You can then edit the object. Clicking again on the object displays the transformation handles, which let you interactively transform the object. Once a child object is selected, you can use the Shape tool to edit the nodes or otherwise reshape the object.

Once a child object is selected, you can move it to modify its physical relationship to other objects. You can also change attributes such as the fill or outline of the object. You can't, however, move a child object up or down in the hierarchy of the group.

Summary

Mastering the basics of manipulating objects within your drawing is an important part of an organized approach to creating documents. As objects are added to your drawing, you can modify the objects and use Draw's wide variety of organization tools to assemble your drawing. These tools let you transform, edit, and determine the relationship between objects in your drawings. In this chapter, you learned to:

✦ Use the Pick tool to interactively position and transform objects in your drawing

✦ Perform precision placement and transformations using the Transform dockers and the Property bar

✦ Use the Undo, Redo, and Repeat commands

✦ Cut, copy, and paste objects in your drawings

✦ Duplicate, clone, and delete

✦ Maintain the relationship between objects using the Group command

✦ Prevent alteration of individual objects and groups by using the Lock command

✦ Work with child objects

✦　　✦　　✦

Using the Shape Tool

◆　　◆　　◆　　◆

In This Chapter

Editing geometric
objects

Modifying objects
with the Shape tool

Using the Node Edit
docker and the
Property bar

◆　　◆　　◆　　◆

Paths, nodes, and line segments define the skeletal
structure of any object. Unlike transforming objects
interactively with the Pick tool, the Shape tool is used to
modify the shape of objects. The type of object determines
the way in which the Shape tool can modify the shape of the
object. You can modify curve objects in a freeform style,
changing portions of the object, while leaving the rest of the
object unchanged. Geometric objects, such as rectangles,
ellipses, and polygons, are constrained to mirror editing that
maintains their symmetry. As you change one portion of a
geometric object, the rest of the object is modified to *reflect*
the change.

Editing Geometric Objects

Draw's geometric objects — ellipses, rectangles, and
polygons — are not considered curve objects. Their vector
descriptions are based upon precise geometry rather than
upon points. The Shape tool performs differently with
rectangles and ellipses than it does with other objects.
Geometric shapes have nodes and line segments, but don't
have control points. You can use the Shape tool to round the
corners of a rectangle, create arcs and wedges from an ellipse,
or modify the geometry of a polygon. Draw lets you create
geometric objects with these effects when you are drawing the
object. If you discover that you need these effects later in the
drawing session, it's useful to be able to edit existing objects,
rather than having to redraw them. Geometric objects edited
in this manner still retain their shape attributes.

Note   If you need to modify a geometric object more extensively,
you will have to convert it to a curve object (see the sidebar later in this chapter on converting geometric objects to
curves). Except for applying the Undo command, converting a geometric object to a curve object is a one-way street.
You can't convert it back to a geometric object. Once an

object is converted to a curve object, you can't perform the standard editing that you could before the object was converted.

Creating arcs and wedges

At the top of every ellipse is a control node. Using the Shape tool, you can click and drag this control node to create arcs and wedges (see Figure 3-1). If you create an arc or wedge from an ellipse, the object is still an ellipse. The exterior dimensions of the modified ellipse are still the same as those of the full ellipse before editing.

To create an arc or wedge from an ellipse:

1. Select the Shape tool and click the ellipse to select it and to display the control node at the top of the ellipse.

2. Click and drag with the mouse pointer outside the ellipse to create an arc.

3. Click and drag with the mouse pointer inside the ellipse to create a wedge.

 Tip   You can quickly edit the nodes of objects with the Pick tool as well as the Shape tool. When the Pick tool is active, it temporarily functions as the Shape tool when you pass over a node on an object. Click and drag nodes to perform editing actions, as you would with the Shape tool.

The total number of degrees of the resulting angle is displayed in the status bar. If you press Ctrl while dragging the control node of an ellipse, the degree of change is constrained. The default is 15 degrees. You can modify this setting in the Options dialog box.

Cross-Reference   For information on modifying the settings in the Options dialog box, see Chapter 2.

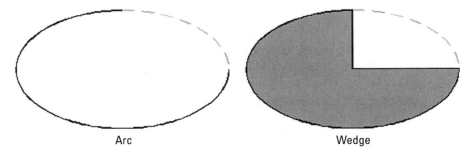

Arc   Wedge

Figure 3-1: Click and drag the control node at the top of an ellipse to create an arc or wedge. The dotted line indicates the original ellipse.

Dimensions of Objects

When you select an object with the Pick tool, it's possible for the handles to appear farther away from the object than the object's visible edges. Similarly, if you move the object, you may notice that the bounding box of the object seems much larger than the object. This is because the handles and bounding box encompass both the object's visible edges and the control points that define the object.

This is also true when you create arcs and wedges. The handles and bounding boxes that define the dimensions of an arc or wedge encompass the same dimensions as those of the original ellipse. This can cause objects to not align properly when the Align command is used. It can also cause the bounding box for EPS exports to be considerably larger than the object itself. For more information about exporting objects, see Chapter 8.

Rounding the corners of a rectangle

When you select a rectangle with the Shape tool, a node appears at each corner of the rectangle. Rectangles employ mirror editing. This means that when you round one corner of a rectangle, the other three corners are rounded identically. The status bar displays the radius of the curve, giving you better control over the amount of the curve. Similar to ellipses, rectangles edited with the Shape tool are still rectangles. You can re-edit them at any time.

New Feature   You can now round corners of a rectangle independently, using settings on the property bar (see Chapter 2 for more information).

To round the corners of a rectangle:

1. Select the Shape tool and click the rectangle to select it and display its control nodes.

2. Click and drag one of the nodes away from the corner until the corners are rounded to the desired amount (see Figure 3-2).

Tip   You can create arcs and wedges and round the corners of rectangles by adjusting the settings on the Property bar.

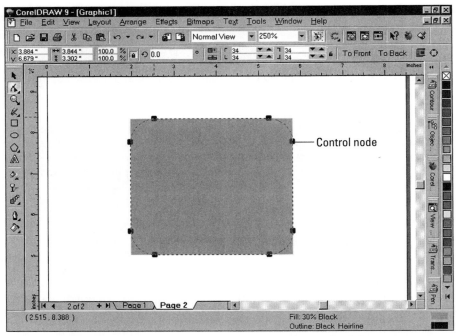

Figure 3-2: Click and drag a control node of a rectangle to round the corners.

Editing polygons and stars

Like ellipses and rectangles, Draw restricts the way polygons and stars are edited with the Shape tool. Draw confines you to these procedures when editing a polygon or star:

✦ Repositioning line segments and nodes

✦ Adding and deleting nodes

✦ Changing a line segment's attributes

✦ Changing node attributes

Polygons and stars retain their symmetry when you edit them with the Shape tool. Similar to rectangles, these shapes are restricted to mirror editing. If you need to edit a polygon or star extensively, you must covert the shape to curves.

Shortcut

You can apply the convert to curves command by pressing Ctrl+Q.

Converting Geometric Objects to Curves

As mentioned in the previous section, editing geometric objects with the Shape tool is restricted to mirror editing. To reshape one of these objects more extensively, you have to convert the object to curves. To convert an ellipse or rectangle to a curve object, select Arrange ➪ Convert to Curves, or click the convert to curves button on the Property bar.

Once a geometric object has been converted to a curve object, you can edit it as you would any other object. The Convert to Curves command can't be reversed. You can apply Undo only if you have sufficient levels of undo configured in the program to include the point at which you converted the geometric object to a curve object.

Understanding mirror editing

The nodes of an object created with the Polygon tool are linked with one another. All the corner or point nodes of a star are linked, and all of the interior nodes are linked. What this means is that if you edit a node of an object created with the Polygon tool, all of the linked nodes reflect the changes to maintain the symmetry. This type of editing is known as mirror editing.

A 5-point star has 10 nodes. Five of the nodes define the points; the other five nodes define the interior angles. If you moved one of the point nodes with the Shape tool, the other point nodes would move identically. The interior nodes would remain unaffected. In Figure 3-3, the original object is shown as a dotted line. The colored area is the edited star and shows the nodes defining the points of the star. The nodes that define the points of the star are linked together. If you edit one of them, all of the linked nodes are edited in the same fashion. Similarly, the interior nodes are linked and any editing affects them all.

If you don't want the changes you make to one node to be reflected in all the linked nodes, or if you want to edit the shape more extensively, you can convert the polygon to a curve object. Like other geometric shapes, you can't reverse this action. Once you do this, you can no longer edit the shape as a symmetrical object. You can edit it as you would any other curve object.

Moving segments and nodes

Moving segments and nodes allows you to refine the shape of a polygon. As mentioned in the previous section, nodes on objects created with the Polygon tool are linked and use mirror editing when they are manipulated with the Shape tool. In the following exercises, you create and edit a polygon.

To create and edit a polygon:

    1. Select the Polygon tool.

    2. On the Property bar, set the number of sides at five.

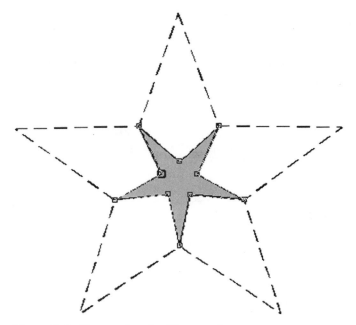

Figure 3-3: The results of editing a polygon.

3. Click and drag in the drawing window to create a pentagon. Pentagons have 10 nodes. Five of the nodes define the points of the shape; five of the nodes reside at the center of each side (see Figure 3-4).

4. Select the Shape tool.

5. Click and drag one of the side nodes, stretching the shape outward as shown in Figure 3-5. All of the side nodes and the associated line segments move in the same manner as the node that you drag. Save the resulting image on your hard disk as **poly1.cdr**.

You aren't restricted to moving the nodes outward. You can move them in any direction you desire to achieve the effect you want. You can also move the nodes using the Nudge and Super Nudge commands. These commands let you tweak your polygon if you only need a small amount of correction.

Adding and deleting nodes

When you add or delete a node from a polygon, mirror nodes are either created or deleted in the object. Open poly1.cdr if it's not already open.

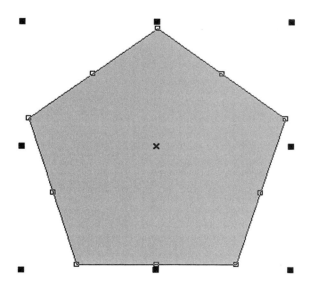

Figure 3-4: A pentagon is created with the Polygon tool.

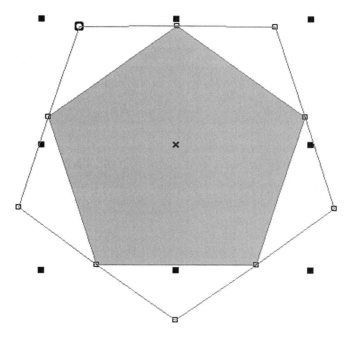

Figure 3-5: Click and drag one of the side nodes outward.

To add and delete nodes from a polygon:

1. Select the Shape tool and click one of the outside nodes to select it.

2. Press Delete. All of the outside nodes are deleted, leaving a polygon with five nodes. Alternatively, you can click the delete node button on the Property bar or Node Edit docker.

3. Select one of the remaining nodes and press the plus (+) key on your keyboard. Nodes appear halfway between each pair of nodes. Alternatively, you can click the Add Node button on the Property bar or Node Edit docker. Save the file.

Tip   Nodes that you add to a polygon are linked in the same way as other nodes in a polygon. If you edit one of the new nodes, the editing changes apply to the linked nodes as well. Using this method, you can quickly add nodes at symmetrical points on a polygon, as well as edit the nodes as a *batch*.

Modifying line segment properties

Normally, polygons have straight sides. Draw, however, lets you modify a polygon so that it has curves by changing the line segment properties.

To change the properties of line segments:

1. Open poly1.cdr if it's not already open.

2. Select the Shape tool.

3. Click a point on one of the line segments, in between the nodes, to select a line segment.

4. Click the To Curve button on the Property bar or Node Edit Docker. Control points appear from the associated node (see Figure 3-6). Although not visible, control points have been added to all of the associated line segments.

Figure 3-6: Click the To Curve button to change the line segment's properties.

5. Drag the control points outward to curve the line segment. All associated line segments curve as well, while nonassociated line segments remain the same (see Figure 3-7). Save the file.

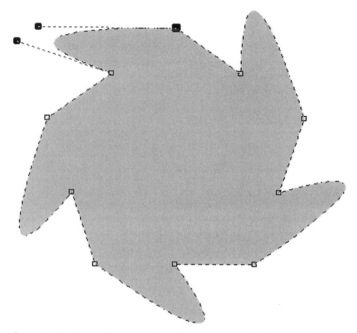

Figure 3-7: Drag the control points to curve all the associated line segments of the polygon.

Modifying node properties

You can change the node properties of a polygon to cusp, smooth, or symmetrical. To change the nodes, the associated line segments must be curved, as shown in the previous section.

To change a node's properties:

1. Open poly1.cdr if it's not already open.
2. Select the Shape tool and click one of the nodes to select it.
3. Click the cusp, smooth, or symmetrical button on the Property bar to change the node's properties. (You can only choose symmetrical if all of the line segments have been changed to curves.)
4. Click and drag the control handles of a node to see the effects of your editing. The type of property selection you make determines the effect on your object.

Modifying Objects with the Shape Tool

Curve objects drawn with the Freehand tool, Bézier tool, Spiral tool, or Natural Pen tool can be edited with the Shape tool. Text and objects created with the Rectangle, Ellipse, or Polygon tool must be converted to curves before you can alter their basic shape. In a production environment, it's frequently faster and easier to create a rough shape and then refine it by editing the object with the Shape tool. Curve objects created with the Freehand tool are rougher by nature, and generally contain more nodes than are required to define the shape. Using the Shape tool, you can delete the extra nodes to give the object a smoother appearance. A direct correlation exists between the number of nodes an object has and the file size of your finished image. Keeping the number of nodes required to a minimum reduces the file size, and increases the performance of Draw by improving the screen refresh time.

Understanding the anatomy of an object

Imagine the frame of a house. The exterior shell consists of studs, beams, trusses, and other structural components that define the shape. The interior walls are substructures of the basic shell. A curve object in Draw is similar to the frame of a house. When you create a curve object in Draw, you define the shape or frame by drawing line segments connected by nodes. Nodes are the points on a path that determine its shape. A curve object has one or more paths. The basic floor plan in Figure 3-8 is a multipath object with 34 nodes on 6 subpaths.

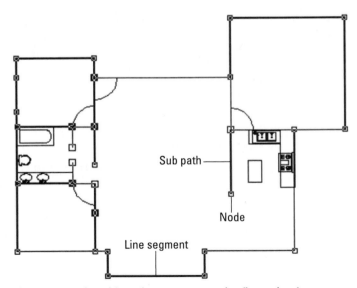

Figure 3-8: The object that represents the floor plan is a multipath object.

Refining shapes

A curve object can be any shape. In addition to line segments and nodes, curve objects have control points. These points look like handles that extend from nodes (see Figure 3-9). Control points refine the shape of a curve object. If you manipulate the nodes and control points, you change the object's shape.

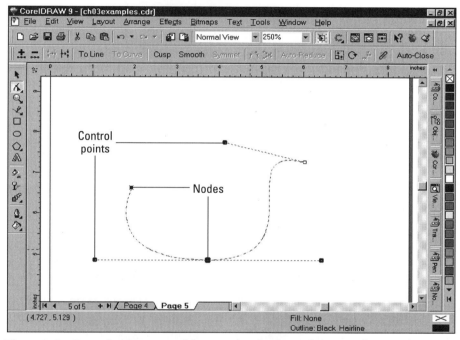

Figure 3-9: Control points extend from nodes, further refining an object's shape.

Open and closed paths

Objects in Draw can have open or closed paths (see Figure 3-10). Every path has a start point and an end point. In a closed path, the start and end points are connected to surround a specified area completely. Although you can apply a fill to an open path, the fill isn't visible. Only closed paths can have a visible fill.

Selecting nodes and segments

Before a shape can be edited, you need to select the nodes or line segments that you want to edit. When you select a node, the line segment that precedes it is also selected. Any changes that you make to that node also affect the line segment. To begin the tutorial exercises, start Draw, if it's not already running. For the sake of speed and to conserve resources, close any open documents before starting this tutorial.

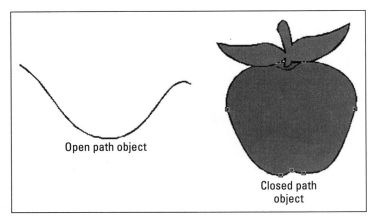

Figure 3-10: Only closed objects can have a visible fill.

In this and the next few sections, you work with boat1.cdr, which is located in the tutorial\ch03 folder on the companion CD-ROM.

To select nodes and line segments:

1. Select File ➪ Open to display the Open Drawing dialog box.

2. Select the D:\ drive (where D is your CD-ROM drive).

3. Select tutorial ➪ ch03 ➪ boat1.cdr to display the document in the file name box. Click Open to open the image in Draw (see Figure 3-11). Boat1.cdr was created using the Natural Pen tool.

4. Select the Zoom tool from the toolbox. Click and drag a bounding box around the boat hull to zoom in on that section of the image.

5. Select the Shape tool from the toolbox.

6. Click the hull of the boat with the Shape tool to make the nodes visible. If the status bar is visible, it displays information about your selection. The hull of the boat is a curve with 10 nodes.

7. Nodes are selected by clicking them with the Shape tool. Select the node at the top left of the hull (see Figure 3-12); the node changes from a hollow to solid black. The control points for a node become visible when it is selected.

8. Press Shift and click another node. When multiple nodes are selected, the control points for those nodes are not visible.

9. Click and drag a bounding box around the nodes to marquee-select all the nodes in the hull.

10. Click anywhere along the edge of the hull between the nodes. A small circle appears to indicate that you have selected a line segment (see Figure 3-13).

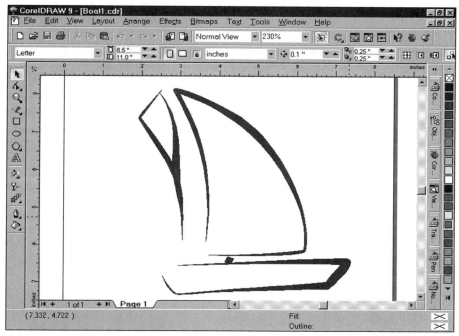

Figure 3-11: Open boat1.cdr in Draw.

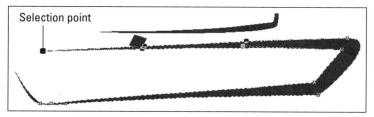

Figure 3-12: Selecting a node displays the control points associated with that node.

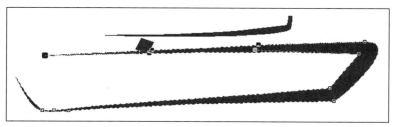

Figure 3-13: When you select a line segment, a small circle appears at the selection point.

Tip Marquee-selecting nodes is useful when you have a number of nodes that you want to edit at one time. Marquee selection also prevents the possibility of moving a node accidentally instead of selecting it. Once the nodes are selected, press Shift and click to add or remove nodes from the selection.

Moving nodes, segments, and control points

Line segments, nodes, and control points offer varying degrees of fine-tuning to a shape. Moving segments allows for crude shaping of a curve. Repositioning a node allows for finer control; moving a control point allows for minute adjustments to a curve. The way nodes, segments, and control points interact with one another is dependent upon which one you move. As you learn to use the Shape tool, you will learn to predict the way that these elements interact with one another to modify the shape of an object. If you move a node, the line segments on either side of the node are affected. The control points associated with the node, however, are not affected. They remain at the same angle extending from the node. Similarly, moving a line segment affects the control points but not the associated nodes. The nodes remain in the same position as they were prior to moving the line segment. If you move a control point, the associated line segment is affected, but the node remains in the same position.

To move nodes, line segments, and control points:

1. Open boat1.cdr if it is not already open.

2. Click and drag the bottom-left node of the mainsail to extend the shape past the end of the hull (see Figure 3-14).

3. Extending the sail makes that section of the sail appear too thin. Select the node to the right of the previous node selection. Move it up and toward the middle of the sail to thicken the bottom of the sail (see Figure 3-15).

4. Reshape the line segment to give it a more curved appearance by moving the control point upward, toward the center of the sail (see Figure 3-16).

The Pick tool can be used as a temporary *shape* tool by moving the Pick tool cursor over a node of a selected object.

In addition to moving control points and nodes, you can also move a line segment by clicking and dragging it to a new location. Using this method, you can easily make fine adjustments to objects. You might find this process easier if you zoom in on the area that you want to adjust.

You can use Draw's nudge feature to move nodes by pressing the appropriate cursor key for the direction in which you want the node to move.

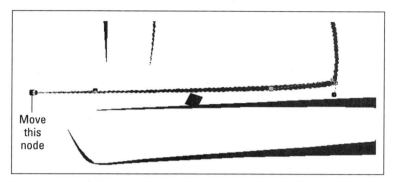

Figure 3-14: Extend the shape of the mainsail by clicking and dragging the bottom-left node.

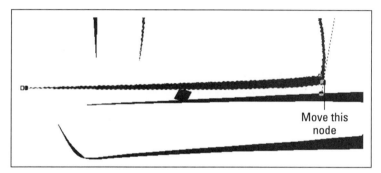

Figure 3-15: Thicken the bottom of the mainsail by moving the node up and toward the middle of the sail.

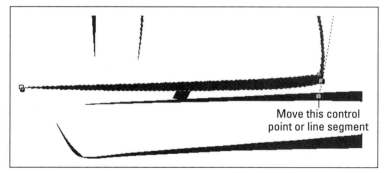

Figure 3-16: Curve the bottom of the mainsail by moving the control point.

Nodes and Control Points

A control point can lie above or below a node, making it difficult to select. If it is above the node, click and drag it to move it off the node. If it is below the node, press Shift while clicking and dragging to move the control point.

The size of nodes and control points can make it difficult to tell which is on top. You may have to try both methods to move the control point.

Adding or removing nodes and segments

Adding nodes to an object allows you to add to or further refine the shape by adding line segments. Conversely, removing nodes lets you smooth the shape, reduce the file size, or delete part of a shape. In the next exercise, you add a stripe to the sail of the boat.

To add or remove nodes and segments:

1. Open boat1.cdr if it's not already open.

2. Select the Shape tool from the toolbox.

3. Add a node on the interior line segment of the mainsail by clicking a point about halfway up the sail and pressing the plus (+) key on your keyboard. Add two more nodes on either side of the node you just added (see Figure 3-17).

4. Click and drag the center node of the three nodes you added, down and across the sail to add the stripe (See Figure 3-18).

To remove a node from an object, select the node and press Delete. Removing a node sometimes distorts the image or a line segment. This occurs because the type of node you are deleting is different from the nodes on either side of it. If this happens, select Undo, reselect the node, and change it to a cusp node. You can then safely delete the node without distorting your image.

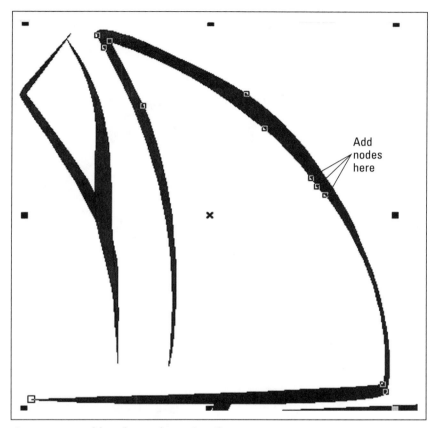

Add
nodes
here

Figure 3-17: Add nodes to the mainsail.

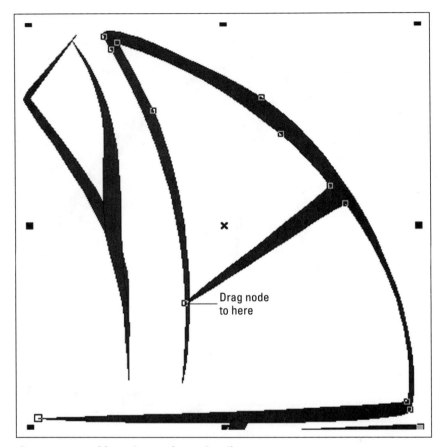

Drag node
to here

Figure 3-18: Add a stripe to the mainsail.

Using the Node Edit Docker and Property Bar

The Node Edit docker and Property bar provide the tools to perform editing functions on an object. The functions available on the Node Edit docker and on the Property bar are identical. Use whichever works the best for you. To display the Node Edit docker, either double-click a node or select View ➪ Dockers ➪ Node Edit. Table 3-1 shows the command buttons and the actions they perform.

Shortcut

Ctrl+F10 displays the Node Edit docker.

Table 3-1
Node commands

Button	Action
	Adds a node at the selected location
	Deletes the selected node
	Joins the selected nodes
	Breaks the curve at the selected node
To Line	Converts the selected segment to a line
To Curve	Converts the selected segment to a curve
Cusp	Changes the selected node(s) to cusp nodes
Smooth	Changes the selected node(s) to smooth nodes
Symmet	Changes the selected node(s) to symmetrical nodes
	Closes a curve by adding a line segment
	Extracts the selected line segment from a curve

Continued

	Table 3-1 (continued)	
Button	**Action**	
Auto-Reduce	Automatically reduces the number of nodes to smooth an object	
	Stretches or scales the curve associated with the selected nodes	
	Rotates or skews the curve associated with the selected nodes	
	Aligns the selected nodes	
	Toggles elastic mode off and on	
Auto-Close	Automatically closes the selected curve	

Joining nodes

Every path, even if it is closed, has a starting and ending node. The starting node appears slightly larger than the balance of the nodes. If the starting and ending nodes of an open path are close together, the object can appear closed, though it is open (see Figure 3-19). You can quickly find the starting and ending nodes of an open path. If you press Home on your keyboard, the starting node is highlighted; if you press End, the end node is highlighted. To close an object, select the start and end nodes of the path, and click the join button on either the Property bar or the Node Edit docker. The Property bar also has an Auto-Close feature. If you click this button, Draw locates the starting and ending nodes of the selected object and automatically closes the object. Auto-Close and the Extend Curve to Join button work the same way in that they extend the curve by adding a line segment between the starting and ending nodes. The difference between the two is that Extend Curve adds a line segment to join the end nodes, where Auto-Close moves the end node to the location of the starting node to close the curve. When you join nodes by selecting them and clicking the join button, the two selected nodes become a single node.

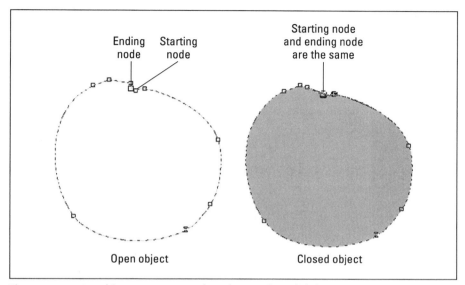

Figure 3-19: An object can appear closed even though it is open.

Reducing nodes

Reducing the number of nodes in an object to the minimum required to define the shape reduces the file size of your document. You could delete the excess nodes one at a time by selecting them and pressing Delete. If the object contains a large number of nodes, and is pretty rough, that's an extensive undertaking. Traced objects, for example, typically have significantly more nodes than are required to define the shape. The hieroglyphic shown in Figure 3-20 was originally created in a bitmap program, then run through Corel OCR-TRACE to yield the image you see. The selected portion of the shape has 131 nodes on 2 subpaths, which is far more than is required to define the shape.

Draw's Auto-Reduce reduces the number of nodes in a selection automatically. The extent of the reduction is determined by settings that you specify in the Shape tool settings of the Toolbox property sheet.

To specify the Auto-Reduce setting and reduce the number of nodes:

1. Select Tools ⇨ Options to display the Options dialog box, and expand the General and Toolbox categories by clicking the plus (+) signs beside their names. Click the Shape tool entry on the list.

Figure 3-20: Excess nodes increase the file size of an image.

2. The default Auto-Reduce setting is 0.004 inches. This is a reasonably low setting and doesn't reduce the number of nodes substantially. This setting deletes excess nodes that are within 0.004 inches of one another. I specified a setting of 0.05 inches. This is a medium setting, which reduces the number of nodes in a traced image without compromising the shape. Specify the setting you want in the Auto-Reduce box and click OK to complete the operation and return to the drawing window.

3. Select the Shape tool.

4. Marquee-select the nodes you want to reduce. You may want to select all the nodes in the object.

5. Click Auto-Reduce on the Property bar.

You can choose higher settings, up to 1 inch. If the setting is too high, however, the shape is distorted and doesn't resemble the original shape. You may need to try a couple of settings to see what works best for your image. Figure 3-21 shows the results of a 0.05-inch setting on the traced image. The nodes are reduced to 66 nodes on 2 subpaths. After reducing all the objects in the image, the file size is 67K smaller than the original file.

Figure 3-21: The image with the number of nodes reduced.

Breaking a path

Breaking a path is useful if you need to rejoin the nodes in another way to achieve a particular effect. When an object has subpaths, the paths aren't attached to one another (see Figure 3-22). By breaking the paths, you can rejoin the subpaths to give them a single path. In this figure, the paths were broken and rejoined to create the stylized C shape.

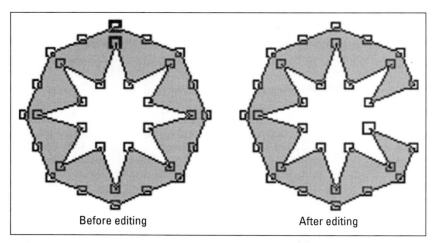

Before editing   After editing

Figure 3-22: Breaking and rejoining paths lets you create a single path from subpaths.

Breaking and rejoining paths is also a method for creating a pierced effect in an image. To begin the tutorial exercises, start Draw if it's not already running. For the sake of speed and to conserve resources, close any documents that you may have open before starting this tutorial.

On the CD-ROM   In this section, you work with pierce1.cdr, which is located in the tutorial\ch03 folder on the companion CD-ROM.

To break a path:

1. Select File ➪ Open to display the Open Drawing dialog box.

2. Select the D:\ drive (where D is your CD-ROM drive).

3. Select tutorial ➪ ch03 ➪ pierce1.cdr to display the document in the file name box. Click Open to open the image in Draw.

4. Select the Shape tool and then the arrow to display the nodes. You may want to zoom in on the point at which the arrow crosses the left side of the circle.

5. Click a point on the arrow where the top line segment touches the inner edge of the circle (see Figure 3-23). Click the break button either on the Node Edit docker or the Property bar. Repeat for the bottom line segment of the arrow. When you break the arrow path, the fill disappears. It's not really gone; it will reappear when the nodes are reconnected.

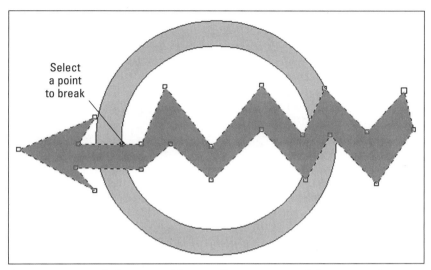

Figure 3-23: Break the top and bottom line segments of the arrow where they touch the inner edge of the circle.

6. Click the node at the top breakpoint of the arrow, and drag it until it touches the outside edge of the circle. Repeat with the node at the bottom breakpoint of the arrow.

7. Marquee-select the top and bottom nodes on the arrow as indicated in Figure 3-24.

8. Click the Extend Curve to Close button on either the Node Edit Docker or the Property bar. A line appears between the two nodes, closing that section of the arrow.

9. Repeat steps 7 and 8 for the two nodes that touch the outer edge of the circle (see Figure 3-25). If you selected the break points correctly, the arrowhead should appear to go behind the circle. You may need to modify the curves that were added to rejoin the nodes.

Although subpaths of an object normally lie in close proximity or are superimposed, they can reside anywhere on a single page of a drawing. A set of lines used for cross-hatching might be separate subpaths of a single object. When breaking and joining the nodes of subpaths to create a larger subpath or a single path object, it's important to align the nodes first. Joining nodes that aren't touching can yield unexpected results. When nodes are joined, one node moves to meet the other. If the nodes aren't touching or in close proximity, this can alter the shape dramatically.

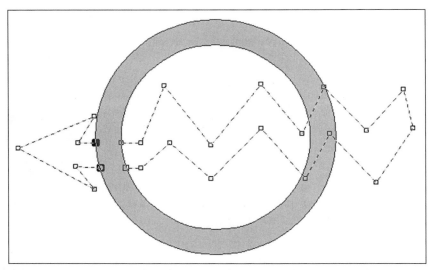

Figure 3-24: Marquee-select the two nodes that touch the inner edge of the circle.

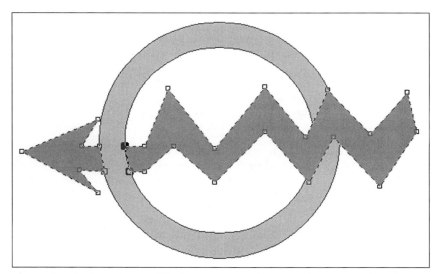

Figure 3-25: Close the modified arrow using the Extend Curve to Close button.

Modifying a node's properties

Draw curve objects can have three types of nodes: cusp, smooth, and symmetrical (see Figure 3-26). Each type has different attributes that affect its behavior. Choosing the desired attributes for a node gives you more control when reshaping an object.

To change a node's attributes, select the node and click the desired node-type button on either the Node Edit docker or the Property bar. The node's current type appears grayed out. Use these descriptions of the node attributes to guide your selection:

✦ **Cusp nodes:** Cusp nodes are used to make an extreme change in direction. A cusp node has two control points that move independently of one another. You can reshape the line segment on either side of the node without affecting the opposing line segment.

✦ **Smooth nodes:** Smooth nodes are used to create flowing transitional curves between line segments. A smooth node has two control points that lie on a straight line. If you move one of the control points, the corresponding control point moves proportionately to maintain the smoothness of the curve. Smooth nodes are frequently used as a transition between a straight line and a curve. When used in this manner, only the curved side has a control point, and movement of the control point is restricted to bidirectional movement along the same plane as the line.

✦ **Symmetrical nodes:** Symmetrical nodes are used to connect two curved line segments, while maintaining symmetry at the node. A symmetrical node has two control points that lie on a straight line equidistant from the node. If you move one of the control points, the opposing control point moves to maintain both the straight line and the distance from the node. Symmetrical nodes can't be used to connect a straight-line segment with a curved-line segment.

Modifying a line segment's properties

Line segments in Draw are either straight or curved lines (see Figure 3-27). You can change a straight line to a curved line and visa versa. Curved-line segments are affected by their associated nodes; straight-line segments aren't affected by their associated nodes. To change a line's properties, select the line and then click either the To Line or To Curve button on the Property bar or Node Edit docker.

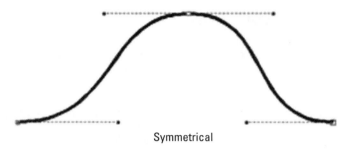

Symmetrical

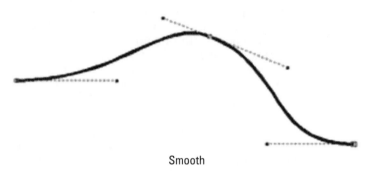

Smooth

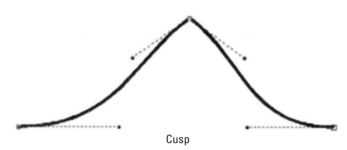

Cusp

Figure 3-26: Each node type has different attributes.

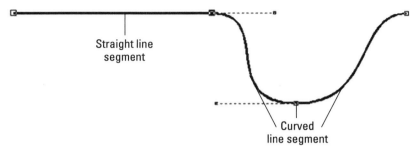

Figure 3-27: Straight- and curved-line segments.

Using Elastic mode

Elastic mode affects how nodes behave when they are moved. If a single node is selected, Elastic mode has no effect. When multiple nodes are selected, the nodes and control points move in proportion to the nodes, giving curves an elastic feel. The nodes move incrementally in relationship to the node being moved. The further away a node is from the one being moved, the less it will move in relationship.

In some instances, the nodes may behave as if they are anchored in place. In Figure 3-28, the solid lines represent duplicates of the original lines. The dashed lines represent the lines after the nodes were moved. For both situations, the three right-hand nodes were selected and the center node of the three was moved while pressing Ctrl. Note the difference between having Elastic mode enabled and disabled. The resulting lines look quite different.

Aligning nodes and control points

Aligning nodes and control points is an important skill. It ensures that objects will abut one another and reduce the possibility of white space appearing between objects when your image is printed. Commercial offset printing depends on trapping to prevent this white space. Other industries, such as the imprinted media industry, or people who use alternate output devices, such as routers or embroidery machines, need a very tight registration on the objects in an image. Without a tight registration, gaps appear between objects. Using the Shape tool, you can align nodes and control points so that two objects fit tightly against one another. In this section, you work with face1.cdr, which is located on the companion CD-ROM. To begin the tutorial exercises, start Draw if it's not already running. For the sake of speed and to conserve resources, close any documents you may have open before starting this tutorial.

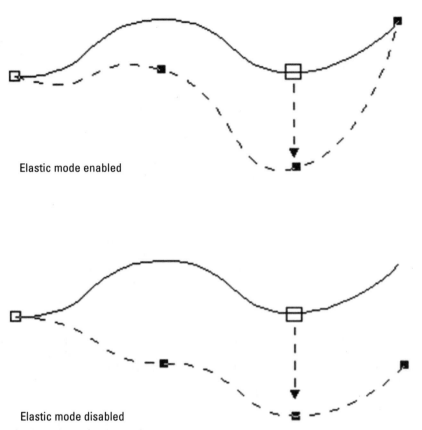

Elastic mode enabled

Elastic mode disabled

Figure 3-28: Elastic mode versus normal editing.

Cross-Reference   For more information on the use of Draw in preparing for the commercial printing process and other output media, see Chapter 16.

Face1.cdr is an illustration of an impressionistic face. The image is constructed of two objects that contain different fills. The goal of this exercise is to fit the two objects together so that they appear seamless. The Shape tool only allows you to edit a single object at a time. Face1.cdr is two objects. You need to combine the two objects into a single multipath object to complete the editing. As with all the tutorials, if you need to stop at some point in the exercise, be sure to save the image in a folder on your hard disk.

To align nodes and control points:

1. Select File ➪ Open to display the Open Drawing dialog box.

2. Select the D:\ drive (where D is your CD-ROM drive).

3. Select tutorial ➪ ch03 ➪ face1.cdr to display the document in the file name box. Click Open to open the image in Draw.

4. Using the Pick tool, select the two objects. Select Arrange ➪ Combine to create a single multipath object (see Figure 3-29). The single object assumes the attributes, including the fill, of the last object selected.

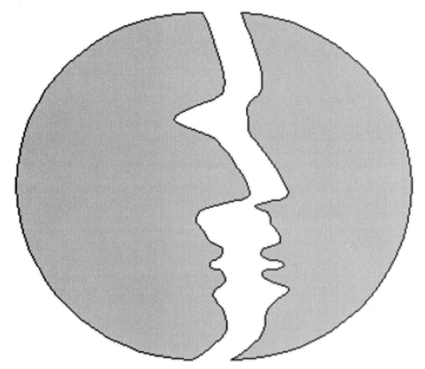

Figure 3-29: Use the Combine command to create a single multipath object.

Pressing Ctrl+L combines selected objects into single multipath objects.

5. Select the Shape tool.

6. Select the top node on the right half of the image. Press Shift and select the top-right node of the left half of the image. It's important that you select the right nodes first. The goal is to get the right image to meet the left image. The node that you select first is the node that moves.

7. Click the node align button on the Property bar or on the Node Edit docker. The Node Align dialog box appears (see Figure 3-30).

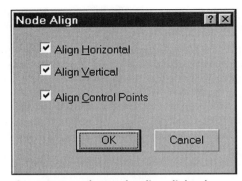

Figure 3-30: The Node Align dialog box.

8. By default all of the options are selected. Select align vertical nodes only and click OK. The right node moved to meet the left node (see Figure 3-31).

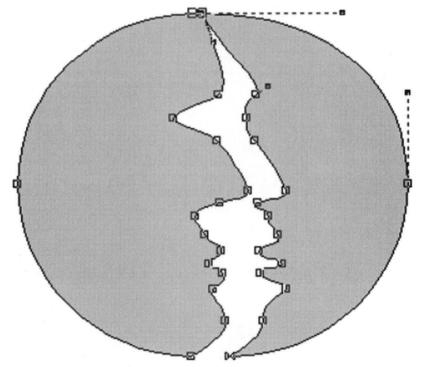

Figure 3-31: The first two nodes are aligned.

9. To continue aligning the rest of the nodes, select the next right-hand node down the object, press Shift, and select the left-hand node.

10. With both nodes selected, click the node align button. When the Node Align dialog box appears, accept the defaults to align the horizontal nodes, vertical nodes, and control points (see Figure 3-32).

11. Repeat steps 6 and 7 for all but the last pair of nodes. Repeat step 5 for the last pair of nodes (see Figure 3-33).

12. Select the Pick tool.

Shortcut

You can switch to the Pick tool when using any other tool, except the Text tool, by pressing the spacebar. To switch to the Pick tool from the Text tool, press Ctrl+ spacebar. To return to the tool you previously used, press spacebar again.

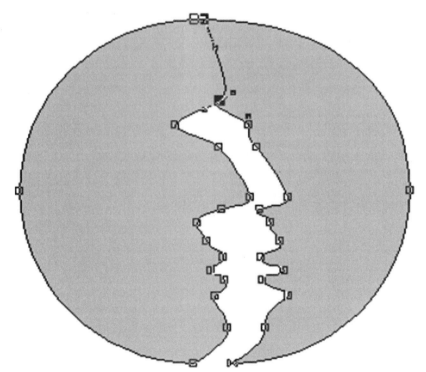

Figure 3-32: Align the second pair of nodes.

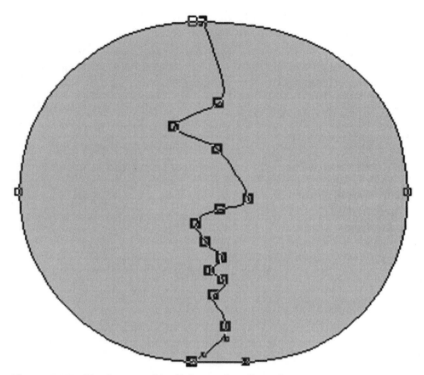

Figure 3-33: The image with all the nodes aligned.

13. Select the image. Select Arrange ➪ Break Apart to reseparate the two objects. You can reapply fills and other attributes once they are broken apart (see Figure 3-34).

Shortcut

Press Ctrl+K to apply the Break Apart command.

When you apply the Break Apart command to multipath objects, the new objects have the attributes of the original object. If you want the objects to have unique attributes, such as a fill, you need to apply them after breaking the object apart. The object fills in Figure 3-34 were changed for illustration purposes.

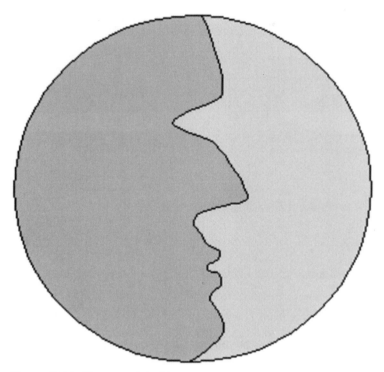

Figure 3-34: The completed image.

Extracting a subpath

In the previous exercise, you broke an object into two paths. Objects can contain several subpaths. Even if an object has several subpaths, you can break it apart into several objects. What happens if you only want to remove one subpath from an object with many paths? You could break the whole object apart, or you could extract just the path that you want to remove from the object. When you extract a path, the path you remove from the original object becomes an independent object. It's no longer a part of the original object. Figure 3-35 shows a before and after illustration of extracting a subpath. The original object on the left had three sub-paths. The object at the top right represents the object after the path at the bottom right was removed.

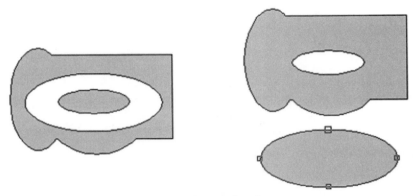

Figure 3-35: The results of extracting a subpath.

To extract a subpath:

   1. Select the Shape tool and click the object to select it and to display the nodes.

   2. Select the nodes on the path to extract.

   3. Click the extract button. The path is extracted and is the selected object.

The new object may be hidden behind the original object. Because it retains any fill and outline attributes, the new object may be difficult to see. To move it so that it's separate from the other object, press Shift+PgUp to bring the object to the top. You can then move it as desired.

Transforming portions of a curve object

Draw lets you transform curves as you would an object. The advantage of transforming a curve is that you can alter part of an object, while the rest of the object remains the same. You can rotate, skew nodes, stretch, and scale nodes to reshape an object. When transforming an object, you must select multiple nodes.

Stretching or scaling parts of a curve object

When you stretch or scale a curved object, the unselected nodes remain in their original position. The associated control points move in proportion to the selected nodes that are transformed. Figure 3-36 shows the effects of scaling and stretching portions of a curved object. The original object is represented by a dotted line.

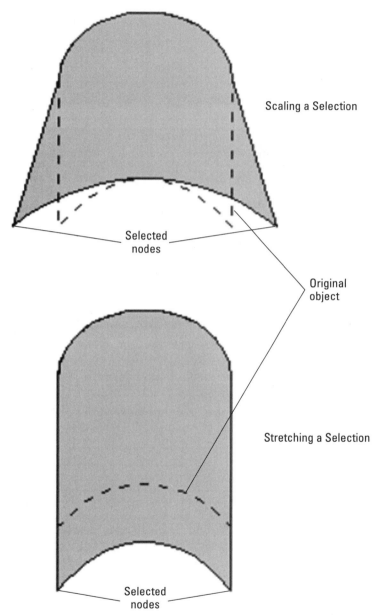

Figure 3-36: The results of scaling and stretching a selected portion of a curve object.

To stretch or scale the nodes of a curve:

1. Select the Shape tool and click the object to select it and to display the nodes.

2. Select the nodes to stretch or scale.

3. Click the Stretch and Scale button on either the Property bar or the Node Edit dialog box. Handles appear around the selected nodes.

4. To stretch an object, click and drag one handle in the direction you want to stretch the selection.

5. To scale an object, press Shift while dragging one handle in the direction you want to scale the selection.

Rotating or skewing parts of a curve object

Similar to scaling and stretching, when you rotate or skew a portion of a curve object, the unselected nodes retain their position. Only the selected nodes and associated control points move to deform the object. Figure 3-37 shows the effects of rotating and skewing portions of a curved object. The original object is represented by a dotted line.

To rotate or skew the nodes of a curve:

1. Select the Shape tool and click the object to select it and to display the nodes.

2. Select the nodes to rotate or skew.

3. Click the Rotate and Skew button on the Property bar or the Node Edit dialog box. Handles appear around the selected nodes.

4. To rotate a selection, click and drag one corner handle in the direction that you want to rotate the selection. You can constrain the rotation amount to specified increments by pressing Ctrl while dragging. The default constraint is 15 degrees.

5. To skew a selection, click and drag one side handle in the direction that you want to skew the selection. You can constrain the skew amount to specified increments by pressing Ctrl while dragging. The default constraint is 15 degrees.

Rotating and skewing selected portions of an object lets you distort the object in a controlled manner. You can create effects such as making objects appear to wrap around other objects or *drip* off a surface.

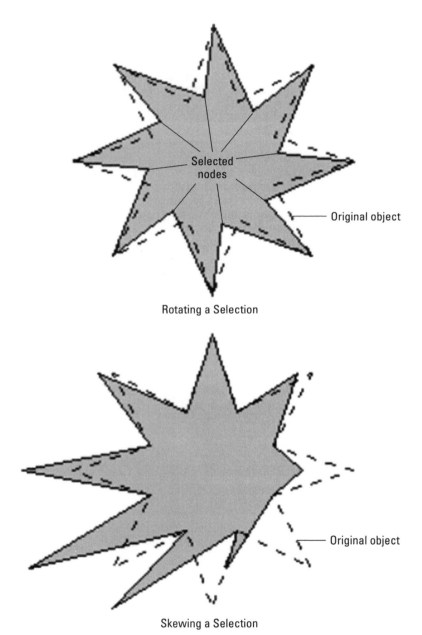

Selected
nodes

Original object

Rotating a Selection

Original object

Skewing a Selection

Figure 3-37: The results of rotating and skewing a selected portion of a curve object.

Summary

The Shape tool is one of the most frequently used tools in Draw. As a fine-tuning tool, this tool lets you make subtle changes in the smoothness of an object. The Shape tool can be used to modify a curve object substantially, changing the object's entire appearance. In this chapter, you learned to

✦ Modify the shape of geometric figures

✦ Change the basic shape of curve objects

✦ Change a node's properties

✦ Align nodes and control points

✦ Stretch, scale, skew, and rotate selected portions of an object

✦ Extract a subpath from a curve

✦ Modify the properties of a line segment

✦   ✦   ✦

Adding Text to Documents

You don't have to think much to realize how much the world has changed in the past 200 years. A letter used to take several weeks to travel from one country to the next. Just 20 years ago, home computers were in their infancy, and if you'd told someone about e-mail, they probably would have thought you'd dropped over the edge of reality. Today, my computer converts text to 0s and 1s, and whisks it electronically around the world in less time than it takes to walk to the mailbox.

Indeed, a great deal has changed. What hasn't changed — and won't — is the impact the written word has on our lives. Draw gives you the ability to create text that has impact. Artistic text lets you add an infinite variety of text effects to your documents. Paragraph text can be formatted using traditional layouts or made to flow around graphics and as fill objects.

Choosing a Text Type

Draw sees Artistic and Paragraph text differently. Paragraph text is viewed as a block of text, whereas Artistic text is seen as individual text objects. As with all objects in Draw, you can transform and add special effects to Artistic text, turning plain text into word art. Adding Artistic text enlivens and adds a creative touch to your documents. If you are creating a document with lots of text, such as a booklet or catalog, Paragraph text is a better choice. Both text types have unique properties and advantages that recommend them for specific applications.

Artistic text

Artistic text offers more graphic options than Paragraph text. In addition, it's ideal for banners, headlines, captions, and any other situation where you need small amounts of text. When creating Artistic text, you can enter a text string with a maximum of 32,000 characters. You can say a great deal in 32,000 characters, although I don't recommend extremely long strings of Artistic text. Because Draw treats Artistic text as it does other graphics objects, entering long strings of Artistic text can put a strain on your system resources and cause a loss of performance. Artistic text does not support text wrap, which means you must manually insert line breaks. The formatting options for Artistic text are limited, as well. For example, you can't indent or tab with Artistic text. If you want to simulate these functions, you have to use the spacebar. This can cause alignment problems and can cause your document to look unattractive.

Paragraph text

Draw offers features similar to those found in most popular word processing programs for use with Paragraph text. These features include extensive formatting options as well as the capability to wrap text around graphic elements in your document. The flexibility of Paragraph text makes it ideal for text-intensive documents. With Paragraph text, you can flow text from one frame or page to the next. You can quickly add indents, tabs, bullets, and columns to your documents.

Draw also lets you transform Paragraph text. Unlike Artistic text, some transformations apply to the text frame only and have no effect on the text itself. For example, if you skew Paragraph text, the frame skews and the text alignment adjusts to the reshaped frame. The text itself doesn't skew, however.

A question of style

Although styles can be created in and applied to both Artistic and Paragraph text, the style options available for Paragraph text are more diverse. Unlike Artistic text, which supports most of Draw's special effects, the graphics options available for Paragraph text are limited. You can apply envelopes to Paragraph text, which makes the text usable as a fill for other objects.

The Text tool

In Draw, you create both Paragraph and Artistic text with the same tool. Using a single Text tool permits quick and efficient switching between the two text types. Your action determines whether you enter Artistic or Paragraph text. If you click in the drawing window and enter text, the Text tool behaves as an Artistic Text tool. If you click and drag a frame, the Text tool behaves as a Paragraph Text tool.

A Few Text-Handling Drawbacks

Technically, in Draw, you can create a document with 998 pages, or 32,000 frames with 32,000 paragraphs that each contain 32,000 characters, whichever is less. That's a lot of numbers, none of which you really need to remember. What is important to remember, however, is that Draw is a graphics program. Although it has a wealth of text features, it is *not* a dedicated word processor or page layout program. Those programs are designed to handle a large volume of text efficiently.

In Draw, such documents are unwieldy and cause screen refresh to slow to a crawl. If your system has limited resources, it could also cause system performance problems and memory errors. Consider using a page layout package such as Corel Ventura if you're creating a long document that contains a lot of text but has few graphical elements.

Using Artistic Text

Artistic text can be placed anywhere on the drawing page or in the drawing window. This flexibility is useful when adding text to an existing graphic image. You can create the text in the desktop area and then move it into position. Text is easier to see while typing if no graphic exists behind it.

Adding text to your documents

Draw provides two ways of adding Artistic text to documents. You can add the text interactively in the drawing window, or you can use the Edit Text dialog box. Adding text interactively lets you immediately view how your text appears with other elements in your drawings. The Edit Text dialog box is especially useful when you are dealing with small font sizes that may be difficult to view without zooming in on the text area of the drawing window.

Shortcut

F8 selects the Text tool.

Entering text interactively

To interactively enter Artistic text:

1. Select the Text tool from the toolbox.

2. Click an insertion point in the drawing window. The way Draw places text in relationship to the insertion point depends on the alignment options you specify. By default, Draw left-aligns text, and the insertion point indicates the left boundary of the text (see Figure 4-1).

3. Enter the desired text. For multiple lines of text, press Enter to start a new line. Text appears in the default font and size as you enter it. Draw uses 24-point AvantGarde Bk BT as the default font. Later in this chapter, you learn to change the default font and other text attributes.

4. To start a new text string, click another insertion point in the drawing window.

Figure 4-1: Click the Text tool in the drawing window to specify an insertion point and to enter your text.

If you need to enter a long string of Artistic text, or need to use smaller point sizes, it may be easier to enter the text in the Edit Text dialog box. One advantage of using the Edit Text dialog box is that you can quickly change the font, size, and alignment while you are editing your text.

Shortcut

Ctrl+Shift+T accesses the Edit Text dialog box.

Using the Edit Text dialog box

To enter text in the Edit Text dialog box:

1. Using the Text tool, click in the drawing window to place an insertion point for your text.

2. Select Text ➪ Edit Text to display the Edit Text dialog box (see Figure 4-2).

3. Specify the alignment, font, and size to use.

4. Enter the text in the entry window.

5. Click OK to return to the drawing window.

You can mix fonts and sizes in a string of Artistic text. Just *swipe* (click and drag to highlight) the text, and select the font and size to use. You can't mix the alignment of Artistic text. The alignment you specify applies to the entire string of text.

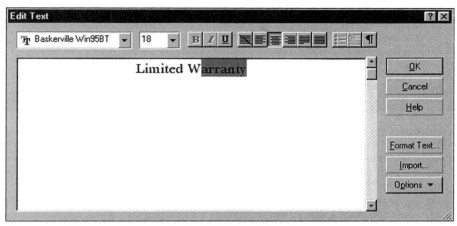

Figure 4-2: You can enter text in the Edit Text dialog box.

Note

Draw supports text transferred via the Windows clipboard. You can paste text from other applications when you edit text interactively or in the Edit text dialog box. The pasted text assumes the default font, alignment, and text attributes that you specified for Draw.

Editing Artistic text

You can edit text interactively in the drawing window or by using the Edit Text dialog box. The Text tool is used to swipe text in the drawing window to replace the text, or to click an insertion point to add or delete text. The Backspace and Delete keys are active when you edit text, and behave as they would in a word processor. You can use either the Text or the Pick tool to access the Edit Text dialog box. Either select the text with the Pick tool, or click an insertion point in the text and then select Text ⇨ Edit Text. When the dialog box appears, you can edit the text as you would in a word processor.

Shortcut

Double-clicking an unselected text string in the drawing window switches to the Text tool. If you want to switch back to the Pick tool, press Shift+spacebar.

Converting text to curves

Although you can apply many of Draw's special effects to Artistic text and still retain the ability to edit the text, sometimes it's desirable to convert the text to curves. Converting text to curves is useful if you need to share your document with others or send it to a service bureau that may not have the fonts contained in your document.

Ctrl+Q applies Convert To Curves.

Once text is converted to curves, you can reshape the individual characters of the text in the same manner as you would reshape any curve object. To convert a selected string of Artistic text to curves, select Arrange ⇨ Convert To Curves or click the Convert To Curves button on the Property bar.

Converting text to curves is a one-way trip. Once the text is converted, you can't revert the resulting graphic object to text beyond the levels of Undo that you've specified. If you need to convert the text to curves, I recommend that you retain a backup copy of your document with editable text, using the Save As command to create another file. By keeping an editable copy of your document, you can change the text later if needed.

Using Paragraph Text

Paragraph text offers more options when you need to add larger blocks of text to your documents. It's ideally suited to newsletters, invoices, and other forms that require columns and formatting options unavailable with Artistic text. Paragraph text can flow from one page to the next in multipage documents. You can also specify that Paragraph text fit inside a specified frame.

Navigating multipage documents

Draw provides two quick ways to navigate through multipage documents. You can click the page navigator at the bottom of the drawing window. In addition, extending from the sides of the pages are blue arrows and boxes that show the previous and following pages (see Figure 4-3). By clicking one of these boxes with the Pick tool, you can quickly move to that page.

Entering Paragraph text interactively

Paragraph text is entered in a text frame. Draw lets you create fixed and variable text frames. The size of a fixed frame corresponds to the frame size you draw in the drawing window. By default, when you click and drag a text frame in the drawing window, you create a fixed text frame. Variable text frames increase and decrease vertically in size as you enter or remove text. Choose a frame type based on the text restrictions of your document. A variable text frame is a good choice if you have reasonably unlimited vertical space or expect to flow text from one frame to the next. If you need to fit your text into a restricted amount of space, choose a fixed frame size. You may need to alter the font size to fit the frame if you choose a fixed frame. Regardless of which frame type you choose, you aren't permanently bound to your decision. You can easily change a frame from one type to the other.

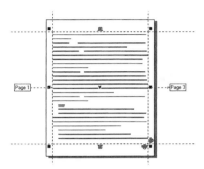

Figure 4-3: Quickly move through a multipage document by clicking a blue page box that extends from the side of the drawing page.

In a fixed frame

To enter text in a fixed frame:

1. Select the Text tool from the toolbox.

2. Click and drag to draw a text frame in the drawing window. When you release the mouse button, the frame appears in the drawing window with a dotted border. A text cursor appears in the top left corner of the frame indicating the insertion point.

3. Enter your text in the frame (see Figure 4-4). A Formatting bar appears in the rulers at the top of the drawing window. Later in this chapter, you learn to interactively adjust indents, tabs, and margins using the Formatting bar.

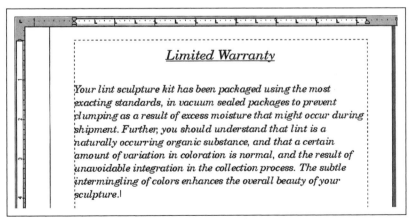

Figure 4-4: The text appears in the frame as you type, using the default font and font size.

Note You can show the frame of unselected text in the drawing window. Clicking the Show Text button on the property bar displays a dotted line around the frames of unselected text. If you want to hide the frame, click the button again.

If your text fills the text frame you created, it may be difficult to visibly discern the difference between a fixed and variable frame. If the text you enter exceeds the space allowed by a fixed frame, it'll appear truncated in the frame. You can alleviate this problem either by switching to a variable frame or by reducing the font size of your text.

In a variable frame

To enter text in a variable frame:

1. Select Tools ⇨ Options and expand the Workspace and Text categories by clicking the plus (+) sign beside their names. Choose Paragraph to display the Paragraph text options page.

2. Enable Expand and Shrink Paragraph Text Frames to Fit Text to specify that you want to use a variable frame, and click OK to return to the drawing window.

3. Select the Text tool from the toolbox.

4. Click and drag in the drawing window to draw a frame of the correct width.

5. Enter your text in the frame. As with entering text in a fixed frame, the text appears as you enter it, and a formatting bar appears in the ruler at the top of the drawing window. As you enter text, the frame expands vertically to accommodate your text.

A variable frame is useful if you have text that you may want to edit or append later. If you were creating a catalog, for example, and specified that you wanted to wrap text around graphic elements in your document, a variable frame would let you update the text while ensuring the tightest frame around your text. Using variable frames in this way lets you easily edit documents that change frequently.

Note Expand and Shrink Paragraph Text Frames to Fit Text will not autoflow multipage documents from one page to the next. If you use this option, you must manually flow the text into other pages.

Formatting Paragraph text

Paragraph text offers formatting options that are unavailable for Artistic text. With Paragraph text, you can specify all character properties and formatting options either interactively or in the Format Text dialog box. Paragraph formatting options include

✦ Columns

✦ Tabs

✦ Indents

✦ Automatic hyphenation

✦ Bullets

✦ Drop caps

✦ Horizontal and vertical alignment

✦ Spacing before and after paragraphs

✦ Additional options for the full and force justify horizontal alignment settings

✦ Wrapping Paragraph text inside objects

Adding and editing indents and tabs

Tabs are left aligned by default. You can change the alignment type in the Alignment column of the Format Text dialog box to add center, right, or decimal tab stops. Text is aligned with the tab, according to the alignment options you set. For example, left-aligned tabs cause the left edge of the first character of text to abut the tab and flow to the right. Center alignment causes the line to be centered over the tab. You can also add tabs interactively by clicking in the ruler to add tabs at the points you click.

Adding tabs

To add tabs:

1. Using the Pick tool or the Text tool, select the text to format.

2. Click the Format Text button on the Text toolbar or the Text property bar to display the Format Text dialog box.

3. Click the Tabs tab (see Figure 4-5).

4. Either click the ruler to place a new tab at that position or click the Add Tab button and enter a value in the tab column.

5. If you want to set tabs at regular intervals, enter a value in the box beside Set Tabs Every. Click the Set Tabs Every button to set the tabs as specified.

6. If you want to remove tabs, click the Delete All button to remove all tab stops. To remove selected tabs, select a tab and then click the Delete button.

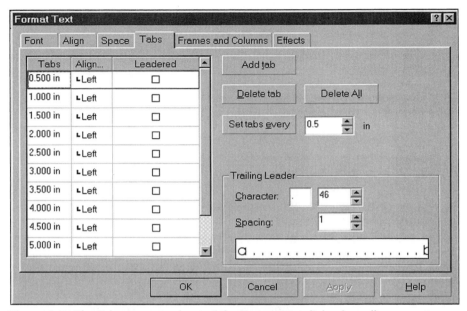

Figure 4-5: The Tabs property sheet of the Format Text dialog box allows you to specify tab settings for your document.

Spacebar Versus Tab

One of the most common mistakes people make when creating documents is to use the spacebar instead of tab. This is a holdover from a time when typewriters created documents with a monospace font. Today's fonts are rarely monospace, and using the spacebar instead of tab can result in poorly aligned text.

If you aren't in the habit of using tab to indent or move text horizontally across your document, it's a good habit to develop. Tabs are designed to ensure that your document has an ordered appearance by guaranteeing the alignment of your text. When specifying tab options for your document, you can change the alignment to right, center, or decimal.

Aligning tabs
To change tab alignment:

1. Using the Pick tool or the Text tool, select the text to format.

2. Click the Format Text button on the Text toolbar or the Text property bar, and then click the Tabs tab.

3. Click the tab alignment that corresponds to the tab to change.

4. Click the down arrow and choose an alignment.

5. Click OK to return to the drawing window.

Inserting leader characters

Draw also lets you specify a leader character for Paragraph text. By default, tabs are left aligned and are not leadered. Leaders are typically a row of dots placed between text objects to help the reader follow a line across white space. Leaders are often used in tab stops, especially before text that is flush right, such as in a list or table of contents. The leaders can be changed to any character in the current font.

To add tabs with leader characters:

1. Follow steps 1 through 3 from the preceding set of instructions.

2. Click the leader box beside the tabs to which you want to add leaders.

3. Click the up and down arrow beside the leader number to choose the character you want to use as a leader. A preview of the leader appears in the small window (see Figure 4-6). You can specify the spacing of leaders by dragging the spacing slider, clicking the up and down arrows, or by entering a value from 0 to 10 in the spacing box. If you compare the leader spacing in Figure 4-5 and Figure 4-6, you can see a preview of the difference that character selection and spacing makes in your document.

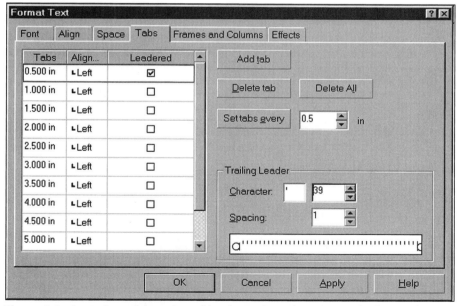

Figure 4-6: A preview of the selected leader and spacing appears in the window.

Working with hyphenation

Draw offers the capability to use automatic hyphenation in documents. Ideally, if you know you will be hyphenating text, you should set autohyphenation as the default before you place text in your document. You can apply automatic hyphenation for selected paragraphs or all paragraphs in a Paragraph text frame. Automatic hyphenation automatically places hyphens in words that can be hyphenated, as defined by Draw's hyphenation dictionary, and are forced to wrap to the next line.

Autohyphenating Paragraph text

To set automatic hyphenation for Paragraph text:

1. Using the Pick tool or the Text tool, select the text that you want to hyphenate. If you use the Pick tool to select the text, hyphenation is applied to all the paragraphs in the frame. If you use the Text tool to select the text, you can specify which paragraphs to hyphenate.

2. Click the Format Text button on the Text toolbar or the Text property bar to access the Format Text dialog box. You can also select Text ➪ Format Text to access the Format Text dialog box.

3. Click the Spacing tab.

4. Enable Use automatic hyphenation (see Figure 4-7).

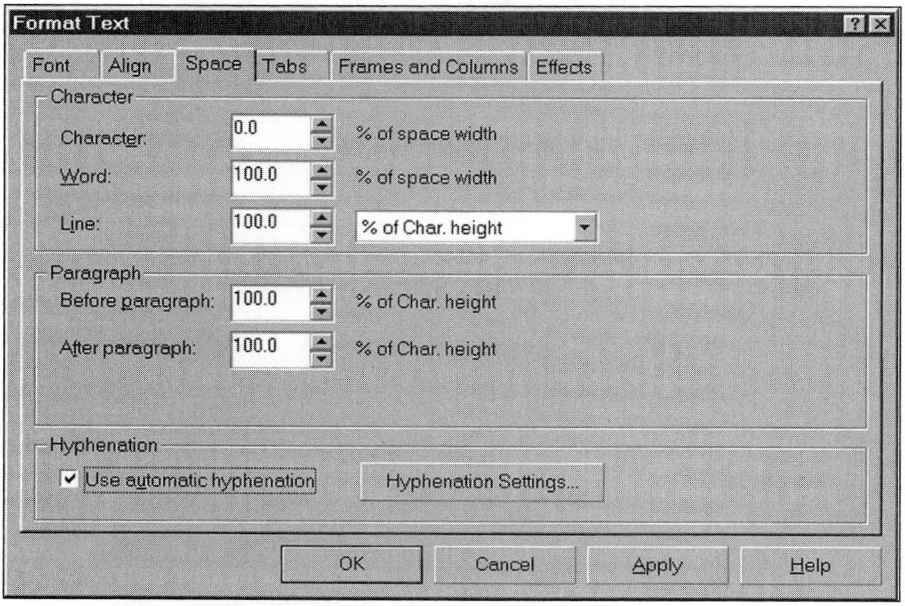

Figure 4-7: Enable automatic hyphenation.

5. By default, Draw does not hyphenate words that begin with capital letters or that contain strictly capital letters. If you want Draw to hyphenate such words, click the Hyphenation Settings button and enable Break capitalized in the Hyphenation Settings dialog box (see Figure 4-8).

6. Using the Hyphenation Settings dialog box, you can also specify the minimum word length, minimum characters before a hyphen, and the minimum characters after a hyphen. Specify the settings you want by entering values in their respective boxes.

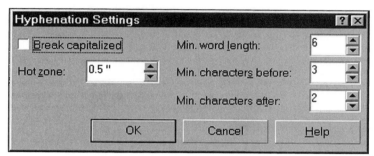

Figure 4-8: The Hyphenation Settings dialog box.

Setting the hot zone distance

You can set the distance in the Hyphenation Settings dialog box by entering the distance in the Hot zone box. A *hot zone* is the distance from the right margin where you want Draw to start hyphenating words.

Setting autohyphenation as the default

If you know you want to use hyphenation in your document, the best idea is to set automatic hyphenation as the default for your document. To set automatic hyphenation as the default for the document:

1. Deselect any text objects in your document by clicking the desktop or pressing Esc.

2. Select Text ➪ Format Text to display the Text Attribute dialog box.

3. Enable Paragraph text and disable Artistic text, and then click OK. The Format Text dialog box appears, which lets you set default formatting for Paragraph text.

4. Click the Space tab and enable Use automatic hyphenation.

5. Click OK to complete the operation and to return to the drawing window. The existing text in your document remains unaffected. Only subsequent frames that you create will use automatic hyphenation.

Tip
Specifying default settings before you create a document saves time and lets you work more efficiently. You can save a variety of default settings as a style so that they are ready to use in subsequent Draw sessions (see the section on using text styles, later in this chapter).

Creating columns

The use of columns provides a means of attractively placing text when producing a text-intensive document. Magazines, catalogs, and newsletters all benefit from the use of columns in layouts by making the text easy to follow and read. Using Paragraph text, you can create columns of equal or varying widths and spacing. After you add columns, you can change their width interactively in the drawing window.

Of equal width

To add columns of equal widths:

1. Using the Pick tool, select the Paragraph text frame to which you want to add columns.

2. Select Text ➪ Format Text, or click the Format Text button on the Text toolbar or the Text property bar to display the Format Text dialog box.

3. Click the Frames and Columns tab and enter the number of columns you want in the Number of columns box (see Figure 4-9).

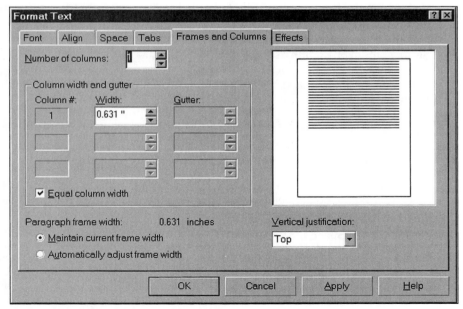

Figure 4-9: Specify the number of columns to use.

4. You can specify that the frame width remains the same (even if you add or delete columns) by enabling Maintain current frame width on the Frames and Columns property sheet.

5. You can specify that the column width remains the same (even if you add or delete columns) by enabling Automatically adjust frame width on the Frames and Columns property sheet. With this option enabled, if you add or delete columns, the frame will adjust accordingly, while leaving the column width the same.

6. Enable Equal column width and click OK to complete the operation and return to the drawing window. The text reformats and flows into the columns you specified (see Figure 4-10).

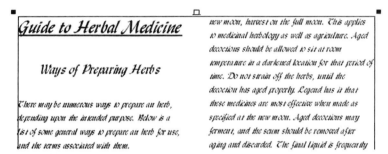

Figure 4-10: The text is reformatted in two columns.

Changing column widths interactively

You can modify column widths interactively in your document. This capability is useful when you place a graphic in your document, for example, and want the column width to match that of the graphic. To edit columns of equal widths interactively:

1. Click inside the Paragraph text with the Text tool.

2. The top ruler displays the widths of the columns and gutters in the selected frame. Place the mouse pointer over the gutter in the ruler. The gutter is the space between the two columns of text. The pointer changes to a double-headed arrow.

3. Drag the pointer until the columns are the size you desire (see Figure 4-11).

Specifying varying column widths

Documents such as newsletters and invoices typically require columns of varying widths and gutters. Using the settings on the Frames and Columns property sheet, you can specify variable columns widths.

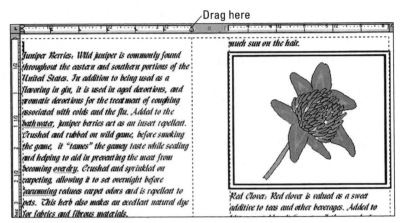

Figure 4-11: Adjust the column width interactively by dragging the gutter in the ruler at the top of the drawing window.

To add columns of varying widths and gutters:

1. Using the Pick tool, select the Paragraph text to which you want to add variable-width columns and gutters.

2. Select Text ➪ Format Text, or click the Format Text button on the Text toolbar or the Text property bar.

3. Click the Frames and Columns tab and enter the number of columns you want in the Number of columns box.

4. Disable Equal column width and enter a value in the Width box beside each column.

5. Enter a value in the Gutter box to specify the amount of space you want between each adjacent pair of columns. Click OK to complete the operation and to return to the drawing window.

Tip

Columns help organize information in an easily read format, and let you guide the reader's eye through a document. The number of columns you use is dependent upon the type of document and the amount of information to be organized. While six columns might be very appropriate for an invoice, six columns would appear confusing in a newsletter. Assess the needs of your document before choosing to add columns.

Adding bullets

Bullets set nonsequential lists of information apart from the body of your text and can be simple, whimsical, or informative. The font of the paragraph determines a bullet's size, style, and position relative to the other text characters. You can change any of these settings to suit your purposes. Draw provides a series of predefined bullet styles for you to apply to Paragraph text, or you can create your own styles and apply them. You can't apply bullets to Artistic text. If you want to apply bullets to a string of Artistic text, first convert the text to Paragraph text. The quickest way to create a bulleted list is to select the paragraphs to format and click the bullet button on the Text toolbar or the Text property bar. You can also apply and modify bullets using the Format Text dialog box.

Creating a bulleted list

To create a bulleted list:

1. Using the Pick tool or the Text tool, select the paragraphs to which you want to add bullets.

2. Select Text ➪ Format Text, and then click the Effects tab to display the effects property sheet, or click the bullet button on the Text toolbar or the Text property bar (see Figure 4-12). If you click the Bullet button on either the Text toolbar or the Text property bar, the bulleted list is automatically generated with the default bullet. To change the bullet, use the Format text dialog box.

3. Enable bullets by clicking the Bullet button.

4. Choose a bullet category from the Bullet Category list box and choose a symbol in the preview window.

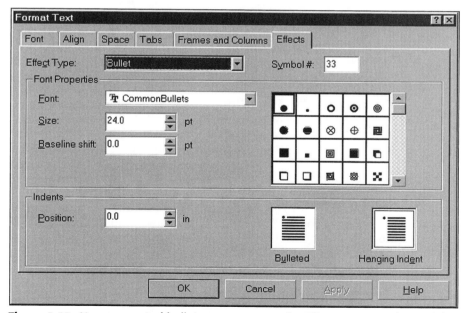

Figure 4-12: You can control bullet appearance on the Effects property sheet of the Format Text dialog box.

5. Click OK to complete the operation and to return to the drawing window. Draw formats the selected text with the bullet you selected (see Figure 4-13).

6. You can remove bullets by choosing No Effect as the Effect Type on the Effects property sheet of the Format Text dialog box.

Infusion: To make an infusion, boil one or two cups of water, and remove the water from the heat. Pour the water into a non-metallic container, and add 1-2 tsp. of the desired herb. Allow to steep for 2-5 minutes and strain off the herbs. Never use a metallic container to make infusions or decoctions as it can adversely alter the effectiveness of the herb.

Decoction: To make a decoction, boil one or two cups of water, preferably in a non-metallic container. Add 2-3 tsp. of the desired herb, and continue to boil for 2-5 minutes. Strain off the herbs.

Legend has it that these medicines are most effective when made as specified at the new moon. Aged decoctions may ferment, and the scum should be removed after aging and discarded. The final liquid is frequently mixed with alcohol, such as whiskey, at a 4:1 ratio, to preserve the decoction for future use.

Aromatic Decoctions: Aromatic decoctions are made by doubling the amount of herbs. The steam rising from the boiling liquid is inhaled. Another method is to soak a cloth in the decoction and place it over the nose, to allow the vapors to be inhaled.

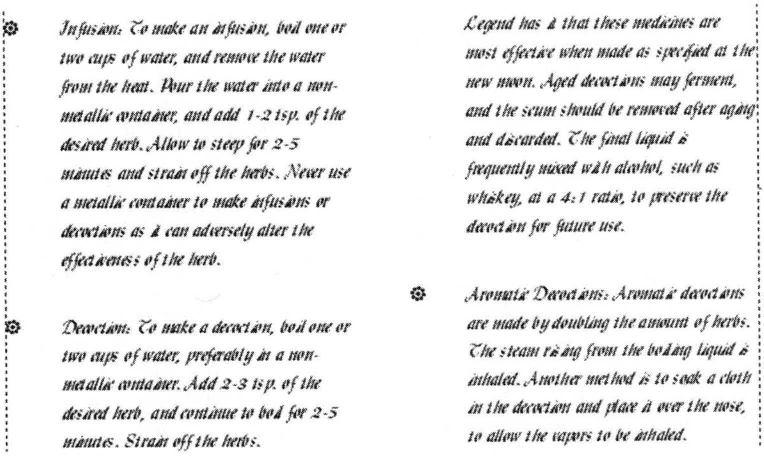

Figure 4-13: Custom bullets added to Paragraph text.

Customizing the bullets

Using the Format Text dialog box, you can customize several bullet attributes, including size, style, position, and spacing. Bullet sizes correspond to the font size of your text. Sometimes they appear small, making custom bullets lose their detail. It's useful to increase the size of the bullet. Once you increase the size of a bullet, you may need to alter the bullet's spacing and position as well, to ensure a consistent look.

To customize bullets:

1. Using the Pick tool or the Text tool, select the bulleted text whose bullets you want to customize.

2. Select Text ➪ Format Text and click the Effects tab to display the Effects property sheet of the Format Text dialog box.

3. Choose bullet from the drop-down list.

4. To change the bullet size, enter a new value in the Bullet Size box.

5. If you want to change the bullet style, select a new symbol from the preview box to use as a bullet.

6. If you need to alter the bullet's vertical position in relationship to your text, enter a new value in the Baseline shift box. Entering a negative value lowers the bullet's position; entering a positive value raises a bullet's position.

7. If you want to set the bullet apart from your text with a hanging indent, click the Hanging Indent button to enable this option and enter a value in the Bullet Indent box.

Changing bullet-to-text spacing

You can also change the amount of space between a bullet and the text. The capability to change the amount of space is critical when you use a bullet whose horizontal dimension exceeds its vertical measurement, such as with a pointing hand. Such bullets tend to lie too close to the text, resulting in a cluttered appearance. To change the space between the bullet and text:

1. Using the Pick tool or the Text tool, select the text whose bullet spacing you want to modify.

2. Select Text ➪ Format Text or click the Format button on the Text toolbar or the Text property bar.

3. Select the Tabs tab to display the Tabs property sheet.

4. In the Indents section, type a value for the amount of space that you want between the bullet and the text in the First Line box.

5. In the Rest of Lines box, type the same value as in the First Line box.

Tip   The amount of space required between a bullet and the text varies with the selected bullet. For the most part, you need to make an aesthetic decision. Some bullets look better set farther apart from the text. Others need to be closer. You can readjust the setting until you are satisfied with the visual results.

Adding a drop cap

Drop caps add impact to your documents. Generally, you add drop caps to the initial paragraph in a document or section. They are especially effective when set in a font that enhances the body of the text. The font need not be the same as the rest of the text.

Using the Text property bar

To add a drop cap using the Text property bar:

1. Using the Pick tool or the Text tool, select the text to which you want to add a drop cap. If you want to apply a drop cap to a specific character, highlight that character with the Text tool.

2. Click the Drop Cap button on the Text property bar. The text reformats with a drop cap as the initial character in the text frame (see Figure 4-14).

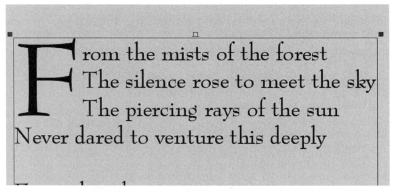

Figure 4-14: You can add a drop cap like this by clicking the Drop Cap button on the Text property bar.

Customizing a drop cap

You can customize the appearance of the drop cap by wrapping the text around the character or by using a hanging indent to offset the initial character from the body of the text. To customize a drop cap:

1. Using the Pick tool or the Text tool, select the text to which you want to apply a customized drop cap.

2. Select Text ⇨ Format Text and click the Effects tab to display the Effects property sheet.

3. Select Drop Cap.

4. Enter a value to specify the number of lines of text that you want to appear beside the dropped letter in the Dropped Lines box.

5. Enter a value for the amount of space you want between the dropped letter and the body of text in the Distance from Text box.

6. Choose a placement option. You can choose to wrap the text around the dropped letter as in Figure 4-14. You can also choose to apply a hanging indent to offset the initial character from the body of the text (see Figure 4-15).

Tip   Drop caps are an effective means of adding drama to your documents. Drop caps, however, are *not* a case of "if a little does a little good, a lot will do a lot of good." This effect can be overdone very quickly, thereby losing its effectiveness. As a point of good design, avoid starting every paragraph with a drop cap. If your document has multiple sections or chapters of unique information, you might want to use a drop cap at the beginning of each section. This identifies an information change to the reader, and is an effective use of a drop cap.

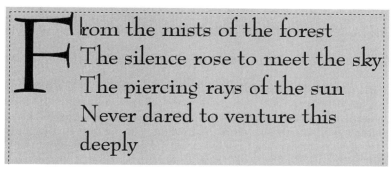

Figure 4-15: The effect of a drop cap with a hanging indent.

Linking Paragraph text frames

If your document has more than one Paragraph text frame, you can link them together to direct the flow of text. When two frames are linked, text flows from one frame into the other if the amount of text is greater than the size of the initial frame. The text flow tabs at the top or middle-bottom handles indicate the direction of text flow in linked frames. To select the starting frame, click the bottom-middle tab and then click the frame into which you want the text to flow. The Paragraph text icon that appears at the top of the second frame indicates that text overflows into it. The two frames are now linked. If you shrink or enlarge one frame or change the size of the text, the amount of text in the next frame adjusts automatically. You can remove links or change the direction of flow if you change your mind later.

When you select one of the linked frames with the Text tool, a blue arrow appears between the two frames indicating the direction of text flow. If the linked frame is on a different page, the page number appears beside the blue arrow (see Figure 4-16). When you import text files longer than a single page, Draw automatically creates new pages and flows the text into frames on those pages.

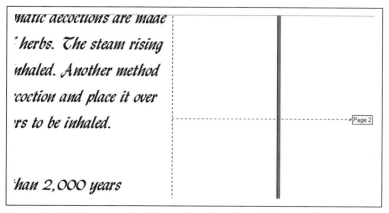

Figure 4-16: The arrow indicates the direction of the text flow onto another page.

To create links

To link frames together:

1. Using the Pick tool, select the starting frame.

2. Click the flow tab at the bottom-middle of the frame. The cursor changes to an arrow.

3. Click the outline of the frame to which you want to create the link. If the frame resides on another page, click the navigator at the bottom of the drawing window to move to that page, or enter the page number. Click the frame you want to link to the previous frame.

4. If you want to change the text flow to another frame, click the flow tab at the bottom of the frame whose link you want to change. Using the Pick tool, select the new frame into which you want to continue the text flow.

To remove links

You can remove links between Paragraph text frames if you make changes in the layout of your document. When you break a link, text flows back into the originating frame if it is linked to one frame only. If the frame is linked to additional frames, the text flows into the next linked frame.

To remove links between frames:

1. Using the Pick tool, select the frame to separate from the link.

2. Select Arrange ⇨ Separate to remove the link.

Linking frames helps you work efficiently with your documents by allowing text to flow from one frame to the next with ease. If you need to change a section of a document, you can remove the link between the frames, replace the section you want to change, and relink the frames. The text flow is reestablished, ensuring the consistency of your layout and document.

Specifying frame options

The Options dialog box lets you specify options for Paragraph text frames. When you apply formatting to a frame, the formatting applies to the paragraphs contained in that frame and in subsequent frames that you create, unless you specify otherwise in the Options dialog box.

To specify Paragraph text frame formatting options:

1. Select Tools ⇨ Options and expand the Workspace and Text categories by clicking the plus (+) signs beside their names. Choose Paragraph to display the Paragraph options page.

2. Enable Show Linking of Text Frame to display the direction of text flow between linked frames.

3. You can specify how formatting changes apply to frames by choosing one of the paragraph formatting options. If you choose All Linked Frames, any formatting changes that you make will apply to all of the text contained in the associated linked frames. Enabling Selected Frames Only applies formatting changes only to those frames that you specifically select. If you choose Selected and Subsequent Frames, formatting changes apply to the selected frame and all the frames that follow it in the document.

Specifying Text Attributes

The content of your document is important, whether it presents just a little bit of text or is almost exclusively text. It takes an investment of time and thought to put words into a good written format for others to read. Your words deserve your effort to make them look good. Your words mean little if the text gets lost in the graphics or are too small to read. Specifying character attributes defines some of the elements that determine the readability of your document. A good document becomes a great document by the thoughtful selection of character attributes.

Character attributes refer to the font, type size, weight, alignment, spacing, and placement of the text. The following exercises teach you to choose and apply character attributes to your documents. To begin the tutorial exercises, start Draw (if it's not already running). For the sake of speed and to conserve resources, close any documents that you may have open before starting this tutorial.

On the CD-ROM

For these exercises, you use dragtxt1.cdr, which is found on this book's companion CD-ROM.

To open the tutorial document:

1. Select File ➪ Open to display the Open Drawing dialog box.

2. Select the D:\ drive (where D is your CD-ROM drive).

3. Select Tutorial ➪ Ch04 ➪ dragtxt1.cdr to display the document in the file name box.

4. Click Open to open the image in Draw.

Tip

For the sake of speed, you might want to save this file to your hard disk by using the Save As command.

The following exercises are sequential. If you can't complete them all in one Draw session, save the document as you move through the exercises. Using this method, you can pick up the exercises where you left off at a later time.

Working with fonts

Draw comes packaged with a vast library of fonts from which to choose. These fonts range from traditional typefaces to whimsical and exotic typefaces. Font selection is a matter of aesthetics. It's difficult to choose a font from such a wide selection. The easiest way to apply a font is via the Text property bar or Text toolbar. You can enable the Text toolbar by selecting View ➪ Toolbars and enabling Text. Fonts are selected for both Paragraph and Artistic text by the same method.

To choose and apply a font:

1. Using the Pick tool, select the text in dragtxt1.cdr. The Text property bar and status bar change to display information about the text (see Figure 4-17).

2. Click the down arrow on the font name box to display a list of available fonts. A sample of the font, using a portion of your text, appears in a preview window.

3. Scroll through the list and select a font. I used BernhardMod BT. If this font isn't installed on your system, select another font.

4. Save the file to your hard disk as dragtxt2.cdr. This file is used in exercises that appear throughout this chapter.

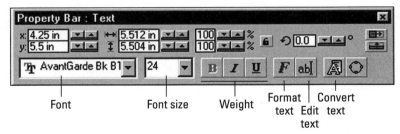

Font   Font size   Weight   Format text   Edit text   Convert text

Figure 4-17: The Text property bar displays information about the selected text.

Tip

You can perform identical text editing functions using either the Text property bar or the Text toolbar. When a text object is selected, these two toolbars are interchangeable. The property bar is interactive and updates to reflect the active tool. If you are working consistently with a large amount of text, you might find it useful to enable the Text toolbar and leave it displayed in the drawing window. The Text toolbar contains most of the controls for editing and formatting text. To enable the Text toolbar, select View ➪ Toolbars and click to enable Text.

Despite the large number of fonts available for your use, you should limit the number of fonts in any given document as a principle of good design. Using too many fonts in a document makes it difficult to read and detracts from the overall appearance. As a general rule of thumb, a document shouldn't require more than three fonts, and one font would probably do the job.

Tip Fonts come as serif, such as Times Roman, or sans serif, such as Futura. As a rule sans serif fonts make better headlines, whereas serif fonts work better as body text. Florid fonts, such as Cloister Black or Flemish Script, should be used sparingly, and never in large blocks of text. They are difficult to read in large blocks of text and are better suited to short text strings, such as an invitation. Check the preview of your document. Some of Draw's fonts, such as the script fonts, are unattractive and unreadable when you enter the text entirely in caps.

Specifying a type size

Draw lets you specify any size font up to 3,000 points. You must specify whole points; Draw does not permit fractional points. The appearance and suitability of a font at any given size varies from one font to the next. Some fonts make great headline fonts but are poor choices in smaller sizes. Other fonts look good at a popular size, such as 12 points, but are hard to read at 4 points and seem to get lost in sizes over 72 points. To change a font size, click the down arrow next to the font size on the Text toolbar or the Text property bar and choose a size from the list. If the font size you want is not displayed, you can highlight the value in the font size box and enter a font size.

Shortcut You can change the font size of selected text using shortcuts: Ctrl+numpad 4 decreases the font to the next size in the font size list; Ctrl+numpad 6 increases the font to the next size in the font size list; Ctrl+numpad 2 decreases the font by 1 point; and Ctrl+numpad 8 increases the font by 1 point.

Greeking

Small text sizes are difficult to render to screen because of the quantity of minute details contained in some typefaces. By default, Draw greeks text under five pixels in size to conserve memory and speed refresh. *Greeked text* appears as small rectangles in full-page view. If you zoom the page view, the actual text characters become visible.

You can adjust the default pixel size of greeked text by selecting Tools ➪ Options and expanding the Workspace category by clicking the plus (+) sign beside its name. Click Text. Specify the value you want in the Greek Text Below entry box by clicking the up or down arrow or highlighting the box and entering a new value.

Determining text spacing

The spacing options available for Artistic text vary compared to those available for Paragraph text. You can specify the character, word, and line spacing for Artistic text (see Figure 4-18). Paragraph text offers more spacing choices. In addition to the spacing options available for Artistic text, Paragraph text offers Before and After paragraph spacing (see Figure 4-19). To display the spacing options for selected text, select Text ⇨ Format Text or click the Format Text button on the Text toolbar or Text property bar.

Shortcut   Ctrl+T accesses the Format Text dialog box, where you can specify formatting options for Artistic and Paragraph text.

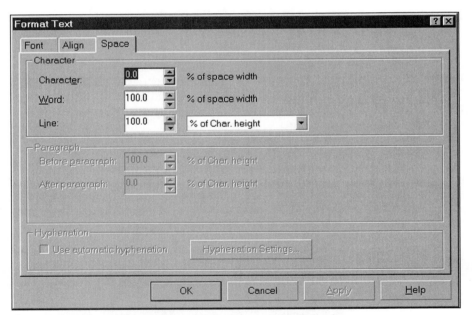

Figure 4-18: The Artistic text view of the Format Text dialog box.

General spacing options

This list outlines the options for setting spacing options for both Artistic and Paragraph text:

✦ **Character:** The Character setting determines the percentage of space between characters within a word. The default setting is 0 percent. Character spacing is based on the letter *m*. The exact amount of space depends on the font you select and the way it kerns.

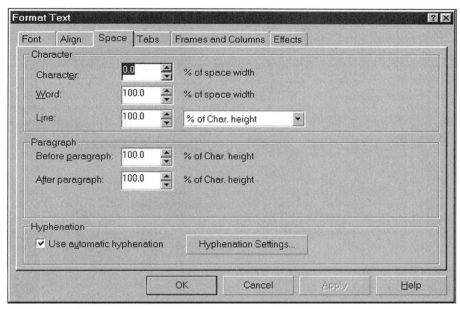

Figure 4-19: The Paragraph text view of the Format Text dialog box.

✦ **Word:** The Word setting determines the amount of space between words. The default setting is 100 percent. Word spacing is proportionate to character spacing and uses that information to calculate the space.

✦ **Line:** The Line setting determines the amount of space in between lines of text. Draw calculates the space based on the choice shown in the list box beside the line value. By default, Draw uses a percentage of the character height. The character height is determined by adding the percentage of the first line's *descender* and the second line's *ascender* (see Figure 4-20). If you choose to specify the line setting based on point size, Draw subtracts the font's point size from the value in the line box to determine the amount of space. If you choose percentage of point size, Draw bases the calculation on the point size of the largest letter in the second line.

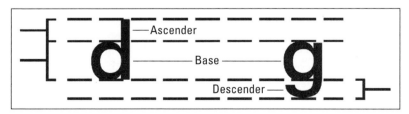

Figure 4-20: A font's ascender, base, and descender areas.

Paragraph text spacing options

This list outlines the options for setting spacing options for Paragraph text only:

✦ **Before Paragraph:** Lets you specify the amount of space before each paragraph.

✦ **After Paragraph:** Lets you specify the amount of space after each paragraph.

Draw uses a percentage of the character height as the basis for calculating Before and After paragraph settings. As with the line setting, the character height is determined by the sum of the percentage of the first line's descender and that of the second line's ascender. You can choose Before paragraph, After paragraph, or both. If you specify both settings, Draw uses the greater of the two to determine the space between paragraphs.

Hard and Soft Returns

Each time you press Enter, you place a *hard return* to create a new paragraph. Pressing Shift+Enter creates a soft return. A *soft return* is useful if you want to force text to the next line without creating a new paragraph. You can identify the end of a paragraph by selecting Text ➪ Show Non-printing Characters or by clicking the Non-printing Characters button on the Text property bar. If Show Non-printing Characters is enabled, a paragraph symbol appears at the end of each paragraph.

When you use a soft return, Draw uses interline spacing, which is much smaller than inter-paragraph spacing. This is useful if you have a limited amount of space in which to place several paragraphs of text.

Applying bold and italic effects

You can apply both bold and italic effects to text by highlighting the text and clicking the appropriate buttons on the Text toolbar or Text property bar. Some fonts don't support bold or italic effects, however. If these effects are not supported, the option is grayed out.

Tip

If you want to apply bold effects to text but the font does not support a bold style, apply a hairline outline to the text instead. Choose the Behind the Fill option from the Outline Pen dialog box. When you choose Behind the Fill, only half of the outline width is visible. The other half of the outline is behind the text fill. This lets you simulate a bold font without losing the details of the typeface shape. You can also simulate italic effects by selecting individual characters with the Shape tool and applying a 10-degree negative skew value.

Applying overline, underline, and strikeout effects

You can apply underlines, overlines, and strikeouts, and change any of the line styles in the Format Text dialog box. You can also use the property bar or the Text toolbar to underline text quickly. Overlining, underlining, and strikeout effects are useful for adding emphasis to text or when proofing text. As with all text formatting, if you select the text with the Pick tool, the formatting choices you make will apply to all the text in the frame or Artistic text string. If you use the Text tool, you can apply the formatting to the selected text only.

Underlining text

To underline text:

1. Using the Text tool or Pick tool, select the text to underline with the Text tool.

2. Click the Underline button on the Text toolbar or the Text property bar. Alternatively, click the Format button and apply the underline in the Format Text dialog box by choosing an underline thickness from the drop-down list.

Overlining and strikeout text

Overlining and strikeout effects can't be applied using the Text toolbar or the Text property bar. They are applied in the Format Text dialog box. To apply overline or strikeout effects:

1. Using the Text tool or Pick tool, select the text to overline or strike out.

2. Click the Format button on the Text toolbar or the Text property bar. Alternatively, you can select Text ➪ Format Text.

3. Enable the overline or strikeout effect by choosing a line thickness from the drop-down list box.

4. Click OK to complete the operation and return to the drawing window.

Editing line thickness

To edit a preset line thickness:

1. Using the Text or Pick tool, select the text that contains the line to edit.

2. Click the Format button on the Text toolbar or the Text property bar to display the Format Text dialog box.

3. Click the Edit button next to the associated line effect to display the Edit Strikeout dialog box (see Figure 4-21).

4. Change the line thickness as desired and click OK to return to the Format Text dialog box. Click OK again to return to the drawing window.

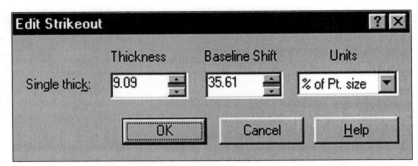

Figure 4-21: The Edit Strikeout dialog box lets you specify a line thickness for strikeout lines.

Adjusting and removing line effects

The line-editing dialog box also lets you adjust line positioning. Line-position editing options are adjusted similarly to line spacing, based on the ascender and descender of a font. Adjusting the baseline shift changes the amount of space between the line and overlined and underlined text. To remove line effects, select None as the line thickness in the Format Text dialog box.

Superscript and subscript

Draw lets you apply superscript and subscript effects to text. These effects are useful for mathematical notations, scientific notations, and for designations such as trademarks. Superscript effects appear above the text; subscript effects appear below the text.

To make text superscript or subscript:

1. Using the Pick tool or the Text tool, select the text to which you want to apply superscript or subscript effects.

2. Click the Format Text button on the Text toolbar or the Text property bar to display the Format Text dialog box.

3. Click the effect you want to apply and click OK to return to the drawing window.

Basic Text Formatting

So far you've learned to format text using the Text property bar and the Text toolbar. These two formatting aids contain the most frequently used formatting options available in Draw. If you require advanced editing capabilities, you can access the Format Text dialog box by clicking the Format button on either bar, or by selecting Text ➪ Format Text.

Choosing default formatting properties

If you are going to be working with the same formatting options for most of your text, it's easier to change the default text attributes than to continually have to specify settings. In a production environment, this translates into saving time. As with other formatting options, you can save the defaults as a style for later use.

To change the default text attributes:

1. Deselect all the objects, including text, in the drawing window by clicking a blank space on the desktop or by pressing Esc.

2. Select the Text tool and click a formatting option, such as an alignment option, on the Text property bar. The Text Attributes dialog box appears (see Figure 4-22).

3. Click the checkbox to specify to which text types the new attributes will apply.

4. Click OK to complete the operation and return to the drawing window.

Figure 4-22: Select a text type to receive the new text attributes.

If you only want to set the defaults for one type of text, specify only that text type in the Text Attributes dialog box. It's not uncommon to use different defaults for Artistic and Paragraph text, especially if Artistic text will be used strictly for headline purposes.

Specifying text units

By default, Draw uses points as the measurement unit for text. Points are the most common unit of measurement for typefaces and fonts. You can change this setting for the current and all subsequent documents you create in Draw.

To specify default text units:

1. Select Tools ➪ Options and expand the Workspace category by clicking the plus (+) sign beside its name. Click Text to display the Text options page.

2. Click the down arrow on the Default Text Units box to display and select a new unit of measurement.

3. When you are satisfied with your choices, click OK to return to the drawing window.

Deciphering Font Sizes

Although points are a precise unit of measurement, the actual size of a particular font might be different from that of another font at the same point size. The reason for the deviation has to do with the way type is measured. Type is usually measured using the M character as the standard. The measurement extends from the baseline (bottom of the character) to the top of the character.

This measurement doesn't allow, however, for differences in design or the ascending and descending portions of the character, which vary from one font to the next. If you need two fonts to be precisely the same size in your document, it's a good idea to print a sample of each font, compare them, and adjust the size of each accordingly.

Changing the text case

Draw lets you format text as small caps or all caps. This formatting effect gives selected text emphasis, and is useful when creating banners and headlines. Some fonts are already all caps, and the All Caps option won't have any effect on these fonts.

Tip All caps can be difficult to read if you have a long text string or multiple lines of text. If you use small caps in these situations, the text will be easier to read.

To specify small caps or all caps:

1. Select the text with the Pick tool or Text tool. If you use the Pick tool, all of the text is formatted; if you use the Text tool, you can choose to format only the selected text.

2. Click the Format Text button to display the Format Text dialog box (see Figure 4-23).

3. On the Font property sheet, click the down arrow next to Uppercase and choose either Small CAPS or All CAPS.

4. Click OK to complete the operation and return to the drawing window.

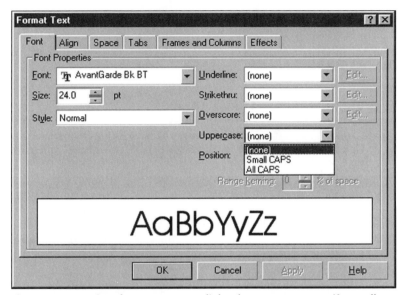

Figure 4-23: Using the Format Text dialog box, you can specify small and all caps.

Small caps work well in a body of text, when you want to emphasize text without overpowering the balance of the text body. The effect varies from one font to the next, so it's a good idea to test several fonts to find the effect you want. This effect doesn't work well with florid or scripted fonts.

Aligning text

Artistic and Paragraph text differ in the way they align. Paragraph text aligns in relationship to its frame; Artistic text aligns with its initial insertion point. Paragraph text can also be aligned vertically within its frame. You can't vertically align Artistic text. Both types of text can be aligned using the Text toolbar, the Text property bar, or the Format Text dialog box.

Aligning text helps ensure a balanced appearance in your documents. In addition, it can be used to create visual impact, and organize the information that you want to present. When combined with Draw's Align and Distribute commands, you can specify alignment that suits nearly any purpose.

Cross-Reference For more information on the Align and Distribute commands, see Chapter 3.

Aligning Artistic text

The easiest method of aligning Artistic text is to use the text view of the Property bar. You can also align Artistic text using the Format Text dialog box. The advantage of using the Format Text dialog box is that in addition to aligning the text, you can also specify other options such as choosing a font or size at the same time. Both methods are described in the following sections.

Using the Property bar

To align text using the Property bar:

1. Using the Text tool, select the text to align.

2. Click one of these alignment buttons:

    - **None:** If none of the characters in the text string have been shifted horizontally, choosing None is the same as left alignment.

    - **Left:** Aligns the text to the immediate right of the initial insertion point (see Figure 4-24).

    - **Center:** Centers the text on the initial insertion point.

    - **Right:** Aligns the text to the immediate left of the initial insertion point.

    - **Full Justify:** Aligns selected text with even left and right margins.

    - **Force Justify:** Aligns selected text with even left and right margins. Unlike full justify, force justify also stretches the last line of a selection.

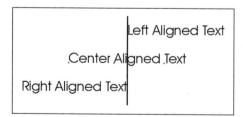

Figure 4-24: Aligning Artistic text.

Using the Format Text dialog box

To align Artistic text in the Format Text dialog box:

1. Using either the Pick tool or the Text tool, select the text to align.

2. Select Text ⇨ Format Text or click the Format Text button on the Text property bar.

3. Choose the Align tab to display the alignment property sheet.

4. Select the type of alignment you want to use and then click OK to complete the operation and return to the drawing window. The alignment options behave the same, whether you use the property bar or the Format Text dialog box.

Tip If you intend to apply special effects, such as envelope effects, to Artistic text, center align the text first. If you need to edit or change the text later, the new text appears perfectly aligned, maintaining the appearance of the effect.

Aligning Paragraph text

Draw lets you align Paragraph text both horizontally and vertically in its frame. You can choose to align all of the paragraphs or selected paragraphs in the frame. Dragtxt2.cdr, which you created in a previous exercise, contains Artistic text. In the following exercise, you convert the text to Paragraph text, and work with Paragraph text alignment.

Horizontal alignment

To align Paragraph text horizontally:

1. Start Draw if it's not already running, and open dragtxt2.cdr.

2. Using the Pick tool, select the text and click the Convert Text button on the property bar (see the "Convert Text" sidebar for more information). The text is converted to Paragraph text with a soft return at the end of each line.

3. Select the Text tool from the toolbox. The tool you use to select text is important when you want to format Paragraph text. If you use the Pick tool to select the text, any formatting options you set are applied to all of the paragraphs in the frame. If you use the Text tool, you can choose to format all of the paragraphs or specific paragraphs in the frame.

4. Click the Center Align button on the Text toolbar or Text property bar to change the alignment of the entire block of text (see Figure 4-25). Alternatively, you can change the alignment in the Format Text dialog box, just as you would for Artistic text.

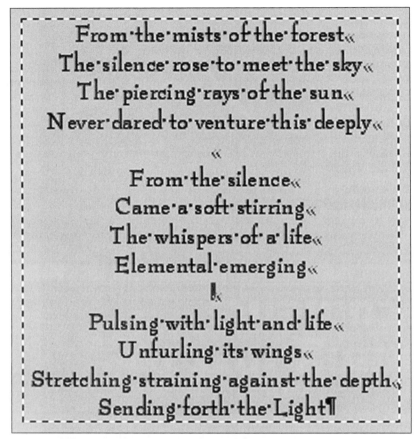

Figure 4-25: Center align the text by clicking the Center Align button on the Text property bar.

Converting Artistic to Paragraph Text

Convert Text is a toggle button. This means that clicking the button swaps between Artistic and Paragraph text. When you convert several lines of Artistic text to Paragraph text, Draw treats the returns as soft returns. Any formatting options that you apply are applied to all of the text. If you want to apply formatting to specific paragraphs only, you have to manually change the soft returns to hard returns. If you convert Paragraph text to Artistic text, any paragraph-specific formatting is lost. If you have several paragraphs, each with a different alignment, Draw changes the alignment of all the paragraphs to the alignment of the first paragraph.

You can also convert using the Convert command in the Text menu. You can't, however, convert Paragraph text to Artistic text if the frame that contains the Paragraph text is linked to other frame(s), if the Paragraph text has special effects applied to it, or if the Paragraph text extends beyond the frame that contains it.

Vertical alignment

To align Paragraph text vertically:

1. Using the Pick tool, select the frame of the text.

2. Select Text ⇨ Format Text, and then choose the Frames and Columns tab to display the Frames and Columns property sheet (see Figure 4-26).

3. Click the down arrow on the Vertical Justification box and select Full. The drop-down list box offers you the choice to vertically justify text at the top, center, or bottom of the page, or full page. The default is to justify the text vertically at the top of the page.

4. Click OK to complete the operation and return to the drawing window (see Figure 4-27). The text appears vertically aligned down the full length of the page. Save the dragtxt2.cdr file for future reference, if you want.

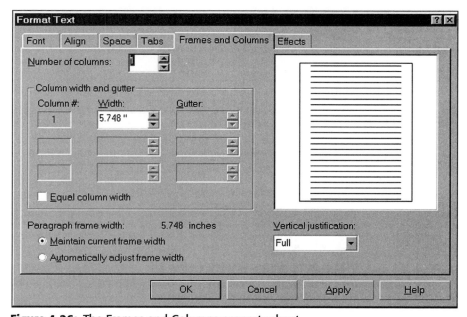

Figure 4-26: The Frames and Columns property sheet.

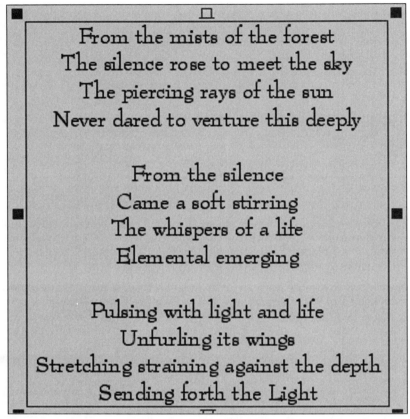

Figure 4-27: The text appears vertically aligned down the full length of the page.

Customizing Text Commands

Draw provides the capability to customize text properties to meet your needs. Using the Customize dialog box, you can add buttons to toolbars for quick access to text commands. Customizing Draw's text properties let you work more efficiently and help you maintain a consistent appearance in your documents.

Adding the Fit Text to Frame button

Fit Text to Frame automatically adjusts the point size of Paragraph text so that it fits inside a fixed frame. To add Fit Text to Frame functionality to a toolbar:

New Feature   The Fit Text to Frame command is new to Draw 9.

Tip

Although you can add buttons to any toolbar, it's a good idea to organize buttons by functionality. The Fit Text to Frame button works well on either the Text toolbar or the text view of the Property bar. If you want to add the button to the Property bar, select the text in your document to display the text view first.

1. Select View ➪ Toolbars, and select the toolbar to which you want to add the Fit Text to Frame button. The selected toolbar appears in the drawing window.

2. Select Tools ➪ Options, and expand the Workspace and Customize categories by clicking the plus (+) signs beside their names. In the Commands window, expand the Text category and then click Text formatting to display the Text formatting toolbar options page.

3. Select the Shrink or Expand Text to Fill the Frame button. The Shrink or Expand Text to Fill the Text Frame Button, as well as the other formatting buttons, appears in the Buttons section. The Fit Text to Frame button is highlighted (see Figure 4-28)

4. Click and drag the button to the toolbar or property bar.

5. Click OK to return to the drawing window.

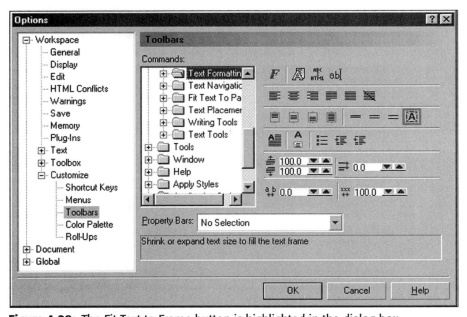

Figure 4-28: The Fit Text to Frame button is highlighted in the dialog box.

Tip

If you forget to display the toolbar to which you want to add the new button, you can click the Toolbars button on the Toolbar property sheet, and select the toolbar you want from the list. Click OK to display the toolbar in the drawing window.

Adding the Extract and Merge Back buttons

The Extract and Merge Back commands, available in previous versions on the Text menu, have disappeared. If you use these commands, you can add the functionality of Extract and Merge Back by customizing the Text toolbar. You can add the Extract and Merge Back buttons using the method above for Fit Text to Frame. The buttons for both commands appear in the Text Tools command category (see Figure 4-29).

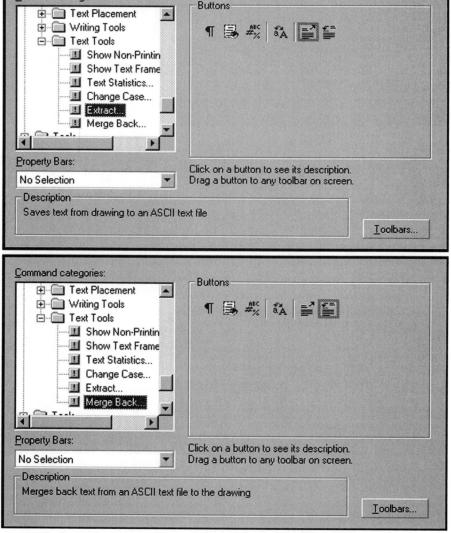

Figure 4-29: The Extract and Merge Back buttons appear in the Text Tools command category and are highlighted when you select them.

Using Extract and Merge Back

Extract and Merge Back let you edit text in an external text editor and remerge it with your document. The Extracted text is saved as an ASCII text (.txt) file in the folder of your choice. These commands are useful if you want to edit a large quantity of text externally in a word processor or the Windows notepad.

Using Extract means that any formatting that you applied in Draw is not preserved when you save the file. Similarly, any formatting that you apply in an external editor is not preserved when you merge the text back into your document. Plain text (ASCII) does not support formatting. When you merge the text into your document, it assumes the formatting attributes you specified in Draw for the text body into which the text is being placed.

Editing Paragraph Text

As it does for Artistic text, Draw offers two ways to edit Paragraph text: interactively in the drawing window and in the Edit Text dialog box (see Figure 4-30). Large blocks of text, such as multipage documents, are easier to edit in the Edit Text dialog box.

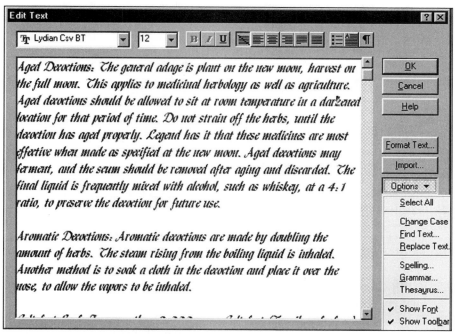

Figure 4-30: The Edit Text dialog box.

Using either method, you can edit text by either highlighting a section of text to be changed or deleted, or by clicking an insertion point and modifying the text. The Edit Text dialog box also has options for editing character properties, such as the font, size, and style for Artistic text, and includes other formatting options, such as indents, tabs, and bullets for Paragraph text. From the Edit Text dialog box, you can import text, change text case, and access these writing tools (which are covered in detail later in this chapter):

✦ Spell Checker

✦ Grammar Checker

✦ Thesaurus

✦ Type Assist

Using the Windows Character Map

The Windows Character Map provides a reference that lists the extended characters available for any installed font, along with their associated code numbers. To use the Character Map, select Start ➪ Programs ➪ Accessories ➪ Character Map. Select the font whose characters you want displayed from the drop-down list.

When you click a character, the keyboard code number is displayed. You can copy the character and paste it into your document, or you can enter the code numbers directly as you are entering text by pressing Alt while entering the numbers.

Working with interactive text editing

Editing text onscreen gives you the advantage of being able to control and view text changes as they are being made. You can click an insertion point and add text, or highlight text and replace it, much as you would in a word-processing program. In addition, you can adjust spacing, such as kerning, interactively. *Kerning* refers to the space between the characters in a word. The goal of kerning is to make the characters in a word appear evenly spaced and balanced, based on a percentage of the letter *m*. Badly kerned text may appear to break a word into parts because the spacing is not even. Every font kerns a bit differently. Some fonts, such as Century Schoolbook, kern nicely, have an easy-to-read and pleasing look, and are traditional favorites. Other fonts, such as some novelty fonts, kern poorly, making them difficult to read, especially when used in large blocks of text.

Adjusting character spacing

To adjust character spacing interactively:

1. Using the Shape tool, select a string of Artistic or Paragraph text. You can select either a single line or multiple lines. A kerning arrow appears at the bottom of the text (on the right side of the selected text).

2. Drag the kerning arrow to adjust the spacing between the characters. If you drag the arrow to the right, the spacing increases; if you drag the arrow to the left, the spacing decreases (see Figure 4-31). As you increase character spacing, the words may seem to flow together. You can adjust the word spacing to compensate for this effect.

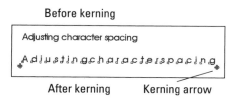

Before kerning

Adjusting character spacing

Adjusting character spacing

After kerning   Kerning arrow

Figure 4-31: Drag the kerning arrow to increase or decrease the amount of space between characters.

Adjusting the kerning lets you balance text, create a point of emphasis, or create effects. Generally, if you adjust the space between characters, you also need to adjust the space between words to prevent the words from appearing to run into one another.

Adjusting word spacing

To adjust the spacing between words interactively:

1. Use the Shape tool to select a line of Artistic or Paragraph text. A kerning arrow appears at the bottom of the text (at the right end of the selected text).

2. Press Ctrl while dragging the kerning arrow to adjust the space between the words. If you drag the arrow to the right, the spacing increases; if you drag the arrow to the left, the spacing decreases (see Figure 4-32).

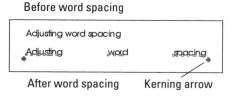

Before word spacing

Adjusting word spacing

Adjusting   word   spacing

After word spacing   Kerning arrow

Figure 4-32: Press Ctrl while dragging the kerning arrow to increase or decrease the amount of space between words.

Adjusting the spacing between characters and words lets you create an effect similar to justified text. The largest difference is that when you justify text, the text spreads across the entire page to maintain even margins. When you adjust the character and word spacing, you control the amount of the spread and, in the case of Paragraph text, the width of the text frame. You can also adjust the line spacing, which is frequently called leading.

Adjusting line spacing

To adjust the spacing between lines interactively:

1. Use the Shape tool to select a line of Artistic or Paragraph text. A line-spacing arrow appears at the bottom of the text (at the left end of the selected text).

2. Drag the line-spacing arrow to adjust the spacing between lines. Dragging the arrow down increases the space; dragging the arrow up decreases the space (see Figure 4-33).

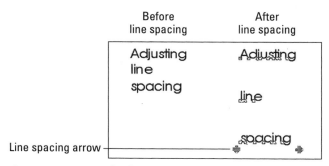

Figure 4-33: Drag the line-spacing arrow to increase or decrease the amount of space between lines of text.

When you adjust the spacing between lines of text, the spacing increases or decreases evenly between all the lines. You can't adjust the spacing between portions of text interactively. As with the spacing between characters, if you adjust the spacing between lines of text, you probably also need to adjust the spacing between paragraphs.

Adjusting paragraph spacing

To adjust the spacing between paragraphs interactively:

1. Use the Shape tool to select a line of Artistic or Paragraph text. A line-spacing arrow appears at the bottom of the text (at the bottom-left corner of the selected text).

2. While pressing Ctrl, drag the line-spacing arrow to adjust the spacing between paragraphs. Dragging the arrow down increases the space; dragging the arrow up decreases the space (see Figure 4-34).

Figure 4-34: Press Ctrl while dragging the line-spacing arrow to increase or decrease the amount of space between paragraphs.

Selecting individual characters

Draw lets you easily select and edit the attributes of individual characters. Once characters are selected, you can change their color, angle, height, and spacing, as well as other attributes. To select individual characters:

1. Using the Shape tool, select the block of text. When you select a block of text with the Shape tool, a small node appears at the bottom left of each character. You can use these nodes to select the individual characters.

2. To select an individual character, click its associated node. If you press Shift while making your selection, you can select multiple characters. You can also click and drag the Shape tool to marquee-select the nodes.

3. To move the selected characters, click and drag the nodes as desired. If you press Ctrl while dragging, you constrain the characters to the baseline (see Figure 4-35).

Figure 4-35: Drag the selected nodes to move their associated characters, or apply a rotation to shift the characters.

Tip   It can be difficult to select the individual nodes of text when using the default view. To reduce this problem, use the Zoom tool to enlarge the view of the text. In addition to being difficult to select individual nodes at reduced views, it's easy to accidentally shift a character when selecting a node by clicking the node. Marquee-selecting a group of nodes and then deselecting nodes that you don't want to change is one solution to this problem. Enabling Snap To Objects can also reduce the possibility of accidentally shifting a node. To enable Snap To Objects, select Layout ⇨ Snap To Objects.

Using Find and Replace

The Find and Replace command lets you search for and replace text and objects within your document. You can save your search criteria for later use, or use the basic default searches. The Replace Wizard provides commonly requested troubleshooting operations, such as finding and replacing colors, color models, outline pen properties, and text properties. The Replace Wizard is ideal for service bureaus or graphics professionals who need to troubleshoot documents or who need to globally change certain object properties.

To use the Find and Replace command:

1. Using the Text tool, select the text to search.

2. Select Edit ⇨ Find and Replace. (You can also choose to find words by selecting Edit ⇨ Find. This is useful for finding a point from which to edit the text.)

3. Enter the word or words you want to find in the Find What box, and then enter the replacement text in the Replace Text box (see Figure 4-36).

4. Click Find Next or Replace All. If you click Find Next, Draw finds the next instance of the text you entered. If you click Replace All, Draw finds all the instances of the text and replaces it.

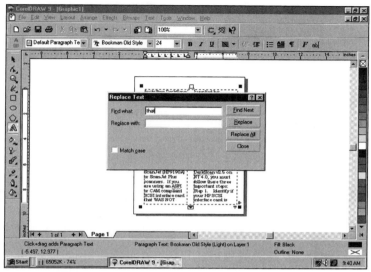

Figure 4-36: Find and Replace lets you find text within your documents and replace it with text you specify.

As a proofing tool, Find and Replace can be invaluable, especially when working with multipage documents. You can search for single words or phrases. If you are searching for instances of a word that normally appears with another word or words, entering the phrase as opposed to just the single word tightens the search parameters, letting you work more quickly through your document.

Tip

We all have our fumble-fingered moments, as well as words that we either consistently misspell or tend to type incorrectly (e.g., becasue instead of because). In the process of using Find and Replace, you may discover words that fall into these categories. Consider using Draw's Type Assist feature to help prevent errors you commonly make (see the section on using the writing tools, later in this chapter).

Importing Text into Draw

You can place text created in other applications in your Draw documents using one of three basic methods: importing, pasting, and using OLE (Object Linking and Embedding) functions. You can also edit imported, pasted, and OLE-inserted text. The following sections show you how.

To import text

When you import text, Draw by default places the text as Paragraph text in a new frame. To import text:

1. Select File ➪ Import to display the Import dialog box (see Figure 4-37).

2. Select the folder and file to import.

3. Click Import to complete the operation and return to the drawing window. The text file appears in your document in a text frame centered horizontally on the drawing page.

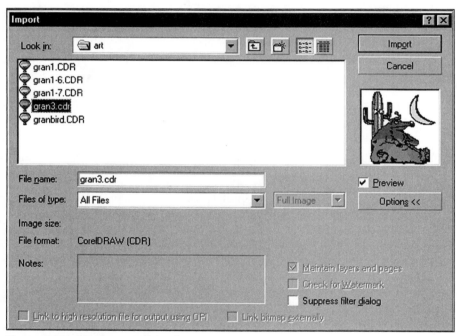

Figure 4-37: The Import dialog box.

Draw supports a variety of imported text formats. During the Draw installation procedure, you were given an opportunity to specify which text format filters you wanted installed. If the file format you want to import doesn't appear in the Import dialog box and it's one of the supported formats, you can go back and install just that filter without reinstalling the entire program.

Pasting text in Draw

Pasted text can come from any source that supports the Windows clipboard. By default, pasted text is placed as Paragraph text in a new frame. When you paste text from another application into Draw, the contents of the Windows clipboard is inserted into your document. If you've set an insertion point, the text is pasted at that location, using the default font and attributes. If no insertion point is specified, the text appears centered on the page as a document object.

If you want to paste text as Artistic text, click the Text tool on the page where you want to insert the text, and choose paste from the Edit menu. You can then edit, format, and modify it as you would text you created in Draw.

To paste text:

1. Open the source application and text file that you want to place in your draw document.

2. Select the text to place, and copy the text to the Windows clipboard.

3. Start Draw if it is not already running.

4. Select Edit ⇨ Paste. The text appears in the drawing window as a document object (see Figure 4-38).

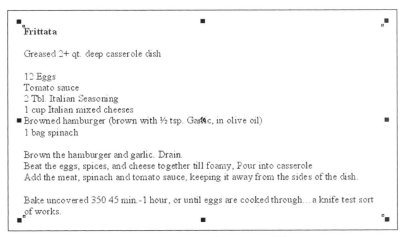

Figure 4-38: Pasted text appears as a document object.

Using the OLE functions

When you place text using OLE functions, the text is either pasted using the Paste Special command or inserted using the Insert Object command.

The Paste Special method

To paste text using Paste Special (OLE):

1. Open the source application and text file you want to place in your Draw document. To use Paste Special, the source application must be OLE-compliant. If you aren't sure whether an application is OLE-compliant, consult the user's manual for your source application. If your source application isn't an OLE-compliant application, Paste Special is grayed out and you can't insert an object using this method.

2. Select the text to place, and copy the text to the Windows clipboard. *Do not close the source application*. If you close the application before the object is inserted in your Draw document, the object is pasted as Paragraph text but isn't inserted as an OLE object. You lose the functionality of OLE.

3. Start Draw if it isn't already running.

4. Select Edit ⇨ Paste Special to display the Paste Special dialog box (see Figure 4-39).

5. Choose either Paste or Paste Link and select the source application from the As box. If you choose Paste Link, a *pointer* is saved with your Draw document rather than the object itself (the pointer "points" to the source file). The next time you open the document, Draw reads the source file and updates the object to include any editing changes made to the source file. Using Paste Link reduces the file size of your Draw document. Choose Paste if you want to embed the text in the document. When you embed an object, it is saved with your Draw document. The object is not automatically updated each time you open the file. Both choices let you open the source application from within Draw so you can edit and update the object.

6. Once you've made your selections, click OK to complete the operation and return to the drawing window.

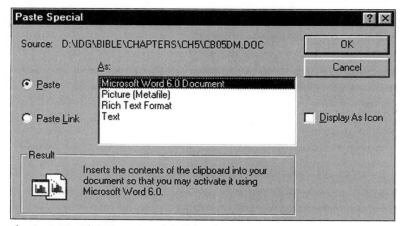

Figure 4-39: The Paste Special dialog box.

Caution If you link an object and then move or delete the source document, the link is broken and the object cannot be updated in the source application from Draw. Draw must be able to find the source document. To reduce the possibility of broken links, store the source file and your Draw file in the same location. If you need to transport the file to another system, be certain to include the linked source document with your Draw document.

The Insert New Object method

To insert a text object using Insert New Object:

1. Select Edit ⇨ Insert Object to display the Insert New Object dialog box (see Figure 4-40).

2. Choose an object type from the list box. If you don't see the object type that you want in the box, you may not have an OLE-compliant application capable of producing an OLE-type object. Either choose another object type or click Cancel to exit the dialog box. Check to make sure the desired source application is OLE-compliant before retrying to insert an object using the Insert New Object command.

3. Choose either Create New or Create from File and click OK. If you choose Create New, Draw opens the associated source application so you can create the object you want to insert. Save the document in your source application and close the application to return to Draw. Draw inserts the document object into a new frame as Paragraph text. If you choose Create from File, Draw prompts you for the location and name of the file, and then places the document object in your Draw document. The text appears as Paragraph text in a new frame.

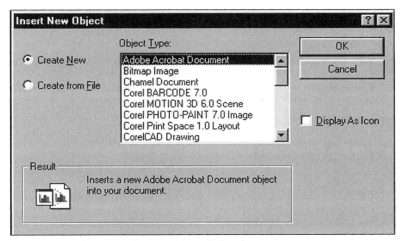

Figure 4-40: The Insert New Object dialog box.

Tip

By displaying both your OLE-compliant source application and Draw side-by-side on your monitor, you can click and drag OLE objects from the source application to your Draw document. This method of placing text and objects in Draw is basically an OLE shortcut that lets you bypass menus. This method *moves* the text from the source application to your Draw document as Paragraph text and places it in a new frame. OLE objects placed in this manner are removed from the source document. If you want to copy the text into Draw instead of moving it, press Ctrl while dragging the text.

Editing pasted and OLE text

If you are pasting text between Draw documents or within a Draw document, the text is editable text. You can edit and format the text as you would any text in Draw. Document objects can't be edited in Draw, however, because Draw sees them as embedded OLE objects (see the sidebar "Why Use OLE?"). You can double-click document objects to edit them. Draw opens a small window linked to the originating application, such as WordPerfect, in which you can edit the text. Clicking off the window closes the window and updates the text.

Why Use OLE?

OLE is, without a doubt, one of the most confusing subjects about Windows and Windows-compatible programs. The best way to understand it is to use it. It helps, though, if you first understand why you might want to use OLE. When you import or export a file or object, it must be converted into a format supported by the application in which it is to be placed. This means you have to have a filter installed on your system for every individual file format.

When you use OLE, file formats are not a consideration. The information is transferred via the Windows clipboard from the source application to the destination application. In Draw, an OLE object is identified on the status bar along with its associated application. If you double-click an OLE document object while in Draw, a small editing window appears in your Draw window with the text. The editing window represents your source application, where you can edit the text. When you've completed the editing, click outside the editing window to update your Draw document. For more information about OLE, see Chapter 8.

Using Text Styles

A style is a set of instructions that determine the appearance of an object. Sometimes called tags, these attributes reduce layout time and ensure that your document has a consistent appearance. In Draw, you can define and apply styles for Artistic text, Paragraph text, and graphic objects. Text styles contain instructions for such attributes as font, alignment, indents, and tabs. Draw provides a set of templates that contain popular layout styles, or you can define and create your own. When you change a style, text that uses that style is automatically updated to incorporate the change.

Applying a text style

Draw offers three methods for applying styles. You can choose a style from the Text toolbar or the Text property bar, or you can right-click an object to display the right-button menu. Select a style from the Styles submenu (see Figure 4-41).

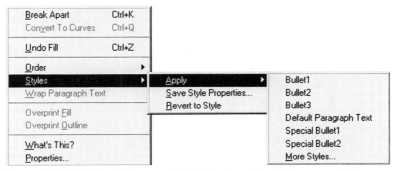

Figure 4-41: Right-clicking an object displays the right mouse button menu from which you can select styles.

Another method is to select a style from the Styles manager. To access the Graphic and Text Styles Docker, select Layout ⇨ Docker ⇨ Graphic and Text Styles (see Figure 4-42).

Shortcut

Pressing Ctrl+F5 displays the Graphic and Text Styles docker.

Using the Text toolbar or Property bar

To apply a text style using the Text toolbar or Text property bar:

1. Using the Text tool, select the text.

2. Select a text style from the drop-down menu. Be sure to choose a style that's consistent with the type of text. For example, you can't apply a Paragraph text style to Artistic text.

Note

When you apply a style to text, the text assumes those attributes that are defined in the style. For example, if the style defined the alignment, but not a font, your text would change to reflect the alignment style, while your font would remain the same.

Using the Graphic or Text Styles docker

To apply a style to text using the Graphic and Text Styles docker

1. Use the text or Pick tool to select the text.

2. Select Layout ⇨ Docker ⇨ Graphic and Text Styles to display the Graphic and Text Styles docker.

3. Double-click the style you want to apply.

Similarly, you can apply a style using the right-button menu by displaying the menu and selecting a style that's appropriate for either Paragraph or Artistic text.

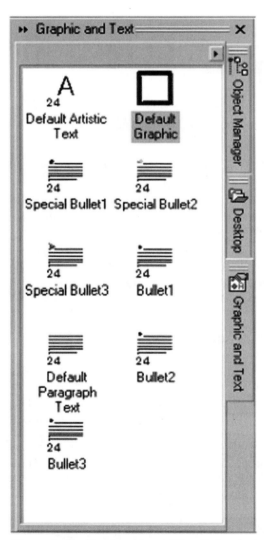

Figure 4-42: The Graphic and Text Styles docker.

Applying a style from another template

You can apply styles from other templates to your text. Draw comes bundled with a selection of templates. You can choose one of the bundled templates, or apply a style from one of your own templates. To apply a saved style:

1. Using the Pick tool, select the text to change.

2. Open the Graphic and Text Styles docker and click the right arrow.

3. Select Template ⇨ Load and choose the name of the template you want to use.

4. Click Open to display the template's styles in the Graphic and Text Styles docker.

5. Apply the style you want as shown in the previous exercise.

Note

The text updates to reflect the changes you selected. If you don't select a text object, the style change applies to *all* the text that uses the previous style.

Restoring a style

If you accidentally apply a style to text, you can either use the Undo command or select the text, and apply the Revert to Style command. To restore the previous style of a text object, right-click the text and select Styles ⇨ Revert to Style.

Creating a text style

Text styles are sets of attributes that you can use to control the appearance, attributes, and formatting of a selected text object. You can create both Artistic and Paragraph text styles. When you first start Draw, it applies a default style to your text. You can create new styles based upon the default text style, based on an existing object, or using the Graphic and Text Style docker.

Based on an object

To create a style based on an object:

1. Create the text you want to use as a basis for your style.

2. Using the Pick tool, right-click the text, then select Styles ⇨ Save Style Properties.

3. Enter a name for the style in the Name box. You can use up to 31 characters including spaces.

4. Leave the name of the style unchanged to overwrite the existing style.

5. Enable and disable the style attributes as desired.

6. Click OK to return to the drawing window.

Draw adds the style to the current template and to the list of styles in the Graphic and Text Styles docker. You can rename a style by clicking its nametag and entering a new name. Press Enter to complete the name change.

Caution   It's not a good idea to overwrite Draw's default style and template. You may want to use that style later. Be sure to enter a new name for the style to avoid overwriting the default style.

Using the Graphic and Text Styles docker

To create a style using the Graphic and Text Styles docker:

1. Using the Pick tool, click the desktop to deselect any selected objects.

2. Select Layout ➪ Docker ➪ Graphics and Text Styles to display the Graphic and Text Styles docker.

3. Click the right arrow and select New from the flyout menu.

4. Select the text style icon to indicate what type of style you want to create. A new style appears in the docker.

5. Select the new style icon.

6. Click the right arrow and select Copy Properties From from the flyout menu. A large arrow appears when you move back over the drawing window.

7. Click the text from which you want to copy the style attributes.

A new style icon appears in the docker. You can change the name of the style if you want.

Tip   By default, Draw saves new templates and styles in the draw\template folder. It's a good idea to make an archive copy of the templates in this folder. Doing so prevents the loss of your templates and styles if you need to uninstall or reinstall Draw.

Editing a style

You can edit styles at any time. Draw automatically updates the style unless you rename it. You can edit a style based upon changes you make to an object, or by modifying the attributes of the style. Editing existing styles is a good way to quickly create new styles.

Based on an object's changes

To edit a style based on an object's changes:

1. Modify the object as desired.

2. Right-click the object and select Styles ⇨ Save Style Properties.

3. Check the style attributes to confirm that the style attributes are the ones you want to use, then click OK.

If you want to use this as a new style, be sure to rename the style before closing the document and ending your Draw session. If you don't rename the style, *all* the text objects that use that style will be updated the next time you open the document, by modifying its attributes.

To edit a style by modifying the attributes:

1. Open the Graphic and Text Styles docker and select the style to edit.

2. Click the right arrow and select Properties.

3. Click the Text tab and change the attributes as desired.

4. Click OK to return to the drawing window.

 Tip   In addition to specifying text attributes, you can also specify other properties, such as a fill and outline, if desired.

Viewing Text Statistics

Draw provides a means for viewing information about your document. Perhaps you're a student who has to write a 300-word essay and chose Draw so that you could add graphics to your paper. Maybe you just have a burning curiosity to know the statistics associated with your document. The capability of viewing statistics about a file is useful when your offset printer calls and wants a list of the fonts in the file. If you're creating a 50-page catalog that incorporates several styles, it helps ensure consistency if you have a list of the styles. Regardless of your reason for wanting to know, the Statistics dialog box maintains a count of the number of words, lines, paragraphs, and characters in your document. The statistics dialog box also displays a list of the font(s) and styles used.

To count text elements for selected objects:

1. Using the Pick tool, select the text about which you want information.

2. Select Text ⇨ Statistics to display the Statistics dialog box (see Figure 4-43). If you enable Show Style Statistics, the Statistics dialog box also displays font and style information. If you don't have text selected, the Statistics dialog box displays information about the entire document.

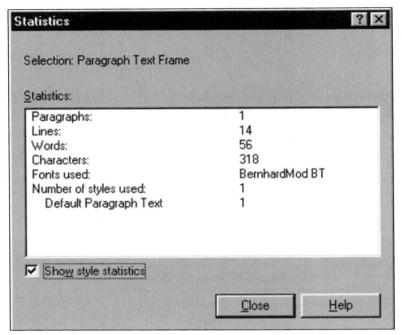

Figure 4-43: The Statistics dialog box.

Using the Writing Tools

It's an imperfect world. If you are similar to me, then writing tools were designed with you in mind. Draw provides a full complement of popular writing tools that assist you in creating your documents. These writing tools include

✦ Spell checker

✦ Thesaurus

✦ Grammar checker

✦ Type Assist

Spell checker

You can check the spelling of an entire document or selected words. By default, Draw uses automatic spell checking. When Draw finds a word it doesn't know, the automatic spell checker underlines the word with a red squiggly line in the drawing window. If you right-click a word that the automatic spell checker doesn't find, a dialog box appears displaying a list of alternatives from which you can choose. You can choose one of the alternatives or ignore the message and keep the original spelling. You have the option of enabling or disabling automatic spell checking on the Spelling tab in the Options dialog box.

To enable or disable automatic spell checking:

1. Select Tools ➪ Options and expand the Workspace and Text categories by clicking the plus (+) sign beside their names. Click Spelling to display the Spelling options page (see Figure 4-44).

2. A checkbox indicates whether automatic spell checking is enabled or disabled. Click the box to enable or disable the spell-checking feature.

3. Specify in which frames you want errors to be highlighted. Enabling Show errors in all text frames highlights all the errors in your document. Enabling Show errors in selected text frame only highlights the errors in the selected frame.

4. To set the maximum number of alternate word suggestions that Draw displays, enter a value in the Display spelling suggestions box.

5. If you have a word that you frequently misspell and want Draw to automatically correct for you in the future, enable Add corrections to type assist.

6. Enabling Show errors which have been ignored highlights all the words you ignored and that Draw still does not recognized after the document has been checked for spelling errors.

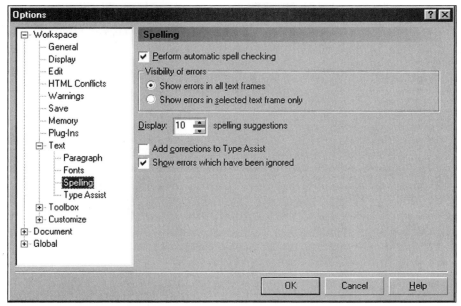

Figure 4-44: The Spelling options page lets you specify the settings to use when spell checking your documents.

Spell checking a large multipage document can take some time if you select Show errors in all text frames. If you only want to check the spelling of a single word, double-click the word you want to check and then open the spell checker (see Figure 4-45).

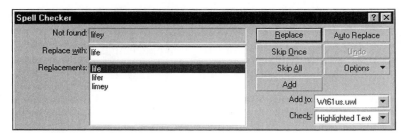

Figure 4-45: The word and possible replacement suggestions appear in the Spell Checker dialog box.

Thesaurus

The thesaurus displays a list of suggested alternative words for words selected in your document. You can view synonyms, antonyms, definitions, and examples of usage for words. If you select a word and then use the Thesaurus command, a synonym and its definition appear for the selected word. If you use the Thesaurus command with no text selected, you can enter a word for which you want to find definitions and alternatives. You can specify whether the thesaurus looks up synonyms, antonyms, or related words. You can also specify that the thesaurus display spelling suggestions when you type a word it doesn't have in its database.

To customize the thesaurus:

1. Select Text ➪ Writing Tools ➪ Thesaurus to display the Thesaurus dialog box (see Figure 4-46).

2. Click the Options button to display a drop-down list of options. A check mark beside the options indicates that the option is enabled. Select those options you want to use with the thesaurus from the drop-down list (see Figure 4-47).

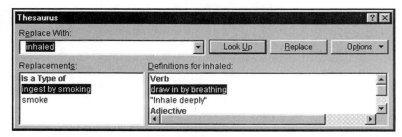

Figure 4-46: The Thesaurus dialog box.

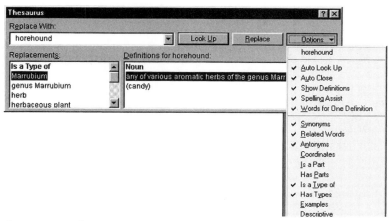

Figure 4-47: Thesaurus options.

When you open the thesaurus, it automatically looks up the word at the insertion point, and it closes automatically when you click Replace or Insert. You can customize the thesaurus to meet the needs of your document.

Grammar checker

The grammar checker lets you proof your document for spelling, grammar, and punctuation errors. The method Draw uses to flag errors is determined by the style you specify. You can specify a grammar level appropriate for the type of document you're creating (see Figure 4-48). For example, you would use a different style of writing and grammar for a formal business letter than you would for a casual letter to a member of your family.

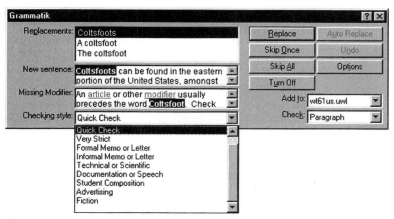

Figure 4-48: Draw flags errors based on the grammatical style you chose.

How it works

When the grammar checker finds a grammatical error, it offers you the option of replacing the error with an alternative it suggests. You can also skip the error for this time only, or skip the error for the rest of the proofreading session. You can also disable the rule associated with the error, so that the grammar checker ignores all errors of the same type. To check grammar: select Text ⇨ Writing Tools ⇨ Grammar Check. The Grammatik dialog box appears only if it finds errors in your document or the selected text. Choose whether you want to accept the suggested correction, or ignore the error. If you change your mind, you can click Undo to reverse changes you've made. You can add the flagged text to the user word list by clicking the Add button.

Specifying options

Choosing grammar-checking options can help you maintain a consistent tone in your documents. The styles used in a formal business letter vary greatly from the casual annual holiday letter. When you use Grammatik to check your documents, you can choose one of the preset grammar styles, or you can customize a style to fit your specific needs.

To specify options for the grammar checker:

1. Select Text ⇨ Writing Tools ⇨ Grammatik.

2. Click the Options button to enable the options that you want to use with the grammar checker. You can enable options such as Suggesting Spelling Replacements or Auto Start. Options are enabled if a check mark appears beside them.

3. To select a grammar style, click the down arrow beside Checking Style and choose a style from the drop-down list.

4. If you want to customize a style, choose a base style to modify and click the Edit button. Enable the rules you want to include when you grammar check your document.

Saving grammar styles

If you want to save a grammar style for future use, click Save or Save As. I recommend you choose Save As because it preserves the original style for future use. Enter a name that helps you identify the style later.

Type Assist

Type Assist automatically corrects selected typographic errors, misspellings, and abbreviations that sometimes occur when you enter text. For examples, Draw replaces "asap" with "as soon as possible," and replaces "hte" with "the."

To specify Type Assist options:

1. Select Text ➪ Writing Tools ➪ Type Assist.

2. Enable the options that you want to use for automatic correction in your documents (see Figure 4-49).

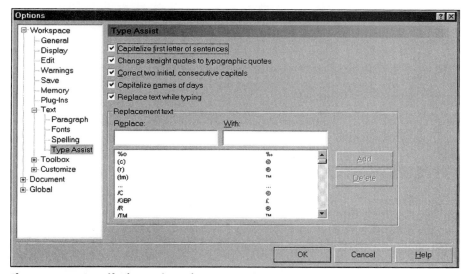

Figure 4-49: Specify the options that you want Type Assist to use.

You can use Type Assist to capitalize certain words. With Type Assist you can also replace text, punctuation marks, and change letter case automatically. By entering phrases or alternate spellings in the Replacement window, you can speed the creation of your documents by adding your own personal shorthand for words. For example, you could have the word "draw" automatically replaced with "CorelDRAW 9" each time you enter the word "draw" in your document.

Transforming Paragraph Text

You can also change the frame itself by applying transformations such as rotating and skewing. When you apply transformations, you can choose to wrap the lines of text to accommodate the frame's interior shape or resize the text along with the frame.

Adjusting the size of a paragraph frame

Draw treats Paragraph text frames similarly to other objects in a document. For example, you can size frames in the same way you size other objects. You can size a frame independently of its contents, or you can size the frame and the text it contains proportionately.

To increase or decrease the frame size:

1. Select the frame with the Pick tool.

2. Click and drag the handles to increase or decrease the frame size. The text rewraps in proportion to the increase or decrease in the frame size.

3. If you want to resize the text as well as the frame, press Alt while dragging the handles.

Tip   You can also apply Fit Text To Frame to selected text, if you have specified a fixed frame. To apply Fit Text To Frame, select Text ⇨ Fit Text To Frame.

Moving Paragraph text frames

Paragraph text frames are like other objects in Draw. To move a frame, simply click and drag it to a new location. The text moves with the frame. You can reposition a frame anywhere on the page. Note that only the portion of the text that falls within the printable page will print.

Summary

Learning to work with text and text options is the first step to creating layouts that are clear, yet have impact. Adding text to documents, as well as editing and formatting text, are basic Draw skills that are essential to creating many documents. Some formatting options, such as drop caps and bullets, let you enhance the appearance of text in your document. Columns let you organize text in clear, concise blocks that are easy to read. In this chapter, you learned to:

✦ Choose between Artistic and Paragraph text

✦ Add text interactively and in the Text Edit dialog box

✦ Specify default text settings

✦ Format text

✦ Specify text attributes

✦ Align Text

✦ Transform text

✦ Use writing aids

✦   ✦   ✦

Editing Objects

I n Chapter 2, you learned the basics of transforming and manipulating objects. Draw's wealth of editing tools goes far beyond those you explored. Draw 9's features include several twists on familiar tools, as well as editing tools that let you expand your creativity. The Transform toolbar and Free Transform tools give you increased flexibility in transforming objects in your drawings. You can also reshape objects and create new elements using the Weld, Intersect, and Trim commands. Draw 9 supports 3D objects. Draw's 3D tools let you manipulate imported VRML (Virtual Reality Modeling Language) objects in the drawing window. Together, these editing tools let you enhance and refine your images.

Using the Transform Toolbar

The Transform toolbar contains all of the transformation commands. Unlike the Transform docker, the Transform toolbar provides a slim appearance and takes up less screen real estate (shown in Figure 5-1). In addition, the Transform toolbar is dockable, which means that you can drag it to any side of the drawing window and it will expand and stick to the side. The Transform toolbar has three views: floating toolbar, top or bottom docked, and side docked.

Tip   Maintaining the maximum amount of space for drawing is one of the most desirable goals when configuring your workspace, especially if your monitor is small. Side docked and floating toolbars interfere the least with the drawing area. Floating toolbars can be resized, and moved out of the way when needed.

You can perform the same functions with the Transform toolbar, regardless of which view is active in the drawing window. When you use a side-docked view of the Transform toolbar, clicking a tool displays the associated flyout menu so that you can specify the parameters to use. Table 5-1 displays the Transform tools in all views, a description of each, and how to apply the function to a selection.

Table 5-1
The Transformation Toolbar

Tool	Description	Action
x =564 " y =402 "	Object's position: Positions the object relative to the rulers	Enter new values in the horizontal and vertical position boxes to reorient the object relative to the rulers in the drawing window.
↔ 3.568 " ↕ 3.064 "	Object's size: Object's horizontal and vertical dimensions	Enter new dimensions for the object.
100.0 % 100.0 %	Scale factor	Enter new scale values for the object.
	Nonproportional sizing	Enable this button if you want to be able to apply nonproportional transformations.
	Mirror	Click either the horizontal or vertical buttons to mirror the selected object.
↻ 0.0 °	Angle of rotation	Enter the angle of rotation you want to apply to the selection. Positive values rotate the object in a counterclockwise direction; negative values rotate the selection in a clockwise direction.
x 4.304 " y 5.986 "	Center of rotation position	Enter values in the horizontal and vertical boxes to change the object's center of rotation relative to the rulers.
1 0.0 ° ↙ 0.0 °	Skew angle	Enter values to specify the horizontal and vertical slant you want to apply to a selection.
	Apply to duplicate	When this button is enabled (depressed), the transformation settings that you enter are applied to a duplicate of the selection. This button is a toggle. If it is disabled (up), the actions apply to the selected object.
	Relative to object	Enter values to reposition the object relative to its current position.

Working with the Free Transform Tools

The Free Transform tools let you rotate, skew, scale, and mirror selected objects in relationship to the objects' anchor points, other objects, or a position in the drawing window. You can specify the anchor point anywhere in the drawing window. The amount of transformation is determined by the direction of your mouse movement and the distance you move the mouse. To use one of these tools, choose the Interactive Transformation tool from the Shape tool flyout menu (see Figure 5-1). The Property bar changes to display the controls for transforming selected objects in the drawing window (see Figure 5-2).

Interactive Transformation Tool

Figure 5-1: The Interactive Transformation tool works with controls on the Property bar to let you interactively transform selected objects in the drawing window.

Free Skew Tool
Free Scale Tool
Free Angle Reflection Tool
Free Rotation Tool

Figure 5-2: Choose the type of transformation you want to perform from the Property bar.

Maintaining Outline Proportions When Resizing Objects

Draw doesn't automatically resize the outline width with an object when the object is sized, stretched, or scaled. If you want the outline to be resized in proportion to size changes that you apply to a selected object, enable Scale with Image in the Outline dialog box. When an outline is not resized with an object, detail within the object can be lost.

To access the Outline Pen dialog box, right-click the object and select Properties from the right mouse button menu. Click the Property tab and enable Scale with Image. Alternatively, you can select the Outline Pen dialog box icon from the Outline tool flyout menu or press F12.

Using the Free Rotate tool

When you use the Free Rotate tools a blue outline appears that allows you to view the rotation of the object (see Figure 5-3). A blue dashed line extends beyond the rotation. To Rotate objects with the Free Rotate tool:

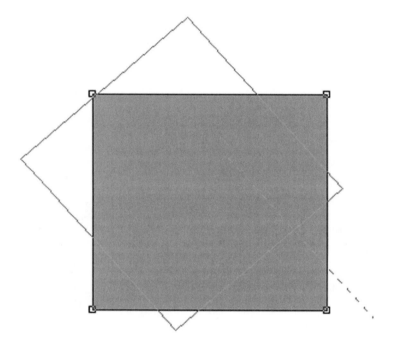

Figure 5-3: When you interactively rotate an object, a blue outline appears to show you the new orientation.

1. Choose the Free Transform tool from the toolbar and then choose the Free Rotate tool from the Property bar.

2. Select the object to rotate.

3. Click in the drawing window to specify an anchor point, and then drag the mouse pointer to specify the distance and direction in which you want to rotate the object.

The closer you move the cursor to the anchor point along the angle line, the more sensitive the rotation is to movement of the mouse. As the cursor moves further away from the anchor point, the rotation is smoother.

Tip Snap-To options make it easier to control the position of your anchor point.

Using the Free Angle Reflection tool

The Free Angle Reflection tool lets you create a mirror image. The angle and the anchor point of the reflection are determined by clicking and dragging the mouse cursor in the drawing window, as you did with the Free Rotate tool. To reflect objects with the Free Angle Reflection tool:

1. Choose the Free Transform tool from the toolbar and then select the Free Angle Reflection tool.

2. Select the object to reflect.

3. Click in the drawing window and drag to specify the anchor point and angle of the reflection (see Figure 5-4).

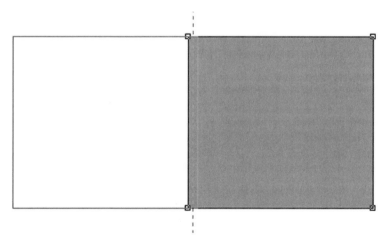

Figure 5-4: Click and drag in the drawing window to specify the anchor point and angle of the reflection.

As you click and drag in the drawing window, your graphic appears in the drawing window, letting you visually specify the reflection. The location of the anchor point specifies the distance between the object and the line of reflection. You set the angle of reflection by clicking and dragging the reflection line.

Using the Free Scale tool

Using the Free Scale tools, you can scale a selection both horizontally and vertically in one step. Like other Free Transform tools, the scaling behavior is based upon the location of the anchor point. When you click inside the object, Draw scales the object from its center. If you click to set an anchor point outside the object, the scaling and location of the object changes to reflect the angle and distance you drag the mouse cursor (see Figure 5-5). To scale objects with the Free Scale tool:

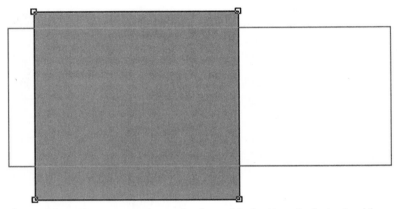

Figure 5-5: When you scale a selection with the Free Scale tool, a blue outline of the object appears to assist you in positioning and sizing the selection.

1. Choose the Free Transform tool from the toolbar and then select the Free Scale tool.

2. Select the object that you want to scale.

3. Click in the drawing window and drag to specify the anchor point and angle of the scaling.

Using the Free Skew tool

The Free Skew tool lets you skew objects horizontally and vertically in one step. The skewing is relative to the anchor point. You can skew the object from the center by clicking inside the bounding box of the object, or you can click outside the object to specify another anchor point. To skew objects with the Free Skew tool:

1. Choose the Free Transform tool from the toolbar and then select the Free Skew tool.

2. Select the object to skew.

3. Click in the drawing window and drag to specify the anchor point and angle of the skewing. As you click and drag, Draw displays a blue dashed outline of your object (see Figure 5-6).

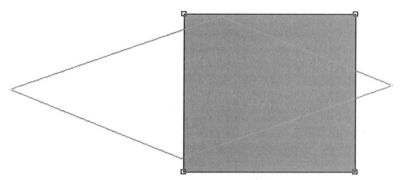

Figure 5-6: As you click and drag, Draw displays a blue outline of your object.

Understanding the Eraser and Knife Tools

The Eraser and Knife tools let you split objects into separate objects or subpaths, without the use of the shape tool. When you use the Eraser or Knife tool, Draw automatically converts the object to a curve object. This means that you don't have to convert Artistic text and geometric objects to curves before you use either of these tools. The Eraser tool functions much like a real-life eraser. The Knife tool creates separate objects or subpaths by cutting through to quickly open a closed path.

Erasing portions of an object

The Eraser tool's adjustable width makes it easy to remove portions of a selected object. As you drag the tool over the object, you erase portions of the object. The action breaks the path that defines the object; Draw, however, automatically closes the path. If you weld the object completely, the result is a single object with multiple subpaths (see Figure 5-7). You can use the Break Apart command on the resulting object to create independent objects.

Using the Eraser tool

To use the Eraser tool:

1. Using the pick tool, select the object from which you want to remove portions.

2. Choose the Eraser tool from the Node Edit flyout menu.

3. Click and drag across the object to erase portions of the object. It might take some practice to use the eraser with accuracy. You can't constrain the movement of the eraser, as you can some of Draw's other tools.

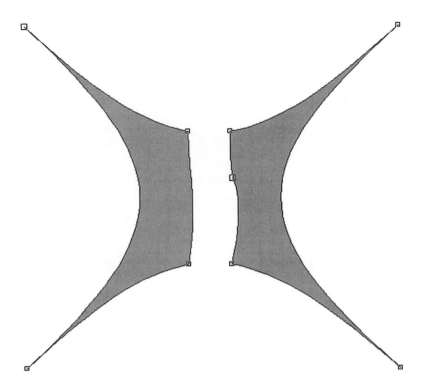

Figure 5-7: The Eraser tool lets you remove portions of an object, splitting an object into multiple subpaths.

Adjusting the Eraser tool's width

You can adjust the width of the Eraser tool to any width from 0.001 inches to 100 inches. The capability to adjust the width gives the tool the flexibility to create subtle changes in an object. The Eraser tool can erase shapes within an object, allowing objects below to show through the removed areas. To adjust the width of the Eraser tool:

1. Select the Eraser tool from the toolbox.

2. Select Tools ➪ Options. Click the plus (+) icon beside Workspace and then Toolbox to display the tools in the window. Select the Eraser tool to display the options for the Eraser tool (see Figure 5-8). Alternatively, you can right-click the Eraser tool icon in the toolbox and select Properties from the right mouse button menu to display the options for the Eraser tool.

3. Click the up and down arrows in the thickness box, or highlight the value and enter a new value.

4. Enabling Auto-reduce nodes of resulting objects eliminates extra nodes to help smooth the edges of the erased area.

5. Click OK to complete the operation and return to the drawing window.

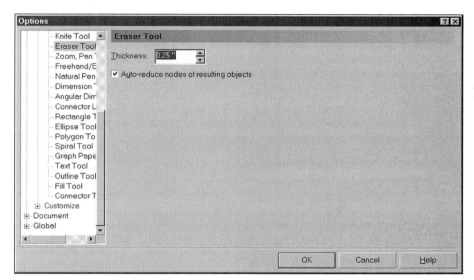

Figure 5-8: You can adjust the width of the Eraser tool on the toolbox property sheet in the Options dialog box.

Tip You can adjust the width of the Eraser tool on the Property bar when the Eraser tool is active.

Using the Knife tool

The Knife tool is similar to the Eraser tool in that it divides an object into multiple parts. Unlike the Eraser tool, the Knife tool doesn't remove a portion of the object. By default, Draw closes each of the open paths to create a separate and individual object. You can specify that Draw creates a single object with multiple subpaths. When you use the Knife tool with an open path, Draw divides the path into a single object with multiple subpaths.

To create separate objects

To split an object with the Knife tool into separate objects:

1. Choose the Knife tool from the Node Edit flyout menu.

2. Click the Automatically Close Object button on the property bar. Alternatively, you can right-click the Knife tool and select Properties from the right mouse

button menu, or select Tools ⇨ Options. Click the plus (+) icon beside Workspace and then Toolbox to display the tools in the window. Select the Knife tool to display the options for the Knife tool (see Figure 5-9). In the knife options window, enable Automatically Close Object. Be sure that Leave as one object is disabled.

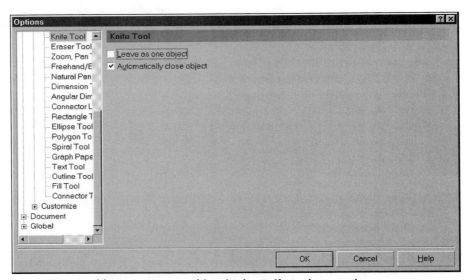

Figure 5-9: Enable Leave as one object in the Knife tool properties.

3. Click the outline of the object at the first point where you want to split the object. Note that the knife cursor turns point down when you are over the outline of an object. For the Knife tool to work, you must click the outline portion of an object.

4. Click the outline at the second point where you want to split the object. Draw closes both of the paths, dividing the object into two separate objects with identical attributes (see Figure 5-10).

To create a multipath object

To split an object with the Knife tool into a multipath object:

1. Choose the Knife tool from the Node Edit flyout menu.

2. Enable Leave as one object on the Property bar.

3. Disable Automatically close object on the Property bar.

4. Click the outline of the object at the first point where you want to split the object. If the original object was an open path, you don't need to select a second point. If you want to close the path later, select the object with the pick tool and click the Auto-Close button on the Property bar.

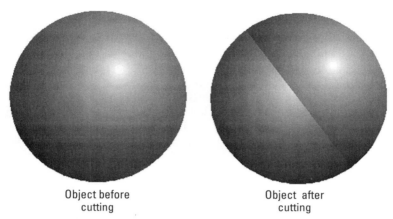

Object before
cutting

Object after
cutting

Figure 5-10: With Automatically close object enabled, the Knife tool creates separate objects with identical attributes.

5. Click the outline of a closed object at the second point where you want to split the object. Draw splits the object into multiple subpaths of a single object; the attributes, such as the fill, still cover the full extent of the object.

Using Intersect, Weld, and Trim

The Intersect, Weld, and Trim commands let you modify multiple objects to create new shapes. The Intersect command creates a new shape from the overlapping portions of multiple objects. The Weld command fuses multiple objects together, using the perimeter outline as the new shape. Any intersecting lines are removed, creating a single object. The Trim command removes the area that overlaps between objects.

Understanding target and other objects

The key to the successful use of the Intersect, Weld, and Trim commands is an understanding of what constitute a *target object* and *other objects*. Imagine that you intend to paint a wall. Before beginning to paint, you select a can of paint and choose the wall to paint. In Draw, the other object is the paint or the object being applied. The wall is the recipient of the paint or the target object. You can select multiple objects with which to apply the command. You choose a single object to receive the command.

Applying the Intersect command

The Intersect command is applied using either the Intersect docker or the Property bar. When you intersect an object using the Intersect docker, the newly created object assumes the attributes of the target object. If you use the Property bar to intersect an object, the attributes of the new object are determined by the method of selection you use. If you marquee-select the objects, the new object assumes the attributes of the bottom-most object. If you use Shift to select multiple objects, the new objects assume the attributes of the last object selected. You can't create intersected objects using Paragraph text, groups, dimension lines, master objects associated with clones, or objects that don't overlap. You can, however, create intersected objects using clone objects.

Using the Intersect docker

To intersect an object using the Intersect docker:

1. Using the Pick tool, select the objects to use for the intersection.

2. Select Window ➪ Dockers ➪ Shaping ➪ Intersect to display the Intersect docker (see Figure 5-11).

3. Enable Target Object if you want to keep a copy of the target object.

4. Enable Other Objects if you want to keep a copy of the other selected objects.

5. Click Intersect With.

6. Click the target object in the drawing window. You can click one of the objects you selected. Draw creates a new object from the overlapping areas of the selected objects (see Figure 5-12).

Using the Property bar

To intersect an object using the Property bar:

1. Using the Pick tool, select the objects to use for the intersection.

2. Click the Intersect button on the Property bar.

When you use the Property bar to create an intersection, Draw automatically intersects the objects, if you have two or more objects selected. The resulting object is the shape created by the space where all of the selected objects overlap. If you select more than two objects, where only two objects intersect at any one point, Draw applies the intersection to the first two objects created.

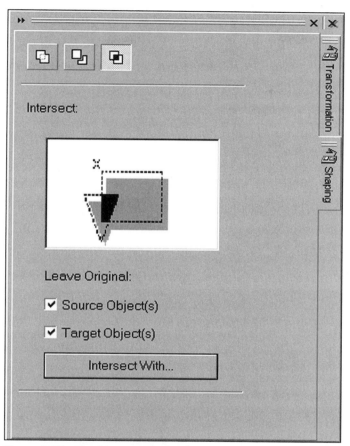

Figure 5-11: The Intersect docker lets you specify which objects are left in the drawing window when you apply the Intersect command.

Applying the Weld command

Welding fuses multiple objects together to create a single object. Unlike using the Combine command, overlapping objects don't create clipping holes. Instead, Weld creates a new outline from the perimeter of the selected objects and removes any internal lines. If the objects don't overlap, Weld behaves much like the Combine command to bind the objects into a weld group that behaves like a single object with multiple subpaths. You can also apply Weld to a single object that contains multiple subpaths. In this case, however, you must remove the internal lines manually. It's easier if you apply the Break Apart command first to separate the individual objects, and then apply the Weld command. Like the Intersect command, you can't apply Weld to Paragraph text, groups, dimension lines, or master objects associated with clones. You can apply Weld to clone objects, however. Welded objects assume the attributes of the target object. You can apply the Weld command using the Weld docker or the Property bar.

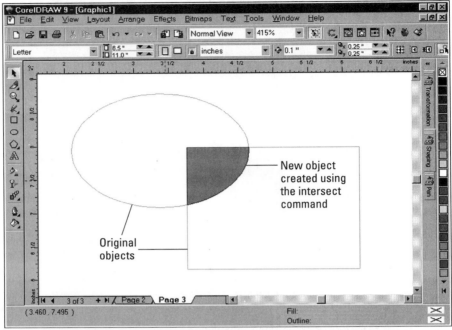

Figure 5-12: Intersect creates a new object from the overlapping area of selected objects. The gray outline indicates the original objects.

Using the Weld docker

To weld selected objects using the Weld docker:

1. Using the Pick tool, select the objects to weld.

2. Select Window ⇨ Dockers ⇨ Shaping ⇨ Weld to display the Weld docker (see Figure 5-13).

3. Enable Target Object if you want to keep a copy of the target object.

4. Enable Other Objects if you want to keep a copy of the other selected objects.

5. Click Weld To.

6. Click the target object in the drawing window. You can click one of the objects you selected. Draw creates a new object from the perimeter of the selected objects (see Figure 5-14).

Using the Property bar

To weld objects using the Property bar:

1. Using the Pick tool, select the objects you want to use for the weld.

2. Click the Weld button on the Property bar.

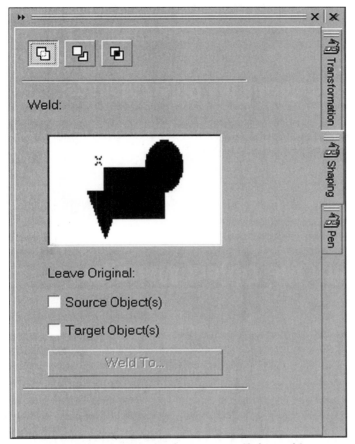

Figure 5-13: The Weld docker lets you specify how objects are to be welded.

Draw creates the weld object or weld group automatically. The method you use to select the objects determines the attributes the new object or group assumes. If you use the Shift-Click method to select the objects, Draw uses the last object selected to determine the attributes. If you marquee-select the objects, Draw uses the bottom-most object to determine the attributes.

Applying the Trim command

The Trim command removes overlapping areas of selected objects to create a new object. The resulting object retains the attributes of the target object. Like Intersect and Weld, you can't use Trim with Paragraph text, groups, dimension lines, or masters of clones. You can trim clone objects, however. You can use the Trim docker or the Property bar to apply the trim command.

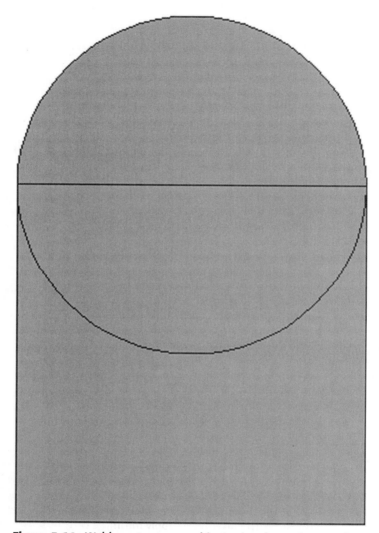

Figure 5-14: Weld creates a new object using the perimeter of overlapping objects to determine the shape. The outlines indicate the original circle and rectangle used to create the new object.

Using the Trim docker

To trim an object using the Trim docker:

   1. Using the Pick tool, select the objects to trim.

2. Select Window ➪ Dockers ➪ Shaping ➪ Trim to display the Trim docker (see Figure 5-15).

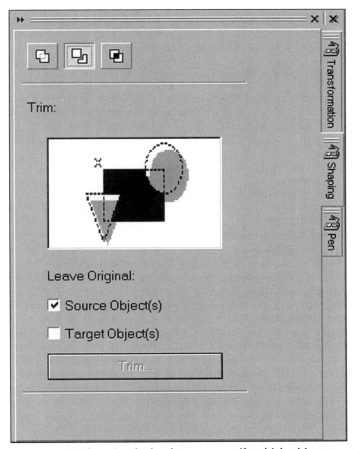

Figure 5-15: The Trim docker lets you specify which objects are to remain in the drawing window when you apply the Trim command.

3. Enable Target Object if you want to keep a copy of the target objects.

4. Enable Other Objects if you want to keep a copy of the other selected objects.

5. Click Trim.

6. Click the target object in the drawing window. You can click one of the objects you selected as the other object. Draw removes overlapping areas to create a new object (see Figure 5-16).

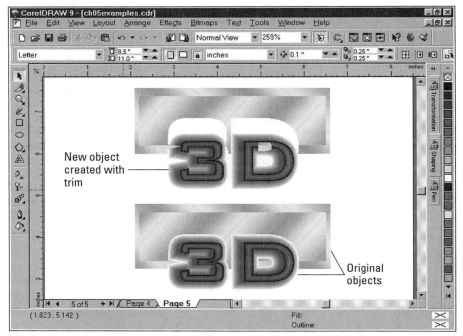

Figure 5-16: Trim removes overlapping areas to create a new object.

Using the Property bar

To trim an object using the Property bar:

1. Using the Pick tool, select the objects you want to use for the trim.

2. Click the Trim button on the Property bar.

Draw automatically trims the objects. The last object selected is trimmed by default. If you marquee-select objects, the bottom object is trimmed.

Tip   You can also use Weld, Intersect, and Trim with groups of objects.

Working with 3D Objects

Illustration and paint applications have historically been 2D applications. In most cases, you could simulate the third dimension, but you couldn't really manipulate 3D objects. Draw 9 has added 3D functionality. You can now import and manipulate 3D objects in your documents. Draw supports .3dmf, .b3d, and .wrl file formats. When you work in 3D, you can view an object from any angle with the 3D viewport.

You can also magnify a view, much as you would any other image. The viewport is your home base for manipulating 3D objects, and presents an alternate view of the drawing window (see Figure 5-17). Objects are viewed as if through a camera. Using the viewport you can:

✦ Change the viewing angle

✦ Reposition the object in the viewport and in your document

✦ Rotate the object on 3D axes

✦ Resize 3D objects

✦ Add lighting effects

✦ Modify camera settings

✦ Specify the settings for rendering the 3D object

Figure 5-17: An alternate view of the drawing window appears when you use the 3D viewport.

Importing 3D objects

You can import 3D objects into the drawing window using either the Import dialog box or the Scrapbook docker. The advantage the Scrapbook docker is that you can view all the thumbnails in a folder, as opposed to a single thumbnail in the import dialog box. To import a 3D object into the drawing window:

1. Select Tools ➪ Scrapbook to display the Scrapbook docker (see Figure 5-18).

2. Select the folder to view in the Scrapbook.

3. Click and drag the 3D object you want to use from the Scrapbook to the drawing window.

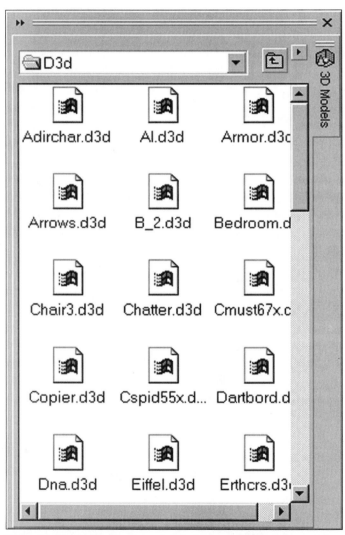

Figure 5-18: Using the Scrapbook docker to import images is quick. The Scrapbook docker also lets you view all the images in a folder.

Using the 3D viewport

Table 5-2 lists the 3D viewport controls, a description of the controls, and how to manipulate objects in the viewport using the controls. You can resize and move the viewport if you want. To reposition the viewport in the drawing window, click and drag the border to a new location. Like other objects in Draw, clicking and dragging the handles resizes the viewport.

**Table 5-2
3D Viewport Controls**

Control	Action	Usage
	Object Select tool	Lets you select a 3D object for manipulation.
	Object Rotation tool	Lets you interactively rotate the object in the viewport on all axes by clicking and dragging the rotation widget in the viewport.
	Camera Zoom tool	Zooms the view of the object in the viewport.
	Camera Slide tool	Clicks ands drag the object along the x and y axes.
	Camera Walk tool	Lets you adjust the camera's view point.
	Camera Pan tool	Lets you adjust the camera angle.
	Camera Rotation tool	Lets you rotate the camera around your 3D text.
	Camera Revolve X axis	Rotates the camera around the x axis.
	Camera Revolve Y axis	Rotates the camera around the y axis.
	Camera Revolve Z axis	Rotates the camera around the z axis.
	Camera Rotation box	Specifies the amount of camera rotation.

Adjusting the camera

When working in the viewport, 3D objects are viewed from a camera's point of view. By adjusting the camera, you can view the 3D object from an infinite number of perspectives and angles. You can also change the degree of magnification and zoom in on the object in the viewport. Camera settings are used to frame and scale the object in the viewport. For example, by adjusting the camera you can make objects appear to be far away, or you can adjust the camera to display only a portion of the object.

Magnifying objects

To magnify 3D objects:

1. Select the Camera Zoom tool from the toolbox.

2. In the viewport, click and drag upward to zoom in on the 3D object or click and drag downward to zoom out.

Alternatively, choose one of the preset magnification views from the Property bar.

Resizing the viewport

Zooming in on the 3D object changes the framing. The view displayed in the viewport is the same as the one Draw renders in the drawing window when you've completed manipulating the object. If the entire object doesn't appear in the viewport, it won't appear in the 2D rendering. Only that portion of the object that falls inside the visible frame is rendered. This can cause the finished object to look truncated or cropped (see Figure 5-19). Resize the viewport as desired to provide the view you want to use. You can also position the camera to adjust the viewpoint of the object (see the next section).

Positioning the camera

To position the camera:

1. Select the Camera Slide tool from the Camera tools flyout menu, and drag along the *x-y* plane in the viewport to adjust the horizontal and vertical view of the object.

2. Select the Camera Walk tool from the Camera tools flyout menu, and drag upward in the viewport to move the camera toward the object. Dragging downward in the viewport moves the camera away from the object.

Alternatively, you can choose one of the preset *walk* levels from the Property bar. These walk levels adjust the distance between the camera and the object. In addition to adjusting the position of the camera, you can also change the angle from which the object is viewed.

Figure 5-19: If the object falls beyond the boundary of the viewport, it will appear truncated or cropped when it's rendered.

Adjusting the camera angle

To adjust the camera angle:

1. Select the Camera Pan tool from the Camera tools flyout menu.

2. In the viewport, click and drag to change the direction of the camera.

When you adjust the camera angle, you change the direction that the camera is pointing, rather than move the camera to a new location. You can also reorient the camera by moving it to a different viewpoint, effectively rotating it around the object. Draw lets you rotate the camera either interactively or by specifying settings on the Property bar.

Rotating the camera around 3D text

To rotate the camera around 3D text:

1. Select the Camera Rotate tool from the Camera tools flyout menu.

2. Choose a rotation plane from the Property bar and drag the rotation widget in the viewport to adjust the rotation of the camera. You can also select one of the camera rotation buttons on the Property bar and either enter a value in the Camera Rotation box or drag the Camera Rotation slider. Press Enter after entering a value or dragging the slider.

Tip

Dragging the rotation widget requires practice. If you click and drag inside the widget, you can rotate the camera view along any of the planes; if you click and drag outside the widget, you are restricted to rotating the camera view along the selected plane. The widget is very sensitive. A small movement can change the view dramatically. I recommend using the camera rotation settings until you are familiar with interactively adjusting the rotation.

Manipulating 3D objects

You can reposition and rotate your 3D object in the viewport. Unlike reorienting the camera, changing the orientation and position of your 3D object changes the object itself. You can choose one of the preset views of the object, display a grid, or display a 3D axis to assist you in positioning your object. Table 5-3 shows the view controls and their use.

Once you have finished manipulating an object, you can return to Draw's regular drawing window. Draw renders the 3D object as a 2D bitmap in the drawing window, but you can edit the object in 3D at any time by double-clicking the object to return to the viewport.

| | Table 5-3 | |
| | **View Controls** | |
Control	*Name*	*Description*
	View Top	Toggles the view to display the top of the object.
	View Bottom	Toggles the view to display the bottom of the object.
	View Front	Toggles the view to display the front of the object.
	View Back	Toggles the view to display the back of the object.
	View Left	Toggles the view to display the left side of the object.

Control	Name	Description
	View Right	Toggles the view to display the right side of the object.
	View Director	Toggles the view to a 3D view of the object.
	Display xyz coordinates	Displays the axes coordinates in the viewport.
	Display home grid	Displays the *floor* grid in the viewport.
	Camera view	Displays the view as seen through the current camera settings.

Positioning objects in the viewport

To position objects in the viewport:

1. Using the Object Select tool, click the object in the viewport to select it. The object appears with a 3D bounding box around it (see Figure 5-20).

2. Drag the object along the *x*- or *y*-axis to a new location in the viewport. If you press Ctrl, you can reposition the object on the *z*-axis.

Alternatively, you can use the position boxes on the Property bar to reposition your object with precision, by highlighting the value to change and entering a new value. Press Enter to move the object to the new location.

Tip   If changing the position of the object in the viewport doesn't display the view you want of your objects, you can rotate the object to display a new view (see the next section).

Rotating objects in the viewport

Like positioning objects, you can rotate objects either interactively or by entering values in the rotation boxes. To rotate objects in the viewport:

1. Using the Object Rotate tool, click the object in the viewport to select it. The 3D rotation widget appears around the object in the viewport (see Figure 5-21).

2. Click and drag the handles on the widget to rotate the object as desired.

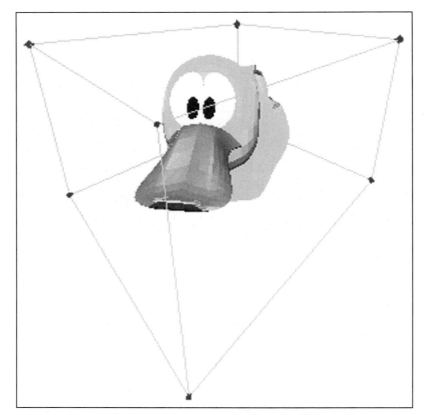

Figure 5-20: When an object is selected in the viewport, a 3D
bounding box appears around it.

Tip

The 3D rotation widget is much like a virtual onscreen trackball, but like the camera rotation widget, it tends to be very sensitive. Learning to operate in 3D space is one of the most difficult computer graphics skills to master. If you aren't familiar with operating in 3D, I recommend that you use the rotation boxes to reorient objects in the viewport.

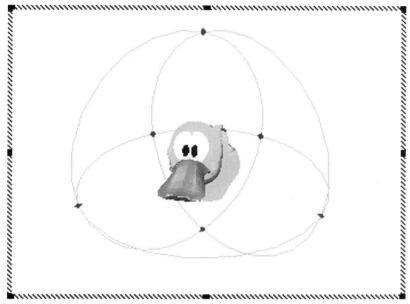

Figure 5-21: Use the 3D rotation widget to interactively rotate your object in the viewport.

Adding lighting to objects

Lighting lends a feeling of realism to 3D objects by adding highlights and shadows to the objects. When you first import a 3D object, it may appear dark or even black because imported objects contain little or no lighting information. You can add as many lights as you want to objects in your drawing. There are four types of lights available to use with 3D objects:

✦ **Ambient:** Ambient light is similar to full daylight and is uniform. It has no specific origin and does not add shadowing to objects. Generally, ambient lighting is the first light you should specify. Specifying ambient lighting is essential for viewing your objects, particularly if you don't use other lighting types.

✦ **Distant:** Distant light casts direct light on your object. Although the light is directional, the amount of light is softened because the virtual source of the light is remote.

✦ **Point:** Point light, like ambient light, casts light in all directions. This is a good choice for brightening your entire object.

✦ **Spot:** Spot lighting is specific. It focuses on a single area of your object. You can change the location and angle of spot lighting.

Note It takes longer for Draw to render your 3D objects as the number of lights increase.

Setting ambient lighting

To set ambient lighting:

1. Click the Distant/Ambient button on the Property bar to display the Illumination dialog box, and then click the Ambient Light tab (see Figure 5-22).

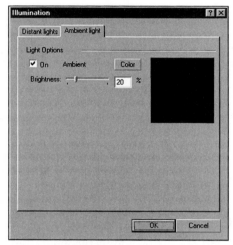

Figure 5-22: You can specify ambient light settings in the Illumination dialog box.

2. Click the On checkbox and click the color swatch to choose a color for your light.

3. Move the Brightness slider to the right to increase the overall brightness of your object; move it to the left to decrease the brightness of your object.

Tip Adding too much ambient light tends to flatten images. I recommend using a lower setting and adding other types of lights to create a higher contrast and give your 3D objects a more realistic feel. You can also use the other lighting types exclusively by turning off the ambient light setting.

Adding distant, point, and spot lighting

To add distant, point, and spot lighting:

1. Determine the type of lighting you want to add, and then do one of the following:

   • Click the Distant/Ambient button to add distant lighting.

• Click the Add Point Light button to add point lighting.

• Click the Add Spot Light button to add spot lighting.

2. In the Illumination dialog box, choose a color for the added light and select Front or Back lighting (see Figure 5-23).

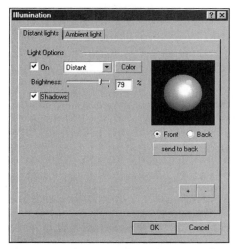

Figure 5-23: You can specify settings for your lights in the Illumination dialog box.

3. Adjust the light's intensity and specify the angle and drop off for the lighting, if any.

4. Click Apply to return to the drawing window.

Using the angle settings

The angle settings adjust the deflection of the light. If you accept the default settings, the light shines directly at the object. When you specify drop-off settings, you adjust the amount of feathering on the edge of the light, narrowing the beam of light. For most purposes use the default settings for both the angle and drop-off of the lighting. Once you add point and spotlights, you can adjust the position of the lights in the viewport by dragging the lights with the Object Select tool. You can also adjust the rotation of spotlights using the Object Rotate tool. Click and drag to adjust the orientation of the selected spotlight.

Once you are satisfied with the light settings, click outside the viewport to return to the main drawing window. Draw renders the object to screen. Rendering the objects may take a few minutes depending on the size of the object and the settings you specified in the viewport.

Summary

The ability to edit elements of a drawing is an essential part of any powerful
drawing package. Draw 9 expands your editing abilities by providing the editing
tools required to control the appearance of objects in your drawings. In this
chapter, you learned to

✦ Use the Transform toolbar to quickly apply transformations to objects in your
  drawings

✦ Work with the Free Transform tools to simultaneously transform objects both
  horizontally and vertically

✦ Erase portions of objects and cut objects into parts

✦ Weld, trim, and intersect objects to reshape existing objects and to create new
  objects from objects in your drawing

✦ Manipulate 3D objects in the drawing window

✦   ✦   ✦

Draw 9 in the Works

Managing Documents

Draw lets you organize your document by managing the objects and styles contained in your drawing. It may seem like file and object management are tedious jobs — basically akin to electronic paper shuffling — but it's not time-consuming and the investment is worthwhile. Keeping track of the elements in your image and the file itself reduces frustration and saves time. The bonus is that good object management helps maintain a consistent appearance in your images and improves the overall quality of your documents.

Planning Ahead

The task of finding a single file can be difficult. To make matters more complicated, the eight-character acronym that made so much sense a month ago frequently becomes as cryptic as hieroglyphics. Another act guaranteed to create confusion is creating multiple versions of an image, then naming them myfile1.cdr, myfile2.cdr, and myfile3.cdr. Unless your memory is far better than mine is, as time passes, it's hard to remember the difference between version files if the names are similar.

Every Draw document evolves from a working environment determined by the page setup, style, view, and settings that you specify for measurement and alignment tools. Each of these elements has default settings that you can accept, or you can specify custom settings to meet your layout requirements. If you were creating a document for the World Wide Web (WWW), for example, you would want to choose pixels as your unit of measurement. Choosing pixels would assist in creating images scaled to fit your Web page. If you are simply playing with Draw, the default settings are probably acceptable.

It's best to plan ahead, and Draw provides these solutions, which are covered in detail throughout this chapter, to prevent problems before they occur:

✦ **Adding keywords and notes:** Both Windows 95 and Windows NT let you give files long filenames, which helps alleviate cryptic file-naming problems somewhat (see the sidebar on long filenames later in this chapter). Over time, however, even a long filename might not conjure a mental image of a document. In Draw, you can avoid the confusion by adding keywords and notes to your drawings when you save them.

✦ **Specifying the layout first:** If you have a specific task in mind, such as a catalog or other document, it's a good idea to specify the layout settings first. It's frustrating to invest hours into a design, only to find that it needs to be reworked to meet specific printing or style requirements. Retrofitting a document is a thankless and time-consuming task. Predetermining your environment lets you devote yourself to the creative side of Draw.

Using the Draw 9 Save Features

I live in an old home in eastern Tennessee. It's beautiful here, but there are some drawbacks. One of the drawbacks is the lack of reliable power. Weather tends to be very harsh here, and the power can go down without warning. I have all kinds of insurance for power outage problems, such as a UPS (uninterruptible power supply), but nothing replaces the policy of saving files, and saving often. Anyone who works with graphic programs should adopt this as a personal mantra. Here are a few guidelines:

✦ **The Auto-Backup feature:** Replicating work is nearly impossible at times. If you are inclined to forget to save files, you can tell Draw to do it for you. Draw has an Auto-Backup feature that you can set to create a backup of your file at specified intervals. Draw can also create a backup file of your drawing every time you save the file. This provides you with a file to which you can revert if the changes you make are not what you wanted or if the program should close unexpectedly, leaving you with unsaved changes.

✦ **The Save As feature:** If you are working on a large file, and want to try several effects or create a what-if scenario, consider working with a copy of the file, rather than the original image. The Save As command lets you work with a copy, or save a different version of your file. Save As is also useful for saving selected objects in your drawing as a separate file, if you want to include them in another image. (See the section on Save As later in this chapter for detailed instructions.)

For more information on Draw 9 Save As features, see Chapter 1.

✦ **Document closing options:** If you close a drawing that hasn't been recently saved, Draw asks if you want to keep any changes, such as additions to your drawing or property changes, that have yet to be saved. You have three choices: Yes to save the latest changes, No to lose them and close the drawing, or Cancel to indicate that you've changed your mind and want to keep working on the drawing. If you try to close a drawing that has no name assigned to it, Draw asks if you want to save it under a new name. If you answer Yes, a dialog box appears to enter the name. Draw saves the contents, using the name you specify. The program also saves any settings you made and then closes.

Using Save As

To use Save As:

1. Select File ➪ Save As to display the Save Drawing dialog box (see Figure 6-1).

2. Select a location for your document, and enter a file name. If you're editing a file, and want to keep the original, or if you want to save the file in a different location, you can make a copy of the file by saving it under a different name in another drive or directory.

3. If you only want to save the objects that are selected in your image, enable the Selected Only box.

4. Enter any keywords and notes that you want to add.

5. Click Save to complete the operation. If you change your mind, you can click Cancel at anytime, and back out of the Save Drawing dialog box.

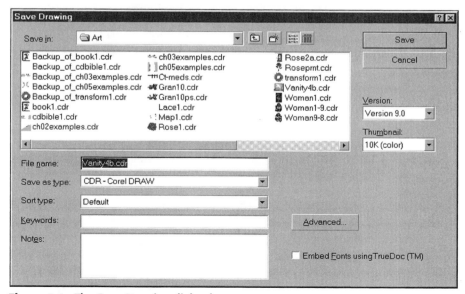

Figure 6-1: The Save Drawing dialog box.

Using Save All

To save all the open documents in Draw, select File ⇨ Save All. If the drawing hasn't been previously saved, the Save Drawing dialog box appears, allowing you to enter a location and file name for your drawing.

Caution   When you select Save All, Draw automatically presumes that you want to use the existing filename of your documents. It's easy to accidentally overwrite files that you intended to save under another filename. If you create version files where each file is a bit different, be sure to save the file using Save As, instead of Save All, to prevent overwriting your file.

The Trouble with Long Filenames

Windows 95 lets you create filenames with up to 255 characters, including spaces. You can include any character with the exception of these: \ / : * ? < > |. While that may seem to solve all of your file-naming and search problems, you should use long filenames with caution. If you need to share files with another person, send files electronically, or use a service bureau, there's no guarantee that the other person's system will support long filenames. They may not be able to read your file. Problems occur, for example, if you have multiple versions of Draw on your system. Version 5 and previous versions of Draw don't support long filenames. In addition, if you need to record your files on a CD-ROM, some recording standards, such as ISO 9066, support only DOS 8-3 (i.e., an eight-character name plus a three-character extension).

Another problem situation occurs if Windows 95 ceases to operate properly and it needs to be reinstalled. On some systems, files with long filenames tend to appear corrupted when Windows 95 has to be reinstalled over an existing but nonfunctional copy of the program. If you have any doubts whether a long filename is appropriate for your image, name files using the conventional method of eight characters with a three-character file extension.

Saving to other version formats

You can save your drawing so that it can be used in versions 5, 6, 7, or 8 of Draw. This is useful if you need to share files with another person who does not have Draw 9. To save a file in another version format:

✦ Click the down arrow next to the version, and select the version that you want to use. If your drawing contains text in a typeface that is not supplied with a previous version and the font is not installed on the system to which you are transferring the file, convert the text to curves using the Convert to Curves command before you save the file.

Caution   If you intend to use a service bureau to process your file, or if your file is being transferred to a Macintosh, you should export your document in .eps format, and specify that you want the text converted to curves. Employing this method for transferring your file for printing avoids potential problems. For best results, I recommend that you contact your service bureau or commercial printer. They will guide you through the process while ensuring successful output.

✦ If you create and use a custom TrueType font in your image, enable Embed Fonts using TrueDoc. This feature is also useful if you are sharing files with someone, and you're not sure that they have the font you specified in your image. If your service bureau does not possess an Adobe Type 1 equivalent of your font, enable this feature to ensure that your document prints as expected. If you are uncertain about font compatibility, contact your service bureau or commercial printer.

Using advanced save settings

You can control the file size and versatility of your document when you save an image. The advanced settings in the Options dialog box let you control the way Draw saves files, such as compression, special effects, and presentation data. To access the advanced settings options, click Advanced in the Save Drawing dialog box (see Figure 6-2). Select the options you want to use and click OK to return to the Save Drawing dialog box. Use the following as a guide to selecting advanced save options:

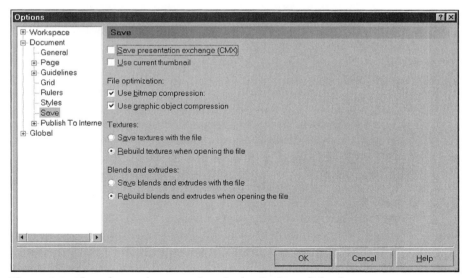

Figure 6-2: The advanced save settings in the Options dialog box.

✦ **Save presentation exchange (CMX):** The Corel Metafile Exchange (CMX) format is a file format that is supported across all of Corel Corporation's products. Files saved in this format can be opened in any application made by Corel Corporation, such as Corel PhotoPaint. Metafiles are a type of vector file format that is used to facilitate the exchange of information among applications. When you enable this feature, you ensure that your file can be exchanged between Corel products. Files saved with presentation data are significantly larger than files saved without this option and take longer to save and open. If you have limited storage space on your hard disk, I don't recommend enabling this feature unless you must be able to exchange data between Corel products.

✦ **Use current thumbnail:** By default, Draw saves a copy of the thumbnail with your image. Thumbnails are small graphics files that are created from the image header of your file. The thumbnails allow you to select a file visually by providing a representative image in the preview window of the Open Drawing dialog box. More information about using thumbnails appears later in this chapter.

✦ **Use bitmap compression:** By default, Draw uses bitmap compression when it stores a document that contains a bitmap. Using compression reduces the file size of your document. Draw uncompresses the file when you reopen the drawing.

✦ **Use graphic object compression:** When Use graphic object compression is enabled, Draw compresses the entire document for storage, reducing the file size. Compressed drawings take longer to open and save.

✦ **Save textures with the file:** Enabling this option lets Draw save any texture fills with your image, exactly as you created them. If you need to share your document with others, this ensures your document will look exactly as you created it when it is opened later. Files that contain texture effects tend to be larger than those without such effects. If file size is a critical issue, you may want to disable this option by selecting Rebuild textures when opening the file.

✦ **Rebuild textures when reopening the file:** This option saves the texture information for associated objects without saving the texture itself. Although this reduces the file size of your document, your image takes longer to open, and may appear different than when you first created it. This is because the texture has to be rebuilt each time the image is open.

✦ **Save blends and extrudes with the file:** This option is similar to textures in that saving extrudes and blends with your image increases your file size, but you can ensure the appearance of your image.

✦ **Rebuild blends and extrudes when opening the file:** This option reduces the file size by saving blend and extrusion information about associated objects without saving the finished appearance of the object. Like Rebuild textures, files take longer to open because Draw has to rebuild each blend and extrusion in your drawing.

Working with archives

Draw offers version control with Corel Versions. This feature lets you archive successive versions of your drawings. Version control gives you access to previous versions of your documents, while controlling which versions are archived. Because your files aren't archived automatically, you can choose which versions of your document are saved as an archive. For example, version control was used to create the steps for the tutorials in this book. Although I tend to save frequently, not every saved file represented a step in an exercise. Using version control, I archived only those versions of the documents that represented an exercise step. You might choose to archive files that had major changes, or that had a specific purpose, such as a proof version of your drawing for a printer.

Note When you save an archive of your document, you use the File ⇨ Version Control command instead of the Save command. Draw prompts you to also save the changes to the original file.

Archived files can be temporary or permanent. Temporary versions are replaced by newer versions once the maximum number of temporary versions is reached. Permanent versions are kept until you decide to delete them. When you use version control, you specify the folder where Draw is to save the file. You can choose to save your versions in the same folder as the original file, or in another folder created specifically for that purpose. A version file might look a bit confusing at first, if you view it using the Windows Explorer. Instead of seeing multiple files, all of your versions are saved as a single file. It contains all the information for each version you save. Additionally, a Versions filename is always the same, and is expressed as the full path of the original file with all special characters such as ":", "\", or "." being replaced with a $. For example, if you saved a file named "mylogo" in the d:\office folder, but the Versions archive folder was e:\archive, the filename for the Versions file would be d:\office\mylogo\cdr.cv.

Caution Versions files are dynamic. That means if you delete or move the file or folder in which the original or versions file resides, the link to the original file will be broken and all of your versions lost. Use extreme caution when moving or deleting files. Although Draw lets you retrieve a file from an archived location, both the original file and the archive file must be in the correct locations with their original names.

Enabling version control

Before you can use Corel Versions, you need to enable version control in the Windows control panel and specify its settings. To enable version control, from the Windows desktop, select Start ⇨ Settings ⇨ Control Panel to display the Windows control panel. Double-click Corel Versions to display the New Version dialog box. Enable Version Control and specify the location where you want to save your archived files. If you don't set a specific location, the Versions file is saved in the same folder as the original file. Set the number of temporary versions you want to keep, and click OK to return to the Windows desktop. You can close the Control Panel if you want.

Archiving files

To archive files using version control:

1. Select File ⇨ Version Control ⇨ Archive Document to display the New Version dialog box (see Figure 6-3).

2. Enter the maximum number of temporary versions you want Draw to make before it starts overwriting previous temporary versions.

3. Enable the permanent option if you want this version of the file to be retained permanently.

4. Enable Use compression if you want to compress your saved files. This option saves disk space but lengthens the time it takes to save and retrieve the file.

5. Enable Archive to Single Location if you want all of your Corel Versions files to be saved in the same place. If you leave this option disabled, your Versions files are stored in the same location as the original files.

6. Click OK. Draw prompts you to save the original file, if the current view of the file hasn't been saved. You must save your file for Versions to work.

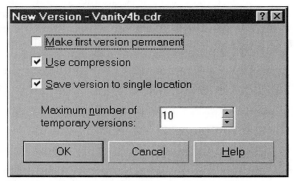

Figure 6-3: The New Version dialog box lets you specify how archived files are to be saved.

Note

Permanent Versions files that you create don't affect the number of temporary versions you can have. If you allow for ten temporary versions and save eight temporary versions and two permanent versions, you can still save two more temporary versions before Corel Versions starts to overwrite files. You can also have a mix of temporary and permanent versions in the same Versions file. They won't be overwritten if you exceed the maximum number of temporary versions that you specified.

Making backups

Draw lets you create a backup of your document each time you save it. By default, the backup copy is stored in the same folder as the original file. This feature is useful if you need to revert to the previous version of a drawing. In addition, you can specify that Draw back up your file at specified time intervals. As mentioned earlier in this chapter, if you tend to forget to save frequently, this option can be invaluable. Backup options are specified in the Options dialog box (see Figure 6-4).

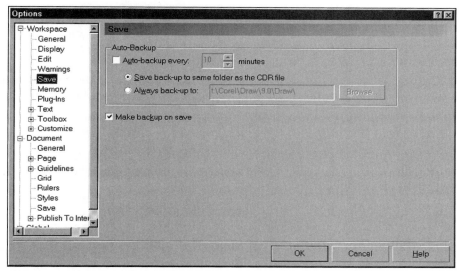

Figure 6-4: The Save page of the Options dialog box lets you specify how to save your documents.

Specifying backup options

To specify backup options:

1. Select Tools ⇨ Options to display the Options dialog box. Expand the Workspace category and click Save to display the Save page.

2. Enable Auto-Backup, if desired. By default, this option is enabled and set to create a backup of your image every 10 minutes. You can change the amount of time by clicking the up and down arrow or by highlighting the amount of time and entering a new value. If you don't want Draw to create a backup file at specific times, disable this option.

3. If you want Draw to create a backup of your file every time you save the file, enable Save Back-Up to Same Folder as the CDR file, or Always back-up to.

Tip

When specifying a location for backup files, it's convenient to have a specific folder where you store all of your backup files. If you choose to use this method of storage, enter a location in the entry box. By default, the corel\draw folder appears in this entry box. It's not a good idea to save files in application directories. If you do and need to uninstall or reinstall an application, your documents could be lost.

Clicking the Browse button lets you locate the folder where you want to store your backup files. When Draw creates a backup file, it stores it under the filename Backup_of_*filename* (where *filename* is the name of your drawing).

Archiving Files for Long-Term Storage

Long-term storage space is problematic for nearly all computer users. Even the largest hard drives become full rapidly when you create a lot of illustrations. Graphics files can be monstrous in size, and unless you are keen on frequently upgrading your storage space, this is a problem. You can't leave your image files on your system forever. They take up too much space, and should your hard drive crash, you could lose months' worth of work.

The obvious solution is to back up your files to storage media for archiving purposes, and delete them from your hard drive. When it comes to archiving media, you have a variety of choices. You can use floppy disk, tape, magneto optical, zip drives, or CD-ROM media. While floppy disks are inexpensive and better than not archiving your files at all, they are not a good choice. Frequently, files won't fit on a single floppy disk, even if the files are compressed. Over time, floppy disks become unreliable. Tape backup units are economical and more reliable than floppy disks, but they, too, suffer from a limited amount of space. Magneto optical and zip drives are more costly than tape backups, but they provide an adequate amount of space and are reliable.

The best choice is to create a CD-ROM of your files. CD-Rs (CD-ROM recorders) have become more affordable, are fairly easy to operate, and are the best archiving choice. CD-Rs hold in excess of 600MB and are far more durable than other forms of media. They also have the advantage of recording to media that allows you to retrieve files easily. Regardless of what media you choose, however, creating an archive of your files is the best insurance against the loss of data.

Rescuing data

In addition to making backup files, Draw creates temporary files that it stores in your Windows Temp directory. Draw creates one temporary file for each level of undo and redo that you specify. For example, if you have specified four levels of undo, Draw will create a temporary file for each of four consecutive steps.

If you are an experienced computer user, you know that computers can make your life very interesting. If your system or a program crashes unexpectedly, you can lose hours of work in the blink of an eye. The temporary files that Draw creates can save a lot of frustration during these moments. It's possible to resurrect most, if not all, of your work using these files.

To restore a document from a temporary file:

1. On the Windows desktop, double-click My Computer (or whatever you call your computer, if you have renamed it).

2. Switch to the drive that contains your Windows Temp directory, locate the temporary folder, and open it.

3. Select a temporary file. By default, Draw's temporary files are easily identified by their balloon icons.

4. Click the file once, and select File ⇨ Rename. Rename the file, using .cdr as the extension. You can then open the file in Draw.

Tip If you select View ⇨ Details, you can view the date and time associated with each file.

If you were saving the file when the system or program crashed, the most recent file may not have the most complete data. If that is the case, rename and open the previous file.

Using Revert

Revert is the ultimate oops insurance, and it allows you to specify less Undo levels. As mentioned previously, it's not a good idea to specify too many levels of Undo. Each level of Undo and Redo requires swapfile space and a pointer that's retained in physical memory. Revert lets you reopen the last saved version of your drawing, regardless of Undo settings. To Revert the drawing window to the last saved version of your document, select File ⇨ Revert.

Adding notes and keywords to a file

When you add notes and keywords to a file, it makes finding the file later much easier. When you open a file to which you've added notes and keywords, the information you entered appears in the Open Drawing dialog box if you highlight the file. To add keywords and notes to a file:

1. Select File ⇨ Save if you are saving the file for the first time. Select File ⇨ Save As if you want to add notes and keywords to a file you saved previously.

2. In the Notes box, enter the information that you want to record about the file.

3. Add keywords by entering a word in the keyword box. You can add as many words as you want, separating each pair of words with a comma (see Figure 6-5).

4. Click Save to complete the operation and return to the drawing window.

You can add as many keywords as you require to identify the file. Notes automatically wrap to the next line as needed. In addition to making it easier to find specific drawings, you can add information about the document, such as a client's name or contact phone number. With this method, information can be at your fingertips whenever you open a drawing.

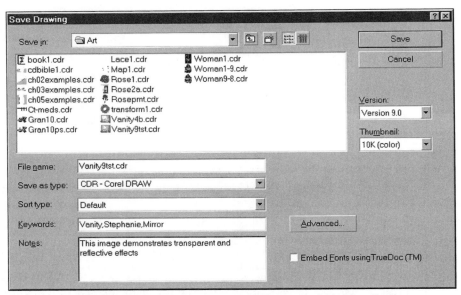

Figure 6-5: Entering keywords and notes can help you quickly identify files.

Choosing a thumbnail size

Thumbnails, like keywords and notes, help you find your files faster. When you've assigned a thumbnail to an image, the thumbnail appears in the preview box of the Open Drawing dialog box when the file is highlighted. Draw offers some options regarding the way thumbnails are displayed. You can choose no thumbnail, black and white (monochrome 1K), 5K color, or 10K color. By default, Draw assigns a 10K thumbnail to your drawings. If you save a file in another version, the thumbnail options change to reflect the version you chose.

To assign a thumbnail to your image:

1. Select File ➪ Save if you are saving the file for the first time. Select File ➪ Save As if you want to add notes and keywords to a file you saved previously.

2. Choose the thumbnail type from the thumbnail list box.

3. Click Save to complete the operation and to return to the drawing window.

Tip

When I have a multipage document that contains several views of an image, I frequently add an additional page as page one. On that page I place a smaller version of the image, *and* a logo or name that identifies the client or project. In the Notes box, I add a note about the number of pages. This method lets me visually identify multipage documents that contain multiple versions of an image.

Getting document information

Draw lets you display useful information about your documents. Selecting File ➪ Document Info displays the Document Information dialog box, where you can find information about your image, such as file size, location, and types of objects (see Figure 6-6). You can save this information as a text file for future reference, or print the file by clicking the Print button. If you save hard copies of your files for reference, you might find it useful to print a copy of this information to store with the hard copy of your image.

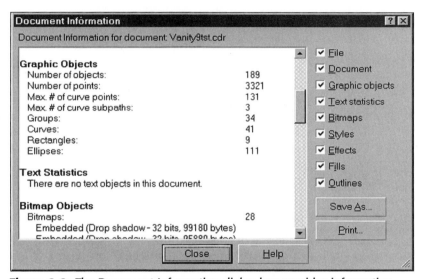

Figure 6-6: The Document Information dialog box provides information about your document, such as the file size and the types of objects that are contained in it.

Using the Object Data Feature

The object data feature is one of the most powerful, but least understood, features in Draw. Using the object data feature, you can create a database about the objects in a drawing. Why would you want to create a database of your objects? Suppose you created a multipage document that contained several similar designs for a silk screen application. One design might be sized to print as a pocket design, another design sized to print on the front of a child's shirt. A third design might be sized to print on an adult shirt. Using the object data feature, you could create a database that included information about the size, cost per shirt, an item number, and other information. You can also print a hard copy of the object data summary. This is useful if you want to add a hard copy to your permanent records.

You create the database by entering information for specific objects on the Object Data docker. This information is set up on a datasheet called the Object Data Manager, with categories of information organized in columns. Using the example above, you might have sizes in one column, an item number in another, and cost in a third. You can enter information about groups of objects or about individual objects. For each element in the drawing, you enter the same categories of information.

After creating a database, you can view information on any object in list or datasheet form. The Object Data docker displays a list of all the information you've assigned. The Object Data Manager displays this information in a formatted datasheet. Draw provides basic functions for formatting and manipulating information in the database. You can add and delete columns, indent rows to show hierarchical relationships, and summarize data for selected objects. Using the Windows clipboard, you can copy data to different locations within the datasheet or between datasheets for different Draw documents. You can also use the Windows clipboard to copy data to and from other Window databases or spreadsheet programs, such as Quattro Pro and Microsoft Excel.

Working with data fields

The first step to creating an object database is to determine the fields and formats that you want to use. By default, Draw creates four data fields: Name, Cost, Comments, and CDRStaticID. You can edit, delete, or rename the first three fields. You can't edit or delete the CDRStaticID, however. Draw requires the field to identify objects in your image. You can create custom fields by defining their formats, using the controls in the Format Definition dialog box. You can choose one of four basic formats: General, Date/Time, Linear, and Numeric. Each of these basic formats offers a set of presets from which you can choose. If none of the formats is suitable for your application, you can modify the format by assigning a set of variables. For example, if none of the preset Date/Time formats is suitable for your application, you can create a custom Date/Time format. You can create and assign as many data fields as you want, as long as they use the allowable format variables.

Creating data fields

To create fields:

1. Using the Pick tool, select an object or group of objects.

2. Select WindowTools ➪ Dockers ➪ Object Data Manager or Tools ➪ Object Data Manager to display the Object Data docker. The fields initially displayed in the docker represent Draw's default fields.

3. Click the right arrow near the top of the Object Data docker and select Field Editor from the flyout menu to display the Object Data Field Editor dialog box (see Figure 6-7).

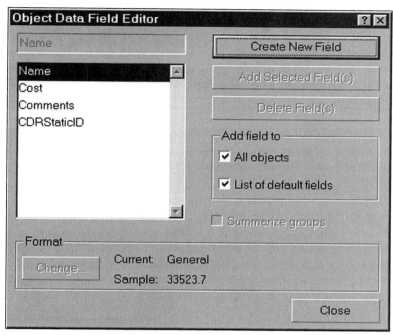

Figure 6-7: The Object Data Field Editor dialog box lets you specify data fields for your document.

4. Once the field editor is displayed, you can create a new field by clicking the Create New Field button. Enter a name for the new field in the Name entry box.

5. You can also add a new field from those listed in the field list by selecting the field you want to add and clicking the Add Selected Field button. This button appears grayed out if only Draw's default fields are listed in the field list.

6. If you want to change the format for a field, click once on the field to select it and then click the Change button in the Format section. The Format Definition dialog box appears (see Figure 6-8). Choose a format from the listed formats, or create a new format by entering the parameters in the Create entry box (see the section on creating a custom format later in this chapter).

7. Once you are satisfied with your field choices, click Close to return to the drawing window.

Note   You can't combine two or more different types of data formats in a single field. You can, however, correlate data between two fields. When you correlate data between fields, changing a value in one field updates the values in related fields.

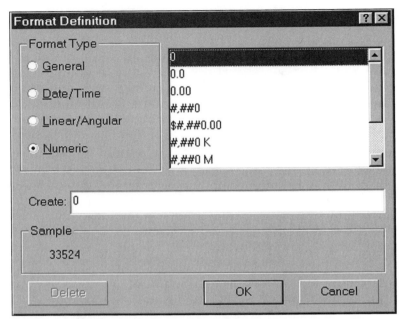

Figure 6-8: The Format Definition dialog box lets you choose a format for your data type.

Deleting fields

You can delete any field with exception of the CDRStaticID field. Remember that deleting a field also deletes all the data in the field. Deleting superfluous fields that contain no data, or data that won't be used, is a matter of good housekeeping. Your data is better organized, and you can produce tidier summaries. To delete a field:

1. Repeat steps 1 to 3 of the previous exercise to display the Object Data Field Editor dialog box.

2. Select the field you want to delete from the field list, and click the Delete Field(s) button.

3. Click Close to return to the drawing window.

Caution   Be careful deleting fields. Deleting a field also deletes all the data in the field, and is not a good method of clearing or editing entries in a field. If you don't want to lose the data, consider renaming the field or editing the data in the field.

Renaming fields

Using the Object Data Field Editor dialog box you can also rename a field. If you want to rename a field, click the field to rename, which will display the field in the entry box at the top. Enter a new name and click in the list box. The new name will appear in place of the old name.

Reordering fields

While collecting and entering data is an important process, it's meaningless unless it's organized in an understandable manner. You can reorder the fields in the Object Data Field Editor dialog box by clicking and dragging the field to a new location in the field list. The capability to reorder fields allows you to create the fields in any order you choose and organize them later. You can also use this method to organize new fields that you add to your object database.

Creating a custom format

You can create custom formats for each of the four main formats: General, Date/Time, Linear/Angular, and Numeric. Each allows a specific set of parameters. Those who are familiar with spreadsheets and databases will recognize these formats. If you are new to this type of information, this is not a complete reference on formats. If you need a complete reference on creating formats, I recommend consulting a spreadsheet or database reference.

Note   You can change the format of a field by selecting the field in the Field Editor and clicking the Change button. Select or enter a new format and click Close to return to the drawing window.

Specifying a General format

General formats display object data text and numbers in the same format that you enter them. Numbers appear without extra zeros preceding or following the number. Numbers also don't use digit-grouping symbols. For example, 001.23 would appear as 1.23, and 2,457 would appear as 2457. If the number exceeds 1,000,000, it is converted to an exponential or shortened number. For example the integer, 123,456,789, appears as 1.23457e+008.

Draw allows the use of the ampersand (&) in formats to indicate a variable value. The variable is replaced by the data you assign to the field. For example, the format "The pay scale for this employment level is" & "per hour." displays the data entry $6.50 as: The pay scale for this employment level is $6.50 per hour.

Note   The information on both sides of the ampersand must be enclosed in quotes to indicate variable data.

Specifying a Date/Time format

Draw uses Windows' current regional settings to determine the way it displays dates and time. To modify these settings, change the regional settings in the Windows Control Panel. Table 6-1 shows the Date/Time formats that you can use in your object databases.

	Table 6-1 Date/Time Formats	
Symbol	**Displays**	**Example**
d	Displays the day of the month as an integer with no preceding zero placeholder	June **10** 1997
dd	Displays the day of the month with a preceding zero, if the integer is a single digit	10/**04**/97
ddd	Displays an abbreviation for the day of the week	Monday = **Mon**
dddd	Displays the full name of the day of the week	**Tuesday**
M	Displays the month as an integer with no preceding zero	February = **2**
MM	Displays the month as an integer with a preceding zero if the integer is a single digit	March = **03**
MMM	Displays an abbreviation for the month	October = **Oct**
MMMM	Display the full name of the month	**July**
yy	Displays the year as two digits	1998 = **98**
yyyy	Displays the year as four digits	**1998**
h	Displays the hour as an integer with no preceding zero	9 AM = **9**
hh	Displays the hour as an integer with a preceding zero, if the integer is a single digit	9 AM = **09**
mm	Displays the minutes with a preceding zero, if the integer is a single digit	10:04 PM = 10:**04** PM
ss	Displays the seconds with a preceding zero if the integer is a single digit	10:04:09 PM = 10:04:**09** PM
am or AM	Displays the time using 12-hour time, with an am or pm symbol	10:04 **PM**

In addition to the format symbols shown in Table 6-1, Draw lets you use other symbols in your formats. You can use a space, tab, or any characters enclosed in quotation marks. These extra characters let you add information that is specific to the data you are using.

Note   If you want to incorporate information enclosed inside quotation marks that is bracketed by quotation marks as formatting symbols, you must precede the first quotation mark with the escape (\) character.

Linear and angular formats

You can display values accompanied by units of measurement. Linear formats display values, using the imperial and metric systems. You can also use picas, points, ciceros, and didots as units of measurement. Angular formats cover any angle measurement in degrees. Draw's built-in linear/angular object data formats combine these units with many of the numeric formats, providing effective display and easy conversion from one type of measurement to another. If the available presets don't meet your needs, you can create your own custom format by making two entries. The first entry is used for the major unit, such as yards; the second entry is a corresponding minor unit, such as inches.

When you create a custom linear or angular format, you must use one of the measurement formats supported by Draw. You can't combine any two systems, such as feet and kilometers. Table 6-2 shows the allowable format symbols, unit of measurement, and example of its use in a format.

	Table 6-2	
	Linear and Angular Data Formats	
Symbol	**Unit of Measurement**	**Major Unit / Minor Unit**
mi	miles	miles/feet
yds	yards	yards/inches
ft or '	feet	feet/inches
km	kilometers	kilometers/meters
m	meters	meters/centimeters
cm	centimeters	centimeters/millimeters
picas	picas	picas/points
points or pts	points	points/picas
ciceros	ciceros	ciceros/didots
didots	didots	didots/ciceros
degrees	degrees (angular)	degrees/no minor unit

Numeric format

Numeric formats let you display nonlinear numeric formats, such as currency. As with the general format, numbers exceeding seven places are displayed in exponential format, unless you specify a format that displays values in thousands or millions. Table 6-3 shows the allowable formats, a description of the formats, and an example of each format.

Table 6-3
Numeric Object Data Formats

Format	Description	Example
0	Used as a placeholder. Draw replaces each incident of the placeholder with a digit from the specified value. If the number has fewer digits than the number of zeros in the format, Draw displays the extra zeros.	If the format is 00.00, the value 5.75 is displayed as 05.75.
#	Used as a placeholder for a digit grouping symbol.	If the format is #,##0, the value 2222.22 is displayed as 2,222.
, (comma)	Used as a digit-grouping symbol.	1234 is displayed as 1,234.
. (period)	Used as a digit-grouping symbol.	1234 is displayed as 12.34.
$	Currency symbol.	12.00 is displayed as $12.00.
/?	Expresses a number as a fraction with the denominator of "?". Draw automatically converts the value to a fraction with the specified denominator, then reduces it to the smallest fraction.	If the format is #,##/16, the value 8 is displayed as 1/2.
K	Expresses a value in units of one thousand.	If the format is 0.0 K, the value 234567.89 would be displayed as 23.4 K.
M	Expresses a value in units of one million.	If the format is 0.0 M, the value 2,345,678.9 is displayed as 2.3 M.
%	Expresses a value as a percentage.	If the format is 0.0%, the value 2.34 is displayed as 234%.
E+00, e+00	Expresses a value in scientific notation.	If the format is 0.00e+00, the value 1234.56 is displayed as 1.23e+03.
- (dash)	Indicates the placement of a negative symbol in the format string.	If the format is #,##0-, the value 12,345.67 is displayed as 12,345-.

Note   Some characters, such as the comma and period, can be modified on the Number property sheet of the Regional Settings, which is found in the Windows control panel. For example, you can specify the number of places to use to the right of the decimal.

Creating an object database

Once you have all the fields you want for your drawing, you're ready to start adding information about your objects. You can use the Object Data Manager to access all the commands you need to add and edit your object information. The Object Data docker is best for entering data for single objects or groups and is accessible from the Tools or View menu. The Object Data Manager is best for entering and editing data for multiple objects, and is accessed by clicking the Object Data Manager button in the upper-left corner of the Object Data docker. You can add information to any selected cell. Table 6-4 shows the various methods of selecting a cell or range of cells using the Object Data docker.

| Table 6-4 |
| **Selecting Cells in the Object Data Docker** |

To select	*Do this*
A single cell	Either click the cell or press the cursor keys to move to the cell.
A range of visible cells	Click and drag from the first cell in the range to include the last cell in the range.
A large range of cells, whether they are visible or not	Click the first cell, press Shift, and then use the scroll bars to move to the last cell in the range and click it.
A row	Click the row heading.
A column	Click the column heading.
A range of contiguous rows and columns	Click and drag across the range of rows and columns.
All of the cells	Click the button in the upper-left corner of the summary sheet.

Once you select a cell or range of cells to receive information, enter the information you want to assign to the selected cells in the entry boxes of the Object Data Manager. To access the Object Data Manager, click the Object Data Manager in the Object Data docker.

The Object Data Manager provides the commands and functions you need for editing and formatting your object data summary (see Figure 6-9). For example, you can add and delete columns, indent rows to show hierarchical relationships, and summarize data for selected objects. You can also print part or all of the database. Cells are selected in the same manner as for the Object Data docker. Once a selection is made, you can enter information in the entry box at the top of the Object Data Manager.

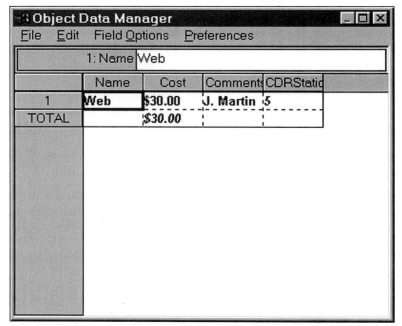

Figure 6-9: The Object Data Manager lets you add information to the fields in your database.

Deleting entries

You can clear the entries in a selected field or in all the fields for a selected object. When you delete an entry in the Object Data docker, the data is removed for the selected object only, and doesn't change the data for other objects. You can also remove cells in the Object Data Manager by selecting the cells and pressing Delete.

To delete entries in the Object Data docker:

1. Using the Pick tool, select the object that has the data to remove.
2. If you want to clear all the fields, click the right arrow in the Object Data docker and select Clear All Fields.
3. If you want to clear a specific field, select the field to clear in the Object Data docker and then select Clear Field from the flyout menu.

The data in the selected fields are removed from the selected object. The field itself is not removed. You can add new data in that field for the selected object.

Copying data

Once you define the data for an object, you can copy data from that object to another. Copying data saves entry time, especially if you have several fields assigned to objects. You can modify the data later for individual fields where the data varies between the objects.

To copy data from one object to another:

1. Select the object to which you want to copy the data.

2. In the Object Data docker, click the right arrow and select Copy Data From. When you move your cursor back over the drawing window, it changes to a large arrow.

3. Click the object from which you want to copy the data. The data is copied to the desired object and appears in the Object Data Manager.

If you want to change the data for a cell, you can click the cell to highlight it and enter the new information. In Figure 6-10, the data was copied from the first object on the list to the other objects, then the objects were renamed in the Name field to B2 and B3.

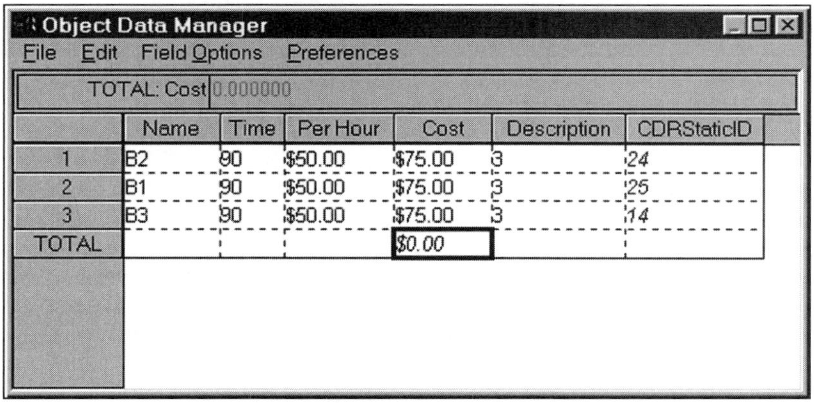

Object Data Manager
File   Edit   Field Options   Preferences

TOTAL: Cost 0.000000

	Name	Time	Per Hour	Cost	Description	CDRStaticID
1	B2	90	$50.00	$75.00	3	24
2	B1	90	$50.00	$75.00	3	25
3	B3	90	$50.00	$75.00	3	14
TOTAL				$0.00		

Figure 6-10: The data appears in the fields for the selected object.

Creating data summaries

You can create a summary, using the Page Setup dialog box, in the Object Data Manager. The Page Setup dialog box lets you specify how your summary is to appear when printed.

To specify a page setup for your summary:

1. Using the Pick tool, select the objects to include in your summary.

2. Select WindowTools ➪ Dockers ➪ Object Data Manger, or Tools ➪ Object Data Manager, to display the Object Data Manager docker.

3. Select File ➪ Page Setup (see Figure 6-11).

4. Click the associated checkboxes to enable or disable printing of grid lines, column headers, and row headers.

5. Enter values in the Left and Top boxes to specify the left and top page margins. Select a unit of measurement if you don't want to use the default unit of measurement.

6. Click OK to complete the operation and to return to the Object Data Manager. Select File ➪ Print to print your summary.

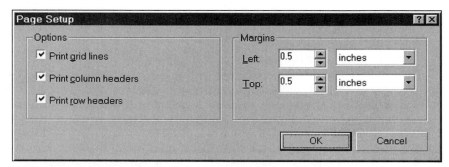

Figure 6-11: The Page Setup dialog box lets you specify how your object data is to print.

Specifying Page Properties

One of the first steps in creating your layout involves determining the page setup for your document, such as the page size, orientation, and layout style. Once you specify the page settings and return to the drawing window, the drawing page updates to reflect the current size and orientation. Draw lets you select from layout styles for creating single- and multiple-page documents. If you chose to start a new drawing based upon a template, some of these settings may already be in place. You can specify page property settings in the Page views of the Options dialog box or on the Property bar.

Accessing the dialog box

To access the Page views of the Options dialog box, select Tools ➪ Options to display the Options dialog box. Expand the options in the left window by clicking the plus (+) beside Document ➪ Page. Clicking the desired option lets you specify settings for your document:

✦ **Size:** Specify the size, orientation, and resolution for your document.

✦ **Layout:** Choose the layout for your document from the presets, such as full-page or booklet.

✦ **Label:** Choose from a variety of label templates or create your own custom template.

✦ **Background:** Specify a background for your document.

Shortcut

You can also open the Page view of the Options dialog box by double-clicking the outline or shadow that indicates the drawing page.

Choosing a page size

Draw provides a plethora of preset page sizes, including standard North American sizes, such as letter and legal, as well as European sizes, such as A4 and German Fanfold. When you make a page size selection, the preview window updates and displays a representation of your selection. If one of the 40 page sizes doesn't meet your needs, you can either specify a custom page size or have Draw adjust the page size to match the active printer. Specify the unit of measurement to use. If you define a page size using one unit of measurement and then switch to another unit of measurement, Draw automatically makes the conversion for you. Table 6-5 shows the different methods you can use to choose a page size for your document.

Table 6-5 Specifying a Page Size	
To choose this type of page size	**Do this**
Choose a preset page size	Click the down arrow in the Paper box to display the list of preset page sizes. Note that page sizes are listed by name, not by measurement. Once you select a size, the actual measurement of the page appears in the Width and Height boxes.
Set the page size using the active printer	Click the Set From Printer button. The page size updates, automatically, to reflect your selection. When you select Set From Printer, Draw sets the page size to match the active printer. If you have more than one printer connected to your computer, be sure you have the printer you want to use selected in the Print Setup dialog box (see Chapter 16).
Define a custom page size	Choose Custom from the Paper list box and then enter the horizontal and vertical page dimensions in the Width and Height boxes.
Choose a page size using the Property bar	Deselect the objects in your drawing and then select a paper size from the list box on the Property bar, or specify a custom size by entering values in the Width and Height boxes.

New Feature Multipage documents can now contain pages of varying sizes and orientation.

Using the Width and Height boxes

If you enter the page dimensions in the Width and Height boxes, Draw automatically changes the entry in the Paper list box to match the dimensions. If it is one of the preset page sizes, the name appears in the Paper box. Otherwise, Custom appears in the Paper box.

Specifying units of measurement

Draw lets you specify the units of measurement in the Page Setup dialog box and on the Property bar. You select a unit of measurement by clicking the down arrow in the units box. You can choose from inches, millimeters, picas/points, points, centimeters, pixels, ciceros/didots, or didots. If you choose pixels as the unit to define your page size, you can specify the resolution in the Resolution setting box. Then check your page size to make sure it matches the size you desire for your drawing. More information about specifying units of measurement appears later in this chapter in the section "Specifying Units of Measurement."

Using the Property bar

Using the Property bar to specify the dimensions and orientation of your document offers the advantage of allowing you to choose different dimensions and orientations for multipage documents. To use the Property bar to specify page properties, you need to deselect all of the objects in your document by clicking on the white space in the drawing window or by pressing Esc. The Property bar then displays the page properties. If you want to vary the orientation and size of different pages in a multipage document, click the lock icon next to the page orientation buttons to disable the default page settings. You can now specify a different orientation and size for the active page without affecting the other pages of your document.

Note When choosing varying orientations and dimensions in multipage documents, you must disable the default page settings for each of the pages you want to vary.

Paper size versus printable area

The variety of printers and output devices in the marketplace today is overwhelming. They all share one thing in common, though. With rare exception, there's not a printer that prints edge to edge, covering 100 percent of the paper. Even printers capable of printing full-bleed images, such as the Seiko 800 series, have a portion of the paper that is designated as a gripper, which allows the paper to feed through the printer.

When you are creating graphics in Draw, it's important to remember that the paper size and the printable area of the paper are *not* the same. The dimensions are different. It's not important to remember what the printable dimensions are for your printer, however. Draw calculates the printable area based upon the active printer specified in the Printer Setup dialog box. You can display the printable area on the drawing page (see Figure 6-12). This nonprintable guide helps ensure that your image falls within the printable area, and that it will appear on the hard copy once it's printed. To display the printable area, select View ➪ Printable Area. The printable area is displayed in the drawing window as black dotted lines. If you select a paper size that is smaller than that of the printer's settings, the lines may appear outside the boundaries of the drawing page.

Figure 6-12: Displaying the printable area ensures that all of your image will print.

Note Your printer settings determine the way the printable area is displayed. If your printer is set to print using a portrait orientation, the printable area is displayed as portrait even if your document uses a landscape orientation. To change the printable area display to match the orientation of your document, you must change your printer setup (see Chapter 16 for details).

Creating labels

Draw now supports label formats for many popular label manufacturers. If you choose Labels from the Page category of the Options dialog box, the label view appears at the right side of the Options dialog box. This list uses a file and folder setup to provide access to more than 800 predesigned label formats from numerous label manufacturers. The label formats are arranged alphabetically by manufacturer. The preview window lets you view how the labels fit on a printed page.

Note   Draw supports more than 800 preset label formats and has templates to assist you in creating labels for a variety of applications.

Preset label styles

To specify a preset label style:

1. Select Tools ➪ Options and expand the Document and Page categories. Click Page ➪ Label to display the Label view of the Options dialog box.

2. Click the Labels radio button.

3. Choose the label style that you want from the list that appears below the preview box. When you select a label style, a representation of the label layout appears in the preview window.

Tip   If you don't see a label style that meets your needs, you can modify an existing style or create and save your own custom label (see the following section). You can also remove any label style from the list.

Custom label styles

To add a custom label style:

1. Click the Labels radio button from the Label view of the Options dialog box.

2. Choose the label style closest to the one you want from the list that appears below the preview box.

3. Click the Customize Label button to display the Customize Label dialog box (see Figure 6-13).

4. Adjust the label size, margins, gutters, and the number of labels that appear on each sheet by entering values in their respective boxes.

5. Click the Add (+) button to display the Save Settings dialog box (see Figure 6-14).

6. Enter a name for the new label style and click OK.

7. You can delete a custom label by selecting it from the Label Style list box and clicking the Delete (–) button.

8. Click OK to exit the Customize Label dialog box and to return to the Label view of the Options dialog box.

Your custom label appears in the label list. If you click the label, a thumbnail appears in the preview window.

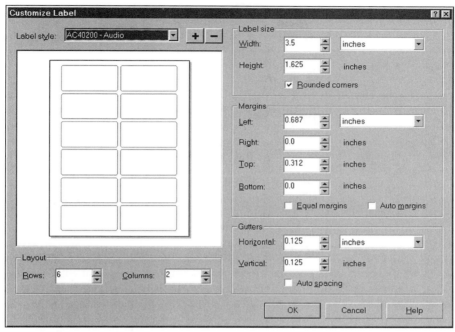

Figure 6-13: The Customize Label dialog box.

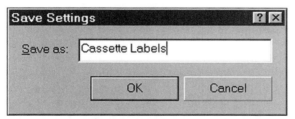

Figure 6-14: Enter a name for your custom label in the Save Settings dialog box.

Selecting an orientation

Draw lets you choose either a portrait or landscape orientation for your image. Portrait orientation means that the height of the paper exceeds the width. Landscape orientation means that the width of the paper exceeds the height. You can set the orientation and size manually, or have Draw automatically match the page orientation to the current output device settings. If the paper size and orientation don't match the printer's current settings, a message appears when you print your document. This message asks whether you want Draw to match these settings automatically.

To set the page orientation:

1. Select Tools ⇨ Options and expand the Document and Page categories. Click Size to display the Size page.

2. By default, Draw uses a portrait orientation. Click the Landscape radio button if you want the width of the page to be greater than the height.

3. Click Set From Printer if you want Draw to automatically adjust the size and orientation of the drawing page to match your output device.

Tip   You can also set the page orientation using the Property bar by first deselecting all of the objects in your drawing. Click the white space in the drawing window, or press Esc to deselect everything in the drawing window, and then click the Portrait button to set the height of the paper as greater than the width, or click the Landscape button to set the width of the paper as greater than the height.

Selecting a layout style

Draw offers layout options for single- and multiple-page documents such as books, booklets, and pamphlets. When you work in Draw, pages appear sequentially in the drawing window. If your document is going to a commercial printer, the pages don't necessarily print sequentially, however. To take advantage of the best use of paper, printers create an *imposition*. An imposition places the pages in the proper sequence to use the paper in the most efficient means possible. It also ensures that the pages appear in the proper order when you bind and trim the publication.

Cross-Reference   For more information about printing options, see Chapter 16.

Figure 6-15 shows a typical layout for a four-page booklet. Pages 1 and 4 print on a single sheet of paper, and pages 2 and 3 print on the back side of the same sheet. Regardless of the style you choose, you edit each page in an upright orientation in the drawing window. Draw autom atically does the impositions for you when your document is printed. You can choose from these preset layout styles:

✦ Full Page

✦ Book

✦ Booklet

✦ Tent Card

✦ Side-Fold Card

✦ Top-Fold Card

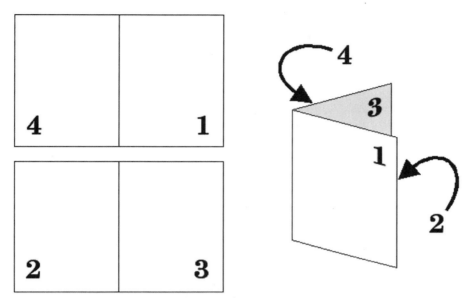

Figure 6-15: Typical page imposition for a four-page booklet.

To specify a layout style:

1. Select Page ➪ Layout from the expanded Document category of the Options dialog box to display the Layout settings.

2. Choose a layout style from the Layout list box. Each layout style is accompanied by a short description, just below document dimensions. A representation appears in the preview box.

Caution If you choose a layout style when specifying Page setup options, the appropriate layout style is automatically selected in the Print Options dialog box. If you change the layout style in the Print Options dialog box, your image may not print correctly.

Selecting a background

The Background view of the Options dialog box lets you specify a background so that you can see what your document would look like printed on colored paper or published on the Web. The Background settings dialog box lets you choose the type of background to use behind the objects in your drawing. The Background settings offer these choices:

✦ **No Background:** This option makes the background behind the objects in your drawing transparent. This is a good option if you are creating graphics for the Web or for export into other applications, such as PhotoPaint.

For more information about using backgrounds for Web documents, see Chapter 17.

✦ **Solid:** This option lets you select a solid-colored background behind the objects in your drawing. This option is a good choice for simulating colored paper and for creating solid-colored backgrounds for use in Web documents.

✦ **Bitmap:** This option lets you specify a bitmap for use as a background. When you select this option, you can specify how you want the bitmap displayed in your document.

Choosing a simulated color

Choosing a simulated color for your page is helpful for selecting a paper color when you specify the paper for output. You can ensure that your document has the proper amount of contrast and is not overwhelmed by the paper. If you choose a background for a multipage document, the background appears on all of the pages in your document. To choose a simulated paper color:

1. Select Tools ➪ Options and expand the Document and Page categories. Click Background to display the Background page (see Figure 6-16).

2. Click the color chip next to Paper Color and choose the color you want. If you don't see the color that you want, click Others and select a color as you would any uniform color in Draw.

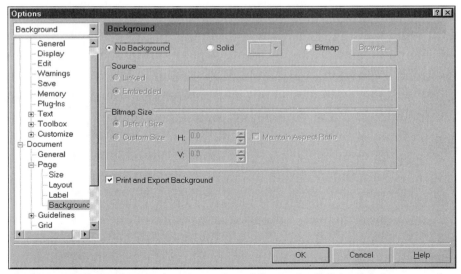

Figure 6-16: The Background settings page of the Options dialog box lets you select a background for your document.

3. Click OK to return to the Page Setup dialog box, then click OK again to return to the drawing window. The background you selected appears in the drawing window.

By default, the simulated color appears only on your monitor for display purposes. It doesn't appear on printed copies of the document, unless you specify that you want the background to print and export with your image. If you select Print and Export Background, the background you choose prints the same as other objects in your drawing.

Caution   Enabling Print and Export Background is not the same as adding a Page Frame to your document. You can't move or edit the background in the drawing window. If you need the background to be an editable object, use the Page Frame feature.

Using bitmap backgrounds

Draw lets you use bitmaps, as well as solid colors, for your backgrounds. As with a solid-color background, you determine whether the bitmap background is printable. If the default size of your bitmap, shown on the Background page, is smaller than the drawing page size, the background tiles to fill the drawing page. To select a bitmap as a background:

1. In the Background settings, select Bitmap and click the Browse button.

2. Choose the image to use as a background from the Import dialog box.

3. Click Open to open the image and return to the Page Background dialog box. The file name and path for the image you selected appears in the Source section of the dialog box.

4. Select either Linked or Embedded for the bitmap source.

5. Select a Bitmap Size. By default, Draw uses the original dimensions of the bitmap. You can specify a custom size by entering new values in the Height and Width boxes.

6. By default, the background you choose won't print. It's for viewing only. If you want the bitmap to print, enable Print and Export Background.

7. Click OK to return to the Background settings, then click OK again to return to the drawing window. The background appears in the drawing window.

Using bitmaps as a background for your documents lets you add subtle background effects to your documents, such as a faded logo. The image behaves like it's part of the Master layer in that it appears on all of the pages in your document. If you turn off the Master layer for a page, the image is still visible, however. Like other imported files, you can choose to embed or link the bitmap file, which lets you quickly update the background image.

Adding a page frame

The Add Page Frame option adds a printable background frame that covers the entire drawing page. The resulting rectangle is sized to fit the page and appears behind all other objects in the drawing. Page frames are treated like any other object in Draw, and assume the default fill and outline. You can change the attributes and manipulate the object. Add Page Frame is also a quick way to add a banner or sidebar to your document. For example, you can resize it vertically to create a banner that fits perfectly across the top of your document (see Figure 6-17).

Tip

You can also add a page frame by double-clicking the Rectangle tool.

To add a printable background frame:

1. Select Tools ⇨ Options and expand the Document and Page categories. Click Size to display the Size page.

2. Click the Add Page Frame button.

3. Click OK to add the page frame and to return to the drawing window.

Page frames always appear behind the other objects in your drawing, although you can move them up in the hierarchy of objects. This makes them useful for quickly creating backgrounds filled with pattern, fountain, or texture fills.

Hiding and displaying a border

The page border is the rectangle with the drop shadow that represents the drawing page in the drawing window. It reflects the dimensions and orientation that you specify in the Display settings of the Options dialog box. Although it is displayed by default, you can hide the page border while you work if you find it distracting. You should display the border, before printing, to ensure your document fits the page.

Tip

You can display the printable area of your document, even if you have the page border disabled. This ensures that your image fits the page without the distraction of the page border. To display the printable area, select View ⇨ Printable Area.

To hide or display the page border:

1. Select Tools ⇨ Options and expand the Document category. Choose Page to show the Page settings.

2. Disable or enable the Show Page Border by clicking the checkbox beside it. If a check mark appears in the box, the page border is enabled and is displayed in the drawing window.

3. Click OK to return to the drawing window.

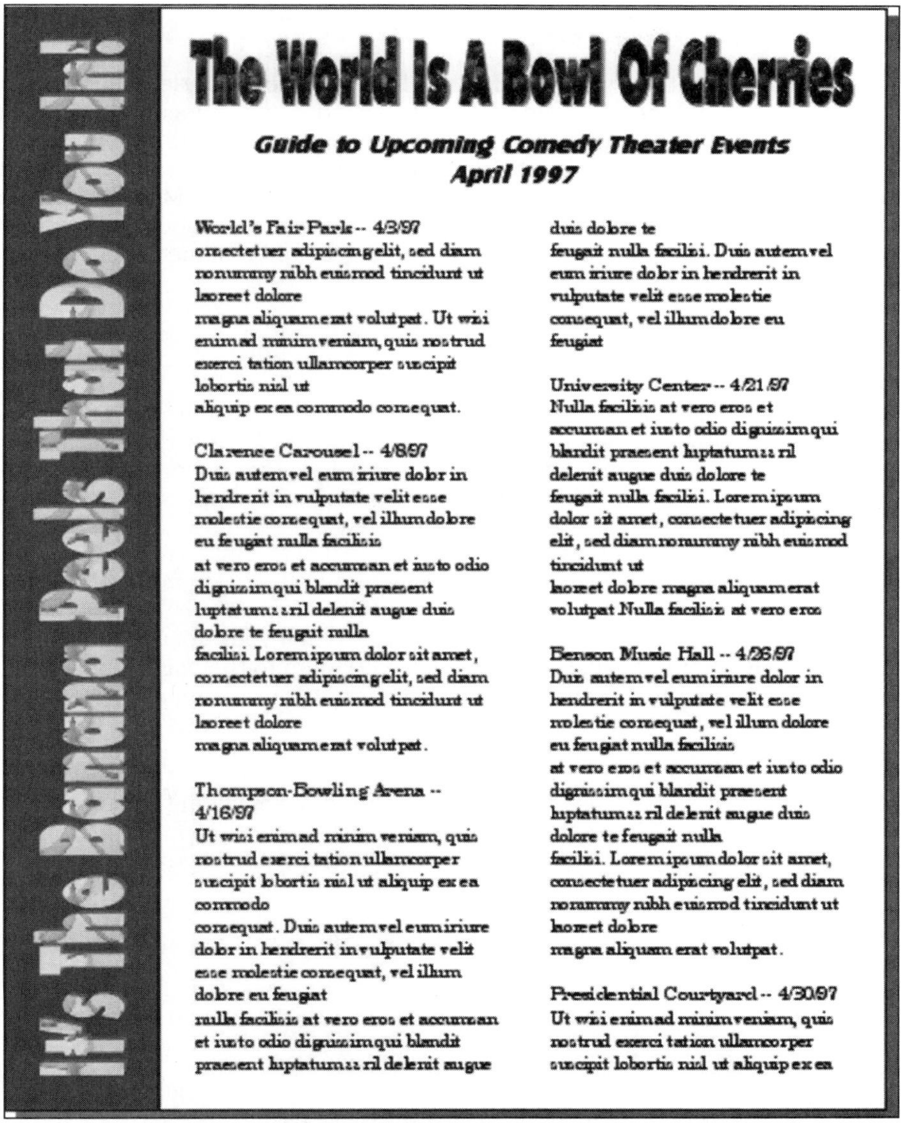

Figure 6-17: The banner in this illustration was created by resizing page frames to fit across the top and side of the document.

The page border is never printable. Your decision whether to display or hide the page border is a matter of personal preference. If you are new to Draw, or inexperienced with printing in Draw, I recommend that you display the page border as a visual guide to help maintain the scale and balance between your objects and the drawing page.

Managing Multipage Documents

The Layout view of the Options dialog box lets you select a variety of multipage layouts. For these to be visible in the drawing window, your document must have more than one page. If you are setting up a new document, your multipage options appear once you add pages to your document. Draw provides two methods for managing multipage documents: the Navigator and the Object Manager. By using these methods, you can go from one page to another in your document, as well as add pages. The Object Manager also lets you delete and rename pages in your document.

Moving from page to page

The Object Manager and the Navigator both allow movement from one page to another in a multipage document. They differ, however, in how they work. Navigator allows you to move through the pages by either panning through the pages one at a time or by clicking one of the visible page flippers to move to its associated page. If your document contains a few pages, this is a quick method of moving from one page to another. It's also useful if you want to review your pages one at a time. You can also click a page name in the Object Manager to move to that page. The layout menu offers the option of going to a specific page with the Go To Page dialog box. The Go To Page dialog box is useful if your document has a substantial number of pages, because it lets you jump to the page you want without having to pan through all the intermediate pages of your document.

With the Go to Page dialog box

The Go to Page dialog box is the preferred method of navigating large multipage documents, such as a 50-page catalog, because it's faster than moving from one page to the next using the Navigator. To move to a specific page using the Go To Page dialog box:

1. Select Layout ➪ Go to Page to display the Go To Page dialog box (see Figure 6-18).

2. Enter the number of the page to which you want to go in the entry box.

3. Click OK to go to the page in the drawing window.

Tip   Clicking the page counter displays the Go To Page dialog box, which lets you move to a specific page.

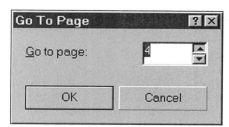

Figure 6-18: The Go To Page dialog box lets you navigate large documents with ease.

With the Navigator arrows

The page counter in the Navigator displays the current page, as well as the total number of pages in your document. Clicking the right or left arrow on the Navigator lets you view additional page flippers. When you click a flipper, it may take Draw a moment to load the contents of the page. The amount of time that's required to load a page is dependent on the complexity of the page's contents and the available resources on your computer.

Working with page names

When you first create a multipage document, Draw names the pages Page 1, Page 2, and so forth. The names appear in the Navigator. These names aren't very descriptive, however. You can rename the pages to provide more information about the contents of the page, which will help you navigate through your document more quickly. You can use up to 32 characters and spaces in a page name.

Tip

When I create a complex image, I frequently try a lot of *what if* scenarios, which leads me to generate multipage documents. Naming the pages to identify their content helps me quickly get to the page I need. If you update images regularly, this feature is also useful for identifying pages in documents, such as catalogs, that are organized by contents.

Renaming your pages

To rename a page:

1. Click the Navigator to make the page to be renamed the active page.

2. Select Layout ➪ Rename to display the Rename Page dialog box (see Figure 6-19). Alternatively, you can right-click a page flipper on the Navigator and choose Rename from the right mouse button menu to access the Rename Page dialog box.

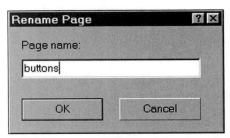

Figure 6-19: Using the Rename Page dialog box to give the pages of your documents meaningful names helps you navigate your document with greater ease.

3. Enter the new name in the entry box and click OK to return to the drawing window. The name that you entered appears on the page flipper.

Resizing the Navigator

You can resize the Navigator to display greater or fewer page flippers. The Navigator size is variable, and you can resize it to any size between the navigational controls and the right side of the drawing window. Resizing the Navigator also resizes the horizontal scroll bar in the drawing window. To resize the Navigator:

1. Move the mouse pointer to the right border of the Navigator. It appears as a thin line between the right edge of the Navigator and the left arrow on the scroll bar. The mouse pointer changes to a double-headed arrow.

2. Click and drag the border until the Navigator is the right size. Release the mouse button.

Caution

I recommend moderation when resizing the Navigator, because as it gets larger, the scroll bar gets smaller. The smaller the scroll bar is, the more sensitive it is to movement. If you greatly reduce the scroll bar size by extending the Navigator, the slightest nudge of the scroll thumb could make your image disappear from the drawing window. Your image is still there; it's just to the right or left of the drawing window. If you accidentally send your drawing on a trip, don't panic. The easiest way to find your image is to zoom out, find your image, recenter it in the drawing window, and then zoom back in to display the image at the level you want.

Adding and deleting pages

The Navigator lets you add new pages at the beginning and end of your document. You can quickly add blank pages without interrupting your work as well as add and delete pages without leaving the drawing window. In addition to the Navigator, the commands that are found on the Layout menu let you add pages to the middle of your document and delete pages in your document. You can also delete pages by right-clicking a page flipper on the Navigator and selecting Delete from the right mouse button menu.

Using the Insert Page dialog box

To add pages using the Insert Page dialog box:

1. Change to the page where you want to add new pages to your document.

2. Select Layout ⇨ Insert Page to display the Insert Page dialog box.

3. Enter the number of pages to add in the Insert Page dialog box.

4. Click Before or After to specify where you want to add the page(s) relative to the active page.

5. Click OK to complete the operation and to return to the drawing window. Draw places the specified number of pages in your document.

Caution   When you insert pages in documents that have linked paragraph text frames, the text doesn't flow into the new pages. For example, suppose you have a 20-page text document where the text flows from one page—or linked Paragraph text frame—to the next. If you insert two pages between pages 1 and 3, your text continues to flow between the Paragraph text frames, but pages 2 and 3 are now blank. The text stops at the end of page 1 and continues on page 4.

Using the Navigator

To add pages to your document using the Navigator:

1. If you want to add pages to the beginning of your document, go to the first page of the document; if you want to add pages to the end of your document, go to the last page in the document. You can use Navigator's First Page and Last Page buttons to move to the beginning or end of your document.

2. Click the Add New Page button (+) to add a new page.

3. To insert a page in-between two pages, go to the page where you want to insert the new page.

4. Right-click the page flipper and select Insert Page Before or Insert Page After from the shortcut menu.

Deleting pages

You can use the Delete Page dialog box to delete pages in your document. If the pages you delete fall in the middle of linked Paragraph text frames, the information contained on the deleted pages isn't lost; it flows to the next linked Paragraph text frame. You can also delete the active page by selecting Delete Page from the right mouse button menu.

To delete pages from your document using the Delete Page dialog box:

1. Select Layout ⇨ Delete Page to display the Delete Page dialog box.

2. Enter the number of the page to delete in the Delete Page box. By default, Draw enters the current page number. If this is not the page that you want to delete, highlight the number and enter a new number.

3. If you want to delete a range of pages, enter the number of the first page in the Delete Page box. Enable the Through To Page checkbox and enter the number of the last page in the Through To Page box.

Caution When you delete pages in your document, Draw also deletes the contents of those pages. Be sure you move any objects or other information that you want to keep from those pages prior to deleting the pages.

Viewing facing pages

The Facing Pages option, in the Layout view of the Options dialog box, lets you display two consecutive pages on the screen at the same time. You can access the Layout page of the Options dialog box by selecting Tools ➪ Options and expanding the Document and Page categories. Click Layout to display the Layout page. This is especially useful when you want to add an image that spans two facing pages to your document. Click the arrow next to the Start On list box to indicate whether you want Draw to start the document on a right- or left-facing page. The Left Side option is only available for the Full Page and Book layout styles.

To use the Facing Pages option, your document must contain more than one page. You must also have specified a page layout that supports multipage documents, such as one of the card or the book layouts. If needed, exit the Layout settings and add pages to your document before enabling this option.

Note If Facing Pages is enabled, the printable area and bleed area views are disabled.

Specifying Units of Measurement

When you specify a unit of measurement in the Size view of the Options dialog box, you're telling Draw that you universally want to use that unit of measurement for all of the alignment aids in your document. Settings that you specify in the Size settings are reflected in the rulers, grid, and guidelines setup. Using these settings, you can specify global measurements and other parameters for your drawing. To access the Size page, select Tools ➪ Options and expand the Document and Page categories. Click Size to display the Size page. You can also specify units of measurement in the Grid & Rulers dialog box, as shown later in this chapter.

Working with rulers

Draw's onscreen rulers assist in sizing and positioning objects in your drawing. Rulers are a movable reference, which gives them extra functionality by allowing you to reposition them anywhere on the drawing window. To display the rulers, select View ➪ Rulers. A check mark beside the command indicates that the rulers are enabled. If you want to hide the rulers, click the command again to remove the check mark. As you move your mouse pointer or drag an object, a dotted line appears across the rulers to show you the current position of your mouse pointer relative to the origin of the rulers (see Figure 6-20). The origin is the location where the rulers' 0 points intersect. The status bar also displays the mouse pointer's position.

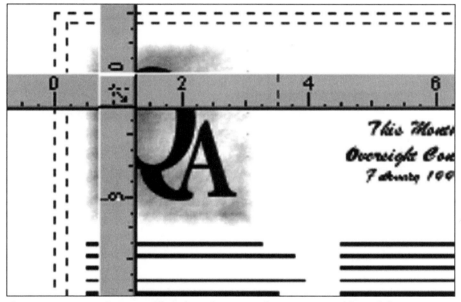

Figure 6-20: Draw's moveable rulers show you the current position of the mouse pointer relative to the origin of the rulers. The dotted line displayed at 3.5 inches on the horizontal ruler is the current horizontal location of the mouse pointer.

Repositioning rulers

Repositioning the rulers in the drawing window is an alternative to zooming in to a magnified view, in that it lets you bring the rulers closer to your work. This makes it easier to interactively position and size elements in your drawings. To reposition the rulers in the drawing window:

1. While pressing Shift, click and drag either the vertical or horizontal ruler to any location in the drawing window. The origin of the rulers remains unmoved, but the reference points where the rulers intersect update automatically to reflect the change.

2. If you want to move both rulers simultaneously, click and drag from the point where the rulers intersect while pressing Shift.

Changing a ruler's origin

Sometimes it's useful to reset the origin of the rulers. For example, if you wanted to position objects in your drawing based upon the center of the page, you could specify the origin as the page center. This would allow you to position objects relative to that location much more easily. You can set the origin interactively in the drawing window, or you can specify the origin in the Rulers settings of the Options dialog box. To return the rulers to their default positions, press Shift and double-click either on the ruler or on the ruler intersection point.

If you want to reset the rulers' origin interactively, click and drag from the rulers' intersection point to the desired location in the drawing window. When you release the mouse button, the rulers update to reflect the new settings. While this is a good method of changing the rulers' origin, it lacks the precision available using the Rulers settings of the Options dialog box.

To change the rulers' origin using the Rulers settings of the Options dialog box:

1. Access the Rulers settings view of the Options dialog box by doing one of the following:
   - Double-clicking on the rulers
   - Select Tools ⇨ Options and expand the Document category. Click Rulers to display the Rulers page.
   - Right-clicking a ruler and selecting Ruler Setup.

2. Select a unit of measurement from the drop-down list box. Enable Same Units for Horizontal and Vertical Rulers if you want to use the same unit of measurement for both rulers.

3. Change the origin by clicking the up and down arrows in the Horizontal and Vertical Origin boxes. Alternatively, you can highlight the value in the boxes and enter new values.

4. Enable Show Fractions if you want to show measurements as fractions instead of decimals.

5. Choose the number of incremental tick divisions that you want between each pair of whole units on the rulers.

6. Click OK to return to the drawing window. The rulers update to reflect the change you specified.

You can change the origin of the rulers at any time during a Draw session. You can also change the ruler units, using the units list box on the Property bar. The units list box appears only when no objects are selected in the drawing window.

Setting up for Web documents

Internet graphics are measured in pixels, the native unit of measurement for all onscreen graphics. If you're creating an image for use on the Web, using pixels as your unit of measurement can speed the creation process, as well as ensure that your image will fit on your Web page. When you specify pixels as the unit of measurement, you can also specify the resolution of your image. After you specify pixels as the unit of measurement and set the resolution, check the Page Setup dialog box to ensure that your page size is correct for the image that you want to create.

More information about resolution appears in Chapter 16.

To specify measurement and resolution for Web documents:

1. Select Rulers settings from the expanded Document category of the Options dialog box.

2. Choose pixels as the unit of measurement in the Horizontal list box.

3. Enable Same Units for Horizontal and Vertical Rulers.

4. Click the Resolution button to display the Edit Pixel Resolution dialog box.

5. Enter the horizontal and vertical resolution that you want to use for your image. Enable Identical Values if you want the horizontal and vertical resolution to be the same.

Resolution and Internet Graphics

A small amount of planning can go a long way when creating graphics for the Web. If you intend to print your image, as well as publish it on the Internet, the best idea is to create two different files: one for the Internet and one for print. Here's why. Pixels are a variable unit of measurement. In other words, a 1-inch by 1-inch square could be any number of pixels in either dimension.

IBM-compatible computers have a maximum effective screen display of 96 ppi (pixels per inch). This screen display resolution is static, regardless of whether you are using a 640x480 display or a 1280x1024 display (or any display in between). Macintosh computers have a default screen display of 72 ppi. Images produced for screen representation look great on the monitor but look horrible when printed. The resolution is too low, and the images look pixelated and choppy.

Continued

(continued)

That problem is not an issue, however, with Draw. You can avoid resolution problems using this method:

✦ First, create your image for the Web. Set the unit of measurement as pixels and specify identical horizontal and vertical resolutions of 96 ppi. This resolution gives the best display on IBM–compatible computers. Macintosh computers will automatically reduce the amount to 72 ppi for display. Any resolution over 96 ppi causes file bloat, and is wasted, because both platforms reduce the resolution – for screen representation anyway.

✦ Once you've created your image, save it with a name that designates it for screen or Internet use only. You might want to add a note or keywords to help you identify it later.

✦ After you save the file, reset the unit of measurement as inches or another defined unit of measurement. Draw automatically converts the image from one unit of measurement to the other, preserving the physical size of your image.

✦ Use the Save As command to save the file with a new name, designating it for print use.

Global measurements

Draw lets you set global measurements for your drawings. Global measurements are useful, when you need to create scaled illustrations, such as a technical drawing of a large object. Setting a drawing scale lets you simulate real-world distances in your documents by having the rulers display the unit of measurement that best suits your image.

Setting a drawing scale

To specify a drawing scale:

1. Select Guidelines settings from the expanded Document category of the Options dialog box.

2. Click the Edit Scale button to display the Drawing Scale dialog box (see Figure 6-21).

3. Choose either custom or one of the typical scales from the Typical scales list box. If you choose one of the typical scales, the Page distance and World distance settings are automatically calculated and entered in their respective boxes.

4. If you choose custom, enter the page distance to use as the base increment in the Page distance entry box. Choose a unit of measurement and then enter the actual distance represented in the World distance entry box.

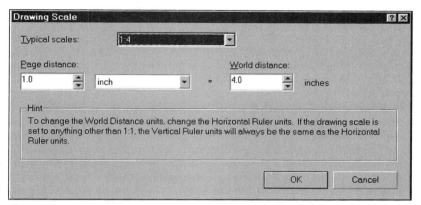

Figure 6-21: Set global measurements in the Drawing Scale dialog box.

The World distance is expressed in terms of the selected unit of measurement. In Figure 6-21, the scale is set at ¼ inch equals 1 foot. This is a common scale and one that is used for the creation of house plans and other structural blueprints. Note that the World distance has been calculated using the scale to display the equivalent measurement that equals one inch in page distance. If you want to change the World distance units later, you can change the horizontal ruler units. When the drawing scale is set to any scale other than 1:1, the vertical ruler units are always the same as the horizontal ruler units.

Specifying grid parameters

Draw's grid system works with the rulers to align and position objects accurately. When you change ruler units, you should also specify new grid frequencies and parameters. Draw displays the grid as a series of intersecting dotted lines spaced according to the settings specified in the Grids settings of the Options dialog box. Displaying the grid provides an easy and accurate way to position objects relative to one another and to the drawing page. To display the grid, select View ➪ Grid or enable Show Grid in the Grid settings of the expanded Document category found in the Options dialog box. You can use Draw's Snap To Grid command, found on the Layout menu, to ensure that objects automatically align with the grid as you move them.

To specify grid parameters:

1. Select Tools ➪ Options and expand the Document category of the Options dialog box (see Figure 6-22). Click Grids to display the Grids properties page.

2. Enable either the Frequency or the Spacing option.

3. If you enable the Frequency option, enter the number of grid lines you want horizontally and vertically per unit of measurement in the Frequency list boxes.

4. If you enable Spacing, specify how far apart you want the grid lines in the horizontal and vertical entry boxes.

5. Enable Show Grid and Snap To Grid, if desired. Click OK to complete the operation and to return to the drawing window.

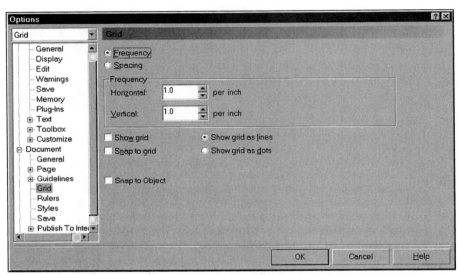

Figure 6-22: Set the grid frequency or spacing on the Grid settings page.

Note   If the grid lines are close together, Draw's default view may not display the frequency of the entire grid. If you zoom in on an area of your drawing, however, the frequency becomes visible. You should note that whether the frequency is visible or not, objects still snap to the grid when Snap To Grid is enabled.

Working with guidelines

Guidelines are lines that you can place anywhere in the drawing window to help align and position image elements. You can use any number of horizontal, vertical, or diagonal lines, as well as specify that Draw save the guidelines with your document. Diagonal guidelines are useful when used in conjunction with Snap To Grid and Snap To Guideline features. They allow you to evenly position objects in a staggered or stairstep manner (see Figure 6-23). By default, guidelines are nonprintable, and don't appear when you print your image. Guidelines can be added interactively or by using the Guidelines setup dialog box.

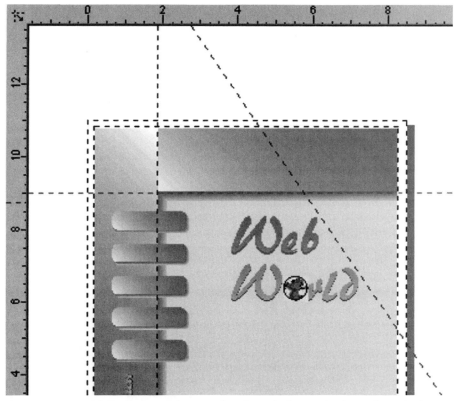

Figure 6-23: Guidelines appear in your drawing window as horizontal, vertical, or diagonal dotted lines.

Adding guidelines interactively

Here are some ways to interactively add guidelines to your drawing:

✦ Click and drag from either the horizontal or vertical ruler to place a guideline at the location you want. A dotted line appears as you drag across the drawing window.

✦ To reposition a guideline, click the guideline and drag it to a new location. You should avoid clicking the guideline where it crosses an object, because you could accidentally move the object instead of the guideline.

✦ To interactively create a diagonal or slanted guideline, click and drag a guideline from either ruler into the drawing window. If you click a guideline twice, movement handles appear on the guideline. You can then move your cursor to an end of the guideline and drag the line diagonally, which lets you set it at any location in the drawing window.

✦ To remove a guideline, either click and drag it back to the ruler, select it and press Delete, or right click it and choose Delete from the pop-up menu.

When you specify diagonal guidelines, you can specify one or two points to set the guideline. If you specify a single point, you set the location where the guideline crosses the horizontal ruler; if you specify two points, you also set the vertical location. When you specify the values for a single-point diagonal guideline, you need to set the angle of the diagonal guideline. If you specify a negative angle, the bottom of the guideline slants away from the vertical ruler. If you specify a positive angle, the bottom of the guideline slants toward the vertical ruler.

Using the Guidelines setup dialog box

To specify guidelines using the Guidelines setup dialog box:

1. Select View ⇨ Guidelines Setup to display the Guidelines page of the Options dialog box (see Figure 6-24).

2. Click the vertical or horizontal tab to display its respective property sheet.

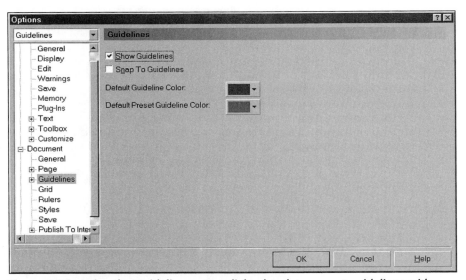

Figure 6-24: Using the Guidelines setup dialog box lets you set guidelines with precision.

Tip

You can also access the Guidelines setup dialog box by double-clicking the guideline with the Pick tool (provided the Master Guidelines layer is both editable and visible).

3. Enter a location for the guideline. The position of guidelines is relative to the 0 point for horizontal and vertical rulers, respectively. Entering a negative number places the guideline either to the left or below the 0 point.

4. Click the Slanted tab to set diagonal guidelines, then do one of the following:

   • Set two points by specifying the x and y coordinates for both endpoints relative to the 0,0 position on the rulers, and then click Add.

   • Set a single point by specifying the x and y coordinates for the point and by specifying an angle. The guideline passes through that coordinate at the angle you specify. Click Add.

5. To move a guideline, select the guideline in the list box that you want to move and enter new coordinates for the guideline. Click Move.

6. To delete a guideline, highlight the guideline to remove and click the Delete button. Clicking Clear clears all the guidelines of that type, such as all of the horizontal guidelines, while leaving the vertical and slanted guidelines in place. Clicking Clear All removes all the guidelines from your drawing.

7. Enable Show Guidelines or Snap To Guidelines, if desired.

8. You can add as many guidelines to your drawing as you wish by specifying the location for each and clicking Add. When you've set all the guidelines you want to add, click OK to complete the operation and to return to the drawing window.

To adjust the appearance of a guideline, you can select the guideline in the Object Manager, right-click, and choose properties. Any object you place on the Guidelines layer becomes a nonprintable "sticky" guide.

Tip You can use diagonal guidelines to set reference points that identify the exact center of any area by placing opposing guidelines from corner to corner. For example, you could identify the center of a square by dragging guidelines and placing them so that they intersect adjacent diagonal corners of the square. The location where the two guidelines intersect is the center of the square.

Selecting a View

Draw lets you adjust how elements are displayed in the drawing window by the setting of view quality. View quality is video- and system memory-dependent. Display selections affect the screen refresh speed and the performance of Draw itself. Each view quality displays elements determined by complexity level from outlines to bitmaps. You can specify the view quality by selecting View ➪ [*the view quality you want to use*] or by making a selection from the standard toolbar above the drawing window. The view quality does not affect the output of your image; the view quality only affects the image's display for editing purposes. Use the following list as a guideline to specifying a view quality:

✦ **Simple Wireframe:** This view quality is the best choice for slower computers or when making selections in complex images. Any fills, intermediate blend steps, contours, and extrusions are hidden, making it easier to choose control objects. Monochrome bitmaps are displayed; color bitmaps are not supported in this view.

✦ **Wireframe:** This view quality is a good choice for slower computers or for making selections in complex images. Fills and color bitmaps are hidden. Contours, extrusions, and intermediate blend steps appear as outlines. Monochrome bitmaps are displayed.

✦ **Draft:** This view quality allows for rapid screen refresh. This is useful when editing object shapes in complex images. PowerClip contents are hidden. Bitmap and vector fills are shown as solid colors, as are any lens effects. Solid fills, fountain fills, low-resolution texture fills, and low-resolution bitmaps are displayed normally.

✦ **Normal:** This view quality displays all fills, objects, and high-resolution bitmaps. Normal view is a good choice for most image editing.

✦ **Enhanced:** This view quality uses 2X oversampling to achieve the best display quality. Enhanced view is memory intensive and affects speed and performance.

Creating Effective Layouts in Draw

Draw is undoubtedly the most powerful illustration package available. It possesses unparalleled versatility, and offers a broad variety of features and effects. All of this capability adds up to a strong temptation to abuse good design principles, especially for novice users or those without a background in design. A good design is one that is clean and balanced. By clean I mean that the design doesn't confuse the eye by overwhelming the viewer with clutter. This isn't to say that your document can't have a large quantity of objects. Creating a clean and balanced design is like conducting an orchestra. If each instrument plays different music, the result is likely to be noise rather than music. If each instrument plays its part of the same music, the results are more harmonious and effective. Use the following tips to help you get the most from Draw's design capabilities and features:

✦ **Plan ahead:** If you are just playing in Draw, this doesn't matter a great deal. However, if you are designing a document with a goal, such as an ad, take the time to consider your audience, budget, output, and theme.

✦ **Be consistent:** Documents have a flow. As the artist, you guide the eye through the drawing or document. Maintaining a consistent feel by repeating design elements, colors, and styles increases the effectiveness of your document. Consider placing objects on the Master layer to set a repeating consistent theme throughout your document. If you are going to break with consistency, do it with purpose and in an obvious way. If done sparingly, startling the viewer by suddenly introducing an incongruent element can be a good way to draw the eye to an element of a design.

✦ **Use fonts as indicators:** Select fonts with care and use them repetitively throughout your document. For example, you might use one font consistently for a headline and another font to indicate the description of a product. Draw comes with a wide variety of fonts. One of the worst design mistakes an artist can make is to include too many different fonts in the same document. Generally, three or four fonts are sufficient to create a clean design.

✦ **Use color wisely:** Select colors and palettes designed for your project. The colors you choose for a Web document are going to be different than those you might choose for a printed document.

✦ **Choose the right layout:** Specifying the correct layout, units of measurement, and background can go a long way toward reducing frustration and the need to redo portions of your image.

This list of tips is by no means complete. These and others tips are discussed in more detail throughout this book. When creating the layout for your document, it's important to keep these concepts in mind. If you preplan your layout and design, your documents will be more effective and your Draw sessions more productive.

Summary

File management is more than a matter of good housekeeping. It can save time and hassles when you are working with Draw documents. File management is more critical if you create a lot of images or work in a production environment. Keeping track of images can be a major project. Draw provides the tools needed for file and object management. Additionally, determining your drawing environment at the beginning of each document saves time and helps ensure consistency in your images. Although you can add pages and make changes on the fly in Draw, you save time and make the creation process easier if you specify the basics beforehand. This chapter taught you to

✦ Use advanced save features

✦ Use Corel Versions for archiving documents

✦ Rescue data

✦ Create an object database

✦ Specify page properties, such as page size, orientation, and layout style

✦ Navigate your document

✦ Add and remove pages

✦ Use alignment aids such as rulers, guidelines, and a grid

✦ Employ design tips

✦   ✦   ✦

Orchestrating Objects and Layers

When you create a drawing, Draw remembers the location of each object. Not only does it remember its horizontal and vertical position in relationship to the rulers, it also remembers a third relationship — its stacking order or hierarchy. Objects are added back to front, and have a specific order in the scheme of things. If you could look behind the scenes at the program code of a saved drawing, you would see that each object is assigned an order number, according to its addition to your drawing. *No two objects have the same order number or same place in the hierarchy of the drawing.* You can change both the position and stacking order of objects in your drawing, but only one object at a time can occupy a plane on the stacking order.

You could say that each object resides on its own layer, but the term layer has a very specific meaning in Draw, and should not be confused with the hierarchy of the objects in your drawing. A layer functions as a container for objects, and lets you organize and manage even the most complex drawings. Like objects, each layer has its own place in the hierarchy of your image.

Managing Objects and Styles

Looking at a completed drawing, it's difficult to visualize the hierarchy of objects. The Object Manager offers an alternate view and lets you perform many of the tasks that you can perform in the drawing window. Draw provides two other organizational tools for managing objects in your drawings, the Graphic and Styles Manager and the Color Styles Manager.

Styles are the basic foundation upon which all drawings are created. They are an instruction set that contains the attributes for objects and text. At their most simplistic level, they provide Draw with instructions about the default fill, outline, font, and formatting attributes. You can modify these styles, however, to control a broad variety of object and text attributes. The ability to apply styles to objects in your drawings increases your productivity and helps provide your documents with a consistent appearance.

Working with the Object Manager

Draw's Object Manager provides an alternate view of your drawing that allows you to see and work with the hierarchy of objects, as well as with the layers and pages in your drawings. When you select an object in the Object Manager, it's automatically selected in the drawing window. Once objects are selected, you can perform organizational tasks, such as copying, combining, and grouping your objects. The Object Manager can help organize your entire document.

Note   Do not confuse the Object Manager with the Object Data Manager. The Object Data Manager deals with information assigned to objects in your drawing.

Opening and closing the Object Manager

The Object Manager deals with the objects themselves by displaying the sequence of objects, layers, and pages in your document. To display the Object Manager, select Window ➪ Dockers ➪ Object Manager (see Figure 7-1).

If you want to close the Object Manager, click the X in the upper right-hand corner or right-click the name tab on the side and choose Close from the right mouse button menu.

Adjusting the view and display

The double-arrowheads in the title bar of the docker collapse and expand the docker. By toggling the display of the Object Manager, you can work in the drawing window, while having the convenience of maintaining the Object Manager onscreen.

When working with the Object Manager, you determine how much of your file you want displayed in the Object Manager's window. By default, Draw displays the pages, layers, and objects in your document. The minus (–) and plus (+) signs beside each entry allow you to specify how much is displayed in the Object Manager. Clicking the minus (–) sign contracts the view one level for the selected entry; clicking the plus (+) sign expands the level for that entry. The capability of expanding and contracting the levels of the view makes editing your document easier. You can display only those objects or groups that you want to edit. You can toggle the display of objects' properties by clicking the Show Properties button at the top of the Object Manager (see Figure 7-2).

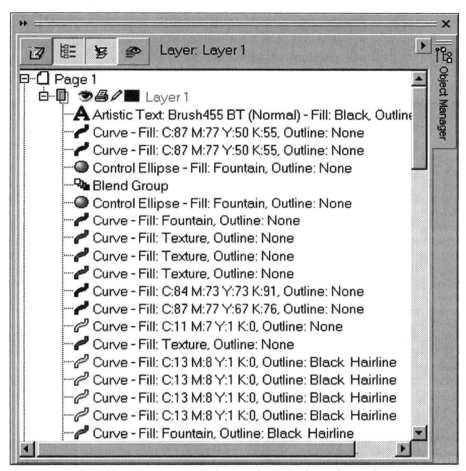

Figure 7-1: The Object Manager provides an alternate view of your drawing.

For each object, the Object Manager displays a small page icon and a brief description indicating the object's basic fill and outline properties. These icons are interactive, which means that you can use the Object Manager to control the layering and arrangement of the objects in your image. The Object Manager basically provides a written view of your document.

Note You can also select objects in the Object Manager and edit them as you would in the drawing window. The editing changes you make in the Object Manager are reflected in your drawing.

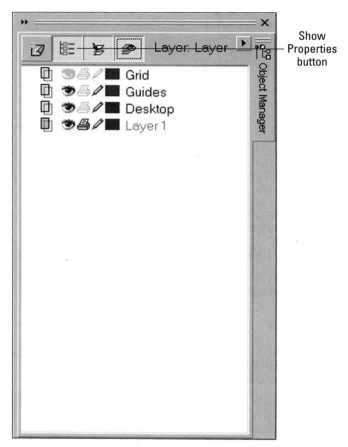

Show
Properties
button

Figure 7-2: Clicking the Show Properties button lets
you choose the type of object properties to display.

Proofing Your Image with the Object Manager

The Object Manager is one of the best proofing tools in Draw. You can check your drawing for color consistency and spot potential printing problems before they occur. Open paths, for example, are problematic if fills are assigned to them. They can cause PostScript errors.

Using the Object Manager, spotting an open path with a fill is significantly faster than tabbing through the objects in your drawing. By giving you a linear representation of your image, you can view the order of the elements in your image and the attributes of the objects.

Selecting objects and groups

Objects and groups are selected in the Object Manager by clicking either on their names or on their associated icons. When you select an object or group, it is highlighted and the object is selected in the drawing window. The eye icon beside a layer entry toggles its visibility. If the icon is grayed out, the associated groups or objects aren't displayed in the drawing window. This is useful for temporarily *removing* elements from your drawing so that you can edit other elements more easily. The objects aren't really gone. They are just invisible.

Similarly, if you click the pencil icon beside a layer, you toggle whether the objects and groups contained on that layer can be selected or edited. Objects can only be edited if the associated layer pencil icon is not grayed out. Turning off the editing capability of layers prevents inadvertently selecting the objects on that layer, making the editing of other objects easier. The printer icon toggles whether a layer is printable.

Manipulating objects and groups

You can perform a number of actions on both individual and grouped objects in the Object Manager. The actions you can perform on grouped objects are limited to some extent, however. For example, you can't align or distribute objects within a grouped object. To perform those commands, you must first ungroup the object. When you select an object or group of objects in the Object Manager, the Property bar changes to reflect those commands that are available for the selected element. For example, if you select a group, the Property bar changes to reflect the change. You can choose to ungroup the element, ungroup all of the grouped elements, move the group to the front, or move the group to the back.

When you select individual objects in a drawing, you can perform all of the actions available for the given object, including applying transformations, alignment, and attributes. The Object Manager also supports drag-and-drop actions (which are described in detail in the next exercise). Basically, you can perform these actions:

- ✦ Order objects within and between layers
- ✦ Apply color, graphics, and text styles
- ✦ Group and ungroup objects
- ✦ Edit fill and outline colors
- ✦ Create and edit PowerClips
- ✦ Control layer properties

Using drag and drop

In this exercise, you create a series of objects. Using the drag-and-drop functionality of the Object Manager, you modify the objects' attributes and their relationship to one another. To perform drag-and-drop functions in the Object Manager:

1. Start Draw if it's not already running. Choose to create a new drawing.

2. Draw a rectangle, an ellipse, and a polygon on the drawing page.

3. Assign each object a different color fill from the onscreen color palette.

4. Remove the outline from one object by right-clicking the X on the color palette. Change the outline color of another object with a color that contrasts with its fill. It doesn't matter which colors you select for the fill and outline of these objects.

5. Select Window ⇨ Dockers ⇨ Object Manager to display the Object Manager. By default, the Object Manager docks to the right side of the drawing window. The image remains on the left. Click the plus (+) sign next to Layer 1 to expand it. The three elements that you created are displayed in the Object Manager, along with their attributes (see Figure 7-3).

Figure 7-3: The Object Manager displays the elements of your drawing, along with their respective attributes.

6. Select ellipse in the Object Manager by clicking it. Then right-click and drag the ellipse to the rectangle. A rectangle appears over the icon of the object to which you are dragging. When you release the mouse button, a menu appears that lets you apply the attributes of one object to another or change the order of the objects.

7. Choose Copy Fill from the menu. The rectangle assumes the fill of the ellipse.

8. While pressing Shift, select the rectangle and the ellipse, and drag them over the polygon. As you drag, a small group icon appears. When you release the mouse button, the three objects appear as a group.

9. To ungroup objects, expand the group to display the individual elements by clicking the plus (+) sign beside the group. Click and drag one of the grouped elements, up and to the left of the layer icon. Release the mouse button to ungroup the objects.

This exercise demonstrated a small number of the actions and commands that you can apply using the Object Manager.

Managing Layers and Pages

Imagine a stack of paper with each successive sheet of paper superimposed over the previous sheet. Each sheet of paper contains information that makes it unique from the other sheets of paper, and is independent of the others. You can change the information on one sheet without changing its order in the stack of paper. If you were to bind the stack of paper into a book, the unique nature of each sheet wouldn't change. You'd simply be containerizing the paper into a collection.

Objects you create in Draw are similar to this stack of paper. As mentioned in the previous section, each successive object that you create lies above the previous object in the stacking order. When you first begin to work with Draw, all of your objects are usually contained on a single layer. In Draw, layers are similar to the chapters of the book in the preceding example. You containerize your objects on different layers, much like the pages in a chapter. The layers stack one atop the other, just as objects stack successively.

Devising an organizational system

The Object Manager's contents can be based on any organizational system that works for you. You can work with one or more layers at a time, thus simplifying the creation process. For example, if you were creating an ad, you might want to place all the background elements on one layer, photos on another, and prices on a third. Layers can help keep a drawing's distinct elements separate, while acting as a hierarchy that determines the vertical arrangement, or stacking order, of a drawing's elements. Using the Object Manager, you can lock individual layers, make them invisible, and specify which layers to print.

Note   Remember that objects and layers are stacked in the order of their appearance in your drawing, from back to front. If you create an object later in your drawing session, and place it on a lower layer than the current layer, it could disappear behind another object.

Naming layers, and placing similar elements on appropriate layers, helps you maintain control of your drawings and identify objects more quickly. To gain a concept of how layers work, complete the exercise in the next section.

Working with layers

Assigning a layer name helps you locate and edit objects in your drawing. By default, layers are named simply "Layer" with a number following the name. Although you can accept the default name that Draw gives each layer, it's a good idea to name the layers. A Draw document can contain well over a thousand objects. Committing the layer on which each object resides to memory is a formidable task. While you might be up to the challenge, it's easier to give each layer a more meaningful name. You can use up to 32 characters, including spaces, to name a layer.

Draw provides a variety of methods for naming and renaming layers. You can use the same procedures to name new layers and rename existing layers. Remember, however, that you can't rename the Grids, Guidelines, or Desktop layers of a document. In the following exercises, you create and name layers, as well as add objects to the layers, to organize the elements of city1.cdr.

City1.cdr is located on your companion CD-ROM in the tutorial\ch07 folder.

Naming and renaming a layer

To name and rename a layer:

1. Open city1.cdr in Draw.

2. Open the Object Manager to display the default layers. Layer 1 is highlighted to indicate that it's the active layer.

3. Click the name Layer 1 twice to select it and to display a box around the name. The text appears highlighted. Enter a new name and press Enter. Alternatively, you can right-click the name and choose Rename from the right mouse button menu.

4. Enter **frame** in the text box, and press Enter. The new name appears in the Object Manager (see Figure 7-4).

You can also name or rename a layer in the Layer Properties dialog box. To access the Layer Properties dialog box, right-click a layer name and choose Properties from the right mouse button menu.

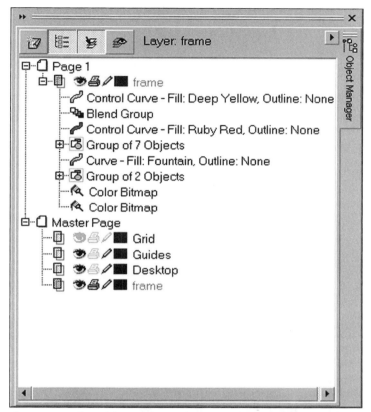

Figure 7-4: The Object Manager lets you rename the layers of your document.

Understanding the Role of Default Layers

Every new document in Draw contains four default layers: Grid, Guides, Desktop, and Layer 1. The Grid and Guides layers are used to place control and guide objects in your drawing. The Desktop layer is a holding area for objects that fall outside of the printable page of your document.

Normally, these layers aren't printed when you print a drawing. Layer 1 is the default drawing layer.

Creating a new layer

When you add a new layer, its printing, editing, and display properties are enabled, and its master layer property is disabled. You can change these properties in the

Layer Properties dialog box (see the section "Setting Layer Properties" later in this chapter). To add new layers:

1. Open city1.cdr, if it's not already open.

2. Select Window ⇨ Dockers ⇨ Object Manager to display the Object Manager.

3. Click the right arrow near the top of the Object Manager and select New Layer from the flyout menu. A new layer appears in the Object Manager as the top layer and becomes the active layer.

4. Name the layer **rose**.

5. Add two more layers by clicking the New Layer button in the Object Manager. Name them **door** and **backgrnd**, respectively (see Figure 7-5).

6. Save the drawing to your hard disk.

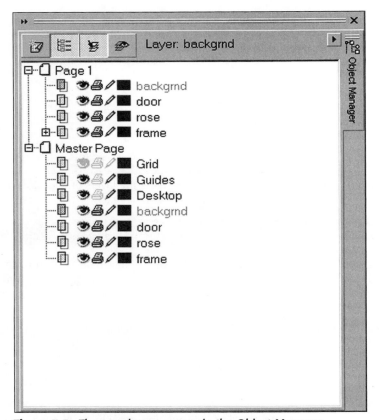

Figure 7-5: The new layers appear in the Object Manager.

At the moment, the three new layers are empty. The entire image resides on the frame layer. You need to reorder the layers, and then move the objects to their respective layers.

Tip If you right-click in the Object Manager, the right mouse button menu appears, enabling you to choose from the most commonly used layer and page commands. You can add a new layer using this method.

Reordering layers

The list in the Object Manager displays the order in which the layers are stacked in your drawing. The first layer shown in the list is the top layer; the last layer shown in the list is the bottom layer. If you change the order of the layers in the list, you change the vertical order in the drawing. The objects contained on a layer move with the layer to reflect the change. To change the layer order:

1. Open city1.cdr, if it's not already open.

2. Select Window ⇨ Dockers ⇨ Object manager to display the Object Manager.

3. Click and drag each layer's name, in the layer list, to invert the order of the layers (see Figure 7-6). An arrow appears as you drag the name, indicating the layer's position.

4. Save the file.

Tip When you added and named the layers to city1.cdr, I had you name them in an inverse order, from top to bottom, to illustrate reordering layers. Before creating and naming layers, it's a good idea to think about your drawing and create the layers from bottom to top. This method reduces the possibility of *misplacing* objects behind other objects.

Layers and Layer Order

If you had placed the objects in city1.cdr on their new layers before reordering the layers, you would have been in for a surprise. Some of the objects would have been hidden beneath other objects. When you added the layers in the previous exercise, each successive new layer became the top drawing layer — remember working from back to front? The order of the layers is inverted, so that what should be the bottom drawing layer, backgrnd, is shown as the top layer.

This is one of the most common errors new Draw users make when arranging objects on layers. If objects seem to disappear when you experiment with your own drawings and layers — *Don't Panic!* The objects are still there. As you reorganize the layers, the objects will return to their proper order.

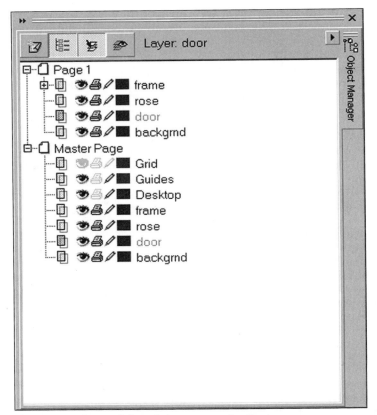

Figure 7-6: If you click and drag to reorder the layers, you can invert the order of the objects in your drawing.

Copying and moving objects between layers

When all your objects are on a single layer, creating a drawing can be like trying to sort grains of sand. As the drawing grows in complexity, the risk of inadvertently selecting the wrong object increases. If you want to marquee-select multiple objects without including others nearby, the task becomes more unwieldy. This problem highlights one of the advantages of working with layers. The capability to edit objects across layers can be enabled and disabled, allowing you to work with a single layer at a time.

The Move To and Copy To commands on the Object Manager flyout menu let you move or copy a selection of objects to a new layer. When you use the Move To command, Draw moves the object to the layer you select. When you use the Copy To command, Draw creates a copy of the selection, and places it on the layer you select. If you move or copy an object to a layer below its current layer, the object becomes the top object on the new layer. Similarly, if you move or copy an object to a layer above its current layer, the object becomes the bottom object on its new layer. In the next exercise, you assign the objects of city1.cdr to the appropriate layer.

To move objects to other layers:

1. Open city1.cdr, if it's not already open.

2. Using the Pick tool, select the skyline background object in the drawing.

3. Select Window ⇨ Dockers ⇨ Object Manager to display the Object Manager.

4. Click the right arrow near the top of the Object Manager and select Move To. A large arrow appears, taking the place of your cursor.

5. Click the nametag backgrnd to move the bitmaps of the city skyline to the bottom layer.

6. Repeat steps 2 through 5 to select the door bitmap and move it to the door layer.

7. Press Shift and click the stem, leaves, and bud of the rose to select them. Move them to the **rose** layer.

8. Save the file.

Note   Both the Edit Across layers and Layer Manager View buttons must be selected in the docker for the Copy and Move functions to be active on the pop-up menu.

The procedure for copying objects between layers is similar to moving objects from one layer to another. After selecting the objects you want to copy, select Copy To from the flyout menu and then click the layer to which to copy the object. When you copy objects to another layer, the copy and original object are directly superimposed. The top copy of the object hides the one below it. If you want to view the bottom-most object, you have to move the top object.

Adding new objects to layers

You can specify the layer on which you want to draw or add objects. Before adding objects to a layer, you must make the layer active. Once active, a layer is ready to receive any new objects you draw, import, or paste onto it. The Object Manager highlights the active layer. When you first start a drawing, Draw creates Layer 1 as the default layer.

To change the active layer:

1. Select Window ⇨ Dockers ⇨ Object manager to display the Object Manager.

2. On the Object Manager, click the name of the layer to activate. When you import or otherwise add objects to a drawing, Draw automatically puts them on the active layer.

You can place objects on the active layer by drawing an object, pasting an object, or importing an object. You can't place objects on inactive or locked layers (more information about locking layers appears in the section "Setting Layer Properties" later in this chapter). To place an object on an active layer, do one of the following:

✦ Draw a new object or create text.

✦ Select Edit ⇨ Paste to paste the contents of the Windows clipboard into your drawing.

✦ Select File ⇨ Import to display the Import dialog box. Select a file from your hard drive and click Import to place the file in your drawing.

Ordering objects on a layer

Draw provides two basic methods for ordering objects on a layer. You can either use the Order commands or use the Object Manager to move the objects. The Order commands — To Front; To Back; Forward One; Back One; In Front Of; Behind; and Reverse Order — also enable you to change the stacking order of objects on a layer. Table 7-1 shows the Order commands, what each does, and the keyboard shortcut for each. To change the hierarchy of a selected object on a layer, select Arrange ⇨ Order and choose one of the commands.

Table 7-1
The Order Commands

Command	Action	Keyboard shortcut
To Front	Moves a selection to the front of a layer.	Shift+PgUp
To Back	Moves a selection to the back of a layer.	Shift+PgDn
Forward One	Moves a selection one position up in the stack order.	Ctrl+PgUp
Back One	Moves the selection one position down in the stack order.	Ctrl+PgDn
In Front Of	Moves the selection in front of another object. Draw prompts you to click the object in front of which you want to place your selection.	No shortcut
Behind	Moves the selection behind another object. Draw prompts you to click the object behind which you want to place your selection.	No shortcut

In addition to the order commands found in Table 7-1, you can reverse the stacking order of a series of objects in your drawing. Reversing the stacking order of selected objects alters the appearance of your drawing (see Figure 7-7). Other objects in your drawing are unaffected by the command.

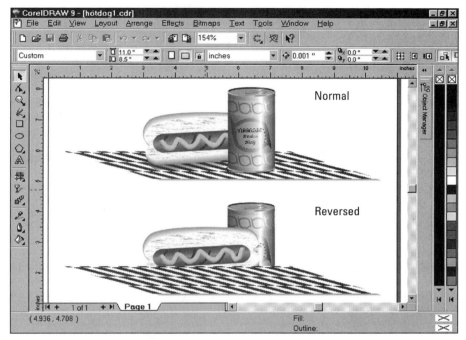

Figure 7-7: The Reverse Order command inverts the order of objects on a layer.

To reverse the stacking order of objects on a layer:

1. Using the Pick tool, press Shift and select the objects whose order you want to reverse. Alternatively, you can marquee-select the objects whose order you want to reverse.

2. Select Arrange ⇨ Order ⇨ Reverse Order. The order of the selected objects will be reversed.

You can also access the Order command by right-clicking an object to display the right mouse button menu. The To Front and To Back commands are also available on the property bar when an object is selected.

Deleting a layer

Draw lets you remove layers from your drawing using the Delete command. You should exert caution when you delete a layer, however. The Delete command removes not only the layer, but all of the layer's contents as well. If you want to keep the objects contained on the layer you plan to delete, be sure to first move or copy the objects to another layer. You can't delete a locked layer or any of the special default layers — Grid, Guides, and Desktop.

To delete a layer:

1. In the Object Manager, highlight the layer to remove by clicking its name.

2. Click the right arrow near the top of the Object Manager and select Delete from the flyout menu. The layer and its contents are removed from the drawing.

Setting layer properties

The Layer Properties dialog box lets you specify settings that control the individual layers in your drawing. To access the Layer Properties dialog box, right-click the layer and select Properties from the flyout menu. The dialog box appears and displays information about the highlighted layer in your document (see Figure 7-8).

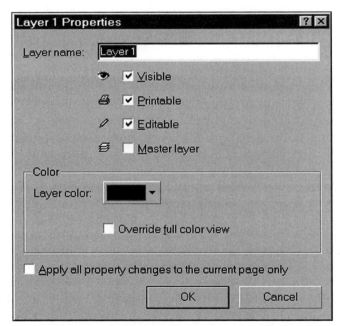

Figure 7-8: The Layer Properties dialog box lets you specify settings that control the individual layers in your drawing.

The Layer Properties dialog box lets you control these options, which are related to the selected layer (more information about each of these options appears later in this chapter):

✦ The layer's name

✦ Whether the layer is visible

✦ Whether the layer is printable

✦ Whether the layer is locked or unlocked (editable or uneditable)

✦ Whether the master layer is enabled

✦ Whether to use color override

✦ Whether to limit layer changes to the current page

Note   Once in a while a client calls me, alarmed about a document he or she hasn't opened recently. They feel really foolish when they discover that they last closed the document with options disabled in the Object Manager. If you open a drawing and objects appear to be missing, or you can't select objects, or if the drawing doesn't print correctly, don't be alarmed. Check the options in the Object Manager. You may have a locked layer, or the visibility or printing options may be disabled.

Showing and hiding layers

You can determine the visibility of the layers in your drawing. When the Visible option is enabled in the Layer Properties dialog box, the objects contained on the specific layer are visible. Similarly, if the option is disabled, objects are invisible. Disabling the visibility of selected layers is useful when you need to edit portions of a complex image. This removes the distraction of other objects, while improving the screen refresh time. You can also click the eye icon in the Object Manager to toggle the visibility of a layer. When a layer is invisible, the eye icon is grayed out.

Enabling and disabling printing

Draw lets you print selected layers of your documents. When the Printable option is enabled in the Layer Properties dialog box, the layer is printable. This option is useful for proofing portions of your document. By making selected layers unprintable, you can print just selected portions of your drawing. Objects residing on unprintable layers won't appear in the printed copy of your document. In the Object Manager, you can also toggle whether a layer prints or not by clicking the printer icon beside the layer name. When a layer is set as nonprinting, the printer icon appears grayed out. Unprintable layers don't appear in full-screen preview.

Locking and unlocking layers

When the Editable option is enabled in the Layer Properties dialog box, you can modify the objects residing on that layer. Similarly, disabling the option locks the layer. Locking layers is useful when you need to perform detailed editing in a complex image. Objects residing on locked layers are held in place and can't be selected or modified. This behavior makes the selection and editing of unlocked layers easier. If the Edit Across Layers option is enabled in the Object Manager, you can select objects on any layer that isn't locked. If the Edit Across Layers option is disabled, you can only select objects on the active layer.

You can also lock and unlock layers by clicking the pencil icon beside the layer name in the Object Manager. When the layer is locked, the pencil icon is grayed out.

You can't lock or unlock the Grid layer. For example, if you wanted to edit only the rose layer, you could lock the rest of the layers and make them invisible. This lets you edit the rose without risk of disturbing the other layers. Making the rest of the layers invisible also speeds the screen refresh, letting you work more quickly.

Understanding the Master layer

By default, the Master layer option is disabled. When this option is enabled, objects placed on this layer appear on every page of a multipage document. If you needed to place a company logo on every page of a document, you could place copies of the object on every page, thereby increasing the file size. By enabling the Master layer and placing the logo on this layer, the logo would appear at the same location on every page. This way, a single logo serves the same purpose as multiple copies of the logo.

You can create a Master layer using the Layer Properties dialog box or by right-clicking the layer icon beside the layer name in the Object Manager and choosing Master from the right mouse button menu. The word "Master" appears beside the layer on the Master page, and the layer is removed from other pages in the Object Manager. To create a Master layer:

1. Select Window ➪ Dockers ➪ Object Manager to display the Object Manager.

2. In the Object Manager, right-click the layer icon of the layer that you want to make a Master layer. Select Properties from the right mouse button menu.

3. In the Layer Properties dialog box, enable Master Layer.

4. If you want to hide Master layer objects for the current page of a multipage document, enable Apply Property Changes to the Current Page Only. Note that you must be on the page for which you want to disable Master layer objects.

Using master layers lets you add elements that lend a consistent appearance to multipage documents. You might want to consider adding a Master layer object to documents such as newsletters to give them a polished appearance.

Using Grids and Guidelines

Draw offers an assortment of alignment aids to assist you in positioning objects in your drawings. Two of these, grids and guidelines, have their own layers, which are always part of the Master layer. Here's how they work:

✦ **Grids:** These are configured according to the unit of measurement used in your drawing. By default, all editing, printing, and visibility controls are disabled for the Grid layer. You can use the Object Manager to set the visibility and toggle printing for the Grid layer. The Grid layer, however, isn't editable in the Object Manager. You can modify the grid in the Grid setup.

✦ **Guidelines:** These are horizontal, vertical, or diagonal lines that you add to your drawing to help you align objects. Similar to grids, when you add guidelines to your drawing, they are visible on every page. By default, printing is disabled for the Guides layer, and editing and visibility are enabled.

You can use the Layer Properties dialog box to change the color of the Grid or Guides layers (as described in the next section).

Changing the color of grids and guidelines

To change the color of the Grid or Guides layer:

1. Select Window ➪ Dockers ➪ Object Manager to display the Object Manager.

2. Right-click either the Grid or Guides layer and choose Properties to display the Layer Properties dialog box.

3. Click the color chip and select a color from the palette. I recommend you select a color other than white that is not commonly used in your drawing.

See Chapter 6 for more information about modifying the way the grid is displayed.

Placing objects on the Guides layer

Although guidelines reside on their own layer, not everything on the Guides layer needs to be a guideline. One of the most useful features of the Guides layer is the capability of placing objects on the layer. You're probably wondering why you'd want to place an object on a layer that generally isn't printed. But there's a good reason.

Draw provides three snap-to features: Snap To Grid, Snap To Guidelines, and Snap To Objects. Snap-to features let you align objects more easily. When you enable snap-to objects, the selected object snaps to the nodes of other objects as you move it. The problem with this feature is that objects also snap to themselves, much like plastic wrap tends to cling to itself better than to other objects. You have to apply the force of a large move to interactively move an object when Snap To Objects is enabled. You can avoid this problem by placing a copy of the object, to which you want to align your selection, on the Guides layer.

You can toggle Draw's snap-to features by selecting them from the View menu or on the default view of the property bar, which appears when no object is selected.

When you place an object on the Guides layer, it appears as an outline in the same color as guidelines. Any fills that the object contains are ignored. Once you've placed the object on the Guides layer, select View ➪ Snap To Guidelines to enable the snap-to feature. Once enabled, you can interactively position your selection, easily and perfectly, each time. You can also align objects on the drawing layer with objects placed on the Guides layer using the Align commands.

Editing multiple layers

Draw lets you determine how much of your drawing is editable at one time. Locking and unlocking layers toggles between the layer being editable or uneditable. You can also toggle between the capability to edit and not edit layers by enabling or disabling Edit Across Layers. When Edit Across Layers is enabled, you can edit objects on any unlocked layer, or move and copy objects between layers. If Edit Across Layers is disabled, you can only work with objects residing on the active layer and on the Desktop layer.

To enable and disable editing of all layers:

1. Select Window ➪ Dockers ➪ Object Manager to display the Object Manager.

2. Click the right arrow near the top of the Object Manager and select Edit Across Layers to enable the feature (if it is disabled). As with all of Draw's features, when an option is enabled, a check mark is displayed beside the option. To disable the option, click to remove the check mark.

Note Although you can move or copy objects from the active layer to unlocked inactive layers, you can't select or edit objects that reside on inactive layers. If you want to edit objects on another layer when Edit Across Layers is disabled, you must first make the layer active.

Using color override options

The capability to lock layers and make them invisible is invaluable. What happens, though, if you need to see those objects to position other elements in your design? This is the point when color override becomes a handy tool. When Override Full Color View is enabled, Draw displays the selected layer's contents as colored outlines. Fills and outlines assigned to the objects are ignored in the display. Using color override options lets you identify objects on different layers and increases screen refresh performance. Color override doesn't affect any object's actual appearance; it only affects the way objects are displayed on your monitor.

Tip Color override is especially useful when you are editing complex images such as technical diagrams or blueprints. By placing similar elements on different layers and using color override, you can assign a unique color to each layer. This makes the creation and editing of subsequent layers easier.

Figure 7-9 shows three views of the same drawing. One view shows the complete image. The Object Manager shows that the drawing contains several layers. Another view shows the same image, with color override enabled on several of the layers. The final view shows an enlarged portion of the castle, displaying the quantity of detail in the drawing.

Complete image

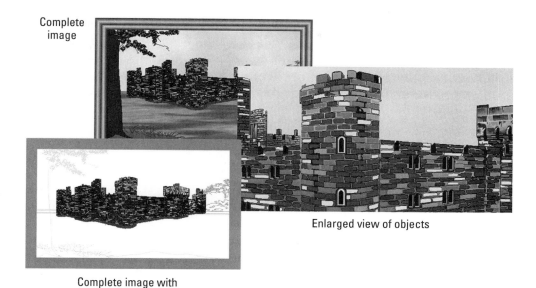

Enlarged view of objects

Complete image with
color override enabled

Figure 7-9: Color override lets you create and edit complex images more easily.

To override a layer's fill and outline attributes:

1. Select Window ➪ Dockers ➪ Object Manager to display the Object Manager.
2. Display the Layer Properties dialog box by right-clicking the layer to override.
3. Enable Override Full Color.
4. Click the color chip and choose the color you want to use for the objects on the selected layer.
5. To redisplay a layer's normal fill and outline attributes, disable Override Full Color View in the Layer Properties dialog box.
6. To change the color associated with a layer, select the layer and click the color chip at the bottom of the Layer Properties dialog box. Choose a color from the palette.

Note

I like to put a lot of detail in my drawings. The image shown in Figure 7-9 contains 4,867 objects. Of those objects, 3,849 are the stone blocks on the castle. Each stone block was separately drawn, not copied. Draw's layer and color override features were critical to the creation of the image.

Moving and copying between layers and pages

The Object Manager provides the quickest way to move and copy objects between layers and pages. The clean visual interface is coupled with interactivity to simplify tasks and improve efficiency. You can see how actions will affect the drawing's hierarchy, which gives you better control.

Moving an object to another layer

When you last worked with city1.cdr, you placed the entire rose on the rose layer of the drawing. In the following exercise, you move the stem of the rose to another layer to create the illusion of the rose protruding through the door.

City1.cdr is located on your companion CD-ROM in the tutorial\ch07 folder.

To move an object to another layer:

1. Open city1.cdr.

2. Select Window ➪ Dockers ➪ Object Manager to display the Object Manager in the drawing window. This may take a moment while Draw examines your document.

3. In the drawing window, use the Pick tool to select just the stem of the rose. Handles appear around the stem, and the stem is highlighted in the Object Manager to indicate that it's the selected object.

4. In the Object Manager, click and drag the stem icon to the icon representing the door layer. When you release the mouse button, the stem appears behind the door (see Figure 7-10).

5. Save the file.

When clicking and dragging objects between layers, it's important to remember the way Draw deals with the hierarchy of layers. If you drag an object from a higher layer to a lower layer, the object appears at the front of the other objects on its new layer. If you drag an object from a lower layer to a higher layer, the object appears behind the other objects on its new layer. Once it is positioned on a layer, you can drag it to a new position on the layer.

Moving and copying with the flyout menu

In addition to dragging objects from one layer or page to another, you can use the commands found on the flyout menu in the Object Manager to move or copy an object to another layer or page.

To move or copy an object using the flyout menu commands:

1. In the drawing window or in the Object Manager, select the objects to move.

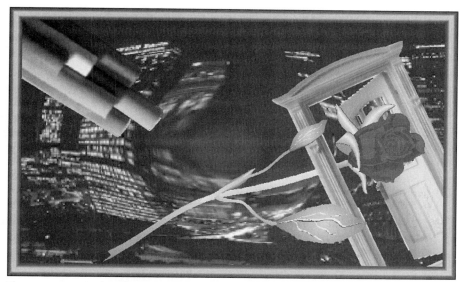

Figure 7-10: Moving the stem to the door layer places the stem below the door, to create the illusion of the rose protruding through the door.

2. In the Object Manager, click the right arrow and select Move To or Copy To from the flyout menu. An arrow appears when you move the cursor back over the Object Manager.

3. Click the layer or page where you want to move the objects.

Pasting objects from the Windows clipboard

You can use the Windows clipboard functions in conjunction with the Object Manager to paste objects to layers or pages in your drawing. The objects can be selected in the Object Manager and copied or cut to the Windows clipboard, or they can come from another source. Using this method, you can quickly place objects in your document. To place the contents of the clipboard on a layer or page, click the layer or page name to highlight it, then select Edit ➪ Paste. The object is copied to the layer or page you specified.

Note

When you copy an object from one layer to another, the object's position on the drawing page doesn't change. Only the order changes. This means that the copied object lies either directly above or directly below the original object. The new object, which is positioned directly above the original object, may hide the original object. If you want the bottom object to be visible, you must move the top object.

Using Graphics and Text Styles

The Styles Manager is one of Draw's productivity tools. Although it may seem transparent, every Draw document that you create is based on a template. A template is a set of instructions that govern the text, formatting, and graphics in your drawing. Each template contains style instructions that determine the outline, fill, format, and text instructions. For example, when you specify the default fill and outline, you're are modifying Draw's default template. When you apply a style to an object, the object assumes the appearance specified by the style. Using templates lets you maintain a consistent appearance in your document by controlling the attributes of the objects contained in the drawing. Draw lets you use the styles contained in any of Draw's templates, or you can create, save, and use your own custom styles.

In Chapter 4, you worked with text styles. This section deals primarily with graphics styles, although the principles are the same.

Understanding styles and templates

As you learned in Chapter 4, styles reduce layout time and ensure a consistent appearance in your documents. Styles have long been a feature of word processing and page layout packages. Draw lets you use styles in conjunction with graphics objects. A graphic style can include fill and outline attributes, transformations, and certain special effects. When you apply styles to objects in your drawing, they are saved with the document, so that they are ready for use the next time you open the drawing. You can also save or copy the style for use in other documents. If you change a style in a document, the style is automatically applied to every object in the drawing that uses that style. Here's a brief overview of what you can do with styles and templates (see the sections that follow for more detailed explanations):

✦ **Choosing and modifying a template:** When you first start Draw, you are given the opportunity to create a new drawing based upon the default template, a preset template, or a template you've created. By default, if you choose a new drawing instead of one based upon a stored template, Draw uses coreldrw.cdt. Coreldrw.cdt is a blank drawing template that contains one style for graphics, one for Artistic text, and four for Paragraph text. In addition to the default template, Draw comes with a library of preset templates appropriate for a series of common applications, such as a business card template. You can use the template as is, or you can modify the template to suit your needs. You can modify a template by changing the styles contained in the template. Once you've changed the styles, you can save the template for future use.

Like the Object Manager, you can dock the Styles Manager on any of the four sides of the drawing window.

✦ **Applying styles:** You can apply a style using one of two basic methods. If you right-click an object, either in the drawing window or in the Object Manager, the right mouse button menu appears, letting you choose a style from the

Styles submenu. You can also apply a style using the Graphic and Text Styles docker. To display the Graphic and Text Styles docker, select Tools ➪ Graphic and Text Styles or Window ➪ Dockers ➪ Graphic and Text Styles (see Figure 7-11). Throughout this section, you'll work with the file, card1.cdr, and its associated template, cards.cdt, to learn how to use styles in your drawings.

You can access the Graphic and Text Styles docker by pressing Ctrl+F5.

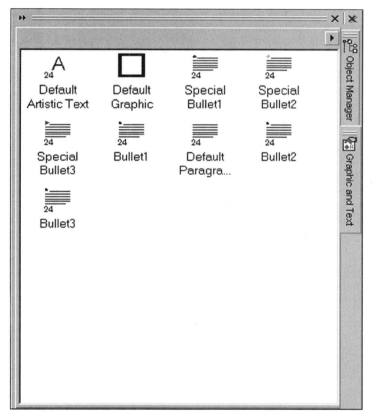

Figure 7-11: The Graphic and Text Styles docker lets you apply styles to objects in your drawing.

Using the Template Customization Wizard

Before you begin to work with the styles for cards1.cdr, you need to load its template. Draw lets you add the templates that you use frequently to the Template Wizard list. The Template Wizard is a convenient way to manage templates. Using the Wizard you can add, remove, and rename templates. Although you can load cards.cdt directly off the companion CD-ROM, the next exercise teaches you to add the template to the Template Wizard list and to save the template to your hard disk.

On the CD-ROM
Cards.cdt is located on the companion CD-ROM in the template folder. Using Draw's Template Wizard you can install this and the other templates in this folder to your hard disk.

To add templates to the Template Wizard list:

1. Start Draw, if it's not already running.

2. Select Tools ➪ Scripts ➪ Script and Preset Manager. The Script and Preset Manager appears docked in the drawing window (see Figure 7-12).

3. Double-click the Scripts folder and then the Scripts subfolder to display Draw's available scripts. Scroll through the scripts shown in the window, and select the tempwiz script. Either double-click the script icon or click the run button to run the script.

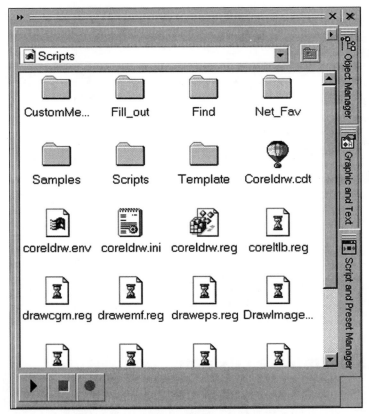

Figure 7-12: The Script and Preset Manager contains scripts that let you automate tasks and run other applications in Draw.

4. When the Template Customization Wizard appears, click Next to start.

5. In the Wizard, select the Add option and click Next.

6. Select Create a New Category and click Add. A dialog box appears where you can name your new category (see Figure 7-13).

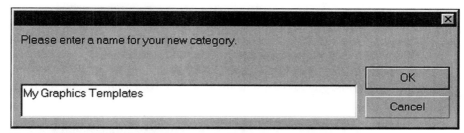

Please enter a name for your new category.

My Graphics Templates

OK

Cancel

Figure 7-13: A dialog box appears that allows you to name your category.

7. Enter the name you want to use for the category and click OK to continue. The new category appears in the Category list.

8. Select your category in the Category list and click Next.

9. In the Wizard, click Add to display a dialog box requesting the location of the template you want to add. Select cards.cdt and click OK.

10. In the Wizard, select Copy Files to the CorelDRAW Template Directory, if you want to store the template on your hard disk. Click Next to continue.

11. The last screen of the Template Customization Wizard appears. Click Finish to return to the drawing window.

Note

If you've already created a personal category for your templates, select Add to Existing Category and click Next. It's not a good idea to add templates to Draw's existing categories. Should you need to reinstall Draw, your templates will be lost.

Once a template is added to the Template Wizard list, you can create new documents based upon the template when you first start Draw. You can also load and apply templates at any time during a Draw session. Storing templates on your hard disk lets you quickly locate and load the templates associated with a file.

Caution

It's a good idea to make a backup copy of all custom templates that you create in Draw. By making a backup, you can ensure that your templates won't be lost if you need to reinstall Draw. Backing up also provides a copy of your template, should it be accidentally overwritten.

Working with templates

Every new drawing you start using the New command uses the default coreldrw.cdt template. If you don't want to use this template, select File ➪ New From Template to choose a different template. If you've already started a drawing and want to change templates, you can load a new template in the Graphic and Text Styles docker. Draw's preset templates and those that you create are, by default, stored in the corel\draw80\draw\template folder.

Loading a new template

In this exercise, you open card1.cdr and use the Graphic and Text Styles docker to load cards.cdt in preparation for the other exercises in this section. To load a new template:

Card1.cdr is located on your companion CD-ROM in the tutorial\ch07 folder.

1. Open card1.cdr.

2. Select Tools ➪ Graphics and Text Styles to display the Graphic and Text Styles docker.

3. Click the right arrow near the top of the Graphic and Text Styles docker to display the flyout menu.

4. Select Template ➪ Load to display the Load Styles From Template dialog box (see Figure 7-14).

5. Select cards.cdt from those listed in the file window. If you stored the template elsewhere on your system, you can change to the folder where the template is stored.

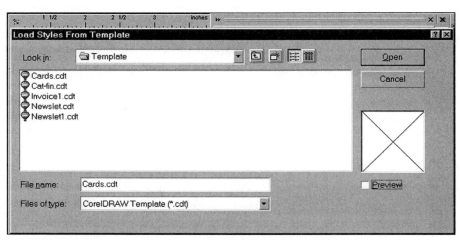

Figure 7-14: The Load Styles From Template dialog box lets you choose the template to apply to your document.

6. Click Open to load the template and to return to the drawing window. Draw loads the template and displays the associated styles in the Style docker (see Figure 7-15).

Note   When you open a file, such as card1.cdr, which is based upon a custom template, the template is embedded in the document and automatically loaded with the file. It's not essential that you load cards.cdt here, but you should be aware that you can load the template separately from the document and can edit the template. If you make changes to the template, you will need to open and apply the updated template to your drawing. You can also apply new templates to existing drawings to change the appearance of your document.

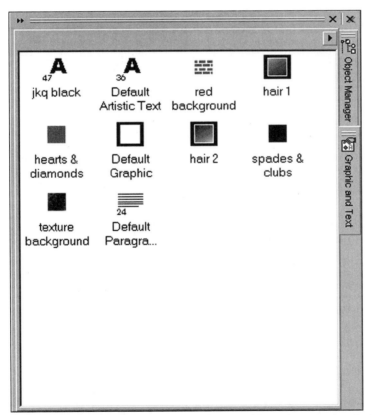

Figure 7-15: The styles displayed in the Graphic and Text Styles docker change to reflect those of cards.cdt.

Once the template loads, Draw looks at the elements in your document. If objects in your document contain styles with the same names as those in the new template, Draw will ask you if you want to apply the new styles to those objects.

Creating a new drawing based on a template

The procedure for starting a new drawing based on a template is similar to loading a template from the Graphic and Text Styles docker. When you create a new template, it's not added to the Template Wizard list until your subsequent Draw session. To create a new drawing based on a template:

1. Select File ➪ New From Template to display the Template Wizard. Click Next to start.

2. Select template category and then click Next to select the folder and template to use.

3. Click Open to complete the operation and to return to the drawing window.

Working with styles

When you apply a style to an object, the object takes on only those attributes that are governed by the style. For example, if you apply a style that controls fill attributes, the object's fill changes while its other attributes stay the same. In the next few exercises, you work with styles to modify the objects in card1.cdr and its associated template, cards.cdt. Card1.cdr has its own style template, cards.cdt, created for the objects in the image.

Applying styles

To apply a style using the Graphics and Text Styles docker:

1. Open card1.cdr.

2. Select the upper-left spade symbol on the card to which you want to apply a style. Note that the status bar indicates this is a control object. The spade in the bottom-right corner of the card is a clone object.

3. From the Graphic and Text Styles docker, double-click the style spades & clubs. The spade symbols on the card turn black (see Figure 7-16).

4. Save the file to your hard disk.

Tip   You can also apply a style to selected objects by clicking the right arrow near the top of the Graphic and Text Styles docker and choosing Apply Style from the flyout menu, or by dragging and dropping the style thumbnail onto the selected object. If you modify or edit a style, objects associated with that style are automatically updated in your drawing. This feature is useful if you need to make global changes in your documents.

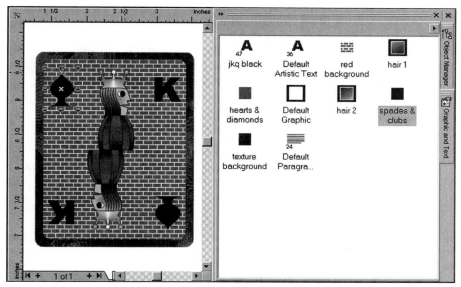

Figure 7-16: Selected objects update to reflect the style that you apply to them.

Assigning shortcuts to styles

Draw lets you assign shortcuts to your styles. Shortcuts permit you to work faster and more efficiently. If you use a style frequently within your documents, assigning and using a shortcut can save a significant amount of time. To assign a keyboard shortcut to a style:

1. Select Tools ➪ Options to display the Options dialog box.

2. Click the plus (+) sign beside Workspace and then Customize to expand the categories. Double-click the Shortcuts folder to display the Commands list. Expand the Apply Styles category from the Commands list (see Figure 7-17).

3. Select jkq black from the styles list.

4. Click inside the Press New Shortcut Key box and press Alt+Shift+B (you don't have to enter the plus (+) keys). If you make a mistake, press Backspace to clear the box so that you can start over. The shortcut can use up to four keystrokes. I recommend using at least three keystrokes, as Draw uses several two-key combinations as shortcuts for its commands.

5. Click Assign to assign the shortcut. You can continue adding shortcuts, or you can click OK to return to the drawing window.

6. In the Graphic and Text Style docker, click the right arrow and select Template ➪ Save As from the flyout menu.

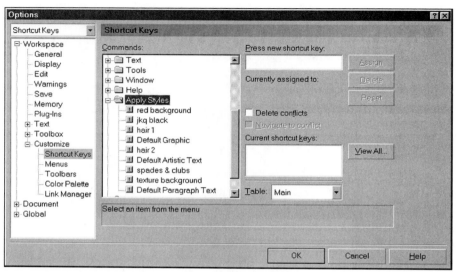

Figure 7-17: The Shortcut Keys page lets you create shortcuts for Draw's commands.

Note   If you stored the template for this exercise in a location other than Draw's default template folder, locate the file before completing step 7.

7. Choose cards.cdt from the list of styles in the file list window and click Save.

Tip   You can also change the shortcut key by right-clicking one of the styles in the Graphic and Text Styles docker and selecting Edit Hot Key.

If the style currently has a shortcut assigned to it, it appears in the Current Shortcut Keys box. To avoid assigning the same keyboard shortcut to two or more commands, enable the Navigate To Conflict checkbox. If you attempt to use a shortcut that is already assigned when this option is enabled, the current one is erased and you are prompted to enter a new one.

Caution   Be careful when you assign styles shortcuts so you don't accidentally overwrite Draw's default shortcuts for other commands. Most of Draw's commands use one- or two-key combinations—Ctrl plus a function key or number. Some include Shift as a third key in the combination. Ctrl+Alt+<*another one or two keys*> make the best combinations, as Draw does not combine Ctrl with Alt in its shortcuts. Avoid using two-key combinations, because they usually are already preassigned to Draw commands.

Working with graphic styles

Graphic styles describe the fill and outline of an object. Draw's default graphic style specifies no fill and a hairline (0.003 inches) black outline. Note that the default outline width does not reproduce well when printed. You should consider increasing the default outline width to 0.015 inches for a better quality of printed output. You can change the default outline and fill, interactively, in the drawing window. You can also change these attributes by either using the Graphic and Text Styles docker or by resaving the style based upon an object. When you change the default graphic style, Draw automatically applies the change to any objects in your drawing that use that style. In addition, any new objects that you create will also have those attributes.

Editing a style

Draw provides two methods for editing the attributes of a style. The first method lets you edit an object that uses the style you want to change and then resave the style. The second method uses the Properties command in the Graphic and Text Styles docker to redefine the style's attributes. Each method has unique advantages.

By changing an object

When you edit a style based upon the changes you make to an object, you can see the effect it's going to have on the overall appearance of your drawing immediately. This allows you to continue to modify the object as desired, prior to changing the style itself. Changes you make to an object don't automatically affect its associated style. To edit a style based on changes to a selected object:

1. Open card1.cdr, if it's not already open.

2. Using the Pick tool, select the texture-filled background of the card.

3. In the color palette, click the white color patch to change the fill to white.

4. With the background still selected, right-click the red color patch to add a red border to the card (see Figure 7-18).

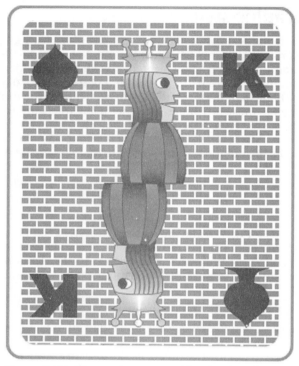

Figure 7-18: The card appears with a bordered white background.

5. Right-click the background to display the right-mouse button menu.

6. Select Styles ➪ Save Style Properties. The Save Style As dialog box appears (see Figure 7-19).

7. Enable the style attributes to include by checkmarking them. The name Default Graphic appears in the Name box. Highlight the name and enter **texture background** in the Name box.

8. Click OK to update the style and return to the drawing window.

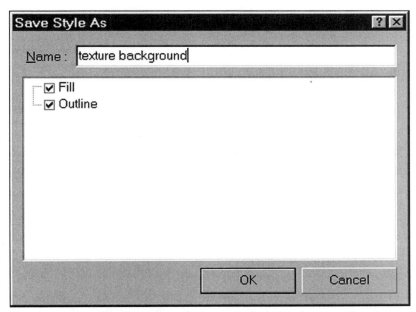

Figure 7-19: Enable the style attributes to include by checkmarking them in the Save Style As dialog box.

Some special effects are also supported as a style. For more information about using special effects as a style, see Chapter 13.

By redefining the style's attributes

Styles can also be edited by redefining the style's attributes using the Style Properties dialog box. Like defining a style based upon changes made to an object, styles that are redefined affect all of the objects that are associated with that style throughout your document. The Style Properties dialog box lets you quickly access fill and outline controls. To edit a style by redefining the style's attributes:

1. Open card1.cdr, if it's not already open.

2. In the Graphic and Text Styles docker, select the style labeled crown1.

3. Click the right arrow on the Styles docker and select Properties to display the Style Properties dialog box (see Figure 7-20). You can also access the dialog box by right-clicking a style and selecting properties from the right mouse button menu.

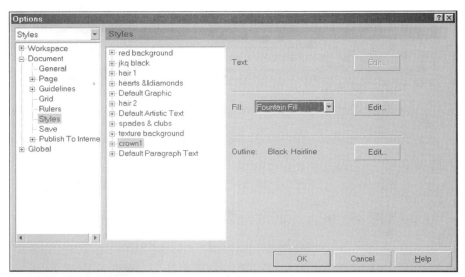

Figure 7-20: The Styles page of the Options dialog box lets you specify the properties of styles within your drawing.

4. Select crown1, if it's not shown as the selected style. Click the Edit button in the Fill section.

5. In the Color blend box, the origination color square is selected. Select a medium gray from the color palette (see Figure 7-21).

6. Click destination color square in the Color blend section and choose the same color gray from the palette. Click OK to return to the Styles page.

7. Click the Outline button to display the Outline property sheet.

8. Click the Edit button next to the Outline. In the Width box, change the value to 0.01 inches. Alternatively, you can highlight the current value and enter a new value (see Figure 7-22).

9. Click OK to complete the changes and to return to the Styles page.

10. Click OK to return to the drawing window. Save the file.

Caution   When you edit a style, its effects are global. What that means is that *all* of the objects that use the style are affected — not only those on the current page of the document, but those on *all* of the pages of a multiple-page document. While this is useful if you want to make global changes to an image, you should exercise caution, especially with multiple-page documents. Be sure that you want to apply the changes to all the objects that use that style.

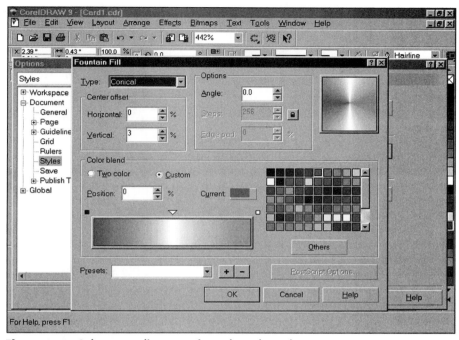

Figure 7-21: Select a medium gray from the color palette.

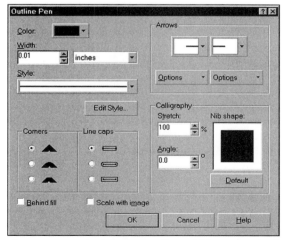

Figure 7-22: Change the outline width to 0.01 inches.

Using Color Styles

If you're an old hand with Draw, odds are that you've tabbed through images to change the colors of individual objects. If your images tend to be large, as mine tend to be, then you know what a tedious task this is. While you can still press Tab to cycle through the objects in your drawing, it's no longer necessary if you want to change the color of several objects in the image. Draw's color styles feature makes tedious color changes a thing of the past. You can now make color design changes in one step, reducing layout time and increasing the consistent appearance within your document.

Understanding parent-child colors

The color styles feature lets you create a family of colors automatically, providing you with a palette containing multiple shades of a particular color. A family of colors is a series of two or more similar solid colors linked together to form a *parent-child* relationship. The parent color is the base color, while the child colors are varying shades of the parent. The parent and child colors share a common hue, forming a link between the colors. You create the different shades by adjusting the amount of saturation and brightness. The result is a range of similar colors. Parent colors are created and applied in the same manner as a uniform fill. You can create a parent color using any color model or color palette. Like graphic and text styles, color styles are saved with the drawing and can be copied to other drawings and documents.

The power of color styles becomes apparent when you understand the relationship between the parent and child colors. For example, presume you drew a car whose body was various shades of red. The color style for the car would use a base color of red as the parent color and several shades of the same red as the children. If you decided later to change the color of the car to blue, you wouldn't have to manually change all the colors. You could simply change the parent color from red to blue. All of the child colors would change automatically, as well. The saturation and brightness values would remain the same, while the hue changed, ensuring that the blue car would have the same highlights, shadows, and subtle shading changes as the original red car. The exercises in this section illustrate how parent and child colors interrelate.

Generating color styles

You can create a new color style, using one of two methods in the Color Styles docker. You can either have Draw automatically create the color styles based upon the objects in your drawing, or you can create a unique style and then apply it to the objects in your drawing. The first method involves selecting objects in your drawing and then assigning the object a color style by clicking the Auto Create Color Styles button. After autocreating a color style, you can edit the hues of the resulting colors within the style to create the color combinations that you want to use in your drawing.

In the following exercises, you use Par_chld.cdr to work with color styles. Par_chld.cdr currently doesn't have any assigned color styles. You add child colors, edit the parent color, create a new parent color, apply a color style, and move a parent color from one style to another.

On the CD-ROM   Par_chld.cdr is located on your companion CD-ROM in the tutorial\ch07 folder.

Automatically

To automatically create parent-child colors:

1. Open par_chld.cdr.

2. Select Edit ⇨ Select All ⇨ Objects to select all the objects on the page.

3. Select Tools ⇨ Color Styles to display the Colors docker (see Figure 7-23).

4. Click the Auto Create Color Styles button.

5. The Automatically Create Color Styles dialog box appears (see Figure 7-24). Accept the default settings and click OK.

6. Save the file to your hard disk.

In a few moments, Draw generates the parent and child colors for the selected objects and they appear in the Colors docker (see Figure 7-25). You can specify whether you want the color styles to be based on fills, outlines, or both. If you enable Automatically link similar colors together in the Automatically Create Color Styles dialog box, Draw associates shades of the hues it finds in your drawing and offers the option of converting child palette colors to CMYK (cyan, magenta, yellow, and black). Move the slider to the left or right to adjust the number of parent and child colors. Moving the slider to the left increases the number of unique hues (parent colors) in the styles. Moving the slider to the right creates more shades (child colors) and associates them with fewer unique hues.

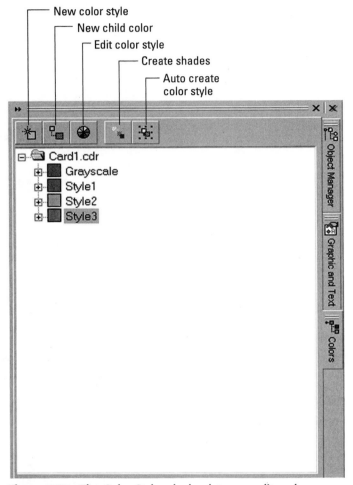

Figure 7-23: The Color Styles docker lets you edit and apply color styles in your documents.

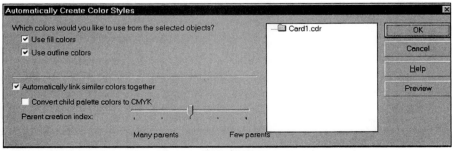

Figure 7-24: The Automatically Create Color Styles dialog box.

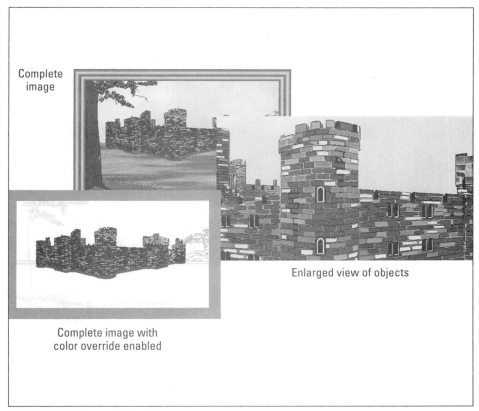

Complete image

Enlarged view of objects

Complete image with color override enabled

Figure 7-25: The Colors docker displays the new parent and child colors.

By creating a new color style

The second method for creating a new color style is to click the New Color Style button. Once you create a color style, you can apply it to objects in your drawing by using the Colors docker. To create a new color style using the New Color Style button:

1. Open par_chld.cdr, if it's not already open.

2. Select Tools ➪ Color Styles to display the Colors docker. The color styles for par_chld.cdr are displayed in the docker window.

3. Click the New Color Style button.

4. The New Color Style dialog box appears and lets you select a color as a new color style (see Figure 7-26). Click and drag the bar and square in the color window to select a blue-green. Alternatively, you can highlight the current CMYK values and enter these values: C: 51; M: 37; Y: 23; and B: 0.

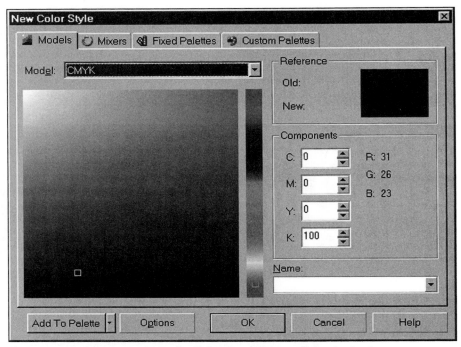

Figure 7-26: The New Color Style dialog box lets you select a color for your new color style.

5. Click OK to return to the Color Styles docker. The Color Styles docker is updated to display the new color style. Click the style label twice and enter **green metallic** to name the new color style.

6. Save the drawing.

Note

The New Color Style dialog box is similar to the Uniform Fill dialog box. Colors, color models, and color palettes are selected in the same manner.

Creating a child color

Once you create a parent color, you can add up to 20 child colors and link them to the parent. Any changes made to the parent color in a style are also reflected in the child colors. Once you define a color style, you can use the Color Styles Manager to apply it to any object. A child color is based on the hue of the parent color. Adjusting the saturation and brightness of child colors lets you create hundreds of variations. You can create child colors one at a time by adjusting the saturation and brightness settings for the color, or you can create a series of shades automatically.

To create a child color:

1. Open par_chld.cdr, if it's not already open.

2. Click the green metallic style.

3. Click the New Child Color button to display the Create a New Child Color dialog box.

4. Click and drag the square in the color window to select a pale gray-green. Alternatively, you can highlight the values in the Saturation and Brightness boxes and enter new values. Enter a value of 5 for the Saturation, and a value of 85 for the Brightness (see Figure 7-27).

5. Click OK to create the new child color and return to the drawing window. The new child color appears in the Color Styles docker.

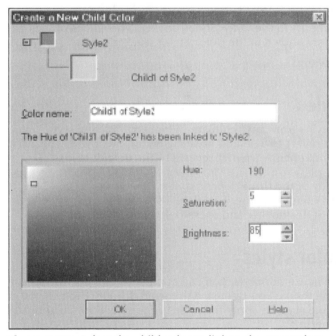

Figure 7-27: Select the child color to link to the parent hue.

You can create child colors to add, and link tints of the parent hue, to a color style. Adding child colors expands the range of colors associated with a hue, which makes it quicker and easier to globally change colors in your drawing. When you apply the color style to an object in your drawing, Draw uses the colors you've specified to fill the object.

Editing color styles

Editing a color style is a quick way of globally changing the colors of objects associated with that style. After selecting a color style in the Color Styles docker, you can modify the color in the Edit Color Style dialog box. To edit a color style:

1. Open par_chld.cdr, if it's not already open.

2. Click the plus (+) beside the Style 1 to display the child color. The child color represents a different saturation and brightness of the parent color, gold.

3. Click the gold parent to select it and then click the Edit Color Style button. The Edit Color Style dialog box appears, which lets you edit the red color style.

4. Select a medium blue color by dragging the color selector in both the color bar and the color window. Alternatively, you can highlight the values in the CYMK boxes. Set the values to C: 80; M: 0; Y: 30; and K: 0.

5. Click OK to return to the Color Styles docker. The colors of the drawing and the child colors shown in the Color Styles docker update.

6. Save the drawing.

Deleting styles

You can remove styles from any template. When you delete a style, objects that use the removed style revert to a default style based on the object type. An object's appearance does not change when it reverts to the default style.

You can't delete any of the three default styles: Default Paragraph Text, Default Artistic Text, and Default Graphic. To delete a style, select the style in the Graphic and Text or Color Styles docker and press Delete.

Applying color styles

Once you create a new color style, you can apply it to objects in your drawing, using one of two methods. You can use a drag-and-drop method or you can double-click the name of the style to apply the style to the selection. To apply a style using the double-click method:

1. Open par_chld.cdr, if it's not already open.

2. Select Tools ⇨ Graphic and Text Styles to display the Graphic and Text Styles docker. Click the Color Styles tab. The color styles for par_chld.cdr are displayed in the property sheet.

3. Using the Pick tool, select the top of the star-shaped polygon.

4. Double-click the name of the green metallic style in the Color Styles docker to apply the style to the background object.

5. Save the file.

When you apply a style by clicking and dragging the style to an object, the mouse pointer changes as it moves over single objects or objects in a group. When it appears hollow, it indicates that the mouse pointer is over an outline; when it appears solid, the mouse pointer is over a filled area. You can't drag a style to a compound object, such as an extrusion or blend. The cone in par_chld.cdr is a compound object (it's an extrusion). If the control object were visible, you could drag the style to the control object.

Note   If you drag a style to an object that is part of a group, the style is only applied to the individual object, not the group.

Moving styles from one parent to another

You can move a parent or child color style and make that style a child of another parent. If the color style has child colors, both the parent and its child colors become child colors of the selected color style.

To move a color from one parent to another:

1. Display the Colors docker.

2. Display the right mouse button menu by right-clicking the name of the color style to move.

3. Select Make Child of an Existing Color. The cursor changes to a large arrow.

4. Click the new parent color to which you want to assign the selected color. If you change your mind, you can press Esc or click outside the Colors docker to cancel this action.

5. If you want to use a drag-and-drop method to move a color style from one parent to another, select the color style and drag it to another location in the Colors docker.

Creating Templates

The styles you create can be applied to any object. You can also create a custom template from a group of styles. By saving different sets and combinations of styles, you can have templates to use with specific types of design projects. If the styles you want to save in the template exist in a drawing, you can save the drawing and all of its associated styles as a template. You can also define the styles in a blank drawing and save the drawing as a template. When you save a template, you can include the objects that formed the basis for the template. This is useful when you want to create a template where portions of the document are used repetitively, such as a newsletter. For example, you could save the newsletter template with its banner and prespecified columns. When you opened the newsletter template to create your monthly newsletter, the elements you saved with the template would already be in place.

To create a template using the Graphic or Text docker:

1. Display either the Graphic or Text docker.

2. Create or add any styles you want to save as a template, using the instructions found earlier in this chapter.

3. If you want to include objects in your template, such as a newsletter banner, place the object in the document and save the formatting and attributes as a style.

4. Click the right arrow near the top of either the Graphic or Text docker and select Template ⇨ Save As.

5. Enter a name and location for your template. Draw stores its preset templates in the corel\draw80\draw\templates folder. Saving your template in the same location as Draw's preset templates isn't a good idea. If you ever need to uninstall or reinstall Draw, your template could be lost.

6. Enable the With Contents checkbox if you want the template to include objects on the active page. If you are creating a multipage document, the template only saves those objects contained on the first page.

7. Click Save to complete the operation and to return to the docker.

Summary

An image created in Draw can have thousands of objects. If you create such a complex drawing, editing the image becomes a management chore that's more technical than creative. You can minimize this troublesome task by using the Object Manager and Snap-To features. These object-management tools provide the controls to easily govern the elements and appearance of your image. In this chapter, you learned to

✦ Use the Object Manager to control objects and their attributes

✦ Specify Master layers

✦ Create and name new layers

✦ Use Snap-To features to position and size objects

✦ Reorder and place objects on layers

✦ Manage layer attributes

✦ Create and apply styles

✦ Create templates

✦   ✦   ✦

Importing and Exporting Elements

Draw's capability to add images to your drawing and then export them to other applications and formats opens the doors to creativity. You can add clipart, images from a variety of software applications, or scanned images. The types of images that you can create with a flatbed scanner are almost endless. When you import or export files between programs, they require a translator in the form of import and export filters, which changes the file format of the image and provides a common format between applications. Fortunately, Draw is an OLE (Object Linking and Embedding)-compliant application. This means that you can use OLE to move images between Draw and other OLE-compliant applications. The advantage of OLE is that it requires no translator or filter for its operation. As long as the applications involved in the transfer are OLE compliant, images can be easily and quickly moved between them.

Importing Images and Text

Importing images and text into your Draw documents is a fairly easy process. Adding images is a similar process. Aside from Draw's native .cmx and .cdr file formats, the program supports a broad range of vector and bitmap file formats that allow you to use images from nearly any source.

Cross-Reference See Chapter 4 for more information on adding text to your documents.

Using the Import dialog box, you can merge existing Draw documents with the active drawing, or import other file formats. To import an image:

Shortcut

1. Select File ➪ Import to display the Import dialog box (see Figure 8-1).

   Ctrl+I accesses the Import dialog box.

2. Click the down arrow next to the Files of Type box and select a file format to import.

3. Choose the folder that contains the image or text to import.

4. Choose the file to import. You can import multiple images by pressing Ctrl while making your file selections. If you want to maintain the layers and pages, enable Maintain Layers and Pages.

5. Click Import. Draw imports the selected image and the Import Placement cursor appears. Click in the drawing window to place your import.

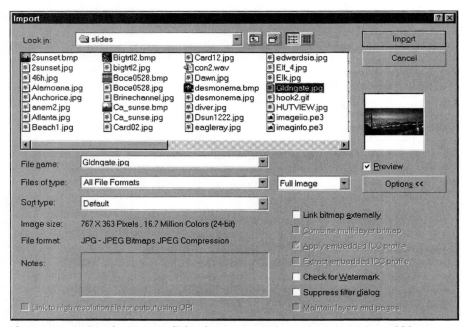

Figure 8-1: Using the Import dialog box, you can incorporate a variety of bitmap and vector images into your Draw documents.

Tip

When you select Maintain Layers and Pages, Draw imports vector files, such as other Draw documents, with their layers and pages intact. All of the layer information is included, and pages are added as needed to accommodate the contents of the file. If this option is disabled, Draw places the entire contents of the file on the active page. The Maintain Layers and Pages option is available for vector imports only. The option is grayed out when you select a bitmap file.

You can click and drag images from the Import dialog box to the drawing window. Draw imports the images when you release the mouse button, and places them at your cursor location in the drawing window.

Note

If you import a 4-bit (16-color) image into Draw, it's automatically converted to an 8-bit (256-color) image.

Understanding file formats

A computer stores data in files using one of a variety of methods. The method that is used to store any one file is known as its file format. Different types of files, such as bitmap, vector, sound, text, and so on, use different formats. A file format is frequently referred to by its extension. The extension is the two- or three-character string that is added to the file when saving it in that format, such as .cdr, .cmx, .bmp, or .doc format. In Windows 95 and Windows NT, different formats use different icons when listed in file managers and dialog boxes such as the Import dialog box in Draw. These icons are associated with specific programs, and you can launch the associated application by double-clicking the icon.

File formats are often proprietary or native only to a specific application. For example, images created in Draw are stored as .cdr files. Some formats are more generic, such as the .txt format, which is an ASCII text file and is not associated with any specific application. Table 8-1 lists the file formats that are supported by Draw's import and export filters.

| Table 8-1 | | |
| **Supported File Formats** | | |
File Format	*Extension*	*Format notes*
3D Model	3dmf/vrml	Objects can be rotated on their 3D axes.
Adobe Illustrator	ai	Imports and exports vector images. These features are unsupported: cropped bitmaps, PostScript, full-color bitmap, two-color bitmap, vector fills, texture fills, interactive and transparency fills, multiple layers, multiple pages, bitmap powerclips, lens effects.
Adobe Photoshop	psd	1-bit, grayscale, and color up to 32-bit CMYK images. All other bitmap import options are available.

Continued

Table 8-1 *(continued)*

File Format	Extension	Format notes
Adobe Portable Document	pdf	These import and export features are unsupported: cropped bitmaps, PostScript, full-color bitmap, two-color bitmap, texture fills, interactive and transparency fills, multiple layers, text fit to path, bitmap powerclips.
Ami Professional	sam	Draw imports this format, ignoring the page size in the original document. The text is fit to the current page size. This may affect the placement of text.
ANSI	txt	ASCII text file. Draw allows a maximum of 8,000 ASCII characters per paragraph of Paragraph text. This format retains no formatting attributes when imported into Draw.
AutoCad	dxf	These import and export features aren't supported: special 3-D shapes, 3-D extrusions, automatic wireframes, hidden lines removal, binary .DXF format, paper space entities, layers.
AutoCad Drawing	dwg	These import and export features are unsupported: cropped bitmaps, PostScript, full-color bitmap, two-color bitmap, vector fills, texture fills, interactive and transparency fills, multiple layers, multiple pages, bitmap powerclips, lens effects.
CALS Compressed Bitmap	cal	Imports images as mono (1-bit) format. All other bitmap import options are available.
Compuserve Bitmap	gif	Files conforming to the 87A and 89A specifications. Image can be multiframe. All other bitmap import options are available.
Computer Graphics Metafile	cgm	Imports vector images. These import and export features are unsupported: cropped bitmaps, PostScript, full-color bitmap, two-color bitmap, vector fills, texture fills, interactive and transparency fills, multiple layers, multiple pages, bitmap powerclips, lens effects.
Corel CMX Compressed	cmx	Draw's native format. Format allows for the exchange of images between Corel applications with no import restrictions.
Corel Photo-Paint 6 Image	cpt	No import restrictions.
Corel Photo-Paint Image	cpt	No import restrictions.

File Format	Extension	Format notes
Corel Presentation Exchange 6/7	cpx	One of Draw's native formats that allows for the exchange of images between Corel applications with no import restrictions.
Corel WordPerfect 4.2	wp4	Draw imports this format with these restrictions: TOC, indices, style sheets, equations, formulas, HLine graphics, and VLine graphics aren't supported; the page size in the original document is ignored. The text is fit to the current page size. This may affect the placement of text.
Corel WordPerfect 5.0–5.1	wp5	Draw imports this format with these restrictions: TOC, indices, style sheets, equations, formulas, HLine graphics, and VLine graphics aren't supported; the page size in the original document is ignored. The text is fit to the current page size. This may affect the placement of text.
Corel WordPerfect 6/7/8	wp8	Draw imports this format with these restrictions: TOC, indices, style sheets, equations, formulas, HLine graphics, and VLine graphics aren't supported; the page size in the original document is ignored. The text is fit to the current page size. This may affect the placement of text.
Corel WordPerfect Graphic	wpg	Graphics text type 2 and WPG Version 2 are not fully supported.
CorelDraw	cdr	Draw's native format. No import restrictions apply.
CorelDraw Compressed	cdx	Compressed Draw format with no import restrictions.
Encapsulated PostScript	eps	Imports files in a "Placeable" format. The applications display the bitmap thumbnail header or preview in the working file, as opposed to the entire file. Used as a placeholder, the file isn't editable in Draw.
Enhanced Windows Metafile	emf	Imports vector images. Multiple pages aren't supported for either import or export.
Frame Vector Metafile	fmv	These import and export features aren't supported: PostScript, full-color bitmap, two-color bitmap, texture and vector fills, interactive and transparency fills, multiple pages, text fit to path, and bitmap powerclips.
GEM	gem	Imports vector images. These import features aren't supported: fills such as grids, hatches, and ball bearings. Objects containing these fills are filled with a solid color representing the hue described by the special fill.

Continued

Table 8-1 *(continued)*

File Format	Extension	Format notes
GEM Paint	img	Supports full imports only.
HPGL Plotter	plt	Imports HPGL and HPGL/2 command set. A stepping factor of 1016 plotter units = 1 inch is used. Color lines are supported.
IBM PIF	pf	Vector graphics created on IBM mainframes. These features aren't supported: background and foreground mixes, call segments, set character sets, paper color, and pattern symbols.
Joint Photographic Experts Group Bitmap	jpg	Compressed file format with no import restrictions. This format is a lossy format.
Kodak FlashPix Image	fpx	Kodak photo image format that offers photo enhancement on import.
Kodak Photo-CD Image	pcd	Digital photo images. All bitmap import options are available, including color correction.
Lotus Pic	pic	Colors are translated to an 8-color palette. Text is editable, but body text is imported as a monospace font.
Macintosh PICT	pct	Imports both vector and bitmap contents of this format. These import and export features are unsupported: cropped bitmaps, PostScript, full-color bitmap, two-color bitmap, vector fills, texture fills, interactive and transparency fills, multiple layers, multiple pages, bitmap powerclips, and lens effects.
MACPaint Bitmap	mac	Imports images as mono (1-bit) format with or without .RLE compression. All other bitmap import options are available.
MET Metafile	met	IBM's Presentation Manager graphics for OS/2. Only basic drawing features are supported, such as solid outlines, solid fills, and both True Type and Type 1 fonts.
Micrografx 2.x–3.x	drw	Clip regions and raster information are not supported. Gradient fills are imported as colored polygons.
Micrografx Designer 6.0	dsf	Clip regions and raster information are not supported. Gradient fills are imported as colored polygons.
MS Word for Macintosh 4.0–5.0	doc	Draw imports this format with these restrictions: footnotes or endnotes aren't supported and the page size in the original document is ignored. The text is fit to the current page size. This may affect the placement of text.

File Format	Extension	Format notes
MS Word for Windows 2.x	doc	Draw imports this format with these conventions: Draw tries to match all the fonts in your document with the same or similar fonts; converts "Normal" text style to a default text style you specify; Symbol or MS Linedraw character sets are converted to the corresponding PC character set entries; indexes aren't supported; fonts are proportionally spaced, and text is reflowed when imported; the page size in the original document is ignored.
MS Word for Windows 4.0–5.5	doc	Draw imports this format with these restrictions: footnotes or endnotes aren't supported, and the page size in the original document is ignored. The text is fit to the current page size. This may affect the placement of text. Draw attempts to match fonts in your document. If it doesn't find them, it substitutes the default font.
MS Word for Windows 6.0/95 Word 6 is the same as Word 95; Word 97 isn't supported	doc	Draw imports this format with these conventions: Draw tries to match all the fonts in your document with the same or similar fonts; converts "Normal" text style to a default text style you specify; Symbol or MS Linedraw character sets are converted to the corresponding PC character set entries; indexes aren't supported; fonts are proportionally spaced, and text is reflowed when imported; the page size in the original document is ignored.
NAP Metafile	nap	Vector file format is used to communicate graphic images between PC and Unix platforms. Only basic drawing features are supported, such as solid outlines, solid fills, and both True Type and Type 1 fonts.
OS/2 Bitmap	bmp	Grayscale and up to 24-bit (16.7 million colors) with or without RLE compression. All other bitmap import options are available.
Paintbrush	pcx	Files can contain 1-, 2-, or 4-color planes. Files containing 3-color planes cannot be imported. All other bitmap import options are available; pcx files are 8-bit color.
Picture Publisher	pp4	Supports mono, color, and grayscale 1- or 8-bit images. All other bitmap import options are available.

Continued

Table 8-1 *(continued)*

File Format	Extension	Format notes
Picture Publisher 5.0	pp5	Mono, color, and grayscale 1- or 8-bit images. All other bitmap import options are available.
Portable Network Graphics	png	Imports up to 24-bit color images. All other bitmap import options are available.
PostScript Interpreted	ps/prn/eps	Imports the PostScript information as a printer would view it. These files can be huge and may not import due to memory limitations.
Rich Text Format	rtf	Retains its formatting attributes when imported into Draw.
Scitex CT bitmap	sct	High-end scanner created 32-bit color or 8-bit grayscale format. All other bitmap import options are available.
Tagged Information File Format	tif	Imports 1-bit, 24- or 32-bit color, and 8-bit grayscale images; the files may be compressed using the CCITT, Packbits 32773, or LZW compression algorithms. All other bitmap import options are available.
Targa Bitmap	tga	Imports 16- and 24-bit images with or without RLE compression. All other bitmap import options are available.
Wavelet Compressed Bitmap	wi	Grayscale and 24-bit (16.7 million colors) images. All other bitmap import options are available.
Windows 3.x/NT Bitmap Resource	exe	Bitmap graphics embedded in executables. These bitmaps are 32 pixels x 32 pixels and no more than 4-bit (16 colors). You can select a color for Transparent and Inverse masks.
Windows 3.x/NT Cursor Resource	cur	Windows cursor file. These bitmaps are 32 pixels and no more than 4-bit (16 colors). You can select a color for Transparent and Inverse masks.
Windows 3.x/NT Icon Resource	ico	Windows icon file. These bitmaps are 32 pixels x 32 pixels and no more than 4-bit (16 colors). You can select a color for Transparent and Inverse masks.
Windows Bitmap	bmp	Grayscale and up to 24-bit (16.7 million colors) with or without RLE compression. All other bitmap import options are available.
Windows Metafile	wmf	Imports vector images. These import and export features are unsupported: cropped bitmaps, PostScript, full-color bitmap, two-color bitmap, vector fills, texture fills, interactive and transparency fills, multiple layers, multiple pages, bitmap powerclips, lens effects.

File Format	Extension	Format notes
WordStar 2000	wsd	Draw imports this format with these restrictions: the page size in the original document is ignored. The text is fit to the current page size. This may affect the placement of text.
WordStar 7.0	wsd	Draw imports this format with these restrictions: footnotes, endnotes, merge dot commands, printer dot commands, and display commands aren't supported; Draw substitutes fonts, and the page size in the original document is ignored. The text is fit to the current page size. This may affect the placement of text.
WordStar for Windows 1.x–2.0	ws1-2	Draw imports this format with these restrictions: footnotes, endnotes, merge dot commands, printer dot commands, and display commands aren't supported; Draw substitutes fonts, and the page size in the original document is ignored. The text is fit to the current page size. This may affect the placement of text.
XYWrite for Windows	xy	Draw imports this format with these restrictions: XYWrite programming language is not supported, and the page size in the original document is ignored. The text is fit to the current page size. This may affect the placement of text.

Adding clipart to your document

Draw's clipart is stored in CDR format on one of the CD-ROMs that came with the program. You can open or import clipart directly, as you would a CDR file. Draw comes packaged with an enormous quantity of clipart. I recommend that you use the clipart catalogue or the scrapbook feature in Draw to preview and select the clipart you want to use. Although the Import dialog box has a preview window, it makes a rather slow browser if you want to view several images. The clipart, located on the CD-ROM, is stored by category to speed the selection process.

Draw's Scrapbook feature lets you preview and select art for your document, instead of using the import dialog box. Icons of the art appear organized on the tab pages of the docker. The Scrapbook lets you browse folders on your computer for your own images, select clipart, add photos, and select from favorite fills and outlines. If you right-click the icon that represents a file, the right mouse button menu offers other options, such as the ability to print, rename, or delete a file. You can add images to the Scrapbook by dragging the image to the Scrapbook. Draw places a thumbnail image of the drawing on the active tab page, and stores the path information for your image.

To use the Scrapbook:

1. Click the Scrapbook button on the Standard toolbar, or select Tools ⇨ Scrapbook and select a category to display the Scrapbook Docker (see Figure 8-2).

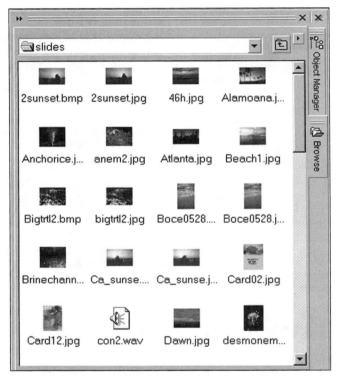

Figure 8-2: The Scrapbook docker lets you preview and import images.

2. Choose the folder and file you want to add to your document.

3. Drag the icon to the drawing page, or right-click the icon and select Import. Draw imports the drawing and places the image in your document.

4. If you want to open the image as a separate document, double-click the icon and select Open from the right mouse button menu, or click the Open button on the toolbar.

Tip

To display the contents of a folder in the Scrapbook, double-click the folder. Click the Up One button in the toolbar to move up one level in the folder hierarchy.

The icons in the Scrapbook are very small. If you have difficulty seeing the contents of a file to select the image that you want, right-click the icon and select Quick View from the right mouse button menu. The Quick View window appears with a low-resolution thumbnail of the image. This option is available only if you have Quick View installed.

Tip You can increase the size of the thumbnails displayed in the Scrapbook docker by either clicking the arrow at the top or by right-clicking in the white space around the thumbnails. Choose View ➪ Thumbnail Size from the menu that appears, and then choose the thumbnail size to use.

Choosing a file format

The list of file formats that Draw is capable of importing is lengthy, as Table 8-1 showed. In the early days of computer graphics, finding a file format common to any two applications was problematic. At that time, most applications used strictly proprietary formats. Very few applications supported generic formats that other applications could read easily. Today, finding a common format is extremely easy. Some formats are better for certain uses, however. If you are preparing a bitmap image in another application for use in a Draw document, or if you intend to export your image as a bitmap, you should consider several factors that affect bitmap files.

Tip Some bitmaps, such as those used in newsletters and catalogues, need to be updated frequently in other programs. If you're creating a document that contains such bitmap graphics, consider enabling Link to External File in the Import dialog box. Each time you open the document, Draw reimports the image, which ensures that your Draw document contains the most current version of the bitmap graphic.

Vector versus bitmap graphics

Vector and bitmap or raster graphics are fundamentally different in how they are created, how they are stored on your hard disk, and how they behave when they are resized or printed. Suppose you drew a red ellipse with a 0.01-inch black outline in the drawing window. When you save the image in a vector format, such as cdr, only the essential information is saved. If you were able to open the file in a text editor and were familiar with graphic-description programming code, you would see that the information for the ellipse contained:

✦ The center of the ellipse relative to the printable page

✦ The distance the ellipse extended on the x and y coordinates from the center of the ellipse

✦ The width of the outline

✦ The CMYK or RGB values for the fill and outline of the ellipse

Vector object information is recorded with mathematical precision. If you resize an object, the values are recalculated and recorded. The quality of the image remains the same. Due to the modest amount of information your computer requires to recreate a vector image, the images create smaller file sizes. Each time you open a cdr file, the objects are recreated from the instruction set stored with the file. Draw then translates the image to create a raster image for screen representation of your graphic. Vector images are device-dependent images. This means that their visible resolution is dependent upon the output device. For example, if you printed a vector image on a 300-dpi (dots per inch) printer, the image would print at that resolution. Similarly, if you printed the image on a 1200-dpi printer, the image would print at that resolution.

When you save an object as a bitmap, the information that's stored on your hard disk is quite different from that of a vector object. A bitmap has four characteristics that describe the image: dimension, resolution, bit depth, and color model. Bitmap images are basically grids. Each square in the grid represents a pixel (see Figure 8-3). The grid of pixels that represents your monitor may be 1280 × 1024, but that does not describe the actual measurement of the image. The number of dots or pixels contained in an inch can vary widely from one device to another. For this reason, the number of dots per inch (dpi) or the number of pixels per inch (ppi) generally describes bitmap graphics.

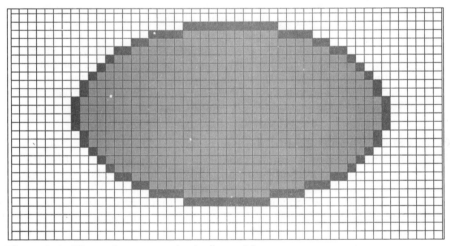

Figure 8-3: Bitmap images are basically a grid.

Bitmap graphics are displayed by turning pixels on or off. If they are turned on, they are assigned a color number to represent them. They can be black, white, gray, or a color. In bitmap data terms, black is 1, white is 0, and so forth. In the case of the ellipse, the pixels would be either red or black. When the file is saved, every individual pixel in the grid must be described. The result is that bitmap files are much larger than vector images.

Compressed file formats

Bitmapped files can be compressed to reduce file size. Some compressed formats, such as jpg files, are *lossy*. Lossy means that information is stripped from the image to create a smaller file size. The result is that the image is degraded and doesn't look as good when printed as lossless files, such as tif format files. You can specify the amount of compression with many compressed formats. As the amount of compression increases, the quality of the image is degraded (see Figure 8-4). Compressed formats, such as jpg, are ideal for onscreen presentation use, such as the Internet, because of the lower resolution supported by monitors. These files may take longer to display because your computer has to uncompress the files before rendering them to screen.

Low Compression   High Compression

Figure 8-4: Lossy compression formats, such as jpg, can cause the quality of an image to degrade.

File formats vary in the manner in which they store data. Draw stores files in a proprietary cdr format, which is generally unreadable by other applications. Other programs store files in more generic formats, such as bmp, which is a Windows or OS/2 bitmap file that can be read by a variety of applications. Some file formats support compression schemes that save storage space on your hard disk.

Note   When importing a compressed file format, Draw must expand the file prior to importing it. Similarly, when exporting an image in a compressed format, Draw must compress the image prior to storing it on your hard disk. The result is that compressed files take longer to read and write to your hard disk.

Importing OPI images

Files created with OPI (Open Prepress Interface) are low-resolution images designed for use as layout placeholders. These images can be placed in large documents to block out text and graphics. The low-resolution tif or ct image is linked to a high-resolution version of the image. When the file is printed, the printing instruction set swaps the high-resolution image for the low-resolution placeholder. Using files created with OPI in your layout speeds the creation of large documents because of the faster screen refresh time. When you import an OPI image, enable Link to High Resolution File for Output Using OPI.

For more information about OPI, see Chapter 16.

Importing Photo CD images

When you choose to import a photo (pcd) image, Draw displays the Photo CD dialog box (see Figure 8-5). The dialog box lets you specify the size, color mode, and color correction for the photo image, prior to importing the image into your document.

You can choose from two methods of color correction: Gamut CD and Kodak. Choosing Gamut CD helps ensure that your image prints accurately by using gamut mapping to adjust the color tones. The Kodak method lets you alter the color tints, as well as adjust brightness, saturation, and contrast in your image. The final output for the image determines the method you choose. If the image will be used for onscreen presentation or the Internet, I recommend the Kodak method. If you intend to print the final image, I recommend the Gamut CD method to ensure the printed output of your image.

Color correcting photo images

To apply color correction to a photo image:

1. Select the image to import using the method outlined earlier. Click the Import button. Note that if you choose to import a photo using the scrapbook, the Photo CD dialog box doesn't appear.

2. In the Image tab of the Photo CD dialog box, choose the size and color depth for your image. If you are going to print the final image, leave the color depth at 24-bit, 16.7 million colors. If you are going to use the image for onscreen presentation, lower that amount to 8-bit, 256 colors.

3. Click the Enhancement tab to display image enhancement options.

4. Choose an enhancement method.

5. Choose a preview method. For most purposes, Fast Preview is sufficient. It provides a quick look at the changes you make to the image. If you require a more accurate preview, choose Best Preview. Best Preview is slower, but displays the most accurate color. Click the Preview button to view the effect of changes you make.

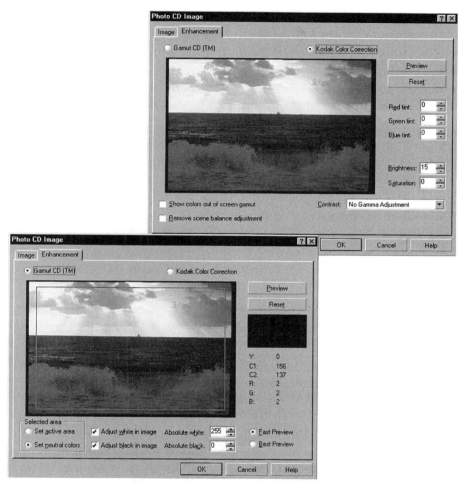

Figure 8-5: The Photo CD Image dialog box.

6. Adjust your photo using the guidelines below for the selected enhancement method. When you are satisfied with the enhancement changes you've made, click OK to complete the operation and to return to the drawing window. Draw makes the enhancement changes to the photo image and imports it into your drawing.

Tip

Choosing an 8-bit color depth decreases the file size and improves the loading performance for onscreen presentation, such as on the WWW (World Wide Web). Another advantage to choosing 8-bit color is that it guarantees the broadest range of audience. Most computers can easily display 256 colors. Some computers may not have the resources to display 16.7 million colors. The online loading time for 24-bit images, using a Web browser such as Netscape, is prohibitive.

Gamut CD correction

To specify Gamut CD correction:

✦ Click the Set Active Area button, and then click and drag in the preview window to select the active area to use for color enhancement. Hint: Consider selecting a small portion of the photo as opposed to selecting most or the entire photo. This is useful if your photo contains an area that needs more color correction than other portions. If you plan to crop the image, you can select the approximate area to which you intend to crop the image. This ensures that the color correction you make will be accurate for that area.

✦ If your image contains white or black, enable the Adjust White and/or Adjust Black options, respectively. Enter new values in the adjustment boxes to define how pure the colors are. Pure white has a value of 255; pure black has a value of 0. Hint: If the image doesn't have white or black, disable the appropriate adjustment option. This helps prevent your image from becoming too light or dark once it's imported. You can use these options to lighten or darken images that don't have these colors. For example, if the image is too dark, enable Adjust White and enter a value less than 255 in the box. Similarly, if the image is too light, enable the Adjust Black option, and enter a value greater than 0.

✦ If your image contains neutral areas (black, gray, or white), choose the Set Neutral Colors option. Click the neutral areas in the preview window. A small plus (+) sign appears at the point you click to indicate your selection. This removes the colorcasts from those areas. Try to select light-colored areas that cover the greatest range of your image.

Kodak color correction

To apply Kodak color correction:

✦ Enable Show Colors Out of Screen Gamut. This helps you make adjustments within the gamut range. Out-of-gamut colors are displayed as red or blue. If these colors appear, readjust the settings to eliminate them. Colors that are out of gamut are outside of the printable range of colors, and don't print correctly.

✦ Adjust the tint by clicking the up and down arrows, or by entering new values in the boxes.

✦ Adjust the brightness by clicking the up and down arrows, or by entering a new value in the box.

✦ Adjust the saturation by clicking the up and down arrows, or by entering a new value in the box. Hint: If the darker areas of your image are displayed as out of gamut, decrease the saturation to correct the problem.

✦ Choose a gamma adjustment from the drop-down list. Positive values darken your image; negative values lighten the image.

✦ When a photo is scanned and placed on a Photo CD, the photo finisher applies a scene balance. The scene balance is an information set that contains the black point, white point, and a median gamma value that are generally acceptable for both display and printing. If you want to disable this feature, enable the Remove Scene Balance Adjustment.

Resampling images while importing

Resampling of bitmap images lets you change the size and resolution of an image with minimal degradation of the image's quality. You can resample a bitmap either during the import or afterwards. If you resample the image during the import, the image is ready to place in your drawing at the size you need. To resample the image during import:

1. In the Import dialog box, click the down arrow next to Full Image, and select Resample from the drop-down list. Draw displays the Resample Image dialog box (see Figure 8-6).

2. Choose the unit of measurement to use from the drop-down list box. The default is pixels, but you can choose other units of measurement to fit your needs.

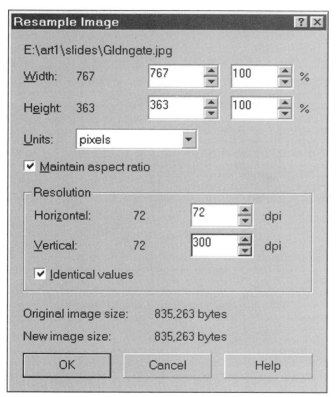

Figure 8-6: The Resample Image dialog box lets you change the resolution and size of your images.

3. Enable Maintain Aspect Ratio, if desired. When this option is enabled, the ratio between width and height is maintained when you change the measurement of either dimension.

4. Enter a new width and height. If you enabled Maintain Aspect Ratio, you only need to enter one dimension here.

5. Modify the resolution, if desired. If you want the vertical and horizontal resolution to be identical, enable Identical Values.

6. Click OK to complete the operation and to return to the drawing window. Draw imports and places the image in your document.

Cropping bitmaps while importing

Draw lets you crop bitmaps either when importing the bitmap or afterwards. When you crop a bitmap in the drawing window, the area that you remove is still there. It's just not visible. If you crop the bitmap when you import the image, however, you reduce the physical size of the image while retaining the resolution. Only the selected portion of the image is imported into Draw. This reduces the file size of your document. To crop an image during import:

1. In the Import dialog box, click the down arrow next to Full Image and select Crop from the drop-down list. Draw displays the Crop Image dialog box (see Figure 8-7).

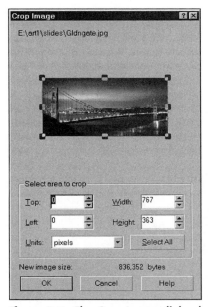

Figure 8-7: The Crop Image dialog box lets you crop unwanted portions of your image when you import the file.

2. Drag the handles in the preview window to crop the image. The area within the bounding box is retained; the area outside the bounding box is removed when the image is imported.

3. If you need to crop a bitmap to a precise size, enter values in the width and height boxes.

4. If you aren't happy with the area that you specified, you can start over by clicking the Select All button.

Exporting Images

Files created in Draw's native cdr format can't be opened directly as .cdr files in bitmap programs. If you want to use an image created in Draw in other applications, such as Photoshop, you must first convert the image to a bitmap format.

Tip If you plan to use your exported image in an OLE-compliant application, consider linking the graphic to that application instead of exporting it. This way, if you change the graphic in Draw, the graphic is automatically updated in the other application.

Exporting Draw to bitmap format

The basic process of converting an image to a bitmap format is identical, regardless of the format you choose. Some formats support other options. Where this applies, additional dialog boxes appear that allow you to choose options associated with that format.

Note Photo-Paint converts a .cdr format file to a .cpt format file when you try to open it. You don't need to convert the file in Draw before opening it in Photo-Paint.

To export a Draw image to a bitmap format:

1. Decide what portion of your image you want to export. If you only want to export a portion of your drawing, select the objects to export. If you want to export the entire drawing, you don't have to perform this step.

2. Select File ➪ Export to display the Export dialog box (see Figure 8-8.)

3. Select a file type for your exported image. If you are exporting to a format with additional options, another dialog box will open listing the filter options associated with that file type. Draw remembers the options you chose for a particular file type. If you generally choose the same options for that file type and you don't need to see the second dialog box, enable the Suppress Filter Dialog checkbox.

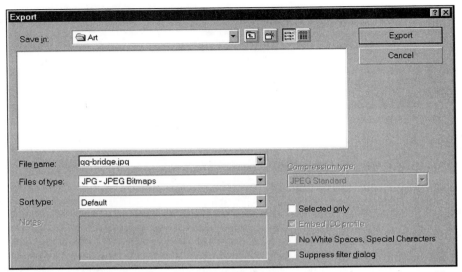

Figure 8-8: The Export dialog box lets you save files in a format that can be read by other applications.

Caution Unless you choose CMX as an export type, only the first page or facing pages of a multipage document is exported. If you want to export the entire document, you must export each page or set of facing pages individually.

4. Choose the folder where you want to store your image, and enter a name for the image in the File Name box.

5. If you are exporting only a portion of your image, enable the Selected Only checkbox.

6. Choose Uncompressed or a compression type from the drop-down list. This option isn't available for some file formats.

Caution Draw uses compression schemes for file formats, such as RLE (Run-Length Encoding) for Windows bitmaps (bmp). These compression schemes may not be supported by the application in which you intend to open your exported image. If you are uncertain whether the compression type is supported, choose Uncompressed.

7. Click Export. If you didn't enable the Suppress Filter dialog box, Draw displays a dialog box with options associated with the export file type (see Figure 8-9).

8. Specify the options you want for your exported image, and click OK when you are satisfied with your choices. The options you select can affect the final file size. Figure 8-9 shows the effect of choosing 16 million colors for the header preview on the projected file size, which is shown at the bottom of the dialog box. If this is an issue, select options that reduce the file size.

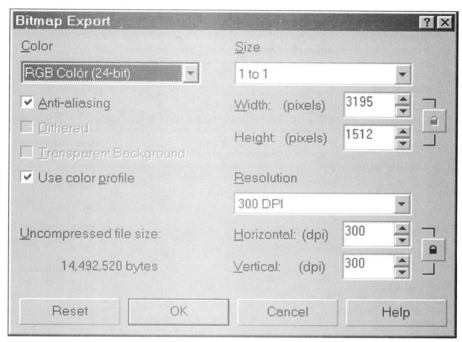

Figure 8-9: You can specify filter options in the filter dialog box associated with the export type you've selected.

The Internet and Anti-Aliasing Options

If you are exporting an image for use on the Internet, I recommend you choose None as the anti-aliasing option. Although anti-aliasing produces a smoother looking edge around graphics, it also can cause ghosting around images with transparent backgrounds that is nearly impossible to remove.

Ghosting is an undesirable condition where there appears to be a one-pixel white border around the image. This border is not actually white, but a very light shade of the adjacent pixels. Against multicolored Web or presentation backgrounds, it makes the image appear as if it were pasted or as if it were floating above the background.

Selecting a file format

Most software applications support a variety of file formats. This support is not to imply that all of the supported formats are the best format for that application. Different applications deal with the formats differently, and some formats support more of Draw's special effects features.

Recommended formats

Table 8-2 lists suggested file formats for a variety of other software programs. These formats are recommended for exporting images from Draw.

Table 8-2 Suggested File Formats for Other Software Applications	
For use in:	**Use this format**
Adobe Illustrator	ai
AutoCad	dxf or hpgl
Arts & Letters	ai
ASCII text	txt or Windows clipboard
Corel applications	cmx
CorelTrace	CorelTrace ai
Gem Artline	gem
Gem Draw Plus	gem
Harvard Graphics	cgm
Lotus 1-2-3	pic
Lotus Freelance	cgm
Macintosh-based vector packages	Macintosh pict or ai
Macintosh-based bitmap packages	tif, Macintosh pict, gif, or jpg
Micrographx Designer	drw or ai
Word Perfect	wpg
Macromedia Director or Authorware, Windows-based	bmp
Macromedia Director or Authorware, Macintosh-based	Macintosh pict or tif
Microsoft products	bmp
Pagemaker	wmf
Alternate output devices, such as vinyl cutters, plotters, and engravers	hpgl or dxf
Film recorders	scodl or eps

Managing import/export filters

Draw lets you manage import and export filters through the Options dialog box. To access the filter management page, select Tools ➪ Options and then expand the Global category. Click Filters to display the Filters page. When you expand the File

Types in any of these categories, Draw displays a list of active filters (see Figure 8-10). Working between the categories and filters lists you can add, delete, and associate file types with Draw (see Table 8-3). Rearranging filters lets you put the filters you use most often near the top and less frequently used filters near the bottom of the list. The capability to associate file types with Draw is useful if you are working with a project where you always want to open or import images into Draw. After associating a file format with Draw, you can open or import the image by double-clicking the file name using Windows Explorer or My Computer.

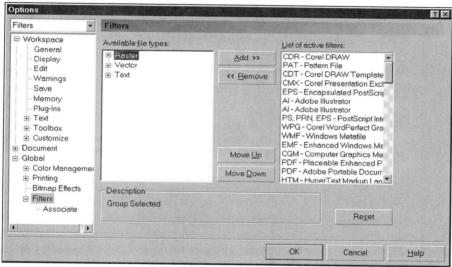

Figure 8-10: The Filters page of the Options dialog box lets you manage the filters associated with Draw.

Table 8-3
Customizing the File Types Dialog Box

To perform this action	Do this
Rearrange file filters	Select the file filter to move (the filter must be installed to use this feature) and then click the Move Up or Move Down arrows to reposition the filter on the filter list.
Add new filters to the list of active filters	Choose a category and filter from the Available File Types box, and then click Add.
Remove filters	Choose the filter to remove from the List of Active Filters box, and then click the Remove button.
Associate a file format with Draw	Click the Associate tab in the File Types dialog box and choose the file format to associate with Draw. Click OK.

Understanding OLE

OLE is an alternate to importing and exporting images from one application to another. Unlike importing and exporting, OLE does not depend upon file filters to move files. The applications involved in the file transfer must, however, be OLE-compliant. First introduced in Windows 3.1, OLE still confuses a lot of users. OLE is actually a powerful extended feature of the Windows clipboard. When you transfer information using this method, the data is temporarily stored on the clipboard and then placed in the destination document. To understand OLE, you need to understand the process and the OLE participants.

Cross-Reference   To learn how to move text from one application to the next using OLE, see Chapter 4.

Servers and clients

An OLE-compliant application can be a server, a client, or both. Server applications let you design objects or text and then transfer them, using OLE, to a client application. Some applications, like Draw, are capable of receiving information as a client and sharing information as a server.

How it works

One of the best examples of OLE is an invoice. Using OLE, you could create invoices that automatically update themselves. Suppose you created a payment entry in a customer's spreadsheet, and created a bitmap image of your corporate headquarters in another application. You intend to create your invoices in Draw, and you want to use the bitmap in the header of your invoice. You also want to use the payment and balance entries you created in the spreadsheet in the invoice. Because both the spreadsheet and bitmap image-editing programs are OLE-compliant, you don't need to worry about importing these two objects. Because the bitmap is unlikely to change, you can embed the image in your invoice. When you embed an OLE object in a Draw document, the information is stored with the file. You want the spreadsheet data to update, however, so when you place the object in your Draw document, you choose to link the object. When you link an object, the object itself isn't stored with your Draw document. Only a pointer is stored. When you open the document, Draw reads the information indicated by the pointer, and places the information in the document. If the information changes, that is, you change the spreadsheet entries, the information is automatically updated in your Draw document.

Inserting objects

You can insert an OLE object in your document by dragging and dropping the object between application windows, if both Draw and the other OLE-compliant application are open. If you press Shift+Ctrl while dragging the object, it becomes a linked object. For more control, right-click and drag objects between application windows; when you release the mouse button, the right mouse menu appears letting you specify how you want to place the object.

You can also place objects by selecting Edit ➪ Insert Object, and selecting a source (see Figure 8-11). The Insert New Object dialog box lets you choose from an existing file, or create a new object in an OLE-compliant server application. If you click Create New, select a server application from the list box below Object Type. Draw reads the OLE-compliant applications from the Windows Registry and lists them in this box. If you choose Create from File, you are prompted to select the location and file to insert in your document. If you enable Link, the file is linked rather than embedded into your document. When you are finished making your selection, click OK. If you selected a file, Draw places the object into your document. If you chose Create New, Draw opens the associated application so that you can create the object to place in your document.

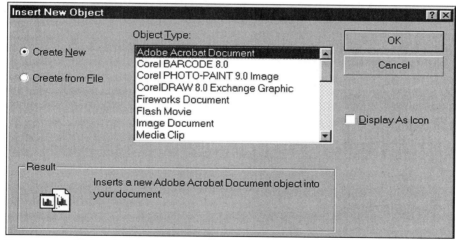

Figure 8-11: The Insert New Object dialog box lets you link or embed objects in your documents using OLE.

Using Paste Special

Paste Special also lets you place OLE objects in your Draw documents. If the server application is OLE-compliant, you are given a choice of whether to embed or to link the object (see Figure 8-12).

To use Paste Special:

1. Open the server application and select the object to place in your Draw document.

2. Copy the object to the clipboard.

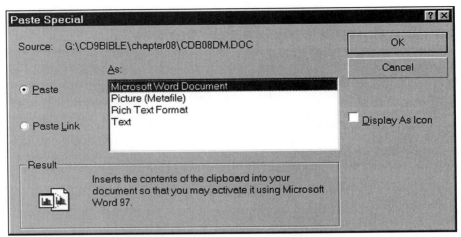

Figure 8-12: The Paste Special dialog box lets you paste OLE objects in your drawings.

3. Open the document to which you want to place the application in Draw.

4. Select Edit ➪ Paste Special.

5. Choose Paste to embed the object. Choose Paste Link to link the object.

6. Click OK to complete the operation and to return to the drawing window. Draw places the object in your drawing.

As a general rule of thumb, you should link objects you update frequently in other applications and embed objects that you are unlikely to change, unless you need smaller file sizes.

Tip

Linked files can make a real difference in the portability of your file. Draw documents with embedded bitmaps can exceed the capacity of a floppy disk. Linking objects lets you restrict the size of your Draw document. You can then store your Draw document on one disk, and linked files on other disks. For best results, place your Draw document and any linked files in the same directory when you move them to another hard disk. If Draw can't find its linked files, your image will be compromised.

Editing OLE objects

When you place an OLE object in a Draw document, Draw remembers that the object was created in another application and stores that information with the document. If you want to edit the object, you can double-click the object, or choose to edit the object using the commands on the Edit menu. Draw opens the originating application, in the background, so that you can modify the object. Your object appears in a box bordered by a thick, diagonal, hatched line. When you are finished editing the object, click outside the box to update your drawing and return to the drawing window. When you close the application, Draw prompts you to save the updated information with your Draw document. Click Yes to update the information and return to Draw.

Working with OLE objects as another type

You can edit an OLE object as another object type or convert an OLE object to another object type. To perform either of these operations you need to start the server application first, by either double-clicking the object or choosing Edit ⇨ Object ⇨ Edit in Draw. If you want to edit the object as another object type, enable Activate As and choose an object type from the Object Type list box. When you edit an object in this manner, it does not change the actual object type. It only changes the way you edit the object. If you want to convert an OLE object to another type, disable Activate As, and choose an object type from the Object Type list box. You can then edit the object as the desired object type.

Changing an OLE server

You can change the source of a linked OLE object. One advantage of changing the source is that it lets you replace one object with another object of the same file type. For example, if you had a bitmap of a building in your Draw document and wanted to replace it with a bitmap of a mountain, you could change the source. Draw places the new source image in the same location as the old source image.

Caution

When changing an OLE source, unpredictable results can occur if the new source object is only a portion of a file or a different file type.

To change the source type of a linked object:

1. Using the Pick tool, select the linked object you want to change.
2. Select Edit ⇨ Links to display the Change Source dialog box (see Figure 8-13).

Breaking an OLE link

When you open a document with a linked OLE object, Draw reads the original file that contains the object, and updates the object as needed in your Draw document. Breaking the link of an OLE object causes the object to behave as an embedded object. Although you can still edit the object, the object is no longer updated. This is useful when you want to freeze the appearance or data contained in an OLE object in your Draw document.

Caution

If you move the original file of a linked object, the link is automatically broken.

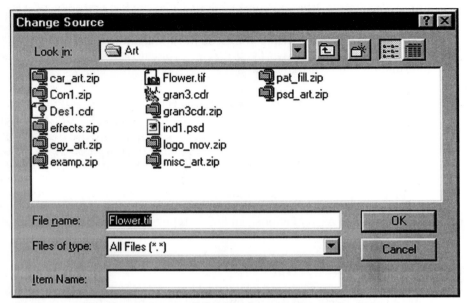

Figure 8-13: The Change Source dialog box lets you change the OLE server application associated with the linked object.

To break an OLE link:

1. Using the Pick tool, select the OLE object whose link you want to break.

2. Select Edit ➪ Links.

3. Choose Break Link.

Once you break a link, the file can't be relinked to your Draw document. If you want to establish another link, you need to replace the object with a copy from the original file. For best results, don't delete the embedded object before inserting the object you want to link. This method lets you use the embedded object for alignment. After aligning the new linked object, delete the older embedded object.

Scanning Tips and Tricks

A few years ago a client came to me wanting to have some promotional materials created for an auto insurance reform group. As we sat over lunch, she handed me some sketches she'd drawn to give me an idea of what she wanted. "Wow . . . cool aardvark," I said, looking at the image in front of me. She replied that the "aardvark" was a car. I recovered quickly by asking her if it was the car *after* the accident. It's no small testimony to her sense of humor that we are still on speaking terms. Most people have that bright shiny car in their mind's eye. They can see the sun glinting off the chrome, and the heat waves rising from the red paint. Moving that image from their mind to a drawing is another matter entirely, however.

Fortunately, despite Draw being an incredibly powerful illustration package, you don't have to be a Rembrandt to create great documents. There are lots of images available out there without you having to draw anything. For the adventurous, here are some easy tricks that can turn your scanner into an art factory:

✦ **Edited images:** If you own a scanner and a bitmapped image editor, such as Photo-Paint or Photoshop, you are more than halfway to obtaining images for your document. You can scan photos and artwork to use as background patterns and custom fills. If your scanner happens to be a flatbed scanner, photos and drawn artwork are just a beginning. You can create really slick backgrounds and custom fills with your scanner by scanning some somewhat unusual objects.

✦ **Scanning your lunch:** Have you ever considered scanning your peanut butter and jelly sandwich? I know it sounds kind of wild, but if you take a few precautions to protect your scanner, you can scan nearly anything that doesn't move. Figure 8-14 shows some of the effects you can get using your scanner and a little thought.

Color versions of the samples shown in Figure 8-14 are included on the CD-ROM for your use.

✦ **Making a mess:** Basically, scannable materials divide into three categories: nonmessy stuff, kind of messy gooey stuff, and truly oozy very messy stuff. Lists divided by category appear later in this section. Once you've scanned these things, you can apply effects to them and use them as backgrounds for your Web pages or apply them as fills to images.

Safe scanning

The basic idea is to do some creative scanning without killing your scanner. The trick to putting these things in your scanner is a trip to your kitchen or local grocery store. Nonmessy stuff can be placed directly on the glass of your scanner with no risk to the scanner. To scan gooey objects, you need to wrap both the body and lid of your scanner with a quality grade of plastic wrap. The clingy quality of this material means that you can smooth it tightly over your scanner glass, without getting air bubbles underneath the plastic wrap. Be sure to overlap the body of your scanner. Using another piece of plastic wrap, cover the lid of your scanner and secure it with tape to the outside of the lid. Place liquids in sandwich bags with a zipper-type closure. Remove any extra air from the bag to ensure successful scanning. You don't need a lot of material in the bag. A couple of tablespoons of liquid does nicely.

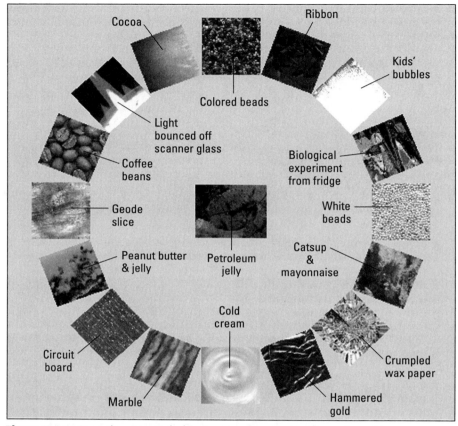

Figure 8-14: Scanning unusual objects opens a new creative-art world.

The following lists are suggestions for things that you can scan. These are not complete lists. I'm sure you can come up with many more. Have some fun with this. You'll have a good time and create some really neat patterns and fills.

Nonmessy stuff

✦ Crumpled wax paper, reflattened

✦ Paper bags

✦ Wrapping paper

✦ Aluminum foil, crumpled and reflattened

✦ Styrofoam

✦ Leaves

✦ Lettuce

✦ Sliced veggies (If these are sticky or leave residue, use glass cleaner on your scanner afterwards, or consider using plastic wrap to protect your scanner.)

✦ Bread, stale (Consider using plastic wrap to protect your scanner or a can of compressed air to remove any crumbs or seeds that might be left behind.)

✦ Fur (I scanned the cat, who'd fallen asleep on my scanner. The bonus is that she hasn't slept there since.)

✦ Wood

✦ Pieces of pottery or glass

✦ Rocks

✦ Bubble pack

✦ Gift ribbons

✦ Fabric

✦ Dryer lint

Kind of messy stuff

Use plastic wrap with these things. Some of them are iffy. If you aren't sure, use a sandwich bag.

✦ Berries — strawberries, blueberries, and so on (squashed to the shape you want)

✦ Lawn clippings

✦ Sliced fruit (Oranges and watermelon with part of the rind showing is good.)

✦ Cheese (Try layering Swiss cheese with something else, or fill the holes with mashed avocado.)

✦ Sand

✦ Rice

✦ Macaroni and cheese or cooked pasta

✦ Toothpaste (The striped stuff is great.)

✦ Marine lubricant (This is usually a marine blue.)

✦ Chocolate

✦ Meat (Chicken skin creates some neat effects.)

✦ Vegetable shortening (butter-flavored and regular)

✦ Peanut butter

✦ Jell-O

✦ Cupcake candies

✦ Bread (Rye bread makes a nice texture.)

Truly messy stuff

You'll want to use sandwich bags for this stuff. Some of these things make great suspension media. You can use them to float other things. To create a suspension medium, place a couple of tablespoons of one of these materials into your sandwich bag, then add whatever you want to float in the media. Using this technique, you can create swirled effects and give the illusion of depth to your pattern.

✦ Food coloring

✦ Mayonnaise

✦ Vegetable oil

✦ Corn syrup (Light works best.)

✦ Whipped cream

✦ Petroleum jelly

✦ Hair-setting gel

✦ Personal lubricant (Suspend other things in this.)

✦ Honey (makes a great suspension media)

✦ Colored water

✦ Pancake syrup

✦ Fruit juice

✦ Motor oil

✦ Tomato sauce or catsup

✦ Bubble bath or liquid dish soap (Try adding a few drops of water to this one, and squishing the bag till you have foamy bubbles to scan.)

✦ Shaving cream

Scanning your pattern

Once you've protected your scanner, you are ready to scan. Don't worry about the size of the object you are scanning. You can crop, scale, and alter the image in your image editor. You do want to keep the image file size small, though, so scanning a 2-inch × 2-inch area works pretty well. Scan the object at 300 dpi. If you want to use the scan in a Web document, you can reduce the resolution later. The instructions below are generic. You can adapt them for most image-editing programs.

To scan your material:

1. Start your image editor and choose Acquire from the File menu to display the scanner dialog box. Note that while you can scan from Draw, the options for editing the resulting bitmap are limited.

2. Set your scanner options for RGB full-color, and click the button for a preview.

3. Adjust the scanning area to include just the portion of the material you want to scan.

4. Click Scan. The image will appear in the image editor shortly, ready for you to modify for use (see Figure 8-15).

Figure 8-15: After scanning, the image appears in the editing window, ready for you to modify for use.

5. Save your scanned image to your hard disk.

6. In your image editor, choose the Crop tool and crop the image if desired.

7. Apply any effects that you want to use. You might want to try applying heat map, blurring, or other effects to your pattern.

8. Resize the image to the size you need. If this causes the image to distort in an undesirable way, consider tiling the pattern to create the needed size. If you want to use the image as a fill, you can apply it to the graphic as is, or you can scale the image for use as a background.

Tip   The average household contains thousands of objects that you can scan to create custom bitmap fills and backgrounds. With a little imagination, you can have a lot of fun, and create a library of scanned images to enhance your documents and Web pages. If you intend to use these images on the Web, consider converting them to 8-bit color for faster downloading.

Deadline scanner blues

Your client wants to see their logo on the Web page that you're creating for them, and you can't draw. Worse yet, their business card is the only copy you have of their logo, and it's on gray paper. Business cards are a nightmare to scan and clean up, especially if they are on colored paper or have raised ink. You could sit for hours editing the scanned image pixel by pixel. You don't have to, though, because you are about to learn a really neat trick for turning that mess into a clean image. These instructions are generic, but you can adapt them for most image-editing programs.

To clean up scanned art:

1. Start your image editor and select Acquire from the File menu.

2. Set the options in your scanning dialog box for RGB or 256 grayscale, and 300 dpi.

3. Preview the image and adjust the scanning size to fit the business card or logo.

4. Choose Scan to scan the card. The image will appear in your editing window shortly. The image probably doesn't look very good at this point. The gray paper makes it look like it snowed in the image, and the logo probably looks just as dirty (see Figure 8-16).

Figure 8-16: Your scanned image in the editing window, ready to be cleaned up.

5. Select Sharpen from the Filter menu, then select Unsharp Mask.

6. Set the percentage of change at 150 percent and the number of levels to 8. You can adjust the number of pixels between 1.5 and 2.5 pixels, until you get the

desired result. What you want to do is smooth the edges of the logo. Unsharp Mask adds anti-aliasing to the edges of selections in the editing window. When you are happy with the results, choose OK to complete the operation and return to the editing window (see Figure 8-17).

Figure 8-17: Applying an unsharp mask adds anti-aliasing to the image, smoothing out the edges.

7. Select Adjust from the Image menu and choose Levels.

8. Click and drag the black slider (arrow) to the right until it's close to the largest clump of lines in the window. The image in your editing window updates to reflect the change. Click and drag the white slider (arrow) to the left, until it's close to the black slider (see Figure 8-18). What you want to do is reduce the number of colors to get a clean black-and-white image of the logo. You can adjust the gray slider until you are satisfied with the results. Click OK to complete the operation and return to the editing window.

Figure 8-18: The cleaned-up logo.

Using this technique, you can clean scanned images quickly, without tedious pixel-by-pixel editing. Once the image is clean, you can add fills or color to the resulting image in an image editor. You can also use CorelOCR-Trace to trace the image for use as a vector object in Draw. Be sure to save your cleaned-up image.

Summary

Importing images into your Draw document broadens the variety of effects that you can achieve. Draw supports a variety of file formats, which gives you flexibility in dealing with your images. In addition, OLE adds the capability to link files from other applications and to ensure that objects are updated as they change globally. The capability to use images from a variety of sources is augmented by adding some scanning magic to your repertoire of skills. In this chapter, you learned to:

✦ Use Draw's click-and-drag functionality to place images in your document

✦ Work with the Scrapbook

✦ Add clipart to your drawings

✦ Specify import and export options

✦ Import and export elements into your documents

✦ Crop and resample images

✦ Select a file format

✦ Manage file filters

✦ Use OLE to link and embed images

✦ Create unique backgrounds using a scanner

✦ Clean up a scanned image

In Chapter 10, you explore the use of bitmaps further as you learn to edit and add effects to a variety of bitmap sources.

✦   ✦   ✦

Manipulating Bitmaps

While you still can't *paint* an image directly in Draw, you can resample, convert, and add effects to bitmapped objects. You can also convert Draw objects to bitmaps, from within the program, without exporting and reimporting the object. Using color masking, you can turn parts of a bitmap transparent, which permits visibility of objects below the bitmap. Effects filters let you apply subtle or dramatic effects to bitmaps.

Bitmap Editing Basics

Before you edit a bitmap, it's a good policy to do a little advance preparation. In the previous chapter, you explored the differences between bitmaps and vector images. Each of the file types has a unique behavior, and each file type lends itself to different editing methods. You can add effects to bitmaps that are unavailable for vector objects and vice versa. In addition, quality bitmaps tend to be large and require significant resources to display on your monitor. Draw lets you change the view to reduce the amount of time it takes to refresh your image after applying a command.

Cross-Reference For more information on bitmaps and vector images, see Chapter 8.

You can create a basic object or an entire drawing using Draw's tools, and then convert the resulting image to a bitmap for enhancement. To work with a bitmap in Draw, you need to select the object first. Depending on what you want to do, you can select a bitmap with either the Pick tool or the Shape tool. With the exception of transformation commands, such as Rotation, you can only edit a single bitmap at a time.

Choosing the Right Tool for the Job

Most digital graphic designers have a variety of software tools at their disposal. At first glance, some of the software may seem redundant. For example, I have five 3D applications, four illustration packages, several image editors, and a variety of multimedia authoring and Web utilities.

Why so many? The answer is really very simple. If you tried to hang a picture with a sledgehammer, you'd probably renovate your home in the process. Similarly, if you tried to drive a large stake into the ground with a tack hammer, you'd be there forever, with little to show for your efforts. Most tasks are easier if you have the right tool for the job.

Software is no different. Each piece of software has unique tools that make it ideal for a specific application. Unfortunately, jumping back and forth between applications is time-consuming. As a partial answer to this problem, Draw lets you enhance and edit bitmaps.

Changing the view

The view mode alters the appearance of bitmapped objects in your Draw document. The view mode does not alter the bitmap itself. It only changes the way it appears on your monitor. You can change the view by selecting View and one of the view modes. In Wireframe or Simple Wireframe modes, bitmaps appear faded and semitransparent and have a bounding box surrounding them. Color bitmapped objects appear as grayscale. Objects below the bitmaps show through, which allows for easy positioning of objects and bitmaps in relationship to one another. In Draft mode, bitmaps appear solid, but at a reduced resolution to speed screen refresh. Normal and Enhanced modes increase the resolution, with Enhanced mode providing the best quality view.

Converting vector objects to bitmaps

You can convert vector objects to bitmaps in Draw. The advantage of using a bitmap versus a vector object in a document becomes apparent in complex drawings. The complexity of your drawing increases, as you create objects and apply effects, such as blend and extrude effects. When several layers of these objects and effects are stacked one upon another, the file becomes larger and Draw has to work harder to render the image to screen. This problem is further compounded by the fact that extremely complex drawings present printing problems.

Suppose you created a full-color pattern fill from an area of an image that contained a complex blend and extrusion. If you added a page frame to another document and filled it with the full-color pattern fill as a background, you might believe that the fill reduced the complexity of the effects. That's not an accurate perception. Although you filled a single object with the pattern, the object would build and render to screen as if the original objects and effects were there! If you then added several other objects and effects to your drawing, there's a distinct possibility that you would experience difficulty printing the document on a PostScript device.

By converting the background object, containing the pattern fill to a bitmap, the complexity of the drawing would decrease dramatically although your file size might increase. The resulting file would be more likely to print.

Note   Converting vector objects to bitmaps is not a batch process whereby you can create several bitmaps at a single time by selecting multiple objects. When you select multiple objects to convert to a bitmap, they become a single bitmap.

To convert a vector object to a bitmap:

1. Using the Pick tool, select the object or objects to convert.

2. Select Bitmap ➪ Convert to Bitmap and choose the number of colors or color depth that you want to use (see Figure 9-1). More information about bit depth and bitmap color models appears later in this chapter.

3. Enabling Dithered improves the transition between colors.

4. Enable Transparent Background, if the bitmap is placed above other objects in your drawing, to prevent blocking the visibility of other objects.

5. Choose a resolution for the bitmap by clicking the resolution box and choosing a resolution.

6. Choose a method of anti-aliasing, using these guidelines:

   • **None:** If you choose this option, Draw applies no anti-aliasing to the object. This is the best choice if the object will be used in an online application.

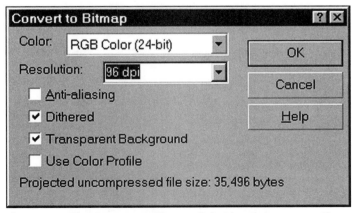

Figure 9-1: The Convert to Bitmap dialog box lets you specify how objects are to be converted into bitmaps.

- **Normal:** Filters and interprets the colors of the bitmap to remove jagged edges from the object by applying intermediate colors or shades of gray.
- **Super-sampling:** Enlarges the size of the vector object, then reduces its resolution to remove jagged edges. This process takes longer, but improves the quality of the resulting bitmap, dramatically.

7. Click OK to return to the drawing window.

Tip

If the object you're converting to bitmap is destined for publication on the Web, selecting a transparent background and deselecting anti-aliasing will yield cleaner graphics and better results.

Bitmap Conversion Tricks

You aren't restricted to converting single objects to a bitmap. If you select multiple objects and apply the Convert to Bitmap command, you can merge the objects and their attributes into a single bitmap. You can also merge vector objects with a bitmap, or multiple bitmaps into a single bitmap. The Convert to Bitmap command also lets you easily create some great special effects. By performing the Convert to Bitmap command multiple times, and adding objects each time, you can create some interesting effects by varying the background. You can choose to leave the background alone, or choose between a dithered or transparent background.

Have you ever wanted to punch a hole in a bitmap, so that the objects below appear through the pierced areas? You could use the bitmap color mask feature to hide some of the colors. This is a start in the right direction, but one that can create a random, speckled effect by removing parts of the image that you want to retain. This is especially problematic with bitmaps that use a wide range of colors distributed throughout the bitmap. To control this effect, draw an object, such as a circle, and apply a uniform fill color that's not used in your bitmap. Remove any outline from the circle. Select the circle and the bitmap, and apply the Convert to Bitmap command. After the circle and bitmap are merged into a single bitmap, apply the bitmap color mask feature to hide the color of the circle. Adjust the tolerance to include the entire circle, but none of the surrounding bitmap. The result is a hole or transparent area in the bitmap.

Cropping and Scaling Bitmaps

Draw lets you crop and scale bitmaps, both before importing and once they are placed in your document. The advantage of cropping and scaling a bitmap in your document is that it lets you adjust your actions in relationship to the other objects in your drawing. If you choose to work in Wireframe or Simple Wireframe view mode, you can see the objects below while you are cropping or scaling your bitmap. This gives you greater control over the final appearance of your drawing. You can also use snap-to aids with bitmaps for even greater precision.

Cropping bitmaps in the drawing window

The Shape tool is used to crop bitmapped images in Draw. When you crop an image in the drawing window, it behaves differently than if you crop the image before importing. Images cropped before importing are actually smaller. The actual size of images cropped in the drawing window does not change. You only change the portion of the image that's visible. If you want to recrop the image later, you can allow more of the image to show in the drawing window. You aren't confined to straight-edge cropping of images in Draw. You can add nodes to the bounding area of the bitmap, and change lines to curves if you want.

To crop a bitmap in the drawing window:

1. Using the Shape tool, select the bitmap to crop. The bitmap appears with handles at the corner (see Figure 9-2).

2. Click and drag the nodes to change the shape of the outline. If you press Ctrl while dragging, the change is constrained to either vertical or horizontal movement.

Figure 9-2: After choosing the Shape tool, the selected bitmap appears with handles at each corner.

3. If you want to crop the bitmap to an irregular shape, you can add nodes to the outline, much as you would to any object in Draw. To add a node, select one of the corner nodes or the outline and click the plus (+) button on the property bar. Alternatively, press the plus (+) key on the number keypad of your keyboard, or right-click the node and select Add from the right mouse button menu.

4. You can also change the attributes of a selected line segment or selected nodes by clicking the To Curve button on the Property bar. You can add, delete, and convert nodes to Cusp, Smooth, or Symmetrical using the same method. Adjust the resulting nodes and handles to create the cropping shape you desire (see Figure 9-3).

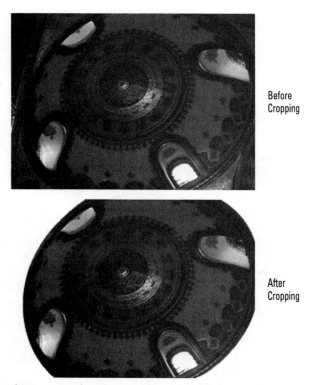

Before Cropping

After Cropping

Figure 9-3: The Shape tool was used to crop the ceiling to reveal only the domed center.

Using this method you can create cropping shapes that add interest to your drawing. If you want to return a bitmap to its original appearance, select all the nodes and press Delete.

Scaling a bitmap in the drawing window

It's important to remember the nature of bitmapped images whenever you scale them. Unlike vector images, which are defined mathematically as points connected by lines and curves, bitmapped images are defined by pixels. Bitmaps have a fixed resolution, which affects the way they behave when they are scaled. When you enlarge a bitmap, you are actually adding pixels to the image. Because the color and placement of the extra pixels have to be interpreted, scaling frequently results in distortion and a jagged appearance. Similarly, if you reduce the size of a bitmap, pixels are removed, which can also cause distortion. Resampling bitmaps, as shown later in this chapter, is a better method of changing the size of a bitmap. It's still not a perfect choice, however. The best solution is to create the bitmap at or near the final size you require, to keep scaling to a minimum.

After selecting the bitmap to scale, you can use the Pick tool to scale the bitmap either interactively in the drawing window, or you can use the Scale view of the Transform docker. Regardless of the method, bitmaps are scaled and sized in the same manner as any other object in Draw.

If you need to resize a bitmap, it's a good idea to resample the bitmap at the size you want. Scaling a bitmap degrades the quality of the image by causing pixelation, especially if you increase the size of the bitmap. If you are using a bitmap from a scanned image, consider rescanning the image at the size you need.

Rotating and Skewing Bitmaps

You can rotate and skew a selected bitmap, as you would any other object in Draw (see Figure 9-4). As you rotate or skew a bitmap, its appearance changes according to the view mode you are using. In Simple Wireframe and Wireframe view modes, the bitmap is displayed inside a gray rectangle. Draft, Normal, and Enhanced modes display the bitmap in color, surrounded by a gray rectangle as it's being rotated or skewed. Draft mode displays the bitmap at a lower resolution of 128×128 ppi during rotation or skewing. If the bitmap is large, consider changing to a lower quality view mode while modifying bitmaps to increase your monitor's refresh rate. You can rotate and skew bitmaps either interactively or by entering amounts in the Transform docker or the Property bar.

Interactive rotation

To interactively rotate a bitmap:

   1. Using the Pick tool, select the bitmap to rotate. Click on the bitmap again to change the handles to the rotation and skew handles.

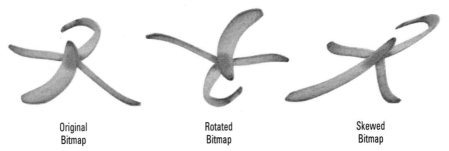

Original   Rotated   Skewed
Bitmap   Bitmap   Bitmap

Figure 9-4: As you rotate or skew a bitmap, the image appears in a gray rectangle.

2. The center of rotation appears at the center of the bitmap. Move the center of rotation, if desired. Press Ctrl while moving the center of rotation if you want it to snap to a side or corner handle.

3. Click and drag a corner handle in the direction that you want to rotate the bitmap. If you press Ctrl while rotating the bitmap, the rotation is constrained to 15-degree increments or to the constraint angle specified in the Options dialog box. Be sure to release the mouse button before releasing Ctrl.

Tip

Draw specifies 15 degrees as the default constraint setting. You can change the amount of the constraint setting in the Options dialog box. Specifying a constraint setting is useful if you need to rotate or skew an object with consistent accuracy.

Skewing interactively

To interactively skew a bitmap:

1. Using the Pick tool, select the bitmap to skew. Click on the bitmap again to change the handles to the rotation and skew handles.

2. The center of rotation appears at the center of the bitmap. Move the center of rotation, if desired. Press Ctrl while moving the center of rotation if you want it to snap to a side or corner handle.

3. Click and drag a side handle in the direction that you want to skew the bitmap. If you press Ctrl while skewing the bitmap, the degree of the skew is constrained to 15-degree increments or to the constraint angle specified in the Options dialog box. Be sure to release the mouse button before releasing Ctrl.

Skewing bitmaps can give them a feeling of depth or motion. You can also use this feature to adjust the orientation of bitmaps you use as the contents of PowerClips. Figure 9-5 illustrates the effects of skewing to create a feeling of motion with the rollerblade bitmap. The wood bitmap in the second image was skewed to match the angles of the sides of the box. The resulting bitmap objects were applied to the sides, using Draw's PowerClip feature.

Figure 9-5: Skewing bitmaps can give the image a feeling of motion.

Editing Bitmap Colors

Draw provides a variety of tools for controlling the color of bitmapped images. These tools let you add color to monochrome images, apply PostScript halftones, and display or hide colors within a bitmap. In addition to the tools created specifically for bitmaps, Draw includes a series of color adjustment tools that you can use to adjust the color of any object in your drawing.

Using the Bitmap Color Mask docker

Draw lets you hide or display up to 10 selected colors in a bitmap, using the Bitmap Color Mask docker. This is useful for masking sections of a bitmap to allow objects below to show. If, for example, you had a bitmap and only wanted an irregular portion of the bitmap to show, you could achieve the same effect as cropping the image by hiding the background color. The portions of the bitmap that are hidden are not removed from the bitmap; they merely appear transparent. You can save a bitmap color mask for later use, but you can't apply more than one mask to a given bitmap.

Hiding and displaying bitmap colors

Hiding and displaying bitmap colors work in an opposing manner. Hiding lets you choose which colors to make transparent; displaying lets you choose which colors to make visible. When you display selected colors of a bitmap, all of the unselected colors become transparent. To hide or display colors in your bitmap:

1. Using the Pick tool, select the bitmap to modify.

2. Select Bitmaps ➪ Bitmap Color Mask to display the Bitmap Color Mask docker (see Figure 9-6).

3. Click either the Hide or Show button. Essentially, both achieve the same effect. Colors in the bitmap are either hidden or visible. Base your choice upon the number of colors you want included in your selection. Choose according to which represents the fewest number of colors. For example, if you only want to hide the black and gray in a bitmap, choose Hide. If you only want the yellow to remain visible and the other colors hidden, choose Show.

4. Click one of the color selection boxes to enable it, and then click the eyedropper.

5. Move the eyedropper over your bitmap, and click to select a color to either hide or show. The color appears in the docker.

6. Adjust the tolerance. When the tolerance is set at 0 percent, Draw selects only that precise color. As you increase the tolerance, a larger range of similar colors is included in the selection. For example, if you selected the color red in a bitmap and increased the tolerance, the selected range of colors might include several shades of pink or orange. Setting the tolerance can take a bit of practice.

7. Continue to add colors to your selection by repeating steps 4 to 6. You can choose to show or hide up to 10 ranges of color.

8. Click Apply to display or hide your selection.

If you later want to edit a color in your color mask, choose the color to edit in the Bitmap Color Mask docker. Then click the Edit Color button. The Select Color dialog box appears, letting you choose a new color.

Removing a color mask

You can remove a color mask from a bitmap at any time, regardless of the levels of Undo you specified. To remove the mask, first select the bitmap. Choose Bitmaps ➪ Bitmap Color Mask to display the Bitmap Color Mask docker. Click the Remove Mask button. The bitmap returns to its original appearance.

Tip   You can't remove a single color of a mask. The entire mask is removed, and the bitmap returns to its original appearance. If you want to reduce the number of colors affected by the mask, highlight one of the mask settings and use the Edit Color feature to change the color to one not contained in your image. You can also adjust the tolerance settings to modify the amount of color affected by the mask.

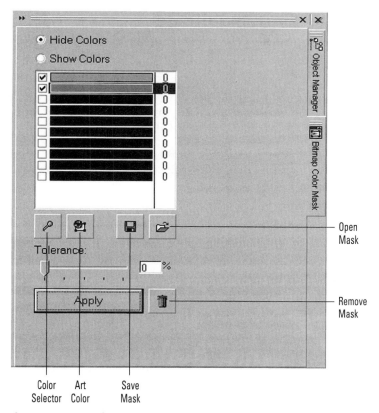

Figure 9-6: Use the Bitmap Color Mask docker to hide or display colors in a selected bitmap.

Saving and opening a color mask

You can save a bitmap color mask for use in other documents. To save a color mask for a selected bitmap, click the right arrow near the top of the Bitmap Color Mask docker and select Save Color Mask from the menu. The Save As dialog box appears, which allows you to save the mask. By default, Draw saves the color mask as an .ini file in the Draw folder. Although you can save the mask in another location, I recommend you accept the default. This guarantees that the mask is easy to find when you want to use it later.

When you want to load the mask for use, display the Bitmap Color Mask docker. Click the right arrow near the top of the docker and select Open from the menu. The Open dialog box appears, with the default Draw folder visible in the window. If your mask is stored elsewhere, choose the folder where the mask is stored. Select the mask you want to open and click Open. The mask settings appear in the Bitmap Color Mask docker, ready for you to apply to a bitmap.

Coloring monochrome bitmaps

You can create some great effects with monochrome bitmaps. Normally, monochrome bitmaps are referred to as black-and-white images or line art. They don't have to be just black and white, though. Draw lets you add color to any monochrome bitmap by changing its foreground and background colors. It further expands this capability by letting you use any type of fill as the background. You aren't restricted to solid color backgrounds. You can use fountain, texture, pattern, or PostScript fills as a background (see Figure 9-7).

Tip   The file size of a bitmap increases as the bit depth increases. Monochrome bitmaps have the advantage of letting you create dramatic effects with bitmaps, yet keep the file size small.

To change the color of a monochrome bitmap:

1. Using the Pick tool, select the bitmap to modify.

2. Apply a color to the foreground (black pixels) by right-clicking a color in the color palette, the same way you would choose an outline color for an object.

3. Apply color to the background (white pixels) by either left-clicking a color from the onscreen palette or by using one of the fill dialog boxes. Alternatively, you can right-click on the object, choose properties from the pop-up menu, and use the Fill tab to access all types of fills.

Tip   Monochrome bitmaps are a low-budget item. You can get a high-impact effect for a very small cost to your resources by using fills. They are especially useful for the creation of elements for the Web because they download more quickly than 32-bit images, regardless of the fills you select. In addition, they provide an easy way of combining diverse types of fills in the same object.

Applying PostScript halftones to bitmaps

Draw lets you apply PostScript halftones to bitmap images. The effect is not visible in the drawing window, however, unless you are in Enhanced View mode. It's only visible in the output from a PostScript printer. Draw's clipart catalog contains a complete set of PostScript halftone thumbnails to aid in selecting the fill to use. To apply a PostScript halftone to a bitmap:

1. Using the Pick tool, select the bitmap to modify.

2. Choose the Fill Color tool from the Fills flyout menu to display the Uniform fill dialog box, and then click the Palettes button.

3. Click the Palettes button and choose Pantone Matching System.

Figure 9-7: You can modify monochrome bitmaps by using any fill type as the background.

4. Click the Options button to display the PostScript Options dialog box (see Figure 9-8).

5. Choose the screen shape you want to use.

6. Enter a value in the Frequency box and the angle of the lines in the Angles box.

7. Click OK to complete the operation and to return to the Uniform Fill dialog box. Click OK again to return to the drawing window.

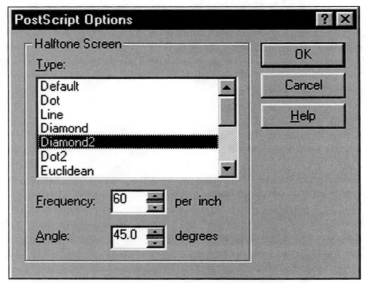

Figure 9-8: Choose a PostScript fill in the PostScript Options dialog box.

Care should be taken when printing bitmaps containing PostScript halftones. If you are printing separations for commercial printed output, you need to specify the screen and angles in the Printing dialog box.

Tracing Bitmaps

Although you can easily convert vector objects into bitmaps, there's no easy way to convert a bitmap into a vector object. You must create the vector objects by tracing the outlines of objects within a bitmap. Draw provides two methods of tracing a bitmap to create vector objects. Both use the Freehand tool. The first method lets you automatically trace sections of the bitmap based upon the amount of contrast between adjoining areas of the image. The second method allows you to manually trace those sections of the bitmap that you want to use. In addition to these two means of tracing bitmaps, Draw provides you with a stand-alone utility called OCR-TRACE. OCR-TRACE creates vector shapes from a bitmap and saves them in a file that you can import and use in your Draw documents.

Choosing a tracing method

Choosing a tracing method is dependent upon the size of the area that you want to trace, the complexity of the image, and the amount of accuracy you require. Here are a few guidelines:

✦ If the area you want to trace is large and complex, use OCR-TRACE to trace the file. Instructions for using OCR-TRACE are included in the manuals that came with the Draw suite.

✦ Choose to Auto-Trace Bitmaps in the drawing window if the area is small, has good contrast, and you don't require a high degree of accuracy.

✦ Manually tracing a bitmap takes longer, but you can control the accuracy, and contrast is not an issue.

Auto-tracing

To Auto-Trace a bitmap:

1. Using the Pick tool, select the bitmap to trace.

2. Select the Freehand tool. As you move back to the drawing window, the Freehand tool cursor changes to a crosshair with a line extending from it.

3. Click the bitmap. If the bitmap has good contrast, Draw will trace the closest section to your cursor, creating a new closed object (see Figure 9-9). Closed objects are filled with the default fill.

4. Continue clicking to trace sections of the bitmap. Draw displays a message box if you click in an area where it can't find an object to trace. Click OK to remove the message box and continue tracing.

5. When you have finished tracing, reselect the Pick tool and click in a blank space in the drawing window to deselect the bitmap.

Note

The Options dialog box lets you adjust how closely Draw follows the original shape when auto-tracing a bitmap. When specifying Auto-Trace settings, higher values produce a smoother outline and less accurate trace. Lower values produce an outline with more nodes, and more closely follow the section of the bitmap.

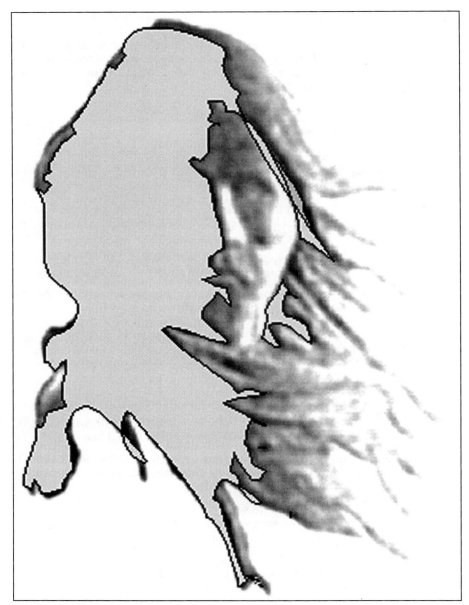

Figure 9-9: Using the Auto-Trace feature, you can trace portions of a bitmap in the drawing window.

To specify Auto-Trace settings:

1. Select Tools ➪ Options to display the Options dialog box, and then expand the Workspace and Toolbox categories by clicking the plus (+) sign beside their names. Choose the Freehand/Bézier tool to display the Freehand/Bézier Tool page (see Figure 9-10).

2. Adjust the value in the Autotrace tracking box.

3. Click OK to complete the operation and to return to the drawing window.

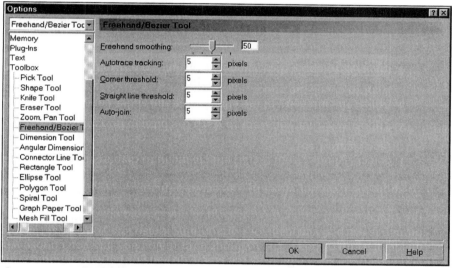

Figure 9-10: Adjust the accuracy of Auto-Trace in the Options dialog box.

Manual tracing

Manual tracing is a good choice if you only want to trace a small portion of a bitmap. Like Auto-Trace, the key to manually tracing a bitmap is to specify the best Auto-Trace options for the bitmap you're tracing. With a little practice, you will be able to determine the best settings for a bitmap at a glance.

Tip   Manual tracing is easier and more accurate if you use the zoom tool to zoom in on the area you want to trace.

To manually trace a bitmap:

1. After making sure that the bitmap is not selected, choose the Freehand tool.

2. Click and drag, drawing on the bitmap, to trace areas of the bitmap.

You can close open objects created when tracing objects by clicking the Auto-Close button on the Property bar. Like other Draw objects, the resulting objects are filled with the default fill when they're closed.

Resampling Images

Resampling bitmaps changes the size or resolution of the bitmap. The advantage of resampling a bitmap, rather than scaling a bitmap, is that resampling lets you correct flaws and minimize the distortion that is common when resizing a bitmap. When resampling, Draw lets you choose from a variety of options that affect the quality of the resulting image. If you are creating an image for display on a monitor, such as a Web graphic, reducing the resolution of bitmaps to a standard screen resolution reduces the size of the file without visibly reducing the onscreen quality. Remember that low-resolution images don't print well, so keep a higher resolution copy of the image for printing.

To resample an image:

1. Using the Pick tool, select the image to resample.

2. Select Bitmaps ⇨ Resample. The Resample dialog box appears (see Figure 9-11).

3. If you want to change the resolution of the image, enter new values in the Horizontal and Vertical resolution boxes. If Maintain Aspect Ratio is enabled, enter a value in either the Horizontal or Vertical resolution box. The other dimension will adjust automatically. To avoid changing the size of the bitmap file accidentally, enable Maintain Original Size.

4. Choose a type of Process. Anti-Alias produces higher quality results, but takes longer to process. Stretch/Truncate is faster, but produces a coarser bitmap.

5. If you want to resize the bitmap, enter new values in the Width and Height boxes, and choose a unit of measurement. Be sure that Maintain Original Size is disabled. Avoid increasing the size of a bitmap if possible.

6. You can reset the values to their original settings by clicking Reset.

Note Although enabling Maintain Original Size ensures that your file size will stay the same, it does change the dimensions of the bitmap if you increase or decrease the resolution of the image. If you increase the resolution, the dimensions become smaller. If you decrease the resolution, the dimensions become larger. Similarly, if you change the dimensions of the bitmap with Maintain Original Size enabled, the resolution will change accordingly.

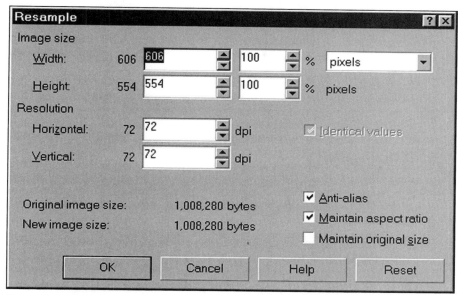

Figure 9-11: The Resample dialog box lets you specify the size and resolution of your bitmap.

Resampling Images for Multimedia Use

When you're creating a multimedia application for distribution, you can't guarantee the type of display the end user has. Older machines, monitors, and those users who have Windows 3.1 may not be able to display 24-bit graphics or higher. They also may not have the memory or resources required for 24-bit graphics.

The best rule of thumb is to consider the lowest common denominator. Determine the minimum system for your application and create your graphics accordingly. If, for example, you are creating graphics that will be later imported into a multimedia-authoring package, such as Macromedia Director or Flash, it's a good idea to choose 8-bit color and a lower resolution of 96 dpi. These graphic elements have a smaller file size, render to screen faster, and animate more smoothly. Because most multimedia applications are intended strictly for screen display, any resolution over 96 dpi is wasted. That's the maximum displayable resolution on a monitor connected to a PC. Computers ignore information that exceeds that amount, but the image takes up more hard drive space and takes longer to render.

Maintaining the aspect ratio

The aspect ratio of a bitmap refers to the relationship between the height and width of the image. You can create interesting effects by altering the aspect ratio. For example, you could reduce the width of a bitmap without reducing the height to distort the bitmap. Similarly, if you changed the resolution in only one dimension, the bitmap would appear distorted. Generally, you should always enable Maintain Aspect Ratio unless you purposely want to distort a bitmap.

Stretch/Truncate versus Anti-Alias

When you increase or decrease the size of a bitmap, you either add pixels or delete pixels from the image. This forces Draw to interpret the color of any added pixels or to determine which pixels to delete. The result of resizing a bitmap can be rough edges called jaggies. Stretch/Truncate and Anti-Alias are designed to help correct flaws created by resizing a bitmap. Stretch/Truncate either expands or reduces the bitmap to try to correct any flaws created in the resampling. Although Anti-Alias is slower, it is more effective in reducing the flaws. Anti-aliasing reads the colors of adjacent pixels. It then creates another pixel that represents the color most evenly between any two adjacent pixels. The result is a smoother edge. Choose the type of process that meets your needs. For printed output, I recommend you choose Anti-Alias. Stretch/Truncate is a better choice for online use.

Working with Bit Depths

Draw lets you convert bitmaps from one bit depth to another. This capability lets you quickly ensure that color palettes are consistent throughout your drawing, and lets you control the file size of your image. To choose between the various bit depths, it's important to understand bit levels and how they affect your document (see the sidebar on understanding color depth). Table 9-1 illustrates a variety of bit depths and the number of colors each bit depth supports. The remainder of this chapter explores the conversion process in detail.

Table 9-1
Bit Depths and Supported Colors

Bit depth	Number of colors supported
1-bit	2 colors (black and white)
2-bit	4 colors (usually black, white, and 2 grays)
4-bit	16 colors
8-bit	256 colors
15-bit	32,000 colors (unsupported by Draw)

Bit depth	Number of colors supported
16-bit	64,000 colors
24-bit	16.7 million colors
32-bit	6.8 billion colors

Understanding Color Depth

A bit is the smallest unit of computer binary data and is described as being either 0 (off) or 1 (on). Each pixel in a bitmap drawing is comprised of these bits of data, and can be black, white, gray, or a color. The most basic of color images are 1-bit images. A 1-bit image contains two colors: white represented by the number 0 and black represented by the number 1. Earlier you learned to apply color to monochrome or 1-bit images. The color that Draw applies is interpreted or translated. In other words, your computer still sees the image as being a 1-bit black-and-white image. To add color to the image, you specify how Draw is to interpret or translate the 0 and 1.

For those of you who are fascinated with the topic of binary data, there is a multitude of programming books that deal with this topic and how it relates to color. It's not necessary to be an expert on binary data to use color in Draw, or to convert bitmaps from one bit depth to another. If you have a basic understanding of bit depth, however, you can make color work for you in ways that enhance your images. This understanding also helps you control the file size of images that contain bitmaps. As the bit depth of a bitmap increases, the file size increases geometrically.

If file size is an issue, reducing the bit depth of a bitmap can represent huge savings in storage space and increase the screen refresh speed of your drawings. Large files take longer to import, load, and render to screen. They may also be larger than required for optimum output. A 32-bit or 24-bit color scanned photo image may look wonderful when it's output to a commercial press. If you intend to place it in a Web page, however, it may be overkill. The Web page will load very slowly. In addition, the browser has to translate the color to a palette supported on the Internet, with unpredictable, and frequently undesirable, results. It's much better to convert the bitmap first, so that you can maintain control over the quality of the appearance and file size.

Converting bitmap depths

To convert a bitmap from one bit depth to another:

1. Using the Pick tool, select the bitmap to convert.

2. Select Bitmaps ➪ Convert To and choose the new bit depth to use from the flyout menu. Use the descriptions (each in their own section later in this chapter) to help you decide which bit depth to use.

3. When you choose 1-bit depth, Draw displays the Convert to 1 Bit dialog box (see Figure 9-12). You can select Line Art, Error Diffusion, Ordered, or Halftone as follows:

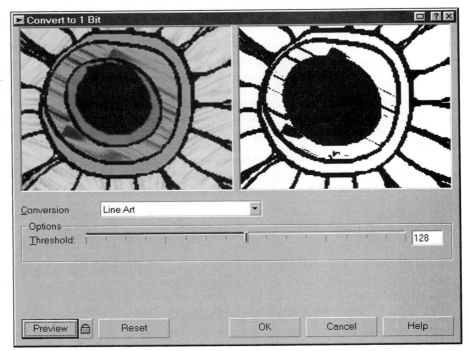

Figure 9-12: The Convert to 1 Bit dialog box lets you specify the parameters for converting your bitmaps to a monochrome image.

- **Line Art:** The Line Art option produces high-contrast black-and-white images without any intermediate colors. You adjust areas of black and white by adjusting the value in the Threshold entry box. All colors below the value you enter appear as black; all colors above the value you enter appear as white.

- **Ordered:** Ordered is similar to Error Diffusion in that it's designed for display on monitors that support fewer than 256 colors. It differs from Error Diffusion in that it uses fixed-dot patterns processed at a higher rate. When applied to lower contrast bitmaps, the results are better than Error Diffusion.

- **Error Diffusion:** Error Diffusion is most effective for display on monitors that support fewer than 256 colors. This dithering method interprets the colors in the image as black or white, and spreads them over several pixels to produce a high-quality screen effect. If the bitmap has poor contrast, the results can be blotchy and dark.

• **Halftone:** Halftone uses a continuous-tone process to produce a near-photo quality image for use in images going to commercial printers. You specify the screen type, lpi (lines per inch), and the angle of the halftone screen. In addition, by choosing halftone screening, you can also specify the type of screen, unit of measurement, frequency, and the angle of the screen.

Caution

The optimum setting for monotone halftone screening is 45 degrees. I don't recommend changing this value if you intend to print your image commercially. Changing the value can cause undesirable results when the image is printed on commercial offset equipment.

Clicking the eye preview icon shows the effects of your choices on the bitmap in the drawing window. Clicking the Preview dialog box icon displays an alternate view of the dialog box with your selection in the preview window and lets you see the effects of changes as they are made.

Grayscale 8-bit

This bit depth produces an image that looks like traditional black and white photography. Draw converts the colors in your image, spreading them across a range of 256 shades of gray. Because the difference between midrange grays can be very subtle, I recommend making any needed color adjustments to your image prior to converting the image to grayscale. This technique helps ensure that the converted image spans the largest number of gray shades possible. The quality of your grayscale image improves as the number of shades of gray increases.

Paletted 8-bit

The paletted conversion option converts images to one of four 8-bit palettes: Uniform, Standard VGA, Adaptive, and Optimized. The final appearance of your bitmap is determined primarily by the palette selection you make. Paletted 8-bit images have a smaller file size than other color palettes, which makes them ideal for online applications, such as graphics for Web pages. When you select this conversion method, Draw displays the Convert to Paletted dialog box (see Figure 9-13).

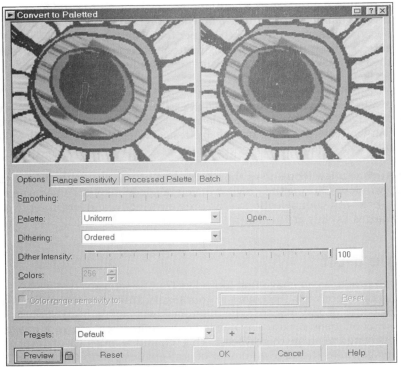

Figure 9-13: The Options property sheet of the Convert to Paletted image dialog box lets you select and preview conversion options for your image.

Choosing a palette option

By clicking the arrow next to the Palette box, you can choose from these palette options:

✦ **Uniform:** The uniform option generates a palette using a range of 256 RGB (red-green-blue) colors. The palette includes the full range of colors regardless of whether they appear in the bitmap.

✦ **Standard VGA:** The Standard VGA option uses the standard 16-color palette, which is common to older, low-end monitors. Because of the limited nature of this palette, colors can shift dramatically in the translation, causing undesirable results.

✦ **Adaptive:** If you choose Adaptive, Draw samples the colors in the bitmap to determine the most frequently used colors and then generates a palette. More infrequently used colors are translated to the closest color in the range of the new palette.

✦ **Optimized:** If you choose Optimized, Draw creates a 256-color palette based upon the entire spectrum of colors contained in the bitmap. Colors that fall outside of the range of the palette are translated to the closest color in the range. Although the differences between the optimized palette and adaptive palette may be subtle, the optimized palette consistently produces a higher quality image.

✦ **Black body:** Creates a high-contrast image based upon the luminescence of the image. Dark colors are converted to black, while light colors such as yellow and white are either ignored or translated to white.

✦ **Duotone:** Translates your grayscale image to contain grayscale plus one to four other colors (spot colors). Duotones are useful for creating the illusion of color in grayscale images while holding the cost of commercial printing to a minimum. Draw lets you specify monotone, duotone, tritone, and quadtone settings.

✦ **System:** System uses the default Microsoft Windows palette. Because of the limited colors in this palette, this is a poor choice for images containing full-color photographs. The image is translated to the closest color of the palette, which can cause sharp changes in color and a banded appearance both onscreen and when printed.

✦ **Microsoft Internet Explorer:** Translates the colors in your bitmap image to those that are specific to Internet Explorer. This palette is useful for previewing the way the colors of your image will be displayed on the Internet when viewed in the Internet Explorer browser.

✦ **Grayscale:** Translates the colors of your bitmap to an 8-bit, 256-grayscale image. If you know your image will be printed in black and white, converting your bitmaps to grayscale beforehand lets you preview the way the colors translate to grayscale. You can then make any color adjustments necessary to ensure the correct translation of your image to grayscale.

✦ **Netscape Navigator:** Translates the colors in your bitmap image to those colors specific to Netscape Navigator. This palette is useful for previewing the way the colors of your image will be displayed on the Internet when viewed in the Netscape Navigator browser.

✦ **Custom:** Translates the colors in your image to those of the custom palette you specify. This option is useful if you have specific palette needs not met by other color palettes.

Choosing a dithering method

Once you've chosen a palette, you can choose a dithering method for your image. Dithering reduces the amount of banding and sharp changes in colors from one to the next. Here's how the dithering methods work:

✦ **None:** Choosing None disables dithering altogether. Although it may create a coarser image, choosing None is the best choice for online graphics. It eliminates anti-aliasing at the edges of the image, which can cause ghosting when a transparent background is applied.

✦ **Ordered:** Ordered dithering employs fixed-dot patterns to simulate the blending between colors. Fountain fills may appear slightly banded with this method of dithering.

✦ **Error Diffusion:** Error Diffusion produces the best results of the three methods of dithering, but takes longer to apply. Transitions between colors are tailored to the type of transition, which creates a smoother-looking image.

Adjusting other settings

In addition to specifying palette and dithering options, you can adjust the settings on the Range Sensitivity, Processed Palette, and Batch property sheets of the Convert to Paletted dialog box. Here's how they work:

✦ **Range Sensitivity settings:** When you choose an optimized palette for your image, you can specify a Range Sensitivity color. By specifying a Range Sensitivity color, you determine how many colors in that range are used in the conversion. As the importance of the color increases, the number of colors in that range decreases. Low-importance settings allow Draw to create a larger range of colors to use in the color conversion.

✦ **Processed Palette tab:** Once you've specified the importance of your target color, you can click the Processed Palette tab to view the palette that will be used to convert your image.

✦ **Batch property sheets:** If you selected multiple bitmaps to convert to a palette, Draw lets you use batch functions to convert the images based upon the settings specified in the Convert to Paletted dialog box. This is useful for insuring that several images use the same palette, increasing the consistency of color in your image.

Saving your palette

Clicking Save lets you save the palette you created for future use. Be sure to give your palette a unique name to avoid overwriting Draw's default palette.

RGB color 24-bit

RGB color represents the broadest range of color displayable on a computer. Only the human eye is capable of discerning more colors than the RGB model can display. Each of the three components that represent the model (red, green, and blue) has 255 levels of intensity ranging from black to pure color. Individual colors are comprised of percentages of each of the components. The RGB color model is the most widely used of the color models, and is the default display model for computers.

Lab color 24-bit

The Lab color model is based upon three components. The first component measures luminance. Each of the other two components measures a range of color. The A component measures the range from green to red. The B component measures the range from blue to yellow. Lab color encompasses the gamut of both RGB and CMYK. Lab color was developed based on the theory about how the human eye interprets color. The goal was to develop a color model that was not device-dependent, because of the inconsistent way devices interpret color. Because no two devices display color in an identical manner, it's nearly impossible to rely upon a device-dependent color model as being absolutely accurate. Lab color isn't widely supported by other software products. If you are creating an image in Draw for export to another software package, be sure it supports Lab color before converting bitmaps to this color model.

CMYK color 32-bit

The CMYK color model was developed for the commercial printing industry. Each of the four colors (cyan, magenta, yellow, and black) represents a color of ink common to the industry. Commercial presses combine percentages of each of the inks to produce a broad range of colors. Despite its greater bit depth, the breadth of the CMYK color model is smaller than the RGB model because ink can represent fewer colors than light. Because of the size difference, CMYK is considered a lossy color model. In other words, if you convert an RGB bitmap to CMYK, a color loss occurs as the colors are translated.

The CMYK color model is device-dependent. That means it derives its color information from an output device in order to measure the percentages of each of the components required to create an individual color. For example, the percentages of each component required to create a baby blue on a commercial offset press might vary from those required to create the same color on a color inkjet printer. No two output devices interpret color in exactly the same way. To convert bitmap images to CMYK in Draw, you must have an active color profile based upon a color printer or output device. Draw uses the information to translate the color to match that device.

Summary

Incorporating bitmaps in your Draw documents broadens the creative possibilities open to you. Draw's bitmap editing and enhancement capabilities make adding and manipulating bitmaps easier and faster. This capability lets you use images from a variety of sources and helps maintain a consistent appearance within your document. You can convert Draw objects on the fly to bitmap images, which can reduce the complexity of a drawing, or you can let additional special effects be applied to the object. In this chapter, you learned to

✦ Choose a view for editing bitmaps

✦ Convert elements of your image to bitmaps

✦ Crop and scale a bitmap image

✦ Transform bitmaps

✦ Edit colors in your bitmaps

✦ Hide and display colors

✦ Apply PostScript halftones

✦ Trace a bitmap

✦ Resample images

✦ Change the bit level of an image

✦   ✦   ✦

Tricks and Tweaks

P A R T

◆   ◆   ◆   ◆

In This Part

Chapter 10
Adding Effects to
Bitmaps

Chapter 11
Creating Word Art

Chapter 12
Designing with Fills
and Lines

Chapter 13
Imagining
Possibilities with
Special Effects

Chapter 14
Customizing Draw

◆   ◆   ◆   ◆

Adding Effects to Bitmaps

Artists trained in traditional media know there's a huge difference between the behavior of oil and acrylic paints. Acrylic paints are more *hard edged* because they dry much faster, making a subtle appearance difficult to achieve. Oil paints dry much more slowly and lend themselves to blending and other soft effects. Similarly, vector images lend themselves to crisp or hard edges, whereas bitmap images let you create more muted and subtle effects. As you learned in the previous chapter, Draw lets you manipulate bitmaps without having to bounce back and forth between the drawing window and a bitmap program such as Photo-Paint. In addition to being able to manipulate bitmap images, you can also apply special effects to give your bitmaps anything from a subtle to a dramatic appearance.

Cross-Reference For detailed information on working with bitmap images, see Chapter 9.

Discovering Bitmap Effects

Draw 9 comes packaged with a variety of bitmap effects for your use. In addition to the filters packaged with the program, Draw supports Photoshop-compliant plug-in filters from third-party companies such as MetaCreations that further expand Draw's bitmap enhancement capabilities.

New Feature Draw 9 offers you more bitmap filters than ever before. The variety of filters available is comparable to those available in many popular bitmap imaging applications.

How filters work

Bitmap filters analyze the colors and position of the pixels in the bitmap, and then calculate the changes you specify in the settings to achieve the effect you desire. You can preview the results of a filter by clicking Preview in the filter's dialog box. This lets you fine-tune the settings you make without having to undo and reapply the filter numerous times. The filter dialog boxes automatically appear in the center of the drawing window. You can click and drag the title bar on the dialog box to move the dialog box out of the way, so that you can see the preview better.

Using the effects dialog boxes

The bitmap effects dialog boxes let you choose from among three types of dialog display (see Figure 10-1): full-screen preview, expanded view, and before and after view. The decision to use original or expanded dialog boxes is mostly a matter of personal preference. The expanded dialog boxes display a smaller version of the image, and generally refresh faster than the image in the drawing window. You can change the display type by clicking the buttons in the upper right-hand corner of the dialog box. Draw displays the full-screen preview mode of the dialog boxes by default. Clicking the X closes the dialog box without applying any effects.

Working with the views

Here's how various views work:

✦ **Full-screen preview:** The full-screen preview mode of a bitmap effects dialog box has the smallest screen display. If you want to preview the effect of your settings on the selected image, click Preview. The effect is applied to the selected bitmap in the drawing window.

✦ **Expanded:** The expanded view of a bitmap effects dialog box displays a preview thumbnail of the selected bitmap in the dialog box. You can see the effects of your settings in the thumbnail prior to applying the effect. When you click Preview, the display in the dialog box updates to reflect the changes you made.

✦ **Before and After:** The before and after view of a bitmap effects dialog box lets you see a thumbnail of the original bitmap in addition to a preview thumbnail that shows you the expected results of the effects settings you make. When you click Preview, the display in the after window of the dialog box updates to reflect the changes you've made.

Bitmap effects tips

✦ Press and hold F2 when using the full-screen preview mode of a bitmap dialog box to temporarily hide the dialog box.

✦ If you have a small monitor, and conserving screen real estate is important, consider using the full-screen preview mode of the dialog boxes.

✦ If you find an effect filter grayed out, the most likely cause is the bit depth of the bitmap. Some of the effects filters packaged with Draw require that your bitmap be an RGB image. To resolve this problem, convert the bitmap to RGB. You can convert it back to another palette later on.

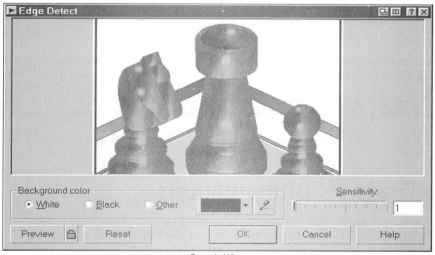

Unexpanded View

Expanded View

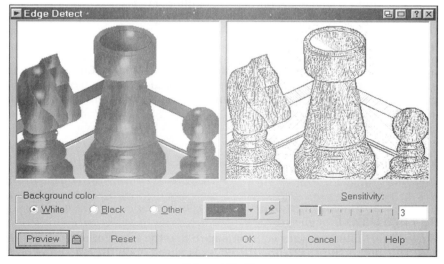

Before and After View

Figure 10-1: Draw lets you choose from among three views of bitmap effects dialog boxes. You can choose the display that suits the way you work.

✦ If you move your cursor over the preview box in the expanded or before and after dialog boxes, the cursor turns into a hand. You can click and drag in the preview box to reposition the image. Double-click to zoom in on a section of the image. Right-click to zoom out on the image.

✦ These same filters are available for use in Photo-Paint, where areas can be selected with masking tools to confine the effects to limited areas of the image.

Autoinflating Bitmaps

DRAW automatically inflates your bitmap to ensure that the effect covers the entire image. Removing the automatic inflate option will truncate effects on your image.

For example, if you apply a blur effect to a rectangle, the corners will be cut off. You can also manually inflate a bitmap by setting the edge value or percentage that surrounds the image.

Using Draw 9's Bitmap Filters

By applying Draw 9's effects filters to bitmaps, you can correct flaws and enhance their appearance. The setting dialog boxes for the filters (each of which is discussed in detail in the following sections) allow you to control the results. By adjusting these settings, you can add both subtle and dramatic effects to your bitmaps. For your convenience, bitmap effect filters are grouped by type.

Adding contour effects

Draw lets you add a variety of contour effects to your bitmaps. Contour effects use variances in luminosity to detect the edges of colored areas of a bitmap. These effects are best suited for high-contrast images. The contour effects include (see Figure 10-2):

✦ Edge Detect

✦ Find Edges

✦ Trace Contour

Using Edge Detect

The Edge Detect filter analyzes your bitmap to find the edges of objects in the bitmap. The method it uses to find the edges is based upon the amount of contrast between objects in the image. The Edge Detect filter is best suited for high-contrast images; it lets you apply outline effects to a selected bitmap image.

Edge Detect   Find Edges   Trace Contour

Figure 10-2: Contour effects emphasize the edges of objects in your bitmap images.

To apply Edge Detect to a bitmap:

1. Select the bitmap to which you want to apply the effect, then select Bitmaps ⇨ Contour ⇨ Edge Detect to display the Edge Detect dialog box (see Figure 10-3).

2. Select a background color from the drop-down color palette. (If you are using the expanded view, you can use the Eyedropper tool to pick up a color in the preview box.) The background color is applied to every part of the bitmap that is not an edge. Edges retain their existing color.

3. Adjust the sensitivity slider to specify the amount of edge enhancement to add. Higher values increase the number of enhanced edges. Click Preview to see the effects of the changes you make.

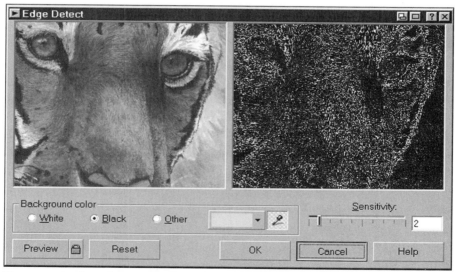

Figure 10-3: The Edge Detect dialog box lets you specify how Draw detects the edges of objects in your bitmap.

4. Click OK to complete the operation and to return to the drawing window. If you want to reset the settings to their original values, click Reset.

The Edge Detect command is an easy way to apply surrealistic effects to an image. If you want to preview the results of your settings, click Preview. By adjusting the sensitivity slider, you can create either subtle or dramatic effects.

> **Tip**
>
> Use the Eyedropper tool in the expanded dialog boxes to *pick up* a color from the bitmap displayed in the preview box by clicking on the color you want to use. The color you select becomes the color selection for the dialog box.

Using Find Edges

The Find Edges effect creates an effect similar to the Edge Detect effect and uses the contrast in the image to determine the final result. Unlike Edge Detect, Find Edges yields better definition, so that the end results more closely resemble the original image. You can choose to apply soft or solid effects, to your bitmap as well as adjust the amount of sensitivity. If you choose soft effects, the resulting image has softer colors and less black. The solid effect choice interprets the image contrast and applies more black to the edges of objects in the bitmap.

To apply Find Edges to a selected bitmap:

1. Select Bitmaps ➪ Contour ➪ Find Edges to display the Find Edges dialog box (see Figure 10-4).

2. Choose either a Soft or Solid effect type.

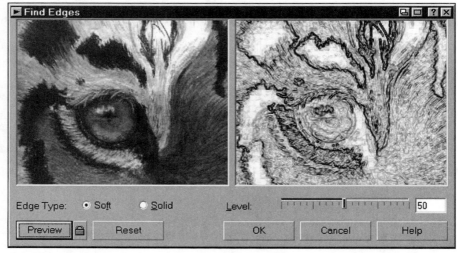

Figure 10-4: The Find Edges dialog box lets you specify the intensity of the edge effects applied to your bitmap.

3. Adjust the sensitivity slider to specify the amount of edge enhancement to add. Higher values increase the number of enhanced edges. Click Preview to see the effects of your changes.

4. Click OK to complete the operation and to return to the drawing window. If you want to reset the settings to their original values, click Reset.

Using Trace Contour

Tracing the edges of objects in a bitmap can be useful when you want to add a subtle hinted effect to an image. By choosing to trace the upper or lower edge of objects in a selected bitmap and adjusting the sensitivity, you can specify the intensity of the effect.

1. Select Bitmaps ⇨ Contour ⇨ Trace Contour to display the Trace Contour dialog box (see Figure 10-5).

2. Choose either Upper or Lower to specify how you want the edges traced.

3. Adjust the sensitivity slider to specify the amount of edge enhancement to add. Higher values increase the amount of edge tracing. Click Preview to see the effects of the changes you make.

4. Click OK to complete the operation and to return to the drawing window. If you want to reset the settings to their original values, click Reset.

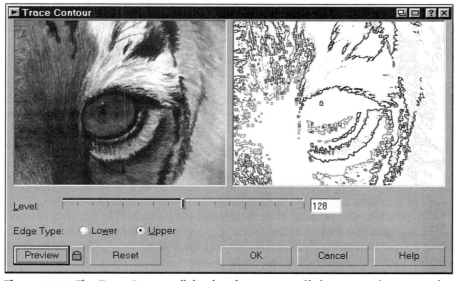

Figure 10-5: The Trace Contour dialog box lets you specify how Draw is to trace the edges of objects in a selected bitmap.

Bitmaps and Resources

I'm writing this book on a fairly high-end computer system. With a very fast processor, a large amount of physical and video memory, and many gigabytes of hard disk space, I have resources to spare. I'm also aware that the average computer system doesn't possess the capabilities of this system. Bitmap files are large, and bitmap filters are very resource-intensive. Depending on the size of the bitmap and the filter you choose, it can take time for Draw to render the final image. I encourage users to use the preview versions of dialog boxes to check the effect of the filters before applying them to a bitmap.

You should also pay attention to the resolution of your bitmap. It's pointless to render a 300 dpi or greater bitmap in Draw if you intend to use the final image on the Web. You may also find it useful to render a low-resolution *copy* of a bitmap while you are creating your document. You can swap the bitmap for a higher resolution copy when your document is done, and recreate the effects by applying the filter settings to the high-resolution version of the bitmap. Using this method of swapping images saves you time overall in your document creation, because Draw doesn't have to render high-resolution bitmap effects every time the screen refreshes.

Applying 3D effects

Seven three-dimensional effect filters are included with Draw (see Figure 10-6). To apply one of these effects, select the bitmap to modify, and then select Bitmaps ⇨ 3D Effects. Choose the effect to apply from the flyout menu, which displays its associated dialog box. You can choose from:

- ✦ 3D Rotate
- ✦ Cylinder
- ✦ Emboss
- ✦ Page Curl
- ✦ Perspective
- ✦ Pinch/Punch
- ✦ Sphere

Figure 10-6: Examples of Draw's seven 3D effects.

Applying 3D rotation

3D Rotate alters the perspective of a selected bitmap so that it appears as if it was mapped to the side of a cube in three-dimensional space. You specify how you want the image to rotate horizontally and vertically. To apply 3D rotation effects to a selected bitmap:

1. Select 3D Rotate from the 3D effects menu to display the 3D Rotate dialog box (see Figure 10-7).

2. Adjust the horizontal and vertical sliders to rotate the bitmap. The preview window in the dialog box displays a 3D representation of a rotated cube to help you specify the rotation. You can also click and drag the image in the preview window to rotate the bitmap.

3. Enable Best Fit if you want the bitmap to be confined within the boundary of the drawing page.

4. Click Preview to view how your settings will affect your bitmap. Click OK to return to the drawing window.

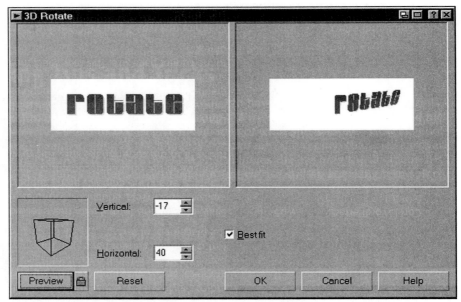

Figure 10-7: The 3D Rotate dialog box lets you specify the orientation of the rotated effect.

You can use 3D rotation as you would use Skew effects to create the illusion of depth with bitmaps. The resulting bitmap can be placed in a PowerClip or used as a bitmap fill.

Adding cylinder effects

The Cylinder filter lets you warp a selected bitmap image so that it appears to either wrap around an object or inside a curved surface. By adjusting the settings, you can create such effects as the labels on cans or perhaps a liquid adhering to the inside of a cup or bowl. The Cylinder filter dialog box lets you choose whether your bitmap is warped vertically or horizontally; it also lets you adjust the intensity of the effect.

To apply the Cylinder effect to a selected bitmap:

1. Select Cylinder from the 3D effects menu to display the Cylinder dialog box (see Figure 10-8).

2. Choose whether you want to warp the bitmap horizontally or vertically.

3. Adjust the intensity of the effect using the slider control. Click Preview if you want to check the effect.

4. Click OK to apply the Cylinder effect and to return to the drawing window.

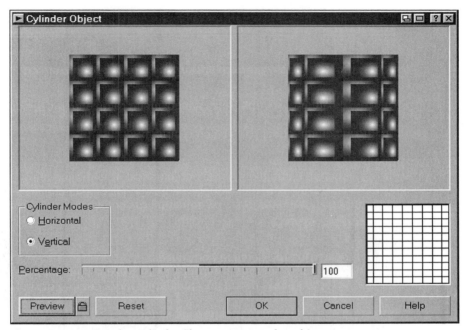

Figure 10-8: Using the Cylinder filter, you can make a bitmap appear to wrap around the outside or inside of objects.

Tip   You can apply this filter multiple times to achieve the amount of wrapping effect you want.

Adding embossing effects

Embossing creates a feeling of depth by adding a relief effect to a selected bitmap. Draw analyzes the contrast of the bitmap to simulate raised and lowered areas in the image. The higher the contrast of the bitmap, the more dramatic this effect becomes. You control the highlighted and shadowed areas of the embossing by adjusting the direction of the lighting source and the depth of the relief.

To apply embossing effects to a selected bitmap:

1. Select Emboss from the 3D effects menu to display the Emboss dialog box (see Figure 10-9).

2. Choose a color to use for the embossed effect:

   - **Original Color:** Uses the colors in the bitmap as an outline and for highlighted areas, while suppressing the color in the lower relief areas

   - **Gray:** Uses shades of gray to simulate raised and lowered areas in the image

- **Black:** Creates a high-contrast embossed effect by using black in the lowered areas, and by adding high-contrast raised areas for dramatic highlights

- **Other:** Uses shades of gray in the lowered areas and creates the highlights and raised areas from the color you choose

3. Adjust the depth slider to increase the height of the raised area.

4. Click and drag the Direction to choose the location of the light source.

5. Click Preview to see the effect of your settings. Click OK to apply the effect and return to the drawing window.

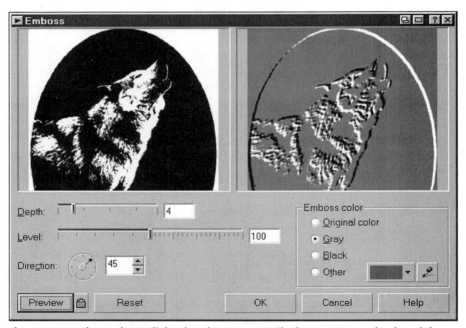

Figure 10-9: The Emboss dialog box lets you specify the amount and color of the embossing effect.

Like many of Draw's bitmap effects, the Emboss effect can add a subtle or dramatic element to your drawing. This effect invites experimentation to create the wanted appearance. The most dramatic embossed bitmaps use settings that create a high-contrast image.

Adding a page curl

The Page Curl filter creates the illusion similar to the corner of a piece of paper that's been curled down. You can curl any corner of a selected bitmap, and you can make the curled area transparent or opaque. If you choose opaque, the curled area has a polished silver metal appearance. Transparent uses the colors in the bitmap to give the illusion of transparency.

To apply the Page Curl effect to a selected bitmap:

1. Select Page Curl from the 3D effects menu to display the Page Curl dialog box (see Figure 10-10).

2. Select the corner of the bitmap to curl by clicking a Page Corner button.

3. Choose the direction in which the bitmap is to curl in the Direction settings. Horizontal curls the page upward or downward; Vertical curls the page from the side.

4. Adjust the curl Width and Height to change the amount of the bitmap that curls.

5. Select a color for the curl and background if desired. By default, Draw specifies two colors of gray, but you can choose any color. If you want to use a color from the image, use the Eyedropper tool to select colors.

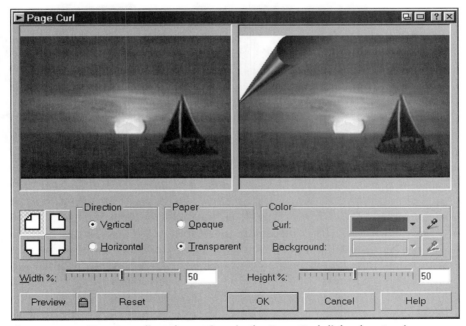

Figure 10-10: You can adjust the settings in the Page Curl dialog box to give your image the appearance of peeling or turning a page.

Tip

The Page Curl effect can be used for more than just *curling* the edge of a drawing of a document page. You can apply this effect to shapes you create in Draw and then convert to a bitmap, such as rectangles. By applying this effect to all the corners of duplicate squares and rotating each 15 degrees, you can quickly create ribbons and bows with a 3D appearance.

Adding perspective

The Perspective filter adds three-dimensional depth effects to a bitmap. The resulting image appears to recede in the distance. You control the direction of the perspective and the amount of distortion. To apply perspective to a selected bitmap:

1. Select Perspective from the 3D effects menu to display the Perspective dialog box (see Figure 10-11).

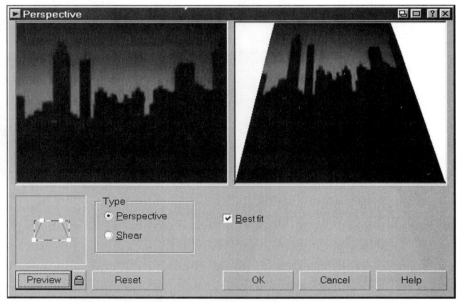

Figure 10-11: Using the Perspective dialog box, you can alter the viewpoint of a bitmap.

2. Choose whether you want to apply Perspective or Shear:

   • **Perspective:** Lets you adjust two nodes in the adjustment window. You can either move them closer together or further apart. The small rectangle shows a representation of the direction and amount the bitmap recedes in the distance. Perspective distorts the bitmap proportionate to the amount of perspective you apply.

- **Shear:** Lets you skew the bitmap by moving the side nodes to specify the amount of depth you want. The side pairs of nodes move in the same direction. For example, if you click and drag the top-right node upward, the bottom-right node moves along with it. The Shear effect maintains the original size and shape of the bitmap, without the distortion of Perspective.

3. Enable the Best Fit option if you want the bitmap to stay within the boundaries of the drawing page.

4. Click Preview to see the effect of your settings. Click OK to complete the operation and to return to the drawing window.

Adding Perspective effects gives bitmaps a feeling of depth and a more realistic look. Bitmap images frequently appear to be floating above the surface of a drawing. Perspective effects can *ground* the bitmap and make it appear to be more integrated with the rest of the drawing.

Using Pinch and Punch effects

Pinch and Punch effects warp your bitmap from the center of the bitmap. This filter creates a symmetrical effect within the bitmap. You choose the type of effect you want by moving the Pinch/Punch slider. If you move the slider toward Pinch, the elements of the bitmap appear to recede toward the center. If you move the slider toward Punch, the elements of the bitmap appear to expand from the center to the edges of the bitmap.

To apply Pinch and Punch effects to a selected bitmap:

1. Select Pinch Punch from the 3D effects menu to display the Pinch/Punch dialog box (see Figure 10-12).

2. Adjust the slider toward Pinch or Punch to specify the type of effect you want.

3. Click Preview to see the effect of your setting. Click OK to apply the effect and to return to the drawing window.

Pinch and Punch effects don't alter the overall dimensions or perimeter shape of the bitmap. If your bitmap has a solid-colored background, such as the white background shown in Figure 10-12, the effect is only noticeable on the contrasting portions of the bitmap. Draw calculates the effect based upon the center of the bitmap. You can change the center of the effect by clicking the Centering button and then clicking the desired location on the original image in the window.

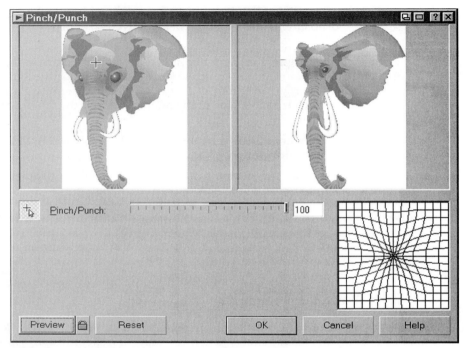

Figure 10-12: The Pinch/Punch dialog box lets you specify how much a bitmap recedes or expands from its center.

Applying Sphere effects

Mapping lets you simulate the effect of wrapping a bitmap around a sphere or cylinder. You can also choose between a horizontal or vertical cylinder. You specify whether the bitmap wraps toward the front, like the label on a beverage can, or toward the back, like the inside of a bowl. To apply mapping effects to a selected bitmap:

1. Select Map to Object from the 3D effects menu to display the Map to Object dialog box.

2. Choose a mapping mode. For this example, I've chosen a sphere effect.

3. Adjust the percentage slider to determine the amount and direction the bitmap wraps (see Figure 10-13). Negative values create a concave appearance; positive values create a convex appearance.

Figure 10-13: The Sphere dialog box (accessed via the Map to Object dialog box) lets you specify the wrapping options to use.

The effect of Map to Object is calculated on the center of the bitmap you are distorting. You can change the center of the effect by clicking the Centering button and then clicking the desired location on the original image in the window. Small percentages of change affect only the center of the bitmap. As the percentage increases, the radius for the area of change increases, creating a greater feeling of wrapping.

Applying Artistic Stroke effects

Draw 9 lets you enhance your documents by applying artistic stroke effects to selected bitmaps. Artistic Stroke effects filters mimic traditional media in the results they produce. The variety of effects you can obtain with this assortment of filters is nearly limitless. Each Artistic Stroke filter has settings for specifying the intensity of the effect as well as controlling elements such as the brush size and color. The available filters include

✦ Charcoal

✦ Conté Crayon

✦ Crayon

✦ Cubist

✦ Impressionist

✦ Palette Knife

✦ Pastels

✦ Pen & Ink

✦ Pointillist

✦ Scraperboard

✦ Sketch Pad

✦ Watercolor

✦ Water Marker

✦ Wave Paper

Tip   As with other bitmap filters, you can choose the display type of the dialog box to suit the way you work. For ease of use, I recommend a dialog box type that lets you preview the results using a thumbnail image. Bitmap enhancement filters are resource-intensive and the preview dialog boxes let you work faster because fewer resources are required to render a thumbnail than the entire image in the drawing window.

Applying Charcoal effects

Charcoal effects convert images to black-and-white images, much as if you were using charcoal to sketch an image on a drawing pad. You can specify the size of the stroke and the hardness of the edges in the resulting image by adjusting the settings in the Charcoal effects dialog box. Lower settings create more subtle effects, while higher settings create more dramatic results. To apply Charcoal effects to a selected bitmap:

1. Select Bitmaps ➪ Artistic Strokes ➪ Charcoal to display the Charcoal dialog box (see Figure 10-14).

2. Adjust the Size and Edge settings to create the effect you want. Click Preview to see the results of your settings.

3. Click OK to apply the filter and to return to the drawing window.

Charcoal effects are useful when you want to add a muted effect to an image. When combined with color adjustment controls, you can fade the effect as a background for other elements in your document. Charcoal effects work well when you need single-color output of your document, such as laser output.

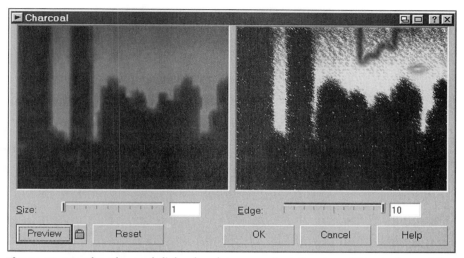

Figure 10-14: The Charcoal dialog box lets you adjust the size of the stroke and the hardness of edges in the effect.

Applying Conté Crayon

Conté Crayon adds a soft diffused effect to bitmaps in your document. By selecting a crayon color and a paper color, you can determine the amount of *warmth* in the image. Lighter colors increase the feeling of warmth. Adjusting the pressure and size of the stroke determines the softness of the effect. Higher settings increase the intensity of the effect. To add Conté Crayon effects to a selected bitmap:

1. Select Bitmaps ⇨ Artistic Strokes ⇨ Conté Crayon to display the Conté Crayon dialog box (see Figure 10-15).

2. Select the color of the paper and Conté Crayon to use.

3. Adjust the Size and Pressure settings to create the effect you want. Click Preview to see the results of your settings.

4. Click OK to apply the filter and to return to the drawing window.

Conté Crayon softens the details of a bitmap, resulting in an image that appears as if it were viewed through frosted glass. It's most effective when applied to bitmaps that are light or contain shades of brown.

Figure 10-15: The Conté Crayon dialog box lets you adjust settings to add soft effects to bitmap images.

Applying Crayon effects

Crayon produces a fused effect that maintains the colors of your bitmap. You can adjust the size of the stroke and the quantity of outlining in the image. As the stroke size is increased, the intensity of the effect becomes more dramatic. Higher outline settings allow more of the image's detail to appear. To apply Crayon effects to a selected bitmap:

1. Select Bitmaps ➪ Artistic Strokes ➪ Crayon to display the Crayon dialog box (see Figure 10-16).

2. Adjust the Size and Outline settings to create the effect you want. Click Preview to see the results of your settings.

3. Click OK to apply the filter and to return to the drawing window.

The Crayon filter is most effective when applied to bitmaps that have few details. The distortion of the filter doesn't affect the results as dramatically when the filter is applied to bitmaps containing a lot of detail.

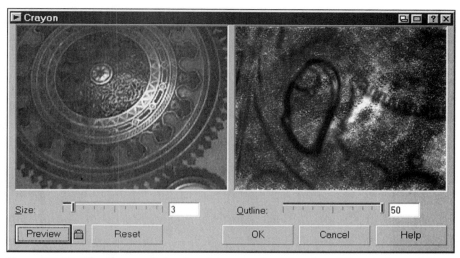

Figure 10-16: The Crayon dialog box lets you adjust the size of the stroke and the quantity of outlining in the effect.

Applying Cubist effects

Cubist effects fragment the bitmap and can be used to add a screened or block-stamped effect to an image. The paper color you choose shows through the final image and can be used to increase or decrease the intensity of the effect. Lighter-color paper selections create more subtle effects. As you increase the Size and Brightness settings, the effect becomes softer.

To apply Cubist effects to a selected bitmap:

1. Select Bitmaps ➪ Artistic Strokes ➪ Cubist to display the Cubist dialog box (see Figure 10-17).

2. Select a paper color. You can use the eyedropper to pick up a color from the original image if you want.

3. Adjust the Size and Brightness settings to create the effect you want. Click Preview to see the results of your settings.

4. Click OK to apply the filter and to return to the drawing window.

Adjusting the settings to lower amounts gives bitmaps a stippled screen effect. When applied to a low-contrast image, the stippled effect is useful for creating background tiles for Web pages and other documents.

Tip

All of the bitmap effects dialog boxes let you specify settings by entering numeric values, as well as by adjusting the control sliders in the dialog boxes.

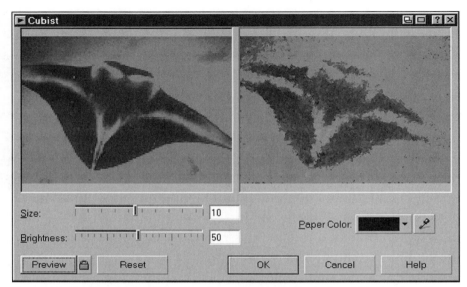

Figure 10-17: The Cubist dialog box lets you create stippled and block print effects.

Applying Impressionist effects

The Impressionist effect analyzes the color of the pixels in your bitmap and shifts them to distort the image. You specify the stroke size, coloration, and brightness settings. You can also choose between stroke and dab types of distortion. The settings roughly correlate to the distance in pixels that Draw uses to shift the colors. Lower settings retain much of the details of the original bitmap, while higher settings create more distortion.

To apply Impressionist effects to a selected bitmap:

1. Select Bitmaps ➪ Artistic Strokes ➪ Impressionist to display the Impressionist dialog box (see Figure 10-18).

2. Choose the stroke or dab as the distortion type.

3. Adjust the Stroke, Coloration, and Brightness settings to create the effect you want. Click Preview to see the results of your settings.

4. Click OK to apply the filter and to return to the drawing window.

When using Impressionist effects, remember that Draw increases the dimensions of the bitmap to include the total effect. The amount of distortion determines the difference in size between the original and enhanced bitmap. Use the Shape tool to crop the bitmap or resample the bitmap if you need to reduce its physical size.

Figure 10-18: The Impressionist dialog box lets you specify the amount and type of distortion you want in the final image.

Applying Palette Knife effects

The Palette Knife filter lets you add a *stucco* effect to bitmap images in your drawing. You can specify the angle of the strokes, as well as the blade size and the softness of the edge. Choosing a smaller blade size increases the roughness of the effect. To apply Palette Knife effects to a selected bitmap:

1. Select Bitmaps ➪ Artistic Strokes ➪ Palette Knife to display the Palette Knife dialog box (see Figure 10-19).

2. Specify the angle you want to use.

3. Adjust the Blade Size and Soft Edge settings to create the effect you want. Click Preview to see the results of your settings.

4. Click OK to apply the filter and to return to the drawing window.

The settings you make determine how much of the details found in the original image appear in the final effect. Higher settings reduce the amount of detail by increasing the distortion and smoothness of the image.

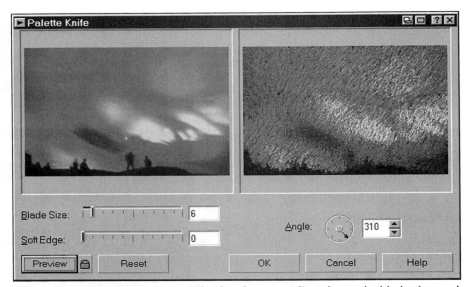

Figure 10-19: The Palette Knife dialog box lets you adjust the angle, blade size, and edge softness of the effect.

Applying Pastel effects

The Pastel filter lets you soften the details of a bitmap. There are two methods of creating the distortion: Soft and Oil. Soft adds subtle distortion to the bitmap, whereas Oil creates more pronounced distortion. By adjusting the Stroke Size and Hue Variation, you can determine how much of the original appearance of the bitmap is retained. Higher settings create more distortion and variation in color.

To apply Pastel effects to a selected bitmap:

1. Select Bitmaps ➪ Artistic Strokes ➪ Pastel to display the Pastel dialog box (see Figure 10-20).

2. Select either Soft or Oil as the method type.

3. Adjust the Stroke Size and Hue Variation settings to create the effect you want. Click Preview to see the results of your settings.

4. Click OK to apply the filter and to return to the drawing window.

Pastel effects are useful when you want to soften the appearance of an image. The result gives the appearance of a blurred image. Lower Hue Variation settings retain the colors found in the original bitmap, whereas higher settings shift the colors, adding interest to the bitmap.

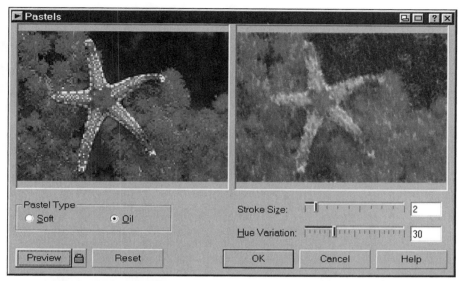

Figure 10-20: The Pastels dialog box lets you add soft, muted effects to bitmaps.

Applying Pen and Ink effects

The Pen & Ink filter lets you choose whether to use cross-hatching or stippling to render your bitmap. The filter analyzes the luminosity of your bitmap and renders the results in black and white. You can adjust the density and number of ink pools to control the final effect. Higher settings produce a more dramatic effect. To apply Pen & Ink effects to a selected bitmap:

1. Select Bitmaps ➪ Artistic Strokes ➪ Pen & Ink to display the Pen & Ink dialog box (see Figure 10-21).

2. Choose either Crosshatch or Stippling as the rendering method.

3. Adjust the Density and Ink Pools settings to create the effect you want. Click Preview to see the results of your settings.

4. Click OK to apply the filter and to return to the drawing window.

Pen & Ink effects mimic traditional pen and ink media, letting you give your bitmaps a hand-drawn effect. This filter is most effective when applied to bitmaps that have objects with defined edges or a great amount of contrast.

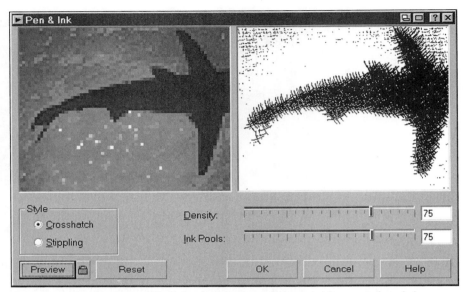

Figure 10-21: The Pen & Ink dialog box lets you give your bitmaps a hand-drawn appearance.

Applying Pointillist effects

Pointillist effects use dots to represent the objects in a drawing. When you apply this filter to a bitmap, Draw interprets the colors in the bitmap as dots. You can specify the size of the dots and the amount of brightness you want in the final rendered image.

To apply Pointillist effects to a selected bitmap:

1. Select Bitmaps ➪ Artistic Strokes ➪ Pointillist to display the Pointillist dialog box (see Figure 10-22).

2. Adjust the Size and Brightness settings to create the effect you want. Click Preview to see the results of your settings.

3. Click OK to apply the filter and to return to the drawing window.

When applying the Pointillist effects filter, specifying increased brightness reveals fewer details and reduces the impact of the effect. This is useful when you want to hint at an image rather than include a lot of sharp detail.

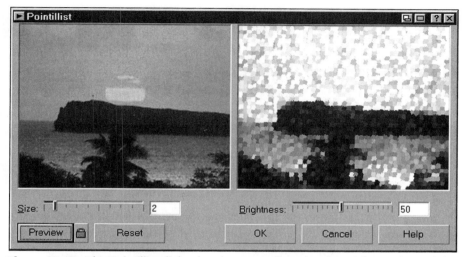

Figure 10-22: The Pointillist dialog box lets you adjust the size of the stroke and the hardness of edges in the effect.

Applying Scraperboard effects

In traditional media, color is scraped off a scraperboard to reveal the black board beneath. The Scraperboard filter lets you apply a similar effect to your bitmaps. You determine whether the image is rendered in black and white or the original colors of the image. Additionally, you determine how much of the color is retained by adjusting the Density and Size settings. Higher settings leave more color or white and reveal less of the black *background.*

To apply Scraperboard effects to a selected bitmap:

1. Select Bitmaps ⇨ Artistic Strokes ⇨ Scraperboard to display the Scraperboard dialog box (see Figure 10-23).

2. Choose either the Color or White method of rendering.

3. Adjust the Density and Size settings to create the effect you want. Click Preview to see the results of your settings.

4. Click OK to apply the filter and to return to the drawing window.

Scraperboard effects are useful for creating a dramatic counterpoint in your document. The intensity of the contrast between black and either color or white adds interest that draws the eye to that point in your image.

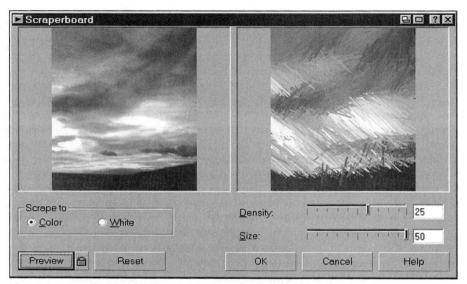

Figure 10-23: The Scraperboard dialog box lets you adjust the amount of black that is revealed in your image.

Applying Sketch Pad effects

The Sketch Pad filter dialog box lets you specify whether to have your bitmaps appear as if they were sketched with a graphite pencil or with colored pencils. By adjusting the Style, Lead, and Outline values, you determine the intensity of the effect. Higher values increase the effect of the filter.

To apply Sketch Pad effects to a selected bitmap:

1. Select Bitmaps ⇨ Artistic Strokes ⇨ Sketch Pad to display the Sketch Pad dialog box (see Figure 10-24).

2. Adjust the Size and Edge settings to create the effect you want. Click Preview to see the results of your settings.

3. Click OK to apply the filter and to return to the drawing window.

The loose style and primitive appeal of a pencil sketch can enhance a document without overpowering other elements on the page. Sketch Pad effects are especially useful for adding interest to text-heavy documents.

Figure 10-24: The Sketch Pad dialog box lets you specify settings that give your bitmap the appearance of having been sketched with a pencil.

Applying Watercolor effects

The Watercolor filter adds a diffused appearance to your bitmaps. The Watercolor dialog box provides a variety of controls for adjusting the amount of distortion, roughness, and brightness of the image. The Brush Size, Water Amount, and Bleed controls alter the amount of distortion. The Granulation setting controls the roughness, and higher settings produce lighter results. You can adjust the lightness of the final result by adjusting the Brightness setting.

To apply Watercolor effects to a selected bitmap:

1. Select Bitmaps ➪ Artistic Strokes ➪ Watercolor to display the Watercolor dialog box (see Figure 10-25).

2. Adjust the settings to create the effect you want. Click Preview to see the results of your settings.

3. Click OK to apply the filter and to return to the drawing window.

The muted appearance of watercolors is useful for creating backgrounds and images that don't require a high degree of detail. This filter lends itself more to pastel colors, creating a soft appearance, than to bright colors.

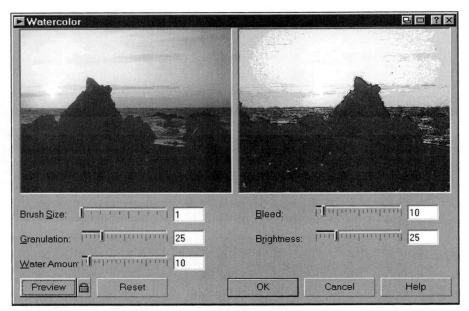

Figure 10-25: The Watercolor dialog box lets you add watercolor effects to your bitmaps.

Applying Water Marker effects

The Water Marker filter creates a speckled effect. You can choose Default, Order, or Random as the method of distortion. Order creates the least distortion, and Random creates the greatest distortion. You can further control the distortion and color variation by adjusting the Size and Color Variation settings.

To apply Water Marker effects to a selected bitmap:

1. Select Bitmaps ➪ Artistic Strokes ➪ Water Marker to display the Water Marker dialog box (see Figure 10-26).

2. Choose the method of distortion to use.

3. Adjust the Size and Color Variation settings to create the effect you want. Click Preview to see the results of your settings.

4. Click OK to apply the filter and to return to the drawing window.

The Water Marker filter is best suited for occasions when details are not desired in the final image. The effect creates too much distortion for small details to remain visible.

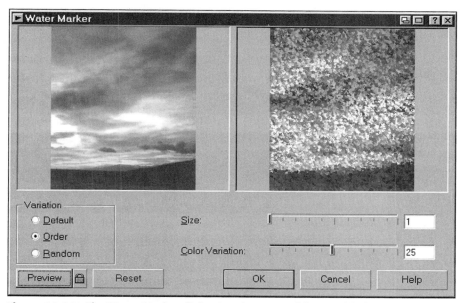

Figure 10-26: The Water Marker dialog box lets you add a speckled effect to your bitmap.

Applying Wave Paper effects

The Wave Paper filter lets you give your bitmap the appearance of having been drawn on textured paper. You can choose whether the final image is rendered in color or black and white. By adjusting the brush pressure, you can change the intensity of the paper effect. Higher settings allow less of the *paper* to show.

To apply Wave Paper effects to a selected bitmap:

1. Select Bitmaps ➪ Artistic ➪ Wave Paper to display the Wave Paper dialog box (see Figure 10-27).

2. Choose the color rendering method you want to use.

3. Adjust the Brush Pressure setting to create the effect you want. Click Preview to see the results of your settings.

4. Click OK to apply the filter and to return to the drawing window.

The nearly monochrome effect of the Wave Paper filter lets you add subtle effects to your document. By adjusting the brush setting to control the amount of the paper effect, you can control the roughness and how much color is applied to the final image.

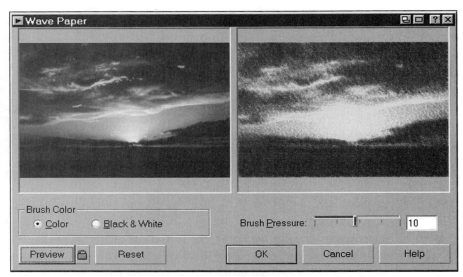

Figure 10-27: The Wave Paper dialog box lets you adjust the brush pressure and color-rendering method of the Wave Paper effect.

Adding blur effects

Blurring softens and blends pixels in a bitmap, smoothing the appearance of the image. You can also apply blurring to add the illusion of motion to a bitmapped image. As with other bitmap effects, blur effects are applied by first selecting the bitmap using the Pick tool and then selecting Bitmaps ⇨ Blur to display the flyout menu listing the blur effects. Draw provides these blur filters:

- ✦ Directional Smooth
- ✦ Gaussian Blur
- ✦ Jaggy Despeckle
- ✦ Low Pass
- ✦ Motion Blur
- ✦ Radial Blur
- ✦ Smooth
- ✦ Soften
- ✦ Zoom

Applying a Directional Smooth effect

The Directional Smooth effect applies small amounts of blurring to an image. Draw determines the direction and variation of the smoothing by analyzing pixels with similar tonal values. The final effect subtly smoothes your image.

To apply a Directional Smooth effect to a selected bitmap:

1. Select Directional Smooth from the Blur effects menu to display the Directional Smooth dialog box (see Figure 10-28).

2. Adjust the Percentage slider to set the amount of the effect. Higher values result in greater blurring of the bitmap.

3. Click Preview to see how the settings will affect your bitmap. Click OK to apply the effect and to return to the drawing window.

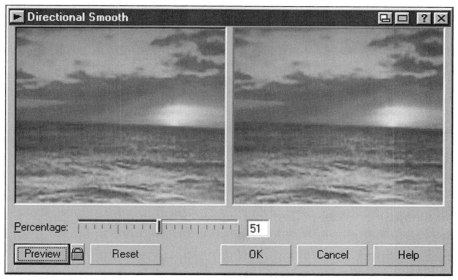

Figure 10-28: The Directional Smooth dialog box lets you specify the amount of blurring to apply to your bitmap.

Directional Smoothing is useful when you have a small amount of roughness to correct in an image. You can apply the filter multiple times, if needed, to smooth tones in your images. This filter is especially effective with portrait images for smoothing skin tones.

Applying a Gaussian Blur

Gaussian Blur adds a fuzzy effect to a bitmap by manipulating the pixel information using Gaussian distribution. Unlike other blurring effects, which calculate the blending of pixel information using a straight line or circle, Gaussian Blur uses a bell-shaped curve to distribute the pixel information. The result is a smooth blending of the pixels.

To apply a Gaussian Blur to a selected bitmap:

1. Select Gaussian Blur from the Blur effects menu to display the Gaussian Blur dialog box (see Figure 10-29).

2. Adjust the Radius slider to set the amount of the effect. The value you enter represents the number of pixels to include in each calculation sample. Higher values result in greater blurring of the bitmap.

3. Click Preview to see how the settings will affect your bitmap. Click OK to apply the effect and to return to the drawing window.

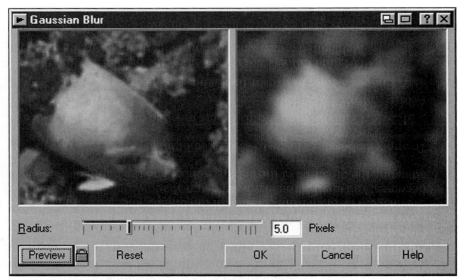

Figure 10-29: The Gaussian Blur dialog box lets you specify the amount of blurring to apply to your bitmap.

Gaussian Blur is useful for improving the quality of images containing undesirable sharp edges. You can use it to simulate *feathering* on the edges of irregularly cropped bitmaps by applying a small amount of Gaussian Blur to the bitmap.

Using the Jaggy Despeckle filter

The Jaggy Despeckle filter applies a soft, blurring effect to an image to reduce the jagged edges frequently associated with bitmaps that have been resized or resampled. It can also be used to remove or minimize dust and scratch marks on a scan. By specifying the Width and Height, you set the number of pixels affected by the filter.

To apply a Jaggy Despeckle to a selected bitmap:

1. Select Jaggy Despeckle from the Blur effects menu to display the Jaggy Despeckle dialog box (see Figure 10-30).

2. Adjust the Width and Height sliders to specify the range of the effect. The value you enter represents the number of pixels to include in each calculation sample. Higher values result in greater blurring of the bitmap.

3. Click the Symmetric box if you want the Width and Height to have identical values.

4. Click Preview to see how the settings will affect your bitmap. Click OK to apply the effect and to return to the drawing window.

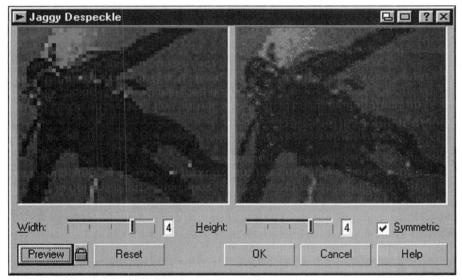

Figure 10-30: The Jaggy Despeckle dialog box lets you specify the amount of blurring to apply to your bitmap.

The Jaggy Despeckle filter is especially effective on high-contrast images. When applied to low-contrast images, the effects are very subtle and may not be discernible.

Note   The Jaggy Despeckle effect supports all color modes except Paletted and Black-and-White.

Applying a Low Pass effect

The Low Pass effect removes sharp edges and detail from an image. It lets you soften images, and can be used to counteract slight defects caused by resizing a bitmap. You specify the number of pixels Draw evaluates to calculate the amount of blurring.

To apply a Low Pass effect to a selected bitmap:

1. Select Low Pass from the Blur effects menu to display the Low Pass dialog box (see Figure 10-31).

2. Adjust the Percentage slider to set the amount of the effect. Higher values result in greater blurring of the bitmap. Adjust the Radius slider to specify the width of the sampling used in the effect.

3. Click Preview to see how the settings will affect your bitmap. Click OK to apply the effect and to return to the drawing window.

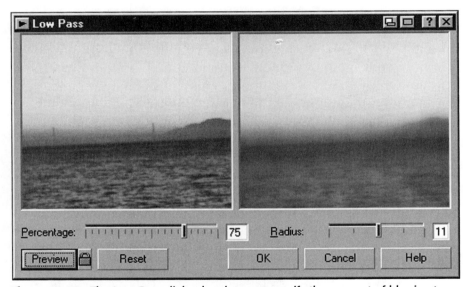

Figure 10-31: The Low Pass dialog box lets you specify the amount of blurring to apply to your bitmap.

When adjusting the setting for Low Pass, remember that higher settings reduce harsh transitions between shadows and highlights but may erase the details of an image. For this reason, Low Pass is best suited for when retention of detail isn't important to the final image.

Using motion blurring

Motion blurring creates the illusion of speed and motion in a bitmap. You specify the direction of the motion, as well as the intensity of the effect. Motion blurring is especially effective with bitmap images of sporting events, by creating a feeling of action.

To apply motion blurring to a selected bitmap:

1. Select Motion from the Blur effects menu to display the Motion Blur dialog box (see Figure 10-32).

2. Click and drag the Direction dial to select a direction for the blurring. Alternatively, if you need a specific angle, enter the value in the entry box.

3. Adjust the Distance slider to specify the amount of blurring. Higher values increase the blurring and illusion of speed.

4. Click Preview to see how the settings will affect your bitmap. Click OK to complete the operation and to return to the drawing window.

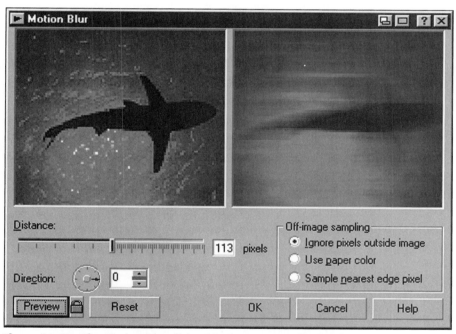

Figure 10-32: The Motion Blur dialog box lets you specify the direction and amount of blurring to apply to your bitmap.

Motion blurring can also be used to give bitmaps a brushed or windswept appearance. The setting for the Distance slider determines the distance the pixels are shifted when the effect is applied.

Applying a Radial Blur effect

The Radial Blur effect creates a circular, swirled, blurred effect. Draw uses the center of the bitmap to calculate the effect, but you can change the center of the effect. The center is protected from change. The effect radiates from the center to become more prominent as the distance increases away from the center.

To apply a Radial Blur effect to a selected bitmap:

1. Select Radial Blur from the Blur effects menu to display the Radial Blur dialog box (see Figure 10-33).

2. Click the Set Center button and then click the point on the original image that you want to use as the center of the effect.

3. Adjust the Amount slider to set the amount of the effect. Higher values result in greater blurring of the bitmap.

4. Click Preview to see how the settings will affect your bitmap. Click OK to apply the effect and to return to the drawing window.

Figure 10-33: The Radial Blur dialog box lets you specify the center and degree of blurring to apply to your bitmap.

The amount of blurring you specify correlates to the number of pixels Draw displaces when calculating the effect. You can apply subtle *swept* effects to images by using lower settings. Higher settings remove the details from images, and are useful for modifying images that you want to use as a custom fill.

Tip　Double-clicking on the original image in one of the preview-style dialog boxes lets you zoom in on your image. Right-click to zoom out on the image. When the Set Center tool is active, you can't use the zoom feature. Deselect the Set Center tool to use the zoom feature.

Using a Smooth effect

Smooth subtly evens the tones between adjacent pixels. The changes it makes to a bitmap may not be readily apparent because they are so slight. Zooming in on the bitmap helps improve the ability to view the changes.

To apply Smooth effects to a selected bitmap:

1. Select Smooth from the Blur effects menu to display the Smooth dialog box (see Figure 10-34).

2. Adjust the Percentage slider to specify the intensity of the effect.

3. Click Preview to see how the settings will affect your bitmap. Click OK to complete the operation and to return to the drawing window.

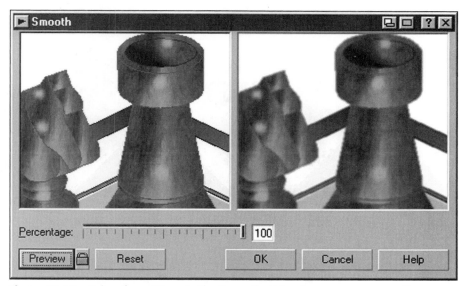

Figure 10-34: Using the settings in the Smooth dialog box, you can smooth an otherwise grainy photo image.

Smooth is an excellent choice if you need to smooth a bitmap but want to do it in tiny increments. You can adjust the intensity of the effect, but you may want to reapply the effect several times to achieve the appearance you want. Each time you apply the effect, Draw recalculates the change in the adjacent pixels. The result is that a 10-percent change that you apply twice has a far more subtle effect than a 20-percent change that you apply once.

Using a Soften effect

The Soften effect lets you add a slight blurred effect to an image while retaining the majority of the detail. You specify the amount of blurring to add. Draw uses the value you specify to soften your image.

To apply Soften effects to a selected bitmap:

1. Select Soften from the Blur effects menu to display the Soften dialog box (see Figure 10-35).

2. Adjust the Percentage slider to specify the intensity of the effect.

3. Click Preview to see how the settings will affect your bitmap. Click OK to complete the operation and to return to the drawing window.

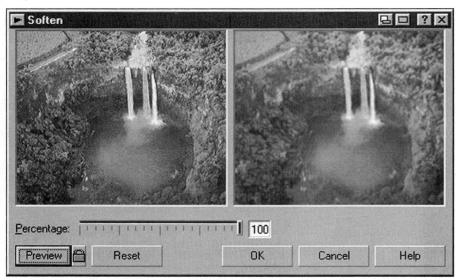

Figure 10-35: By Using the settings in the Soften dialog box, you can subtly smooth an image.

Soften is useful when you have a detailed scanned image that has slight defects. It lets you reduce the impact of the defects without losing the detail in your image.

Using a Zoom effect

The Zoom effect blurs an image progressively outward from the center. By default, Draw calculates the blurring based upon the center of the bitmap; you can, however, change the center of the blurring using the Set Center option. The pixels nearest to the center blur the least. You can control the amount of blurring by adjusting the Amount slider to achieve subtle or dramatic effects.

To apply a Zoom effect to a selected bitmap:

1. Select Zoom from the Blur effects menu to display the Zoom dialog box (see Figure 10-36).

2. Click the Set Center button and then click the point on the original image that you want to use as the center of the effect.

3. Adjust the Amount slider to set the amount of the effect. Higher values result in greater blurring of the bitmap.

4. Click Preview to see how the settings will affect your bitmap. Click OK to apply the effect and to return to the drawing window.

Figure 10-36: The Zoom dialog box lets you specify the center and degree of blurring to apply to your bitmap.

The Zoom filter lets you call attention to a specific portion of a bitmap by blurring other portions of the image. You should note that as the value increases the number of pixels affected by the filter also increases, and the quantity of protected pixels is reduced.

Using color transformation effects

Draw provides color transformation filters that you can apply to bitmaps. These color transformation effects modify the colors in your bitmap. The filters create dramatic effects that you control by adjusting the threshold levels. To apply color transformation effects, select the bitmap you want to modify, using the Pick tool.

Then select Bitmaps ➪ Color Transform and choose the effect you want to apply. The effects are:

- ✦ Bit Planes
- ✦ Edit Duotone
- ✦ Halftone
- ✦ Psychedelic
- ✦ Solarize

Adding Bit Planes effects

The Bit Planes effect reduces the colors in an image to basic RGB color components and displays tonal changes in the image using solid colors. Draw uses the saturation of color to analyze the colors in your image. You can specify the effect that you want by adjusting the Red, Green, and Blue sliders in the dialog box.

To apply a Bit Planes effect to a selected bitmap:

1. Select Bit Planes from the Color Transform effects menu to display the Bit Planes dialog box (see Figure 10-37).

Figure 10-37: The Bit Planes dialog box lets you convert the colors in your bitmap to their basic RGB component colors.

2. Adjust the color sliders to specify the intensity of the effect. To specify equal values in each box, click the Apply To All Planes checkbox.

3. Click Preview to see how your settings will affect your bitmap. Click OK to apply the effect and to return to the drawing window.

The Bit Planes effect is useful for analyzing image gradients. Specifying higher values creates a coarser appearance and more large flat areas in the final image. Specifying lower values creates an image with more tonal variations and gradations.

Using the Edit Duotone filter

The Edit Duotone filter lets you modify the color and tonal curve of a selected duotone bitmap. You can change the colors of the duotone or adjust the tone curve settings to lighten or darken the effect of the duotone.

To edit the duotone effects of a selected duotone bitmap:

1. Select Edit Duotone from the Color Transform effects menu to display the Duotone dialog box (see Figure 10-38).

2. Select the number of enhancement colors you want to use from the drop-down menu.

3. Double-click a color to select a new color for the duotone.

4. Adjust the tone curve as desired. Enable the Show All box to display all of the ink tone curves at once. In general, decrease the amount of black ink in the midtones and replace it with color by increasing the amount of the second color ink in the midtones. Click Null to reset the ink tone curves to their default positions.

5. Click Preview to see how your settings will affect your bitmap. Click OK to apply the effect and to return to the drawing window.

A duotone bitmap is a grayscale image that has been enhanced with up to four additional colors. Duotones are useful for adding a touch of color to predominantly grayscale documents.

Note   The Edit Duotone filter is only available when a duotone bitmap is selected. First convert the image to duotone using Bitmap ⇨ Mode ⇨ Duotone, and then you can edit the duotone using the Edit Duotone filter.

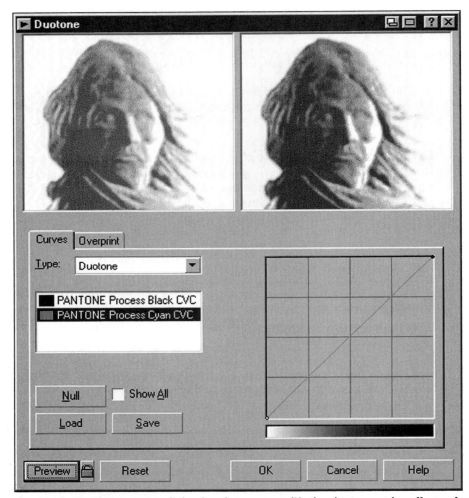

Figure 10-38: The Duotone dialog box lets you modify the duotone color effects of a duotone image.

Understanding the Tone Curve

The Tone Curve is a color grid that displays the ink curves used in a duotone image. Here's how it works:

- The horizontal plane, or *x* axis, displays 256 possible shades of gray. Black is represented by 0, and white is represented by 256.

- The vertical plane, or *y* axis, displays the intensity of ink as a percentage to be applied to the corresponding grayscale values.

- As you adjust the curve, the amount of ink applied to the duotone changes to increase or decrease the appearance of the effect on your grayscale image.

Adding Halftone effects

The Halftone effect gives an image the look of a color halftone. A color halftone is an image that has been converted from a continuous tone image to a series of dots of various sizes that represent different tones.

To apply Halftone effects to a selected bitmap:

1. Select Halftone from the Color Transform effects menu to display the Color Halftone dialog box (see Figure 10-39).

2. Adjust the Max Dot Radius slider to specify the radius of the halftone dot.

3. Adjust the colorsliders to specify the angles of the CYMK colors.

4. Click Preview to see how your settings will affect your bitmap. Click OK to apply the effect and to return to the drawing window.

Color halftones add interest to a document. They are also useful when the original scanned image is grainy or has moderate defects. Using the Halftone filter lets you purposely coarsen the image, minimizing the impact of any flaws contained in the original image.

Adding Psychedelic effects

Psychedelic effects convert the colors in your image to bright vibrant colors that give a bitmap a surreal, high-contrast appearance. This effect is useful for creating a high-impact appearance in your document, or to add a whimsical effect to bitmaps. You adjust the levels to specify how many colors contained in your bitmap you want included in the transformation.

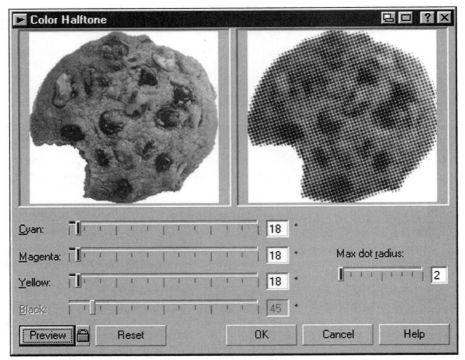

Figure 10-39: The Color Halftone dialog box lets you apply color halftone effects to your bitmaps.

To apply psychedelic effects to a selected bitmap:

1. Select Psychedelic from the Color Transform effects menu to display the Psychedelic dialog box (see Figure 10-40).

2. Adjust the Level slider to specify the intensity of the effect. As the value becomes higher, more colors in your bitmap are included in the effect and the changes are more radical.

3. Click Preview to see how your settings will affect your bitmap. Click OK to apply the effect and to return to the drawing window.

The colors Draw uses to create the psychedelic effects are based upon a traditional color wheel. Draw replaces colors with their complementary or inverse color. A complementary color is either of two colors that when added in the right proportion to the second color produces white or gray. For example, red and green are complementary colors. If you add the correct amount of red to any green, the result would be gray.

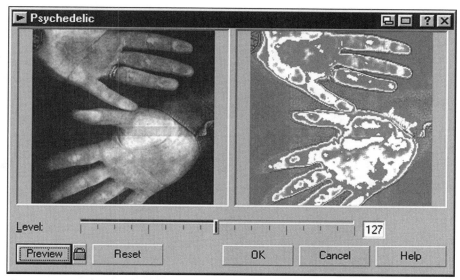

Figure 10-40: The Psychedelic dialog box lets you apply surreal effects to your bitmaps.

Adding a Solarize effect

Solarize effects transform the colors of your bitmap to resemble those of a photonegative image. The resulting high-contrast image is useful when you need to add a feeling of drama to your document. Like the Psychedelic effect, you control the intensity of the effect by adjusting the threshold levels.

To apply a Solarize effect to a selected bitmap:

1. Select Solarize from the Color Transform menu to display the Solarize dialog box (see Figure 10-41).

2. Adjust the Level slider to specify the intensity of the effect. As the values become higher, more colors in your bitmap are included in the effect and the changes are more dramatic.

3. Click Preview to see how your settings will affect your bitmap. Click OK to apply the effect and to return to the drawing window.

Unlike Psychedelic effects, Solarize effects are based upon the luminescence of the image rather than the precise hue of the colors within the image. Dark colors become light, while more luminescent or light colors become dark. The actual replacement hues are the exact luminescent opposite of the hues contained in the image.

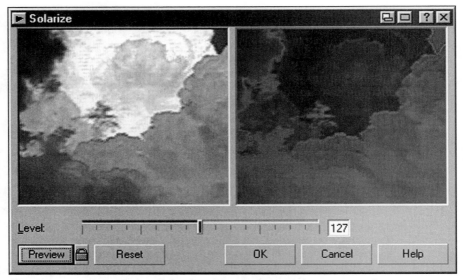

Figure 10-41: The Solarize dialog box lets you control the amount of contrast.

Using creative effects

Draw 9 provides a variety of filters that allow you to modify and distort bitmaps. Unlike the Artistic effects filters, which distort images by applying a variety of *brush* effects, the Creative effects filters turn bitmaps into patterns or add texture to the image. The variety of effects that you can create is virtually limitless. Creative effects filters include

✦ Crafts

✦ Crystalize

✦ Fabric

✦ Frame

✦ Glass Block

✦ Kid's Play

✦ Mosaic

✦ Particles

✦ Scatter

✦ Smoked Glass

✦ Stained Glass

✦ Vortex

✦ Vignette

✦ Weather

Applying Crafts effects

Crafts effect filters use the shapes of common objects to modify your bitmaps. Draw analyzes the colors in your bitmap and applies the effect using those colors. You specify the type and size of the objects used to create the final image. You can also adjust a filter's Complete setting to determine how much of your bitmap is included in the final image. By adjusting the Brightness and Rotation settings of the objects, you can further enhance the bitmap. Draw provides these styles from which to choose:

✦ Puzzle

✦ Gears

✦ Marbles

✦ Candy

✦ Ceramic Tile

✦ Poker Chips

To apply the Crafts effect to a selected bitmap:

1. Select Crafts from the Creative effects menu to display the Crafts dialog box (see Figure 10-42).

2. Choose a Style from the drop-down list box and adjust the size of the objects. The Size setting specifies the number of pixels in the diameter of each object.

3. Adjust the Complete, Brightness, and Rotation settings as desired.

4. Click Preview to see how your settings will affect your bitmap. Click OK to apply the effect and to return to the drawing window.

Draw uses a black background behind Craft effects. If you rotate an asymmetrical pattern, such as the puzzle pattern, the pieces won't fit together tightly and more of the black background appears. Similarly, if you choose a Complete setting of less than 100 percent, more of the black background becomes visible.

Applying Crystalize effects

The Crystallize effect fragments your bitmap into irregular pieces. You specify the size in pixels to use as the diameter of each piece. At a very low setting, such as 5, much of the detail in your image is retained and objects appear to have particles around their edges. The larger sizes cause considerable distortion to the original image.

Figure 10-42: The Crafts dialog box lets you change your bitmap into a pattern of common shapes.

To apply the Crystallize effect to a selected bitmap:

1. Select Crystallize from the Creative menu to display the Crystallize dialog box (see Figure 10-43).

2. Adjust the Size setting as desired.

3. Click Preview to see how your setting will affect your bitmap. Click OK to apply the effect and to return to the drawing window.

Draw calculates the colors of the Crystallize effect based upon the colors in the bitmap. This effect can create dramatic results when applied to high-contrast bitmaps or to those that contain vibrant colors.

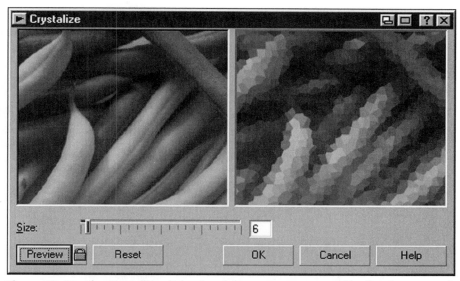

Figure 10-43: The Crystallize dialog box lets you create a crystallized or fragmented pattern from a selected bitmap.

Applying Fabric effects

The Fabric effect enhances bitmap images by giving them the appearance of textile patterns. Draw lets you specify the appearance of the pattern by choosing the type, size, and brightness of the effect. You can also rotate the pattern and choose the percentage of the original bitmap that you want affected by adjusting the Complete setting. These styles are available:

✦ Needlepoint

✦ Rug Hooking

✦ Quilt

✦ Strings

✦ Ribbons

✦ Tissue Collage

To apply the Fabric effect to a selected bitmap:

1. Select Fabric from the Creative menu to display the Fabric dialog box (see Figure 10-44).

2. Choose a Style from the drop-down list box and adjust the size of the objects. The Size setting specifies the number of pixels in the diameter of each object.

3. Adjust the Complete, Brightness, and Rotation settings as desired.

4. Click Preview to see how your settings will affect your bitmap. Click OK to apply the effect and to return to the drawing window.

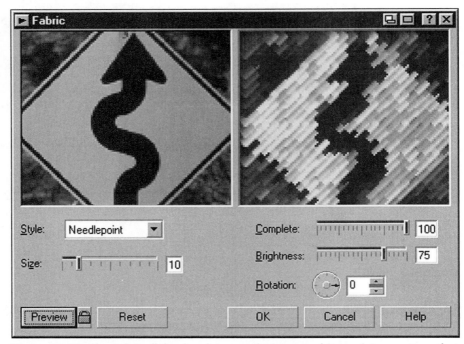

Figure 10-44: The Fabric dialog box lets you change your bitmap into a pattern that has a textile appearance.

The textile patterns you create using the Fabric effects filter are useful for creating quick backgrounds for use on the Web. Draw calculates the effect using the colors contained in the original bitmap plus a black background as the base color. The results can either be subtle or dramatic, depending on whether you apply the effect to a low- or high-contrast image, respectively.

Applying Frame effects

The Frame filter lets you frame your bitmap image. Draw provides a variety of preset images from which to choose. Additionally, you can modify an existing frame or create a new one from another bitmap image and save it as a preset. Table 10-1 lists the modifications that you can make to a frame.

Table 10-1
Frame Modifications

Control	Adjusts
Color swatch	Click this swatch to select a color for your frame from the color palette.
Eyedropper	Click the Eyedropper and then a location on the original image to pick up a color for your frame.
Opacity	Adjusts the opacity of your frame. Lower settings create a more transparent frame; higher settings create a more solid frame.
Blur/Feather	Adjusts the opacity at the edges of the frame in pixels. The amount of feathering increases proportionate to the value you specify for this setting.
Blend	You can choose Normal, Add, or Multiply. Normal places the selected color on top of the existing bitmap. Add analyzes the colors in the bitmap and adds the values of the selected color to create the frame. The color may vary from one location on the frame to another. Multiply analyzes the colors in the bitmap and multiplies the values by those of the selected color, and then divides the resulting value by 255. This generally darkens the bitmap in the affected areas. When applied over white areas, however, the color remains unchanged. If you select black as your frame color, the result is always black, regardless of the color of the bitmap beneath it.
Horizontal Scale	Adjusts the percentage of the total width of the bitmap that will be affected by the filter.
Vertical Scale	Adjusts the percentage of the total height of the bitmap that will be affected by the filter.
Rotate	Rotates the frame by the value you specify.
Flip	You can flip the frame horizontally and/or vertically.
Align	Lets you specify the center of the effect by clicking on the original image.
Re-center	Returns the center of the effect to the default location of the center of the original bitmap.

To apply the Frame effect to a selected bitmap:

1. Select Frame from the Creative menu to display the Frame dialog box (see Figure 10-45).

2. Click the Select tab and choose a preset frame from the selection window. Alternatively, click the Load button to the right of the selected file to display the Load Frame Shape File dialog box. Choose the file you want to use as a frame and click Open to return to the Frame filter dialog box. The file you selected appears in the frame list, and a preview appears in the preview window.

3. If you want to modify the frame, click the Modify tab and use Table 10-1 as a guide to adjusting the settings.

4. Click Preview to see how your settings will affect your bitmap. Click OK to apply the effect and to return to the drawing window.

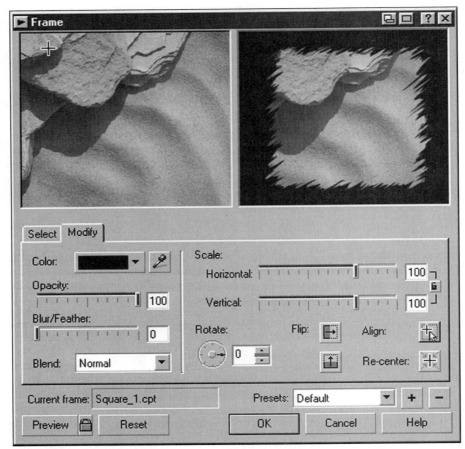

Figure 10-45: The Frame dialog box lets you change your bitmap into a pattern of common shapes.

You can modify an existing frame by adjusting the settings on the Modify tab. Click the Add Preset button if you want to save the changes for future use, and enter a name for the frame in the Save As dialog box. For best results, choose a file that contains sections of white when you use an existing bitmap for your custom frame. White areas appear transparent to the filter so that your original bitmap is visible.

Tip

When customizing and saving frames, give the frame a unique name to prevent overwriting an existing frame. As with all custom files, you should make a backup copy of the file in another location so that you won't lose the frame if you need to reinstall Draw.

Applying Glass Block effects

The Glass Block effect gives an image the appearance of being viewed through thick glass blocks. The results can be subtle or dramatic, depending upon the settings you specify. You specify the height and width of the blocks. Higher settings create a refracted appearance, as if the bitmap were being viewed through a prism. Lower settings give the bitmap a pixelated appearance.

To apply the Glass Block effect to a selected bitmap:

1. Select Glass Block from the Creative menu to display the Glass Block dialog box (see Figure 10-46).

2. Adjust the Block Height and Block Width settings to specify the dimensions of the blocks.

3. Click Preview to see how your settings will affect your bitmap. Click OK to apply the effect and to return to the drawing window.

Figure 10-46: The Glass Block dialog box lets you specify the intensity of prismatic effects.

The Glass Block effect divides a bitmap into tiles or a grid. Although there is a small amount of repetition on the edges of the tiles, the overall image isn't repeated. The amount of distortion increases as the number of tiles increases.

Applying Kid's Play effects

The Kid's Play effect transforms a bitmap image into whimsical shapes. You can specify the type and size of the shape. By adjusting how much of your image is included in the final effect using the Complete setting, you can further enhance the bitmap. You can also specify brightness and rotation settings to further customize the effect. Draw includes these Kid's Play effects:

✦ Lite Pegs

✦ Building Blocks

✦ Finger Paint

✦ Paint By Numbers

To apply the Kid's Play effect to a selected bitmap:

1. Select Kid's Play from the Creative menu to display the Kid's Play dialog box (see Figure 10-47).

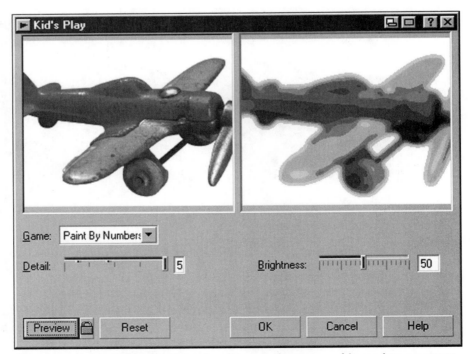

Figure 10-47: The Kid's Play dialog box lets you change your bitmap into a pattern that has a playful appearance.

2. Choose a Game from the drop-down list box and adjust the settings. The Detail setting specifies the number of pixels in diameter of each object.

3. Adjust the Brightness setting as desired.

4. Click Preview to see how your settings will affect your bitmap. Click OK to apply the effect and to return to the drawing window.

The playful nature of the patterns created with the Kid's Play filters make them ideal for creating patterns and custom fills for text and banners on a child-oriented Web page. You might also want to consider using muted tones such as grays and tans with the Building Block filter to create a *techno*-type background for a Web page.

Note

The Paint By Numbers effect varies a bit from the other filters in the Kid's Play group in that you can only specify the brightness and the amount of detail that you want included in the final image.

Applying Mosaic effects

The Mosaic effect uses the colors in your bitmap to fragment the image into pieces similar to ceramic tile. You can choose the size of the mosaic tiles to use, as well as the background color that serves as the *grout* between the tiles. If you enable the Vignette option, your image is framed by the background color you chose.

To apply the Mosaic effect to a selected bitmap:

1. Select Mosaic from the Creative menu to display the Mosaic dialog box (see Figure 10-48).

2. Adjust the size to specify the diameter of the tiles.

3. Click Preview to see how your settings will affect your bitmap. Click OK to apply the effect and to return to the drawing window.

The Mosaic effect adds interest to bitmaps. By adjusting the size of the tiles, you can specify how much detail is retained in the final image. The Vignette option lets you blend the bitmap with background colors while calling attention to a section of the bitmap.

Applying Particles effects

The Particles effect lets you add bubbles or stars to a bitmap image. You can choose the size of the individual particles, as well as specify the density of the particles. You can further enhance the bitmap by specifying the coloration, transparency, and rotation of the particles. Low coloration values yield white particles, whereas high coloration values incorporate more color.

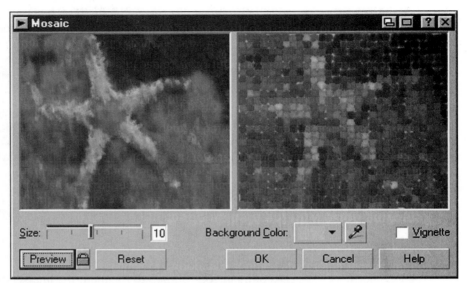

Figure 10-48: The Mosaic dialog box lets you specify the settings for creating an image with a tiled appearance.

To add Particle effects to a selected bitmap:

1. Select Particle from the Creative menu to display the Particles dialog box (see Figure 10-49).

2. Choose either Stars or Bubbles as the style of particles to use.

3. Adjust the values to specify size, density, coloration, transparency, and rotation of the particles.

4. Click Preview to see how your settings will affect your bitmap. Click OK to apply the effect and to return to the drawing window.

When you adjust the rotation setting, you change the direction of the reflective light on the particles. Using this setting, you can add subtle lighting effects to a bitmap that has an otherwise flat appearance.

Applying Scatter effects

The Scatter effect distorts images by letting you scatter the pixels horizontally and vertically. You can specify a distortion between 0 and 100 pixels. The settings roughly correlate to the distance in pixels that Draw uses to shift the colors. Lower settings retain much of the details of the original bitmap, whereas higher settings create more distortion.

Desert Dusk

One of my favorite drawing subjects is the desert. The primitive beauty and vivid spectrum of colors capture my imagination and remind me of a living watercolor painting. Reproducing the colors and textures of a desert vista is also a challenge. I employed the Eraser and the Interactive Fountain Fill tools to create the variety in the butte shown in the image, *Desert Dusk*.

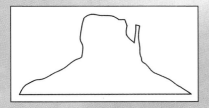

I started by drawing the outline of each butte using the Beziér Pencil tool. One butte I filled with a solid color, and the second butte I filled with a simple fountain fill. I wanted one butte to be prominent and display the riot of colors at dusk. The single outline of the butte didn't allow me to control the fill to achieve the effect I wanted.

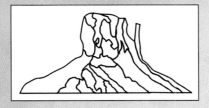

Draw provides a variety of approaches to dividing a single object into multiple objects. I chose the Eraser tool because it allowed me to quickly draw rough irregular lines, carving the butte into pieces. I didn't want to leave wide gaps between the objects, so I set the eraser width on the Property bar to 0.001 inches.

Once I'd drawn all my divisions, I applied the Break Apart command to allow the pieces to behave independently of one another. Using the Interactive Fill tool, I applied a fountain fill to each of the pieces, adjusting the color and the fill mode from one piece to the next. I used a circular fountain fill for most of the objects, with colors selected from Draw's default palette.

The resulting pieces were grouped and positioned in the image.

Castle

Castle is an image revisited. When I first created *Castle* in the stone
and chisel days of Draw, it was done in grayscale on a 386 computer
that fairly groaned under the weight of this large file. The image contains
4867 objects. Of those objects, 3849 are the stone blocks on the castle.
Each of the stone blocks was separately drawn, not copied. Those
numbers are nothing by today's standards, but back then that meant a
lot of waiting. While I waited for the screen to slowly refresh after every
action, I thought a great deal about Draw. "If Draw could only. . . ."

I wanted speed, texture, rich color, and perspective drop shadows back
then. Draw 9 allowed me to add the textures and drop shadows shown in
the image; here's how.

✦ Originally the castle rose out of the water with no apparent land beneath it. To get the effect I wanted, I added a freeform object with the Beziér tool, placing the object beneath the castle and applying a texture fill.

✦ I wanted to apply a shadow that darkened the water around the land without darkening the background. To achieve this I needed to use a perspective fill, so that I could closely control the direction of the shadow. The problem with this is that I either could darken the water to the right or to the left.

✦ The solution was to create two shadows, using the Interactive Shadow tool. Because you can only apply one shadow to an object, I duplicated the land object and superimposed the shadows so that one resided directly below the other.

Woman in Blue

Capturing a moment in time is a difficult task for an illustration program
such as Draw 9. Generally, this type of
image is either photographic or created
in a bitmap program, such as Photo-
Paint. *Woman in Blue* was created in an
effort to capture a personal moment
that is the essence of women. My
heartfelt thanks go to one of my best
friends, Debra Norris, for providing the
inspiration for this drawing.

The draped blue silk lends softness to
the drawing to complete the image. The
folds in the silk were created using the
Interactive Fill tool to modify one of
Draw 9's texture fills. After selecting
one of the objects to receive the draped
silk, I selected the texture fill icon from
the Fill tool flyout menu. The fill was
Texture #8890, Fold of Silk, from the
Samples 7 library of texture fills. I
accepted all the default settings for
the fill, and then clicked OK to apply
the fill.

With the object still selected, I clicked the
Interactive Fill tool to select it and to
display the adjustment handles for the fill.
By dragging the adjustment handles, I
turned, skewed, scaled, and positioned
the fill to create the illusions of soft folds
in the object.

Pour Toujours

Pour Toujours is reminiscent of a rainy day in spring with a single rosebud appearing through the window. Although the image is fairly complex because it uses a variety of Draw's special effects, it also illustrates how to get the most from the simplest of objects. The lacy curtains were created using a tiled symbol from one of Draw's symbol libraries.

After selecting a symbol from one of the libraries, I selected the tiling option and specified three columns and eight rows as the number of repetitions. I grouped the resulting 24 symbols so that the Envelope effect would be applied to the group rather than to each individual symbol.

Using the Interactive Envelope tool, I selected Unconstrained mode to edit the envelope. Once the curtain was the shape shown here, I placed it in front of the rest of the objects and set the outline to white.

Album

Album was created to illustrate one way of combining vector graphics and bitmap photo images. Whether you are creating a Web page or outputting the results to a printer, using Draw to create a layout for your photos provides the opportunity to truly show off your images.

✦ The first step to creating the layout is to scan your photos and to perform any corrections to the image. Both of the photos used in this image were very old and showed signs of damage and fading. They were also black-and-white photos. After scanning the images, I applied Duotone effects to them to give them a little more life.

✦ Then I started Draw, created the rectangles for the background, and filled them with a texture fill. I used Utah Stone #7792. Both background rectangles use the same fill. The large rectangle was darkened by specifying −10 percent in the Texture Fill dialog box. Similarly, I lightened the small rectangle by specifying 10 percent brightness.

✦ Then I added two smaller rectangles to frame one of the images, and two ellipses to frame the other image. The larger framing rectangle and ellipse are 0.25 inches larger than the two smaller frames.

✦ Selecting both small framing objects and the large background rectangle, I used the Combine command to create a mask with two holes. Then I selected the large framing objects and the small background rectangle, and repeated the Combine command. The masks allow the bitmap images to show through the holes. I used the Order commands to stack the images with the bitmaps below the resulting objects.

✦ I duplicated and offset the text slightly to create a title for the image. The lower string of text is filled with black, and the upper string of text is filled with the goldplate preset fountain fill.

✦ I then created the gold border using two new rectangles, one slightly larger than the other. Like the frames, they were combined to create a thin border object and filled with gold to match the text.

Ride in Time

Ride in Time steps back to the era of coal-fueled trains making their lonely trek across the countryside and rivers. In those days, their whistles could be heard and their smoke seen for miles, as almost a herald of the bonding between large cities and small rural towns. Capturing the essence of the train represented some challenges for me as a computer artist. The softness of smoke is very difficult to create in a vector package, which by its nature lends itself to hard-edged objects. The smoke is easier to create when you combine the power of Draw's blend effects and a trick for softening the edges of an object.

The smoke object is created using four freeform objects that have been stacked and offset. The top object contains a texture fill that incorporates the colors contained in the final blend object. This object was not included in the compound blend. It only overlaps the blend group.

The trick to softening the edge of the smoke comes from the color of the bottom object in the blend group. Its shape is identical to the object directly above it, but it has been filled with the same color as the sky and offset to the left. As the offset and number of steps increase, the amount of softness also increases.

The remaining three objects were blended together using the Interactive Blend tool. I used the default setting of 20 steps between each pair of objects. The offset and steps were enough to soften the edge and give the illusion of the smoke blending into the sky while allowing it to retain its identity as a distinct object.

Vanity

The inimitable talent of Stefanie Rowland is showcased in *Vanity*. Stefanie combines a scanned photo image with Draw's Lens effects to create the reflection of the woman in the mirror. Here's how she did it.

◆ Stefanie first worked on the mirror by filling a rectangle with a fountain fill, using contrast and highlights to give the fill a reflective appearance.

◆ The photo was scanned and imported into Draw. She created an outline of the body and space inside the elbows. Using Draw's PowerClip feature, Stefanie placed the bitmap inside the outline of the body, and trimmed the resulting object with the elbow space outlines she created.

◆ The PowerClip containing the image of the woman was placed on the mirror.

◆ The mirror object was copied and placed on top of the resulting image, and a Transparency Lens set at 37 percent was applied to the duplicate mirror.

Eyelevel

Eyelevel presents a surreal perspective of Arizona's parched desert world. It combines bitmap effects with a variety of Draw's vector effects to create the final image. The shiny, domed appearance of the head itself was created using Contour effects.

Starting with a circle, I used the Shape tool to edit the shape to a half circle, and then filled the resulting object with a cyan-to-magenta circular fountain fill.

Selecting the Interactive Contour tool, I used the settings on the Property bar to create a contour to the center of the object.

I inverted the colors to go from magenta to cyan. This gave the resulting object a shiny and rounded 3D appearance.

Old Town

I love to draw architecture, especially old buildings and houses. They have character and impart a nostalgic feeling. Architectural drawings also present a challenge to most people. The keys to creating an accurate rendering of a building are to maintain the perspective and lighting effects. *Old Town* captures the imperfect rugged feeling of adobe and clapboard buildings, while maintaining the perspective that gives the image a sense of reality

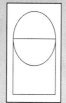

The arches in this image were the pivotal objects around which the rest of the drawing was created. I started with an ellipse and a rectangle, using the Weld command to combine the two into a single object.

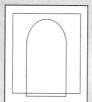

The next step was to use the object to cut the arches out of a rectangle using the Trim command, and to overlap the objects slightly.

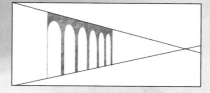

I selected Surface #7767 to fill the arch wall. I changed the colors in the Texture dialog box to a medium gray and pale pink to create the adobe color. I used the guidelines to create a vanishing point (shown by solid lines in this example), and applied the Perspective command to set the wall at an angle.

The Interactive Extrusion tool was used to give the arch wall a 3D appearance. I used the Back Parallel setting, and chose to fill the extrusion with the object fill.

The resulting object needed lighting for the archways to be visible. Using a single light set at 100 percent intensity, I placed the light to create the shadow effects of the archways.

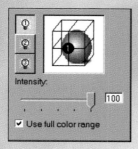

In the Balance

Probably one of the toughest objects to draw is glass. The trick is to create sharp contrasts of light and dark. Because glass refracts and reflects light, a glass object may appear white or dark, rather than transparent, in areas. Draw's Transparency Lens makes the task of letting things show through glass images easier. *In the Balance* uses Draw's Transparency Lens and Extrusion effects to create the sphere balanced on a fingertip.

The imported map of the globe provided the beginning for the image.

The idea was to make the map appear to be a raised portion of the glass, rather than as if it was inside the glass. Selecting the Interactive Extrusion tool, I chose the small back setting on the Property bar, and extruded the map slightly by clicking and dragging on the map.

I separated the extrusion because I wanted to make the original map surface somewhat transparent, yet keep the extrusion opaque. Then the extrusion was filled with a single lighting source in mind. I wanted the light to appear to come from the lower left. I filled parts where the light would be the most intense with white, while those parts that would receive very little light I filled with varying shades of blue.

I filled the original map surface with a white-to-cyan fountain fill, and applied a 50 percent Transparency Lens. The map and extrusion were grouped so they could be moved as one object later.

The Ellipse and Beziér tools were used to create the sphere. Two identical circles were superimposed, and then one was flattened to give the appearance of the glass being thicker at the top and bottom. Selecting the unmodified circle I copied it to the clipboard for later use, and then combined the two ellipse shapes. I filled the object with a white-to-cyan fountain fill and applied a 50 percent Transparency Lens. Using the Beziér tool, I drew the highlight at the lower left of the sphere and applied a 50 percent white transparency lens.

The map was centered over the sphere, and I pasted the circle I'd placed on the clipboard back into the drawing. I applied an 80 percent white Transparency Lens to the pasted circle, and grouped all of the objects so that they could be positioned in the final image.

Elk

The difference between a flat, uninteresting drawing and one that appears more realistic is the interplay of light and shadow. *Elk* was created using two custom wood-grain fills to create the contrast that forms the shape of the elk head.

To finish the drawing, I added a lighting effect that highlighted a portion of the plaque. Draw doesn't have a light command, but you can create the illusion of light using the Interactive Transparency tool.

To create the effect, I duplicated the background ellipse, filled it with white, and superimposed it on top of the rest of the objects. Although you can apply a transparency to a group of objects, it causes the resulting image to be complex and can cause printing problems, because it applies the transparency to each of the individual objects. It's preferable to apply the transparency to a single object that covers all the objects you want affected.

Once the white ellipse was in place, I selected the Interactive Transparency tool, and chose Square as the fill mode. I clicked the white object and dragged up and to the right to create a small white opaque area over the rest of the objects.

This finished image has a starburst lighting effect in the upper right of the plaque. By adjusting the size of the transparency area and the median slider, you can specify how much opaque light appears in the image.

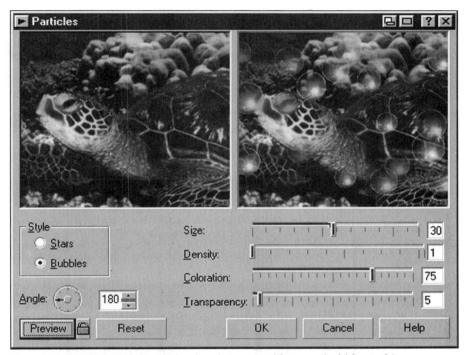

Figure 10-49: The Particles dialog box lets you add star or bubbles to bitmap images.

To apply the Scatter effect to a selected bitmap:

1. Select Scatter from the Creative menu to display the Scatter dialog box (see Figure 10-50).

2. Adjust the Horizontal and Vertical sliders to adjust the amount of distortion you want in the final effect. The Horizontal slider shifts the pixels right and left; the Vertical slider shifts the pixels up and down. Enable the Symmetrical option, by clicking the padlock, to make the horizontal and vertical values identical.

3. Click Preview to see how your settings will affect your bitmap. Click OK to apply the effect and to return to the drawing window.

Caution

The Scatter effect can be used to give bitmap images a soft, diffused effect by setting the horizontal and vertical settings to low values. High values produce a significant amount of distortion, and details are lost.

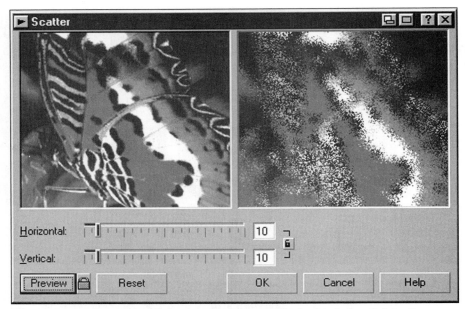

Figure 10-50: The Scatter dialog box lets you specify the intensity of distortion you want in your final image.

When using scatter effects, remember that Draw increases the dimensions of the bitmap to include the total effect. The amount of distortion determines the difference in size between the original and enhanced bitmap. Use the Shape tool to crop the bitmap or to resample the bitmap if you need to reduce its physical size.

Applying Smoked Glass effects

The Smoked Glass effect lets you give your bitmaps the appearance of being viewed through smoked or colored glass. You can specify the amount of the tint and blurring of the original image.

To apply the Smoked Glass effect to a selected bitmap:

1. Select Smoked Glass from the Creative menu to display the Smoked Glass dialog box (see Figure 10-51).

2. Move the Tint and Blurring sliders to adjust the intensity of the effect.

3. Click Preview to see how your settings will affect your bitmap. Click OK to apply the effect and to return to the drawing window.

The Smoked Glass effect is useful for adding the appearance of a color overlay to a bitmap. As you increase the tint amount, the selected color becomes more opaque, obscuring more of your bitmap.

Figure 10-51: The Smoked Glass dialog box lets you specify the intensity of the color overlay effect.

Applying Stained Glass effects

The Stained Glass effect gives your images the appearance of stained glass. The pieces are bordered by edges that resemble the solder between stained glass pieces. You can specify the color and thickness of the edges. The Light Intensity value determines how much light appears to show through the effect.

To apply the Stained Glass effect to a selected bitmap:

1. Select Stained Glass from the Creative menu to display the Stained Glass dialog box (see Figure 10-52).

2. Adjust the Size to specify the diameter of segments, and specify the Light Intensity value. Enable 3D Lighting to add a 3D effect to your image.

3. Choose a color for the solder. By default, Draw uses black, but you can select another color from the palette or use the Eyedropper to pick up a color from your original bitmap.

4. Click Preview to see how your settings will affect your bitmap. Click OK to apply the effect and to return to the drawing window.

The Stained Glass filter is best suited for bitmaps that contain vivid colors and a large degree of contrast. The amount of distortion this filter creates makes it unsuitable if your bitmap contains a large amount of detail that you want to retain.

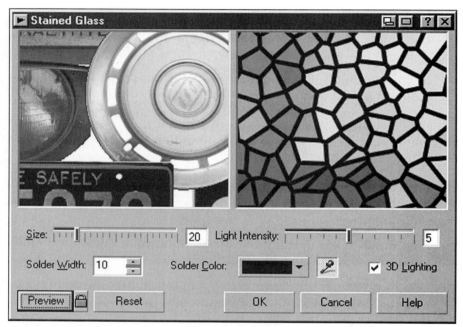

Figure 10-52: The Stained Glass dialog box lets you add a stained glass effect to your bitmap image.

Applying Vignette effects

Vignette creates an oval frame around your bitmap, masking the outer edges of the bitmap in the process. You specify the size, color, and amount of fading to include in the frame. Vignette effects let you give your image an antique or ethereal quality.

To apply the Vignette effect to a selected bitmap:

1. Select Vignette from the Creative menu to display the Vignette dialog box (see Figure 10-53).

2. Choose a color for the frame. You can choose black, white, or specify another color.

3. Adjust the Offset slider to specify the size of the frame. Higher values decrease the size; lower values increase the size.

4. Adjust the Fade slider to specify the transition between the frame and the rest of the bitmap. Higher values increase the softening effect, causing the frame to fade gradually into the bitmap. Lower values produce a harder edge between the frame and the bitmap.

5. Click Preview to see how your settings will affect your bitmap. Click OK to apply the effect and to return to the drawing window.

Figure 10-53: The Vignette dialog box lets you specify the parameters for framing your bitmap image.

The Vignette effect is useful when your bitmap contains a central focal point, such as a portrait. It lets you block out unwanted portions of the background, while drawing attention to the point of interest in the image.

Tip | Before applying Vignette effects to a bitmap, crop the bitmap to center the focal point of the image. This increases the balance of the image, and results in a more pleasing appearance.

Applying Vortex effects

The Vortex filter creates a swirled effect in your bitmap. By default, Draw calculates the effect around the center of the bitmap, but you can specify a new center to alter the appearance of the final image. You adjust the settings to determine the size of the stroke and the direction of the distortion for the pixels central to and peripheral to the specified center. In addition to controlling the intensity of the effect, you can choose one of these distortion styles:

✦ Brushed

✦ Layered

✦ Thick

✦ Thin

To apply the Vortex effect to a selected bitmap:

1. Select Vortex from the Creative menu to display the Vortex dialog box (see Figure 10-54).

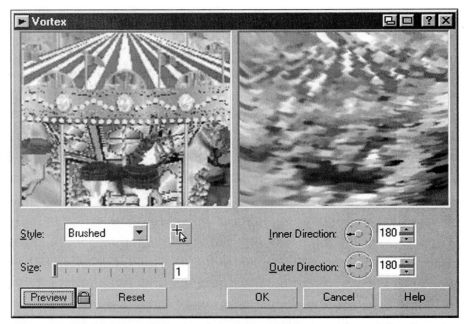

Figure 10-54: The Vortex dialog box lets you specify the intensity and direction of the swirled distortion in your final image.

2. Choose a Style from the drop-down list box. Enable the Set Center option if desired and click on the original bitmap to specify the center of the effect.

3. Adjust the Inner Direction and Outer Direction settings to create the effect you want to use.

4. Click Preview to see how your settings will affect your bitmap. Click OK to apply the effect and to return to the drawing window.

The Vortex effect can be used to give your bitmap a feeling of motion by blurring the details in a direction you specify. The various styles help you determine the intensity of the effect and the amount of distortion in the final image. The effect is intensified if your bitmap contains a large quantity of detail.

Applying Weather effects

The Weather effect applies the appearance of weather conditions to a bitmap image. Each effect is unique in the type of distortion it adds to your bitmap. You can specify the intensity of the effect by adjusting the Strength and Size controls. The weather conditions are:

✦ Snow

✦ Rain

✦ Fog

To apply the Weather effect to a selected bitmap:

1. Select Weather from the Creative menu to display the Weather dialog box (see Figure 10-55).

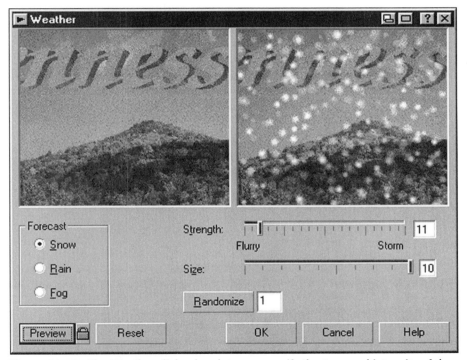

Figure 10-55: The Weather dialog box lets you specify the type and intensity of the Weather effect on your bitmap.

2. Choose a type of weather condition for the effect.

3. Adjust the Size and Strength sliders to specify the intensity of the effect. Enabling the Randomize option lets you add variety to the effect.

4. Click Preview to see how your settings will affect your bitmap. Click OK to apply the effect and to return to the drawing window.

The Snow option adds the appearance of white snowflakes to your image. You can use this effect to add drama to a winter scene or a surreal effect to images that depict springtime. Rain adds a white, streaked effect to your bitmap that can vary from light drizzle to a virtual downpour. The Fog effect adds a light white haze to an image or gives it the appearance of being behind a cloud. While all three weather conditions can nearly completely obscure your bitmap, they are best suited for applying subtle effects to an image.

Using the Distort effects

Draw's capability of distorting bitmap images is useful for a variety of applications. For example, you can use Draw's distortion filters to create custom fills, backgrounds, or just to put a new twist on a common theme. Each of Draw's distortion filters transforms your bitmaps without adding light or shadows that create a feeling of depth. The Distort effects are

- ✦ Blocks
- ✦ Displace
- ✦ Offset
- ✦ Pixelate
- ✦ Ripple
- ✦ Swirl
- ✦ Tile
- ✦ Wet Paint
- ✦ Whirlpool
- ✦ Wind

Applying Blocks effects

The Blocks effect breaks an image into chunks. You specify the dimensions of the individual pieces and the amount of offset you want to use. Choosing one of the following options from the Undefined Areas list box lets you control the appearance of any empty spaces created by the effect

- ✦ **Original Image:** Fills the empty space with the original image
- ✦ **Inverse Image:** Fills the empty space with a color inverse of the original image
- ✦ **Black:** Fills the empty space with black
- ✦ **White:** Fills the empty space with white
- ✦ **Other:** Fills the empty space with a color you choose from the color picker

To apply the Blocks effect to a selected bitmap:

1. Select Blocks from the Distort menu to display the Blocks dialog box (see Figure 10-56).

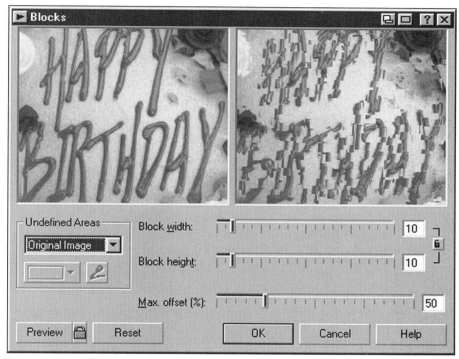

Figure 10-56: The Blocks dialog box lets you specify the size, offset value, and the background color of the distortion.

2. Choose a background option from the Undefined Areas list box. You can use the Eyedropper tool to pick up a color from the original bitmap image.

3. Adjust the settings to specify the width and height of the individual pieces.

4. Specify the maximum amount of offset between the pieces.

5. Click Preview to see how your settings will affect your bitmap. Click OK to apply the effect and to return to the drawing window.

The value you specify for the maximum offset determines the amount of distortion in the final image. Higher values create larger amounts of distortion, while lower values retain much of the appearance of the original bitmap. Like many of the bitmap filters, the Blocks effect is useful for adding interest to your documents.

Applying Displace effects

The Displace filter uses two images to create distortion in your bitmap: the selected bitmap in your document and a second bitmap that you load in the Displace dialog box. Draw analyzes the color values of a second image to create a displacement map. A displacement map is simply a pattern created by the variations of color in an image. After creating the displacement map, Draw uses the information to shift the pixels in your original bitmap to match the pattern. You can adjust the amount of distortion by adjusting the horizontal and vertical scaling. Additionally, you can choose Tile, which causes the distortion pattern to repeat throughout the image, or you can choose Stretch to Fit, which distributes the distortion across the entire bitmap.

The setting you specify in the Undefined Areas section determines how Draw treats areas that are left empty by the distortion. The Repeat Edges option stretches the edges of the image to fill in any empty areas. The Wrap Around option fills the empty areas, like a label wraps around a bottle or can, with the opposite side of the image.

To apply the Displace effect to a selected bitmap:

1. Select Displace from the Distort menu to display the Displace dialog box (see Figure 10-57).

2. Select a file from the file selection area to use as a displacement map. If you don't see the image you want to use in the drop-down list box, click the Load button to choose another image.

3. Chose either Tile or Stretch to Fit as a Scale Mode.

4. Adjust the Horizontal and Vertical scaling to specify the amount of distortion to apply to your image.

5. Click Preview to see how your settings will affect your bitmap. Click OK to apply the effect and to return to the drawing window.

The Displace effect is similar to the Bump Map effect available in bitmap imaging and 3D programs. Unlike bump maps, which add light and shadowing to give an image a 3D textured effect, the Displace filter retains the colors of the original bitmap. This is useful when you need to maintain a consistent color theme in your documents.

Applying Offset effects

The Offset filter shifts the bitmap within the perimeter boundary of the bitmap size. You can specify the color to use in the empty border, as well as in the empty space that was created when the bitmap shifted.

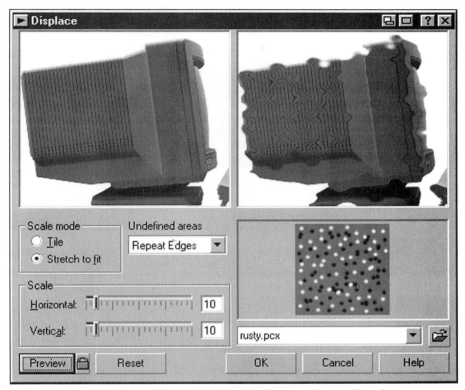

Figure 10-57: The Displace dialog box lets you distort an image based upon a pattern created from another image.

To apply an offset to a selected bitmap:

1. Select the Offset filter from the Distort menu to display the Offset dialog box (see Figure 10-58).

2. Move the horizontal and vertical sliders to specify the amount of the offset. Enable Shift value as % of dimensions if you want to adjust the values using percentages versus actual measurements. Click the Dual View button if you want to see a representation of both the original bitmap and a view that displays the changes.

3. Choose the method you want to use to fill the empty spaces. You can choose Wrap Around or Repeat Edges, or you can choose a color using the Color Picker.

4. Click Preview if you want to see the effect your settings have created. Click OK to apply the effect and to return to the drawing window.

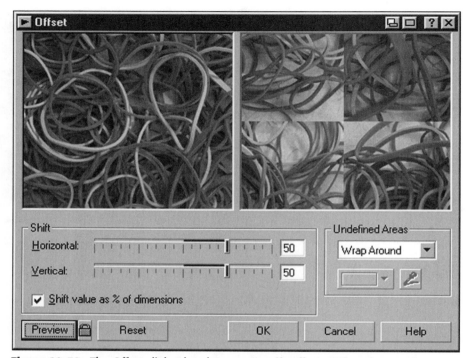

Figure 10-58: The Offset dialog box lets you specify offset settings for your image.

The Offset Edge command lets you create tiled effects using any bitmap. You determine the type of tile effect by selecting the method to use.

Applying Pixelate effects

Pixelate splits a bitmap image into square, rectangular, or circular cells. If you choose the square or rectangular options, the resulting image looks like an overenlarged bitmap. The radial option creates a circular mosaic appearance. You can also adjust the transparency of the effect. At lower settings, the pixelation appears ghosted and overlays the original image.

To apply the Pixelate effect to a selected bitmap:

1. Select the Pixelate filter from the Distort menu to display the Pixelate dialog box (see Figure 10-59).

2. Choose the type of pixelation to use, and adjust the dimension settings of the blocks. If you choose Square, the Height and Width settings are locked to identical values.

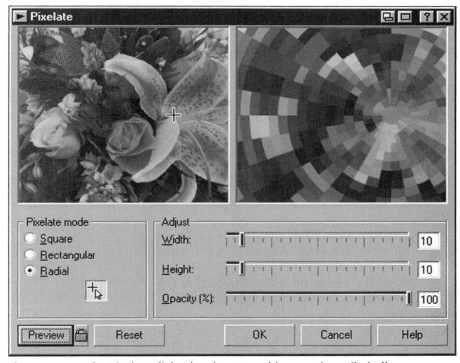

Figure 10-59: The Pixelate dialog box lets you add a mosaic or tiled effect to your bitmap images.

3. If you choose the radial option, you can specify the center of the effect by clicking the Set Center button and clicking the center location you want on the original image.

4. Adjust the amount of transparency. Higher settings are more opaque; lower settings are more transparent.

5. Click Preview to view the results of your settings. Click OK to apply the filter and to return to the drawing window.

You can use the Pixelate effect to give a bitmap the appearance of being viewed through beveled glass or glass blocks. The type of pixelation and the amount of transparency that you specify determine the muted effect.

Applying Ripple effects

The Ripple effect distorts an image by adding a wave. The strength of the first wave sets the warping of the image, while adding an additional perpendicular wave increases the distortion. By adjusting the Period, you can set the span of the wave. The Amplitude setting specifies the height of the wave.

To apply the Ripple effect:

1. Select the Ripple filter from the Distort menu to display the Ripple dialog box (see Figure 10-60).

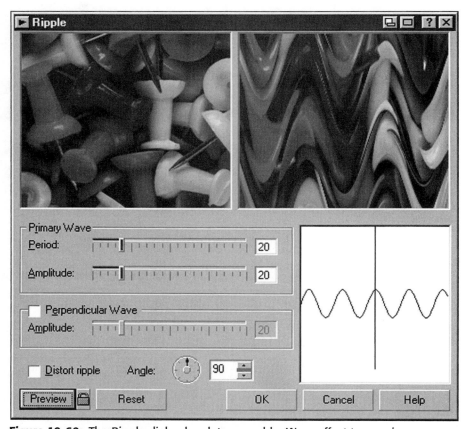

Figure 10-60: The Ripple dialog box lets you add a Wave effect to your image.

2. Adjust the Primary Wave values to specify the first wave. If you want a vertical wave as well as a horizontal wave, enable the Perpendicular Wave option and specify the amplitude of the perpendicular wave.

3. By default, Draw creates a smooth wave. If you want to distort the wave, enable the Distort Ripple option.

4. Specify the angle of the wave.

5. Click Preview to view the results of your settings. Click OK to apply the filter and to return to the drawing window.

The Ripple filter can be used to create both subtle and dramatic effects. As the span of the wave increases because of using higher Period values, the effect of the distortion is decreased. Similarly, lower Amplitude settings create more subtle changes.

Applying Swirl effects

Swirl effects distort your bitmap by blending the pixels in the direction and angle you specify. The resulting image spins around the center point of the bitmap in either a clockwise or counterclockwise direction. You specify the number of rotations you want to use. Lower settings create a spiraled swirl effect. At higher values, the image starts to break up, creating a swirling dust effect, using the colors in the bitmap.

To apply the Swirl effect to a selected bitmap:

1. Select Swirl from the Distort menu to display the Swirl dialog box (see Figure 10-61).

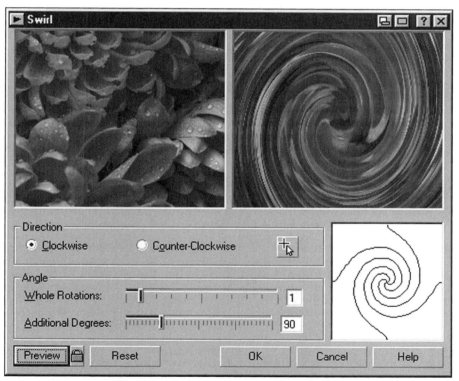

Figure 10-61: Using the Swirl dialog box, you can add spiraled effects to your bitmaps.

2. Choose Clockwise or Counter-Clockwise to specify the direction of the swirl.

3. Specify the number of rotations.

4. Adjust the Additional Degrees slider if you want to rotate the swirl by an additional portion of a full rotation. For example, if you specified a 180-degree additional angle, the bitmap would turn an additional half turn.

5. Click Preview to view the results of your settings. Click OK to apply the filter and to return to the drawing window.

The Swirl effects command is great for creating background images for documents and Web use. You can also use it to create custom bitmap fills for objects that you create in Draw. Consider combining this effect with color adjustment features to create faded and other effects.

Applying Tile effects

The Tile filter lets you create tiled images from your bitmap. You can specify the number of horizontal and vertical tiles you want in the final image. Draw repeats the image in each of the tiles.

To apply the Tile effect to a selected bitmap:

1. Select Tile from the Distort menu to display the Tile dialog box (see Figure 10-62).

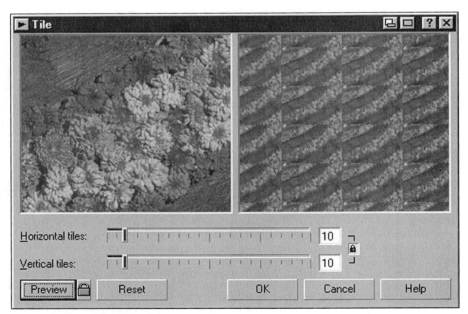

Figure 10-62: With the Tile dialog box, you can create tiles of your bitmaps.

2. Specify the number of Horizontal and Vertical Tiles you want in your final image.

3. Click Preview to view the results of your settings. Click OK to apply the filter and to return to the drawing window.

The Tile effect reproduces an image as a series of tiles and is especially useful for previewing tiled backgrounds for Web pages. Using this filter, you can check whether your background tiles have a seamless appearance.

Note

When you apply a bitmap filter to an image, Draw uses the entire bitmap to calculate the effect. Any cropping that you performed with the Shape tool is ignored. If you want Draw to consider only a portion of your bitmap, crop the image when you import the bitmap.

Applying Wet Paint effects

The Wet Paint filter creates a variety of effects, from a subtle, slick, wet paint appearance to an overbrushed or scrubbed paint appearance. You control the effect by specifying the angle and percentage of wetness.

To apply the Wet Paint effect:

1. Choose Wet Paint from the Distort menu to display the Wet Paint dialog box (see Figure 10-63).

2. Adjust the Percent slider to specify the size of the drips of paint.

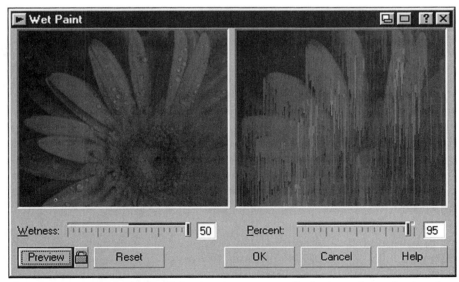

Figure 10-63: The Wet Paint dialog box lets you specify the intensity and color of the Wet Paint effect.

3. Adjust the Wetness slider to specify what colors appear to run. Positive values cause the lighter colors to run; negative values cause the darker colors to run.

4. Click Preview to view the effect of your settings. Click OK to complete the operation and to return to the drawing window.

The Wet Paint effect can be combined with halftone effects to *age* an image. Choose a halftone that creates a rough texture, and then apply slight Wet Paint effects to the image. The combination gives bitmaps an aged or antique appearance.

Applying Whirlpool effects

The Whirlpool effect creates a swirling pattern from your bitmap image. You can choose a preset whirlpool style or you can create custom whirlpool styles. You specify the Smear Length, Spacing, Twist, and Streak Detail of the Whirlpool effect. Use the following as a guideline:

✦ **Spacing:** Sets the distance in pixels between the swirls of the effect

✦ **Smear Length:** Specifies the length of the streaks

✦ **Streak Detail:** Specifies the amount of smearing

✦ **Twist:** Sets the whirl method

To apply the Whirlpool effect to a selected bitmap:

1. Select Whirlpool from the Distort menu to display the Whirlpool dialog box (see Figure 10-64).

2. Choose Style of Whirlpool effect to use from the drop-down list box.

3. Adjust the Spacing, Smear Length, Streak Detail, and Twist values to achieve the effect you want.

4. By default, Draw creates a smooth pattern when it creates the Whirlpool effect. If you want to distort the whirls, enable the Warp option.

5. Click Preview to view the results of your settings. Click OK to apply the filter and to return to the drawing window.

The Whirlpool effect is similar to the Swirl effect in that it creates a circular pattern from your bitmap. Unlike the Swirl effect, the Whirlpool effect creates a spiral similar to water going down a drain. Higher values make the fluid flow around the swirls like whirlpools; lower values make the fluid flow out of the whirls like fountains. You can save custom whirlpool styles for future use by clicking the Add (+) button and naming the style. To remove a style, select the style from the list box and click the Remove (−) button.

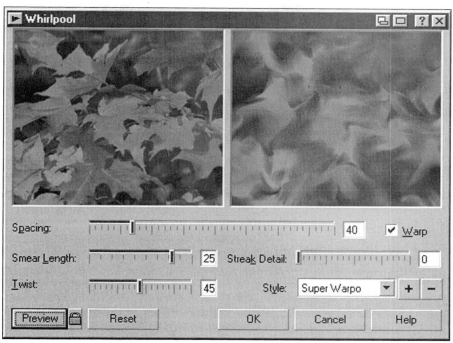

Figure 10-64: The Whirlpool dialog box lets you specify the type and intensity of the Whirlpool effect on your bitmap.

Applying Wind effects

The Wind effect creates a streaked effect and gives images a windswept appearance. You specify the amount of your bitmap that's affected by the filter by adjusting the Strength value. You can also control the opacity and angle of the effect.

To apply the Wind effect to a selected bitmap:

1. Choose Wind from the Distort effects menu to display the Wind dialog box (see Figure 10-65).

2. Adjust the Strength slider to specify the amount of your bitmap you want affected by the filter.

3. Specify the angle and opacity to use for the effect.

4. Click Preview to view the effect of your settings. Click OK to complete the operation and to return to the drawing window.

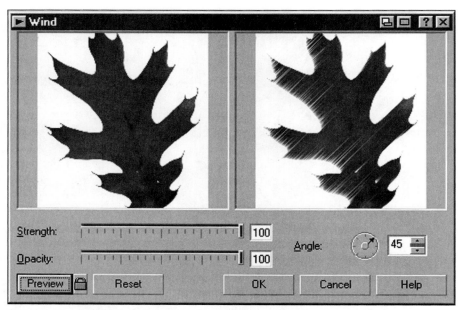

Figure 10-65: The Wind dialog box lets you give your bitmap a windswept appearance.

The Wind filter is useful for adding a grainy appearance in a specified direction. Applying the filter multiple times using varying angles simulates the weave of fabric or the grain in paper. Higher values produce visible distortion and blurring; lower values produce a more subtle effect.

Adding and removing noise

Noise effects can add interest to your images and correct flaws created by scanning or over-blending of colors. Draw provides these Noise effects:

✦ Add Noise

✦ Diffuse

✦ Dust and Scratch

✦ Maximum

✦ Median

✦ Minimum

✦ Remove Moiré

✦ Remove Noise

Adding noise

Adding noise to your bitmap can improve the appearance of an image that appears flat or too smooth. Noise creates the illusion of texture and can be used to add a grained look to objects that have a coarse appearance in real life. You can choose to add three types of Noise to your bitmaps: Gaussian, Spike, and Uniform. To apply Noise to a selected bitmap:

1. Select Add Noise from the Noise effects menu to display the Add Noise dialog box (see Figure 10-66).

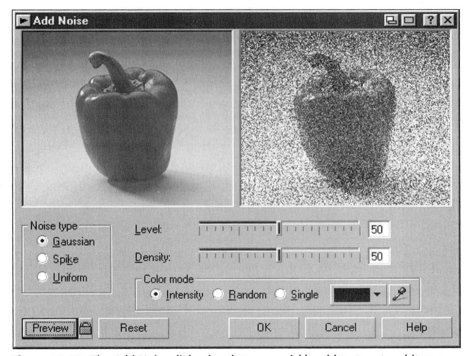

Figure 10-66: The Add Noise dialog box lets you quickly add texture to a bitmap.

2. Choose the type of Noise effect to add using this list as a guide:

   • **Gaussian:** Produces a more intense effect than Spike or Uniform Noise. Draw analyzes the colors in the bitmap and orders them based upon luminescence and the frequency with which the color occurs in the bitmap. The colors are then arrayed on a Gaussian curve to determine the distribution of color. While the colors of the noise are similar to those already in the image, Gaussian Noise adds high contrast to the bitmap.

- **Spike:** Uses a narrower curve than the Gaussian curve to add a smaller and lighter grain to your image.
- **Uniform:** Applies noise randomly to add an overall grainy appearance to your bitmap.

3. Adjust the Level slider to specify the range of colors to use as noise. Higher values increase the number of colors.

4. Adjust the Density slider to specify the number of noise pixels per inch to add. Higher values increase the amount of noise in your image.

5. Choose a color mode. Intensity adds the most noise of the three choices based upon the luminosity in the image. Random adds a variety of colored pixels. Single lets you choose a color. You can use the Eyedropper to pick up a color from the original image.

6. Click Preview to see how the settings will affect your bitmap. Click OK to complete the operation and to return to the drawing window.

Noise is especially effective with grayscale and 1-bit images. When applied to color images, the effect has a more psychedelic appearance and can distort the image to the point where you can't recognize the subject in the bitmap. Noise creates a granular effect that adds texture to a flat or overly blended bitmap.

Diffusing noise

The Diffuse effect removes noise by spreading out the pixels in an image to fill in blank spaces. This effect also smoothes and blurs your image.

To apply the Diffuse effect to a selected bitmap:

1. Choose Diffuse from the Noise effects menu to display the Diffuse dialog box (see Figure 10-67).

2. Adjust the Level slider to specify the intensity of the effect.

3. Click Preview to view the effect of your settings. Click OK to complete the operation and to return to the drawing window.

The Diffuse effect is useful when you need to repair minor flaws in a scanned image. Because the effect also blurs the image, it might not be suitable for severely flawed images.

Using Dust and Scratch effects

The Dust and Scratch effect reduces the amount of noise in an image. You specify the color threshold that Draw is to use to calculate the effect. Draw analyzes your image for marked color variations and uses the Radius setting to identify imperfections in your image. The imperfections are then blended with the surrounding pixels to reduce their visibility.

Figure 10-67: The Diffuse dialog box lets you specify the intensity of the effect.

To apply the Dust and Scratch effect to a selected bitmap:

 1. Choose Dust & Scratch from the Noise effects menu to display the Dust & Scratch dialog box (see Figure 10-68).

Figure 10-68: The Dust & Scratch dialog box lets you remove minor flaws such as dust from scanned images.

2. Adjust the Threshold slider to specify the number of color levels that Draw is to use in calculating the effect.

3. Set the Radius to specify the number of pixels to include in each sampling.

4. Click Preview to view the effect of your settings. Click OK to complete the operation and to return to the drawing window.

The Dust and Scratch filter is useful for eliminating flaws created during film processing or scanning. Generally, a setting of 1 to 3 pixels eliminates most of these flaws without obscuring the detail in your image.

Using Maximum effects

The Maximum effect removes noise by adjusting the color value of a pixel based on the maximum color values of its neighboring pixels. This effect causes a mild blurring or distortion if applied in large percentages, or if applied more than once to a bitmap.

To apply the Maximum effect to a selected bitmap:

1. Choose Maximum from the Noise effects menu to display the Maximum dialog box (see Figure 10-69).

2. Adjust the Percentage slider to specify the intensity of the effect.

Figure 10-69: The Maximum dialog box lets you remove noise and smooth images based upon the maximum difference in tonal values.

3. Specify the Radius you want Draw to use in each sample.

4. Click Preview to view the effect of your settings. Click OK to complete the operation and to return to the drawing window.

The Maximum filter is most effective when applied to images that contain few small details. When applied to images with a significant amount of small details, it frequently results in the distortion of the image because the small details are eliminated from the image. If you apply the filter to bitmaps with large areas that contain similar colors, the result is a smoother looking image with balanced tonal values.

Removing noise with the Median effect

The Median effect removes noise by averaging the color values of the pixels in an image. You specify the size of the sample that you want Draw to use when calculating the effect by adjusting the Radius value. The amount of blurring increases proportionately with the size of the sample.

To apply the Median effect to a selected bitmap:

1. Choose Median from the Noise effects menu to display the Median dialog box (see Figure 10-70).

2. Specify the Radius that you want Draw to use in each sample.

3. Click Preview to view the effect of your settings. Click OK to complete the operation and to return to the drawing window.

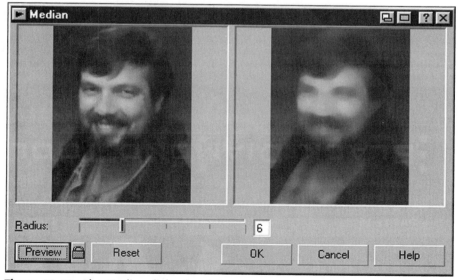

Figure 10-70: The Median dialog box lets you remove noise by averaging the tonal values in an image.

The Median effect blends the tonal values of the pixels in your image. This effect is a good choice if you want to dramatically soften an image. It makes your bitmap appear as if it were behind diffused glass.

Removing noise with the Minimum effect

The Minimum effect removes noise by darkening the pixels in an image. You specify the intensity of the effect by adjusting the Percentage slider. Higher values darken an image dramatically and reduce the tonal variations that define the details in your image.

To apply the Minimum effect to a selected bitmap:

1. Choose Minimum from the Noise effects menu to display the Minimum dialog box (see Figure 10-71).

2. Adjust the Percentage slider to specify the intensity of the effect.

3. Specify the Radius that you want Draw to use in each sample.

4. Click Preview to view the effect of your settings. Click OK to complete the operation and to return to the drawing window.

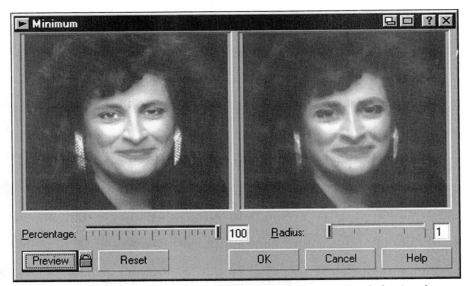

Figure 10-71: The Minimum dialog box lets you remove noise by darkening the pixels in your image.

The Minimum filter is useful when you want to remove noise from images that are too light or that are overexposed. You can lose a significant amount of detail if the original image is darker, or if you specify higher intensity values.

Removing Moiré patterns

Scanned photographs usually let you create high quality bitmap images with ease, because you are starting with an image that is a continuous tone or of photographic quality. But you can't always guarantee that you will have a photo original from which to scan. You may need to scan an image from a newspaper or magazine. The problem with scanning printed media is that the printing process that created the image used halftone screening. When you scan a halftone image it can create patterned noise, which is called *moiré*. The Remove Moiré effect lets you remove this type of patterned noise.

To apply the Remove Moiré effect from a selected bitmap:

1. Choose Remove Moiré from the Noise effects menu to display the Remove Moiré dialog box (see Figure 10-72).

2. Adjust the Amount slider to specify the intensity of the effect.

3. Choose either Better or Faster as the Quality and enter the Output resolution to use.

4. Click Preview to view the effect of your settings. Click OK to complete the operation and to return to the drawing window.

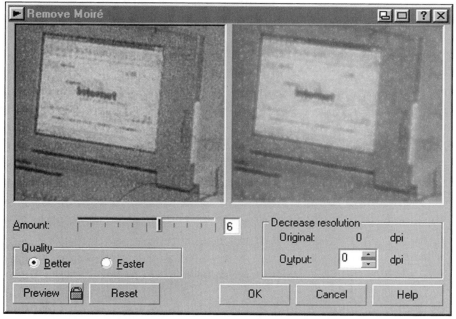

Figure 10-72: The Remove Moiré dialog box removes patterned noise created by scanning halftone images.

Tip   For best results, scan the original image using a resolution of 300 dpi and set the output resolution to 200 dpi in the Remove Moiré dialog box. The output dpi should be approximately two-thirds of the original dpi.

Applying the Remove Noise effect

Removing noise from a bitmap can reduce flaws and the speckled appearance that sometimes occurs when scanning images or making digital captures. This effect is controlled by the luminescence of your bitmap. Draw analyzes adjacent pixels and calculates an average. Pixels that exceed the threshold you specify are removed from the image.

To apply the Remove Noise effect to a selected bitmap:

1. Select Remove Noise from the Noise effects menu to display the Remove Noise dialog box (see Figure 10-73).

2. Enable Auto if you want Draw to calculate the effect based upon the average luminescence.

3. If you want to manually control the threshold, disable Auto and adjust the Threshold slider. Lower values increase the amount of noise removed; higher values restrict the amount of noise removed.

4. Click Preview to see how the settings will affect your bitmap. Click OK to complete the operation and to return to the drawing window.

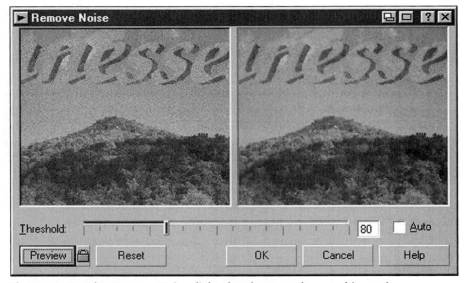

Figure 10-73: The Remove Noise dialog box lets you clean up bitmap images.

Tip

Specks of dust and small scratches on a photograph can adversely affect a digital image. Photo imaging tends to be somewhat unforgiving in this area, and the speck you didn't notice before scanning the image can stick out like a sore thumb on the scanned image. The Remove Noise command can help improve small defects and minimize the need to rescan the image.

Using Sharpness effects

Sharpness effects let you add definition to the edges of elements in your bitmap. Draw analyzes the pixels in your bitmap to determine the edges and background areas based upon the contrast in the bitmap. The program then accentuates the edges by increasing the contrast between the two elements. Draw provides these sharpening filters for your use:

✦ Adaptive Unsharp

✦ Directional Sharpening

✦ High Pass

✦ Sharpen

✦ Unsharp Mask

The Adaptive Unsharp effect

The Adaptive Unsharp effect enhances detail in your bitmaps by analyzing the values of neighboring pixels. The effect increases the contrast at the edges of objects to make them appear sharper and more focused. You specify the intensity of the effect by adjusting the Percentage slider.

To apply the Adaptive Unsharp effect to a selected bitmap:

1. Select Sharpen from the Sharpness effects menu to display the Sharpen dialog box (see Figure 10-74).

2. Adjust the Percentage slider to specify the amount of enhancement to be applied to the edges of elements in your bitmap.

3. Click Preview to see the effect of your settings. Click OK to apply the effect and to return to the drawing window.

Adaptive Unsharp is useful for enhancing the details in most bitmap images, but its effect is more apparent in high-resolution images. The effect also becomes more pronounced as the Percentage value entered here increases.

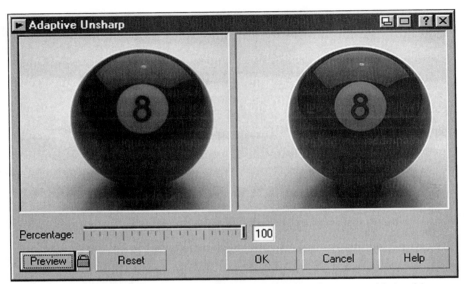

Figure 10-74: The Adaptive Unsharp dialog box lets you sharpen and bring bitmap images into focus.

The Directional Sharpen effect

The Directional Sharpen effect analyzes the luminosity of pixels near the edges of objects to determine the direction in which to apply the greatest amount of sharpening. Draw applies the greatest sharpening on low-contrast areas and the least in areas of high contrast. This effect uses subtle sharpening to enhance the edges of objects without giving the image a grainy appearance.

To apply the Directional Sharpen effect to a selected bitmap:

1. Select Directional Sharpen from the Sharpness effects menu to display the Directional Sharpen dialog box (see Figure 10-75).

2. Adjust the Percentage slider to specify the amount of enhancement to be applied to the edges of elements in your bitmap.

3. Click Preview to see the effect of your settings. Click OK to apply the effect and to return to the drawing window.

The Directional Sharpen filter is useful for increasing the crispness of edges in low-contrast images or when there is a variable amount of contrast within the image. It's especially well-suited for enhancing the edges between an object and the object's shadow. Because the degree of enhancement is subtle even at higher values, this filter is a good choice when you only need to apply small amounts of sharpening to improve the quality of an image.

Figure 10-75: The Directional Sharpen dialog box lets you specify the amount of sharpening in low-contrast areas of your bitmap.

The High Pass effect

The High Pass effect removes image detail by emphasizing the highlights and luminous areas of an image. You specify the intensity of the effect by adjusting the Percentage setting. Draw calculates the effect based upon the size of the sample you specify in the Radius setting.

To apply the High Pass effect to a selected bitmap:

1. Select High Pass from the Sharpness effects menu to display the High Pass dialog box (see Figure 10-76).

2. Adjust the Percentage slider to specify the amount of enhancement to be applied to the edges of elements in your bitmap.

3. Adjust the Radius to specify the size of the sample.

4. Click Preview to see the effect of your settings. Click OK to apply the effect and to return to the drawing window.

The High Pass filter decreases the amount of color as it reduces the details in your images. Gray replaces colors where the intensity of the effect is the greatest. Higher values remove most of the image detail, leaving only the edge details clearly visible; lower values emphasize highlights only. Higher settings can also give brighter colors a halo effect.

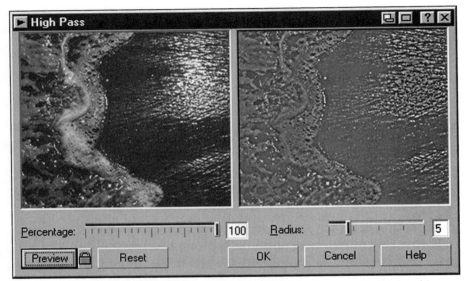

Figure 10-76: The High Pass dialog box lets you reduce the quantity of detail in your images based upon luminosity.

Sharpening a bitmap

When you apply Sharpen effects to a bitmap, the edges of elements in the bitmap are enhanced. Sharpen effects are useful for bringing elements of a bitmap into focus. Draw analyzes the bitmap for contrasting areas and then increases the contrast of adjacent pixels. The result is to reduce the effects of anti-aliasing within the image.

To apply Sharpen effects to a selected bitmap:

1. Select Sharpen from the Sharpness effects menu to display the Sharpen dialog box (see Figure 10-77).

2. Adjust the Edge Level (%) slider to specify the amount of enhancement to be applied to the edges of elements in your bitmap. The effect becomes more pronounced as the value entered here increases. Enable Preserve Colors if you want Draw to retain the colors in the original bitmap.

3. Adjust the Threshold slider to specify how much you want the sharpening to affect the background pixels in the image. Higher values have more impact on the background pixels.

4. Click Preview to see the effect of your settings. Click OK to apply the effect and to return to the drawing window.

Figure 10-77: The Sharpen dialog box lets you sharpen and bring bitmap images into focus.

Take care when applying sharpening effects. Oversharpening can cause a halo effect outside of the enhanced edges, as well as add unwanted contrasting pixels. Fine-tuning the amount of sharpening helps avoid this problem and optimizes the amount of focus that is added to your bitmap.

Using the Unsharp Mask effect

The Unsharp Mask effect enhances the edges of a bitmap much like Sharpen. They differ in how they deal with the background pixels, however. Unsharp Mask limits the amount of sharpening it applies to the background.

To apply the Unsharp Mask effect to a selected bitmap:

1. Select Unsharp Mask from the Sharpness effects menu to display the Unsharp Mask dialog box (see Figure 10-78).

2. Adjust the Percentage slider to determine the amount of sharpness to apply to the edges and background of your bitmap. Higher values increase the amount of enhancement that's applied to the image.

3. Adjust the Radius slider to specify the number of pixels to include in the radius of each sharpening evaluation that Draw makes.

4. Adjust the Threshold slider to specify the number of color levels to include in the Unsharp Mask sampling. Higher values include more colors in the effect.

5. Click Preview to see how your settings will affect your image. Click OK to apply the effect and to return to the drawing window.

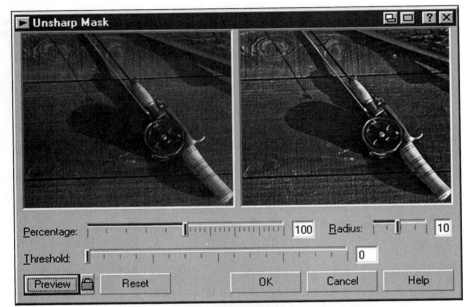

Figure 10-78: The settings in the Unsharp Mask dialog box can help you remove the effects of a blurred image.

When you apply Unsharp Mask to a bitmap, Draw analyzes the image to find areas of contrast. Like sharpening effects, the amount of contrast is increased between contrasting adjacent pixels. Unlike sharpening effects, however, Draw interpolates the adjacent pixels to add anti-aliasing, making the contrast changes subtler.

Using Add-Ons and Plug-Ins

Draw provides a broad assortment of filters for enhancing your bitmapped images. In addition to these filters, a growing number of third-party companies are making effects and plug-ins available for those who work with images.

To add or remove a plug-in:

1. First install the plug-in according to the manufacturer's instructions. Remember where the files were installed.

2. Select Tools ➪ Options to display the Options dialog box. Expand the Workspace category and click Plug-Ins.

3. To add a plug-in to the Bitmaps/Plug-in menu in Draw, click the Add button. Use Browse or enter the path for the location of the plug-in filter to add. If more than one filter is located in that folder, all of the plug-ins will be added.

4. To remove a plug-in, highlight the folder in the list box where the plug-in to remove is located. Click Delete.

5. Click OK to close the Options dialog box and to return to the drawing window.

Plug-ins are named for the way they are accessed in other programs. Generally, a plug-in is not a standalone piece of software. It hooks to another piece of software that supports plug-ins, such as Draw. You can add and remove plug-ins from Draw. When you add a new plug-in, it appears at the bottom of the Bitmaps menu, in the Plug-ins flyout menu. These miniprograms can be used to enhance, refine, correct, and add effects to your bitmaps.

Summary

Bitmapped images can enhance your Draw documents. Because bitmaps create larger file sizes than vector images, they should be used judiciously if file size is a factor. Bitmap effects filters can be used to correct a host of flaws in scanned photographs. For example, you can use filters to brighten an image that's too dark, or smooth an image that has speckles from dust. Effects filters can be used individually or successively to apply both subtle and dramatic effects to your documents. Your bitmap library can be expanded with the addition of plug-in filters. In this chapter, you learned to

✦ Apply 3D effects

✦ Enhance your bitmaps using artistic stroke effects

✦ Blur and smooth images

✦ Add and remove noise in your images

✦ Add Distortion effects to your images

✦ Use color transformation effects

✦ Apply creative effects to bitmaps

✦ Use plug-ins to enhance images

✦   ✦   ✦

Creating
Word Art

Draw provides the tools to explore and create text as art. You can add special effects to Artistic text and mold Paragraph text frames to a variety of shapes, adding dynamic momentum to your documents. Draw's large symbol library provides characters that can be used alone, incorporated with other graphics, or used as fills.

Discovering the Difference: Artistic and Paragraph Text

Draw treats Artistic and Paragraph text differently. Artistic text is considered a text object. Like any other multipath object, you can apply a variety of special effects that enhance Artistic text. These effects, such as Blend and Extrude, are discussed later in this book. In addition to the effects that apply to nearly any object, you can add effects that are somewhat specific to text. You can flow text along a shape or line using the Fit Text to Path feature, create unusual banners, add drop shadows, use text as a mask, or manipulate text to enhance your documents.

The number of effects that you can apply to Paragraph text is limited. You can apply envelope effects to Paragraph text frames, which lets you use Paragraph text as a fill, or shape the frame to any shape. You can also wrap Paragraph text around graphical objects. It's important to remember that when you apply effects to text, that it still remains text, unless you convert it to curves. This means that you can edit the text to add, remove, or replace portions of the text.

The Advent of Text as Art

People have been communicating ideas with text and symbols for centuries. Long before written languages, societies used symbols to record stories and events. In the mid-fifteenth century, text and symbols took on another dimension with the advent of typefounding.

By the twentieth century, text had become more than just words; it had become an art form in its own right. Computers have enhanced text as an art form, as text has become an integral part of design. One of the most important features of Draw is that the program lets you quickly and easily apply special effects to text. Some industries, such as the screen printing industry, rely heavily on text effects.

Fitting Text to a Path

One of the most popular and frequently used text effects is Fit Text to Path. Fit Text to Path lets you place text on an open or a closed object. Using this command, you can create effects such as placing text around a circle. Once limited to Artistic text, you can now place Paragraph text using the Fit Text to Path command.

Placing Artistic text on a path

You can make text an integral part of the artwork in your drawing, using Fit Text to Path. A path can be either a curve or an object (see Figure 11-1). Draw has two methods of fitting text along a path. You can either type directly on the path or use the Fit Text to Path command. You can fit text to any path except another string of text. After Artistic text is fitted to a path, the Fit Text to Path settings on the Property bar provide several options for changing the position of text. The settings on the property bar let you specify placement, orientation, and the distance from the path.

Tip　You can't directly fit text to another text string. If you want to fit a string of text to the shape of another text string, convert the text that you want to use as a path to curves. You can then apply Fit Text to Path, using the converted text as the path. Once you convert text to curves, you can no longer edit the text as a text object.

Flowing directly along a path

To flow text directly along a path:

1. Create the path along which you want the text to flow.

2. Using the Text tool, move the cursor close to the path until the cursor changes to a text cursor (see Figure 11-2). Click to set an insertion point.

3. Enter the text you want to flow along the path. The text flows onto the path as you enter the text string.

Figure 11-1: Using Fit Text to Path, you can make text follow another object.

Figure 11-2: As you move the cursor close to the object, it changes to a text cursor.

Once the text is in place, you can alter its orientation and distance from the path using the Property bar. More information about modifying text on a path appears later in this chapter.

Tip   Before applying a special effect to Artistic text, center-align the text. This guarantees that the text retains the same basic shape, without distortion, if you need to edit or replace the text later.

Using the Fit Text to Path command

To use the Fit Text to Path command:

1. Using the Pick tool, select the text to fit to path. With the text selected, press Shift and click the path you want to use (see Figure 11-3).

2. Select Text ➪ Fit Text to Path. The text automatically flows along the path you specify (see Figure 11-4).

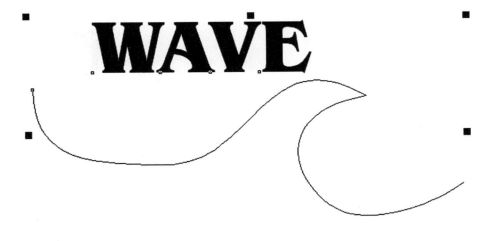

Figure 11-3: Select the text and path along which you want to place the text.

Tip   To edit text that flows along a path, press Ctrl and click the text to select it. The text can then be edited directly using the Text tool, or by selecting Text ➪ Edit Text to open the text in the Edit Text dialog box.

Fitting Paragraph text to a path

Draw lets you fit Paragraph text to a path. You can flow text along multiple paths, or use portions of a Paragraph text block like a fill. Like Artistic text, you can use the Fit Text to Path command to fit Paragraph text to path. Unlike Artistic text, however, you can't flow the text directly onto the path as you enter the text.

Figure 11-4: The completed Fit Text to Path effect.

Determining path and formatting attributes

Paragraph text also behaves differently than Artistic text when fitted to path. The type of path and the formatting attributes of the Paragraph text determine how Draw flows Paragraph text along a path. If the path is open, Draw flows the text along the path like Artistic text, *until* it encounters the first hard return. Text that follows the first hard return is still there, although you can't see it (see Figure 11-5). Clicking the bottom text handle lets you move the balance of the text to a linked text frame by clicking elsewhere in the drawing window.

 Note   Draw ignores soft returns (Shift+Enter) when it places text using the Fit Text to Path command. If Draw encounters a soft return, it continues to flow the text as if a return did not exist.

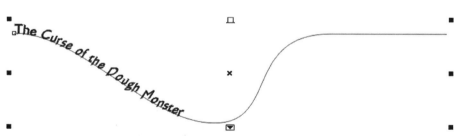

Figure 11-5: When you flow Paragraph text on an open path, only the text prior to the first hard return is visible.

If you click the white space in the drawing window, the balance of the text is placed in a regular Paragraph text frame. You can also flow the balance of the text along another path or fill a closed object with the text by clicking an object. Figure 11-6 shows a block of Paragraph text after applying the Fit Text to Path command to flow the text along multiple open paths. Note the lines showing the links between the Paragraph text frames.

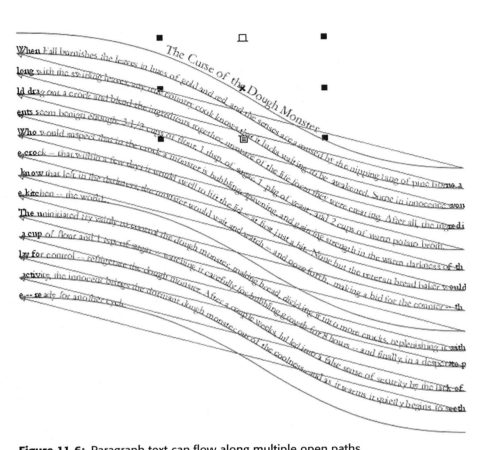

Figure 11-6: Paragraph text can flow along multiple open paths.

Fitting to multiple paths

To fit Paragraph text to multiple paths:

1. Create the paths and the Paragraph text that you want to Fit to path

2. While pressing Shift, select both the Paragraph text and the path.

3. Using the Pick tool, select Text ➪ Fit Text to Path. Draw automatically flows the text along the path until it encounters the first hard return.

4. Press Ctrl and select just the text. Draw displays Paragraph text handles at the top and bottom of the text to show that it's selected.

5. Click the down arrow at the bottom of the text. When you move your cursor away from the arrow, a page icon with an arrow appears, indicating the remaining Paragraph text.

6. Move your cursor until it is over the next open path along which you want to flow text. As you move over objects, the cursor changes to a large arrow. Click the path. Draw applies text along the path until it either runs out of path or encounters the next hard return.

7. Repeat steps 4 through 6 to place the remaining text along other paths. Be sure that when you select the text you select the last block of text you place on a path.

You can add extra paths as needed to accommodate the amount of text you have, and then continue flowing text to the new paths. The Property bar displays the way the text is placed on the path. If you aren't pleased with the results of the default placement, you can alter the way the text is placed on the path. You can place Paragraph text on any combination of open and closed paths.

Working with closed and open objects

Applying Paragraph text to a closed object places the text either along the path or inside the object. The placement is determined by a series of factors. If the object is a geometric object, such as a star or circle, the text is placed inside the object. If the object is a curve, Draw places the text as if it was Artistic text until it encounters the first hard return. If your text exceeds the amount of text you can place, you can flow the balance to another object. If that object is closed, Draw places the balance of the text inside the object (see Figure 11-7). Using this method, you can alternate between closed and open objects until all the text is placed.

Tip

You can tweak the appearance of text inside an object by clicking the text and selecting Text ⇨ Fit Text to Frame. Draw resizes and flows the text to fit perfectly inside the frame.

Editing a Fit Text to Path group

When you fit text to a path, the resulting object becomes a text-path group. Draw lets you edit the elements of a text-path group separately or in relationship to one another. You can select a single element for individual editing by pressing Ctrl while clicking that element. In addition, using the Property bar lets you specify the orientation, horizontal position, and vertical position of your text in relation to the graphical element of the group. You can also separate the elements within the group, yet have the text retain the shape of the path to which it was fitted.

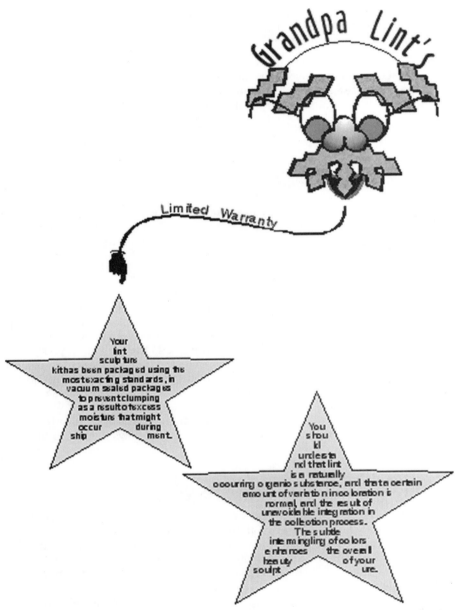

Figure 11-7: Draw places the Paragraph text along a path until it comes to a hard return. If you choose a closed object as the path for the balance of the text, Draw places the balance as a fill.

Specifying the orientation

To specify the orientation relative to the path:

1. Using the Pick tool, select the text-path group.

2. On the Property bar, click to select an orientation (see Figure 11-8). You can choose to have the letters stand upright, remain perpendicular to the path, have the baseline of the letters follow the path, or rotate the characters along the path.

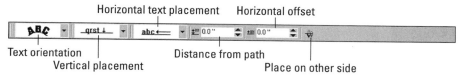

Figure caption labels: Horizontal text placement, Horizontal offset, Text orientation, Vertical placement, Distance from path, Place on other side

Figure 11-8: You can select the orientation of your text using the settings on the Text to Path view of the Property bar.

Choosing an orientation for your text is mostly a matter of aesthetics. As a general rule, text looks better on a curved path if you choose to have the baseline of the letters follow the path. Depending on the font, characters may appear to overlap or collide if the text remains perpendicular to the path. Try different orientations until you find one you like.

Specifying vertical placement

Fonts can vary a great deal in appearance. Draw centers text vertically on the path by default. If your text string has characters with descenders, such as the tail of the "g," the descenders extend across the path. You can specify how Draw places text vertically in relationship to the path.

To specify the vertical placement:

1. Using the Pick tool, select the text-path group.

2. On the Property bar, select a vertical placement for your text from the Vertical Placement drop-down menu.

Draw displays the vertical placement choices as examples of how the text will look placed on the path. You can choose to center the text on the path, place the text above the path, place the text below the path, or choose to customize the distance from the path.

Adjusting the vertical position

If you choose to customize the distance from the path, adjust the values in the Vertical Placement box.

To adjust the vertical position or distance from the path:

1. Using the Pick tool, select the text-path group.

2. On the Property bar, click the up and down arrows or enter a new value in the Vertical Placement box to specify the vertical distance from the path that you desire for the placement of your text. If you click the arrows, the distance changes automatically.

3. If you enter a new value, press Enter to apply the change.

Moving the text away from the path helps create a balanced appearance. This option is especially useful when the graphical element is closed, such as a circle. Sometimes when you fit text to a closed path, a word will split to wrap around the corner of the object, or the text overlaps when the text string is longer than the object around which it's being fit. You can adjust the placement on the path and the distance from the path to compensate for this problem (see Figure 11-9).

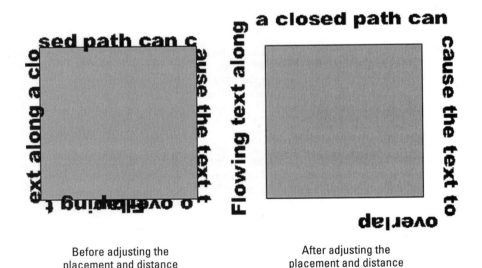

Before adjusting the
placement and distance

After adjusting the
placement and distance

Figure 11-9: Adjusting the distance from the path and the placement along the path helps text fit closed objects better.

Specifying the horizontal placement

When you place text on a path, Draw aligns the text to the left side of an open path by default. You can specify whether you want text to be left-, right-, or center-aligned on an open path.

To specify the horizontal placement:

1. Using the Pick tool, select the text-path group.

2. On the Property bar, select a horizontal placement for your text from the Horizontal Placement drop-down menu.

Adjusting the horizontal position

Once you make your selection, Draw automatically adjusts the text on the path. You can also fine-tune the adjustment to move the text along the path to achieve the effect you want.

To adjust the horizontal placement of text along a path:

1. Using the Pick tool, select the text-path group.

2. In the Horizontal Offset box on the Property bar, click the up and down arrows or enter a new value to adjust the text on the path. If you click the arrows, the distance changes automatically. If you enter a new value, press Enter to apply the change.

By adjusting the horizontal placement on the path, you can modify the balance of the effect. This is especially useful when the path has an irregular shape or when fitting text to a closed shape.

Fitting text to a closed path

Draw treats the placement of text differently when you fit the text to a closed path versus an open path. When text is fit to a closed path, Draw centers it at the top of the object by default. Enabling Place on Other Side flips the text vertically and horizontally, and places it on the other side of the object (see Figure 11-10).

To fit text to a closed path:

1. Using the Pick tool, select the text to fit to path. With the text selected, press Shift and click the path you want to use.

2. Select Text ➪ Fit Text to Path. Draw automatically centers the text at the top of the closed object (see Figure 11-11).

Note

You can also apply text to a path by first selecting the text and then choosing Fit Text to Path. An arrow appears that lets you choose the object along which to place the text.

Figure 11-10: Place on Other Side mirrors the text object and places it on the other side of the object.

Figure 11-11: Draw centers the text at the top of the object.

Choosing a quadrant

Once the text is initially placed, you can change the quadrant where the text appears, the text orientation, and the vertical and horizontal placement of the text. When you choose a quadrant, Draw moves the text as if the object were rectangular, regardless of the actual shape (see Figure 11-12).

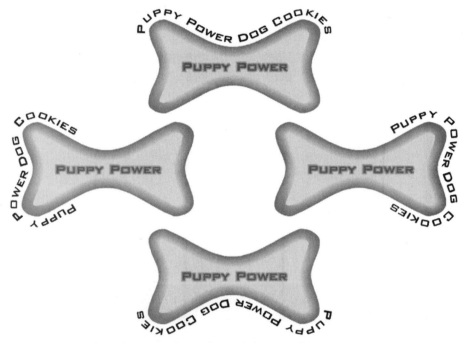

Figure 11-12: Choosing a quadrant changes the text placement.

To change the text location on a closed object:

1. Using the Pick tool, select the text-path group.

2. Choose a quadrant from the Text Placement drop-down menu on the Property bar. Draw automatically repositions the text on the path.

3. Click the Place Text on Other Side button to move the text inside the path (see Figure 11-13).

You can separate text from a text-path group and return it to its original shape. Separating text from a path is useful when you want to shape text but don't want to add a graphical object to your drawing. Once the text-group is separated, you can delete the graphical object without compromising the shape of the text, or you can choose to straighten the text.

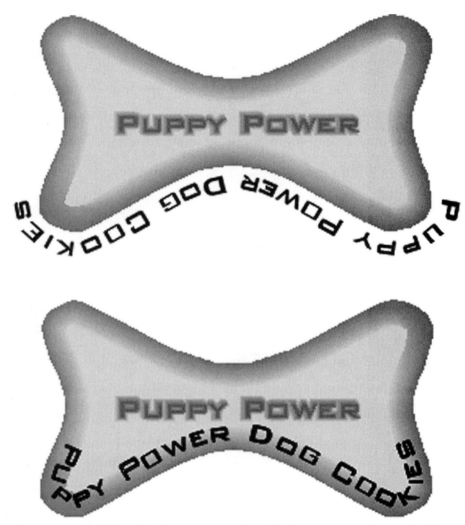

Figure 11-13: Clicking the Place Text on Other Side button moves the text inside the path.

Separating text from a text-path group

To separate text from a text-path group:

1. Using the Pick tool, select the text-path group.

2. Select Arrange ➪ Separate. The text retains the shape of the path, but the elements are no longer part of a group.

3. If you want to straighten text that's been separated from a text-path group, select Text ➪ Straighten Text. The text returns to its original appearance (see Figure 11-14).

Figure 11-14: You can straighten text to return it to its original appearance.

Embedding Graphics in Text

Word art is the definitive term for this new Draw 9 feature. You can now insert graphic objects into strings of Artistic text (see Figure 11-15). When you insert a graphic into your text, Draw automatically resizes the object to the size of the text. This feature is especially good for Web use and banner text.

L⚭⚭KIN' G⚭⚭D!

Figure 11-15: You can insert graphic objects into text, and Draw automatically resizes the objects to match the text size.

Note Draw lets you insert graphic objects into strings of Artistic text to further enhance your documents. You can't add objects to Paragraph text.

To insert a graphic object into strings of Artistic text:

1. Create the string of Artistic text in which you want to insert an object.

2. Copy the graphic to insert to the Windows clipboard by pressing Ctrl+C.

3. Using the Text tool, click an insertion point or highlight the text to replace with a graphic object.

4. Press Ctrl+V to paste the object into the text.

You can also enter the text to the point where you want to insert the object and then paste the object in place. After pasting the object, continue entering the rest of the text string.

Creating Collegiate-Style Text

Collegiate text is a favorite effect of screen printers and others who create drawings for institutions such as universities. This text is usually three superimposed layers, with each layer filled with a different color (see Figure 11-16). You could use the contour command to create the effect, but you would have to separate the resulting object to fill the objects. You also could not edit the individual layers as text. You can create collegiate text simply, while retaining the ability to edit each layer of text. You can select any colors you want. Just make sure that the outline color matches that of the fill.

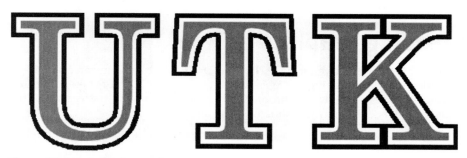

Figure 11-16: Collegiate-style text.

To create collegiate-style text:

1. Using the Text tool, click an insertion point on the drawing page and enter the text that you want to use. Center-align the text. You should choose a large font size, such as 72 points or greater; otherwise, the outline will overwhelm the text, making it difficult to read.

2. Using the Pick tool, select the text and choose the Outline Pen dialog box from the Outline Pen flyout menu (see Figure 11-17). Fill the text with the color you want to use by clicking a color swatch in the onscreen palette. For this example, select maroon.

Shortcut

If you hold down Shift and press the spacebar, you can quickly switch from the text tool to the Pick tool.

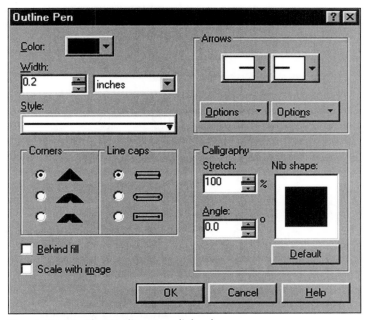

Figure 11-17: The Outline Pen dialog box.

3. Change the outline pen width to 0.2 inches. Click OK to apply the outline and to return to the drawing window (see Figure 11-18). If the characters overlap, adjust the character spacing in the Format Text dialog box to 50 percent of the space width. Adjust the word spacing to 200 percent.

4. With the text still selected, hit the plus (+) key on your keyboard keypad to duplicate the text and place it directly over the original text string. Fill the duplicate with white by clicking the white color swatch in the onscreen palette.

Arizona State University

Figure 11-18: Add a 0.2-inch outline to the text.

5. With the new text string selected, open the Outline Pen dialog box and change the outline color to white. Set the outline width to 0.1 inches (see Figure 11-19).

Figure 11-19: Apply a white outline 0.1 inches wide to the duplicate text string.

Ctrl+F12 accesses the Outline Pen dialog box.

6. Repeat steps 4 and 5, except fill the new text string with gold.

7. Right-click the X in the onscreen palette to remove the outline from the new text string. The finished effect appears as shown in Figure 11-20.

Figure 11-20: Remove the outline to finish the effect.

Collegiate text is frequently used for banners and imprinted media. For best results, select contrasting colors and a font that is either bold or sans serif. This effect does not work well with scripted fonts.

Adding Drop Shadows and Highlights

Drop shadows and highlights can give text depth. You can easily create the effect of raised text, similar to what you might find with a raised button. These effects add interest to your documents, and work well as banners or headlines. Creating both effects in Draw is easy.

 Tip

When you create effects in which the placement relative to other objects is critical to the effect, group the resulting objects to prevent them from being accidentally shifted away from one another.

Creating a Drop Shadow effect

To add a drop shadow to text:

1. Using the Text tool, click an insertion point on the drawing page and enter your text.

2. Hit the plus (+) key on the keypad to duplicate the text, superimposed directly over the original text.

3. Fill the new text object with gray. Gray colors from 10 to 30 percent work best.

4. Click and drag the gray text string down and to the right, as shown in Figure 11-21.

5. Select Arrange ➪ Order ➪ Back One to move the gray text behind the original text (see Figure 11-22).

 Shortcut

Ctrl+PgDn moves objects back one. Shift+PgDn moves objects to the back of the active layer.

Figure 11-21: Fill the duplicate text string with gray.

Figure 11-22: Move the gray text string behind the original text string.

You can also add drop shadows using the Drop Shadow tool. One advantage of creating a drop shadow using the method above is that you can edit the shadow independent of the original object. Another advantage is that unlike Draw's new Drop Shadow feature, this method of adding a drop shadow creates a vector object instead of a bitmap object.

Tip   Bitmap objects increase the file size of your document. If you need to maintain a small file size, consider using this method of creating a drop shadow.

Creating a 3D Raised Button effect

To create a 3D Raised Button effect:

1. Using the Text tool, click an insertion point on the drawing page and enter your text (see Figure 11-23).

2. Select the Fountain Fill dialog box from the Fill tool flyout menu (see Figure 11-24). By default, Draw specifies black and white as the fountain fill colors, and the angle as 0 degrees. Change the angle to 90 degrees and click OK to apply the fill and to return to the drawing window.

3. Select Tools ➪ Options and click the General tab. Set the nudge value at 0.01 inches and click OK to return to the drawing window.

4. Hit the plus (+) key on the keypad of your keyboard to duplicate the text and superimpose it directly over the original text.

5. With the duplicate text selected, open the Fountain Fill dialog box and change the fill angle to 45 degrees. Change the black to 70 percent gray and the white to 20 percent gray. Click OK to apply the changes and to return to the drawing window (see Figure 11-25).

6. Select Arrange ➪ Order ➪ Back One to move the duplicate text object behind the original text string.

7. While holding down Shift, press the right arrow (fi) and then the up arrow (>) one time each to offset the duplicate text object. This offsets the object using Draw's Super-Nudge feature.

Figure 11-23: Enter the text to use as a button.

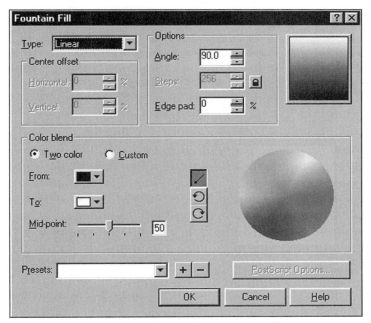

Figure 11-24: Apply a black-to-white 90-degree fill to the text string.

Figure 11-25: Apply a 70 percent gray to 20 percent gray 45-degree fill to the duplicate text string.

8. Reselect the original text string and repeat steps 4 through 6, except set the angle of the fountain fill to –135 degrees.

9. While pressing Shift, press the left arrow (<) and then the down arrow (fl) one time each to offset the second duplicate text object (see Figure 11-26).

Tip The finished effect is a 3D button in the up position. If you invert the highlight and shadows, you can create the button in the down position. Two-state (up and down) buttons are useful for creating Web pages and are essential for multimedia applications. With a little practice, you can create a wide variety of two-state 3D buttons.

Figure 11-26: Use Super-Nudge to offset the duplicate text object.

Using Text as a Mask

A mask is a combined object that leaves clipping holes. If, for example, you were to place an ellipse in the center of a rectangle and combine the two objects, the result would be a rectangular frame. The elliptical area in the center would behave like a hole in the rectangle. Any object residing below the hole would be visible. Similarly, you can combine text with other objects to create a variety of masking effects. Only areas that overlap appear transparent. You can overlap the text slightly to create a partial mask, or overlap the text completely to create a full mask effect. Figure 11-27 shows text combined with a rectangle to create a mask. The finished mask was used as a container for a PowerClip to add the photograph that appears around the text.

Figure 11-27: Text combined with other objects lets you create mask effects.

To create a mask with text:

1. Using the Pick tool, select the text. Press Shift and click the graphics object that you want to combine with the text. For best results, the text should be a bold font and the graphics object should be larger than the text (see Figure 11-28).

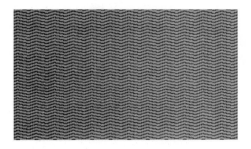

Figure 11-28: Select the text and graphic object that you want to combine.

2. If you want the text and graphics object directly superimposed, use the Alignment command to arrange them.

3. Select Arrange ➪ Combine to combine the text and graphics object (see Figure 11-29). The resulting object appears with the fill of the graphics object because you selected it last. The text appears as a hole cut in the object.

4. In the example used for these instructions, a contrasting rectangle and fish were placed behind the mask object. Portions of the rectangle and fish appear through the clipping holes created by the text (see Figure 11-30).

Caution   Once text is combined with another object, you can't edit it as text. It becomes a curve object. If you later break the object apart using the Break Apart command, the graphics object and each character of the "text" is a separate curve object.

Clipping holes in objects lets you create masks that block portions of objects lying below. This effect can also be used to create the illusion of picture frames around your finished image. If you are creating a frame that surrounds your entire image, make sure that the final exterior dimensions of your image, including the frame, fit within the printable area of the drawing page.

Figure 11-29: Apply the Combine command to merge the text with the graphic object.

Figure 11-30: Objects placed behind the mask object appear through the clipping holes created by the text.

The Anatomy of Text/Curve Objects

The Combine, Weld, Intersect, and Trim commands change the nature of text. Applying these commands to text automatically converts the text to curves. The result is a multipath graphical object that can no longer be edited as text. The letter "D," for example, becomes an object with two paths. The first path describes the outer shape of the character; the second path describes the center or transparent space of the character.

If you apply Break Apart to the resulting object or one of the effects that converts text to curves, the multiple paths become separate objects. Each object is filled with the same color as the combined object, which can make portions of the object seem to disappear.

If the object contained a nonuniform fill, such as a texture fill, the superimposed objects increase the complexity of your document. Smaller objects may also reside below other objects making them difficult to select. You can use Tab or Draw's Digger function to select objects that are hidden by other objects to reposition or manipulate them. To use the Digger function, press Alt while clicking an object. Draw selects the next object down in the hierarchy of objects. Each successive click moves down one level to select the next object in the hierarchy. If you press Alt+Ctrl while clicking object groups, the Digger function selects the next child object down in the hierarchy of objects.

Putting a Spin on Text

The Blend effect lets you add a 3D appearance to selected text. When you apply Blend, you control the number of steps, as well as the way the intermediate steps appear in your drawing. Draw also provides options that let you control the palette, blend objects along a path, and rotate objects as they are blended.

Cross-Reference For more information about blending objects, see Chapter 15.

This exercise uses two duplicate strings of text to create a rotated blend:

1. Using the Pick tool, select the two text objects to blend together. These may be duplicate text objects or two different strings of text. These two objects become the control objects for your blend (see Figure 11-31).

2. Select the Interactive Blend tool from the toolbox.

3. On the Property bar, enter **20** for the number of steps in the blend.

4. Enter **360** for the number of degrees of rotation and enable Loop.

5. Click and drag between the two objects. Draw blends the two text objects while creating a loop effect (see Figure 11-32).

Figure 11-31: Select the two text objects to blend.

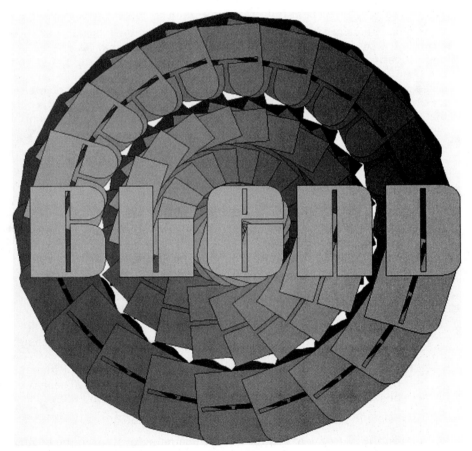

Figure 11-32: Blended text with a 360-degree loop.

You can achieve a variety of results by applying blend effects to text. In Figure 11-33, one string of text was rotated 90 degrees. Then, the two text strings were selected and blended 90 degrees, with Loop enabled.

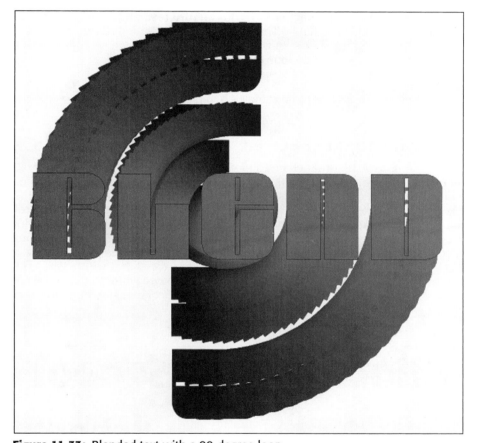

Figure 11-33: Blended text with a 90-degree loop.

Tip When blending text objects, consider either applying an outline to the text or placing the objects in close proximity to one another. These two methods produce the best results when you want to create a blend with legible text. Without an outline, blended text can be difficult to read if the control objects are placed further apart.

Shaping Text with Envelopes

Draw provides the capability of shaping text while retaining the capability to edit the text, either directly or using the Edit Text dialog box. Draw's Envelope features let you shape text in a variety of ways. The shape of the envelope and the mapping mode you choose control the distortion. You can select from a preset envelope, use another object as an envelope, or create your own by dragging the bounding handles of the envelope. Using Draw's Envelope features lets you control the maximum amount of space text occupies, distort text, or use text as a fill for other objects. With a little experimentation, you can turn text into artistic logos, banners, or nearly any shape imaginable. This section is not intended to be a definitive lesson in the use of envelopes, but showcases the unique and wonderful effects possible when you apply envelopes to text.

Cross-Reference   Envelopes are covered more completely in Chapter 15.

Controlling text space

Laying out Artistic text that changes monthly can be a chore, unless you create a template. Another problem occurs when you have a specific amount of space in which to place text that changes. Your options are limited. You can change the font size, adjust the kerning, or you can control the text using an envelope. Controlling the maximum space using an envelope lets you edit the text within the envelope without changing the amount of space it occupies. If, for example, you commonly used a banner at the top of your document that was six inches wide, this technique lets you guarantee that your text string will never exceed that width. Figure 11-34 shows three strings of text. Note that the characters are shifted or compressed to fit the same amount of space. In addition, the strings of text stay perfectly aligned on the page.

Clinton High School
Oak Ridge High School
Oliver Springs High School

Figure 11-34: Control the page alignment and maximum space text occupies by applying an envelope to the text.

Tip   You can control the alignment and amount of space text occupies by applying an envelope to the text. Later, if the text is edited, the new text occupies the same amount of space, while retaining its alignment.

To use envelopes to control Artistic text spacing:

1. Create a text string that approximates the maximum width you anticipate using. Center-align the text.

2. Using the Pick tool, select the text string.

3. Select the interactive Envelope tool from the Interactive tool flyout on the toolbar. The Property bar changes to display the Envelope settings (see Figure 11-35), and envelope handles appear around your object.

4. Click the Straight-line Envelope button. Because you are applying a constraining envelope, you don't want to move any of the envelope handles that appear around the object. Draw automatically applies the effect.

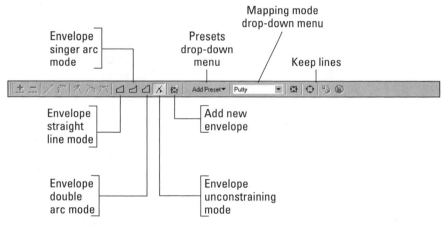

Figure 11-35: The Envelope view of the Property bar lets you choose the Envelope effects to apply.

Tip This technique for controlling text space is useful for newsletters or the drop names that are popular in the silk-screening industry. Centering the text lets you change the text later and still ensure that the new text maintains the correct spacing and alignment within the envelope.

Warping text using envelopes

When you warp Artistic text using an envelope, Draw treats the text like any other graphical object. Because of the basic nature of text, there is a difference in the way text behaves, however. The mix of uppercase and lowercase characters, the active font, and the character attributes all contribute to the final results. Before applying an envelope to text, it's important to understand the flexibility of this feature.

Choosing an editing mode type

In addition to preset envelopes and creating envelopes from graphical objects, you can use these editing mode types for envelopes (see Figure 11-36):

Figure 11-36: Envelope editing modes.

✦ **Straight Line:** You drag nodes horizontally or vertically to shape the sides of the envelope. The resulting envelope retains straight sides.

✦ **Single Arc:** You drag nodes horizontally or vertically to shape the sides of the envelope. The resulting envelope curves in only one direction per side.

✦ **Double Arc:** You drag nodes horizontally or vertically to shape the sides of the envelope. The resulting envelope curves in two directions per side.

✦ **Unconstrained:** You drag nodes or node handles to create irregular shapes. You can change the properties of the nodes, add nodes, or delete nodes as you would any curve object.

Choosing a mapping mode

The flexibility of envelopes does not stop with choosing an editing mode. Draw also lets you choose a mapping mode, which controls the way the text fits inside the envelope. You can choose to use horizontal, original, putty, or vertical mapping modes. If you are working with Paragraph text, you can also choose to work with a text-mapping mode. Working with mapping modes and text requires some experimentation. Text can become illegible when placed in some envelopes.

Remember that you can always use the Undo command if the results are not what you want. Use these guidelines to choose a mapping mode (see Figure 11-37):

Figure 11-37: Envelope mapping modes.

✦ **Horizontal:** This mapping mode stretches the text to fit the basic dimensions of the envelope, then compresses the text horizontally to mold it to the shape of the envelope. This mode can render text illegible.

✦ **Original:** This mapping mode reshapes the bounding box of the text to match that of the envelope. The text is mapped in a straight line along the edge of the bounding box.

✦ **Putty:** This mapping mode resembles the original mapping mode in that it matches the corners of the text's bounding box to that of the envelope. This mapping mode produces less dramatic effects, however, by softening or curving edges of the text, rather than producing a hard edge.

✦ **Vertical:** This mapping mode stretches the text to fit the basic dimensions of the envelope, then compresses the text vertically to mold it to the shape of the envelope. This mode can render text illegible.

✦ **Text:** This mode is only available when you apply an envelope to Paragraph text. By default, it is associated with an unconstrained editing mode that lets you mold the Paragraph text frame to any shape.

Creating an envelope

To create an envelope:

1. Using the Pick tool, select the text to fit to an envelope.

2. Select the interactive Envelope tool from the Interactive tool flyout on the toolbar. The Property bar changes to display the Envelope settings and envelope handles appear around your object.

3. Choose the editing and mapping modes you want to use. Enable Keep Lines if you want to prevent Draw from modifying the straight lines of text to curves.

Note   The effect of enabling Keep Lines is more noticeable with some fonts than with other fonts.

4. Click Add New.

5. Click and drag the handles as desired in the drawing window.

6. Click Apply. Draw applies the envelope to the text. You can add other envelopes to the text, if you want, to combine the effects of two or more envelopes. Figure 11-38 was created by applying a straight-line envelope and then adding an unconstrained envelope to fine-tune the shape.

Tip   If you press Ctrl while dragging, the adjacent node moves an equal amount in the same direction. If you press Shift while dragging, the adjacent node moves an equal amount in the opposite direction.

Using text as a fill

Creating Paragraph text that fits into neat rectangular frames and columns makes Draw a great layout package for small documents. Remember, though, that Draw is an illustration package. What if you want to shape the text so that it fits on a banana peel or an oval label on a can (see Figure 11-39)? Draw lets you fill objects with Paragraph text. You can also shape the text frame by selecting a preset envelope shape or by manually editing the shape of the frame.

When you apply an envelope to Paragraph text, the envelope is applied to the frame. Unlike Artistic text, it does not reshape the text itself. It alters the layout of the text to fit inside the envelope. You can fill an object with Paragraph text interactively in the drawing window.

To interactively fill an object with Paragraph text:

1. Using the Text tool, press Shift and click the outline of the object to fill with Paragraph text. A Paragraph text frame appears that is the shape and size of the object.

2. Enter the text to use as a fill.

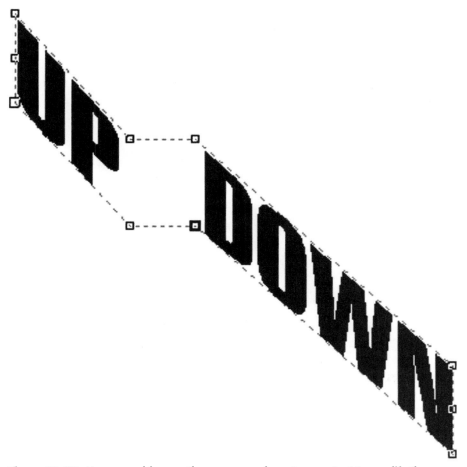

Figure 11-38: You can add more than one envelope to your text to modify the shape.

Text Fill Creativity

The creative uses for text as a fill are numerous. As a single feature, you can flow a list of names into shapes to create a customized list of acknowledgements or credits.

Perhaps you might want to convert other text, such as the numbers for a class year, into curves, and flow the class member's names into the shapes. Combining it with other features, such as flow text around graphics, lets you create a mapped pierced effect that allows other elements to show through text mapped to a 3D object. You can still format the text as Paragraph text, which lets you enhance the text further by changing attributes, such as font, sizing, and other paragraph and character attributes.

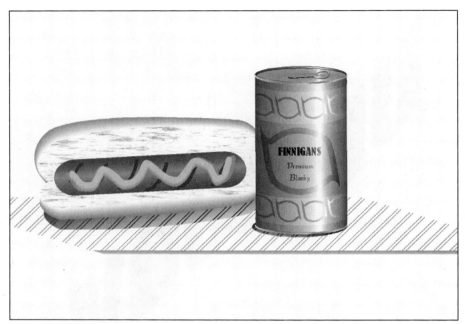

Figure 11-39: You can use Paragraph text as a fill for other objects, such as can labels.

Flowing Text Around Graphics

Draw gives you the ability to flow Paragraph text around graphics, allowing you creative control over the balance between text and graphics in your document. When you flow Paragraph text around the graphics in your drawing, the text becomes an artistic element that enhances the appearance of your drawing (see Figure 11-40). You can choose to flow existing text around the graphics in your drawing, or you can create new text that flows as you enter the text.

To flow text around a graphic element:

1. Using the Pick tool, right-click the object around which you want your text to flow. Select Properties to display the Object Properties dialog box (see Figure 11-41). Click the General tab.

2. Enable Wrap paragraph text and enter the amount of Text wrap offset you want.

3. Click OK to return to the drawing window. If you are flowing existing text around a graphic, drag the text frame over the object and skip the next two steps.

Figure 11-40: Flowing text around graphics lets you add text as an artistic element in your documents.

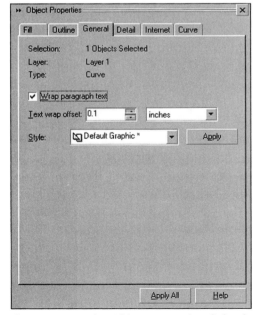

Figure 11-41: The Object Properties dialog box.

4. Using the Text tool, create a paragraph frame on top of the object around which you want to wrap the text.

5. Enter the text to use. As you enter the text, it flows around the graphic, leaving the space occupied by the graphic plus any offset blank.

The capability of flowing text around graphics has long been a feature of most layout packages. Using this feature enhances documents, such as newsletters and catalogs, by letting you merge text and graphics with creativity.

Adding Symbols

Symbols are a quick way to add art to your drawings. You can use symbols as stand-alone art, as the basis for more elaborate objects, or as a background pattern in your documents. You can also add symbols to both Artistic and Paragraph text objects. Symbols are edited as you would edit any other graphical object. Draw provides a wide array of symbol libraries from which to choose. Symbol libraries are added when you install Draw, but you can add more libraries later, or create your own symbols (see the later section "Creating New Symbols").

Symbols are accessed using the Symbols docker. To display the docker, either click the Symbols Docker button on the toolbar, or select Tools ➪ Symbols and Special Characters (see Figure 11-42).

Ctrl+F11 accesses the Symbols docker.

To your drawings

To add a symbol to your drawing:

1. Click the down arrow near the top of the docker to choose a symbol library from the drop-down list.

2. Enter a size in the size box. By default, the size shown is 2 inches. This is the size of the symbol at its widest dimension.

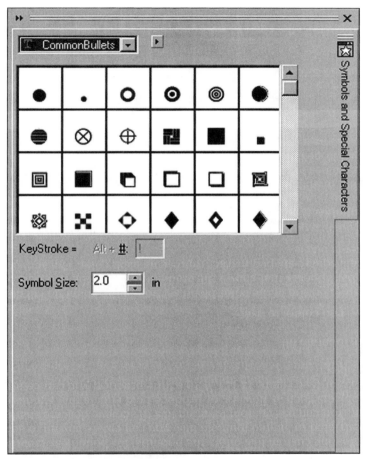

Figure 11-42: The Symbols docker.

3. Choose the symbol you want and then click and drag it to the drawing window. Alternatively, you can enter the number for the symbol in the number (#) box. Each symbol has a unique number (a list of the symbols and their associated numbers appears in the Draw Libraries Catalog). The symbol appears in the drawing window (see Figure 11-43). Draw uses the default fill and outline to determine the attributes of the symbol.

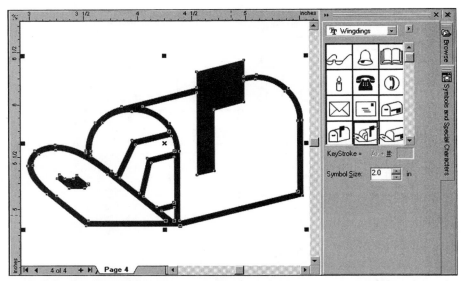

Figure 11-43: The symbol appears in the drawing window with the default fill and outline attributes.

To text objects

To add a symbol to a text object:

1. Using the Text tool, select the text to which you want to add a symbol. Click an insertion point where the symbol is to appear.

2. Specify the size of the symbol to use.

3. Double-click the symbol to insert in the text. The symbol appears at the insertion point (see Figure 11-44).

Figure 11-44: Double-clicking a symbol adds the symbol at the insertion point of selected text.

As background patterns

You can add a background pattern composed of symbols to your document. Background patterns are especially effective on forms, coupons, or other documents where you want a subdued effect behind your text and graphics. To create this effect, simply fill the symbols with a light gray or other light color. When you add a background pattern of symbols to a drawing, it automatically appears within the printable area of the page.

To add a background pattern to your drawing:

1. Click the Symbol Docker button in the toolbar or select Tools ⇨ Symbols and Special Characters to display the Symbols and Special Characters docker.

2. Select the library to use from the drop-down list.

3. Enter a size for the symbol.

4. Enable Tile.

5. Click the Tile Options button to view the Tile Options dialog box. Specify the horizontal and vertical grid settings to use. Enabling Identical Values ensures that the grid has the same horizontal and vertical values. Click OK to return to the docker.

6. Choose the symbol to use and drag it to the drawing window. Draw duplicates and arranges the symbols on the page to form the background pattern (see Figure 11-45).

Tip   When you tile symbols, they appear as individual objects on the page. To prevent displacing one of the symbols accidentally, select all the symbols and group them.

Creating new symbols

Creating a custom symbol is a great way to add company logos, modified characters, or other graphics to symbol libraries where they are quickly accessible. Symbols that you create become a TrueType font and are added either to an existing library or to one that you create. Observing these rules and hints guarantees the successful creation of a custom symbol:

Caution   It's a good idea to add symbols to a library that you create rather than to an existing library. By using this method and backing up your custom library file, you prevent Draw from overwriting the library should you ever need to reinstall Draw.

✦ You can only create a symbol from a single object. You can't create a symbol from a group or multiple objects. If you want to include multiple objects in your symbol, they must be combined into a single object using the Combine command.

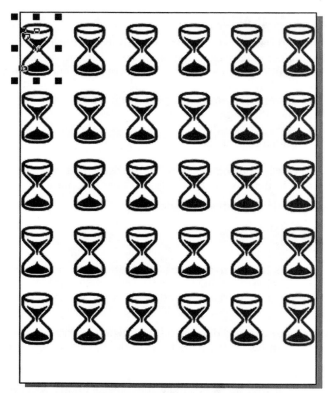

Figure 11-45: Draw duplicates and arranges the symbols on the page to form the background pattern.

✦ The object must have a closed path.

✦ If you want to create a symbol based on a modified character, you must use TrueType fonts to create the symbol.

✦ For best results, create the symbol in a large size. Draw a 6-inch by 6-inch square on the drawing page as a guide for creating the symbol at the correct size. Although you can create the symbol at any size, this technique yields the smoothest appearance at most sizes. Draw automatically resizes the symbol to match the proportions of other symbols in the library.

✦ If your object is too complex, you may receive an error message when you add the symbol to your library using the Create Symbol command. If this occurs, use the Break Apart command to separate the object into its individual elements. Simplify the object and then apply the Combine command to recreate a single object.

To create and add a symbol to a symbol library:

1. Using the Pick tool, select the object from which you want to make a symbol.

2. Select Tools ➪ Create ➪ Symbol to display the Create Symbol dialog box (see Figure 11-46).

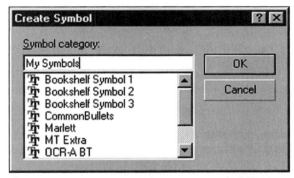

Figure 11-46: You can create a new symbol library and add symbols using the Create Symbols dialog box.

3. Enter a new name for your symbol library or select an existing library from the list.

4. Click OK to add the symbol and to return to the drawing window (see Figure 11-47).

Note

Your symbol may appear more than once in the library. This is normal. Draw allows up to 220 symbols in a library, and fills the extra spaces with the first symbol as placeholders. As you create new symbols, they replace the placeholders.

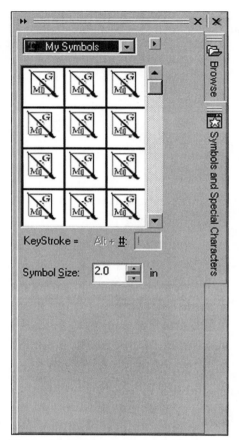

Figure 11-47: Your new symbol appears in the Symbols docker.

Summary

When I walk past a magazine rack these days, I'm struck by the special effects race displayed before me. Plain text just isn't good enough for the sophisticated palette of today's viewer. This doesn't mean, however, that you want to bury your document in an avalanche of fonts and text effects. With some careful planning, you can insert text effects that grab the attention of the viewer without overwhelming the viewer. In this chapter, I brushed the surface of some of the effects that you can create with text. I say brushed because you can create a nearly infinite variety of effects by expanding on the techniques illustrated in this chapter. Fit Text to Path and envelopes let you reshape text while retaining editing control. Using these two effects, you can create eye-catching looks that range from the whimsical to the exotic. Drop shadows and highlights let you add depth to your text, making it seem to pop off the page, while masking techniques let you subtly hint at objects beneath. In this chapter, you learned to

✦ Fit Artistic and Paragraph text to a path

✦ Work with 3D text

✦ Embed graphics in text

✦ Create collegiate-style text

✦ Add Blend effects to text

✦ Shape text using envelopes

✦ Use text as a fill

✦ Wrap text around graphics

✦ Create new symbols

✦ Embed graphics in text

✦ ✦ ✦

Designing with Fills and Lines

Choosing and applying fills and outlines in Draw is similar to working in pen and ink. The onscreen color palette is the most basic of fill tools in Draw. You can apply light and shadow effects that lend subtle depth to objects in your drawing or that make text stand out in your documents. Draw provides a wide variety of fills from which you can choose, or you can create and save your own custom fills.

Cross-Reference   See Chapter 1 to learn how to apply a fill and outline color using the onscreen color palette.

Choosing a Fill

Throughout this chapter I share the technical information required to select and apply fills. That's the easy part. The process of making a decision about which fill to use is one of the most difficult tasks in Draw — and is often an aesthetic choice. Initially, the situation is like a child with a full box of crayons. With all of the colors, everything is possible. I'm about to make it even more difficult — or easier, depending upon your point of view. You need to consider several questions before selecting a fill. Appearance might seem to be the determining factor, but it isn't. The purpose of any fill is to meet your needs while maintaining or creating an attractive appearance. Answering these questions makes your fill choice easier.

♦ *Who is your audience?* If you are creating an in-house newsletter, your audience and requirements differ from those associated with a billboard design. Similarly, if you are creating graphics for a Web page, fill choices differ from those needed for graphics in a high-resolution art book. Some fills that look great in a coffee-table book look horrible when displayed on the World Wide Web.

✦ *What is your output device?* The number of colors and type of fill vary according to the output device. If you are creating a newsletter to be printed on a black-and-white laser or inkjet printer, you need to select colors and fills that translate well into grayscale. You may need to restrict the number of colors if you intend the design for T-shirts and other silk screen applications. If you're using a router or other inscribing device, any color or fill you choose is mostly for your own information, because they are ignored by the output device.

✦ *What is your budget?* Your in-house printer and the Web are the cheapest output devices available; color and fill choices you make aren't affected by your budget. At the other end of the spectrum, if you plan on having your document commercially printed on offset or lithographic equipment, your budget becomes critical in selecting fills and colors.

✦ *Do file size restrictions exist?* When you create documents for commercial printing or in-house printing, file size is generally not a factor beyond storage limitations. Documents that contain fractal and fountain fills are larger and take longer to display. If you are creating images for recording to a CD-ROM, file size is important. (Although it seems that a CD-ROM has a lot of room, a certain amount of that room is required for overhead, and the point of using a CD-ROM is to avoid compressing the files. EPS files can be huge — in excess of 50MB each — so file size clearly matters.) If Draw isn't the final stop in the creation trip, and your image is destined for the WWW or another software application, such as Macromedia Director, file size and fill selection are critical. Some of these files can be humongous.

✦ *What are the object's requirements?* How realistic do you want the object to appear? Realistic objects have fill effects that create the illusion of lighting, depth, transparency, texture, and reflection. The choices you make determine the success of the effect you're trying to achieve.

✦ *What are the document's requirements?* Fills can overwhelm a document. This is especially true for documents that contain lots of text. If your document intends to relay information, it's a mistake to make the text difficult to read or to distract your audience from the goal.

One of the worst nightmares a commercial artist can have occurs when the artist's concept and the final output don't match. Aside from the potential expense of having to reprint something, there's the task of disassembling a drawing to replace colors or fills. By considering the foregoing questions before you create a document, you can save a lot of time, as well as make the project easier.

The Roots of Digital Artistry

The term *artist* covers a lot of territory. It could refer to a musician, poet, actor, or a plethora of others, including those who create visual art. Although most people immediately think of painters when you say *artist*, it encompasses a wide range of media in the graphic or visual arts alone.

One of the most demanding of the visual arts media is pen-and-ink drawing, if for no other reason than one cannot simply erase one's mistakes. Beyond that, the artist is limited to black ink and, usually, a white sheet of paper. Every dot, dash, and line means something in the larger scheme of the drawing. The artist painstakingly uses the concept of negative space to create *fills* that express light and shadow, giving objects depth.

Applying Uniform Fills

Uniform (solid color) fills are the foundation of Draw's color system. Solid color fills can be applied to selections in the drawing window, or can be designated as the default fill and automatically applied to each new object drawn. In Chapter 1, you learned the basics of applying a simple uniform fill interactively to objects. You can apply a uniform fill using any of these methods:

✦ **Interactively, using the onscreen palette:** The easiest method of applying a fill is to do it interactively. You can choose a color from the displayed color palette (see Chapter 1). If you click and hold the mouse button down briefly over a color in the onscreen palette, Draw displays a *ramp* of similar colors from which to choose.

✦ **Uniform Fill dialog box:** The Uniform Fill dialog box lets you select and customize colors from a variety of color models and palettes. Using the dialog box, you can create custom palettes and mix colors. See "Using the Uniform Fill Dialog Box" later in this chapter for more information about how to use this dialog box.

✦ **Fill and Outline Property bar, using the Interactive Fill tool:** When you select the Interactive Fill tool, the Property bar changes to display fill choices. Using the settings on the Property bar, you can quickly add or change the fill types of selected objects.

The selected object, the fill type, and your own personal preference determine the method you use to apply a fill. Most users develop their own personal approach to applying fills according to the fill type. In a production environment, I find myself whipping through shortcut keys or applying fills interactively because of the requirement for speed.

Tip By default, Draw displays its own custom palette in the drawing window. You aren't limited to this palette, however. You can change the palette that appears in the Drawing window by selecting Window ➪ Color Palettes and then selecting a palette from the flyout menu. Each palette has attributes that recommend it for a specific purpose. For more information about color palettes, see Chapter 14.

Using the Uniform Fill dialog box

The Uniform Fill dialog box lets you apply solid color fills using precise percentages of selected values to describe a color. Aside from this precision, using the Uniform Fill dialog box has many advantages. You can

✦ Convert the fill of an object from one palette to another

✦ Choose fills from several palettes and color models in one location (this gives you the capability of comparing colors)

✦ Create custom colors and palettes and save them for future use

✦ Adjust a color

✦ Search for colors

✦ Match colors

✦ Name colors

✦ Adjust the tint of spot colors

✦ Blend colors to create new colors

✦ Determine the color of a selected object

Draw provides a broad variety of color models and palettes from which to choose. To ensure consistency, it's a good idea to use one color model or palette for an entire document, if possible. When you create images that will be printed, remember that screen representations of color are approximate. An understanding of color palettes and the application of color management help improve the results of your printed images.

Cross-Reference For more information about color palettes and color management, see Chapter 14. I recommend that you refer to that chapter before choosing a color palette in the Uniform Fill dialog box.

To use the Uniform Fill dialog box:

1. Using the pick tool, select the object to fill.

2. Click the Fill tool button to display the Fill tool flyout menu (see Figure 12-1). Click the Uniform Fill button to access the Uniform Fill dialog box. Expand the dialog box by clicking More.

3. If the object currently has no fill, the Uniform Fill dialog box displays black in the Reference Color box (see Figure 12-2). Click and drag the slider in the color selection bar at the right to select a color. Then select a color from the color selection window by dragging the square in the large color selection window to choose a shade of the selected color.

4. To search for a specific color, enter the color name in the Search box. If a color has a specific name, that name appears in the Name box. Clicking the down arrow next to the Model box lets you select the color model to use.

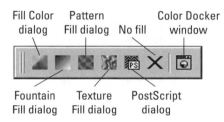

Figure 12-1: The Fill flyout menu provides a number of different types of fills.

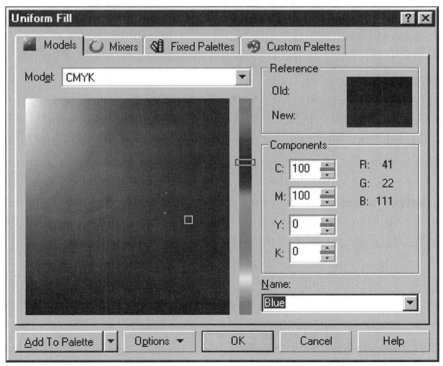

Figure 12-2: The Uniform Fill dialog box displays the reference color and the controls for changing the color of your fill.

Pressing Shift+F11 accesses the Uniform Fill dialog box.

When you are satisfied with your color selection, click OK to apply the fill and to return to the drawing window.

You can also enter values in the palette value boxes, such as the CMYK value boxes. Entering values lets you fine-tune a color. You can apply values that make subtle or dramatic changes to a color.

Be careful when modifying or selecting a color. The color you choose could be out of gamut, which means that the output device will substitute the closest color it recognizes in the place of the color that you selected. In addition, if your image is going to be displayed on the WWW, the color you select may change to reflect the default color palette of the browser. For more information about color palettes, see Chapter 14.

Setting the Default Fill

You can set the default fill that appears when you first draw an object. To specify the default fill, deselect all the objects in your drawing by clicking the desktop or by pressing Esc. Choose the uniform fill icon from the Fill tool flyout menu. A dialog box appears that lets you specify the object types to which you want to apply the new fill. Select the options you want and click OK.

The Uniform Fill dialog box appears, letting you make the selections you desire. When you are satisfied with your choices, click OK to return to the drawing window. When you draw a new object, the fill is automatically applied. The new default fill remains in effect until you change it.

Selecting colors using color models

You can choose to display other color models or palettes, use the Color Blender feature, or use the mixing area. Color model mode is the default method of selecting colors. You can modify a color directly by changing the values in the value boxes below the Model box. The value headings for these boxes change to reflect the selected palette or color model. For example, if you select a CMYK palette, an entry appears for each of these four colors: Cyan, Magenta, Yellow, and Black.

A list of approximate values for other color models appears beside the value boxes. These values are a great reference for selecting matching colors across color models. If you switch between palettes, Draw approximates the existing color using the new color model.

Once you select a color, you can add the color to the palette by clicking Add. If you change to another view of the Uniform Fill dialog box and want to change back to the color viewer, click the Viewers button.

Click the Options button to display a drop-down menu with options related to using color models for color selection. Table 12-1 lists the menu options associated with using color Models.

Table 12-1
Color Models Menu Options

Selecting this option	Performs this action
Value 2	Lets you choose from a list of color models for the New color.
Swap Color	Swaps the selected color with the Reference color.
Gamut Alarm	Warns you when a selected color falls outside the range of color that your printer can produce.

Click the Options button to display a drop-down menu with options related to using fixed color palettes for color selection. Table 12-2 lists the menu options associated with using Fixed Palettes.

Table 12-2
Fixed Palettes Menu Options

Selecting this option	Performs this action
Value 1	Lets you choose from a list of color models for the Reference color.
Value 2	Lets you choose from a list of color models for the New color.
Gamut Alarm	Warns you when a selected color falls outside the range of color that your printer can produce.
Show Color Names	Shows the names, if any, of select colors in the Name box.
PostScript Options	PostScript options are grayed out unless you have selected one of the spot color palettes. PostScript fills that you specify here are created from the selected spot color.

Using mixers

Draw provides two methods of mixing custom colors: Color Blend and Color Harmonies. These methods offer a unique way of creating color for objects in your drawing. To choose a color mixing method, click the Mixers button in the Uniform Fill dialog box, and then click to select a method from the menu.

Blending colors

Draw's Color Blender feature let you create a ramp of four colors from the RGB (Red, Green, Blue), CMYK, or HSB (Hue, Saturation, Brightness) color models. A ramp of colors is a blended range between two or more colors. Click the arrow on the Mixers button, and choose Color Blend to change to the color blend view of the Uniform Fill dialog box.

The color selection window changes to display a blend of the colors shown in each corner (see Figure 12-3). To change color models, click the down arrow next to Model and select a color model from the list. You can change the four control colors in the color selection window by clicking the down arrow on the color chip and choosing a color from the palette. The blend in the color selection window updates as you select control colors. If you want to add the color to the palette, click Add.

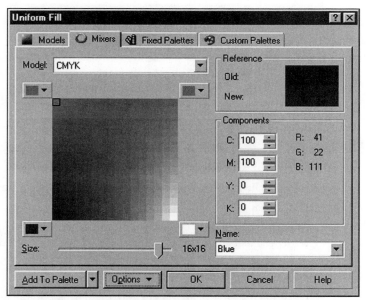

Figure 12-3: The Color Blender view of the Uniform Fill dialog box lets you select colors from a range between two or more colors.

Click the Options button to display a drop-down menu with options related to using the color Mixers view for color selection. Table 12-3 lists the menu options associated with using color Mixers.

Table 12-3 Color Mixers Menu Options	
Selecting this option	**Performs this action**
Value 2	Lets you choose from a list of color models for the New color.
Swap Color	Swaps the color with the Reference color.
Gamut Alarm	Warns you when a selected color falls outside the range of color that your printer can produce.
Mixers	Lets you select Color Blend or Color Harmonies style of mixer.

Using Color Harmonies

The Color Harmonies view of the Uniform Fill dialog box lets you select hues of colors and ramped tints of those hues (see Figure 12-4). To access the Color Harmonies view of the Uniform Fill dialog box, click the arrow on the Mixer button and select Color Harmonies from the drop-down menu.

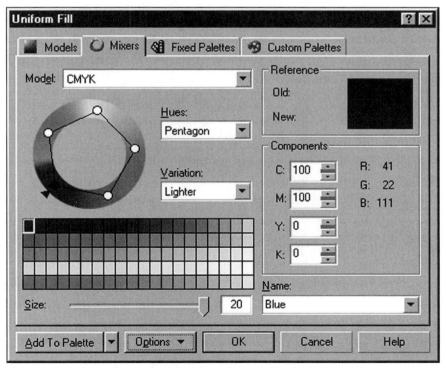

Figure 12-4: The Color Harmonies view of the Uniform Fill dialog box.

The Color Harmonies view appears with a set of triangles inside a color wheel. An interactive hue selection box is displayed over the wheel with circles at each corner. You can click and drag a handle to rotate the color selection. Clicking one of the corner circles selects that color as the New color. The triangles represent the pure hue of each color in the selected color. Clicking one of the triangles changes the selected color to the pure hue of that color. To change to another color harmony, click the down arrow below Hues and select a Harmony from the list. If you want to add a color to the palette, click Add.

Selecting colors using color palettes

When you first open the Uniform Fill dialog box, the uniform fill palette is displayed by default. If you want to use a palette such as the PANTONE Color Matching System for color selection, click the Fixed Palettes tab.

You can change the color palette by clicking the down arrow next to the palette box and selecting a palette from the list. The color selection process is similar to that of the color model method. Select a color from the palette by moving the color slider and then the color-selection square in the color-selection window (see Figure 12-5). If you want to add the color to the palette, click Add.

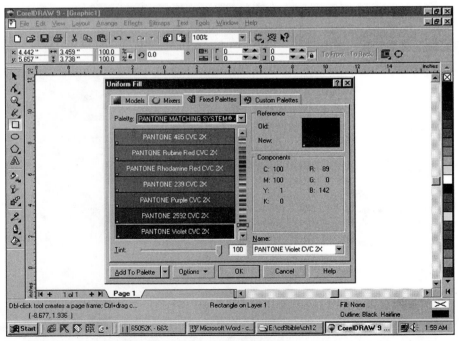

Figure 12-5: Select a color by moving the color slider and then the color-selection square in the color-selection window.

Working with custom palettes

When you first start Draw, it displays its own custom palette (coreldrw.cpl). Using this palette as a base, you can select solid fills for your objects and create your own custom palettes. Click the Custom Palettes button to access the Custom Palettes view of the Uniform Fill dialog box.

Note

To save a custom palette, it needs to be the active palette in the drawing window.

Select a color by scrolling through the color window and clicking the color to use (see Figure 12-6). You can sort the colors by clicking a color and dragging it to a new location in the color window. Clicking the Options button displays a drop-down menu with options related to using the mixing area for color selection. Table 12-4 lists the menu options associated with using the mixing area.

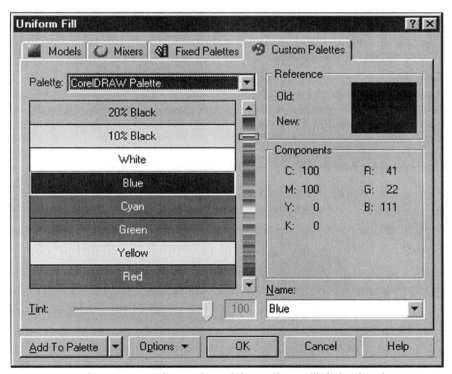

Figure 12-6: The Custom Palettes view of the Uniform Fill dialog box lets you select colors from Draw's default palette.

Table 12-4
Custom Palettes Menu Options

Selecting this option	Performs this action
Value 1	Lets you choose from a list of color models for the Reference color.
Value 2	Lets you choose from a list of color models for the New color.
Gamut Warning	Warns you when a selected color falls outside the range of color that your printer can produce.
Show Color Names	Shows the names, if any, of select colors in the Name box.
PostScript Options	PostScript options are grayed out unless you have selected one of the spot color palettes. PostScript fills you specify here are created from the selected spot color.

Saving a palette

You can add or delete colors from any palette. Once you've created the palette, you can save the palette for future use. The quickest way to save the active palette is to click Save or Save As. I recommend using Save As instead of Save to avoid overwriting one of Draw's default palettes. When the dialog box appears, give your palette a name, and click Save. Draw stores custom palettes in the draw\custom folder. Although you can save a palette anywhere, Draw looks for palettes in this location, and finding a palette saved elsewhere can be time-consuming.

Caution   It's a good idea to create a backup of custom palettes that you create. Creating a backup copy of a palette ensures that your palette won't be lost if you need to reinstall Draw at a later date. For more information about creating and using custom palettes, see Chapter 14.

Using the Color docker

The Color docker provides for onscreen editing of uniform fills and outline colors (see Figure 12-7). This is useful when you don't want to continually access the Uniform Fill or Outline Color dialog boxes. As with all roll-ups, you can leave it in the drawing window in either its closed or open position.

To use the Color docker:

1. Select the object to fill or that contains the fill to edit.

2. Select the Color docker icon from the Fill tool flyout menu.

3. If you want to apply a fill or outline color, select a color model from the drop-down list and click the color to apply. Click the Fill or Outline button to complete the operation.

4. Selecting the Eyedropper from the toolbox and clicking an object updates the Color docker and selects the object's fill as the active color.

Using this method, you can quickly edit the fill using the value boxes or apply the fill to other objects. Right-clicking the color swatch in the docker opens a pop-up menu. Choose Swap Colors, and the active color becomes the new Reference color. The Reference color lets you compare two colors when editing a color. Click the Fill or Outline button to apply the new fill or outline color to the selected object.

Figure 12-7: The Color docker lets you quickly apply uniform fills to selected objects and edit them.

Using the Fountain Fill Dialog Box

Draw lets you interactively apply fountain fills to objects. If you have an irregularly shaped object, the capability of working directly onscreen with a fountain fill is useful for adjusting the fill by eye to suit the object The advantage of working with the Fountain Fill dialog box is that it lets you apply fills with numeric precision. This is useful when you need to apply fountain fills to several objects at one time. To use the Fountain Fill dialog box, select the Fountain Fill option from the Fill tool flyout menu to display the Fountain Fill dialog box.

Shortcut

Pressing F11 accesses the Fountain Fill dialog box.

You can create and save custom fills for future use with other documents or objects. Draw comes with an assortment of preset fills that you can modify or use to quickly apply metallic or other special-effect fills to objects.

Choosing a fill type

The shape of the object and the effect that you are trying to achieve determine the fill type you choose. For example, all of the fill types lend themselves well to metallic effects. If you wanted to apply the effect to a circular shape, however, a radial or conical fill would have more impact than a linear or square fill. Figure 12-8 shows two pentagons. The pentagon on the right has a linear fill and looks flat; the pentagon on the left has a square fill that adds interest, depth, and light to the object. To choose a fill type, click the down arrow next to the Type box and select a fill type from the list.

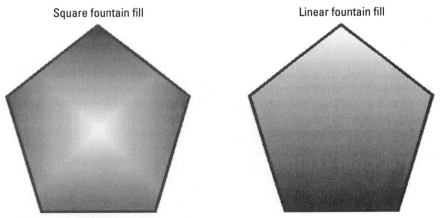

Square fountain fill   Linear fountain fill

Figure 12-8: Square versus linear fountain fill.

Specifying colors

Color selections and settings for your fountain fill are made in the Color Blend section of the Fountain Fill dialog box (see Figure 12-9). Choose a method of color blending. By default, fountain fills are two colors. You can create custom fountain fills that have more than two colors by selecting Custom. Select the colors to use in the fountain fill by clicking the down arrow on the color chips and choosing a color from the palette. The process of selecting or modifying individual colors is the same as for uniform fills.

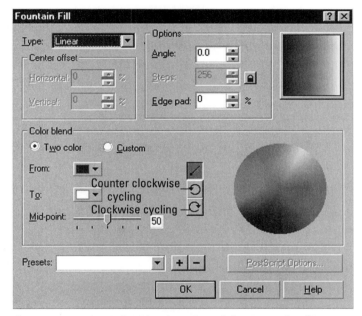

Figure 12-9: The Color blend section of the Fountain Fill dialog box.

Select the application method. The default calculates a direct blend between the two selected colors. Clicking one of the cycling buttons changes the intermediate colors, so that they cycle clockwise or counterclockwise through the color spectrum between the two selected colors. Cycling colors gives your fountain fills a rainbow effect.

Adjusting the fill

Once you've made the type and color selections for a fountain fill, you can adjust the center offset, angle, edge pad, steps, and midpoint of your fill. These settings dramatically alter the appearance of a fill. If an option is not available for the type of fill you've selected, it appears grayed out.

Specifying a center offset lets you apply highlights to selected objects. Highlighted objects gain a feeling of depth and appear 3D. For example, if you apply an offset of 20 percent horizontal and 20 percent vertical to a radial fountain filled circle, the circle acquires the appearance of a highlighted sphere (see Figure 12-10). This setting is not available for linear fountain fills.

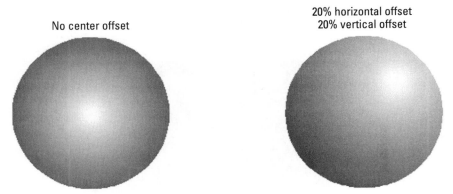

Figure 12-10: Specifying a center offset gives objects a feeling of depth.

To specify a center offset, click the up and down arrows to increase or decrease the horizontal and vertical center offset in increments of 5 percent. Alternatively, you can highlight the value in the box and enter a new value, or you can click and drag in the preview window. You can enter any value from 0 percent to 100 percent.

Customizing fountain fills

The capability of creating custom fills offers the potential for boundless creativity. Instead of being restricted to limited fountain fills, you can create any fill to achieve the effect you want. You can use custom fountain fills to achieve delicate shading effects in organic objects such as flowers, or produce bold effects that simulate lighting with vivid color (see Figure 12-11). With a little practice, you can create the perfect fill for any object.

To create a custom fountain fill:

1. Select the two end colors to use.

2. Click the Custom button in the color blend section of the Fountain Fill dialog box. A color bar appears that shows the gradient between the two selected colors. A small, square-shaped marker represents each color. The active color's marker is black.

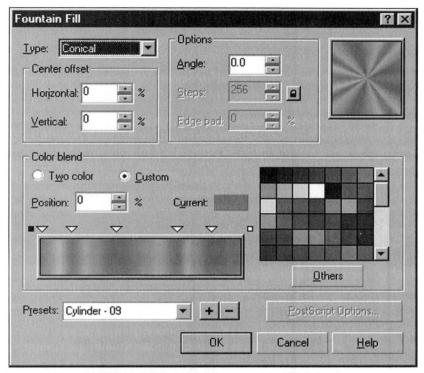

Figure 12-11: The Custom fill view of the Fountain Fill dialog box.

3. To change the end colors, click the marker to make it active and choose a color from the palette, or click the down arrow on the color chip and select a color. Colors are selected and modified using the same methods as with uniform fills.

4. To add a color to the gradient, double-click either of the end colors to add a color. You can also double-click anywhere between the dotted lines to add a new color marker.

5. The default color that you add is the same as the end color you double-click. While the new color is active, you can change the color. If you want to change it later, select it to make it the active color, and then choose a new color from the palette.

6. Drag the new color marker to change its position in the gradient. Alternatively, you can click the up and down arrow or highlight the value in the position box and enter a new location.

7. To remove a color marker from the gradient, double-click it.

8. To save a custom fountain fill for future use, name the fill and then click the plus (+) button next to Presets. The next time you want to use the fill, it will appear in the Presets list.

 Caution   When you add a new fill to the fountain fill presets, Draw saves it in the draw\ custom folder in the coreldrw.ffp file. If you ever need to reinstall Draw, be sure to create a backup of this and other files in this folder. Otherwise, your custom settings will be lost.

Presets are a set of custom fountain fills that you can apply to objects in your image. These fills provide a starter set of custom fills. A wide variety of metallic, cylindrical, rainbow, and other effects are included. As shown in the previous section, you can add your own custom fills to the available presets. To select a fill from the presets, click the down arrow in the Fountain Fill dialog box and choose a fill from the list. You can modify these fills as you choose. If you want to save the modified fill, I recommend renaming the fill before clicking the plus (+) button to avoid overwriting the original preset. You can remove a fill by selecting it from the preset list and clicking the minus (–) button.

Using Special Fills

Solid and fountain fills are just two of the types of fills that you can use with Draw objects. You can also choose from a variety of special fills that let you apply a wider range of effects to objects. By modifying these fills and creating new fills, you can expand your library even further. Each of the special fills has attributes that recommend it for a particular use.

✦ **Pattern fills:** You can choose from three types of pattern fills: two-color, full-color, and bitmap. When you apply a pattern fill, Draw creates tiles of the size you specify to fill the object.

✦ **PostScript fills:** PostScript fills are available when you select a spot-color fill. These fills let you add halftone effects to your documents.

✦ **Texture fills:** Texture fills are pregenerated fractal fills that allow you to add richness, depth, and texture to objects in your drawings.

Applying pattern fills

You can apply repeating patterns as a fill (see Figure 12-12). Two-color fills let you specify a background and foreground color for the repeating pattern. This fill is a good choice for graphs and technical illustrations. Full-color fills use multiple colors and can be used to create simple texture effects and repeating color patterns. Bitmap pattern fills let you apply a bitmapped image as a fill. For example, you could use a scanned bitmap of your favorite photo as a fill.

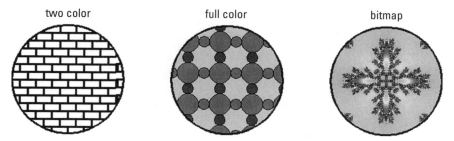

Figure 12-12: You can use pattern fills to add repeating pattern effects to objects.

Pattern fills serve a number of purposes. You can choose from two-color, full-color, and bitmap fills. The two-color pattern fills are especially well-suited for shading technical illustrations and schematics (see Figure 12-13).

Figure 12-13: Two-color pattern fills are useful for shading schematic drawings.

To apply a pattern fill:

1. Using the Pick tool, select the object to fill.

2. Click the Pattern Fill icon on the Fill tool flyout menu to display the Pattern Fill dialog box (see Figure 12-14).

3. Choose the type of pattern fill to use and select a fill by clicking the down arrow on the fill sample and choosing a fill. Click Load if you want to use a previously created custom fill.

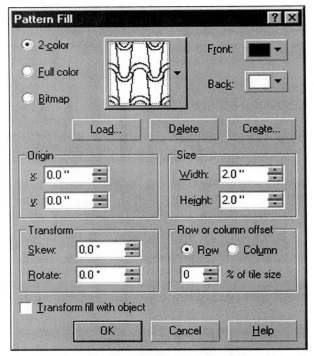

Figure 12-14: The Pattern Fill dialog box lets you specify a type of pattern fill and the fill options to use.

4. Select a tile size from the Size options by highlighting the width and height values and entering a new value. A tile must be a minimum of 0.1 inches.

5. You can offset rows or columns of tiles. To change the tiling options, choose either Row or Column and click the up and down arrow, or enter a new value in the Percentage box.

6. Specifying an origin sets the center of the pattern fill in relationship to the drawing page. To set the origin, click the up and down arrows, or enter new values in the x and y origin boxes.

7. You can rotate and skew pattern fills by clicking the up and down arrows or by entering new values in the Skew and Rotate boxes.

8. Enable Transform fill with object if you want the fill to be responsive to transformations that you apply to the object in the drawing window.

By enabling Transform fill with object, you link the fill to the orientation of the object. If you skew or rotate the object afterwards, the fill adjusts in accordance with the new orientation (see Figure 12-15).

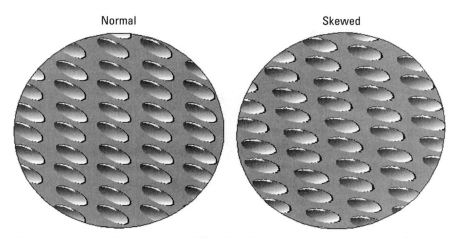

Figure 12-15: Enabling Transform fill with object causes the orientation of the fill to change whenever you rotate or skew the object in the drawing window.

Creating pattern fills

Finding the perfect fill can be an art form in itself. A library of preset pattern fills comes with Draw, but you aren't confined to using those fills. You can create your own fills from any image that you can display in Draw. While the process of creating the actual fill is the same for two-color or full-color files, there are some hints that are specific to each type.

Tip Before creating a pattern fill, use the rectangle tool to create a 1-inch square. Position the square over the area from which you want to create a pattern fill, and remove any fill or outline. Select Layout ⇨ Snap To Object. When you create the fill, Draw snaps to the square you created, enabling you to easily create a 1-inch pattern fill — 1 inch is usually the default size for pattern fills.

To add a pattern fill:

1. Create, open, or import the image from which you want to create a pattern fill.

2. Select Tools ⇨ Create ⇨ Pattern to display the Create Pattern dialog box (see Figure 12-16).

3. Choose either Two Color or Full Color and click OK. If you select Two Color, choose a resolution for your fill.

4. Cross hairs appear in the drawing window. Click and drag to select the area from which you want to create the fill (see Figure 12-17). Release the mouse button to complete the operation. Draw automatically adds two-color fills to its pattern fill file.

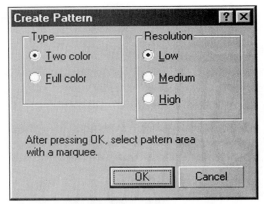

Figure 12-16: The Create Pattern dialog box lets you specify color and resolution options for the pattern fill you are creating.

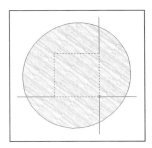

Figure 12-17: Click and drag the cross hairs to select the area you want to use as a fill.

5. If you are creating a full-color fill, the Save Vector Pattern dialog box appears automatically, allowing you to name your fill. Give the fill a name and click Save.

Draw saves full-color pattern fills in the draw\custom\patterns folder. Although you can save your fill anywhere, I recommend saving your pattern fill in the default folder. This allows Draw to easily find your fill, and to display a thumbnail in the Pattern Fill dialog box.

Caution   Draw automatically appends the coreldrw.bpt file when you create a two-color pattern fill. This file is found in the draw\custom folder. I recommend creating a backup of this file so that if you have to reinstall Draw, your custom two-color fills won't be lost. Similarly, if you create a full-color fill, be sure to create a backup of it.

Pattern fills can affect both the file size and complexity of an image. As the complexity of an image increases, the possibility of printing problems also increases. Of the three fill types, two-color fills have the least impact on printing and file size. Full-color and bitmap fills affect the file size and complexity more significantly. Figure 12-18 shows two full-color fills. Full-color fills are unique in that they are vector fills. If you can create an effect as a vector image, you can use it as a full-color fill. The circle on the left is filled with one of the full-color presets and is 92K in size. The fill on the right is a custom full-color fill. The pyramid and sky are blended objects that increase the file size to 1.44MB. A bitmap fill applied to the same object would also be 1.44MB in size, but would not affect the complexity of the image as much as the blended pyramids and sky.

Preset full-color pattern fill: 92K

Custom full-color pattern fill: 1.44MB

Figure 12-18: Full-color pattern fills are vector fills that can impact the file size and complexity of your image.

Bitmap Resolution Magic

Draw lets you create a bitmap fill of any pattern fill. This is great for bitmap pattern fills, because you can increase the effective resolution of the bitmap. Fill a 1-inch square with the pattern or bitmap fill that you want to use. Remove any outline from the square by right-clicking the X in the onscreen palette and select Layout ➪ Snap To Object. Convert the square to a bitmap by selecting Bitmaps ➪ Convert to Bitmap. Adjust the resolution in the Convert to Bitmap dialog box to 300 dpi, and then click OK to convert your selection to a bitmap.

Select Bitmaps ➪ Resample and adjust the size of the square to 2 inches. Leave the resolution at 300 dpi. Select Tools ➪ Create ➪ Pattern, and select the square in the drawing window. When Draw creates the pattern, it reduces the size, internally, to 1 inch. This method increases the effective resolution of the fill to 600 dpi. This method is useful for improving the quality of bitmap fills. You can use this with both preset fills and fills that you create.

Working with PostScript fills and textures

You can add a variety of PostScript textures and fills to your image. PostScript textures are grayscale fills that make excellent backgrounds for other objects in your image (see Figure 12-19). PostScript fills are PostScript screen effects that you can apply to PANTONE Color Matching System colors. Because these textures and fills are interpreted internally in Draw before they are printed, you are not required to have a PostScript device for the output to render correctly. A PostScript device, such as a laser printer, however, will yield a better output. Normally, PostScript textures aren't displayed on screen because they are large and resource intensive. The letters PS are used as the onscreen fill for your object. If your resources enable you to run Draw with an enhanced display, PostScript textures are visible, but the refresh speed may be slower. PostScript effects applied to PANTONE Color Matching System colors are not visible in the drawing window.

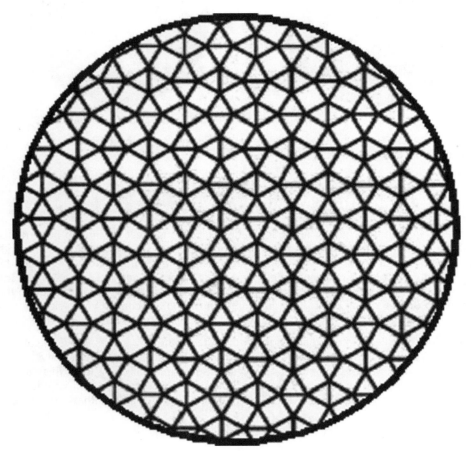

Figure 12-19: PostScript textures are excellent as background fills.

Applying a PostScript fill

You apply PostScript fills and PostScript textures using different methods. PostScript screen effects are only available for PANTONE Color Matching System colors in the Uniform Fill dialog box. PostScript textures can be applied interactively or in the PostScript Texture dialog box.

To Apply a PostScript Fill:

1. Select the Uniform Fill icon from the Fill flyout to display the Uniform Fill dialog box.

2. Click the Fixed Palettes tab of the Uniform Fill dialog box and select PANTONE Color Matching System from the drop-down Type list.

3. Click the Options button, and choose PostScript Options to display the PostScript Options dialog box (see Figure 12-20).

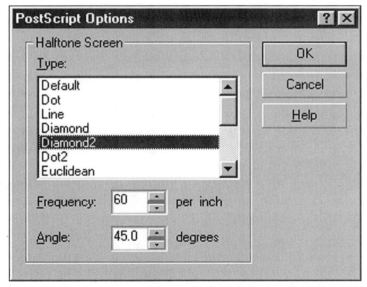

Figure 12-20: You can specify PostScript fills in the PostScript Options dialog box. They add interest to objects in your documents.

4. Select a Halftone screen from the list and adjust the frequency and angle of the screen, if desired.

5. Click OK to return to the Uniform Fill dialog box, and OK again to return to the drawing window.

I don't recommend adjusting the screen frequency and angle. The default settings work well for most purposes and are the optimal settings. You might want to consult your printer before changing these settings. The halftone screen is not visible in the drawing window, but it does appear when printed on a PostScript device.

Note

PostScript options are only available for PANTONE Color Matching System colors.

Applying PostScript textures

To apply PostScript textures:

1. Using the Pick tool, select the object to which you want to apply a PostScript texture.

2. Select the PostScript Fill dialog box icon from the Fill flyout menu to display the PostScript Textures dialog box (see Figure 12-21).

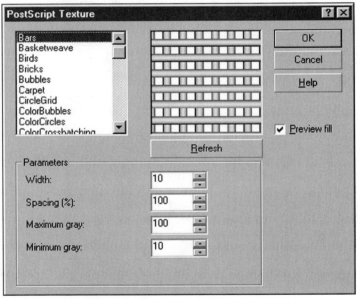

Figure 12-21: Select the PostScript texture you want and click Preview to see a sample of the texture in the PostScript Fill dialog box.

3. Scroll through the texture list and click the texture to apply. Click Preview fill to see a sample of the selected texture.

4. Adjust any of the texture settings that you want to adjust, and click OK to return to the drawing window.

Draw applies the texture to the selected object in the drawing window. Each PostScript texture has settings that are unique to that texture. You can increase or decrease the values to alter the appearance of the fill. When applying PostScript textures, it's better to work in Enhanced view if you need to adjust the settings for a texture. This lets you view the texture as it will look when printed.

Caution   PostScript textures are resource intensive. They create large files and take a significant amount of memory to calculate and to render the image on your monitor.

Using texture fills

Texture or fractal fills are great for adding texture and depth to objects. The variety of fills and variations is endless. Texture fills are basically fractal fills. A fractal fill is a computer-generated pattern based on a set of mathematical formulas. Each texture fill has a set of attributes specific to that fill. If you click Preview, the fill is regenerated based on that fill's formula, and a new view of the fill appears in the window. Because texture fills are created randomly, you might want to write down the file number of fills that you like while browsing the fills. If you want to return to a specific fill, enter the number in the Texture # box.

These fills allow for variable resolution, which lends itself to creating some incredible special effects. Fractal fills do affect both file size and complexity. The circle shown in Figure 12-22 is 924K. If file size is critical, consider applying fractal fills to smaller objects. If you apply a fractal fill to a background the size of the drawing page, the file size becomes prohibitive. When combined with the complexity of the image, it can slow screen refresh and printing speed enormously. For instance, 1 sheet of 10 business cards, each with a very small texture — less than 1 square inch — could cause the rasterize time to go from minutes to almost an hour.

Texture fills can bring objects to life. Such fills let you simulate natural substances or other textures. In the next few exercises, you work with a tutorial file using texture fills to add depth and texture to a plaque.

On the CD-ROM   The tutorial file, duck1.cdr, is located on your companion CD-ROM in the ch12\tutorial folder.

To apply a texture fill:

1. Open duck1.cdr. When you first open the file, the duck is red and the exterior oval is black.

2. Using the Pick tool, select the duck.

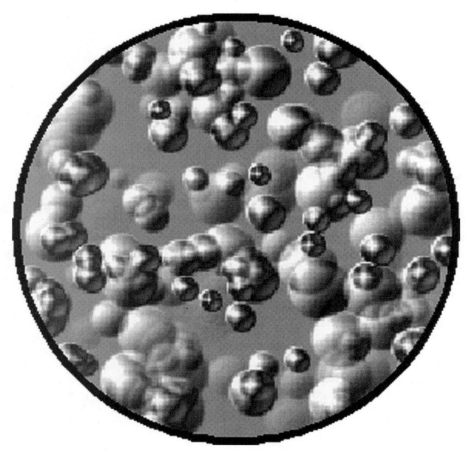

Figure 12-22: Fractal fills let you add texture and depth to your image.

3. Click the Texture Fill icon in the Fill tool flyout menu to display the Texture Fill dialog box.

4. Select the Samples 7 Texture Library. A list of fills associated with that library appears in the texture list (see Figure 12-23).

5. Select Utah Stone from the list. A thumbnail of the fill appears in the preview window.

6. Click OK to apply the fill and to return to the drawing window (see Figure 12-24).

7. Save the file on your hard disk as **duck2.cdr**.

The fill is too dark and seems to disappear into the black background. In the next section, you learn to adjust texture fills to change the brightness and vary the fill.

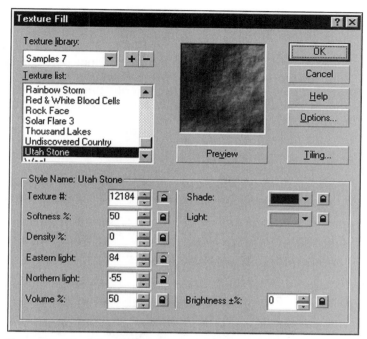

Figure 12-23: A list of fills appears in the Texture list.

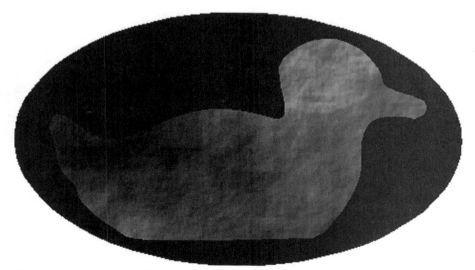

Figure 12-24: Draw applies the selected texture fill to the duck.

Varying texture fills

You can change the colors of the fill by clicking the associated color chip and selecting a color from the palette. As with all fills, colors are selected and modified in the same fashion as for uniform fills. By altering the various parameters, you can change the fill more extensively. The number of permutations on any fill is nearly endless, and it would be impossible to begin to describe them here. In the next exercise, you brighten the fill you applied to the duck and apply a new fill to the background.

To vary texture fills:

1. Open duck2.cdr if it's not open.

2. Using the Pick tool, select the duck and, from the Fill tool flyout menu, select the Texture Fill icon.

3. In the Brightness section, increase the value to 40 percent.

4. Click OK to apply the fill and to return to the drawing window. Draw renders the changes to the duck's fill (see Figure 12-25).

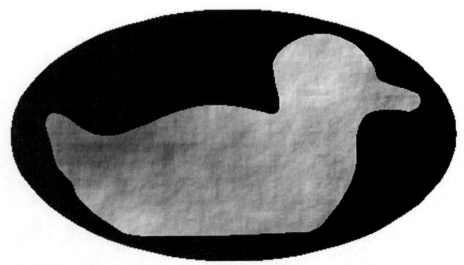

Figure 12-25: The duck's fill becomes lighter, providing more contrast with the background.

5. Using the Pick tool, select the background in the drawing window and open the Texture Fill dialog box.

6. Choose the Samples library and the Soft Water fill.

7. Click the Bottom color swatch and select a dark brown. Choose a cream color for the Surface color.

8. In the Texture # box, enter **27077**.

9. Click OK to apply the fill and to return to the drawing window. The background has the appearance of wood (see Figure 12-26).

10. Save the drawing.

Figure 12-26: The texture fill gives the background the appearance of wood.

These last two exercises just touched the surface of the effects that you can create using texture fills. By varying the fill and modifying fill parameters, you can give the fill an entirely new appearance.

Choosing texture fill options

Clicking the options button in the Texture Fill dialog box displays the Texture Options dialog box, letting you select a tile size and the resolution of texture fills (see Figure 12-27). Texture fills tend to have a grainy appearance if they are printed at a resolution other than the resolution specified for the bitmap. You can change the resolution by clicking the down arrow next to Bitmap Resolution and selecting the value that you want. For the smoothest results, select a resolution that matches your output. You can also change the maximum tile width by selecting a new width from the drop-down list box.

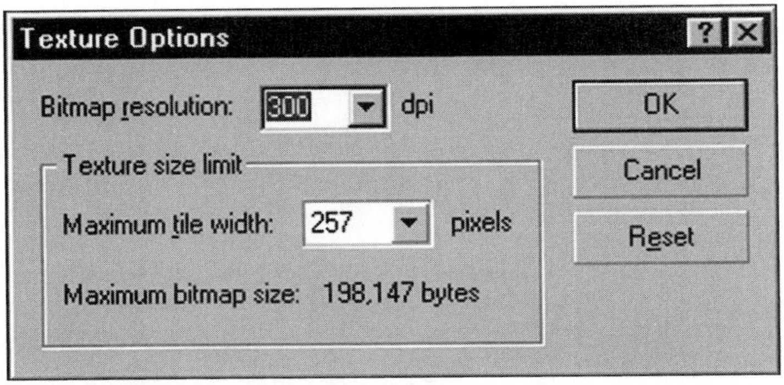

Texture Options

Bitmap resolution: 300 ▼ dpi

Texture size limit

Maximum tile width: 257 ▼ pixels

Maximum bitmap size: 198,147 bytes

OK
Cancel
Reset

Figure 12-27: The Texture Options dialog box.

Changes that you make in the Texture Options dialog box affect the file size of your image. The maximum bitmap size is shown at the bottom of the Texture Options dialog box. This amount is *not* based on the size of your object. It's based on the printable area of your page size. For example, if you have a possible 8 × 10-inch printable area, the maximum bitmap size might be well over 3MB, even though you're only filling a 2-inch object. Draw assumes that you might want to fill an entire page with the fill, although I don't recommend that you do so. The file size would be prohibitive. Similarly, if you are creating an image for the Web or for other onscreen use, the ideal bitmap resolution is either 72 dpi or 96 dpi. It is pointless to choose a higher resolution, because higher resolutions exceed the maximum resolution displayable by a monitor.

Customizing texture fills

Once you've modified a texture fill, you can save it for later use in the Texture Fill dialog box. Creating and saving custom textures lets you expand the texture libraries with frequently used fills. If the custom fill that you want to add to the Texture Library has been applied to an object in your drawing, select the object so that it's displayed in the Preview window when you open the Texture Fill dialog box.

Note   The Styles Library is unique in that you can't add to the textures in that library. You also can't overwrite its existing textures. If your custom texture is based on one in the Styles Library, you can save it to any of the other libraries.

To add a custom texture fill to a library:

1. Open the Texture Fill dialog box. Be sure that the fill you want to add is displayed in the Preview window.

2. Modify the fill, if desired, by adjusting the fill parameters.

3. Select the library to which you want to add the fill.

4. Click the plus (+) button to add the fill. The Save Texture as dialog box appears, with the name of the fill on which your custom fill is based. Clicking the minus (–) button deletes the texture.

5. Enter a name for your fill. You can use up to 32 characters and spaces (see Figure 12-28).

6. Click OK to return to the Texture Fill dialog box. The name you gave your custom texture appears in the texture list.

7. Click OK to return to the drawing window.

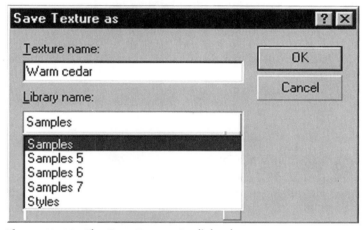

Figure 12-28: The Save Texture As dialog box.

It's a good idea to always give your texture a new name. Although Draw lets you overwrite any of the texture fills, with the exception of those located in the Styles Library, I don't recommend it. If you overwrite the file, its base information won't be available in the future.

Caution   When you save a custom texture, Draw stores the information in the library.txr file found in the draw\custom folder. It's a good idea to create a backup of this file, in case you need to reinstall Draw, so that you won't lose your custom textures.

As with all of Draw's special fills, you can control a texture fill's behavior. You can adjust the tile size, rotate, skew, or make it respond to object transformations. Using the Interactive Fill tool, you also can change the tile's center (see the next section, "Using the Interactive Fill Tool"). Click the Tiling button in the Texture Fill dialog box to rotate or skew the object, or enable Transform fill with object and specify the settings you want, as you would for a Pattern fill. Click the Options button if you want to change the tile size in the Texture Options dialog box.

You can specify any tile size from 0.01 inches to 15 inches. You should note that the tile size values in the Texture Options dialog box are expressed in pixels per inch (ppi). This is because of the direct relationship between the resolution and the actual size of a tile. The actual size of a tile is Pixels/Resolution. For example, if you wanted the tile width to be 2 inches, and your resolution was 300 dpi, you would set the tile width at 600 pixels (600 ppi/300 dpi = 2 inches).

Using the Interactive Fill Tool

The Interactive Fill tool lets you apply any of Draw's fill types to objects in your drawing. When the Interactive Fill tool is selected, the Interactive Texture Fill Property bar is displayed (see Figure 12-29). Using the Property bar, you can apply any type of fill. You can also access the various fill dialog boxes if you need to edit a fill. In Figure 12-29, the Property bar displays the fill settings for the background behind the duck.

Note   For the illustrations in this section, the Property bar and onscreen color palette have been undocked and resized to fit in the drawing window.

Figure 12-29: The Interactive Texture Fill Property bar.

How interactive fills work

The Property bar changes to reflect the current fill of the object. Click the down arrow for the fill type and select Fountain Fill. The object changes to display the controls for a linear fountain fill (see Figure 12-30).

Each type of fountain fill displays a different set of controls specific to that fill type. The same methods, however, are used to modify each fill type. Figures 12-31 through 12-35 show the fill controls associated with each type of fill.

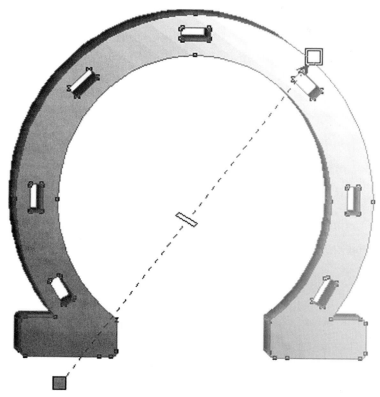

Figure 12-30: Draw displays the controls for a linear fountain fill.

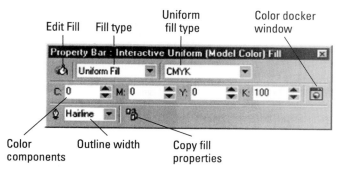

Figure 12-31: Interactive Uniform Fill Property bar controls.

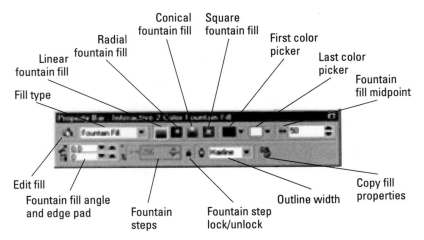

Figure 12-32: Interactive Fountain Fill Property bar controls.

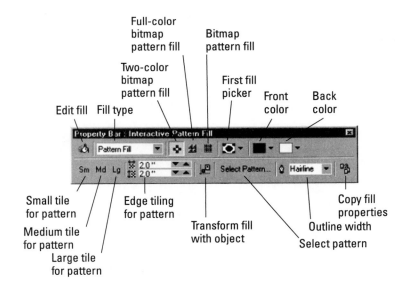

Figure 12-33: Interactive Pattern Fill Property bar controls.

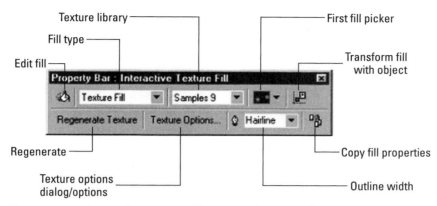

Figure 12-34: Interactive Texture Fill Property bar controls.

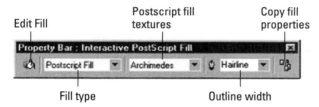

Figure 12-35: Interactive Postscript Fill Property bar controls.

Applying interactive fountain fills

Fountain fills are the most interactive of the fill types. Each fountain fill type has its own unique set of visible controls that it places on an object to let you add colors, adjust the orientation, and adjust the midpoint of the fill. You can apply an interactive fountain fill to objects by selecting the objects with the Interactive Fill tool. The four fountain fill types are shown in Figure 12-36.

To apply and modify a fountain fill:

1. Using the Rectangle tool, create a rectangle in the drawing window. The size and precise shape don't matter.

2. Select the Interactive Fill tool from the toolbox. Click the Rectangle to select it. If you haven't specified a default fill, Draw displays the object as having No Fill on the Property bar.

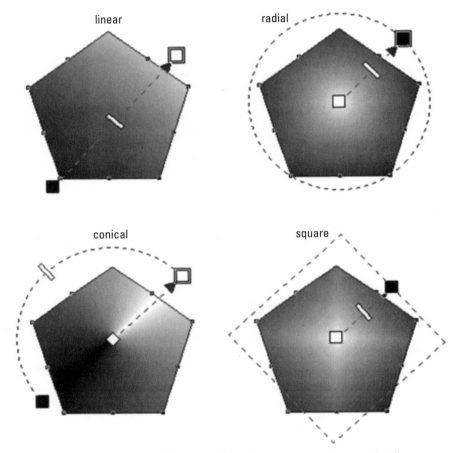

Figure 12-36: The linear, radial, conical, and square types of fountain fill are displayed here.

Note   If you click and drag in the rectangle, Draw automatically applies a linear fountain fill.

3. Select Fountain Fill and click the Linear button. By default, Draw applies a black-to-white linear fill to the selected object.

4. In the drawing window, click and drag the midpoint slider down to increase the amount of white showing in the fill.

5. Adjust the range of the fill by clicking and dragging the end handles of the fill outward from the object (see Figure 12-37).

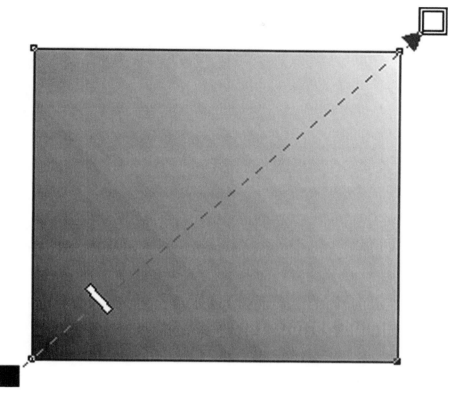

Figure 12-37: You can increase the range of the fill by adjusting the end handles of the fill.

6. Click and drag the end handles of the fill to adjust the angle of the fill. The dotted line indicates the angle of the fill. Alternatively, you can highlight value in the angle box on the Property bar and enter a new angle. Adjust the fill to about 45 degrees.

7. Click the Radial Fill button on the Property bar to change the type of fountain fill.

8. Drag the outside handle of the fill toward the center of the object to add edge padding to the fill (see Figure 12-38). Alternatively, you can highlight the value in the Edge Padding box on the Property bar and enter the amount of edge padding you want.

9. Click the Conical Fill button on the Property bar to change the type of fountain fill.

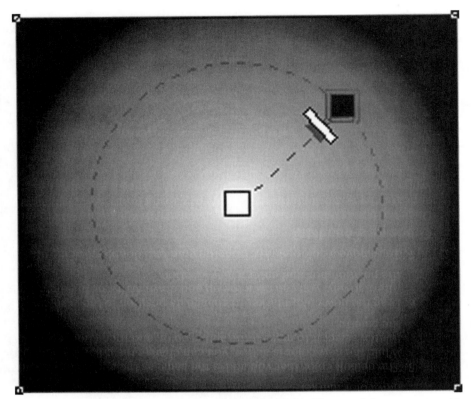

Figure 12-38: Click and drag the outside handle of the fill toward the center to add edge padding to the fill.

10. Click and drag the center handle of the fill to the upper-right corner of the rectangle. On the Property bar, slide the midpoint slider to 1 to display the maximum amount of white, and then drag either of the outside handles counterclockwise to rotate the fill, as shown in Figure 12-39.

11. Click the Square Fill button on the property bar to change the type of fountain fill.

12. Click and drag the outside black handle down and to the left to center the fill vertically in the rectangle (refer to Figure 12-39). Click and drag the white square to rotate the fill to create the diamond shape with a large amount of edge padding.

Tip   If you use the Interactive Fill tool with a fountain fill, then adjusting the position of the dotted box by moving the end squares changes the look of the fountain fill. If you rotate the dotted box by clicking and dragging on the corner circle, you can create tiled blocks with perspective.

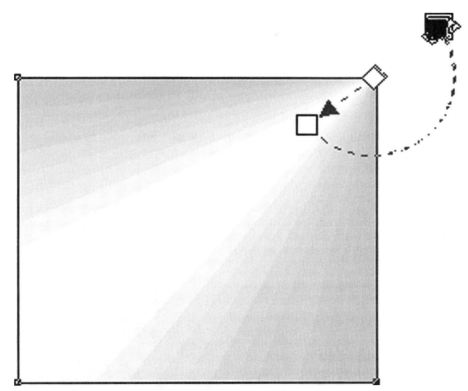

Figure 12-39: By adjusting the position and rotation of the fill, you can modify the amount of edge padding and create shapes within a fill.

The previous exercise showed you how to create just a few of the effects that are possible using the Interactive Fill tool with fountain fills. In the next exercise, you learn to change the color of a fill and to add new colors to give objects a metallic appearance. The horseshoe in hshoe.cdr (on the CD-ROM) is an extruded object. You apply the fill to adjust the control object by dragging colors from the onscreen palette to the fill line of the object. As you drag colors to an object or fill line, the color swatch changes as it passes over objects. As it passes over an area that can be filled, it appears solid; as it passes over an outline that cannot be filled, it appears hollow. This method lets you apply both outlines and fills to objects.

Adding Mesh Fills

You will appreciate Mesh fills if you've ever wished you could bend a fountain fill or found the preset fountain fill modes restrictive. Mesh fills are based on a grid. You specify the number of columns and rows to use. You can interactively add fills to either the nodes for subtle shading, or inside a grid square to cover a larger area.

New Feature   Mesh fills are one of Draw 9's exciting new features. Using the Mesh fill tool, you can blend the color objects interactively with other objects around it, or create a custom multicolor fill.

You can add as many colors as you have nodes and squares when applying a custom fill to the object. You can also move the nodes and change their properties much as you would with the Shape tool. If you want to add another column or row, you can at anytime. This new feature is useful for adding the appearance of a contour and for creating a subtle transition between the selected object's fill and a fountain fill object beneath it (see Figure 12-40).

Figure 12-40: The contours of the woman's face were created using a mesh fill to create subtle transitions between the object and the fill below.

To apply a mesh fill:

1. Using the Pick tool, select the object to which you want to apply a mesh fill. You can also select the object with the Mesh fill tool.

2. Select the Mesh tool from the toolbox. The Property bar changes to display the Mesh tool settings, and a grid is applied to your object (see Figure 12-41).

3. If you want to adjust the number of columns or rows, change the value on the Property bar. Draw updates the grid when you either click another setting or press Enter.

Tip

When applying a mesh fill to an object with an irregular shape, you will find it easier to start with fewer columns and rows, adding them at the locations you desire as needed. It's also easier to edit the grid lines and nodes prior to adding colors.

4. Adjust the grid to create the contour you want. You can change the node and line segment type as you would with the Shape tool by clicking and dragging a node or line. You can also add, delete, and select multiple nodes.

Caution

If you move an exterior node on an object to adjust the fill, you also change the shape of the object.

5. Click and drag colors from the color palette to the grid. As your mouse pointer passes over an area that can receive the fill, the icon changes to a color square. Alternatively, select the nodes that you want to receive a fill and click the fill in the color palette.

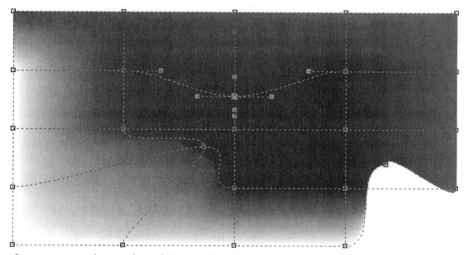

Figure 12-41: The Mesh tool view of the Property bar lets you adjust the object's grid.

Mesh fills are useful for creating fades and other transitional color effects. While you retain total control over the finished fill, these fills can be time-consuming to apply because you can apply a different fill to every node and square in the grid. It's also possible that the grid may fall outside the outline of irregularly shaped objects, or may not appear uniformly spaced across an object. Edit the grid to create the desired effect. You may find it easier to work in a zoomed view when editing the grid.

Note You can't apply Mesh fills to text objects. An object cannot receive both a mesh fill and one of Draw's special effects such as an Extrusion, Envelope, Contour, or Blend effect.

If you want to copy a mesh fill from one object to the next, select the object to which you want to copy the mesh fill and then click the Copy Mesh Fill Properties From button on the Property bar. When you move your cursor back to the drawing window, you can click an object that contains a mesh fill. Draw duplicates both the grid and colors of the original mesh fill as closely as possible to the new object. You can remove a mesh fill from an object by clicking the Clear Mesh button on the Property bar.

Caution Mesh fills are editable in future Draw sessions *only* if you save them as Version 9 files. If you save a document containing a mesh fill as a previous version of Draw, the object is converted to a bitmap and can't be edited as a mesh fill in future Draw sessions.

Creating Special Effects with Fills

Nothing in our existence is a single color. Our perception of depth and reality is linked to the subtle play of light and shadow on the world around us. Draw provides the power to use fills creatively to simulate light and shadow. The results lend realism and depth to objects in your drawings. You can make objects appear rough, smooth, shiny, reflective, or transparent. In the next exercise, you use the Interactive Fill tool to give the horseshoe in hshoe.cdr a metallic fill.

On the CD-ROM The exercise for this section uses hshoe.cdr. This file can be found on your companion CD-ROM in the ch12\tutorial folder.

To add metallic effects interactively:

1. Open hshoe.cdr.

2. Using the Interactive Fill tool, click the horseshoe to select it. You want to select just the horseshoe and not the extruded group. The Status bar indicates that the selected object is a Control object.

3. In the onscreen palette, select a dark blue-gray and drag it to the bottom handle of the fill (see Figure 12-42).

4. Click and drag a lighter blue-gray, white, and the dark blue-gray to locations on the fill line, as shown in Figure 12-43.

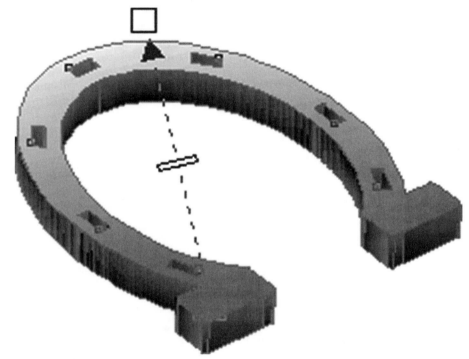

Figure 12-42: Drag a dark blue-gray to the bottom handle of the fountain fill.

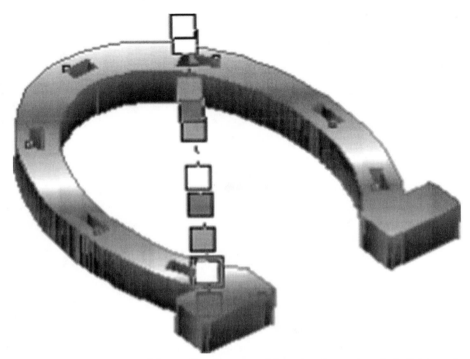

Figure 12-43: You can add metallic effects to objects by alternating dark, light, and medium shades of a color.

Using the Eyedropper and Paintbucket Tools

The Eyedropper and Paintbucket tools make the precise selection of fills and outlines easier (see Figure 12-44). This is especially true if you are trying to match a color from a bitmap or to match a fountain fill that you previously used. The Eyedropper lets you pick up a color from any object, including bitmaps, in your document. You access the Eyedropper and Paintbucket tools by selecting the Eyedropper tool flyout menu. The Eyedropper and Paintbucket tools let you:

✦ Copy a fill, including fountain and texture fills, from an object.

✦ Copy a color from a limited sample area.

✦ Copy the dominant color from a selected area.

✦ Apply the copied fill directly to an object in the drawing window.

Figure 12-44: The Eyedropper and Paintbucket tools make the copying of complex fills easier.

The Eyedropper and Paintbucket tools make matching fills much easier and faster. You can pick up colors with the Eyedropper and then apply them with the Paintbucket to quickly transfer fills and outlines from one object to another.

When the Eyedropper or the Paintbucket tool are active, the Property bar updates to let you specify how the two tools behave. Choose the outline or fill button on the Property bar. Then you can specify the area that the Eyedropper uses to sample colors and fills in your document (see Figure 12-45).

Tip Pressing Shift+Tab toggles between the Eyedropper and Paintbucket tools so that you can select and apply colors quickly.

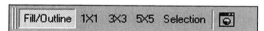

Figure 12-45: The Eyedropper view of the Property bar lets you select the sampling area that Draw uses to determine the selected color.

Use Table 12-5 as a guide for selecting Eyedropper properties. After selecting the settings you want to use, click in the drawing window to select a color.

	Table 12-5 **Specifying Eyedropper Properties**	
Setting	**Selection**	**Suggested use**
Fill/Outline	Selects the fill of a vector object.	Choose this option to recreate a fountain or texture fill.
1 × 1	Selects the color of a single pixel.	Choose this option if the fill you are sampling is from an object that contains a single color.
3 × 3	Selects the dominant color in an area 3 pixels square.	This option is useful if you want to sample a portion of a fountain fill. Draw displays the dominant color of the sample area.

Continued

	Table 12-5 *(continued)*	
Setting	**Selection**	**Suggested use**
5×5	Selects the dominant color in an area 5 pixels square.	Similar to the 3×3 option, this is a good choice for selecting colors from a complex fill. Draw displays the dominant color of the sample area.
Selection	Lets you click and drag to create a selection area. Draw determines the dominant color in the selected area.	Use this option to select the dominant color from an object containing a wide range of colors.

Using the Outline Pen Dialog Box

The Outline Pen dialog box provides access to every attribute control available for an outline (see Figure 12-46). Selecting the Outline Pen icon from the Outline Pen tool flyout menu accesses the Outline Pen dialog box. By specifying settings in the Outline Pen dialog box, you can

+ Create calligraphic effects
+ Choose a corner type
+ Select line caps
+ Add an arrowhead to a line
+ Choose a line style
+ Specify an outline color
+ Select how the outline appears in relation to the fill and image

Shortcut   F12 accesses the Outline Pen dialog box.

Choosing a line width and line style

Draw lets you set a broad range of line widths. You can select any width from 0.00005 inches to 36.0 inches. The default hairline width is 0.003 inches or 2 points. By default, Draw lists outline widths as points, but I recommend changing it to inches, millimeters, or another unit of measure that is more familiar to you. Using a familiar unit of measure lets you work faster and more efficiently. Extremely low values are hard to see, however, and may not print accurately. I recommend specifying a minimum value of 0.014 inches. To specify a line width, click the up and down arrows next to the Width box, or highlight the value in the box and enter a new width. For quick selection, Draw provides some preset line widths, as well as an option for no outline, on the Outline Pen flyout menu.

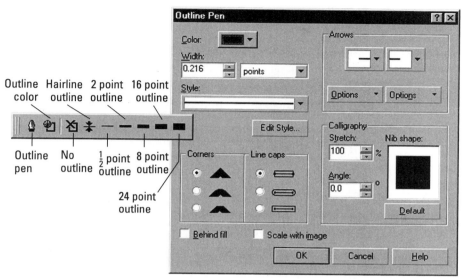

Figure 12-46: The Outline Pen flyout menu and the Outline Pen dialog box.

Clicking the down arrow in the Style box displays the available line styles. In addition to using a solid line, you can use dotted and dashed lines as the object outlines. To select a line style, click the example of the line that you want to use. The width and length of the object's line determines the appearance of these lines. You may have to try more than one of these to get the desired effect.

Choosing corners and end caps on lines

Although they may not be visible at smaller sizes, corners determine the appearance of a line when it takes a sharp turn in direction. Similarly, end caps affect the ends of your lines. At larger line widths, the aesthetic impact of these two style options can be significant (see Figure 12-47). Corner styles have no effect on curved lines. To select a corner or end cap style, click the radio button beside the style you want, using the guidelines that follow.

Figure 12-47: Select a corner and end cap style for your lines.

There are three different types of corner treatments:

- ✦ **Mitered:** Mitered corners have crisp, sharp corners. If the angle where two line segments meet exceeds 90 degrees, the corner changes to a beveled corner. This prevents the line from extending beyond the node where the two line segments meet.

- ✦ **Rounded:** Rounded corners are smooth, curved corners. The radius of the corner depends on the line width and angle of the corner.

- ✦ **Beveled:** Beveled corners cut the corner off at an angle between two connecting line segments. The degree of the bevel is equal to 50 percent of the angle of the corner.

There are three different types of end caps:

- ✦ **Square:** Square end caps are cut flush against the end nodes of a line. This type of end cap produces a clean, precise line.

- ✦ **Rounded:** Rounded end caps have a semicircular tip at the end of the line. The diameter of the end cap equals the width of the line.

- ✦ **Extended:** Extended end caps extend the line beyond the end nodes. The amount of the extension equals 50 percent of the line width.

Setting the Default Outline

You can set the default outline that appears when you first draw an object. To specify the default outline, deselect all the objects in your drawing by clicking the desktop or by pressing Esc. Choose the Outline Pen icon from the Fill tool flyout menu. A dialog box appears, asking you to specify the object types to which you want the new fill to apply. Select the options you want and click OK.

The Outline Pen dialog box appears, letting you make your selections. When you are satisfied with your choices, click OK to return to the drawing window. When you draw a new object, the fill is automatically applied. The new default outline remains in effect until you change it.

Selecting inks

Colors applied to outlines are known as inks. Inks are selected in the same manner as uniform fills. To change the ink color of an outline, click the color chip and select a color from the palette. Alternatively, you can select the Outline Color icon from the Outline Pen flyout menu to display the Outline Color dialog box (see Figure 12-48). This dialog box resembles the Uniform Fill dialog box and behaves in the same manner. Select the color to use and click OK to complete the operation and to return to the drawing window.

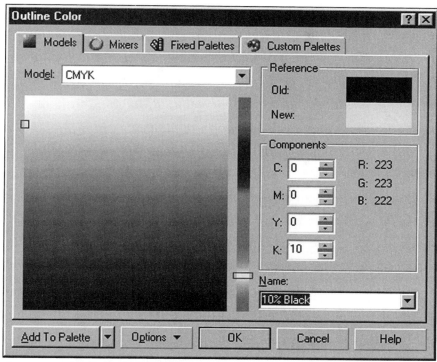

Figure 12-48: The Outline Color dialog box lets you choose a color for your outlines.

Using the Behind Fill option

Enabling the Behind Fill option lets you place the outline behind the fill of an object (see Figure 12-49). The default location for an outline is in front of the fill, which makes the entire width of the outline visible. The outline straddles the line of the object shape. If behind fill is enabled, only 50 percent of the outline width is visible; the balance is behind the fill. This option is useful when working with outlined text, and for manually trapping an image for printing.

For more information about trapping, see Chapter 16.

The details of more florid and intricate typefaces are frequently obscured when an outline is added to the text. Placing the outline behind the fill helps prevent this problem.

Adding an outline to text lets you simulate a boldface type when a bold style is not available. If the typeface is scripted or intricate, enable the Behind Fill option in the Outline Pen dialog box.

In front of the fill   Behind the fill

Figure 12-49: Enabling Behind Fill lets you apply an outline without compromising the details of the object.

Using Scale with Image

One of the advantages of Draw over bitmap image editing programs is Draw's capability to scale objects without a loss in quality. By default, however, outlines don't automatically scale with the object. Enabling Scale with Image solves this problem by instructing Draw to scale the outline proportionately with the image. This is especially useful if the finished design is going to be output at various sizes. Objects maintain their detail regardless of their size. If Scale with Image is disabled, the outline remains the same and may seem to disappear at larger sizes. A wide outline can also conceal most, if not all, of an object that's reduced if Scale with Image is not enabled. If you rotate or skew an image with Scale with Image enabled, the angle and width adjust proportionately to maintain the appearance of the image. This option reduces jagged, or pixelated, edges. In Figure 12-50, the original image size was increased 25 percent. One view shows the increase with Scale with Image enabled; the other shows the increase with Scale with Image disabled.

Converting Outlines to Objects

You can now convert an outline of an existing object to an object. Converted outlines can be manipulated like any closed object. You can apply a fill or edit the outline as you would other objects. When Draw converts an outline to an object, it actually duplicates the outline of the selected object, creating a new closed object that appears to have the same width and shape of the original outline. The new object is superimposed over the existing outline. Unlike duplicating the entire object, only the outline is reproduced.

You can change the width of the new object using the shape tool as you would other objects, by clicking and dragging the nodes. Converting an outline to an object is useful when you want the outline of an object to have the same coloration as the object, such as a fountain fill.

Figure 12-50: If Scale with Image is enabled, the outline is resized proportionately when you scale an object.

Creating with Artistic Media

The Natural Pen tool from Draw 8 has been vastly enhanced in Draw 9 and now sports a new name, the Artistic Media tool, to match its capabilities. Draw provides two methods of working with Artistic Media. You can use the Artistic Media tool to create effects interactively in the drawing window, or you can apply artistic effects to an existing curve using the Artistic Media docker (see Figure 12-51).

New Feature The new Artistic Media features in Draw let you apply a variety of effects to curves.

You can choose an Artistic Media mode that lets you:

✦ **Apply preset pen effects:** Draws curves that change thickness based on preset line shapes that you can choose from the drop-down preset list on the Property bar.

✦ **Work with Brush effects:** Lets you apply shapes or text to a curve. You can select a preset brush from the Brush list or save an object as a brush stroke.

Figure 12-51: Artistic Media can be used to create a variety of pen effects, including the whimsical. The elements of this image incorporate all of the Artistic Media drawing modes.

✦ **Add Object Sprayer effects:** Applies a series of images to a curve.

✦ **Create calligraphic effects:** Draws curves that change thickness based on the direction of the curve.

✦ **Create Pressure Sensitive lines:** Draws curves of variable thickness based on the amount of pressure from a pressure-sensitive pen.

Note   You can apply all of the effects, except the Pressure Sensitive effect, using either the Artistic Media tool or the Artistic Media docker. Pressure sensitivity is interactive and you must use the Artistic Media tool to produce the effect.

Using the Artistic Media tool

The lines you create using the Artistic Media tool can be straight, freehand, or a combination of both. Press Tab to toggle between straight and freehand strokes. Strokes made using Artistic Media effects have two parts: the effect and the control path along which the effect is applied. You can edit the control path. Draw automatically reflows the effect along the modified path.

Tip

As with many Draw tools, you can constrain lines made with the Artistic Media tool in 15-degree increments by pressing Ctrl while drawing the line.

To draw a curve with the Artistic Media tool:

1. Select the Artistic Media tool from the pen flyout menu on the toolbox. The Property bar updates to display the settings and options available for the Artistic Media tool (see Figure 12-52).

 Note

To change the default Artistic Media tool settings, deselect the objects in the drawing window and then specify new settings on the Property bar.

2. Select the mode to use for your curve.

3. Adjust the Smoothness slider. Dragging the slider to the right increases the smoothness of the curve. Similarly, dragging the slider to the left decreases the smoothness of the curve.

4. Choose the other settings specific to the tool (see Table 12-6).

5. In the drawing window, click and drag to create your curve.

Note

If you are using a mouse to simulate pressure-sensitive effects, press the Up Arrow (↑) or Down Arrow (↓) to vary the pen pressure. The Up Arrow (↑) increases the pressure; the Down Arrow (↓) decreases the pressure. As the pressure increases the line becomes wider.

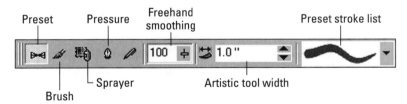

Figure 12-52: The Artistic Media view of the Property bar lets you select the drawing mode and specify the curve settings.

Table 12-6
Specifying Artistic Media Tool Settings

Tool	Available settings	Note
Presets	Choose a Preset pen type from the Presets drop-down list, and then set the maximum width in the Width box.	Presets are closed objects and you can apply fills to them as you would to any object in Draw.
Brush	Choose a Brush type from the drop-down list, and then set the maximum width in the Width box.	You can also create, save, and delete brushes.
Object sprayer	Adjust the spacing between the objects, vary the order of the objects in the curve, adjust the Sprayer to rotate the objects along the curve, and offset the objects from the curve you draw.	You can import bitmaps to use with the Object Sprayer.
Calligraphic	Set the maximum width in the Width box and specify the angle of the pen nib.	As values approach 0 degrees, horizontal lines become narrower and vertical lines become thicker. Conversely, as values approach 90 degrees, horizontal lines become thicker and vertical lines become narrower.
Pressure Sensitive	Set the maximum width in the Width box.	As the pressure of your stylus increases, the line becomes wider.

Editing Artistic Media Strokes

You can edit Artistic Media strokes as you would edit any curve object in Draw. Using the Pick tool, you can interactively scale and stretch the effect. You can also use the Shape tool to modify the path along which the effect is created.

If you want to edit the path and the effect independently, select Arrange ⇨ Separate to separate the path from the effect. This is a one-way street. You cannot reattach an effect to a path beyond the levels of undo that you have specified.

Working with brush strokes

You aren't limited to the preset list of brushes when you use the Brush mode of the Artistic Media tool. You can create your own brush strokes and save them for future use. Your brush stroke can be created from text or an object.

Note   Text that appears as a custom brush is not editable as text.

Custom brushes are a good way to create and save effects that you intend to use repetitively. For example, you could create a logo or signature brush and use it to personalize your documents (see Figure 12-53).

Figure 12-53: You can personalize your documents with a custom brush.

To create a brush stroke:

1. Select the Artistic Media tool.

2. Choose the Brush mode and then select the graphic or text string to use as a brush with the Artistic Media tool.

3. Select the Save button on the Property bar to display the File Name dialog box.

4. Enter a name for your brush and click Save.

Caution   Whenever you create a custom brush or effect and save it for future use, be sure that you back up your custom effects in another location on your hard disk. This ensures that your custom effects won't be lost if you need to uninstall or reinstall Draw.

The new brush appears in the Property bar ready for your use now and in future Draw sessions. When the Artistic Media tool is selected, you can delete a brush by selecting it from the brush list on the Property bar and clicking the Delete button.

Tip You can also create a custom brush stroke in the Artistic Media docker. Select the graphic or text object, and then click the Save button in the Artistic Media Docker. Enable the Brush button to view and use your custom brush.

Working with the Object Sprayer

Object Sprayer mode lets you *spray* a series of objects along a curve. In addition to the preset spraylist, you can apply other objects using the Object sprayer. The objects can include graphic objects, text, and imported bitmap images. You control how objects are applied on the curve by the settings you make.

Settings that you specify are saved to a spraylist. You can change a spraylist, save it, or reset it to its saved settings. You can also choose which objects in a spraylist are applied. For example, if you have a spraylist that contains hotdogs, hamburgers, and french fries, you can choose to spray all of the food products or any one or combination of them.

Caution The Object Sprayer is resource intensive. As the complexity of the spray objects increases, the amount of screen refresh time and file size also increase.

You can also specify the percentage of the original size of the objects to be used for the spray object. If the original object was 1 inch and you specified 50 percent, the resulting spray objects would be 1/2 inch. If you want to vary the size of the objects, click the Incremental Scaling button and enter the value to use as the increment.

Adjusting the Dabs and Spacing settings lets you control the distance between clusters of the effect and the number of objects in each cluster. For example, you could specify 2 Dabs with a spacing of 1 inch apart. Using the food example above, you would have a cluster of two hamburgers with 1 inch between the clusters. You can also adjust the rotation value to vary the orientation of the clusters. Click the Path Based button if you want to rotate the objects in relation to the curve. Similarly, click the Page Based button if you want to rotate the objects in relation to the page.

Specifying the offset value lets you determine how far from the curve the objects are placed. If the Offset checkbox is disabled, the objects closely follow the curve. Choose Alternating if you want the objects to be placed on either side of the curve.

As mentioned earlier, you can create your own spraylists and save them for future use. Adding objects to a spraylist is similar to creating custom brushes.

To create a new spraylist:

1. Select the Artistic Media tool and then choose the Object Sprayer mode.

2. Select New Spraylist from the Spraylist drop-down list box.

3. Click the object to add to the spraylist with the Artistic Media tool and then click Add to Spraylist. Continue adding the objects you want to use in the spraylist.

4. When you're satisfied with your spraylist, click the Save button and enter a name for your spraylist in the File Name dialog box.

You can edit a spraylist by adding objects to the list or by selecting an object in the spraylist and clicking Remove. Selecting an object from the list and clicking the up or down arrow changes the order of the spraylist. You can also reverse the order by clicking the Reverse Order button. Click the Clear button if you want to remove all the objects from a spraylist. Finally, you can reset a spraylist to its saved values or delete a spraylist by clicking the Reset or Delete button, respectively.

Tip You can also create a custom spraylist in the Artistic Media docker. Select the graphic or text object and then click the Save button in the Artistic Media docker. Enable the Spraylist button to view and use your custom brush.

Applying artistic strokes to existing curves

Draw has the capability to apply Artistic Media strokes to existing curves and objects using the Artistic Media docker. Draw uses the outline of the object to determine the placement of the sprayed objects. After you apply a stroke, it appears in the Last Used list. This makes it easier to reapply the stroke to various objects in your document.

To apply Artistic Media strokes to existing objects:

1. Select Effects ➪ Artistic Media to display the Artistic Media docker (see Figure 12-54).

2. Choose the folder that contains the strokes you want to use from the Group list box.

3. Choose the Pick tool from the toolbox and then select the object to which to apply the Artistic Media stroke.

4. Select the stroke to use in the Artistic Media docker and click Apply.

Tip You can also use the Pick tool to click and drag strokes to objects in your drawing. Draw applies the effect when you release the mouse button.

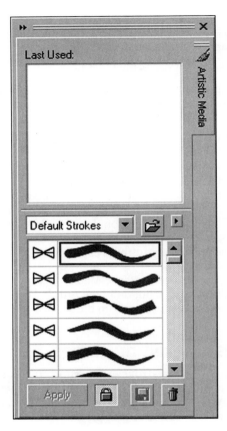

Figure 12-54: The Artistic Media docker lets you apply Artistic Media strokes to existing objects in your drawing.

Using Color Adjustment Tools

Although good color management can go a long way toward ensuring consistent color, sometimes you need to adjust the color of individual elements in your drawings. Draw provides these series of tools, which let you adjust the color of both vector and bitmap objects in your documents:

✦ Brightness-Contrast-Intensity

✦ Color Balance

✦ Gamma

✦ Hue-Saturation-Lightness

✦ Invert

✦ Posterize

Tip

When you specify parameters in a color adjustment tool, the parameters are retained in the dialog box until you change them. This lets you apply the same parameters to multiple objects in your drawing, if the objects aren't part of the original selection. If you don't want to use the values displayed in a color adjustment dialog box, click Reset to reset the parameters to their default values.

Using these tools, you can improve the quality of selected objects by adjusting shadows, midtones, and highlights. These tools are especially useful for improving under- and overexposed bitmap images, or for fine-tuning the color of a vector object in relationship to other objects in your drawings. You can access the Color Adjustment tools by selecting Effects ➪ Color Adjustment and then choosing the tool you want to use. Alternatively, you can select Color Adjustment tools by clicking the Effects button in any of the bitmap effects or color adjustment dialog boxes. If you click the Eye Preview button in a Color Adjustment dialog box, you can preview the effects of your changes prior to applying them. Select Color Adjustment and then click the tool you want to use from the flyout menu.

Note

Color adjustment tools use filters to convert color. These filters won't work with objects containing PANTONE Matching System colors.

Adjusting brightness, contrast, and intensity

The Brightness-Contrast-Intensity tools use HSB (Hue, Saturation, and Brightness) values to adjust the tones of selected objects in your documents. When you adjust the color of an object using this tool, it adjusts all of the colors in the selection equally, without regard to whether the color is a shadow, midtone, or highlight. The Brightness-Contrast-Intensity option is a good choice for adjusting the overall tonal quality of scanned images and photographs.

To adjust the brightness, contrast, and intensity of a selection:

1. Select Brightness-Contrast-Intensity from the Color Adjustment tools to display the Brightness-Contrast-Intensity dialog box (see Figure 12-55).

2. Slide the Brightness slider to the right to lighten the colors in the selection; sliding the Brightness slider to the left darkens the colors.

3. Slide the Contrast slider to the right to increase the contrast, or range, between the darkest and lightest pixels in your selection; sliding the Contrast slider to the left reduces the amount of contrast.

4. Slide the Intensity slider to the right to brighten lighter areas in your selection; sliding it to the left darkens the lighter areas.

Tip

Sometimes, increasing the amount of contrast in a selection reduces the visible detail of lighter and darker portions of your selection, while improving the midtones. You can compensate for this effect by increasing the Intensity.

▶ Brightness-Contrast-Intensity		? ☒
<u>B</u>rightness:		0
<u>C</u>ontrast:		0
<u>I</u>ntensity:		0
Preview 🔒 Reset	OK Cancel	Help

Figure 12-55: The Brightness-Contrast-Intensity dialog box lets you adjust the overall tonal quality of a selection.

Adjusting color balance

The color balance options let you shift the colors of a selection between CMY and RGB values. This tool is especially useful for correcting colorcasts in bitmap photo images when the effects of scanning add too much of a hue to the image. You can apply this filter to an entire image if you need to shift the overall balance of multiple objects in your drawing.

To apply color balance options to your selection:

 Tip

Adjusting the color balance is useful for shifting the overall range of colors in a fountain fill, without adjusting each color separately.

1. Select Color Balance from the Color Adjustment tools to display the Color Balance dialog box (see Figure 12-56).

2. Click the checkbox or checkboxes of the tonal values that you want to correct to enable them. If a tonal range is disabled, the corrections you make won't affect colors that fall within that range. You can correct

   - **Shadows:** Shifts the colors that fall within the darker or shadowed range of colors in your selection.

   - **Midtones:** Corrects the colors that fall within the midtone range of your selection. This option affects the greatest range of colors in most bitmap selections.

   - **Highlights:** Corrects the colors that fall within the lightest or highlighted areas of your selection. This is useful for softening stark white highlights.

   - **Preserve Luminance:** Forces Draw to maintain the brightness level of the selection, regardless of the amount of color correction you apply.

3. Shift the color channel sliders to adjust the individual colors between the CMY and RGB values.

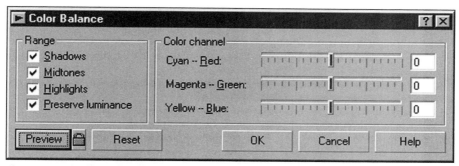

Figure 12-56: The Color Balance dialog box lets you shift the colors of your selection to correct color discrepancies.

Adjusting the color balance of selected objects in your drawings is a quick way to globally change the colors of fills. While it doesn't replace the use of color styles, it does allow you to view changes as you fine-tune the colors in your document.

Adjusting gamma settings

The human eye rarely sees individual colors. It interprets color and luminance based on a gestalt of the color and those colors that surround it. For example, Figure 12-57 shows two polygons with the same midtone fill superimposed on squares. The polygon in the black square is far more vivid and appears darker than the polygon in the white square even though both polygons have identical fills. The reason that the two polygons look different is the difference in the contrast with their surrounding areas.

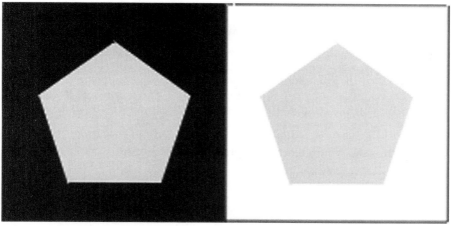

Figure 12-57: The human eye perceives color based on the contrast between adjacent objects.

Objects with midtone fills tend to appear faded when the contrast between the object and adjacent objects is low. When you adjust the gamma of objects in your document, you are adjusting the contrast of midtone colors in relationship to the colors that represent highlights and shadows. Although adjusting the gamma affects all the color values in the selection, gamma calculations are based on a curve that affects midtone colors more significantly. This is useful for improving the detail in low-contrast images, or for creating more subtle effects.

To adjust the gamma of selected objects in your drawing:

1. Select Gamma from the Color Adjustment tools to display the Gamma dialog box (see Figure 12-58).

2. Move the value slider to adjust the gamma curve value.

3. Click OK to apply the effect and to return to the drawing window.

Figure 12-58: The Gamma dialog box lets you adjust the contrast of midtone colors in your drawings.

Tip

Increasing the gamma value improves the quality of low-contrast or dark, under-exposed photo images.

Adjusting the hue, saturation, and lightness

Every color has a specific hue, intensity, and lightness based upon HLS (Hue-Lightness-Saturation) values. Draw lets you adjust these three variables. You can change the color of a selection entirely by adjusting the hue, or you can adjust the intensity and lightness by adjusting the saturation and lightness settings. Additionally, you can change the colors of a specific color channel, or you can adjust the master channel, which adjusts all channels equally.

To adjust the hue, saturation, and lightness of a selection:

1. Select Hue-Saturation-Lightness from the Color Adjustment tools to display the Hue-Saturation-Lightness dialog box (see Figure 12-59).

2. Choose a channel button. You can modify each channel individually. If you choose the Master Channel button, all the channels are modified equally.

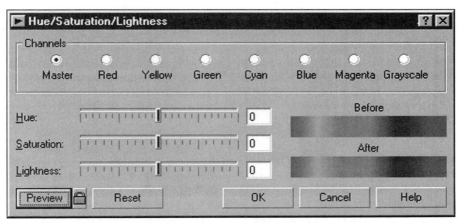

Figure 12-59: The Hue/Saturation/Lightness dialog box lets you adjust the colors of selected objects.

3. Move the hue slider to change the color of the selected channel.

4. Move the saturation slider to adjust the intensity of the color. A negative value of –100 produces a gray monochrome color; a positive value of +100 produces a vivid intense color.

5. Move the lightness slider to adjust the amount of white (positive values) or black (negative values) in the selection.

6. Adjust the sliders for each channel that you want to modify. For the best results, click Preview so that you can preview the changes as you adjust the colors.

7. Click OK to return to the drawing window.

Hue, saturation, and lightness settings are useful for tweaking colors in your drawing. Generally, the settings you specify will be near the middle values. Converting bitmap objects to grayscale using the Convert to command is a more efficient method of obtaining a grayscale bitmap object in your drawings. Additionally, grayscale objects create smaller file sizes than using an extreme negative saturation setting to adjust the color of a 24- or 32-bit bitmap object. While extreme positive saturation settings produce vivid colors, they tend to have an unnatural appearance.

Inverting colors

When you apply the Invert command, Draw changes the colors of the selection to the contrasting color. The color is based on opposing colors on a color wheel. For example black becomes white, blue becomes yellow, and red becomes green. To invert the colors in a selection, select Invert from the Color Adjustment options.

Summary

The variety of effects achievable with fills and outlines is endless. This chapter just scratched the surface of the achievable effects. Draw provides numerous methods for selecting, editing, and applying fills and outlines. I recommend that you try the various methods and work with the one that suits your personal working style. In this chapter, you learned to

✦ Apply and work with solid fills

✦ Use and create pattern fills

✦ Add texture to objects in your drawings

✦ Use the Texture Maker

✦ Add PostScript fills to objects

✦ Apply fills interactively

✦ Choose and modify lines

✦ Apply color adjustment options

✦   ✦   ✦

Imagining Possibilities with Special Effects

Draw provides a wide variety of tools for creating basic and more advanced special effects. These features let you enhance graphic objects and artistic text by taking the ordinary and turning it into the spectacular. Special effects let you enhance your image by adding effects to your drawings, ranging from the subtle to the dramatic. You can apply contour, perspective, extrusion, lense, PowerClip, distortion, envelope, and blended effects to objects. Some effects give your objects a 3D look, while others alter color or create the illusion of airbrushed objects. When combined with other effects, you have the ability to create a nearly infinite range of looks for your documents.

Adding Perspective to Objects

Perspective adds a feeling of depth to objects, making them look more realistic. Draw lets you add both one- and two-point perspectives to objects. Perspective makes objects appear to diminish in size as the view is further away, giving objects a sense of distance (see Figure 13-1). When you apply perspective to objects or a group of objects, you establish an artificial horizon, and give them a 3D feel on a 2D plane. This horizon is generally at the top of the object or group of objects. As objects approach the horizon, they appear smaller.

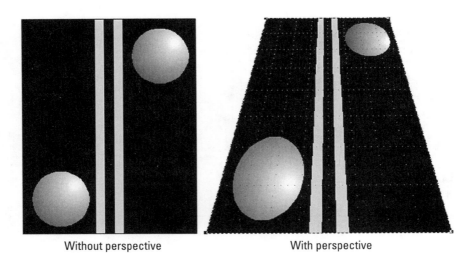

Without perspective   With perspective

Figure 13-1: Using the Perspective command lets you give objects a feeling of depth.

To apply perspective to an object:

1. Using the Pick tool, select the object or objects to which you want to apply perspective effects.

Tip

If you have several objects to which you want to apply the same perspective, group the objects first. Using this method, the objects are guaranteed to use the same vanishing point and maintain their relationship with one another.

2. Select Effects ⇨ Add Perspective. The tool automatically switches to the Shape tool, and a grid appears over the object.

3. Click and drag the corner handles of the grid to reshape the object. If you press Ctrl while dragging, the movement is constrained to a straight line. The result is a one-point perspective effect where the object recedes in one direction (see Figure 13-2). If you don't constrain the movement, the result is a two-point perspective, where the object recedes in two directions.

Note

Ctrl+Shift creates a symmetrical one-point perspective.

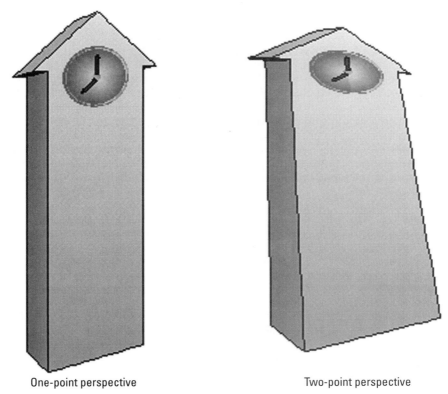

One-point perspective   Two-point perspective

Figure 13-2: You can add one- and two-point perspectives to objects by using the Perspective command.

Modifying Effects Objects

When you add one of Draw's effects to an object, remember that the object is linked to the effect. When you add perspective to a rectangle, for example, it is still a rectangle. If you convert the rectangle to curves, the link to the Perspective command is broken, and you can't edit, copy, or remove the perspective. You can, however, add a new perspective. The same is true for grouped objects. If you apply an effect to a group of objects and then ungroup the objects, you can no longer edit, copy, or remove the effect.

Once you've added perspective to an object, you can edit the perspective by clicking the Shape tool and dragging the corner handles of the object you want to edit. If you press Ctrl, the motion is constrained to a straight line to produce a one-point perspective. If the motion is not constrained, you edit a two-point perspective. To remove perspective from an object, use the Pick tool to select the object, and then select Effects ➪ Clear Perspective. The object returns to its original appearance. To copy the perspective from one object to another, select the object to which you want to apply the perspective effect, and then select Effects ➪ Copy ➪ Perspective From. An arrow appears allowing you to choose the object whose perspective you want to copy.

Adding Blended Effects

The Blend effect lets you morph between two vector objects that are called control objects. When you apply a blend, attributes such as shape, size, color, and outline change gradually over a set of transitional steps from one object to the other (see Figure 13-3). The attributes of the control objects, and the variables that you specify before and after applying the blend, determine the results of the Blend command. In addition to blending two objects, you can create a compound blend by connecting two or more blends. You can also blend objects along a path, and specify the spacing between objects. By default, when you blend two objects, the bottom object is the start object; the top object is the end object. You can reverse the order of a blend, after it's created, if needed to achieve the effect you want.

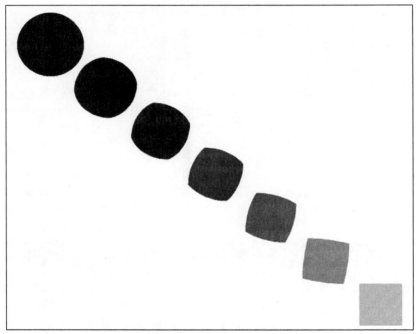

Figure 13-3: Blended objects morph from one object to another through a set of transitional steps.

Blend effects are useful for adding contour and definition to the elements in your drawings. The image shown in Figure 13-4 was created using a number of blends to add depth and contour to the various elements in the illustration. The highlighted veins in the center of the flowers were created by drawing a Bézier curve and breaking it into segments. The segments were assigned different outline colors and then blended together. You can blend objects filled with colors from different palettes, including spot tints. Objects can have an open or closed path.

Figure 13-4: Blend effects let you add contour and depth to objects in your drawings.

 Tip
Draw maps the blend using the starting nodes of the selected objects by default. This can cause a jagged appearance. You can eliminate this problem by mapping the nodes of the selected objects. More information about mapping nodes appears later in this section.

Using the Interactive Blend tool

Draw provides the Interactive Blend tool. To use it:

1. Choose the Interactive Blend tool from the toolbox.

2. Click one of the objects that you want to use as a blend control object and drag it to the second control object in your blend.

3. Release the mouse button to apply the blend.

Tip   Normally, objects blend from the start to the end control object. You can reverse the direction of a blend so that objects blend from the end to the start control object. To reverse the direction, select Arrange ➪ Order ➪ Reverse Order. The blend is redrawn to reflect the change.

Rotating intermediate blend objects

When you create a blend, you can specify rotation settings for the intermediate objects in the blend. By default objects rotate counterclockwise around their own center of rotation. Rotating intermediate objects also lets you specify a loop. The loop option isn't available if you aren't rotating the intermediate objects in your blend. If you enable Loop, objects rotate around a halfway point between the center of rotation for the control objects. You can enter any value between –360 degrees and 360 degrees. When Loop is enabled, objects form an arc as they rotate. The direction of the arc is determined by whether you've entered negative or positive values for the degree of rotation (see Figure 13-5). You can specify rotation settings using the Blend property bar.

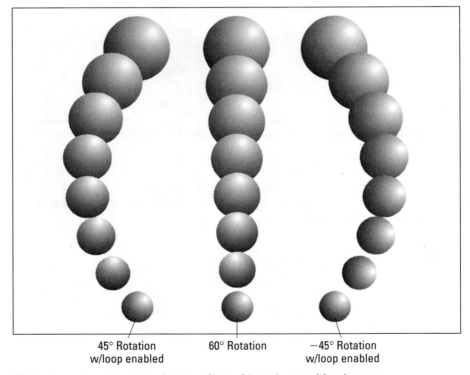

45° Rotation w/loop enabled   60° Rotation   −45° Rotation w/loop enabled

Figure 13-5: You can rotate intermediate objects in your blend groups.

To specify rotation settings:

1. Enter a rotation value in the Rotate box in the Property bar.

2. Enable Loop, if you want to apply an arc to the intermediate objects.

When a blend group or the Interactive Blend tool is selected, the Property bar displays the controls required to modify the blend. Table 13-1 shows the blend controls on the Property bar and a description of the action each performs.

	Table 13-1	
	Blend Controls	
Control	*Control name*	*Description*
x: 3.425 " y: 5.31 "	Object(s) position	Adjusts the object(s) position relative to the rulers.
2.63 " 1.577 "	Object(s) size	Sizes the object(s).
20 1.0 "	Number of steps or Offset between intermediate shapes	Specifies the number of steps between the two control objects, or the amount of space between the intermediate objects in the blend.
0.0 °	Blend direction	Rotates the intermediate objects. Positive values rotate the objects counterclockwise; negative values rotate the objects clockwise.
	Loop blend	Rotates the intermediate objects around a point halfway between the control objects' centers of rotation.
	Direct blend	Fills the intermediate objects with a direct blend between the colors of the two control objects.
	Clockwise blend	Fills the intermediate objects with colors representing a clockwise direction of the color wheel between the two control objects.
	Counterclockwise blend	Fills the intermediate objects with colors representing a counterclockwise direction of the color wheel between the two control objects.
	Blend object acceleration	Adjusts the distribution of objects along the blend path.

Continued

Table 13-1 *(continued)*

Control	Control name	Description
	Blend color acceleration	Adjusts the distribution of colors along the blend path.
	Accelerate sizing for blend	Toggles whether or not blend acceleration affects the size of intermediate objects.
	Link blend accelerations	Toggles whether or not object and color acceleration should be linked.
	Miscellaneous blend options	Accesses the controls for miscellaneous blend options, such as map nodes.
	Start and end object properties	Shows the start and end objects of the blend.
	Path properties	Lets you select path options, such as Show Path.
	Copy blend properties	Copies the blend properties of another blend group to the selected blend group.
	Clear blend	Clears the selected blend.

You can specify rotation settings on the Property bar by first selecting a blend group with either the Pick tool or the Interactive Blend tool. Enter a rotation value in the Blend direction box, and click the Loop button if you want to apply an arc to the intermediate objects in the blend. Draw automatically updates the blend group.

Mapping a blend to a path

Blend to Path lets you map the objects in a blend along a specified path. The path can be any open or closed Draw object. By default, the objects assume the path object's orientation. The objects' center of rotation is used to determine their relationship with the path. You can rotate objects on a path, as well as specify that the objects cover the entire path. In Figure 13-6, the carousel lights that adorn the top and surround the mirrors were placed using the Blend to Path effect.

To blend objects along a path:

1. Using the Pick tool, select the objects to blend.

2. Select the Interactive Blend tool and create a basic direct blend between the objects (see Figure 13-7).

Figure 13-6: Blend to Path lets you place objects along a path you specify.

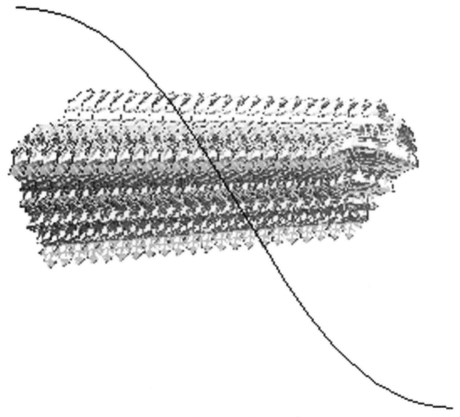

Figure 13-7: Create a direct blend between the two objects.

3. With the blend still selected, click the Path button and select New Path from the flyout menu.

4. Click the path along which to blend the objects.

5. If you want the blend to cover the full path, enable Blend Along Full Path from the submenu, which is accessed from the flyout menu that appears after clicking the Miscellaneous Blend Options button on the property bar (see Figure 13-8).

6. Enable Rotate All Objects to rotate the objects so that they match the shape of the path.

Figure 13-8: Enable Blend Along Full path on the Miscellaneous Blend Options submenu if you want the blend to cover the entire path.

Tip

If you don't want a path to be visible, click the path to select it. You can also choose Show Path from the Path Button flyout menu to select the path. Once the path is selected, right-click the No Fill well on the color palette to make the outline transparent.

Selecting Blends

The Pick tool or the Interactive Blend tool is used to select blend groups. To select a blend group, you must click the group, and either the start or end control objects.

If you click one of the control objects, you can edit that object, but not the blend. If you need to select a single blend group or control object within a compound blend, press Ctrl while clicking the element you need to select.

Specifying blend attributes

You can change the appearance of a blend by altering the blend attributes. The Blend Roll-Up and the Property bar contain a variety of options for modifying blends to create the effect you want. Using these options, you can change a blend's color attributes, modify the spacing, map the nodes of a blend, or accelerate a blend to alter the symmetry or color progression of a blend.

Setting the distance between blend objects

There are two methods by which you can specify the distance between blend objects. The first method is to choose the number of intermediate objects you want in the blend group. You can specify any number of intermediate objects between 1 and 999. The greater the number of intermediate objects, the closer they appear in relationship to one another. The second method is to set the distance between the objects. This option is available only if you are blending objects along a path. You can specify any distance between 0.01 inches and 10 inches. If you are using another unit of measurement, the distance is the equivalent of inches.

Note

The distance you specify is measured between the objects' center of rotation, rather than the edge of the visible object. You can also specify the spacing on the Property bar (see Figure 13-9).

Figure 13-9: You can specify the distance between objects that are blended along a path.

To specify the distance between objects:

1. Using the Pick tool, select the blend group to modify.

2. Enable Fixed Spacing by clicking the button on the Property bar and enter the distance you want between objects.

Specifying color attributes

When you create a blend between objects, Draw, by default, uses the objects' fill and outline colors to determine the color progression for the intermediate objects. Draw has three methods of color progression: direct (the default), clockwise through the color spectrum, or counterclockwise through the color spectrum. You specify a color progression using the Property bar.

To modify the color progression of a blend group:

1. Use the Pick tool or the Interactive Blend tool to select the blend group.

2. Enable the type of color progression you want to use: Direct, Clockwise, or Counterclockwise.

Draw automatically applies the changes to the blend. You can create a rainbow effect in between the control objects by selecting a color progression. The proximity of the two colors that represent the control objects determines whether the effect is subtle or dramatic.

Mapping nodes

When you blend two objects, Draw uses the starting nodes of each object to map the intermediate steps of a blend by default. The result can make the blend look rotated or distorted (see Figure 13-10). To solve this problem, map the nodes of the control objects to alter the points between which the blend is created. Using this method, you can control the blend to achieve the desired results.

Figure 13-10: By default, Draw uses the starting nodes on each of the control objects to map the intermediate steps of a blend.

To map the nodes of a blend group:

1. Using the Pick tool, select the blend group.

2. Click the Miscellaneous Options button on the Property bar to display the Miscellaneous Options menu (see Figure 13-11).

Figure 13-11: The Miscellaneous Options Property menu lets you map the nodes of the control objects in your blend group.

3. Click the Map Nodes button. The cursor ch anges to an arrow in the drawing window, and the nodes of the start object are highlighted.

4. Click the node on the start object that you want to use for the blend. The nodes on the end object are highlighted.

5. Click the nodes on the end object.

Draw rebuilds the blend using the nodes you specified as the mapping points (see Figure 13-12).

Figure 13-12: Draw rebuilds the blend using the nodes you specified as the mapping points.

Using acceleration

When you create a blend, the intermediate objects and the color progression are evenly spaced across the length of the blend. Draw provides controls that let you alter the balance of a blend, so that the progression of objects and colors are closer to either the start or end object (see Figure 13-13).

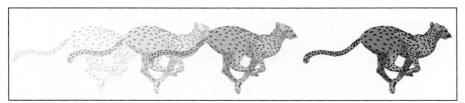

Figure 13-13: Acceleration controls let you alter the balance of a blend toward either the start or the end object.

To accelerate a blend:

1. Using the Pick tool, select the blend group to accelerate.

2. Click the Object and Color Acceleration button to display the Object and Color Acceleration menu (see Figure 13-14).

3. Drag the Object Acceleration and the Color Acceleration sliders to set the direction and the rate of acceleration. If you drag the sliders to the left, the balance of the objects and colors shift toward the start object; if you drag the sliders to the right, the balance of the objects and colors shift toward the end object.

4. Enable Accelerate Sizing for Blend if you want the object size to accelerate at the same rate as the colors or objects. This option is only effective if the start and end objects are different sizes (see Figure 13-15).

5. Enable Link Accelerations if you want the color and object accelerations to change at the same rate. Using this option, you only have to move one acceleration slider to change the rate and direction of acceleration.

Acceleration lets you give blends a feeling of motion and speed. When you combine Apply to Sizing with Acceleration, you can make objects appear to move closer or appear to move away.

Creating a compound blend

Once you create a basic blend, you can add other blend groups to either end of the blend to create a compound blend. Compound blends enhance your drawings, enabling you to expand a blend to include other objects or effects. Although simplistic in its structure, the compound blend group shown in Figure 13-16 illustrates the capability of compound blends to extend blend effects. The basic shapes for the compound blend were taken from the Draw common bullets symbol library. The objects were sized, placed, and filled with solid fills. The two end objects in the back row of symbols were blended together, and then each end was blended with the larger front symbol to create the triangular effect.

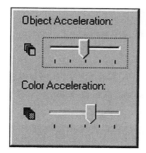

Figure 13-14: The Object and Color Acceleration menu lets you shift the transitional steps or colors toward one of the control objects in your blend group.

Figure 13-15: Enabling Accelerate Sizing for Blend changes the sizing at the same rate as the colors or objects.

Figure 13-16: Even simple objects are enhanced when used to create a compound blend.

To create a compound blend from an existing blend:

1. Using the Pick tool, select either the start or end object of an existing blend (see Figure 13-17).

2. Select the Interactive Blend tool and click one of the control objects and drag it to the second object.

3. Click and drag the Interactive Blend tool to the next control object.

4. Choose the blend options to use to create the compound blend (see Figure 13-18).

Figure 13-17: Select the objects to use for the compound blend. You can select the start, finish, or both objects, as shown here.

Figure 13-18: When you click Apply, the compound blend is created.

Editing blend groups

The Blend properties bar and Effects menu offer a variety of ways to edit blend groups. When you edit a blend group, you modify the basic properties of the blend, which expands the range of effects you can create. Editing a blend group, or either of the control objects, alters the appearance of the blend group. Draw updates the blend to reflect any changes you make. Using the editing controls and commands, you can

✦ Change the start or end object

✦ Edit a blend path

✦ Separate a blend from a path

✦ Specify a new path

✦ Clear a blend effect

✦ Separate a blend into individual elements

✦ Split a blend group

✦ Fuse blend groups

Changing starting and ending blend objects

You can identify and change the start and end control objects in a blend group using the Blend view of the Property bar. Identifying the start and end object is useful if your drawing is complex and you need to edit the object. When you identify either control object, it becomes the selected object, allowing you to make the editing changes you want. You can also change the start or end object to create a variety of effects.

To identify or change the start or end objects in a blend:

1. Using the Pick tool, select the blend group to modify.

2. Click the Starting and Ending Object button and choose the option you want.

3. If you choose New Start or New End, you can select a new object in the drawing window. Draw updates the blend after the new start or end object is selected.

Note   You cannot choose an intermediate step in the selected blend as the new start or end object.

Editing a blend path

You can change the shape, size, or orientation of a blend path. Sometimes it's difficult to gauge the way a blend group will fit in the larger scheme of things. By modifying the path of blend to path groups, you can tailor your blend group to fit your drawing. You can edit a blend path by selecting the blend path. Modify the path as desired. Draw automatically updates the blend.

Separating a blend from a path

Draw lets you separate a blend from its path. This is useful if you are finished editing an image and don't believe that you will need to edit the path. Unless you intend to edit the individual elements of a blend, I don't recommend separating a blend from its path. When I'm creating an image for a company, I tend to need to reuse graphics and modify blends. Once the blend is separated from the path, it can no longer be edited as a blend group.

To separate a blend from a path:

1. Using the Pick tool, select the blend group to separate from its path.

2. Click on the Path Properties button to display the Path Properties menu.

3. Select Detach From Path.

Generally, the reason for separating a blend from its path is to delete the path so that it's not visible. Consider, instead, not giving the path an outline, which will make the path invisible. By using this method, the path is still there if you need to edit the blend later.

Specifying a new path

When you select Show Path from the path button menu, Draw automatically selects the path associated with the selected blend group. You can change this path to a new path in the Blend Roll-Up. This is useful if you need to reshape the blend group to fit your drawing or image, and the current path doesn't achieve the effect you want.

To specify a new path:

1. Using the Pick tool, select the blend group to separate from its path.
2. Click the Path Properties button to display the Path Properties menu.
3. Select New Path.
4. Click the new path to which you want to apply the selected blend group.

Draw automatically transfers the blend group to the new path. Once you've transferred your blend to a new path, you can delete the old path, if you want.

Caution Deleting a linked control object, such as a blend path, breaks the link and can cause unpredictable results when you attempt to modify the blend or associated effect. Be sure to separate the control object from its linked effect *before* you delete the object.

Separating blends

You can separate a blend to break the blend group into its individual elements. When you separate a blend, Draw breaks the blend group into its control objects and a group of objects that contain the intermediate steps of the blend. The number of intermediate blend steps determines the number of objects in the group.

To separate a blend group:

1. Using the Pick tool, select the blend to separate.
2. Select Arrange ➪ Separate. Draw automatically breaks the blend into its individual components.

Separating a blend group is useful for editing the individual elements of the blend without affecting the other elements. Once a blend group is separated, the group cannot be edited as a blend.

Splitting blend groups

When you split a blend, you create a compound blend. By clicking one of the intermediate objects in the selected blend group, you determine the start and end object of the two blend groups. If you edit the object, you affect both of the new blend groups. Splitting a blend is useful if you want to alter the way colors are ramped in the blend, or if you want alter the shape of a blend that's not blended to a path.

To split a blend:

1. Using the Pick tool, select the blend group to split. If the blend group is part of a compound blend, press Ctrl while selecting the blend group.

2. Click the Miscellaneous Options button.

3. Click Split.

4. Click the object in the blend group where you want to split the blend. The object you select becomes the start object of one blend group and the end object of the other blend group.

Note   You can't split a blend by selecting the intermediate object directly next to a start or end control object.

5. Click Apply. Once you've split a blend, you can move the new control object, or change the attributes of the individual blend groups in the compound blend.

Figure 13-19 shows the effects of splitting a blend. The top image is a compound blend, before splitting the blend. The center intermediate object was selected as the split location in the bottom image. After splitting the blend, the object was moved and resized.

Fusing blend groups

The Fuse commands, Fuse Start and Fuse End, let you recombine a split or compound blend into a single blend group. Split and compound blends share a common object that serves as both the start and end object of the individual blend groups. When you fuse a blend, this object reverts to an intermediate object in a continuous blend between the two original control objects.

To fuse a compound or split blend:

1. Using the Pick tool, press Ctrl and click one of the blend groups in the compound or split blend.

2. Click the Miscellaneous Options button to display the Miscellaneous Options menu.

3. Click Fuse Start or Fuse End. Note that only one choice is available here; the other choice appears grayed out. The available choice is determined by the order in which the compound blend was created. If the compound blend shares a single common start or end object, a pointer appears letting you select the intermediate objects where you want the blend to fuse. If they don't share a single common start and end object, Draw automatically fuses the blend together.

Figure 13-20 shows the original compound blend at the top, and the results of fusing the blend back together at the bottom.

Figure 13-19: Splitting a blend lets you change the appearance of a blend group.

Figure 13-20: Fusing a compound or split blend reforms the blend between the original start and end control objects.

Clearing blend effects

You can clear blend effects whenever you want. The Clear Effects command is not tied to the levels of Undo you've specified for Draw. When you clear a blend effect, the blend is removed and the original start and end objects remain. These objects are no longer linked to the effect and can be modified without affecting other elements in your drawing. To clear a selected blend, click the Clear Blend button on the Property bar.

Copying and cloning blends

Two quick ways to reproduce blend effects using other control objects are either to copy or to clone the blend from an existing blend group. The new blend group uses the new objects, but reproduces the attributes of the blend that you copied or cloned. Although both methods reproduce the original blend group's attributes, they vary in how they behave. When you copy a blend, the new blend group is independent of the group from which you copied the blend. If you clone a blend, you create a clone blend group. The blend group from which you cloned the blend attributes becomes the master blend group. Changes you make in the master blend group are replicated in the clone. Figure 13-21 shows a master clone blend and a clone blend.

Figure 13-21: Copying and cloning a blend lets you replicate a blend's attributes in a new blend group.

To copy or clone a blend group:

1. Using the Pick tool, select the two objects to which you want to copy or clone a blend.

2. Select Effects ➪ Copy ➪ Blend From or Effects ➪ Clone ➪ Blend From.

3. Click the blend to copy or clone. Draw automatically blends the two objects you selected.

The acceleration attributes that you apply to the master blend are replicated in the clone blend. If you modify the master blend, the clone blend updates to reflect the changes. Like all clone objects in Draw, you can modify the clone blend independently. If you modify the acceleration or other blend attributes, however, you break the link between the master and clone blends. Future changes that you make in the master blend won't be reflected in the clone blend once the link is broken.

Using the Contour Effect

Contour effects are similar to blend effects in that they employ intermediate steps to create a transitional effect. Unlike blend effects, contour effects are applied to a single object, rather than to two or more objects. The result is a series of symmetrical concentric objects (see Figure 13-22). You can apply contour effects to the outside, inside, or center of an object to add contour and depth to the elements in your drawing.

Applying a contour

To apply a Contour effect to a selected object:

1. Click the Interactive Blend tool and hold the mouse button down to display the flyout menu. Select the Interactive Contour tool (see Figure 13-23).

2. Choose the kind of contour to apply. Use the following list as a guide in making a choice (see Figure 13-24).

   • **Center:** Creates symmetrical concentric objects to the center of the control object. The number of objects created is determined by the amount of offset between the intermediate steps. The more intermediate steps, the smoother the transition appears.

- **Inside:** Creates symmetrical concentric objects using the number of intermediate steps you specify. If the offset is too large to accommodate the number of steps you want to use, the number of steps is reduced proportionately.

- **Outside:** Creates symmetrical concentric objects outside the object. You specify the number of steps and the amount of the offset to use.

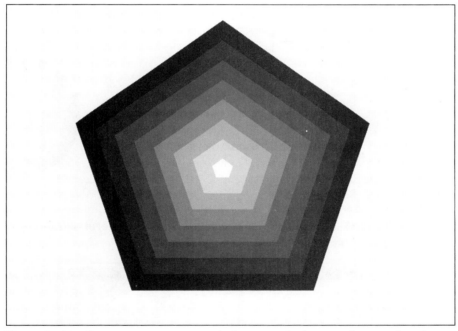

Figure 13-22: Contour creates symmetrical concentric shapes using a series of intermediate steps.

Figure 13-23: Using the Property bar settings for the Interactive Contour tool, you can specify the number of contour steps and the space between the contour steps.

3. Specify the amount of offset to use. By default, the offset is set at 0.1 inches.

5. Choose the color you want as a fill for the final object in the transition. If your control object contains a fountain fill, you can specify originating and destination colors as a fill for the final object in the transition (see Figure 13-25).

6. Choose an outline color, if you desire to add an outline. Use caution when applying an outline to a contour effect. If the offset is a small value, the outline can obscure the fill.

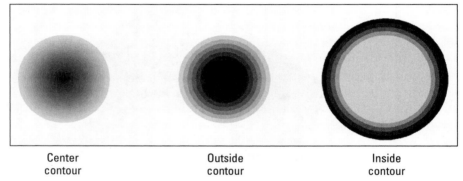

Center   Outside   Inside
contour   contour   contour

Figure 13-24: You can choose to apply a center, inside, or outside contour.

Figure 13-25: The Outline and Fill menus let you choose the fill and outline color of the last object in the contour group.

Working with contours and fountain fills

When applying a contour to an object that contains a fountain fill, Draw, by default, uses a direct progression between the colors. You can specify colors that pass from the control object to the final object through the color spectrum. Choose either clockwise or counterclockwise by clicking the desired directional color spectrum button. You can also specify the last color of the fountain fill by selecting the desired color from the End Fountain Fill Color menu.

Editing contour groups

Once you've created a contour group you can edit the number of steps, offset, or color options using the Property bar. To edit a contour group, select the group with the Pick tool and choose new options for the group. If you want to separate the control object from the contour group, select Arrange ➪ Separate. The contour group is separated, breaking the link between the control object and the transitional steps. The control object reverts to its original status. The transitional objects appear grouped. Once a control object is separated from a contour group, the objects cannot be edited as a contour group beyond the specified levels of Undo.

Using the Interactive Distortion Tools

Draw provides tools for distorting objects — the Interactive Distortion tools. Selecting the Interactive Distortion tool from the toolbox lets you apply three different types of distortions to objects:

✦ **Push Pull:** Pushes the edges in or out of a selection. The direction you drag the mouse determines which edges are affected, and whether they are pushed to the center of the object or pulled to the outside, away from the object.

✦ **Zipper:** Affects the edges of the selection by creating a sawtooth effect. You can adjust the smoothness and intensity of the effect by the settings you make on the Property bar and the distance you drag away from the object.

✦ **Twister:** Distorts selections by rotating portions of the object in the direction you drag. You can choose the direction, number of rotations, and the origin of the rotation.

Note

The Interactive Distortion tool invites experimentation. The effects you can achieve are too numerous to list. The original shape of the object, the distortion tool, the property settings, and the way that you apply the effect all serve to determine the final results. I trust you'll have as much fun experimenting with these tools as I did.

Applying push-pull distortions

Push-pull distortions are applied by clicking and dragging horizontally in the drawing window using the Push Pull Interactive Distortion tool. For the following exercise, use the Ellipse tool to draw a circle in the drawing window. A circle is a good choice for experimenting with all of the Interactive Distortion tools, because it allows you to quickly see the symmetry — or lack of same — in your effect.

To apply push-pull effects:

1. Select the Interactive Distortion tool from the toolbox, and click the Push Pull button on the Property bar.

2. Click the object to distort, and drag left or right to modify the effect. If you drag to the left, Draw pushes the edges of the object toward the center of the object; if you drag to the right, Draw pulls the edges of the object away from the center of the object. When you release the mouse button, Draw applies the effect (see Figure 13-26).

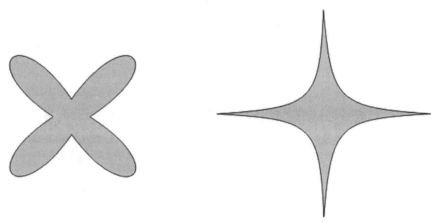

Figure 13-26: A circle with the Push (left) and Pull (right) effects applied.

Note

You can also specify settings by entering values in the Amplitude box.

Applying zipper distortions

Zipper distortions affect the edges of a selection. The effect you apply can be ragged or smooth, depending on the parameters you choose on the Property bar.

To apply zipper distortions:

1. Create a circle.

2. Select the Interactive Distortion tool and click the Zipper button on the Property bar.

3. Choose a distortion type by clicking its associated button. Use this list as a guide:

   • **Random:** Creates a random zipper distortion. The distortion effect is rough and is determined by the starting point you select.

- **Smooth:** Creates a smoother zipper distortion, with more rounded edges.

- **Localized:** Focuses the effect on the area of the object across which you drag the mouse.

4. Click and drag anywhere on the circle to apply the distortion.

5. Press Ctrl+Z to undo the effect, and then enable Smooth distortion and click the Center Distortion button.

6. Click the circle again and drag to the outside edge to create an effect similar to that shown in Figure 13-27. You use this object in the next section to apply a Twister effect.

7. If you can't complete the exercise in the next section at this time, save the drawing to your hard disk as **distort.cdr**.

Figure 13-27: Click and drag to apply a center zipper distortion to the circle.

The zipper effect is useful for creating ragged edge effects around the edge of a background or in combination with other distortion effects to create special effects objects.

Applying twister distortions

Twister distortions create swirl effects when applied to objects. You can choose the direction of the swirl, the number of rotations, and the number of degrees of rotation for effects under a full rotation of the swirl.

To apply a twister distortion:

1. Open distort.cdr if it's not already open.

2. Select the Interactive Distortion tool and click the Twister button on the Property bar.

3. Click and drag counterclockwise until the number of degrees on the property bar says 145 degrees (see Figure 13-28).

Figure 13-28: Dragging the mouse pointer counterclockwise creates a swirled effect.

Working with the Envelope Effect

Draw's Envelope feature provides the tools to reshape and distort objects that you create in the drawing window. Using the Envelope Roll-Up, you can select an envelope type, create an envelope based on an object in your drawing, or apply one of a library of preset envelopes to a selected object or object group. When you add a new envelope to an object, you can reshape the envelope by clicking and dragging the envelope's nodes. When you apply the envelope to your object, Draw reshapes the object to fit within the envelope shape. Once you create an envelope, you can edit the existing envelope, or add a new envelope, to further distort the object.

Cross-Reference In Chapter 11, you learned to apply the Envelope effect to text. This section examines envelopes in more depth, as you learn to distort other Draw objects.

Choosing and applying an envelope

Draw offers an assortment of envelope types and editing modes from which to choose. If you choose to apply an envelope based on an object in your drawing, you can create nearly any shape that you can imagine. In addition, Draw provides a library of preset envelopes that you can use as is, or modify to suit individual requirements. The most commonly applied envelopes are based on one of Draw's four envelope-editing modes. These editing modes start as a rectangular envelope that you can reshape to distort the selected object or group. If you want to create your own envelope, use the following descriptions as a guide to choosing an editing mode (see Figure 13-29):

✦ **Straight Line:** Lets you create an envelope based on straight lines. You can drag an envelope node horizontally or vertically to reshape one side of an envelope. This editing mode is useful for adding perspective-like effects to your objects.

✦ **Single Arc:** Lets you create an envelope based on a single arc. You can drag an envelope node horizontally or vertically to create an arc shape on one side of the envelope. This editing mode is useful for giving objects a concave or convex appearance.

✦ **Double Arc:** Lets you create an envelope based upon a double arc. You can drag an envelope node horizontally or vertically to create an "S" shape on one side of the envelope.

✦ **Unconstrained:** Lets you create a free-form envelope. You can drag envelope nodes and handles freely, in addition to applying any of Draw's node attributes to the envelope.

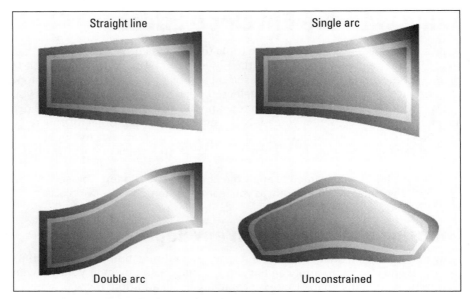

Figure 13-29: Examples of envelope-editing modes.

To add a new envelope:

1. Using the Pick tool, select the object.

2. Click the Interactive Blend tool and hold down the mouse button until the flyout menu appears. Select the Interactive Envelope tool (see Figure 13-30).

Figure 13-30: Using the Interactive Envelope tool, you can specify the type of envelope and the application method to use.

3. Choose the type of envelope or editing mode you want to use and click Add New. Enable Keep Lines if you want to prevent Draw from changing the object's straight lines to curves when you apply the envelope.

4. A red dotted bounding box with nodes appears around your selection in the drawing window. Click and drag the nodes to create the envelope shape you want to use.

Tip

Pressing Shift or Ctrl as you drag moves the adjacent node an equal distance in the opposite or same direction, respectively. Pressing Ctrl+Shift moves all four corner or side nodes, depending on whether you're dragging a corner or side node.

Working with the mapping mode

The options in the Mapping Mode list box let you control how an envelope alters the appearance of an object. You can choose from four mapping modes: Horizontal, Original, Putty, and Vertical. When you apply a new mapping mode, you change the way Draw fits the object to the envelope. It does not change the shape of the envelope itself. Use these descriptions to choose a mapping mode for your envelope (see Figure 13-31):

✦ **Horizontal:** Stretches the object to fit the basic dimensions of the envelope, then compresses it horizontally to fit the shape of the envelope.

✦ **Original:** Maps the corner handles on the object's selection box to the envelope's corner nodes. The remaining nodes are aligned along the edge of the object's selection box.

✦ **Putty:** Maps the corner handles on the object's selection box to the envelope's corner nodes only. The remaining nodes are ignored, producing less dramatic distortions than Original mode.

✦ **Vertical:** Stretches the object to fit the basic dimensions of the envelope, then compresses it vertically to fit the shape of the envelope.

The difference between original and putty is subtle. Putty mode yields smoother, more rounded objects. Original mode causes harder, more dramatic changes in the object's shape.

To change the mapping mode:

1. Using the Pick tool, select the object that has the envelope to modify.

2. Select the Interactive Envelope tool.

3. Choose the mapping mode to use from the Mapping Mode list box.

If you are new to Draw, experiment with the envelope feature and various mapping modes. This will help you learn to predict how an envelope will behave when you apply it to objects in your drawings.

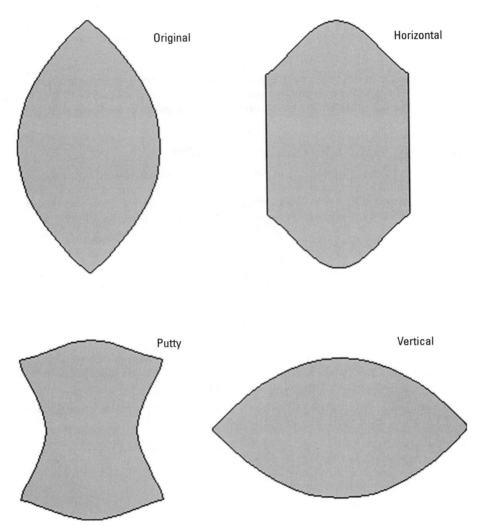

Figure 13-31: Examples of mapping modes.

Using preset envelopes

The Envelope Property bar lets you choose from a set of predrawn envelopes. These shapes include a variety of popular shapes. You can use the shape as is, or modify the shape of a preset envelope after you apply it.

To choose a preset envelope:

1. Using the Pick tool, select the object to which you want to apply an envelope.

2. Select the Interactive Envelope tool.

3. Click the Add Preset button and choose a preset envelope shape from the preset library (see Figure 13-32).

4. Modify the shape and, if desired, select other envelope options.

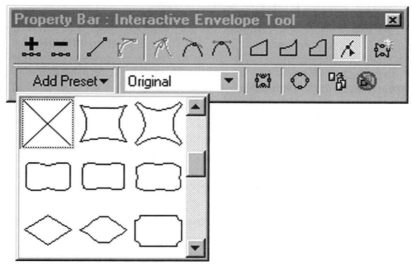

Figure 13-32: Choose a preset envelope shape from the preset library.

Reshaping an envelope

The Envelope nodes can be modified in much the same way that you modify nodes on an object. You can change a node's attributes as you would those of any curve object in Draw. The shape tool lets you modify the shape of any envelope and then apply the changes using the Envelope Roll-Up. Like many of Draw's other effects, however, if you apply other effects after creating the envelope, you have to clear those effects before you can edit the envelope.

To modify the shape of an envelope:

1. Using the Shape tool, click to select the object that has the envelope to modify.

2. Select the Interactive Envelope tool.

3. Click the button that indicates the editing mode you want.

4. Click and drag the nodes or control points to reshape the envelope. If you want to move several nodes at the same time, marquee-select the nodes, then drag one of the selected nodes. Each selected node moves the same direction and distance as the node you drag.

Note When you apply an envelope, Draw automatically activates the Interactive Envelope tool. Changes you make in the envelope are applied automatically.

Copying and cloning envelopes

Like other effects, you can copy and clone envelopes from one object to another. When you copy or clone an envelope, the shape and other attributes are transferred to the new object. The difference between copied and cloned envelopes is in the way they behave after they are applied. Objects containing copied envelopes are independent from the object whose envelope was copied. Objects containing cloned envelopes are linked to the master object whose envelope was cloned. If you update the envelope of a master object, the clone object's envelope is modified in the same manner.

To copy or clone an envelope from one object to another:

1. Using the Pick tool, select the object to which you want to copy or clone the envelope.
2. Click Effects ➪ Copy ➪ Envelope From or Effects ➪ Clone ➪ Envelope From.
3. Click the object whose envelope you want to copy or clone.

Note that if you've applied an effect to the object since you applied the envelope, you won't be able to copy the envelope. Draw automatically applies the selected envelope to the new object.

Removing an envelope

The Clear Envelope command removes envelopes one at a time, starting with the most recently applied envelope. If you've applied several envelopes to an object, for example, you need to apply the command once for each envelope until all of the envelopes are cleared. Once you remove all envelopes applied to a selected object, the object reverts to its original shape. Before clearing an envelope, you must clear any other effects that were applied after you applied the envelope. To remove an envelope, select the object whose envelope you want to clear. With the object selected, select Effects ➪ Clear Envelope. Repeat this action to clear multiple envelopes.

Adding Extrusions

Draw's extrusion feature lets you give a selected 2D object a 3D appearance by extending the object's shape toward a vanishing point that you specify. Using the controls available in the Extrude Roll-Up and on the Property bar, you can manipulate the orientation, vanishing point, and depth of the extrusion. You can also apply and control the extrusion's fill and lighting effects. Like many of Draw's special effects, the elements of an extrusion are dynamically linked to the control object on which the extrusion is based. Dynamically linked extruded surfaces automatically reflect any modifications you make to the control object. For example, if you skew the control object, the extruded surfaces are automatically skewed proportionately to the control object.

Creating and editing extrusions

Draw has the capability of creating two extrusion types using the Extrude Property bar: perspective extrusions and parallel extrusions (see Figure 13-33). Perspective extrusions use both depth and perspective to create the illusions of surfaces appearing to recede towards a vanishing point. The vanishing point is the point where the receding lines would meet if they were extended (see Figure 13-34). When you create parallel extrusions, the lines of the extrusion are parallel to one another and have no vanishing point. Regardless of how far you extended the lines, they would never meet.

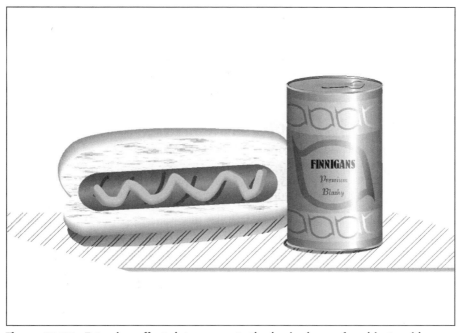

Figure 13-33: Extrusion effects let you create the basic shapes for objects with a 3D appearance.

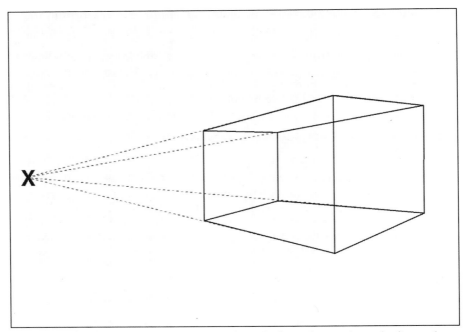

Figure 13-34: The vanishing point of an object is the point X, where the lines of an object would meet if they were extended.

Extruding an object

To extrude an object:

1. Using the Pick tool, select the object to extrude.

2. Click the Interactive Blend tool, hold down the mouse button until the flyout menu appears, and select the Interactive Extrusion tool. The Extrusion view of the property bar appears (see Figure 13-35).

3. Choose an extrusion type from the list box. Use these descriptions as a guide:

   • **Small Back:** Creates an extrusion with the back smaller than the selected object. The extrusion appears behind the selected object.

   • **Small Front:** Reduces the size of the selected object when creating the extrusion. The extrusion's largest dimension is the size of the original text string. The extrusion appears in front of the selected object.

   • **Big Back:** Creates an extrusion with the back larger than the selected object. The extrusion appears behind the original object.

   • **Big Front:** Creates an extrusion in front of the original object. The extrusion is larger than the selected object, which remains at its original size.

- **Back Parallel:** Creates an extrusion behind the selected object. The largest dimension of the extrusion is equal to that of the selected text.

- **Front Parallel:** Creates an extrusion in front of the selected object. The largest dimension of the extrusion is equal to that of the selected text.

4. Choose a vanishing point option from the Vanishing Point Properties list box. If you choose one of the parallel extrusions, this is ignored. Use these descriptions as a guide to choosing a vanishing point:

- **VP Locked To Object:** By default, Draw locks the viewpoint to the object. If you move the object, the viewpoint and extrusion move with the object and appear the same.

- **VP Locked To Page:** If you choose VP Locked To Page, the extrusion of the object is locked to its location on the page. When you move the object, a constant viewpoint is maintained.

- **Copy VP From:** If you choose this option, an arrow appears in the drawing window, allowing you to use the same type of viewpoint as another extruded object.

- **Share Vanishing Point:** This option lets you share the vanishing point with another object. When you choose this option, an arrow appears in the drawing window, which lets you choose the object with which to share a vanishing point.

5. Select a depth. Small Front, Small Back, Large Front, and Large Back let you specify a depth for your extrusion. You can't change the depth of a parallel extrusion. By default, the depth is set at 20. Larger values increase the depth of the extrusion. Smaller values decrease the depth of the extrusion.

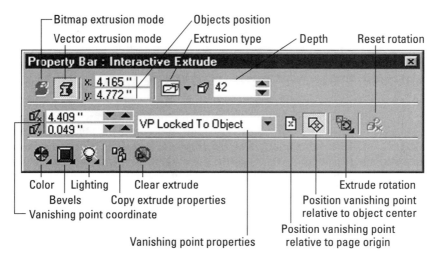

Figure 13-35: The Extrusion Property bar lets you choose an extrusion type, as well as set the extrusion's color, lighting, and rotation parameters.

6. Drag the vanishing point marker (indicated by X) to set the depth and direction of the extrusion. Or click the Page Flipper button to display controls for placing the vanishing point at a precise coordinate.

Editing extrusions

Sometimes it's hard to envision how an extrusion will look once it's applied. The capability of editing extrusion properties lets you try "what if" scenarios without having to start over if the results are not what you wanted. Once you create an extrusion, you can edit or change its properties, using either the Extrude Roll-Up or the Property bar. You can change the type of extrusion, alter the depth, move the vanishing point, or change the type of vanishing point. If you want to move the vanishing point, select the extrusion and either click the edit button on the Vanishing Point property sheet of the Extrude Roll-Up or the Vanishing Point button on the Property bar. When the X appears, click and drag the X to move the vanishing point.

To change an extrusion's properties using the Property bar:

1. Using the Pick tool, select the extrusion to modify.

2. On the Property bar, do one of the following:

   • Choose an extrusion type from the Extrusion Type list box.

   • Enter new horizontal and vertical coordinates in the Vanishing Point Coordinate boxes. Remember that these coordinates are relative to the 0,0 point on the rulers.

   • Enter a new value in the Depth box.

Tip   Sometimes when selecting an extrusion to move the vanish point, the vanishing point appears outside of the drawing window. Either zoom out or pan the drawing window until the vanishing point is visible.

Copying and sharing a vanishing point

If you were creating a street scene with buildings, you would find it useful to have the buildings' extrusions use the same vanishing point. Draw lets you specify that extrusions share a common vanishing point. If you move a shared vanishing point, all extrusions that share that point are updated, automatically. When you copy an extrusion's vanishing point to another object, a new vanishing point is created on top of the existing vanishing point. As a result, both objects appear to recede toward the same point, but the two vanishing points can be edited independently.

Copying from one extrusion to another

To copy the vanishing point to a selected extrusion from another extrusion:

1. Click the Vanishing Point Properties list box.

2. Choose Copy VP From.

3. Select the extruded object from which you want to copy the vanishing point.

Tip   When you rotate an extrusion, using the Extrude Property bar, it can't share a vanishing point with another extrusion. If you want to rotate an extrusion that shares a vanishing point, rotate the extrusion using the mouse or Transformation docker. This lets you modify the extrusion, while maintaining the shared vanishing point link.

Sharing among multiple extrusions

To specify a single vanishing point for multiple extrusions:

1. Using the Pick tool, select the extrusion whose vanishing point you want to change.

2. Choose Shared Vanishing Point in the Vanishing Point Properties list box.

3. Select the extrusion that has the vanishing point that you want to share.

If you are creating a drawing where creating a sense of reality is essential, your extrusions need to share a common vanishing point. For example, if you create a city scene with a building-lined street, specifying a single vanishing point for the buildings lends the drawing a sense of reality. If the buildings don't share a single vanishing point, some buildings may appear to float above the surface of the drawing, instead of contacting the ground.

Printing Extrusions

Extruded objects can cause printing to slow. The reason these objects slow printing is related to the facet size of the object. The facet size is the distance between shades of color in an extrusion. Similar to the number of steps in a fountain fill, as the facet size decreases, the print time increases proportionately. You can specify the facet size used when Draw renders and prints illustrations containing extrusions on the Display property sheet of the Options dialog box. Draw lets you specify any size between 0.001 inches and 36 inches.

Larger sizes print more rapidly, but the quality of the print is compromised. For best results, set the Minimum extrude facet size to a value from 0.001 to 0.5 inches. A higher value of 0.5 inches reduces the screen refresh time while you are creating your drawing. Before you print your drawing, reduce the facet size to 0.01 inch or lower. The new setting affects every extruded object in your drawing. Using this method, you can hit a balance between production speed, while you are creating your image, and quality output.

Applying fills to extrusions

Draw provides three fill options for extruded objects: Use Object Fill, Solid Fill, and Shade. Choosing Use Object Fill applies the control object's current fill to the entire extrusion. If you also enable Drape Fills, the object may lose its definition, if it doesn't have an outline. Use Object Fill is the recommended and default option if your control object has a uniform, fountain, pattern, or texture fill. The Solid Fill option fills extruded surfaces with the solid color you specify. The control object retains the original fill properties, but the extruded surfaces take on the color you choose. The Shade option blends the two colors that you specify along the length of the extruded surfaces. The result is similar to a linear fountain fill. Unlike linear fountain fills, you can't modify the angle or other fill attributes.

To specify an extrusion's fill:

1. Using the Pick tool, select the extrusion to fill.

2. Click the Color Wheel button to display the fill menu of the Extrude Property bar (see Figure 13-36).

3. Choose the type of fill you want to use (see Figure 13-37).

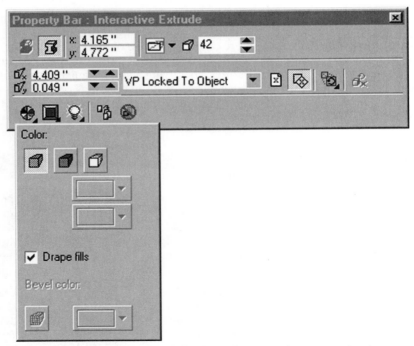

Figure 13-36: The Fill menu of the Interactive Extrude Property bar lets you choose the method that Draw uses to fill the extruded surfaces of your object.

4. Specify the color(s), if you have chosen Solid or Shade as a fill option, by clicking the color chip(s) and choosing a color from the drop-down palette.

5. Enable the Drape Fills checkbox if desired. If your object has a bevel, and you want to use the extrude fill for the bevel, enable Use Extrude Fill for Bevel. You can also specify fills on the Property bar.

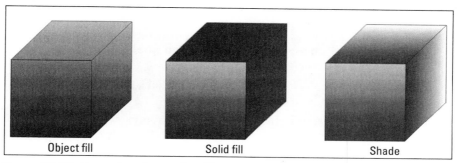

Figure 13-37: Examples of extrusion fills.

When you choose to drape an extrusion fill, the fill becomes uniform throughout the object, as if you wrapped a package with a solid color of giftwrap (see Figure 13-38). Draping fills is especially effective when combined with lighting effects. If Drape Fill is disabled, the selected fill is copied to each of the extrusion's surfaces.

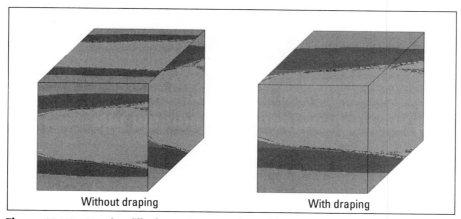

Figure 13-38: Draping fills the entire extrusion with the selected fill.

Adding lighting

The lighting feature in the Extrude Roll-Up lets you further enhance the 3D effect of an extrusion by adding highlights and shadows to your extruded objects. The lighting preview window displays a sphere in a wireframe box. The sphere represents the object being lighted. You can position up to three lights at intersection points of the wireframe box.

To apply lighting to an extrusion:

1. Using the Pick tool, select the extrusion to which you want to apply lighting effects.

2. Select the Interactive Extrude Tool and click the Lighting button to display the Lighting menu (see Figure 13-39).

3. Click up to three of the light buttons to apply one, two, or three light sources. The lights appear as numbered circles in the preview window (see Figure 13-40).

4. Position the light sources by dragging the numbered circles to intersecting points in the display box. Enabling Use Full Color Range makes the shading more realistic.

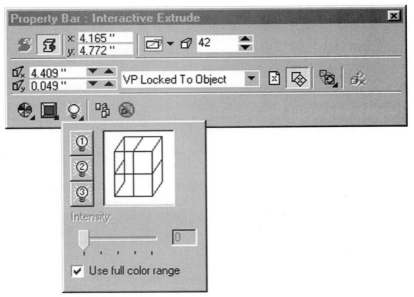

Figure 13-39: Using the Lighting menu of the Property bar, you can specify lighting that enhances the 3D appearance of your object.

5. Adjust the lighting intensity by dragging the Intensity slider. Dragging to the left lowers the intensity, making the extrusion's colors darker. Dragging to the right increases the intensity, making the extrusion's colors lighter. Each light is adjusted independently. Select the light to adjust before dragging the slider.

Figure 13-40: Applying lighting effects gives objects a greater 3D feel.

Adding a bevel

Bevels give objects and extrusions a more polished appearance by creating the illusion of an angled interim edge rather than the hard edge of normal extrusions (see Figure 13-41). When applied to text or other objects, bevels enhance the 3D appearance of elements in your drawing. Using the Bevels button on the Extrude Property bar, you can add a bevel to objects or extrusions. Enter values to specify the bevel angle and depth. A second method lets you interactively adjust the bevel by dragging a handle control within the interactive display box. As you drag the handle, you change the bevel depth and angle. These changes are reflected in the Bevel Angle and Bevel Depth boxes.

To create a beveled extrusion:

1. Using the Pick tool, select the object or extrusion to which you want to apply beveled edges.

2. Select the Interactive Extrude tool and click the Bevels button to display the Bevels property menu of the Property bar (see Figure 13-42).

3. Enable the Use Bevel checkbox.

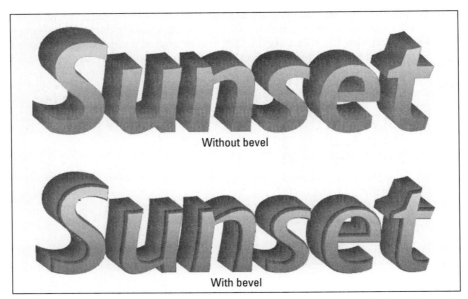

Figure 13-41: Applying a bevel to extruded objects softens the hard edge of extrusions and gives the object a more polished appearance.

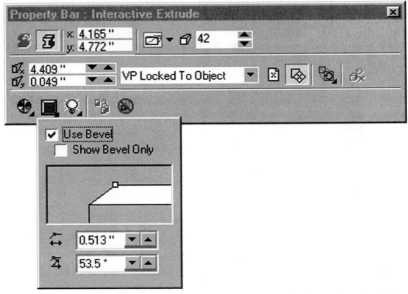

Figure 13-42: The Bevels menu lets you specify the depth and angle of the beveled surfaces.

4. Enable Show Bevel Only if you only want the bevel and control objects displayed. If you choose this option, the extruded elements aren't visible (see Figure 13-43).

5. Enter a value in the Bevel Depth box to specify how deep to make the bevel. You can specify values from 0.001 to 1,980 inches or the equivalent in another unit of measure. Alternatively, you can click-and-drag in the display box to adjust both the depth and angle of the bevel.

6. Enter a value in the Bevel Angle box to specify the angle at which you want to cut the bevel edge. You can specify values from 1.0 degree to 89.0 degrees. Lower values create flatter bevels; higher values create more angled bevels.

Figure 13-43: Enable Show Bevel Only to display only the bevel and the control object.

Copying and cloning extrusions

The quickest way to reproduce extrusions using other control objects is to copy or clone the effect from an existing extrusion. The new extrusion uses the new control objects but reproduces the attributes of the extrusion you copied or cloned. Although both methods reproduce the original extrusion's attributes, they vary in how they behave. When you copy an extrusion, the new extrusion is independent of the group from which you copied the extrusion. If you clone an extrusion, you create a clone extrusion. The extrusion from which you cloned the extrusion attributes becomes the master extrusion. Changes that you make in the master extrusion are replicated in the clone. You can't edit the cloned extrusion's settings using the Extrude Roll-Up. Any changes must be made to the master object.

To copy or clone an extrusion:

1. Using the Pick tool, select the object to which you want to copy the extrusion.

2. Select Effects ➪ Copy ➪ Extrude From or select Effects ➪ Clone ➪ Extrude From.

3. Click the extrusion to copy or clone.

Rotating an extrusion

You can rotate an extrusion in three planes. This lets you create an additional feeling of depth or align the extrusion with other elements in your drawing (this option isn't available if you are creating a parallel extrusion). Using the 3D-rotation view of the Property bar, you can choose one of two methods for rotating the object. You can interactively rotate your object in the drawing window by double-clicking an extruded object to activate the rotation mode. As you drag your object in rotation mode, a wireframe image of your extrusion is displayed in the drawing window so you can preview the changes. You can also specify values on the Property bar from –360 degrees to 360 degrees for each of the rotation planes.

To interactively rotate an extrusion:

1. Using the Pick tool, select the extrusion to rotate.

2. Select the Interactive Extrude tool and double-click the extrusion to rotate. The Property bar changes to the 3D-rotation view, and the object is surrounded by the 3D-rotation control (see Figure 13-44).

3. Click and drag the object to rotate it to a new view. The mouse pointer changes to guide you in the direction of the rotation.

Editing the control object

Generally, you can edit a control object using the Pick or Shape tool as you would edit any object in Draw. The Pick tool lets you scale, rotate, or skew the extrusion. The Shape tool lets you change the basic shape of the object itself or re-kern artistic text. If you've added other effects to an extrusion, such as Perspective or Envelope effects, you have to clear the effects before you can edit the control object using the Shape tool.

Separating and clearing an extrusion

Like many other special effects, extrusions are dynamically linked objects. This means that the extruded surfaces are linked to the control object. In addition, the extruded surfaces form a group of objects. You can separate extrusions into the control object and a group of the extrusion elements. If you want to return the control object to its original state prior to applying the extrusion, you can clear the effect.

To separate an extrusion:

1. Using the Pick tool, select the extrusion you want to separate.

2. Select Arrange ⇨ Separate.

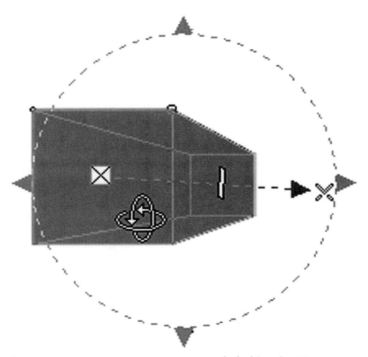

Figure 13-44: You can rotate your extruded object in 3D space.

To clear an extrusion:

1. Using the Pick tool, select the extrusion to clear.

2. Select the Clear Extrude button. The extrusion will be removed, but any bevel that had been applied will remain. Alternatively, you can select Effects ➪ Clear Extrude to clear an Extrude group.

Note

Once you clear or separate an Extrusion effect, the dynamic link is broken and you can no longer edit the object as an extrusion.

Working with Drop Shadows

Shadows give objects a realistic appearance. You can add interactive drop shadows to any Draw object or object group. You can adjust the feathering type, direction, and opacity of a drop shadow. Drop shadows are dynamically linked to the selection, as are many of Draw's special effects. They are unique, however, in that they are bitmap, rather than vector, objects. This is important to remember, because as bitmap objects they can dramatically increase the file size of your document (see Figure 13-45).

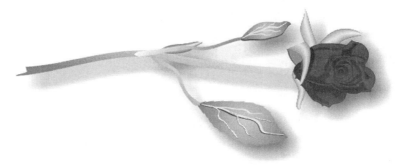

Figure 13-45: Drop shadows can enhance objects in your drawings by giving them a realistic appearance.

Applying a drop shadow

To apply a drop shadow to a selection:

1. Select the Interactive Drop Shadow tool from the toolbox.

2. Click the object to which you want to apply a drop shadow and drag the cursor in the direction in which you want to place the drop shadow. As you drag the mouse, Draw displays the shadow as a blue line to assist you in placing the shadow (see Figure 13-46).

Tip   You can't add drop shadows to dynamically linked groups such as blend groups. If you want to add a drop shadow to such a group, select the group with the Pick tool and apply the Group command. Draw sees groups as an object rather than as a dynamically linked group and lets you apply the drop shadow.

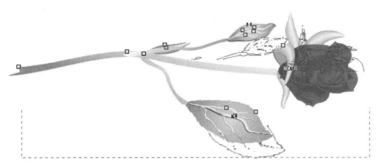

Figure 13-46: As you drag the mouse cursor, Draw displays the drop shadow as a blue line.

Modifying a drop shadow

Once you've applied the basic drop shadow, you can adjust the opacity, the feathering direction of the drop shadow, and the feathering type by modifying the settings on the Property bar. You can also change the color of the drop shadow by dragging a color from the onscreen color palette to the black square of the shadow direction line or by selecting a drop shadow color from the Drop Shadow Color swatch on the Property bar.

To change the feathering properties and opacity of a drop shadow:

1. Create a drop shadow, and with the Shadow tool and object still selected, choose a shadow type from the Drop Shadow Direction box. Use this list as a guide for choosing a feathering type:

   - **Average:** The default feathering direction calculates the shadow based on the average between the inside and outside edges of the control object. The rose example (Figure 13-46) displays an average drop shadow.

   - **Middle:** Calculates the shadow from the center of the control object. In the rose example, the veins of the leaves would be prominent in the drop shadow.

   - **Inside:** Calculates the shadow from the inside edges of the control object. Creates a smaller, subtler-looking drop shadow with less feathering.

   - **Outside:** Calculates the shadow from the outside edges of the control object. Creates a dense, pronounced drop shadow with heavy feathering.

2. If you select a feathering direction other than average, you can also choose a feathering edge style for your drop shadow. Use this list as a guide for choosing an edge style:

- **Linear:** This edge style creates a soft-feathered drop shadow with no prominent edge.

- **Squared:** This edge style has a soft edge with feathering that extends beyond the edge.

- **Inverse Squared:** This edge style has a prominent edge with feathering that extends beyond the edge.

- **Flat:** This edge style has no feathering and produces a dense, opaque drop shadow.

3. To adjust the opacity of the drop shadow, click the up and down arrows in the opacity-setting box on the Property bar, or enter the value to use. You can also drag the midpoint slider on the drop shadow control to alter the amount of opacity.

4. To adjust the amount of feathering, click the up and down arrows in the drop shadow feathering box, or enter the value to use. By default, Draw uses a value of 13 pixels.

You can remove a selected drop shadow using the Clear Effects command from the Effects menu.

Tip   As with many of Draw's special effects, you can use the Copy and Clone commands on the Effects menu to copy drop shadows from one object to another. This lets you give objects within your document a consistent feel.

Creating Lens Effects

Lens effects alter the appearance of objects that reside below the lens. Lenses act like filters on cameras to change your impression of the objects residing below the lens, rather than to change the viewed object itself. Draw provides 12 lenses from which to choose. Each lens produces unique effects when applied to objects residing over vector or bitmap objects. Some lenses, such as the Color Limit lens, modify the color of objects behind them. Others, such as the Magnify lens, distort objects. Lenses can be applied to any closed-path object, including Artistic text. You can't, however, apply lenses to open paths, Paragraph text, or bitmaps. You also can't apply lenses to objects that have dynamically linked effects, such as extrusions or contours. You can apply lenses to grouped objects, but remember that they are applied to every object in the group separately, and not to the group as a whole.

Choosing and applying a lens

Each of the 12 lenses has unique properties that enhance the objects that lie below the lens. Choosing a lens is a matter of aesthetics, as is finding the lens that creates the effect you want (see Figure 13-47). Experiment with the lenses to become familiar with their individual properties. Use the following descriptions as a guide to choosing a lens. The parameters that you can set appear along with the description of each lens:

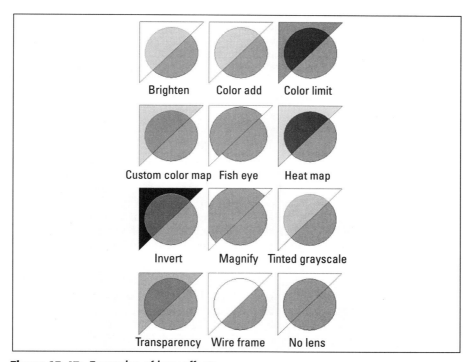

Figure 13-47: Examples of lens effects.

✦ **No Lens:** This lens removes the effects of a lens, returning objects below to their original appearance. The lens object reverts to its original attributes, as well.

✦ **Brighten:** The Brighten lens makes objects below the lens look brighter or darker, as determined by the settings that you specified. The Rate value controls the amount of brightness or darkness created by the lens. You specify a rate between –100 percent and 100 percent. Positive values increase the amount of brightness; negative values increase the amount of darkness.

✦ **Color Add:** The Color Add lens adds the specified color to the objects below the lens. This lens acts as an additive light model. Using red, green, and blue as the *light* colors, areas where the three colors merge result in white light. By setting the rate level to a value between 0 percent and 100 percent, you can control the intensity of this effect. A rate of 0 percent results in no color addition, and the lens appears to have no fill. A rate of 100 percent defines maximum color addition. White light contains all colors of the spectrum. If you place this lens over a white object, the lens turns white, and no color is added.

✦ **Color Limit:** The Color Limit filter makes objects below appear as if they were viewed through a color filter lens on a camera. The Color Limit filter *removes* colors from the object below, displaying all the colors in the object as either black or one other color that you specify. White and light colors in objects beneath the lens appear as the lens color. Dark colors and black appear black. The rate specifies how much of the color to convert to the lens color and black. Higher values increase the number of colors converted to the lens color and black. Lower values apply tints of the lens color and black to the objects below.

✦ **Custom Color Map:** The Custom Color Map lens sets the colors of objects below the lens to a color range between the two colors that you specify. In addition to defining the start and end colors, you can choose the progression between the colors. By default, the lens uses a direct progression between the two colors. You can also specify Forward Rainbow or Reverse Rainbow options. These options map colors using a progression that follows a forward or backward route through the spectrum between the two selected colors. Areas of the lens that do not cover other objects are filled with the color at the end of the color map.

✦ **Fish Eye:** The Fish Eye lens makes objects below the lens appear distorted and either enlarged or reduced in size. The amount of the effect is determined by the setting specified in the Rate box. Lenses with positive rates distort and magnify objects by increasing amounts as their rate setting progresses from 1 to 1,000. Lenses with negative rates shrink and distort objects by increasing amounts as their rate setting progresses from –1 to –1,000. A rate of 0 results in no change to the appearance of objects behind the lens. The Fish Eye lens has no effect on bitmap images.

✦ **Heat Map:** The Heat Map adds infrared effects to objects below the lens. This lens remaps the colors of the objects below the lens, using a limited color palette of white, yellow, orange-red, blue, violet, and cyan. When you adjust the value in the Palette Rotation box, you specify which colors to display as hot, and which colors to display as cool. Values set at 0 percent or 100 percent cause all the colors of the object below to appear as either white or cyan, respectively. A value between these two settings displays colors using the other colors in the palette.

✦ **Invert:** The Invert lens gives the objects below the lens the appearance of a photonegative. This lens displays the colors of objects below as their complementary CYMK color, even if the object uses another color palette. Complementary colors are those that appear directly across from one another on a color wheel.

✦ **Magnify:** The Magnify lens resembles the effect of a magnifying glass. The Magnify lens is transparent, except where objects fall below the lens. Objects below the lens appear magnified by the value you specify. You can specify a value between 1.0 and 100.0 times the original size of the objects below the lens.

✦ **Tinted Grayscale:** The Tinted Grayscale lens gives objects below the lens a sepia or duotone appearance by changing the colors of objects beneath it to their grayscale equivalents and adding a tint. The lens color you specify becomes the darkest color in any object under it. All other colors in the object become lighter shades of the lens's color.

✦ **Transparency:** The transparency lens makes objects below the lens appear as if they were being viewed through tinted glass. You can specify any color for the lens, and set transparency rates from 0 percent to 100 percent. The Rate setting controls the lens's level of transparency. Rates closer to 100 percent are more transparent, while those closer to 0 percent are more opaque.

✦ **Wireframe:** The Wireframe lens makes objects below the lens to appear as an outline filled with the color you specify. If the objects below the lens have no fill, they appear unchanged. You can specify the fill and outline colors to use. If you don't want the lens to affect the outline or fill, disable the appropriate checkbox.

Although the settings available for each lens vary from one lens to another, the basic process of applying a lens is the same for all the lenses.

To apply a lens:

1. Using the Pick tool, select the object to which to apply a lens.

2. Select Effects ➪ Lens to display the Lens docker (see Figure 13-48).

3. Specify the parameters and options to use for the lens.

4. Click Apply.

Caution

Lenses appear as gray objects in versions of Draw prior to Draw 7 because they didn't have lens capabilities.

Figure 13-48: The Lens docker lets you to choose lenses and specify the parameters associated with each lens.

Choosing lens options

The Lens docker offers the capability to select lens options that affect what is displayed in the lens. You can choose from Frozen, Viewpoint, or Remove Face. You can specify these options by enabling the option when you create the lens, or later if you edit the lens. Use these descriptions as a guide to choosing lens options:

> ✦ **Frozen:** The Frozen option fixes the current contents of a lens. You can then move the lens without changing what's displayed through it. Changes made to those objects that are seen through the lens have no effect on the lens contents (see Figure 13-49).

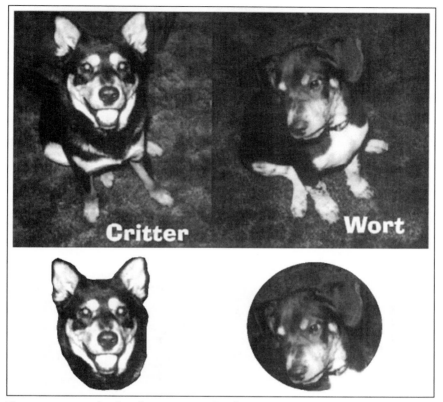

Figure 13-49: Selecting the Frozen option lets you move the circles to which a lens effect has been applied anywhere on the page without changing what's displayed in the lens.

✦ **Viewpoint:** The Viewpoint option lets you display a portion of a drawing through a lens without moving the lens. The viewpoint represents the center point of what is being viewed through the lens, as indicated by an "X" in your drawing. You can position the viewpoint by dragging it to any location in your drawing (see Figure 13-50).

Figure 13-50: You can move a viewpoint to display a selected portion of your drawing.

✦ **Remove Face:** When you enable Remove Face, the lens only shows where it overlaps other objects. It appears invisible where it covers blank space. Remove Face is only available for lenses that alter the color of objects beneath them. If you've chosen another type of lens, the option appears grayed out. Figure 13-51 shows a variety of lenses, each with Remove Face enabled, covering areas of the image below.

Figure 13-51: When Remove Face is enabled, color lenses only appear when they overlap an object below.

Copying lens effects

Like most other special effects, you can copy a lens from one object to another. When a lens is copied, all of the parameters and settings are also copied. This may require repositioning the viewpoint, if that option is enabled.

To copy a lens from one object to another:

1. Using the Pick tool, select the object to which you want to apply the lens.

2. Select Effects ⇨ Copy ⇨ Lens From.

3. Click the object from which you want to copy the lens.

Working with PowerClips

Just for a moment, imagine an 8-by-10-inch oval picture frame. Now imagine that you have a 12-by-14-inch rectangular picture that you need to place in the frame. Obviously, if you don't buy a new frame, you are going to have to trim the picture to fit. In the process, part of the object will be lost. Draw's PowerClip feature is similar to the frame and picture, only much easier. Using the PowerClip feature, you can designate any object you create in Draw, except Paragraph text, as the frame or container in which to hold another object (the contents). This feature is especially useful for placing bitmaps in your drawings. If the contents object is larger than the container object, Draw automatically crops the contents object. You see only the contents that fit inside the container object. The portion of the object that falls outside the container is still there—you just can't see it.

Creating a PowerClip

Draw has two methods for creating a PowerClip. You can create a PowerClip using the commands on the Effects menu, or you can use the Object Manager. While both methods provide the same commands and options, the Object Manager is the more efficient means of creating and editing PowerClips.

To create a PowerClip using menu commands:

1. Using the Pick tool, select the object to place inside a PowerClip.

2. Select Effects ➪ PowerClip ➪ Place Inside Container.

3. Click the object you want to use as the container. By default, Draw centers the contents object in the container.

To create a PowerClip using the Object Manager:

1. Select Tools ➪ Object Manager to display the object manager in the drawing window (see Figure 13-52).

2. In the Object Manager, right-click the object you want used as the contents object and drag it over the object you want used as the container. When you release the mouse button, a pop-up menu appears (see Figure 13-53).

3. Select PowerClip Inside. Draw centers the selected object in the container.

Editing a PowerClip

You can edit PowerClips either in the Object Manager or by using the commands on the Effects menu. Although both methods of editing achieve the same effect, using the Object Manager for editing PowerClips is faster and more efficient.

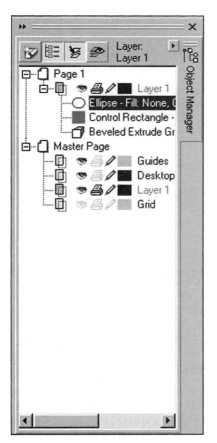

Figure 13-52: You can apply PowerClip effects from within the Object Manager.

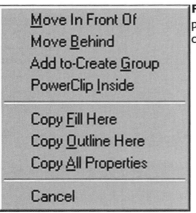

Figure 13-53: The Object Manager pop-up options menu lets you create a PowerClip effect.

Using the Effects menu

To edit a PowerClip using the command on the Effects menu:

1. Using the Pick tool, select the PowerClip to edit.

2. Select Effects ➪ PowerClip ➪ Edit Contents. The PowerClip container and contents appear in the drawing window. The rest of the objects in your drawing are hidden while you edit a PowerClip. The contents of the PowerClip appear as they did prior to being placed in the PowerClip. The container appears as a blue outline. If you have a nested PowerClip, you need to reselect the Edit Contents command until the individual PowerClip that you want to edit is separated from the rest. Choosing Extract Contents from the PowerClip menu removes the contents from the PowerClip and restores the contents and container to their original appearance.

3. Edit the contents as desired. You can reposition the contents or perform any editing options that were available to that object before being placed in the PowerClip.

4. Select Effects ➪ PowerClip ➪ Finish Editing This Level. The contents are returned to the PowerClip.

Using the Object Manager

To edit the contents or container object using the Object Manager:

1. In the Object Manager, select the contents or container object.

2. Right-click and make the desired changes to the object; for example, resize it or change its fill.

Moving the contents

To move the contents using the Object Manager:

1. In the Object Manager, select the contents object.

2. Drag the object from the Object Manager to the drawing window. As you drag, an outline of the contents appears to assist in positioning the contents.

Extracting the contents

To extract the contents using the Object Manager:

1. In the Object Manager, select the contents object.

2. Click and drag the object over the name of the layer that holds the container object. This procedure will not work if the container object is nested in another PowerClip or forms part of a group.

You can also interactively create a PowerClip in the drawing window. Right-click the object that you want to use as the contents of a PowerClip, and drag it over the object that you want to use as a container. When you release the mouse button, the right mouse button menu appears, allowing you to select PowerClip Inside. You can place PowerClips inside other PowerClips to create a nested PowerClip. A nested PowerClip can have up to five nested levels. Additionally, you can choose other PowerClip options from the right mouse button menu, such as editing, extracting, or locking the PowerClip.

Locking and Unlocking the Contents of a PowerClip

You can move a PowerClip to anywhere in your drawing, but when you select a PowerClip, remember that you are selecting the container, not the contents. If the PowerClip is unlocked and you move the container, the contents stay at their current location. The contents don't automatically move with the container. This is useful for quickly changing the position of the container in relationship to the contents.

By default, Draw locks the contents of a PowerClip to the container. This guarantees that if you move the PowerClip, the contents will move with the container. Once you have positioned the contents in a PowerClip, it's a good idea to lock the contents, if they're not already locked. By locking the contents, you guarantee that if you move the PowerClip the contents will move with it. To lock or unlock the contents of a PowerClip, right-click the PowerClip and choose Lock Contents To PowerClip.

Changing the default placement

By default, Draw automatically centers a PowerClip's contents inside its container. You can change the default placement in the Options dialog box. This is useful if you want to offset the contents by a specific amount in relationship to the container. If the contents and container objects aren't superimposed, however, the contents don't appear in the PowerClip object. When you change the default PowerClip setting, the setting that you specify applies to all documents, not just the current document.

To change the default placement of PowerClip contents:

1. Select Tools ➪ Options and expand the Workspace category. Click Edit to display the Edit page of the Options dialog box (see Figure 13-54).

2. Disable Auto-Center New PowerClip Contents.

3. Click OK to complete the operation and to return to the drawing window.

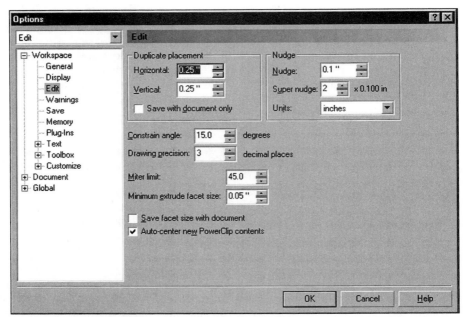

Figure 13-54: The Edit page lets you enable or disable contents centering as a PowerClip option.

Copying a PowerClip

You can copy the contents of one PowerClip to another object container. When you apply the Copy PowerClip From command, Draw duplicates the contents of the existing PowerClip and places the contents in a new container that you specify. The new container's outline and fill settings are not affected by receiving the new contents.

To copy PowerClip contents to another object:

1. Using the Pick tool, select the object to which you want to copy PowerClip contents.

2. Select Effects ➪ Copy ➪ PowerClip From.

3. Select the PowerClip that contains the contents to copy.

Using Presets

Presets are premade CorelScripts. A script is essentially a computer program, written as a text file, that performs a series of specified instructions. Scripts let you apply a series of commands and actions to your drawing in a single step. You can use scripts to perform repetitive tasks or to simplify complicated sets of steps. Although you can write your own scripts, you can use presets even if you have no programming knowledge.

Applying presets

You can apply presets to objects and Artistic text in your drawings (see Figure 13-55). Draw comes with a library of presets that you can use to enhance your documents. You can also create your own presets.

Figure 13-55: Presets let you quickly apply effects to objects and Artistic text.

To apply presets:

1. Select the object to which to apply a preset.

2. Select Window ➪ Dockers ➪ Script and Preset Manager to display the Script and Preset Manager (see Figure 13-56). The preset files are located in a folder called Presets. Double-click this folder to display the contents.

3. Either double-click the preset you want to run, or click and drag the preset from the Script and Preset Manager and drop it on top of the object to which to apply the preset. When the preset is over the object, the icon changes to a small rectangle attached to an arrow.

4. Alternatively, you can use the Pick tool to select the object to which to apply the preset. Then select the preset to apply and click the Play button at the bottom of the Script and Preset Manager.

Caution You can't apply a preset to a group or to multiple selections at the same time. Similarly, you can't apply a preset to a dynamically linked object, such as an extrusion or blend. You must first clear the effects currently associated with the object.

Editing an object after applying a preset

A preset is basically a recording of a series of commands, such as duplicate or extrude, that has been applied to an object. Once you've added a preset to an object, the object becomes like any other object in Draw. By default, Draw groups preset objects. You can edit the various elements as child objects, or ungroup the preset to break it into its basic elements. Many presets use extrusion effects, for example. Once you ungroup a preset, you can see the various elements and commands that went into creating the effect.

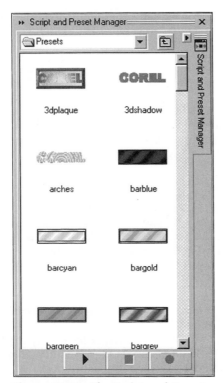

Figure 13-56: The Script and Preset Manager.

Creating new presets

Creating a new preset is essentially recording a script of a series of actions or commands to create an effect. In some cases, you might want to create an object prior to recording the script; in other cases, you create the object as part of the script. If you want to be able to apply the effect to any selected object, such as Artistic text, in the drawing window, create the object before recording the script. Using this method, the actions needed to create the effect are recorded, rather than the object itself, and can be applied to any graphic or text object in Draw. If you create the object during the recording, the object is recreated each time you play the script.

To create an effects script:

1. To be able to apply the effect to any object, create a base object.

2. Click the Recording button in the Script and Preset Manager.

3. Perform the commands to create the effect you want.

4. Click the Stop Recording button in the Script and Preset Manager.

5. A Save dialog box appears. Enter a name for your preset. I recommend allowing Draw to save the preset in its default location so that it's easily available when you are ready to use it.

6. Click Save to complete the operation. Then test your script by applying the script to a new object.

Action scripts that you record are similar to a preset from the Script and Preset Manager. Recording actions is the easiest way to create a script in Draw. The types of scripts that you create this way enable you to automate repetitive tasks, such as alignment and transformations.

Summary

Draw's basic special effects features offer a broad range of tools for enhancing your drawings. This is a world of exploration. Whether you are looking for subtle or dazzling effects, Draw has tools to enhance your documents. The Perspective and Contour commands let you give objects a feeling of depth. The Blend effect possesses the versatility to create a broad variety of effects, including an illusion of depth and speed, with its morphing capabilities. Envelope effects distort the elements in your drawing, letting you add interest or easily modify the basic shape of objects. Like most of the effects in Draw, these effects are capable of producing both subtle and dramatic results. It's impossible to cover either all the uses or the broad range of effects that these features are capable of creating, both singularly or in conjunction with other features. You should explore and experiment with these effects. In this chapter, you learned to

✦ Apply perspective to objects

✦ Create blend effects

✦ Add contour effects

✦ Work with envelopes to distort objects

✦ Use the Interactive Distortion tool

✦ Extrude objects to give them a 3D appearance

✦ Apply drop shadows

✦ Apply lenses

✦ Use PowerClips

✦ Apply and create your own preset effect scripts

✦   ✦   ✦

Customizing Draw

Who are you? How do you work? Are you a person who remembers that saving frequently is one of the Ten Commandments of using a computer, or do you lose track of time and forget? When you first start Draw, what's the first thing you usually do? Do you open a new drawing, open an existing drawing, or use a template? Are you a mouse and button person, or are you a keyboard-shortcut person? What kind of working display do you prefer? This chapter is about you and making Draw work the way you do.

When you customize Draw, you optimize your productivity. Once you specify settings for your work environment, you can forget them and move on with the business of being creative. Draw remembers settings you make, and they become the default settings for every Draw session until you change them.

Configuring Basic Options

Throughout this book you used the Options dialog box to specify tool, text, and other action-based options. The Options dialog box also lets you specify display, backup, and other general options that affect your overall work environment. As you learn to use Draw, you can reconfigure the program for your needs. In some cases, you may find it convenient to configure Draw for a particular document so as to speed the creation process. You can save the settings you make so that they affect new drawings or so that they affect only the current Draw session.

Choosing display options

The Display page of the Options dialog box offers choices that affect the view of your drawing. You can choose how your image displays when using full-screen preview by enabling the view you want. Choosing Normal speeds the screen refresh but doesn't display the most accurate rendering of your drawing. Enhanced view simulates more accurately how your drawing will look after it's printed commercially. If you want an idea of how it fits on the page, choose Show Page Border. In addition to selecting full-screen preview options, you can specify the type of refresh and panning, and whether Tooltips, PostScript fills, and Snap Marks are displayed.

To specify display options:

1. Select Tools ⇨ Options and expand the Workspace category. Click Display. The Display page appears (see Figure 14-1).

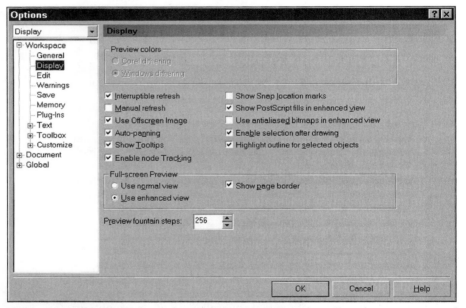

Figure 14-1: The Display page lets you choose options that affect the appearance of the drawing window and full-screen preview.

2. Select the options you want, using these descriptions as a guide:

   • **Interruptible refresh:** Complex drawings can take a long time to refresh on screen. If you enable Interruptible Refresh, you can pause the refresh to make additional changes to your drawing. When this option is enabled, clicking any object in the drawing pauses the refresh briefly to allow you to make changes.

Note

Draw completes rendering the current object to screen before pausing to let you complete another action.

- **Manual refresh:** If you are making minor editing changes and don't want to wait for the screen to refresh, enable Manual Refresh. This lets you stop the screen refresh until you tell the program to update the screen. Ctrl+W refreshes the screen when you are ready to update the screen.

- **Use Offscreen Image:** This lets you copy your work into memory, resulting in no redraw.

- **Auto-panning:** Auto-panning automatically scrolls the drawing window when you drag a tool beyond its borders. This feature is especially useful when you are working in a zoom mode, where all of your drawing is not visible in the drawing window.

- **Show Tooltips:** Tooltips display the names of tools, buttons, and other features when you pause your cursor over a feature location. This option is especially useful if you are new to Draw. It lets you identify the function of Draw's various buttons and commands.

- **Enable node Tracking:** This option lets you select nodes with the Pick tool or any of the basic drawing tools.

- **Show Snap location marks:** If this option and the snap-to features are enabled, Draw displays a small square identifying the point to which your object snaps as you drag the object.

- **Use enhanced view:** You can choose from a variety of views when you are editing a drawing. Although Enhanced View has a slower screen refresh speed, it shows the most accurate view of the drawing.

- **Show PostScript fills in enhanced view:** By default, PostScript fills are only visible on printed output. Enabling this option lets you view PostScript fills when you are using Enhanced View.

- **Use antialiased bitmaps in enhanced view:** This option is handy if you frequently import bitmaps in your work. This option uses 2X oversampling to result in the best possible view.

- **Enable selection after drawing:** This option lets you select an object immediately after drawing it.

- **Highlight outline for selected objects:** Enabling this option creates an outline around selected objects.

3. Click OK to apply the changes and return to the drawing window.

Tip

Clicking the scroll thumb on either scroll bar refreshes the drawing window.

Choosing saving options

The Save page of the Options dialog box lets you determine when and if Draw creates back-ups of your files. You can choose to have Draw automatically create a backup of your file, create a backup when you save the image, and choose where you want to store your backup files.

To specify settings on the Save property sheet:

1. Select Tools ⇨ Options and expand the Workspace category. Click Save to display the Save property sheet (see Figure 14-2).

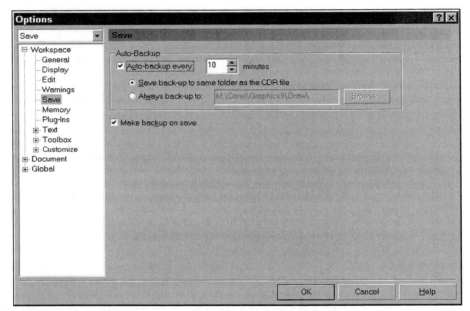

Figure 14-2: The Save page of the Options dialog box lets you specify backup options for your files.

2. Select the options you want, using the following descriptions as a guideline:

- **Auto-backup every:** By default, Draw creates a back up of your drawing every 10 minutes. You can change the amount of time, or disable this feature altogether. Although Auto-Backup is a boon to the forgetful, it can be extremely annoying if you are editing a large file that takes a while to save. While a file is saving, all action is suspended in the drawing window. You can't work, and watching a large file save is tantamount to watching grass grow. Unless you are extremely forgetful, I recommend disabling this feature.

- **Save back-up to the same folder as the CDR file:** This option tells Draw to save any backup files to the same location as the active drawing.

- **Always back-up to:** Using this option, you can specify a folder to contain your backup files.

• **Make backup on save:** This option tells Draw to make a backup of the active drawing when you save a new version. This is extremely useful if you need to resurrect the previous version of an image at a later time.

3. Click OK to apply the changes and to return to the drawing window.

Note   Undo and Redo are durable beyond saving the file. This means you can undo actions you performed after you save the file or Auto-Backup saves the file.

Saving configuration settings

Once you create the environment you want to use for new drawings, it's useful to save those setting for use in future new drawings. Draw remembers some settings automatically when you close a document, for use the next time you start Draw. For example, Draw saves all the settings in the Options with the active document, as well as the appearance of dockers, toolbars, and the active color palette. The Document page lets you save additional settings (see Figure 14-3). Draw determines the settings based on settings that are current in the active drawing.

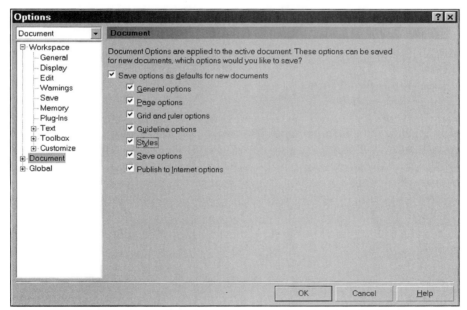

Figure 14-3: The Document page lets you save program settings for future Draw sessions.

To save the active drawing's settings as the default for new documents:

1. Select Tools ➪ Options and expand the Workspace category. Click Document to display the Documents page.

2. Click the Save options as defaults for new documents checkbox. Enable the options you want to use for each new document and click Save Settings as Default for New Documents. Use these descriptions to determine which settings to save:

- **General options:** Saves the Undo and Redo levels.

- **Styles:** Saves the active fill and outline settings as selected on the Styles property sheet.

- **Page options:** Saves the current settings from the Page Setup dialog box, including page size and orientation.

- **Grid and ruler options:** Saves the current grid, ruler, guideline, and scale settings.

- **Guideline options:** Saves the guideline settings on the Guidelines pages in the Options dialog box as default settings for all new documents created.

- **Save options:** Saves the current settings shown on the Edit page. The settings include specifications for saving thumbnails, file optimization, textures, blends, and extrusions.

- **Publish to the Internet options:** Saves the settings for publishing documents to the Internet.

Customizing Shortcuts

Many of Draw's commands and tools have keyboard shortcuts that help you work more quickly and efficiently. Draw lets you modify these shortcuts and add your own. By assigning keyboard shortcuts, you can customize Draw to suit your working style.

You can save and load keyboard shortcut configurations to use with particular documents or types of drawings. For example, you could have one set of keyboard shortcuts designed to work with newsletters and another created for Web pages. You can also edit, remove, or restore the keyboard shortcuts to the default configuration.

Assigning keyboard shortcuts

Keyboard shortcuts are stored in accelerator tables in the draw folder. These tables contain lists of equivalencies for specific mouse operations. When you change the shortcuts that are assigned to keyboard keys, the changes are saved either in the default accelerator table or one you name. To assign a keyboard shortcut to a command or tool:

1. Select Tools ⇨ Options and expand the Workspace and Customize categories. Click Shortcut Keys to display the Shortcut Keys page (see Figure 14-4). In the

Commands box, each folder represents a menu that you can customize to suit your needs.

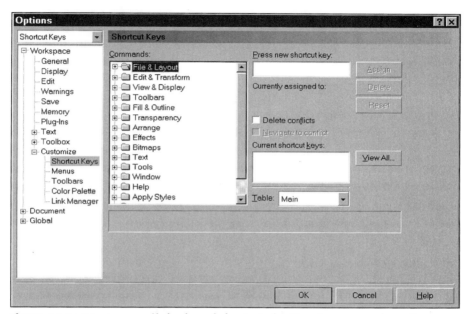

Figure 14-4: You can specify keyboard shortcuts for Draw's commands on the Shortcut Keys page.

2. Double-click the folder containing the command or tool to which you want to assign a shortcut, and choose the command or tool.

3. From the drop-down list, choose the table to change. You can choose from the Main Table or the Text Editing table.

4. Enter the shortcut you want to use in the Press New Shortcut Key box by pressing the characters for the shortcut. Press Backspace if you need to erase the entry and start over. The Current Shortcut Keys box displays any shortcut keys currently assigned to that command or tool. Your shortcut can use up to four different keystrokes.

5. Enable Delete Conflicts to erase an old shortcut key and assign it to a new command or tool. Enable both Delete Conflicts and Navigate to Conflict to erase an old shortcut key and navigate to the command or tool that previously used the shortcut key. After Draw navigates to the old command, enter a new shortcut key for that command. For example, if you assigned Ctrl+S as a shortcut for the Insert Page command, Draw would navigate to the Save command and prompt you to enter a new shortcut.

Tip It's a good idea to enable both Delete Conflicts and Navigate to Conflict until you become familiar with Draw's default keyboard shortcuts. This prevents accidentally reassigning a shortcut that you use regularly.

6. Click Assign to create the new shortcut.

7. Continue to assign keyboard shortcuts. When you are finished, click OK to return to the drawing window.

Tip I typically assign keyboard shortcuts to toolbar commands so that I can hide the toolbar. By using this method, I gain valuable screen real estate for drawing.

Adding or deleting shortcuts

You can modify the shortcuts at any time by adding or deleting shortcuts. Deleting shortcuts you no longer use lets you assign that shortcut to another command.

To delete a shortcut:

1. Follow steps 1 to 3 from the previous section to display the shortcut in the Current Shortcut Keys box.

2. Click the shortcut in the Current Shortcut Keys box to highlight it, and click Delete.

Restoring default shortcuts

Once you delete a shortcut, it's no longer available to use. If you accidentally delete one of Draw's default shortcuts, you can restore the default shortcuts by clicking the Reset button. If you restore the default shortcuts, any shortcuts you created and saved with the default accelerator table are lost. If you want to use them at some time in the future, you will need to recreate them.

Saving your changes

When you are finished assigning shortcuts, Draw automatically saves the changes you make when you close the Options dialog box. If you want to return to the default configuration at a later time, click the Reset button.

Customizing Toolbars

You determine the content and placement of toolbars. Draw provides the tools to add, remove, and rearrange the toolbar controls of any toolbar with the exception of the toolbox. These tools also let you create custom toolbars that contain the controls that you use most often. You can also resize and move toolbars to suit your working needs.

Caution Draw's online Help is written for the application's default settings. If you customize the toolbars, the help topics associated with them do not change to reflect the new toolbar.

Moving and resizing a toolbar

Draw lets you move toolbars anywhere on the screen. If you place a toolbar against any of the four sides, the toolbar docks there. Docking means that the toolbar becomes anchored there. You can also place a toolbar in the drawing window to turn it into a floating toolbar with a title bar. Once a toolbar is floating, you can resize the toolbar to meet your needs.

Moving a toolbar is easy. Simply click the toolbar's border and drag it to a new position (see Figure 14-5). Docking a toolbar is the reverse process. Drag the toolbar back to any of the four sides of the drawing window. As it contacts a border of the window, the toolbar docks to that side.

Figure 14-5: Click and drag a toolbar's border to turn it into a floating toolbar. The toolbox shown here is a floating toolbar.

If you want to resize a toolbar, first turn the toolbar into a floating toolbar. You can then click and drag the edge of the toolbar to the size and shape you want (see Figure 14-6). The controls on the toolbar are rearranged to reflect the new size and shape.

Figure 14-6: Resize a floating toolbar by clicking and dragging the edge of the toolbar to the size you want.

Shortcut Double-clicking a floating toolbar redocks it at its previous docked location.

Why You Should Customize Draw's Features

The choices you make for some customizable features in Draw, such as choosing between two- and three-dimensional color swatch wells, are purely a matter of aesthetics. Display and similar options affect your efficiency in Draw. Other options conserve screen space.

Monitor display sizes vary greatly. If you own a 21-inch monitor, giving up screen space for a collection of toolbars is probably not a problem. If you have a 14- or 15-inch monitor, however, you fight for every square pixel of screen real estate that you can get. Any space that you can save increases your work area, allowing you to work more efficiently.

Creating a custom toolbar

Draw lets you create an almost infinite variety of documents. If you find you frequently create specific types of documents, such as newsletters or Web pages, it's useful to create custom toolbars. Using this technique, you can add buttons for the command that you use most often in connection with the type of document and remove other toolbars from the drawing window. This provides more working space, while keeping handy the tools you use most. Custom toolbars can be deleted at any time, unlike the predefined toolbars provided with Draw.

To create a custom toolbar:

1. Select Tools ➪ Options and expand the Workspace category. Click Customize to display the Customize page. When you click the New button, a new toolbar appears, allowing you to enter a name for your toolbar (see Figure 14-7).

2. Enter a name for the new toolbar. If you click OK, an empty toolbar appears in the drawing window. (By selecting an existing custom toolbar and clicking in its name box, you can rename it.) You can't rename Draw's default toolbars.

3. Select Tools ➪ Options and expand the Workspace and Customize categories. Click Toolbars to display the Toolbars page.

4. In the Commands categories box, click the folder that contains the command you want to add. The buttons associated with that command category appear on the right-hand side of the dialog box (see Figure 14-8).

5. Drag the highlighted button in the dialog box to your new toolbar in the drawing window. When you've finished adding buttons to your toolbar, click OK to return to the drawing window.

Tip   You can also customize existing toolbars by adding, removing, or moving buttons. You can't add or remove buttons from the toolbox or its flyout menus.

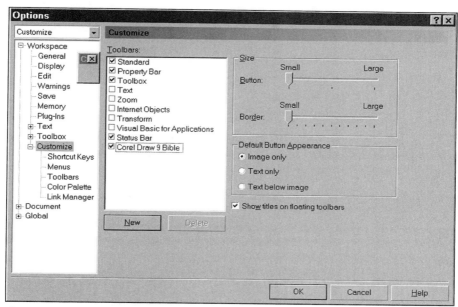

Figure 14-7: Clicking New in the Customize property sheet lets you create a new toolbar.

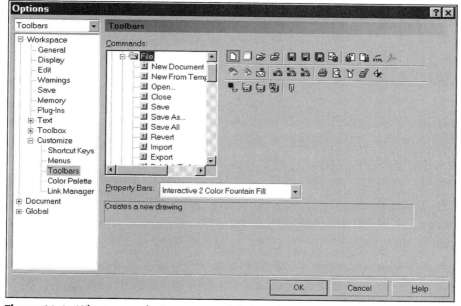

Figure 14-8: When you select a command, button icons appear on the right side of the Customize dialog box.

You can also access the Customize dialog box by right-clicking a toolbar and selecting Customize from the right mouse button menu.

Restoring or deleting a toolbar

You can restore the original configuration of a built-in toolbar or delete custom toolbars on the Customize page.

To restore or delete a toolbar:

1. Display the Customize page in the Options dialog box.
2. Select the built-in toolbar's name and click Reset.
3. If you want to delete a custom toolbar, select the toolbar's name and click Delete.
4. When you are finished modifying the toolbars, click OK to return to the drawing window.

Generally, I recommend creating new toolbars instead of modifying existing built-in toolbars. Then, if you need to reinstall Draw, you are less likely to overwrite your custom environment.

Hiding a toolbar

You can't delete any of Draw's default toolbars. If you don't want them to appear on the screen, you can hide them by selecting Tools ⇨ Options and then Customize, and clicking the box next to the toolbar to remove the check mark. When you return to the drawing window, the toolbar is hidden.

Moving or relocating buttons

While you are customizing a toolbar on the Customize page, you can freely move or remove buttons from the toolbar you're customizing. To move a button, click and drag the button to a new position on the toolbar. If you want to remove a button, drag the button off the toolbar to the drawing window. Once you leave the Customize page, the new toolbar appears in the drawing space. Dock the new toolbar in a position that's conducive to your work habits. You can also remove, copy, relocate, or move a button from a toolbar in the drawing window.

To edit a toolbar in the drawing window, do one of the following:

✦ **Move a button:** Press Alt and drag the button to its new position on the toolbar.

✦ **Relocate a button:** Press Alt and drag the button to another toolbar.

✦ **Copy a button:** Press Ctrl+Alt and drag the button to another toolbar.

✦ **Remove a button:** Press Alt and drag the button from the toolbar to the drawing window.

Modifying toolbar buttons

When you modify toolbar buttons, you can resize the buttons, change the outline size, or change the icons that appear in toolbar buttons. This is useful if you have a button that has text, but would prefer a graphic icon.

Editing buttons

Editing a button icon lets you change icons that look too similar and which are difficult to tell apart at a glance.

To edit toolbar buttons:

1. Select Tools ➪ Options and expand the Customize and Toolbar categories.

2. Move the dialog box so that you can see the toolbar you want to edit, then right-click the toolbar button you want to change on the toolbar. Select Properties to display the Button Properties dialog box (see Figure 14-9).

3. Enable the Show Image button. You can either accept the image as is, or edit the appearance of the button in the editing window.

4. When you are finished editing, click OK to return to the drawing window.

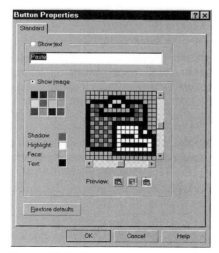

Figure 14-9: You can customize a button using the Button Properties dialog box.

Using this method, you can change the way a button looks. However, you can't change the command associated with a button, nor can you create new buttons.

Resizing and changing button borders

To change the button or button border size:

1. Select Tools ➪ Options and then Customize to display the Customize page.

2. Drag the button slider in the dialog box to resize the button.

3. Drag the button border slider to resize the border.

Caution　Take care when resizing buttons. When you expand buttons, every toolbar is affected, which uses more screen space. Additionally, the button settings you make apply to *all* of the toolbars.

Customizing Menus

Draw lets you customize menus, as well as other features, such toolbars. For example, you can add commands to existing menus or add new menus to the Menu bar. You can also remove menu commands or entire menus. You can also change the name or order of menus and the commands they contain to gain easy access to the commands and options that you use most frequently. In many cases, menus and toolbars duplicate one another. Some users find toolbars easier; others use menus almost exclusively. Your personal style determines which you use more. Like toolbars, the concept behind customizing menus is to allow you to work more efficiently.

Reorganizing menus and commands

You can change the order of menu commands to suit the way that you work. This lets you shuffle the commands on a menu to make the menu more convenient. Perhaps you might want to reorganize a menu so that the commands that you use most appear clustered at the top of the menu. You can also change the order in which they appear in the drawing window.

To change the order of menu commands:

1. Select Tools ➪ Options and expand the Workspace and Customize categories. Click Menus to display the Menus page (see Figure 14-10).

2. In the Menu box, select a menu.

3. Double-click a menu to view its related commands.

4. Select a command. Either drag the menu command to the location on the menu where you want to place it, or click Up or Down until the command is in the correct position.

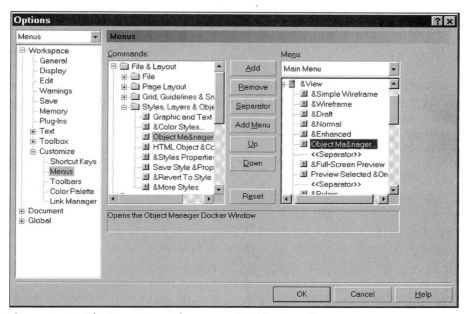

Figure 14-10: The Menus page lets you customize Draw's menus.

Note In addition to moving the commands, you can also move the separators, which allows you to regroup commands to meet your needs. Instructions for moving menu separators appear later in this section.

Changing the order of menus

To change the order of menus in the drawing window:

1. Select Tools ➪ Options and expand the Workspace and Customize categories. Click Menus to display the Menus page.

2. In the Menu box, select a menu.

3. Click and drag the menu to the position you desire, or click Up or Down until the menu is in the desired position.

Tip If you later want to return a menu to its original appearance and configuration, select the menu in menu box and click Reset.

Modifying menu shortcuts

Draw uses a series of shortcuts to access menus and commands. For example, if you pressed Alt+F and then I, you would access the File menu and display the

Import dialog box. You can change the shortcuts used to access Draw's menus and menu commands.

To change a menu command's shortcut:

1. Select Tools ➪ Options and expand the Workspace and Customize categories. Click Menus to display the Menus page.

2. In the Menu box, select a menu or menu command. Click the name again to place an insertion point after the last character in the name.

3. Insert an ampersand (&) before the character that you want to use as a shortcut, and remove any other ampersands in the name.

4. Click OK to complete the operation and to return to the drawing window.

Note   Menu command shortcuts are applied differently than other toolbar shortcuts. These commands are always accessed by pressing Alt plus a character. The shortcut character is always underlined for identification. For example, pressing Alt+F accesses the File menu, and then pressing S saves your file.

Adding and removing commands

The Draw configuration I've used for creating captures for this book is pristine. All of the menus and toolbars appear in their default configuration. I admit that this does not represent an optimum work environment for me. My normal work environment has a single custom toolbar with the menu commands I use most near the top of every menu. Infrequently used commands are moved to submenus of added menu commands. Flexibility is the beauty of Draw. In addition to customizing other features, you can customize your work environment by choosing which commands appear in the menus.

To add a command to a menu:

1. Select Tools ➪ Options and expand the Workspace and Customize categories. Click Menus to display the Menus page.

2. In the Menu box, double-click the menu or submenu to change.

3. Click the menu item above where you want the new command to appear.

4. In the Commands box, double-click the folder that contains the command you want to add, and click the command you want to add.

5. Click Add.

You can also remove a command by selecting the command from the Command box and clicking the Remove button.

Adding, removing, and renaming menus

In addition to modifying the menus themselves, you can further customize Draw by adding or removing menus in the Menu bar, or by renaming the ones that are included. Just as you can create custom toolbars, you can also create new menus that are customized for your use. You should be aware that Draw's help files correspond to the default configuration. If you change the configuration, you can receive erroneous information when you use the What's This help feature.

To add a menu to the Menu bar:

1. Select Tools ⇨ Options and expand the Workspace and Customize categories. Click Menus to display the Menus page.

2. In the Menu box, click the menu at the place immediately above where you want to place the new menu.

3. Click Add Menu. The new menu appears below the selected menu in the dialog box and to the right of the selected menu in the Menu bar (see Figure 14-11).

4. Enter a name for the menu in the Menu box. Be sure to add an ampersand in front of the letter you want to use as the shortcut.

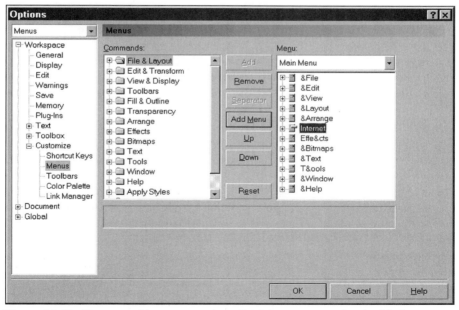

Figure 14-11: You can add menus, such as the Internet menu that I added, as shown.

Adding menus is one way of organizing your workspace efficiently. Once you've created a menu, you can move the commands that you want to group on that menu. For best results, group commands having similar functions on menus. This makes it easier to remember where you placed commands.

To rename a menu:

1. Select Tools ⇨ Options and expand the Workspace and Customize categories. Click Menus to display the Menus page.

2. In the Menu box, to select the menu name to rename, click it.

3. Enter the new name. Be sure to place an ampersand (&) in front of the letter you want to use as the shortcut.

 You can give a menu any name you want. Although you can use up to 255 characters and spaces, I recommend giving your menu a shorter name that indicates the contents of the menu. If your menus extend beyond the width of the drawing window, Draw adds another Menu bar below the default Menu bar.

 When placing the ampersand in front of a letter, be sure that the letter is not already in use as another shortcut to avoid creating a conflict.

To remove a menu from the Menu bar:

1. Select Tools ⇨ Options and expand the Workspace and Customize categories. Click Menus to display the Menus page.

2. In the Menu box, click the menu to remove.

3. Click Remove.

Remember that when Draw removes a menu, it also removes the commands on that menu. Draw asks you to verify that you want to remove the menu and its contents before continuing. If the menu contains one of Draw's default commands, such as Save and Open, they are still available in their original menu.

 While in the Options dialog box, you can also right-click the menu you want to change. You now have the option to Cut, Copy, Rename, or Delete the menu. Choosing Cut or Copy will let you paste the menu in another position or delete it completely.

Adding or removing command separators

Separators appear as horizontal lines between groups of commands in a menu. These lines create visual cues that help you move to the commands you want quickly. You can add or remove a menu command separator, as desired.

To add or remove a menu command separator:

1. Select Tools ➪ Options and expand the Workspace and Customize categories. Click Menus to display the Menus page.

2. In the Menu box, double-click the menu to modify.

3. Click the command above the location where you want to add the separator.

4. Click Separator.

5. If you want to remove a separator, select the separator to remove and click the Remove button.

You can add as many separators as you want to a menu. By clustering like commands and adding separators between the clusters, you make it easier to quickly find and apply commands.

Working with Dockers

Previous versions of CorelDRAW have relied on roll-ups to group like commands and actions in convenient boxes. These roll-ups could be grouped and customized. In Draw 9, dockers have replaced the familiar roll-ups. Dockers are boxes that contain information about objects in your drawing or a list of commands associated with an Effect. Dockers can be attached (docked) anywhere within the Draw window.

Accessing dockers

To access a docker, select Window ➪ Dockers and select the desired docker from the submenu. The selected docker docks itself in the default position at the right side of the drawing window. Drag the docker anywhere in the Draw window that's conducive to your work habits. Dockers can be expanded and collapsed just like the old roll-ups. Dockers can be docked at any corner of the Draw window, or left free floating. Once you close a docker group, Draw remembers exactly where you last placed it. When you reopen a docker group, it appears exactly where you left it the last time.

New Feature If you're a veteran user of Draw, you'll notice the Docker submenu is missing several of the Effects that were roll-ups in prior versions of the program. Don't panic. The effects are still there. You have to customize Draw by adding the desired Effect dockers to a menu.

Adding dockers to submenus

You should consider adding a docker to a menu if you use a particular effect on a regular basis. For example, if you're consistently constraining a text string within an object's outline, have the Envelope docker available. Then it's a simple matter of opening the Envelope docker and grabbing the trusty Eyedropper tool to apply the effect to your text string.

To add a docker to a menu:

1. Select Tools ➪ Options and expand the Workspace and Customize categories. Click Menus to display the Menus page (see Figure 14-12).

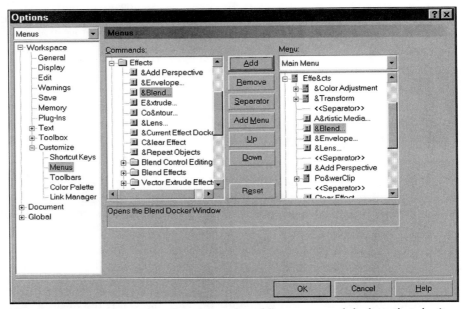

Figure 14-12: You can customize a menu by adding command dockers that don't appear on other menus or toolbars.

2. In the Command box, expand the Command folders until you locate the docker you want to attach to a menu. For example, if you're looking for what used to be the Envelope roll up, expand the Effects Commands menu and locate the Envelope command. Click the command, and in the dialog box below, you'll see the message, "Opens the Envelope Docker." Any command that uses a docker displays a similar message.

3. In the Menu box, double-click the menu you want to add the docker to.

4. Click the command above the location where you want to add the docker.

5. Click Add.

6. After adding the desired dockers, click OK.

Creating a Library of Custom Workspaces

Draw is a diverse program. You can create nearly any kind of document for any use. Unless you have a large monitor (20 inches or greater), you can wind up with a lot of screen clutter between the dockers and toolbars. It is useful to create a library of custom workspaces for specific uses.

Tip

In my library, I have, for example, one configuration for technical drawing and one for creating cartoons. Each workspace has settings that apply specifically to that use. In addition, I've created custom toolbars and menus containing only the features and commands that I use most frequently for that application. By limiting and organizing the features I need for a specific application, I can limit the amount of screen clutter, leaving me plenty of room to create.

To create a custom workspace:

1. Select Tools ➪ Options. The current workspace will be listed, and the available workspaces will be listed in the Workspaces window.

2. Click New to create a new workspace. You can base the new workspace on either the current workspace or on another workspace that you've already saved. A dialog box appears prompting you for a name and a description of the new workspace (see Figure 14-13). Pick a name associated with the application you're creating the workspace for. After entering the name and description, click OK to create the new workspace.

3. To finish creating the new workspace, expand the Customize page. Add and/or subtract toolbars, menus, and dockers as desired for the application you're creating the workspace for.

4. Click OK to apply the changes to the new workspace.

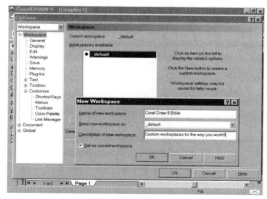

Figure 14-13: You can create a custom workspace to optimize Draw for a frequently used application.

To change from one workspace to another:

1. Select Tools ➪ Options.

2. In the Workspaces window, click the workspace desired.

3. Click Set as current.

4. Click OK to return to the drawing window.

Customizing Filters

Using filters, Draw is capable of importing and exporting a broad variety of file formats. When you first start Draw, all the filters that you installed are active by default. You can customize the list of active filters and the order in which they appear in the Import and Export dialog boxes. Managing filters streamlines the appearance of the Import and Export dialog boxes and lets you select the filter you want to use more quickly.

To manage filters:

1. Select Tools ➪ Options and expand the Global category. Click Filters to display the Filters page (see Figure 14-14). A list of active filters appears in the List of Active Filters box.

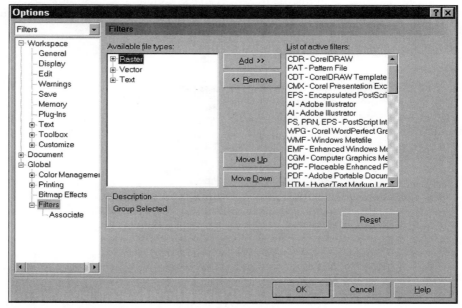

Figure 14-14: The Filters page shows the active filters.

2. In the Available File Types box, select the file type you want to customize, and click the plus (+) beside it to display the available filters. You can choose from Raster (bitmap), Vector, and Text types. A list of available filters appears below the file type.

3. Activate a filter by clicking the filter to add to the list of active filters, and then click the Add button.

4. Deactivate a filter by selecting the filter in the List of Active Filters box and clicking the Remove button.

5. Move a filter up or down in the List of Active Filters box by clicking the Move Up or Move Down button.

When you select a filter, information about that filter appears in the Description section to assist in your decision making. If you deactivate a filter, it's not removed from your system; it just doesn't appear in the Import and Export dialog boxes. You can reactivate filters at any time, or click the Reset button to return the filters to their original installed configuration.

 Tip   Reorganizing the order of filters saves time when you have a number of filters installed by placing the filters you use most near the top of the file type lists in the Import and Export dialog boxes.

Specifying Associations

Draw lets you select which file types are associated with Draw. When a file type is associated with a program, that program is used as the default program to open or import that file type. Windows displays the program icon next to the filename in folders. If you double-click a filename in a folder, the file is opened or imported into the associated program.

To change the association, Select Tools ⇨ Options and expand the Global and Filters categories. Click Associate to display the Associate page (see Figure 14-15). Click a file type to associate it with Draw. A check mark appears beside associated files, and a description of the file type appears in the Description section. Click OK to associate the new file type with Draw. Click the Reset button if you want to restore the associations to their original installed configuration.

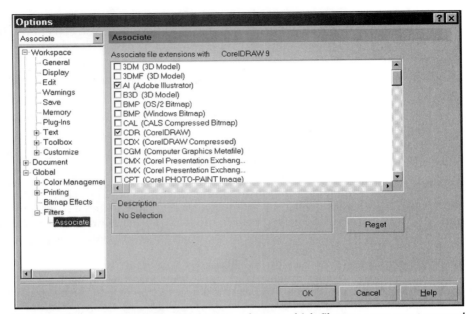

Figure 14-15: The Associate page lets you choose which file types you want opened or imported by Draw.

Customizing Color Palettes

Several preset color palettes are included with Draw. Using the Palette Editor, you can add, delete, and rearrange colors in these palettes, and then save them under a new name. You can modify an existing custom palette or create your own from scratch. You can also add new colors to a palette in the Uniform Fill dialog box.

Opening a custom palette

To open a custom palette:

1. Select Window ➪ Color Palettes and then Open Palette. The Open Palette dialog box appears (see Figure 14-16).

2. By default, Draw stores custom color palettes in the Custom folder. These files have a .cpl extension. Either select a palette from this location or choose the folder where you store your custom palettes.

3. Click Open. Draw opens the custom palette and displays it as the onscreen color palette.

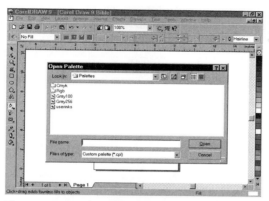

Figure 14-16: The Open Palette dialog box.

Creating a new palette

To create a new palette using the Palette Editor:

1. Select Window ➪ Color Palettes and then Palette Editor to display the Palette Editor.

2. The Palette Editor dialog box opens, allowing you to add to the existing colors in the palette.

3. To edit a selected color, click Edit Color to open the Select Color dialog box. Select one of the four tabs to edit your color. When you're satisfied with the new color, click OK to apply the change.

4. To add a color to your palette, click Add Color to open the Select Color dialog box. Select one of the four tabs and either mix the new color or add a color from one of the other existing palettes. Click the Add button after each selection.

5. When you are finished adding colors, select Save As to display the Save Palette As dialog box (see Figure 14-17). Name the new palette and click OK to save it and to return to the drawing window. Your new palette now appears as the active palette in the drawing window.

Caution When you create a custom palette, Draw saves it in the same location as the rest of its palettes by default. It's a good idea to save a copy of the palette elsewhere, in case you ever need to reinstall Draw. Doing so ensures that you won't lose your custom palettes.

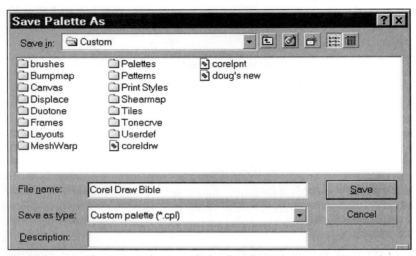

Figure 14-17: The Save Palette As dialog box lets you save custom palettes for future use.

Color Selection Tips and Cautions

You can add colors from any of the palettes, color systems, or color models. The colors don't need to be from the same color collection. Observe, however, these tips and cautions before making your selections:

✦ Adding colors to your new color palette from a number of different color palettes or color models can substantially increase the cost of printing your file if you plan to print your file at a commercial print shop.

✦ For best results and lower printing costs, only add colors from one existing palette or color model in each new color palette.

✦ It's also a good idea to name colors that you add to a palette. Naming makes searching for colors much easier.

Editing existing palettes

Using the Palette Editor, you can edit and create new palettes from existing palettes. The tools in the Palette Editor let you add, remove, and replace colors in a palette. You can also reorganize the colors of a palette either interactively or by sorting them. To reorder colors interactively, click and drag a color in the palette to a new location. If you haven't saved a palette after making changes, you can click the Reset button to restore the palette to the appearance it had when it was last saved.

To sort palette colors:

1. Select Window ⇨ Color Palettes and then Palette Editor to display the Palette Editor.

2. Select the palette to sort to make it active in the Palette Editor.

3. Click the Sort button and choose a sorting method from the drop-down menu.

Draw sorts the colors using the sorting method you choose, and redisplays the sorted palette in the Palette Editor.

Caution

It's not a good idea to overwrite Draw's preset palettes when creating a new palette. If you do, the preset palette will be unavailable for use. Whenever you edit a preset palette, give your palette a new name to avoid overwriting a preset palette.

Using Color Management

If you've ever scanned a color photograph or printed color graphics on a color printer, you've probably discovered a frustrating fact: Digital color doesn't always work the way you want it to. When you send full-color files to a color printer, the colors are always slightly different between the screen and the printed page, and sometimes disastrously different. This is because of a number of complex factors that affect the production of color on your system. Draw has tools for making sure that what you see on the screen closely matches what your viewers ultimately see. The process is far from automatic, and in this section, you learn about managing colors with Draw.

Understanding Color Gamut

A color gamut is the range of colors that can be perceived by a particular device, whether it is the human eye (infrared light is *outside the gamut* of the human eye, while red is not) or an inkjet printer.

Corel's color management tools aim to minimize the discrepancy between what you see on your screen (a very large gamut with millions of visible colors) and what the printer can print (a much smaller gamut of colors).

Working with color profiles

Corel Color Profiles work with Draw to insure that your final output colors are as close as possible to what you see on your monitor and to what is picked up and relayed through your scanner. If you intend to output your file for commercial printing, creating a color profile can make the difference between a successful print job and one that's disappointing. When you use color management, Draw alters the colors you see on the screen to match the input (scanner) and output devices you use.

To select a color profile:

1. Select Tools ↪ Options and expand the Global settings by clicking the plus sign (+) beside the listing.

2. Click the plus sign beside Color Management to expand that heading, and click Profiles to display the Profiles settings (see Figure 14-18).

3. Select the devices you are using from the drop-down list boxes and click OK to return to the drawing window.

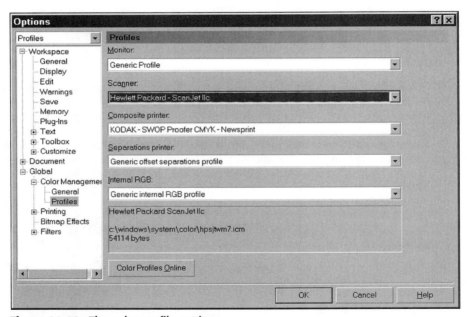

Figure 14-18: The color profile settings.

Tip   If you don't see the devices you're using in the drop-down list boxes, you can click the Obtain Profiles Online button to obtain a color profile for your system.

Once you select a profile, you shouldn't have to do it again, unless you change the hardware associated with the profile. You may choose what type of printer you'd like your monitor to simulate in the way it displays colors. Your choices are Composite or Separations. To choose, click on your selection in the Monitor Simulates section of the Color Management property sheet.

Setting the "out-of-gamut" color

After selecting color management options, Draw can notify you when you've added a color to your document that is outside what your printer can print, even though your monitor can display the color without a problem. Note the menu item Gamut Color at the lower right of the Color Management dialog box. This is the color that Draw displays on your screen any time you try to apply a color that is "out of gamut" (that is, out of the range of colors available to your printer). By default, Draw uses a neon green as the gamut warning color, having determined that this shade of green is not likely to be used in somebody's artwork. This neon green is displayed when an out-of-gamut color is chosen.

There may be times when you need to change the gamut warning color. For example, when designing a picture of a bowl of lime sherbet, you might need to use the neon green as an actual color value in your document. In such a case, click the drop-down menu next to Gamut Color and choose a new color to be the out-of-gamut warning. Don't forget to choose a warning color that is well out of the range of colors used in your document.

Summary

Optimizing Draw's work environment to suit your needs is easy and yields enormous benefits in creating an efficient working environment. Draw's flexibility lets you customize many of the program's features, including display, menus, and toolbars. You can determine both the appearance and behavior of the program, which lets you concentrate on creativity. In this chapter, you learned to

✦ Specify display options

✦ Create shortcuts for menu and toolbar commands

✦ Customize menus and toolbars

✦ Create custom workspaces

✦ Manage filters

✦ Select file associations

✦ Customize color palettes

✦ ✦ ✦

Making It Public with Draw

✦ ✦ ✦ ✦

Using Draw in the Office

You don't have to be a graphic designer to take advantage of Draw's power and flexibility. It resides as comfortably in a small office as it does in a large commercial ad agency. Using Draw, you can create forms, newsletters, catalogues, and masters from which you can have business stationary printed. This chapter is dedicated to the office and creating documents commonly needed in that environment. Once you create a form, save it as a template for future use.

Developing a Common Theme

Business forms come in all shapes and sizes, and fulfill a variety of needs from invoices and letterheads to business cards and fax cover sheets. The key to creating a form is to make elements of the form universal. You save a significant amount of time if you create a series of forms with a common theme, such as a logo.

When you've created the graphic for the logo and selected a font for the text, you can reuse these elements for all of your forms, which allows you to maintain a consistent and professional appearance in your business documents.

Creating an Invoice

An invoice is basic to performing routine business tasks. We all like to get paid for our labor. Most invoices are plain white and tend to get "plain white" attention. I prefer to gain attention by adding a bit of color. The exercises in this section guide you through creating the invoice shown in Figure 15-1. The finished invoice template and the logo used in this section have been created for you, and are stored on the companion CD-ROM.

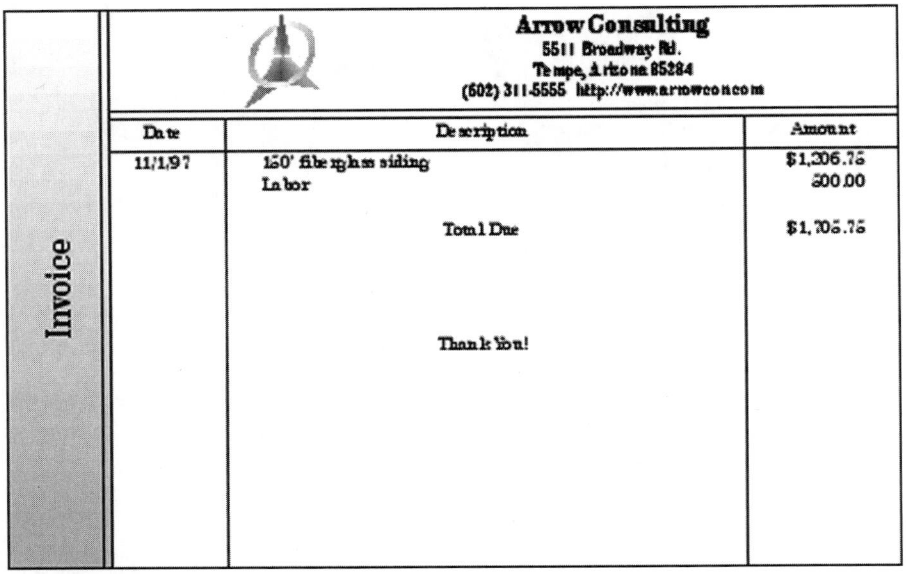

Date	Description	Amount
11/1/97	150' fiberglass siding	$1,206.75
	Labor	500.00
	Total Due	$1,706.75
	Thank You!	

Arrow Consulting
5511 Broadway Rd.
Tempe, Arizona 85284
(602) 311-5555 http://www.arrowcon.com

Invoice

Figure 15-1: An invoice is one of the most basic forms in an office environment.

On the CD-ROM   Although you create the invoice featured in this section, the finished template is available on your companion CD-ROM in the \template folder. Logo1.cdr is also located on your companion CD-ROM in the ch15\tutorial folder.

The first step in creating any form is to specify the page setup and to construct the basic structure and layout. In this exercise, you create the background that serves as the foundation for your invoice.

To create the basic layout for an invoice:

1. Select File ⇨ New to start a new document in Draw.

2. Select Tools ⇨ Options to display the Options dialog box and then expand the Document and Page levels by clicking the plus (+) sign beside them. Click Size to display the Size settings (see Figure 15-2).

3 Click the down arrow next to Paper size and choose Statement/Half and Landscape to specify a document with 8.5-X-5.5-inch dimensions.

4. Click the Add Page Frame button to apply a page frame to the drawing page.

5. Click OK to return to the drawing window.

Basic geometric shapes such as rectangles and ellipses are used to create initial elements for many forms. By using these shapes, you can define separate space in your layout for columns of numbers, product descriptions, or headings.

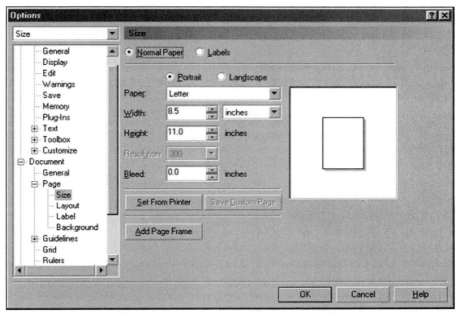

Figure 15-2: The Size setting view of the Options dialog box lets you choose a variety of settings, including the paper size and orientation.

Note
Draw, by default, specifies a resolution of 300 dpi. This resolution is adequate for most printing applications.

Using page frames in layouts

Page frames are useful for quickly creating rectangles that have the precise dimensions of the drawing page. If you need a rectangle that only needs to match the horizontal or vertical dimensions, you can modify the page frame or a copy of the page frame, while ensuring that the resulting rectangle is centered on the drawing page. In this exercise, you create copies of the page frame and resize them in one dimension to create the partitions of the invoice. Draw resizes objects based upon their anchor point. By changing the anchor point, you can resize and place objects in your document in one step.

To divide the invoice into sections:

1. Use the Pick tool to select the page frame in the drawing window.

2. Select Arrange ⇨ Transformation to display the Transformation docker, and click the Size button (see Figure 15-3).

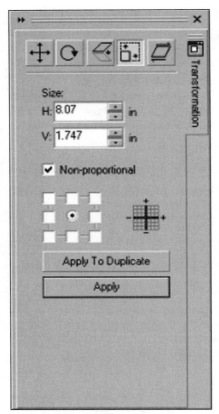

Figure 15-3: The Size page of the Transformation docker lets you resize objects with precision.

3. Click the Non-proportional checkbox to enable it, and then click the top box in the relative positioning section to change the anchor point.

4. Change the value in the vertical dimension box to 1 inch and click Apply To Duplicate. Draw resizes a duplicate of the rectangle and positions it at the top of the drawing page.

5. With the rectangle still selected, reset the anchor point in the Size page of the Transformation docker by clicking the right-hand box. Change the value in the horizontal dimension box to 7.5 inches and click Apply. Draw displays the finished rectangle aligned at the top and right-hand side of the drawing page (see Figure 15-4).

6. Select the page frame again.

7. In the Size page of the Transformation docker, set the anchor for the left side and change the value in the horizontal dimension box to 1 inch.

8. Click Apply To Duplicate. Draw resizes a duplicate of the rectangle and aligns it to the left side of the drawing page.

9. Using the Interactive Fill tool, press Ctrl and then click and drag from the bottom to the top of the rectangle on the left side. Draw fills the rectangle with a fountain fill that goes from black at the bottom of the rectangle to white at the top of the rectangle.

Note   Pressing Ctrl ensures that the angle of your fill remains at 90 degrees.

10. From the onscreen color palette, click and drag the color Light Blue-Green to the black rectangle. The name of the color appears in the status bar when you move your mouse cursor over the color. When you release the mouse button, Draw replaces the black with the new color and updates the fountain fill (see Figure 15-5).

11. Save the file as **invoice1.cdr**.

12. The rest of the partitions are line segments created using the Freehand tool. Consult Figure 15-6 to place these straight lines. They don't have to be placed exactly. You can adjust them later.

Tip   Enabling Snap to Objects helps you place the lines in the invoice with greater precision.

Figure 15-4: The finished rectangle aligns to the top right-hand corner of the drawing page.

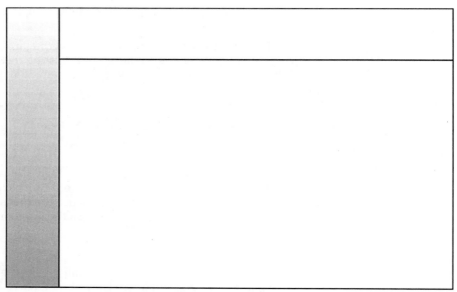

Figure 15-5: Draw displays the modified fountain fill.

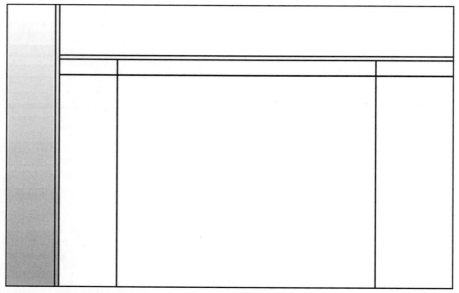

Figure 15-6: Position the lines in your invoice as shown to create the remaining partitions.

Creating a header

Once you've created the background for the invoice, you're ready to place the logo, header, and banner text. For this exercise, I used Century725BnCn as the font for headline text. You can use another font if you want, however.

To add the logo and headline text:

1. Open invoice1.cdr in Draw if it's not already open.

2. Select File ⇨ Import and import logo1.cdr into your document. The import placement cursor appears, allowing you to click the location where the imported file is to appear in your document.

3. Using the Pick tool, click and drag the logo up and into the top rectangle. Precise placement isn't necessary at this point.

4. Using the Text tool, click in the top rectangle to place an insertion point. Before entering any text, select center alignment and specify a 12-point font. Choose Century725BnCn. Enter the text as shown in Figure 15-7.

Arrow Consulting
5511 Broadway Rd.
Tempe, Arizona 85284
(602) 311-5555   http://www.arrowcon.com

Figure 15-7: Enter the name and address for the company.

5. With the Text tool and text still selected, click and drag across the text to highlight the top line of text. Change the point size to 18 points.

6. Using the Text tool, click to set an insertion point somewhere off the drawing page. Enter the word **Invoice**.

7. Using the Pick tool, click and drag the logo to adjust the horizontal space between the logo and the company address.

8. With the logo still selected, press Shift and click the headline text to select both the logo and the text.

9. Select Arrange ⇨ Align and Distribute to display the Align and Distribute dialog box (see Figure 15-8). Choose Center for the vertical alignment, and click OK to align the two objects and to return to the drawing window.

10. With both objects still selected, select Arrange ⇨ Group to group the two objects.

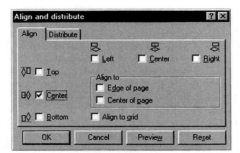

Figure 15-8: Center-align the address and logo vertically.

11. Depress Shift and select the top rectangle. Both the group and the rectangle are selected. Using the Align and Distribute dialog box, center-align the two elements horizontally and vertically.

12. Using the Pick tool, double-click the word Invoice to display the rotation handles. While pressing Shift, click and drag a corner handle counterclockwise to rotate the word 90 degrees.

13. With the text still selected, press Shift and click the sidebar to select both objects. Using the Align dialog box, center-align the two elements horizontally and vertically.

14. Save your file.

Remember that when you align objects, it is their bounding boxes that align, not the objects themselves. You may need to adjust the alignment to ensure a balanced appearance.

Tip   When creating headline text, select center alignment. Then its overall alignment with other objects and the page won't change if you need to change the text.

Using Paragraph text formatting effectively

The main body of the invoice is comprised of two parts: the column headers and the entry area. These two areas are actually two paragraph text frames. The column headers use a three-column format, which allows you to center the headers in each column. The entry body of the text is another paragraph text frame, but instead of having columns, it utilizes custom tab settings that allow for easy keyboard entry of information.

You could use Artistic text or columnar format for the entry area, but entering data wouldn't be as easily accomplished. Artistic text would require that you create three separate and unique text objects for the main body of the invoice. Aligning the text vertically would be difficult, at best, because you would have to select each text object separately in order to enter information in that column. If you wanted to use a columnar format, you couldn't tab from one column to the adjacent column. You'd have to move to the bottom of one column before the cursor would move to the next column.

Inserting column headers

In this exercise, you insert the column headers. Once the column headers are complete, you lock the contents of the invoice to prevent accidental editing of the elements before creating the data entry area of the invoice.

To create column headings:

1. Select View ➪ Snap to Objects.

2. Using the Text tool, click and drag a paragraph text frame to set a one-line frame for the column headers (see Figure 15-9).

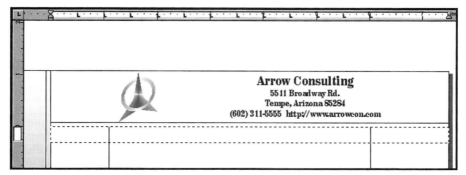

Figure 15-9: Create a paragraph text frame for the column headers.

3. Select Text ➪ Format Text to display the Format Text dialog box, and specify these settings:

   • Click the Font tab and specify 12-point CentSchbook Win95BT

   • Click the Align tab and specify Center alignment

   • Click the Frames and Columns tab and specify three columns. Deselect Equal column width. Set the width of the first column to 1 inch, the second column to 4.5 inches, and the third column to 1.5 inches. The gutters are automatically adjusted to be 0.25 inches each.

4. Click OK to return to the drawing window.

5. Enter **Date** in the first column, and then press Enter to move to the second column.

6. Repeating the previous step, enter **Description** in the second column and **Price** in the third column. The text appears centered in the columns (see Figure 15-10).

7. Select Edit ➪ Select All ➪ Objects to select all the objects in the invoice. Right-click the selection, and choose Lock from the right mouse button menu.

8. Save the file.

Note

You can lock and unlock objects using commands found on the Arrange menu or on the right mouse button menu. Locked objects display small padlocks when you select them, to indicate that the objects can't be edited. To edit a locked object, you must first unlock it.

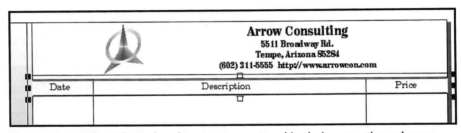

Figure 15-10: The column headers appear centered in their respective columns.

In this exercise, you added a page frame to the invoice and then created the header and banner rectangles from duplicates of the page frame. The original page frame was left in place. The page frame was left to form the exterior border surrounding the entire invoice. Adding a page frame let you use Snap to Object and the original page frame to quickly place the paragraph text frame for the entry area.

Adding a data entry area

In this exercise, you complete the invoice by adding the data entry area and saving the finished invoice as a template.

To add a data entry area:

1. Enable Snap to Object if it's not already active.

2. Using the Text tool, click the lower right-hand corner of the invoice and drag the cursor to the lower left-hand corner of the column headings, creating a paragraph text frame.

3. Using the Text tool, click and drag the left margin marker to 0.25 inches on the horizontal ruler (see Figure 15-11).

4. Click and drag the first tab marker to 1.5 inches on the horizontal ruler.

5. Click and drag the far right tab marker to 7.25 inches on the horizontal ruler (see Figure 15-12).

6. Right-click the right-hand marker and select Right Tab from the right mouse button menu.

7. Remove the excess tabs by clicking and dragging the tab markers into the drawing window.

8. Save the file as **invoice1.cdt**.

Figure 15-11: Drag the left margin marker to 0.25 inches on the horizontal ruler.

Figure 15-12: Drag the right tab marker to 7.25 inches on the horizontal ruler.

The invoice is now ready for the entry of billing information. By saving completed invoices as .cdt files, you can use the template repeatedly.

Designing an Office Newsletter

Like creating the invoice in the previous example, designing a newsletter can be divided into a series of parts: banner, body text, and graphic elements. Creating a template for a newsletter is a good idea if you publish the newsletter frequently. By using a template, you can change the body text and graphic elements, yet retain a consistent feel from one issue to the next. In this section, you create a basic newsletter for a confectioners group.

Although you create the newsletter featured in this section, the finished template is available on your companion CD-ROM in the \template folder.

Preplanning Your Newsletter

You can smooth and streamline the creation of documents, such as a newsletter, with a little advance planning. If you know you will want to use the Nudge command (as you will in this section) or other commands that require presetting a value or preconfiguring, do the presetting ahead of time. Effects that you'll apply later in this section require a nudge value of 0.01 inches, for example, which you specify in the Options dialog box. When you are ready to use the feature, the parameters are already specified.

Advance planning lets you maintain your train of thought, and saves the steps of toggling between dialog boxes and the drawing window, by presetting all of the values you need in the Options dialog box at one time. Additionally, once your template is complete, consider presetting the default font that is used when you first open the template to edit the newsletter contents for a newsletter document.

Creating a banner graphic

The first step in creating the newsletter is to specify the page setup. The base shape for the banner is created from a modified page frame after you have specified your newsletter's page size. Using a letter-size layout is ideal for the small office, or when you need a limited number of copies, because it lets you print the document in-house on inkjet and laser printers.

Creating a banner base

To create the banner base:

1. Start a new document in Draw.

2. On the Property bar, choose Letter as the paper size, and then double-click the Rectangle tool to add a page frame to your document.

3. Select Arrange ➪ Transformation to open the Transformation docker, if it is not already open, and click the Size button to show the Size page.

4. In the Size page of the Transformation docker, set the anchor point at the top.

5. Specify 2 inches in the vertical size box and click Apply to resize the page frame and align it with the top of the drawing paper. Draw resizes the page frame to create the banner for the newsletter.

6. Click the Texture Fill icon in the Fill tool flyout menu. Draw displays the Texture Fill dialog box.

7. Choose Samples 7 as the fill library, and select Aztec Cave Drawing as the fill.

8. Click OK to apply the fill (see Figure 15-13). Right-click the X on the onscreen color palette to remove the outline.

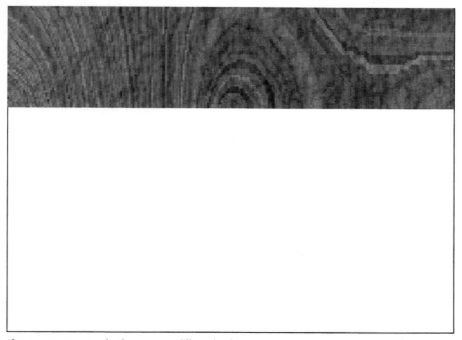

Figure 15-13: Apply the texture fill to the banner.

Adding a blend effect

The base banner is dark and lacks pizzazz. It also seems, at first, like a poor choice for a group of people whose interest is the creation of sweet treats. In this exercise, you spice up the banner by adding a blend effect. This will give it a raised appearance reminiscent of confectionery delights.

To add a blend effect:

1. Using the Pick tool, select the rectangle that you created in the previous exercise.

2. Press the plus (+) key on the numeric keypad of your keyboard (make sure you have Num Lock enabled) to duplicate the rectangle. Draw superimposes the duplicate directly over the original object, so you can't see both objects.

3. Select the Texture Fill icon from the Fill tool flyout menu to display the Texture Fill dialog box. The dialog box displays the active fill (see Figure 15-14).

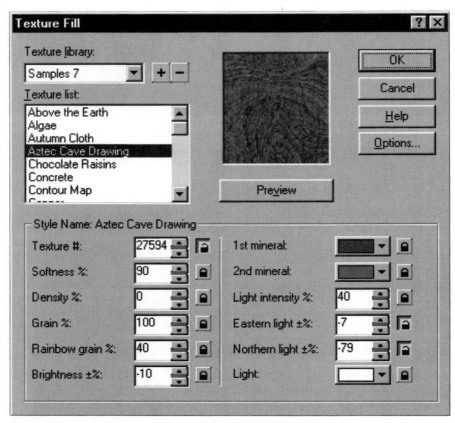

Figure 15-14: The Texture Fill dialog box displays the fill of the selected object.

4. In the Texture Fill dialog box, change the first and second mineral colors to white. Change the brightness value to 10, and click OK to apply the fill and to return to the drawing window. Draw recalculates the color of the fill and updates the rectangle in the drawing window.

5. With the rectangle still selected, select Arrange ➪ Transformation to open the Transformation docker. Click the Size button to display the Size page of the Transformation docker. Set the horizontal value to 8 inches and the vertical value to 1.5 inches. Click Apply. The updated rectangle appears in the drawing window (see Figure 15-15).

6. Select the Interactive Blend tool. Click and drag from the bottom to the top rectangle. Draw blends the two rectangles together to create a raised effect (see Figure 15-16).

7. Change the number of steps to 10 in the Blend View Property bar.

8. Save the file to your hard disk as **newslet1.cdr**.

Caution   Applying the blend command to objects that contain a texture fill is a resource-intensive process. The resulting blend group takes longer to display in the drawing window and creates a large file. If file size is an issue, use this effect sparingly.

Figure 15-15: Resize the rectangle containing the modified fill.

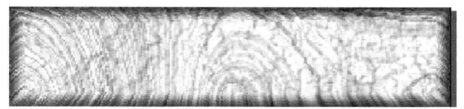

Figure 15-16: The final blend effect.

Adding effects to headline text

Applying blend effects can add drama to your documents or create a subtle transition from one object to another. In the next exercise, you add the headline text to the newsletter. The headline text incorporates the fills used in the banner and blend effects to add a subtle 3D appearance to the headline. The second text string for the headline is filled with the darker texture fill to tie the banner together by providing a consistent color theme.

To add headline text:

1. Using the Text tool, click an insertion point on the drawing page somewhere below the banner. You don't have to be precise, because you move the text into position later.

2. Enter the text **Confectionery Newsletter** and then select the Pick tool. Draw adds the text and applies the default fill to the text string.

3. Select Edit ➪ Copy Properties From, and choose Fill and Outline. Click OK. The cursor changes to a large arrow. Click near the edge of the banner to apply the fill attributes of the original rectangle to the text.

4. With the text string still selected, choose BinnerD from the font list and specify 24 point as the font size.

Note   If you didn't install BinnerD when you installed Draw, you can add the font using Bitstream Font Navigator or substitute a similar font.

5. Using the Text tool, click in the drawing window to set another insertion point and enter the text **Sweet Nothings**.

6. Select Edit ➪ Copy Properties From, and choose Outline, Fill, and Text Properties. Click OK, and then click the text string Confectionery Newsletter to copy the font, font size, fill, and outline attributes to the new text string.

7. With the text still selected, highlight the font size and enter 65 points.

8. Press the plus (+) key to duplicate the text twice. Draw superimposes the two duplicates directly over the original text string, and displays the top copy as the selected text object.

9. Using Copy Properties From, copy the fill from the top control rectangle of the banner blend group to the text (see Figure 15-17).

Figure 15-17: Apply the fill attributes of the top rectangle to the top string of text.

10. Press Tab once to select the next copy of the text down in the hierarchy. While pressing Shift, press the up and right cursor twice to move the text string 0.04 inches up and to the right.

11. Press Tab again to select the next text string down in the hierarchy, and then repeat step 10, except to move the copy down and to the left.

12. With the text string still selected, press Shift and click the top text string.

13. Select the Interactive Blend tool, and click and drag between the two objects. Specify 10 steps in the Blend View Property bar.

14. Press Tab to select the other copy of the text, and then press Shift while clicking again on the top text string.

15. Repeat Step 13. Draw creates the two blends and links them as a single complex blend (see Figure 15-18).

Figure 15-18: The complex text blend.

Tip

When superimposing text on top of a complex object such as the banner background, it's easier to create the text in a blank area of the drawing window. This reduces the amount of screen refresh time by reducing the number of objects that Draw has to render to the screen.

16. Using the Pick tool, click and drag the text blend group and the single string of text, positioning them as shown in Figure 15-19.

17. Save the file.

Figure 15-19: Position the text string and the blend group on the banner.

When selecting textures and fills for elements of a newsletter or other document, it's a good idea to select them with an eye toward maintaining a consistent look throughout your document. Your documents will look more professional, and it makes it easier to use global replacement features if you need to make changes at a later time.

Importing a banner graphic element

The banner for the newsletter is nearly finished. It needs one final touch to complete the theme. In the next exercise, you begin to add graphics to your newsletter by adding a bitmap image to the banner. The Photoshop file used in this exercise has a transparent background.

To add an image to the banner:

New Feature

Draw now supports alpha (transparent) channels during import.

1. Open newslet1.cdr if it's not already open.

2. Select File ➪ Import to display the import dialog box. Select candy2.psd and click Import. Click the drawing page to place the image.

Candy2.psd is located on your companion CD-ROM in the ch15\tutorial folder.

3. Click and drag the candy to the banner and place it as shown in Figure 15-20.

4. You may need to resize the candy a small amount.

Normally, it's a better idea to resample a bitmap rather than to resize it interactively. In this case, however, the amount of change doesn't warrant resampling the bitmap.

Figure 15-20: Place and adjust the bitmap on the banner.

Adding body text

The final step of creating the newsletter is to place the text and graphics in the body of the newsletter. The newsletter has a two-column format and uses 12-point CentSchbook Win95BT as the main text body font. The article heads are 14-point CentSchbook.

To add the body text:

1. Open newslet1.cdr if it's not already open.

2. Using the Text tool, create a paragraph text frame by clicking and dragging a frame from just below the banner to within 0.5 inches of the bottom of the page. Allow a 0.5-inch margin on each side.

3. Select Text ➪ Edit Text to open the Edit Text dialog box. Click the Import button and select sweet.doc.

Sweet.doc is located on your companion CD-ROM in the ch15\tutorial folder.

4. When the text is placed in the Edit Text dialog box, click and drag over all the text to select it.

5. Specify 12-point CentSchbook as the font size and font, and set the alignment to Justify by clicking the Justify button.

6. Click and drag over the phrase Sweet Success, and change the font size to 14 points. Specify a Center alignment.

7. Repeat the previous step to change the font size and alignment for Post-Valentine's Day Stress Syndrome? and The King Lives!

8. Click OK to apply the changes and to return to the drawing window. Draw displays the text in the paragraph text frame.

9. Select Text ➪ Format Text and click the Frames and Columns tab. Specify two columns and enable Equal column width.

10. Click OK to return to the drawing window. Draw displays the imported text in two even columns (see Figure 15-21).

11. Save the file.

Placing text in columns allows you to include a significant amount of information in a document while increasing the odds that it will be read. The human eye follows columnar text more easily, which enables you to better control the order in which the information is read.

Figure 15-21: Draw displays the imported text in two even columns.

Adding graphic elements

Draw enables text to flow around or over graphic elements. The graphic elements designed for the newsletter include a single sucker and a bitmap image of chocolate chip cookies. In this exercise, you place the two elements. The bitmapped suckers are used to call attention to the newsletter articles. After importing the graphic, you duplicate it and place three copies of the graphic in the document using Draw's Text Wrap feature. The cookies are faded, and you place the graphic behind the text without using text wrap features.

To place graphics in a text document:

1. Open newslet1.cdr if it's not already open.

2. Select File ⇨ Import to display the Import dialog box.

3. Press Ctrl and select cookie.psd and candy1.psd. Click Import. Click the drawing page to place the image.

On the CD-ROM   Cookie.psd and candy1.psd are located on your companion CD-ROM in the d:\tutorial\ch15\ folder (where d: is your CD-ROM drive).

4. Using the Pick tool, select the image of the cookies and place it as shown in Figure 15-22.

5. Select Arrange ⇨ Order ⇨ To Back to move the image behind the text.

6. Using the Pick tool, select the sucker. Right-click the image and select Wrap Paragraph Text from the right mouse button menu. Right-click again and choose Properties. Set the Text wrap offset to 0.1-inch and click OK to return to the drawing window. Draw wraps the paragraph text around the image.

7. Press the plus (+) key on the keypad to create two duplicates of the sucker, and place them as shown in Figure 15-22. The text wraps around the two duplicates without adjusting the settings because the duplicates assume the attributes of the original object.

8. Save the file as **newslet.cdt**.

Note   The newsletter used as an example for the previous series of exercises only has a single page. You might want to add extra pages to expand the newsletter.

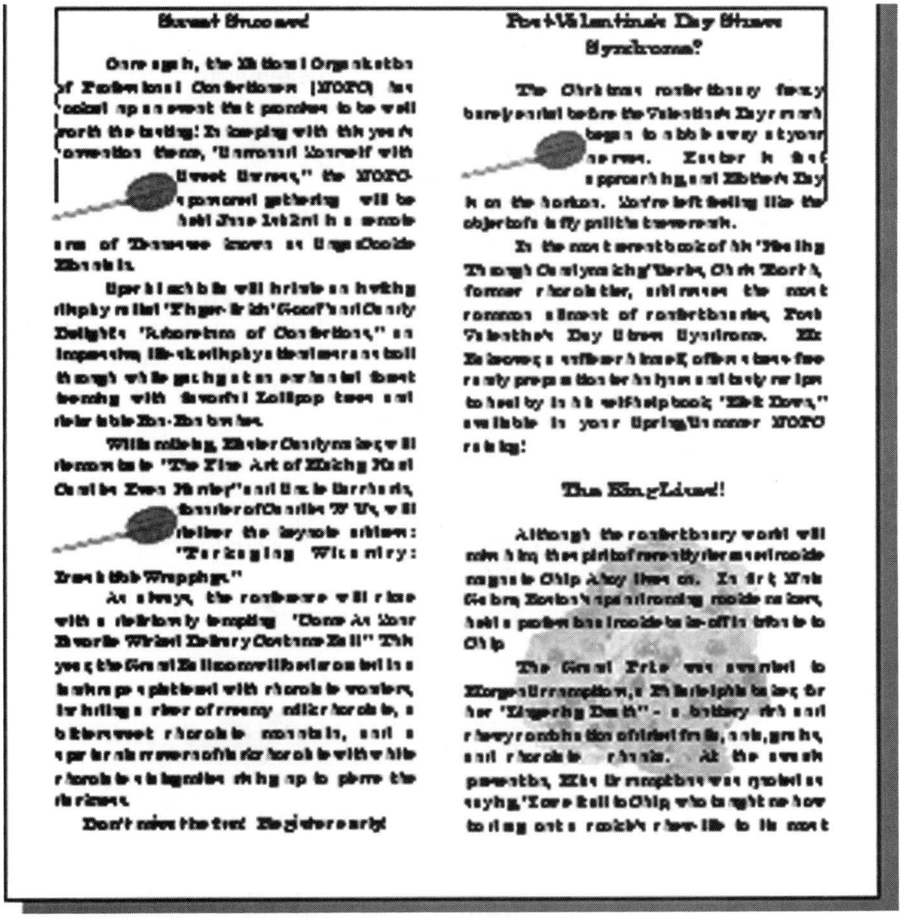

Figure 15-22: Place the graphics as shown in the text body.

Creating a Brochure

Brochure covers a lot of territory. It can be a single page or a large catalogue. The layout can vary from a full page to a trifold. The brochure for a service-based company is quite different from one that advertises specific products and contains pricing. In this section, you create a simple brochure that advertises the showroom of a furniture company, with emphasis on its interior design consultants. Although the example only has two pages, it can be expanded for use as a complete catalogue. While creating the brochure, you work with CorelMedia folders to keep your work organized, and which give you easy access to the brochure elements.

Although you create the brochure featured in this section, the finished template is available on your companion CD-ROM in the template folder.

Creating a master background

The first step to creating the brochure is to specify its page layout and then create a background and place it on the master layer. When you place objects on the master layer, they appear in every page of your document. This reduces the file size while letting you ensure consistency between the pages of your document. As with other documents in this chapter, the brochure starts by using a page frame to quickly create some simple rectangular shapes.

Specifying size and layout settings

To specify size and layout settings:

1. Select File ➪ New to create a new document. When the drawing page appears in the drawing window, double-click the edge of the page border to display the Size page of the Options dialog box (see Figure 15-23).

2. Click Portrait for the orientation and choose Letter size from the drop-down list box. Click the Page Frame button to add a page frame to the document.

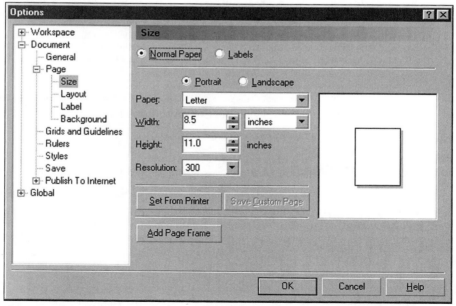

Figure 15-23: Specify the page size settings that you want to use on the Size page of the Options dialog box.

3. In the category window, choose Layout to display the Layout page of the Options dialog box (see Figure 15-24).

4. Select Full Page from the Layout drop-down list box, and enable Facing pages. Normally, documents like brochures start on the right side, but for this exercise select Left Side from the Start On drop-down list box.

5. Click OK to return to the drawing window.

6. Select Layout ➪ Insert page, add one page, select After Current Page, and then click OK.

Note

You can also access the Page setup views of the Options dialog box by selecting Tools ➪ Options and expanding the Document and Page categories by clicking the plus (+) signs beside the names. Choose the page setup functions such as Size and Layout from the expanded list.

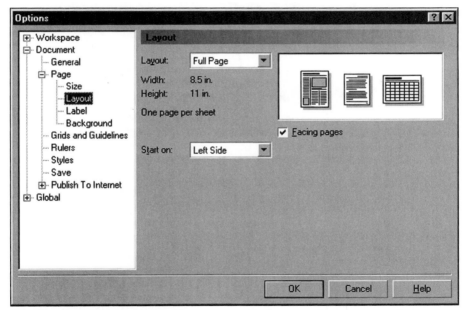

Figure 15-24: The Layout page lets you specify the type of layout to use for your document.

Note

To quickly access the Layout page of the Options dialog box, select Layout ➪ Page Setup.

Your document appears in the drawing window, showing both pages of the document. A page frame appears selected on the left page (page 1).

Adding borders

The brochure uses a pattern fill to create a subtle background for the other elements on the page. To accent the background, add a border to the outside edges of the pages.

To add borders:

1. With the page frame selected, click the Fill tool and choose the Pattern Fill icon from the flyout menu. Choose 2-Color fill and click the down arrow to select the diagonal pattern shown in Figure 15-25. Choose a pale green (ghost green) as the Front color from the drop-down palette, and then enable Transform Fill with Object. Click OK to return to the drawing window. Draw applies the fill to the page frame.

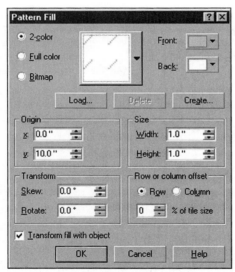

Figure 15-25: Specify a pale green and white diagonal pattern as the fill for the page frame.

2. Press the plus (+) key on your keypad to duplicate the page frame and to superimpose it directly over the original page frame. Using the Pick tool, click and drag the left handle of the duplicate page frame to the right while pressing Ctrl. Drag your cursor past the right handle of the page frame to flip the object horizontally, and place it on page 2 (see Figure 15-26). The duplicate page frame appears on page 2 with the pattern mirrored horizontally.

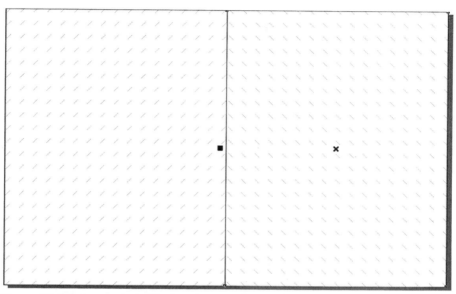

Figure 15-26: Interactively flipping the page frame also mirrors the pattern because Transform Fill with Object was enabled in the Pattern Fill dialog box.

3. Double-click the Rectangle tool to add another page frame to the document, and then select Arrange ⇨ Transformation to display the Transformation docker. Click the Size button to display the Size page of the Transformation docker. Change the anchor point to the left side (see Figure 15-27). Change the value in the horizontal setting box to 1 inch and click Apply. The width of the page frame changes and the new border object appears aligned at the left of the document.

4. With the border object selected, expand the onscreen color palette and apply a pale green (ghost green) fill to the border object. Press the plus (+) key on your keypad to duplicate the object, and then, using the Pick tool, press Shift and select the page frame on page 2. The status bar should show two objects selected. Click the Align button on the Property bar to display the Align and Distribute dialog box.

5. Select Right as the horizontal alignment and click OK. The duplicate border object moves and is positioned at the right side of page 2 (see Figure 15-28).

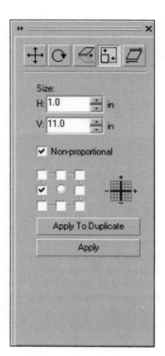

Figure 15-27: Change the width of the page frame to 1 inch and align it on the left of the document in the Size page of the Transformation docker.

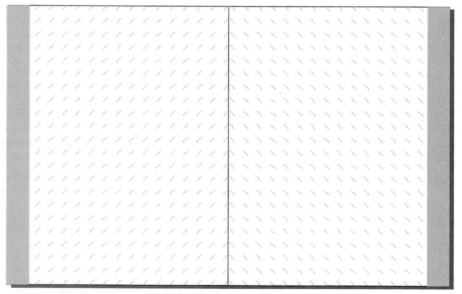

Figure 15-28: Align the duplicate border on the right side of page 2.

6. Select the left border object. Open the Transformation docker, if it is not already open, and click the Size button. Change the anchor to the center position and set the horizontal value at 0.5 inches. Click the Apply to Duplicate button. A new object appears centered horizontally over the left border. Repeat the action for the right border object (see Figure 15-29).

Figure 15-29: Create two new objects, centered horizontally, over the left and right border objects.

7. With the right border still selected, set the anchor for the top in the Size page of the Transformation docker. Change the vertical value to 1.5 inches and click Apply to Duplicate. Draw creates a new object and aligns it at the top of the border. Repeat the action for the left border (see Figure 15-30).

8. Using the Pick tool, select one of the small rectangles you just created and change the corner roundness on the property bar to 25 percent. Repeat the action for the other small rectangle.

9. Deselect all the objects in your document, and set the nudge value on the property bar to 0.1 inches.

10. Using the Pick tool, select the small rectangle on page 2 and press the down arrow (fl) five times while pressing Shift to move the rectangle down 1 inch. Press the right arrow (fi) twice to move the rectangle outward 0.2 inches (see Figure 15-31).

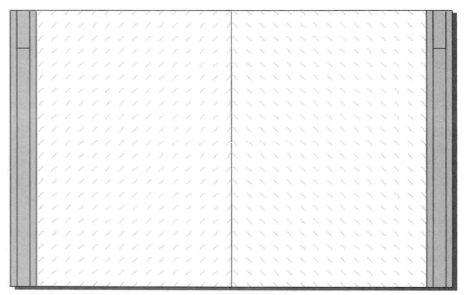

Figure 15-30: Create two new objects and align them at the top of the border using the Size page of the Transformation docker.

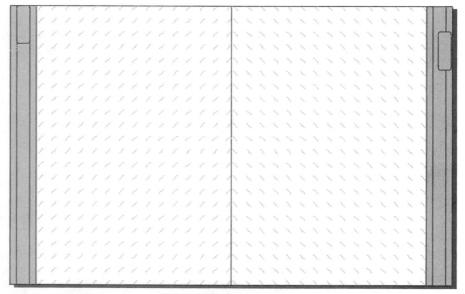

Figure 15-31: Use Super Nudge and Nudge to move the small rectangle down and outward.

11. Using the Pick tool, select the small left rectangle and press the down arrow (ﬂ) and left arrow (<) twice each to move the rectangle down and outward 0.2 inches. With the rectangle still selected, select Arrange ➪ Shaping ➪ Weld to display the Shaping docker, and then click the Weld button. Click Weld and click the narrower of the two border objects to create a single object that resembles a file tab (see Figure 15-32).

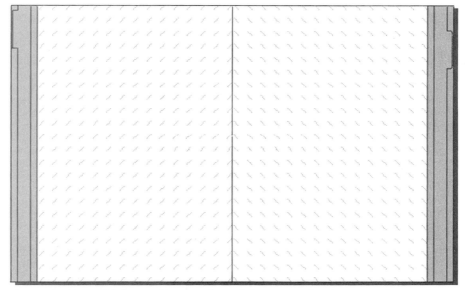

Figure 15-32: Weld the small rectangle and the narrow border rectangle together to create a new object.

12. With the tab object selected, click the yellow color swatch on the onscreen palette to fill it with yellow. Repeat the action to fill the other tab object with yellow.

13. Select Edit ➪ Select All and right-click the X on the onscreen palette to remove the outline from all the objects in your document.

14. Using the Pick tool, select the left tab object and the border beneath it. Use the Align command to right-align the objects. Repeat with the left tab object and border to left-align the objects.

15. Save the document to your hard disk as **broch1.cdr**.

Figure 15-33 shows the completed background. You can add text to the tabs, as I did, by creating two strings of center-aligned Artistic text and rotating them 90 and –90 degrees, respectively.

Figure 15-33: The completed background is ready to receive your graphics and text.

Creating the Master page

In this exercise, you use the Object Manager docker to specify that you want your completed background to be a Master layer so that it appears on every page of your document.

To make the completed background the Master page:

1. Open broch1.cdr in Draw if it's not already open.

2. Select Tools ➪ Object Manager to display the Object Manager docker in the drawing window.

3. In the Object Manager docker, click the plus (+) beside Layer 1 to expand the layer and to display all of the background objects that you created. Right-click the icon beside Layer 1, and choose Master from the right mouse button menu.

4. Save your document.

Making Background Masters and Templates

Creating the basic background for your brochure and placing it on the master page offers advantages. Regardless of how many pages you add to the document, the background appears on every page, removing the need to reproduce the work on every page. You can lock the layer so that any work you do later won't disturb the background.

In addition, it works well as a basic document. You can create a template based on the background, letting you create a variety of documents that use the background as a central theme.

Adding headline text and graphics

Any brochure or advertising document requires headline text. This brochure is not an exception. It has both a headline and a subheadline, as well as a large graphic to lead into the body of the document. Choosing a font for the text in an advertising document can take time, and the vast number of fonts packaged with Draw doesn't make this task any easier. For consistency and ease, I chose to use Garamond throughout the brochure.

Tip

If you haven't installed the Garamond font, I recommend stopping here and installing it. You use this font throughout the rest of the exercises. (The fonts are found on Disk 1 of your copy of CorelDRAW 9.)

For convenience, both the headline and subhead text have been created for you and are located on your companion CD-ROM. Part of creating any document is collecting the elements to include in a centralized location. In addition to the text used in the brochure, all of the graphics required to complete the brochure are also included on the CD-ROM.

On the CD-ROM

The files for this tutorial are located on your companion CD-ROM in the ch15\tutorial folder. I recommend using Windows Explorer to move the entire folder to your hard drive.

To place graphic elements and headline text:

1. Open broch1.cdr, if it's not already open, and click the Scrapbook icon on the main toolbar to display the Scrapbook Docker.

2. Using the navigation tools at the top of the docker, switch to the location where you stored the files for this tutorial.

3. While pressing Ctrl, select htext.cdr, shtext.cdr, and room1.jpg. Drag the three elements to the left page of your document.

Note

Room1.jpg is not a photo. The room and its contents were created in Draw. The fills for the various pieces of furniture, wood, rug, and other elements were created from objects scanned using the techniques shown in Chapter 8. The rug's fill is cooked oatmeal and petroleum jelly. The wood fills are either peanut butter and jelly or peanut butter and automotive oil. The fill for the couch and chair are cupcake candies melted and swirled into personal lubricant. The scanned *trash* was enhanced in Photoshop and imported as bitmap pattern fills in Draw.

4. Using Figure 15-34 as a guide, position the elements on the left page. Use the Align command to align the text with the top of the image.

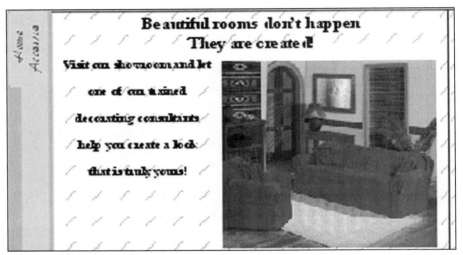

Figure 15-34: Position the elements on the left page of your document.

5. Using the Shape tool, select the subhead text beside the image. Draw displays the kerning and leading handles for the text string.

6. Click and drag the down arrow to adjust the leading of the text so that the bottom of the text aligns with the bottom of the image (see Figure 15-35).

7. Drag ellipse.cdr to your document from the Scrapbook Docker.

8. Using the plus (+) key, duplicate the ellipse group three times, and then position them in the document as shown in Figure 15-36. Each ellipse object is actually a group of two ellipses, which permits easier placement in your document.

9. Using the Pick tool, press Shift and select the four ellipse objects. On the Property bar, click Ungroup All.

10. While pressing Ctrl, select mirror1.cdr, mirror2.cdr, basket1.cdr, and pots1.cdr. Drag them from the Scrapbook docker to the document.

11. Using the Pick tool, select the pots and then select Effects ➪ PowerClip ➪ Place Inside Container. When the large arrow appears, click the white ellipse in the lower right-hand corner of page 2. Draw places the object inside the ellipse.

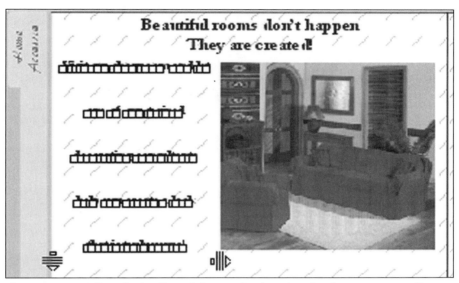

Figure 15-35: Adjust the leading of the text by dragging the down arrow to align the bottom of the text with the bottom of the image.

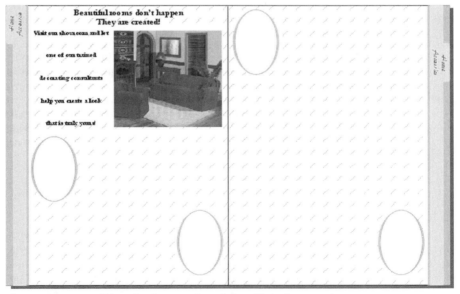

Figure 15-36: Position the four copies of the ellipse in your document.

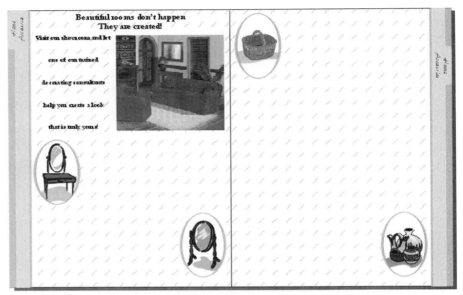

Figure 15-37: Insert the graphic objects into the ellipses using the PowerClip command.

12. Repeat the last step to place the rest of the objects as shown in Figure 15-37 using the PowerClip command.

13. Using the Pick tool, marquee-select a PowerClip and the pale green ellipse behind it. Group the two objects. Repeat this step to group the other three PowerClips with the ellipse beneath each.

Note   The PowerClips both hold and frame the graphic elements. By sizing your graphic elements to fit inside the PowerClips, you control the size of the elements you add to your document. This lets you easily change graphic elements while maintaining a consistent size.

14. Save your document.

Adding body text

The body text of the brochure wraps around the graphic elements in the document. In this exercise, you specify the offset for the text and flow the text into your document. When you specify an offset, you determine the distance you want between a graphic element and the paragraph text. When creating a layout, *ipsum lorem* text is frequently used as a placeholder for other text. *Ipsum lorem* text is basically nonsensical Latin text, but it serves well as a placement object by letting you position paragraph text and text frames.

On the CD-ROM

Lorem1.txt is included on your companion CD-ROM in the tutorial\ch15\ folder.

To specify paragraph text offset values and add body text:

1. Open broch1.cdr, if it's not already open, and display the Scrapbook docker in the drawing window.

2. Double-click lorem1.txt to open the text document in Windows Notepad. Select Edit ➪ Select All to select all of the text, and the press Ctrl+C to copy the text to the Windows clipboard. Close Notepad and return to Draw.

3. Using the Pick tool, right-click one of the ellipse groups that you created in the previous exercise. Choose Properties from the right mouse button menu to display the Object Properties dialog box (see Figure 15-38). Click the General tab.

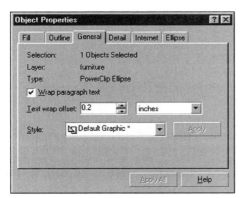

Figure 15-38: You can enable text wrap functions and the amount of offset you want to use in the Object Properties dialog box.

4. Enable Wrap Paragraph Text and click the up and down arrows to specify an offset value of 0.2 inches. Alternatively, you can highlight the value and enter a new value. Click OK to return to the drawing window.

5. Repeat steps 3 and 4 to specify a paragraph text wrap offset for each of the other three ellipse groups.

6. Using the Text tool, click and drag a paragraph text frame to page 1, as shown in Figure 15-39. Draw automatically displays the text wrap offsets in the paragraph text frame, and an insertion point at the beginning of the frame.

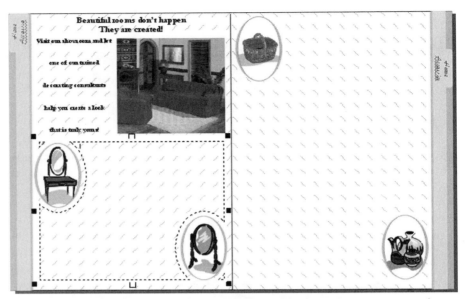

Figure 15-39: Draw displays the text wrap offsets when you create a paragraph text frame.

7. Press Ctrl+V to paste the contents of the Windows clipboard into the paragraph text frame. Draw pastes the text, and wraps it around the graphic elements.

Note

Filling the text frames is the most important concept in this exercise, because the *ipsum lorem* text is used strictly as a placeholder. Once the text is in place, you can adjust the frames to your margin specifications.

8. Using the Text tool, click and drag another paragraph text frame to page 2 as shown in Figure 15-40. Paste the text into that frame as well. If the text doesn't fill the frame, use the Text tool to set an insertion point at the end of the text and paste more text to fill the frame.

9. Save your document.

Tip

If you want to keep this document for future use, use the Save As command to save it as a template (.cdt) file.

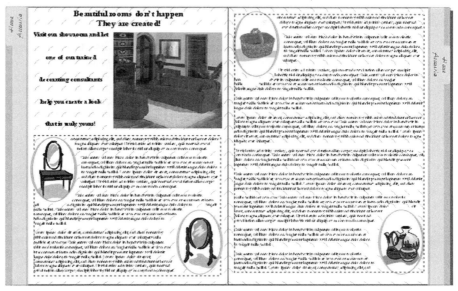

Figure 15-40: Paste the text into the frame on page 2.

Tips for Using Draw in the Office

The documents used around the office are frequently repetitive, such as an invoice or letterhead. When I teach people to create office documents, I make several recommendations that make the creation and use of these documents easier.

✦ Use a theme for your documents: The logo you create for your letterhead works equally well at the top of an invoice, on a business card, or on your company newsletter. Let Draw work for you. Because Draw is vector-based, you can resize and use the same artwork repetitively, without having to recreate it each time. This also gives your documents a consistent and professional appearance.

✦ Add notes and keywords to your documents when you save them: This makes finding the correct document easier, especially if you have multiple versions of the same document.

✦ Create a template of the documents that you revise or use frequently: You can open the template, make the changes you need quickly, and save the document as a .cdr file. To get the most from your templates and to make revising templates easier, create styles for your text and graphic objects. When you revise the template later, you will save time by being able to make global changes.

✦ Keep your design clean and simple: Most office documents aren't designed to show off your artistic ability. They are utilitarian in nature, and the message they contain is the focus of the document, not the artwork.

Summary

The capability to create forms and templates for office use is one of Draw's strong features. Its layout capabilities make it ideal for incorporating graphics and text into booklets, catalogs, and other small documents as well. If you are creating a larger document, such as a book, you'll want to use a more text-intensive layout program such as Corel Ventura, but for most office needs, Draw more than meets the test. In this chapter, you learned to

✦ Use page frames to quickly create banners and sidebars

✦ Create blended text effects

✦ Create the illusion of a raised 3D object

✦ Add paragraph text to documents utilizing snap-to features

✦ Flow text around graphic elements

✦   ✦   ✦

Successful Printing and Output

The topic of printing and output is huge, detailed, and rates several books all by itself. The designated output should be an integral part of the design of any document, and under-standing your output requirements goes a long way toward creating images and documents that print successfully. Draw provides the design and printing tools necessary to create documents for nearly any output imaginable.

Printing Basics

Where Draw is concerned, there's really only one criterion regarding whether you can output to a device. Does the device have a Windows 95, Windows 98, or Windows NT compatible driver? If it does, you can send your file to that device. The range of devices is amazing.

✦ You can send files to any device from an inkjet or laser printer to a computerized router or embroidery machine.

✦ In addition, you can output files to service bureaus, which create films for other output devices, such as commercial presses and screen printers' equipment.

Basically, printing is divided into these categories with a small overlap, and the needs and requirements for each category vary:

✦ In-house printing

✦ Camera-ready laser output

✦ Output to a service bureau

Preparing to print

Draw provides a variety of printing options. Some of these options are specified in the drawing window; others are specified in the Print dialog box. The basic process of printing a file, however, is the same for all types of output.

Determining what to print

Start by determining what to print. You can choose to print the objects selected on a page, the entire page, an entire multipage document, or a range of pages in a multipage document. You can also choose to print specific layers. If you want to print specific objects or layers, printing preparation begins in the drawing window. Using the Pick tool, select the objects to print. You can only select objects on the active page of multipage documents. You have to print selected objects that reside on other pages as separate print jobs.

Preparing specific layers

To prepare to print specific layers:

1. Select Layout ⇨ Object Manager to display the Object Manager docker.

2. Click the printer icon beside the individual layer names (see Figure 16-1) to specify which layers to print. If the printer icon is grayed out, the layer won't print. You can print selected objects from any layer where the printer icon is not grayed out.

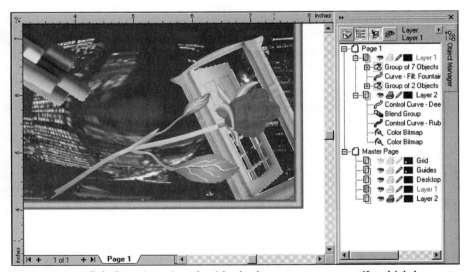

Figure 16-1: Click the printer icon beside the layer names to specify which layers to print. In the example, the frame, door, and background layers of Layer 2 will print. The Master Grid, Master Guides, Desktop, and rose (Layer 1) will not print, even though the rose is visible on the monitor screen.

Layer Printing Tips

If you want to print some objects on a layer, but not others, you may find these tips useful:

✦ Move objects from one layer to another. The easiest way to rearrange objects in your drawing is by selecting the object in the Object Manager and dragging it into the desired layer.

✦ Remember though, that rearranging the objects changes the order of the objects in the drawing. Rearranging overlapping objects may change the appearance of your drawing.

✦ If portions of your drawing don't print, check the Object Manager docker to make sure that the layers have been specified as printable.

Printing your file

Once you've determined what you want to print, you are ready to print. Draw lets you specify the number of copies and the range of pages to print, as well as other options related to printing your document. You can also preview how your document will appear once it's printed.

To print a file:

1. Select File ➪ Print to display the Print dialog box (see Figure 16-2).

2. Choose the printing options that you want to use and enter the number of copies you want (more information about choosing print options appears later in this chapter). Use this Print Range list as a guide to choosing a print range:

   • **All:** Prints all the pages in your document. If you enable collate, Draw prints the entire sequence of a multipage document of each individual copy of a document, before printing the next copy. If collate is disabled, Draw prints all copies of page 1, then all copies of page 2, and so on.

   • **Current Page:** Prints the current page of a multipage document. By default Draw prints the current page only. You can change this setting on the Printing page in the Options dialog box.

   • **Pages:** Prints a selected range of pages in a multipage document. If you don't have multiple pages, this option is grayed out. Information about specifying a range of pages appears later in this chapter.

   • **Selection:** Prints only the selected objects. If no objects are selected in your drawing, this option appears grayed out.

3. Click OK to print your file.

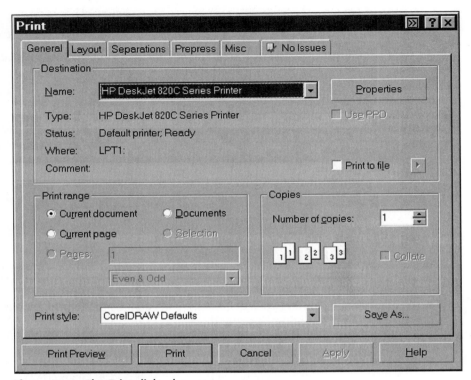

Figure 16-2: The Print dialog box.

Caution   If you have more than one printer, make sure that the printer specified in the printer box is the printer you want to use. When the Print dialog box opens, it displays the Windows default printer as the selected printer. Click the down arrow to select another printer if desired. Selecting the wrong printer wastes time and can cause undesirable results. For example, if you send a PostScript file to a non-PostScript printer, you'll get pages of PostScript description language instead of the image you expect.

Specifying a page range

When you choose to print a range of pages in a multipage document, you can specify which pages to print and the order in which you want them printed. This is useful if you have a large document and want to proof a limited number of pages, or if you want them printed in a specific order.

To specify a page range:

1. Enable Pages in the Print dialog box.

2. Choose whether you want Even Pages, Odd Pages, or Even & Odd Pages to print. This option overrides any page range that you specify. For example, if you specify that you want to print pages 1 through 10 and choose Even Pages, only the even-numbered pages in that page range will print.

3. Enter the pages you want printed in the Pages box. Don't put spaces between your instructions. Use this list as a guide to specifying the pages:

   • Place a dash (-) between numbers to define a range of sequential pages, such as pages 1-10. This setting would print pages 1 through 10.

   • Place a comma (,) between numbers to define a range of nonsequential pages, such as 1,6,9. This setting would print pages 1, 6, and 9.

   • Enter a combination of dashes and commas, if desired. Entering 1-4,6,9 would print pages 1 through 4, as well as pages 6 and 9.

   • Place a tilde (~) between two numbers to print the two specified pages, plus every second page in between. Entering 1~8 prints pages 1, 3, 5, 7, and 8.

Previewing your document

Taking a couple of minutes to preview your document can save a lot of aggravation. The preview window lets you see how your document will look once it's printed, as well as how it fits in the printable area of the page (see Figure 16-3). If you have a multipage document, tabs called page flippers appear at the bottom of the Print Preview window. Clicking the tabs lets you navigate through your document to view each page. In addition, you can select several options in the Print Preview, which are discussed later in this chapter. Select File ➪ Print Preview to preview your drawing. Alternatively, you can click the Print Preview button in the Print dialog box.

Choosing a preview color

Complex images can take time to render to screen. It also takes longer to display color than it does grayscale. You can adjust the speed of the screen refresh in the Print Preview window by choosing a preview color.

To set the preview color:

1. In the Print Preview window, select View ➪ Preview Color and choose one of the preview colors (see Figure 16-4). Use this list as a guide to assist you in your selection:

Tip   A color preview can take twice as long to display than a grayscale preview. If you don't need to check the colors in your image, I recommend choosing a grayscale preview.

- **Auto (Simulate Output):** This option displays the images based on the output device. If the active printer is a monochrome printer, the image is shown in grayscale tones. Similarly, if the active printer is a color printer, the image is displayed in color.

- **Color:** This option displays your image in color and has the slowest rendering time.

- **Grayscale:** This option displays your image in grayscale and has the fastest rendering time. Grayscale is also a good choice for checking color distribution if you have pale colors in your image that might disappear against the white background.

Figure 16-3: Print Preview lets you see how your document will look when printed.

2. Choose Preview Color from the View drop-down menu. Choose the preview color you want and Click OK to apply the change.

Shortcut

If you are in the Print Preview window, Ctrl+O accesses the Misc property sheet of the Print Options dialog box.

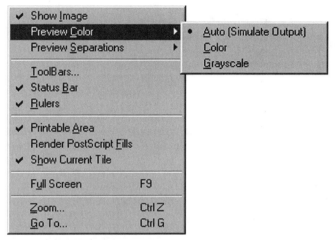

Figure 16-4: You can increase screen refresh in the Print Preview window by selecting how colors will be treated.

Using visual aids in preview

Draw provides a variety of visual aids for your use in the Print Preview window. Visual aids, such as bounding boxes, assist you in adjusting your image prior to printing. You can choose which aids to display. Table 16-1 lists the visual aids that you can use in the Print Preview window, and how to display them.

Table 16-1
Print Preview Visual Aids

Visual aid	Description	Do this:
Bounding Box	This option displays the perimeter dimensions of your image. If you have an image that fades into the paper color, the bounding box assists you in resizing your image.	Click the image. The bounding box is visible, while the mouse button is in the down position.
Printable Area	This option displays the printable area of the page. You can use this visual aid to assist you in resizing your image.	Select View ⇨ Printable Area.
Rulers	This option displays the rulers in the Print Preview window.	Select View ⇨ Rulers.

Continued

Table 16-1 *(continued)*		
Visual aid	**Description**	**Do this:**
Selection Handles	This option displays sizing handles, enabling you to interactively resize your image.	Click the image.
Tiled Page Boundaries	If you have a large image that will be tiled on several sheets of paper, Tiled Page Boundaries shows the location where the image will be tiled.	Click the page in the Print Preview window. This option is available only if you have specified that you want to tile the image.
Top Right Corner Fold	This option lets you view the relationship between your image, and the paper, by displaying the edge. This is useful if you are creating a full-bleed image.	Click the N-up format tool in the toolbar. (More information about the N-up format tool appears later in this chapter.) The image changes to a gray rectangle with the upper right-hand corner turned down.

Using the Zoom tool in print preview

The Zoom tool in the Print Preview window works much like it does in the drawing window. You can choose one of the zoom levels from the drop-down zoom menu, or you can interactively marquee-select the area that you want to view at a zoomed level. This is especially useful for viewing small images, such as logos for letterheads or portions of your drawing (see Figure 16-5).

To magnify the print preview:

1. Click the Zoom tool. You can also marquee-select the area that you want to view.

2. Click the down arrow, beside the Zoom tool, and choose an option from the drop-down menu.

3. To zoom out, right-click your image.

Shortcut

Ctrl+F2 selects the Zoom tool; Ctrl+F3 zooms out; Shift+F2 zooms to selection; Shift+F4 zooms to page; F4 zooms to fit.

Figure 16-5: Use the zoom feature to view a magnified portion of your drawing.

Previewing color separations

The Print Preview window lets you view your image as color separations, if you have Color Separations enabled in the Separations tab of the Print Options dialog box. When you preview your drawing as color separations, it appears on several pages in grayscale. Each page represents a color of ink. Because most images are printed in CMYK, the preview generally displays the colors cyan, magenta, yellow, and black on separate pages. If you have specified PANTONE spot colors, a page appears for every PANTONE spot color that you've used in your drawing.

To preview your drawing as color separations:

1. In the Print Preview window, select View ⇨ Preview Separations and choose a view type. You can choose from these views:

    • **Auto (Simulate Output):** This option simulates the output of the active printer. If the active printer is capable of printing separations, they are displayed in the preview window.

    • **Composite:** This option displays the composite image.

    • **Separations:** This option displays the separations for the image as individual pages. One page per CMYK color and spot color is displayed.

2. Use the page flipper to move from one color separation to the next.

PANTONE Inks and Printing Budgets

The PANTONE color matching system is one of the most consistent and precise color-matching systems available. It has several advantages over CMYK output. CMYK colors are represented by percentages of cyan, magenta, yellow, and black. Several factors can affect the color of CMYK output, which can vary widely from one printer or printing press to the next. Instead, in the PANTONE process, each PANTONE color is assigned an ID name and number. PANTONE colors come in inks, paper, film, color swatches, illustration markers, and a variety of other media. The result of this precision matching system is that regardless of the media, the color is always exactly the same. There are no dye lots, and no deviation. The colors are always predictable. Some industries, such as the screen-printing industry, depend on this color system and premixed inks to ensure consistent color from one job to the next. Draw has three PANTONE color systems: Spot, Hexachrome, and Process. The most commonly referenced is Spot, which offers you precision that is not available using other color palettes or models.

PANTONE's precision has a price, however. When you specify PANTONE inks for a commercial printing job, you pay for the color consistency. You also pay more for the printing process. Here's why. Most printing presses are four-color or two-color presses, and primarily use CMYK values for printing. The inks are calculated as percentages of the four colors and laid down on the paper in one or two passes through the press. (A four-color press uses one pass; a two-color press uses two passes.) If you specify PANTONE inks, each color of ink requires a separate film and plate. Each color also represents a single pass through the press, which must then be cleaned before the next color is laid down. In addition, every pass through the press increases the possibility of registration problems due to shrinkage of the paper and slippage on the press. In other words, printing PANTONE colors is more labor intensive, and therefore costs more money if your print job contains more than two colors. Mixing PANTONE and CMYK colors escalates this problem. Although PANTONE colors are the closest thing to WYSIWYG (What You See Is What You Get), they are costly. You should consider your printing budget carefully, and consult your printer and service bureau before specifying PANTONE colors.

Positioning and sizing your image in preview mode

Draw's full-screen preview lets you view the size and position of your drawing as it will appear when it's printed. You can also modify the size and position, if you are using a Full Page style. When you size or position your image in Print Preview mode, the original drawing remains unaffected. You can fit the image to page, resize an image to specific dimensions, or manually resize an image by dragging its handles. If you have a multipage document, you can also place multiple pages on a single sheet of paper.

Resizing your image

To resize your image in Print Preview:

1. Select Settings ⇨ Layout to display the Print Options dialog box (see Figure 16-6). Click the Layout tab, if the Layout property sheet is not displayed.

2. Enter the values you want to use for width and height in the Size box. If you enable Maintain Aspect Ratio (the lock icon at the far right of the settings dialog determines whether this option is enabled or disabled), you only need to enter a value in the Width box. Draw automatically calculates the proportionate height.

3. Enable Apply Settings to All Pages, if desired. This option only applies to multipage documents and will not appear on the Layout property sheet of a one-page document.

4. Click Close to apply the change and return to the Print Preview window.

Shortcut

If you are in the Print Preview window, Ctrl+L accesses the Layout property sheet of the Print Options dialog box.

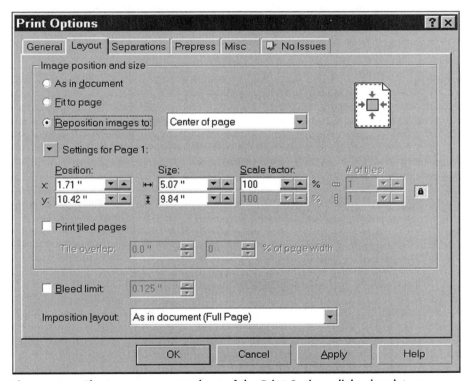

Figure 16-6: The Layout property sheet of the Print Options dialog box lets you adjust the height and width of your printouts.

Note

You can resize an image using this method only if you are using a full-page or manual layout style. If you have rows and columns, you can't use this method to resize your image.

Fitting an image to a paper size

To fit an image to the specified paper size:

1. In the Print Preview window, select Settings ➪ Layout to display the Print Options dialog box. Click the Layout tab, if it's not displayed.

2. Enable Fit to Page. To prevent distortion of your image, be sure to also enable Maintain Aspect Ratio, the button with the lock icon.

3. Enable Apply Settings to All Pages, if desired. This option only applies to multipage documents.

4. Click Close to apply the change and to return to the Print Preview window.

 Tip

Choosing Fit to Page is a convenient way to output an image at multiple sizes according to the output device. If your drawing contains bitmaps, create your image at the largest output size. Reducing a bitmap to fit to page causes less distortion than increasing the size.

Positioning an image on a page

To position an image on the page:

1. In the Print Preview window, select Settings ➪ Layout to display the Print Options dialog box. Click the Layout tab, if the Layout property sheet is not displayed.

 Shortcut

Ctrl+L displays the Layout tab of the Print Options dialog box.

2. Either enter values in the Top and Left boxes or enable Center Image. The top and left values represent distance from the top and left edges of the printable area of the paper, not from the edge of the paper itself. You can also position an image on the page by clicking and dragging it in the Print Preview window to the location you desire.

3. Click Close to apply the change and to return to the Print Preview window.

 Caution

Exercise caution when resizing bitmaps, or images containing bitmaps. Resizing a bitmap can distort the image and cause the print to appear jagged or pixelated. If you need to resize an image containing a bitmap, perform any resizing in the drawing window by resampling the bitmap, as opposed to stretching or scaling it. Resize other elements of your drawing as needed.

Proofing your image

It's frequently useful to proof your image before printing your final drawing. Draw enables you to print portions of your image for proofing purposes. You can choose to print vector objects, bitmaps, text, or a combination of these three object types. Proofing a single object type lets you see how that portion of your image looks in print. This is useful for checking placement on the page, or the attributes of an object type, such as the way a transparency fades into the background.

To print only vectors, bitmaps, or text:

1. Select File ⇨ Print Preview to display the Print Preview window.
2. In the Print Preview window, select Settings ⇨ Misc Options and click the Misc tab. Enable Vectors, Bitmaps, or Text. You can select a combination of these options if you want.
3. Enable Print All Text in Black if you want to print text in black instead of color.
4. Click OK to apply the changes and to return to the Print Preview window. You can then print your file to proof the selected object types.

Printing a proof of an element in your drawing is useful if you want an element, such as the text, to be printed on film by itself. Some industries, such as screen printers, typically create a separate film for the text. This lets them change the text when they screen-print the item, such as a T-shirt. Using this method, the shirts can all have the same graphic image but different text.

Output Considerations

Whenever you create a document, you need to consider the output of the finished document. In fact, you should consider the output before you create a drawing or other document. Simply saying that you intend to print the document is not a sufficient answer. These factors need to be considered before you print your document:

✦ What is the goal of your document?

✦ Who is the intended audience?

✦ Does the document need to serve multiple purposes?

✦ Do you need to print your document at a variety of sizes?

✦ What kind of quality is required?

✦ What are your budgetary requirements?

✦ Will your document be printed in black and white or in color?

To some extent, I'm playing the devil's advocate when I pose these questions. Some of these questions lead to other questions. The reality is that the sooner you get these questions out of the way, the sooner you can move on with the creation process. The answers to these questions provide a framework, or plan, from which you can work. You also increase the probability of your document's success if you answer these questions early in the process. The answers also help you determine the output device your document requires.

Choosing a print quality

When planning the printed output of a document, many of the questions that need to be answered overlap. The first step is to figure out the goal and audience for your document. In most cases, the answers to these two questions provide the answers to other questions. If you are creating an ad, for example, your intended audience and how your ad will be distributed determine the output. A company logo frequently needs to be printed at multiple sizes on a variety of media, and in black and white as well as in color. Once you've determined the goal and audience, you can decide how many copies and the quality you require.

Inkjet printers

If you intend to print a limited quantity of a single page or a small document, such as a flyer, an inkjet printer is a good output choice. Although these printers provide an adequate resolution for general purpose printing, they are not designed to produce camera-ready artwork for commercial printing purposes. The technology is better suited for use in the home or small office. Some inkjets are capable of printing your document in color, and accept a variety of media sizes. The consumables, such as ink, for an inkjet printer are expensive when you consider that most cartridges are only capable of printing between 400 and 500 copies. This amount is determined by the quantity of ink coverage on a page, and can vary from one printer to the next. If you have an inkjet printer, and require many copies of a document, consider photocopying your print or using another type of output device, such as a laser printer.

Desktop laser printers

Laser printers are a variable class of printers, ranging from the office desktop printers that print up to legal size to more expensive large-format printers that can print documents up to 36 inches wide. Much faster than inkjet printers, the average desktop laser printer is capable of printing nearly 5,000 copies per toner cartridge, which makes them more economical than inkjet printers. Most laser printers use PostScript technology to provide clean black-and-white copies of your document. Although several color laser printers are available, they tend to be too expensive for most general-purpose printing. Laser printers are somewhat limited in that most of them are designed to print a single side of a sheet of paper. Generally designed for in-house use, most laser printers can print on a variety of media, such as envelopes, light-weight card stock, and transparency media. Laser printers also produce acceptable separations for modest quality offset printing and screen-printing purposes.

If you print your images on a PostScript laser printer, a printing shop can print your camera-ready images, as long as they don't require complicated color work. Using your laser printer to create camera-ready masters for reproduction on a commercial press is useful if you are printing a large quantity of material, such as a newsletter. Creating a master on a laser printer is less effective, however, for print jobs requiring high-quality color output.

Tip One way to maintain a budget, but get the feel of color, is to use halftones to produce one-color print jobs on colored stock. This method produces excellent effects at a fraction of the cost of full-color. More information about using halftones appears later in this chapter.

Specialty printers

Specialty printers, such as thermal wax, dye sublimation, and Iris printers, use PostScript technology to create color printouts of your images. These printers vary in their capability to handle a variety of print sizes and types of media. Thermal wax and dye sublimation printers create color using rolled inksheets that resemble cellophane wrap permeated with colored dyes or waxes, as opposed to liquid ink or toner. Both of these printers require special media for optimum printing. They also handle transfer media that can be bonded to textiles and other surfaces using heat. Iris printers use liquid inks sprayed in ultrafine droplets. These printers enable you to print on a variety of media, including canvas and plastic veneers. Iris printers frequently enable large-format printing as well.

Specialty printers are not designed for creating large output quantities. The consumables, such as media and inks or inksheets, are too expensive for this purpose. Specialty printers also do not produce camera-ready artwork. Dye sublimation printers, for example, are continuous tone, which means they produce an extremely smooth image. The dots that create halftone screens required for commercial printing purposes aren't visible because they are not used to create an image on these printers.

Service bureaus and commercial printshops

Service bureaus and some printshops use imagesetters to produce high-resolution film output, which is then used to produce printing plates. You generally send your files to a service bureau on disk or via modem. In some cases, you can send the file in its original format. Other service bureaus and printshops require that you print the document to file first. If you require a high-quality print or custom media, such as glossy stock, service bureaus and printshops can provide the required quality.

Tip The most important thing to remember when you want to have an image processed by a service bureau or printshop is to always consult them first. They will be able to provide information about their equipment and file formats that will ensure the success of your print job.

Working with output resolution

Commercial printers calculate and measure resolution in lines per inch (lpi). For most printing requirements, especially monochrome output, a good rule of thumb to use is that the dpi (dots per inch) output should be twice the lpi. Most desktop laser printers are capable of producing adequate results for documents that contain few graphics or nonphotographic images.

Laser printer output

Laser printers aren't adequate if you need a higher quality image or if your document contains complex color or photographic images. The success of your print job is increased if you print to file, as opposed to hard copy, then have it processed commercially. The most frequent problem with laser output is toner density. Most lasers don't produce sufficient toner density to stand up to a camera. Another problem is that most laser printers tend to drop grayscale colors at the ends of the range. It's not unusual, for example, for a laser hard copy to display little discernible difference between 10 percent black and 30 percent black or between 70 percent black and 100 percent black. When film is shot from such hard copies, it contains fading and holes where the toner was thin, or it loses detail where the colors dropped out at the ends of the color range.

Tip   If your commercial printer, or a newspaper where you are placing ads, requires camera-ready prints, you can increase the effective resolution of your laser print by doubling the size of your drawing. If your ad, for example, is 4×3 inches, make it 8×6 inches before printing it to your laser printer. When the printer photographs it and reduces it back to 4×3 inches, a simple job for the printer, the result is equal to 2,400 dpi.

High-quality printed output

If you are creating a table-top book, catalog, or other document that requires high-quality imaging, you need output that includes as much of the 256 grayscale levels as possible. This is especially critical if your document contains bitmaps or photographs. Table 16-2 shows the resolution levels for high-quality printed output. The values in each column represent the maximum levels of gray obtainable using the resolution of various devices at specific screen rulings. The shaded areas represent the optimum combinations to achieve the best results.

Tip   Consult your printshop to determine the resolution required for their equipment and your project. This information lets you work effectively with your laser printer or service bureau.

Preparing the printer

Before you print, you need to select the appropriate printing device and set its properties. The Printer Color Profile helps to ensure accurate color reproduction. You can enable or disable this feature when you print, but you must initially set it up using Draw's color management features (more information about color management appears later in this chapter).

Note   Windows controls printer installation. Every type of printer has different device properties, which you can specify. Refer to the printer manufacturer's documentation and your Windows documentation for more information about installing and setting up your printer.

Table 16-2
Resolution Guide

Resolution of laser printer or imagesetter in dpi	Screen ruling in lpi									
dpi	60 lpi	65 lpi	80 lpi	85 lpi	100 lpi	110 lpi	120 lpi	133 lpi	160 lpi	175 lpi
300	25	21	14	12	9	7	6	5	4	3
400	44	38	25	22	16	13	11	9	7	5
600	100	85	56	50	36	30	25	20	16	12
800	178	151	100	89	64	63	44	36	28	21
1000	278	237	156	138	100	83	69	57	44	33
1270	448	382	252	223	161	133	112	91	72	53
1700	803	684	452	400	289	239	201	163	128	94
2540	1792	1527	1008	893	645	533	448	365	287	211
3250	2943	2500	1650	1462	1056	873	743	597	469	345

Choosing printer options

Draw enables you to choose a printer and specify printer properties. Depending on the printer you choose, you can specify a variety of printing options that are designed for your printer, such as paper size, port, spooling, and whether you want to use a portrait or landscape orientation. When you print an image with an orientation different from the orientation selected in the device properties, Draw displays a warning message, asking you if you want Draw to automatically adjust the orientation of the printer (see Figure 16-7). If you are using a PostScript printer, you can specify the way you want to deal with resident and nonresident fonts. Resident fonts are preprogrammed into your printer's memory; nonresident fonts are downloaded to the printer.

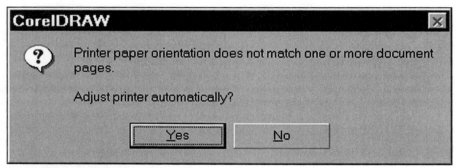

Figure 16-7: Printer orientation warning.

Selecting a printer

To select a printing device:

1. Select File ➪ Print Setup to display the Print Setup dialog box (see Figure 16-8).

Note   You can also access the Print Setup dialog box from the Print dialog box.

2. Click the down arrow next to the printer name to choose a printer or imagesetter from the Name list box. If the device driver you require is not listed, install it following the usual Windows procedure.

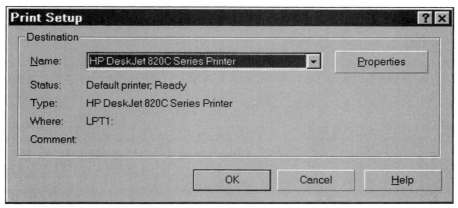

Figure 16-8: The Print Setup dialog box.

Tip

If you're proofing or printing a job in-house, choose the driver for your local printing device. You don't have to personally own a printer to select that printer type, however. If you are creating an image for a service bureau, for example, you can install drivers for that device, and print your image to file. Consult your service bureau for device drivers and setup instructions.

Setting printer properties

To set the device properties:

1. Select File ⇨ Print Setup to display the Print Setup dialog box.

2. Click the Properties button to display the Properties dialog box for the active printer (see Figure 16-9). The Properties dialog box contains several tabs, which allow you to specify printer options. Refer to your printer manual for appropriate time-out and configuration settings.

3. If you're printing to a PostScript device, specify the paper size and orientation. Leave all other options at their default settings. You can specify those in the Print Options dialog box.

4. If you are printing to a non-PostScript device, specify the paper size, resolution, orientation, and any other relevant settings for your printer.

The Properties dialog box may vary for your printer. The dialog box shown in Figure 16-9 is for a Digital DEClaser 1152. Printers, such as the Seiko 835PS and other color printers, frequently have settings that let you select the rendering quality of prints.

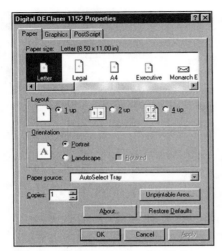

Figure 16-9: The Properties dialog box lets you specify printing options.

Specifying Basic Printing Options

Draw's print dialog box lets you specify a variety of options that are useful for modifying your print job. If you are printing to a non-PostScript printer, you can create separations, as well as specify settings, such as fountain fill steps and proofing options. If you are printing to a PostScript device, you also can specify a variety of advanced PostScript options, such as the way to handle fonts.

Printing tiled images

When you specify the printer properties for your printer, be sure to select the correct size of the paper you're using. If the paper size is inaccurate, it can cause your image to appear offset on the paper. Portions of your document may not print because they fall outside the printable area of the paper. The paper size should be the same as the one specified in the Page Setup dialog box. If your image is larger than the paper on which you are printing, you can tile the image so that it prints across several pieces of paper. Draw prints a small overlap area on each page so that you can assemble the separate pages to create a whole image (see Figure 16-10).

To tile large images when printing:

1. Select File ➪ Print to display the Print dialog box, and then click the Layout tab.

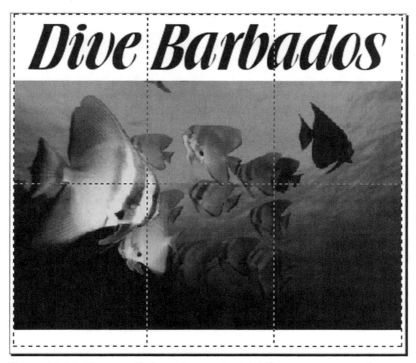

Figure 16-10: You can tile large images to print them across several pages.

2. Enable Print Tiled Pages.

3. Enter the amount you want the tiles to overlap in the Tile Overlap box. You can enter a value or a percentage of the page size.

Tip

> If you are outputting an image for a commercial printer, check the paper sizes that are available. Though the image won't fit the page of your in-house printer, it may well fit the larger output of the commercial printer, making tiling unnecessary.

Placing multiple pages on single printed sheets

Draw enables you to arrange multiple pages of your document so that they print on a single sheet of paper. This feature is useful if you are creating impositions for documents, such as a booklet or catalog. You can also use this feature to arrange several smaller images on larger sheets of paper. Page arrangement options are determined by the settings you specify in the Page Setup dialog box and the size of the paper on which you are printing. If the paper on which you are printing is much larger than the page size in the Page Setup dialog box, then you may be able to fit several pages on a sheet of paper.

You can also reduce the size of the pages if you want to fit multiple pages on a smaller sheet of paper (see Figure 16-11). Each page of your document is placed in a frame, starting from the top left of the sheet of paper. Subsequent pages are placed from left to right and top to bottom. If you use a signature style that already places several pages on a single sheet of paper, such as one of the card styles, the images that would have been placed on an entire sheet of paper are placed in a single frame.

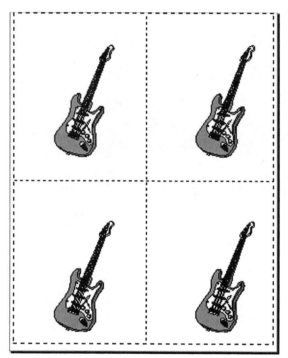

Figure 16-11: You can fit multiple pages on a single sheet of paper.

Note   Draw has a method of printing multipage documents that enable you to choose an Imposition format and a signature layout.

To place multiple pages on a single sheet of paper:

1. Select File ➪ Print Preview to display the Print Preview dialog box (see Figure 16-12).

2. Choose the Imposition Layout tool.

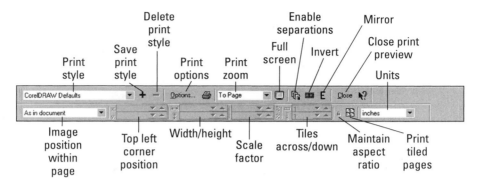

Figure 16-12: The Print Preview Property bar contains the controls for adjusting how your document prints.

3. Choose a format from the Current Imposition Layout drop-down menu. Each page of your document appears in a frame. Alternatively, you can also select an imposition layout from the Layout tab (Ctrl+L) of the Print Options dialog box.

4. After choosing your layout, you have the option to Edit Page Placement. The available placement options are Intelligent Auto Ordering, Sequential Auto Ordering, and Cloned Auto Ordering. How each option places the frames depends on the layout you choose and the number of pages your document contains. For example, if you click the Cloned Auto Ordering button, all the frames on a single sheet of paper contain the same page. If you specified four frames, page 1, for example, would be placed in each of the four frames on the first sheet of paper. Page 2 would appear in each of the four frames on the second sheet of paper, and so forth.

5. To change the margins, select the Edit Margin tool, disable Auto Margins, and enter new values in the margin boxes. You can change the unit of measurement in the Units box, if you desire.

6. If you enable Equal Margins, the left and right margins, as well as the top and bottom margins, become equal.

7. You can adjust the gutters by selecting the Edit Gutters and Finishing tool. Enter values in the Horizontal and Vertical gutter boxes. If you enable Auto Gutter Spacing, Draw automatically calculates the gutter width for you. The gutter is the space between rows and columns.

8. If you enable Maintain Document Page Size, each frame is constrained to the same size as the page size specified for the document. For example, if you create a document on an 8.5 by 11-inch page, the frames are constrained to that size.

9. You can save the layout settings that you specify by clicking the plus (+) next to the Current Imposition Layout dialog box and entering a name. If you select a name, and click the minus (–) button, the selected setting is deleted.

Note   The layout style is not saved automatically. You must specify that Layout Style be saved.

Choosing layout styles

Signature or layout styles, like positioning options, determine how your document is placed on the paper. A booklet or card, for example, frequently places more than one page on a single sheet of paper. You can choose from a variety of preset signature styles in the Print Options dialog box, or you can create a custom style for your document. Generally, you choose the layout style for your document in the Page Setup dialog box when you create a new document. If you selected a layout style using this method, the style appears automatically in the Print Options dialog box. You can change the option in the Print Options dialog box but should use caution when you do.

Caution   Be sure to check the print preview of your document to make sure that the new layout setting doesn't cause a portion of your document to lie outside the printable area of the page.

By default, unless you've specified another layout option, Draw uses the Full Page layout style. If you select another layout style, it affects the printing without changing the original document in the drawing window.

Choosing a signature style

To choose a signature style in the Print Preview window:

1. Select File ➪ Print Preview to display the Print Preview window.

2. Select Settings ➪ Layout and choose a style from the Current Imposition Layout dialog box. Alternatively, you can choose the Imposition Layout tool in the Print Preview window, and choose an Imposition Layout from the drop-down list.

3. Choose an N-up format if you want to change the number of pages printed to a single sheet of paper.

4. Enter the gutter size in the Horizontal and Vertical boxes and choose a unit of measure.

5. Click the arrow in each frame in the preview window to specify the page rotation you desire. The page rotation determines whether a page is printed from top to bottom or from bottom to top (see Figure 16-13).

6. You can print on both sides of the paper by enabling Double-Sided Layout.

Shortcut If you are in the Print Preview window, Ctrl+L accesses the Edit Layout Style dialog box.

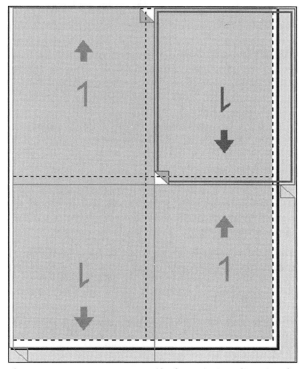

Figure 16-13: You can specify the printing direction by clicking the arrow in each frame of your document while in the Print Preview window.

Creating impositions

If you are printing to a nonduplex printer, the Duplexing Wizard guides you through the process of inserting the pages. Click the Signature Layout flippers at the bottom of the Print Preview window to view each side. Using the method described in the previous exercise, you can create impositions. Imposition refers to the arrangement of pages on a printed sheet, which, when the sheet is finally printed on both sides, folded, and trimmed, will place the pages in their correct order. You can also control which pages are printed in the imposition by clicking the Page Sequence Number arrows on the toolbar. You can also highlight the page number and enter a new number.

Note You can't change the page order unless you have enabled Print All. If you have just Current Page checked, Print Preview will not see any other pages.

Printing color artwork in black or grayscale

When you print your image to a black-and-white printer, such as an inkjet or laser printer, you can specify whether you want solid colors converted to black or a grayscale. Although colored images automatically print in grayscale to a noncolor printer, the printer generally translates the color. If Draw converts the hue of the color to gray, the results are generally a truer grayscale representation of the color. Converting the colors to grayscale also improves the printing time. Printing colors a solid black is useful when you are making separations applications such as screen-printing. This enables you to produce the dense black required to create screens or other applications that require a dense color.

To print color artwork in black or grayscale:

1. Select File ➪ Print Preview.

2. In the Print Preview window, select Settings ➪ Misc Options to display the Misc Options property sheet of the Print Options dialog box.

3. In the Proofing options section, click to enable Full Color, All Colors as Black, or All Colors as Grayscale.

4. Click OK to apply the change and to return to the Print Preview window.

Tip Converting colors to black or grayscale prior to printing on transparency media ensures the density and distribution of color required to stand up to a light source such as an overhead projector or other projection equipment.

Printing bitmaps in chunks

One of the problems that exists when printing to non-PostScript printers is that their memory frequently can't handle a continuous flow of data from your computer. The result is that the images appear choppy or an error occurs, because the stream of data is interrupted while waiting on the printer to catch up. To solve this problem, you can specify that images are sent in chunks of data, rather than a continuous stream. A chunk of data is usually 64K or less. Occasionally, sending data in chunks causes the image to appear to have a grid pattern. If this occurs, you can specify that one chunk overlaps adjacent chunks of data. Overlapping the chunks reduces the grid pattern and produces a better quality print.

To print bitmaps in chunks:

1. Select File ➪ Print Preview.

2. In the Print Preview window, select Settings ➪ Printing Preferences. Select Driver Compatibility to display the Driver Compatibility dialog box.

3. Choose Output Bitmap in 64K Chunks from the Settings list box.

Specifying PostScript Printing Options

The options for PostScript printing devices are more extensive than those for non-PostScript devices. When you specify PostScript options, you can optimize fountain fills, specify font options, and control the way bitmap colors are printed. PostScript settings affect the output of your image, but don't affect the image itself.

Optimizing fountain fills

Fountain fills lend depth and light effects to objects. For fountain fills to effectively create the illusion of depth and light, the transition between colors needs to be smooth. Unfortunately, fountain fills can band, if they aren't optimized. Banding is a condition that occurs when there are insufficient gradient steps to the fill (see Figure 16-14). If the number of transitional steps is too high for the object, the result is a complex object that can cause problems when you try to print the image. If you are printing to a PostScript printer, you can manually modify the number of fountain steps from within the Print Options dialog box. In addition, you can specify that Draw automatically calculate and apply the optimum number of transitional steps. By default, Draw warns you when the number of linear fountain steps is too complex or when there is a risk of banding.

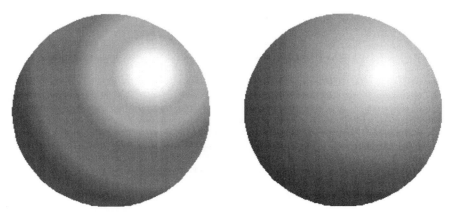

Figure16-14: The object on the left shows the effects of banding; the object on the right has a smoother transition between the colors.

To optimize fountain fills:

1. Select File ➪ Print Preview

2. In the Print Preview dialog box, select Settings ➪ PostScript Preferences to display the PostScript tab of the Print Options dialog box (see Figure 16-15).

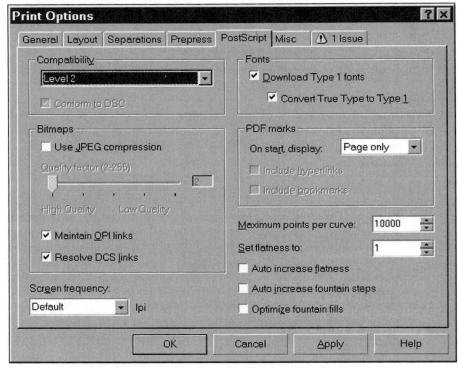

Figure 16-15: The PostScript tab of the Print Options dialog box.

3. Enable the Fountain fill options to use and click OK to return to the Print Preview window. These options are available for PostScript devices only. Use this list of options as a guide in your selection:

- **Banded Fountain Fill Warnings:** When you enable this option, Draw warns you when there is a risk of banding in your image (see Figure 16-16). You can choose to skip the object, continue printing, or cancel the printing operation. If you choose to skip the object or continue, Draw will issue further warnings when it encounters a problem object, unless you enable Disable warnings for this print job. If you choose to cancel the printing operation, you can modify printing options for linear fountain fills to prevent banding problems. No warning statement is issued for radial, conical, or square fountain fills.

- **Auto Increase Fountain Steps:** When you enable this option, Draw automatically increases the number of fountain fill steps to prevent banding. Increasing the fountain steps increases the printing time of your image, but it produces the best printing results.

- **Optimize Fountain Fills:** Sometimes fountain fills create objects that contain too many gradient steps. This happens most frequently with small objects that have custom fountain fills. If you enable this option, Draw automatically decreases the number of fountain fill steps to reduce the complexity of the object and optimize the printed result.

If you are in the Print Preview window, Ctrl+T accesses the PostScript Preferences dialog box.

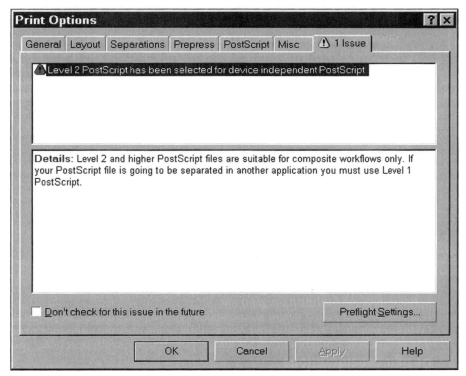

Figure 16-16: Printing alert.

Converting bitmaps to grayscale

By default, color images are sent as grayscale images to black-and-white devices, such as laser printers. Draw converts the image to grayscale at the beginning of the printing process and sends the results to the printer. You can choose to send bitmaps as color images, however, if you want the printer to make the color conversion to grayscale. If you choose this option, the printing time and file size increase. This option is available for PostScript devices only.

To choose a grayscale or color printing option for bitmaps:

1. Select File ⇨ Print Preview.
2. In the Print Preview window, select Settings ⇨ Misc Options to display the Options property sheet of the Print Options dialog box.
3. Choose Grayscale Bitmap Output from the Special Settings list box.
4. Choose either Send Color Bitmaps as Grayscale or Send Color Bitmaps as Color from the Setting list box.

Note
This option can seem confusing to new users. If you are outputting to a color PostScript printer, you don't need to select either of these options. Draw responds to the active printer, so that even if you don't select Send Color Bitmaps as Color, your color bitmaps are printed in color.

Printing color bitmaps as RGB

Some printing devices use a CMY or RGB printing model when printing your document. By default, Draw and PostScript output is normally CMYK. It takes longer for your printer to convert CMYK images to CMY than it does to convert RGB to CMY. You can improve your printing time by sending RGB values to RGB or CMY printers. This option is available for PostScript devices only.

To specify an RGB color model for printing:

1. Select File ⇨ Print Preview.
2. In the Print Preview window, select Settings ⇨ PostScript Preferences to display the PostScript Preferences dialog box.
3. Enable Output color images in RGB and click OK to return to the Print Preview window.

Tip
If you are uncertain whether your printer is CMY, RGB, or both, consult the user's manual for your printer. As a general rule, most desktop laser printers are CMY. Color laser or specialty printers, such as dye sublimation printers, can be either, or they may support both color models.

Downloading Type 1 fonts

Draw downloads Type 1 fonts to PostScript devices by default. When Type 1 fonts are downloaded, Draw automatically converts TrueType fonts to Type 1 fonts for the download. You can specify whether you want Type 1 fonts downloaded, as well as whether you want TrueType fonts converted to Type 1 fonts. If you disable the font-downloading feature, your fonts are printed as bitmap or curve objects. This is useful if your document contains a large number of fonts and your printer has limited memory, or if you want to reduce the download time.

To specify font downloading options:

1. Select File ➪ Print Preview.

2. In the Print Preview window, select Settings ➪ PostScript Preferences and enable or disable Download Type 1 fonts.

3. Click OK to apply the changes and to return to the Print Preview window.

Note

Draw only downloads those fonts that are not resident in your printer. You should only disable the Convert TrueType to Type 1 option if your printer has difficulty interpreting the Type 1 fonts and produces a PostScript printing error. This option is especially useful if you are creating documents that use a large number of different fonts, such as an advertisement or catalogue. The printing time is reduced, and you don't have to be concerned about font availability at your service bureau or commercial printer.

Using Color Management

WYSIWYG (What You See Is What You Get) is a term that's been used a great deal in relation to computer graphics. It's also a myth, and here's why. No two monitors display color in precisely the same way. Like the computers to which they are attached, monitors are like snowflakes. Monitors display RGB color, which is the widest range of discernible color, surpassed only by the capability of the human eye. Most printers and printshops use CMYK colors when they print your image. Software and CMYK printers translate the RGB values to CMYK values at print time. The reality is that the printed image will never be identical to what you see on the monitor. It's not as grim as it sounds, however. If you use color management to calibrate Draw, what you see will be very close to what you get. Good color management is critical, if you don't want to be disappointed when your image is printed.

Specifying color correction

Draw enables you to select the type of color correction to use. You can choose to preview the printer's colors. If you choose Display Simulated Printer Colors, you can choose the printer to simulate. For the results to be accurate, you must first have created a system profile in Draw's color management tools. Draw uses the system profile to change the view you see on your monitor to match the colors of your output device. If you simulate your printer, you can also specify that Draw warn you of colors that are out-of-gamut colors.

Cross-Reference For more information on creating system profiles with Draw's color management tools, see Chapter 14.

To specify color correction:

1. Select Tools ⇨ Options, expand Global, and click Color Management (see Figure 16-17).

2. Choose the type of color correction to use by selecting which type of printer to simulate.

3. Click OK to return to the drawing window. Draw updates your document and the onscreen palette to reflect the change.

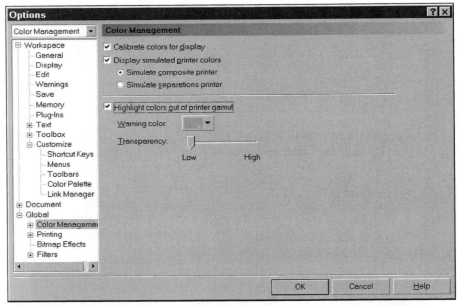

Figure 16-17: You can simulate your printer's colors on the Color Management page of the Options dialog box.

Specifying a gamut color

Gamut is the range of colors your printer is capable of printing. If a color falls outside the range, Draw fills the object with the gamut color you specify. This enables you to choose a different color for your fill. If you don't change the color of an object that's outside the range of gamut, Draw fills that object at print time with the closest viable color.

Working with a Service Bureau

Service bureaus are the best choice if you require high-resolution output for your documents. If your document contains photos or other color graphic elements, and you require a large number of copies, this is your best option. A service bureau outputs your file to film. The film is then taken to a commercial printshop and used to create the plates that are used to print your document. A number of printshops have service bureau capability. Contact your printshop to determine their capabilities.

Communication is essential!

Draw is one of the most flexible graphics programs available. You can customize dozens of features, including printing. The result is that there are few hard and fast rules to operating Draw. One item, however, goes beyond a rule directly to an edict: *Communication is essential when you are using a service bureau!* It's not an option. Failure to consult your service bureau, communicate your needs, and exchange information is inviting disaster.

Choosing a file format

Some service bureaus are capable of processing .cdr files; others are not. If the service bureau you've selected is capable of processing a .cdr file, you only need to verify two factors:

✦ That they are using Draw 9

✦ That they have the fonts specified in your document

With previous versions of Draw

If they are using Draw versions 5 to 8, you can save your file in that format for processing. I recommend saving the file under a new name when you use Save As to create a version 5 to 8 format file. This ensures that your original drawing isn't altered. Due to feature changes, previous versions don't support some of the features that are available in Draw 9, and the appearance of your drawing may be altered.

Tip

An alternative solution to this problem is to export your drawing from Draw as an .eps file. If the service bureau supports .eps files, they can import the file into other applications and output the file to film.

Using PostScript print files

Frequently, a service bureau prefers a .prn file. A .prn file is a PostScript print file. Print files contain all the information, such as font information, required to print your document on a remote device that doesn't have Draw. If you select a service bureau that requires a .prn file, install and configure a device driver for the imagesetter that the service bureau uses, such as a Linotronic imagesetter. Use this checklist as a guide to preparing a .prn file for a service bureau:

Note   This checklist does not eliminate the need to discuss your print job with the service bureau.

✦ Set the resolution in the Printer Properties dialog box as specified by the service bureau.

✦ When you specify a paper size in the Printer Properties, be sure that the width is always the smaller value, then set the orientation. Make sure that the paper size you specify allows enough room for your image, as well as any prepress marks, such as crop marks.

✦ Verify that you have the correct output device selected as the default device, and that Print to File is selected as the port.

✦ If the service bureau uses a Macintosh front-end, be sure that both Print to File and For Mac are enabled.

✦ Enable any required prepress marks such as crop marks or registration marks.

✦ Print out the job information sheet to include with your file.

✦ If the service bureau and commercial printshop are separate businesses, make sure that the service bureau outputs the film in the format that the printshop requires. Some commercial printshops create plates from film positives; others from film negatives.

The Open Prepress Interface

Draw supports open prepress interface. This is a layout and printing method that lets you use low-resolution bitmaps as placeholders in your document and substitute their high-resolution equivalents at press time. When you use OPI (Open Prepress Interface), your service bureau scans two images: a high-resolution image and a low-resolution replica. The service bureau retains the high-resolution image on file, and gives you the low-resolution image to position in your layout. The low-resolution image is called FPO, For Position Only, and is either a .tif or .ct format.

Importing FPO images

FPO resolution isn't high enough to support quality printing, but it's sufficient for placement and proofing of your document. By importing the FPO image for layout placement, you keep your document size smaller and improve screen refresh speed. When you've finished creating your document and are ready to have the films prepared, your service bureau substitutes the high-resolution images back into your document. The result is high quality films with the minimum of impact on your computer's resources.

When using FPO images, remember that:

✦ You need to import the images correctly so that you maintain the OPI link. If the link is broken, your images will not be replaced at print time.

✦ The modifications that you can make to FPO images are limited. You can scale, crop, and rotate FPO images, but you can't apply any other transformations or effects to them.

✦ You *must not* rename these image files. The names establish the link to the high-resolution file.

To import an FPO image into your document:

1. Select File ➪ Import to display the Import dialog box.

2. Choose the file to import and enable Link to high resolution file for output using OPI (see Figure 16-18).

3. Click Import. When an OPI file is imported, the Maintain OPI links option is automatically enabled in the PostScript Preferences dialog box.

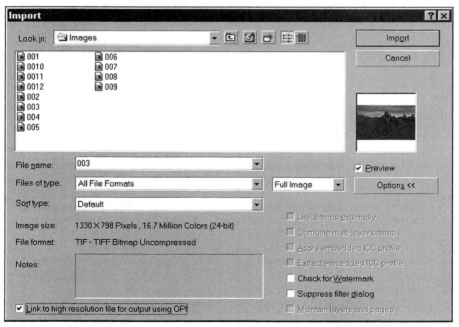

Figure 16-18: Enable Link to high resolution file for output using OPI in the Import dialog box.

Proofing OPI image files

If you want to proof a file that contains OPI images, select Settings ➪ PostScript Preferences in the Print Preview window. Disable Maintain OPI Links. You can then print the file on your desktop PostScript laser printer for proofing. Be sure to reenable Maintain OPI Links when you are finished proofing the image.

Creating Color Separations

When you create a multicolor document to be printed on a commercial press, either you, the service bureau, or the printshop must create separations of the image before it can be printed. The process of creating CMYK (Cyan, Magenta, Yellow, and Black) separations involves analyzing the colors in your image and converting them to percentages of each of the four ink colors. This separates your image into four images, each representing one of the four CMYK process colors. Each process color is printed on a separate sheet of film or paper. Figure 16-19 shows a representation of how each of the four-color sheets would look.

Specifying spot colors

If you have specified spot colors in your image, each spot color is printed on a separate sheet of film or paper. Generally, it's not a good idea to combine spot colors with process color in a single job. An exception to this is when you are preparing a document for a company where a logo or other graphic needs to be a specific color to meet trademark rules. In this case, you are generally dealing with one or two spot colors at the most. I don't recommend using more than two spot colors with a process color job, however. The primary reason is that it increases the number of separations for your document and raises the cost. You can convert spot colors to process colors when you print your document.

Tip

One way to save money on a print job is to choose a single spot color or a single spot color plus black for your document. Use percentages of that color to fill the objects in your drawing. You can make this a simple process by creating a custom palette with a range of percentages of a single spot PANTONE color, and displaying the palette in the drawing window. When the document is printed, it prints on a single sheet of film or paper, saving film and plate costs.

Using the Print Options dialog box

When you create separations for press, Draw enables you to specify a variety of options in the Print Options dialog box. You can access the Print Options dialog box from either the Print dialog box or the Print Preview window. The options you select should be based on the advice of your service bureau or commercial printshop. Select the options to use, and click Close to apply the options and return to either the Print Preview window or the Print dialog box.

Cyan   Yellow

Magenta   Black

Figure 16-19: Each process color of the separation is printed on a single sheet of film or paper.

Applying color options

Draw enables you to specify color options when you print your document. For example, you can print spot colors as CMYK, choose Hexachrome colors, and print color separations. Printing spot colors as CMYK or process colors lets you reduce the cost of your print job by reducing the number of plates required to print the job. Hexachrome color is a PANTONE process color system based on the CMYK color model, but it adds two additional inks, bright orange and green, for a total of six inks and a broader range of colors. Not all printshops support the Hexachrome option. Consult your printshop to inquire if this option is required.

To specify color options:

1. Select File ➪ Print Preview to access the Print Preview window.

2. In the Print Preview window, select Settings ➪ Separations to display the Separations property sheet of the Print Options dialog box (see Figure 16-20).

3. Choose the settings to use and click Close to apply the settings and to return to the Print Preview window.

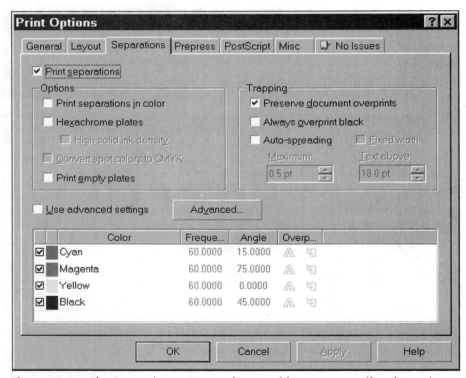

Figure 16-20: The Separations property sheet enables you to specify color options and to print proofs or separations of your images before you send them to a commercial printer.

Tip   Printing color separations is an excellent in-house proofing tool. You can print your separations in color on transparency media, then check the registration and color by superimposing the transparencies.

Working with trapping

Color trapping is essential to compensate for registration problems that appear when your image is printed. Registration problems occur when print plates are not perfectly aligned or slip on the press. The result of poor registration is that the paper color shows between overlapping objects (see Figure 16-21).

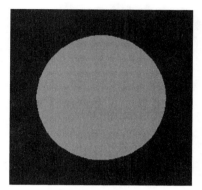

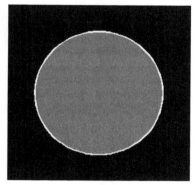

Properly trapped   Without trapping

Figure 16-21: A properly trapped image has no white space between overlapping objects.

Tip   Many service bureaus provide color-trapping services when they create the films of your image. They have software designed for this purpose. Check with your service bureau to determine whether you need to trap your image.

Understanding overprinting

Normally, when an image is separated, the area where objects overlap is not printed. The effect on the separation is that objects that reside below overlapping objects appear trimmed or "knocked out." Figure 16-22 shows the results of normal trapping. The objects have been separated to illustrate how the trapping process trims objects.

In the illustration, the black polygon is the bottom-most object; the rectangle overlaps the polygon. The circle is the top object and overlaps both the rectangle and the polygon. By default, Draw traps objects by overprinting. When overprinting is applied, the top object is superimposed over the object below. The result is that the area of the bottom object that is obscured by an object above prints in its entirety. Using the example shown in Figure 16-22, all of the objects would print as whole objects, instead of being trimmed. This makes it impossible for the paper color to show between the objects.

Figure 16-22: Normal trapping without overprinting.

Overprinting and Imprinted Media Applications

For most purposes, overprinting works as a method of trapping. It does not work well for some applications, such as screen-printing and embroidery applications, however. Screen-printing inks are very thick, and, frequently, lighter inks are laid down after darker, more intense inks. Overprinting to achieve trapping for screen printing applications causes the ink to be too thick, which impairs the drying process, and causes the media, such as a T-shirt, to be unacceptably stiff. The problem is similar for embroidery or similar applications. Overlapping the thread completely would be unacceptable.

To solve this problem, specify that trapping overprint the outline of objects only. The overlap creates the trap (more information about trapping individual objects appears later in this chapter).

Using automatic trapping

To trap your image:

1. In the Print Preview window, select Settings ➪ Separations to display the Separations property sheet of the Print Options dialog box (see Figure 16-23).

2. Enable Auto-spreading. Draw will automatically trap your image. You can specify the amount of the trap by entering a maximum amount for the overlap.

3. If you want to lock the amount of the overlap, enable the Fixed width option for Auto-spreading.

4. Enter the minimum text size you want to trap. The default is 18 points.

5. Click OK to apply the changes and to return to the Print Preview window.

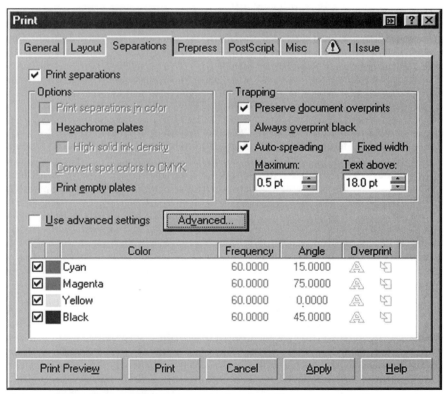

Figure 16-23: The Separations property sheet enables you to specify separation options for printing your document.

Text under 18 points should never be trapped. Trapping smaller text sizes can make the text difficult to read because it obscures the detail of smaller font sizes.

One of the problems associated with autotrapping is that it traps every object in your drawing. This can create a color distortion problem if a light color is applied over a darker or more intense color. It can also create problems with applications that require separations but are not going to a commercial offset press, such as screen-printing applications.

Manually trapping objects

To avoid the problems associated with autotrapping, you can manually trap individual objects or separations—enabling you to overprint an outline or fill of an individual object or selected color separations, or to specify a black overprinting option—as described in the following sections.

Tip

Overprinting black is useful when your document contains a large amount of black text and few overlapping graphics. Overprinting black results in clear text, but should be used with caution when your image contains a large amount of over-lapping graphics with little text.

Overprinting an outline or fill

To overprint an outline or fill of an individual object:

1. Right-click the object to overprint. The right mouse button menu will appear.

2. Select Overprint and then either Fill or Outline.

Tip

If you choose to overprint the outline of an object and it's not the same color as the fill, enable Behind Fill in the Outline dialog box, and double the width of the fill. Generally, a 0.05-inch outline is effective to solve most trapping problems. You may need to adjust the amount of the overlap to suit your application. This enables the outline to overlap both the selected object and any objects it overlaps.

Overprinting selected color separations

To overprint selected color separations:

1. In the Print Preview window, select Settings ⇨ Separations and enable Print Separations and Use Advanced Settings.

2. Click the Advanced Settings button to display the Separations tab of the Print Options dialog box (see Figure 16-24).

3. Choose the color separation to overprint.

4. Enable Overprint Color.

5. Enable Graphics, Text, or both by clicking the appropriate icons, and then click OK to apply the change and to return to the Print Options dialog box. There is also the option to specify halftone types, a topic that is discussed later in this chapter.

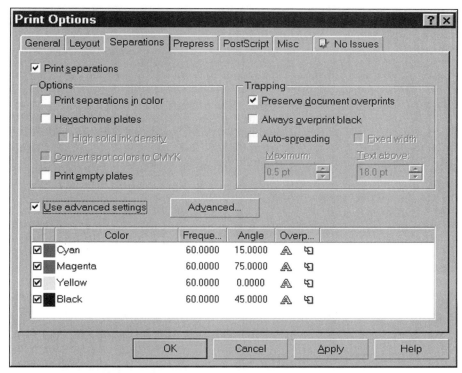

Figure 16-24: The Separations tab of the Print Options dialog box.

Tip

I don't recommend selecting a light color separation, such as yellow. This can cause color distortion, as darker colors will show through the yellow in your final print.

Specifying black overprinting options

To specify black overprinting options:

1. In the Print Preview window, select Settings ➪ Separations and enable Print Separations.

2. To always overprint black, enable Always Overprint Black.

Caution

If your document contains a number of dark objects, selecting Always Overprint Black can cause a color distortion in your image. For best results, consult your service bureau or commercial printer if you aren't sure whether to specify Always Overprint Black.

Specifying Invert and Mirror

Invert and Mirror settings determine the way your image prints on film. If you specify Invert, your image will be printed as a negative on the film. When this option is disabled, your image prints as a positive on the film. Mirror settings determine on which side of the film your image is printed. Mirror is useful when you need to print your image in reverse. For example, if you were printing your image for imprinted media purposes, you would want to print the image in reverse if it contained text. Doing so ensures that your text is correct when it is re-created on the final product.

Note   For most commercial printing purposes, neither of these options needs to be enabled. To determine whether you need to specify either of these options, consult your service bureau or printshop.

To specify Invert and Mirror:

1. In the Print Preview window, click the Invert button to enable it.

2. Click the Mirror button to enable it.

Draw applies your choices, and the image in the Print Preview window changes to reflect the settings.

Using printer's marks

Draw lets you print registration and other printer's marks on your separations. You can choose these marks by selecting the Marks Placement Tool and clicking the Prepress button on the toolbar. Alternatively, in the Print Preview window, you can select Settings ➪ Prepress to display the Prepress tab of the Print Options dialog box (see Figure 16-25). Use these descriptions as a guide in making your selection from among the available Prepress options:

✦ **Print file information:** Selecting this option prints a page containing information about your file.

✦ **Print page numbers:** Prints the page numbers on your document.

✦ **Print crop marks:** Prints crop marks for the printshop. Crop marks note where you want the paper to be trimmed.

✦ **Print registration marks:** Enables the printshop to align the separations of your document by placing alignment marks on the film or paper. These marks can be placed outside the boundary of the image. If you choose this option, be sure to specify a paper size that is larger than the page size you specified in Draw.

✦ **Color calibration bar:** Prints a bar of six colors: red, green, blue, cyan, yellow, and magenta. This option lets the printshop verify the quality of the color.

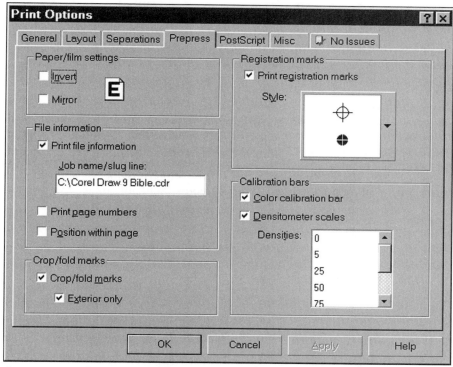

Figure 16-25: The Prepress tab of the Print Options dialog box enables you to print file information and printer's marks on your separations.

- ✦ **Densitometer scales:** Prints a range of grayscale colors that can be measured with a densitometer to gauge the consistency, accuracy, and quality of the output.

- ✦ **Invert:** Prints the image in negative colors, similar to a photonegative.

- ✦ **Mirror:** Prints the image with the emulsion down. The result is that the image appears in reverse. For example, text appears backwards.

Choosing halftone screens

When you print separations, halftone screens are used to simulate shades of color. Halftone screens are made up of regular patterns of dots in varying sizes. As dots increase in size and frequency, the intensity of the color increases, resulting in a darker or more pure shade of the color. If you were creating CMYK separations, for example, each of the four colors would print as a halftone screen. As the image was printed on a press, the superimposed screens would provide the correct blend of overlapping inks to create the colors in your image. The attributes of the halftone screen determine the final color of the print. Each screen is set at a different angle, to prevent moiré patterns. Moiré patterns occur when superimposed halftone screens are set at the wrong angle. The result is a checkered appearance in your final print. Setting the screens at different angles to one another normally eliminates moiré effects.

Draw lets you specify the halftone type, screen angle, frequency, and screen technology of halftone screens. The halftone type of a screen describes the shape of the individual dots. Although the dots are usually round or diamond-shaped, you can change the shape of the dots to another shape. This is useful for creating special effects with halftone screens. The screen angle is the angle of the pattern of the halftone screen. The frequency of a screen is measured in lpi, and is determined by the quality of output desired. Generally, you should not change the screen angle and frequency of the screen, unless your service bureau directs you to do so. You should also check with your service bureau to determine the appropriate screen technology for your image. The screen technology should be set to match the imagesetter used for outputting your film.

To specify halftone screen settings:

1. In the Print Preview window, select Settings ⇨ Separations to display the Separations property sheet of the Settings dialog box.

2. Enable Print Separations and Use Advanced Settings.

3. Click the Advanced button to display the Advanced Settings dialog box. Advanced halftone screen options are available for PostScript devices only.

4. Click the down arrow next to Halftone type, choose a halftone from the drop-down menu, and then click OK to return to the Settings dialog box.

Tip If you are unsure what screen angles and frequency to specify, consult your service bureau, or accept the default screen angle and frequency.

Summary

Printing is a topic that could easily become a book. The variety of output devices and their individual requirements are diverse. This chapter skimmed printing as a topic by showing you how to produce successful output from Draw. Most of the problems associated with printing can be avoided if you configure your in-house output device correctly. If you are sending a file to a service bureau, or the document is going to be commercially printed, communicating your needs to these businesses goes a long way toward avoiding problems. Most service bureaus and printshops are more than willing to assist you in getting the best quality output possible. They possess the specialized technical knowledge necessary, relieving you of the need to become a printing guru. In this chapter, you learned to

✦ Specify printing options

✦ Preview your document

✦ Choose an output device

✦ Work with service bureaus

✦ Apply trapping

✦ Use color correction

✦ Use printer's marks

✦   ✦   ✦

Publishing on the Web

Draw provides the tools to produce single or multipage documents for publication on the World Wide Web (WWW). Using the steps introduced throughout the tutorials in this chapter, you create a Web site for La Aquila Coffee Co. (LACC). Because Draw does not behave like other HTML editing programs, you'll be presented with challenges that are unique to the way Draw creates and publishes Web pages. The LACC Web site will have multiple Web pages, and instead of creating separate documents in Draw, you'll create a single multipage document. Creating a single document ensures that all the pieces relevant to your Web site are contained in the same location in the event that you need to modify the site later.

Creating Images for the WWW

Although the basic layout and design principles required for creating Web documents are not all that different from those required for producing documents for print media, the similarity ends there. Once you get past the issue of portability when creating a document for print media, the size of your document and the quantity of effects it contains don't matter. In the end, it is transferred to film — frequently by an imagesetter — and from there to paper. The end viewer doesn't know, or care, about the size of the file. On the Web, however, the viewer interacts more with the file itself. The file, including all the images, sounds, and, perhaps, interactive elements must be downloaded to the viewer's computer. The download time of Web documents is critical to the success of a Web page. In addition to download time, the author of a Web page needs to pay attention to a variety of design issues for the document to reach the widest audience possible.

Why the World Wide Web?

The WWW is one of the fastest growing and evolving areas in the computer industry. Web surfers can tell you that a broad range of Web pages is available for perusing. These pages range from the simplistic home page to some exotic corporate pages that incorporate animation and audio. The reality is, that for all the sophistication you might see on some Web sites, Web page creation and design is in its infancy.

Interest in the Web comes from all quarters of the global community. It seems that nearly everyone who is an active online computer user has a page, or is planning to create one. As a vehicle for changing the face of our lives, the potential is mind-boggling.

Learning a new language

If you are new to the WWW or to creating Web pages, you're going to discover that there's a whole new language involved. Understanding what some of the terms mean can go a long way toward demystifying creating Web pages. While the following list is by no means a complete listing of all the terms you'll discover during your Web adventure, it serves as a basic list for the terms used both in this chapter and in working with Web documents. Other terms and definitions appear throughout this chapter to help guide you in creating successful Web documents.

✦ **Browser:** A browser is an application that lets you connect via a modem to the WWW, as well as to other services on the Internet. Although a variety of browsers are available, the two most common browsers are Netscape Communicator and Internet Explorer. Browsers let you access URL addresses to view Web pages and FTP sites, as well as manage other Internet tasks, such as mail and newsgroups.

✦ **ISP:** An ISP is an Internet Service Provider. These organizations provide connection services that enable you to connect to the Internet. They can be large providers, such as AOL or CompuServe, or they can be small independent providers that serve your local area. Regardless of the size of the provider, ISPs let you access the Internet and such services as the WWW or e-mail. Some ISPs provide space for their customers to maintain Web pages, and provide CGI scripts that enable Internet objects.

✦ **Bookmark:** A bookmark is a unique name or hyperlink that you can assign to text or graphics in your Web document. A bookmark functions as an address, or URL, for the object to which it's assigned. When the viewer clicks a bookmarked object, the browser moves to the associated object or location. It can be used to access another portion of the same document or a location in another document. You can assign bookmarks to objects using the Internet Objects toolbar, the Internet page in the Object Properties docker window, or the Internet Links submenu in an object's right mouse button menu.

✦ **Uniform Resource Locator:** A Uniform Resource Locator (URL) is an address that defines where a document is found on the Internet, such as `http://www.rainwatermedia.com/cd8bible`. The `http` identifies the type of Internet resource that's being requested, such as the WWW (http) or FTP. The next portion, `www.rainwatermedia.com`, identifies the server where the document is located and is followed by the directory structure, `cd8bible`. Some URLs include another portion, such as `/info.htm`, which identifies a specific filename. When you specify addresses, it must exactly match the URL address to which you want to connect. Because of the way most Web documents are stored, URLs are also case sensitive. To connect to a page, or to a specific location on a page within the document you're browsing, enter the specific address. You can assign URLs to objects using the Internet Objects toolbar, the Internet page in the Object Properties docker window, or the Internet Links submenu in an object's right mouse button context menu.

✦ **Hyperlink:** A hyperlink is a text or graphical hyperlink known as hypertext or hypergraphic, respectively. It is used to change to the URL address associated with the link. Hypergraphics utilize a hotspot to identify the clickable location associated with the address. The hotspot can be an entire graphical object or a portion of a graphical object. You determine whether the hotspot follows the contours of the object or whether the hotspot fills the object's entire bounding box. You can't apply hotspots to hypertext.

✦ **Internet layer:** When you create a Web document in Draw, HTML text and Internet objects, including Java or Barista applets, are placed on a separate layer that resides above all other graphic layers in the document. This layer is called the Internet layer. The Internet layer is created automatically when you add an Internet object or import an object that must be placed on the layer. To function correctly in a Web browser, no object on the Internet layer can intersect or overlap another object on the layer. Graphical objects to which you assign URLs reside on the graphic layers and use image maps to store their Internet properties. These objects are not considered Internet objects.

✦ **CGI:** CGI, or Common Gateway Interface, is a scripting language that enables Internet objects such as forms and other interactive Internet elements. Generally, these scripts are server-side scripts, which means they are put in place by your ISP. It's less common for these scripts to be client-side scripts that reside locally on your computer. Web pages that contain Internet elements requiring viewer feedback, such as order forms, generally employ these scripts to provide an interface for the return of information. For more information about using CGI scripts, I recommend you contact your ISP.

✦ **Internet object:** An Internet object can be a button, user text box, form, or other element that normally returns information from the viewer to you, the author of the Web document. It can also be used as an interactive element to control the events that occur on a Web page. Internet objects can be Java-enabled or can require CGI scripting to control the event.

Caution   Most ISPs use UNIX or LINUX operating systems. The command language for these operating systems is extremely case sensitive. A common mistake that people make when creating Web pages is to name a file or file extension using one case, and specify the filename in the HTML code using another case. To UNIX and LINUX, mixing the cases in this way is the same as misspelling the filename, and causes an error when the file can't be located. To avoid this problem, I recommend you develop a habit of *always* naming files and pages using *only* lowercase letters.

Creating successful Web designs

Earlier in this book I discussed the myth of WYSIWYG (What You See Is What You Get) as it related to printed output. Because Web graphics are designed to be displayed on a monitor and less frequently printed, WYSIWYG approaches reality rather than myth. Unlike printed documents that rely predominantly on text to relay information, the Web's visual nature has different requirements. If you think about the information you want to present, you'll find that you can pack a lot of information into smaller blocks of text intermixed with graphics that help relay the information. Meeting all the requirements that are associated with these factors is a challenging task. Traditional concepts and rules for layout and design have to be revamped for online display.

Design considerations

Although there's no substitute for sound layout and design practices, the rules for creating Web pages require that you rethink some conventional ideas and concepts in order to create successful Web designs. These factors need to be considered when designing graphics for Web use:

- ✦ Layout
- ✦ Unit of measurement
- ✦ Resolution
- ✦ Color depth
- ✦ File size
- ✦ HTML restrictions
- ✦ Image size
- ✦ File format

Tip   When creating documents to publish on the Internet, you make decisions that affect the resolution and display speed of your document by balancing factors such as color depth and the size of images with the speed of Web transmission. Remember that the larger the file size, the longer it takes the user's browser to download and display images contained in your Web page.

Determining the page type

Preplanning is the key to a successful Web page. Determine what elements you want to include on the page, how you want the viewer to navigate through the page, and the type of page you want to create. Draw lets you create three types of Web pages:

Note

You can also create pages that incorporate elements from more than one of these three types of documents.

✦ **HTML:** Standard HTML (Hypertext Markup Language) pages are the easiest to create. HTML is a language of markup tags that describes the layout and elements of a document. Using tags, you can add resources such as images, sound, animation, and video to a Web page. Draw uses a table-type format as the basis for placing the elements in your Web document.

✦ **Barista:** Barista is a Java-based format that lets you save Web documents as Java applets. Java gives you broader formatting control, while still supporting most HTML features, such as tables, hyperlinks, and graphics. When you save a Web image as a Barista file, text is converted to curves and isn't editable within a browser.

✦ **Single-image pages:** Single-image pages generally refer to image maps. Draw lets you turn any drawing into an image map for publication on the Web (see Figure 17-1). You can add hotspots to the document that make calls to other Web pages or to files stored with your Web page.

Caution

Before creating a Web document, read the sidebar "Troubleshooting in Advance." It contains information that is critical to the success of your Web documents.

Publishing Documents on the Web

This chapter is not intended to be the definitive guide to publishing documents on the WWW. Draw automates much of the process for you. Although knowledge of HTML isn't essential to creating Internet documents in Draw, it might be helpful to have a more in-depth understanding of HTML.

Many thousands of pages have been written about publishing documents on the WWW. Extensive *how to* topics, such as coding restrictions and CGI scripting, I've left to the able hands of others. If you need assistance in these areas, or are just getting started with Web design, I recommend these books: *Creating Web Pages for Dummies* (Second Edition), by Bud Smith and Arthur Bebak, and *HTML Publishing Secrets*, by Jim Heid.

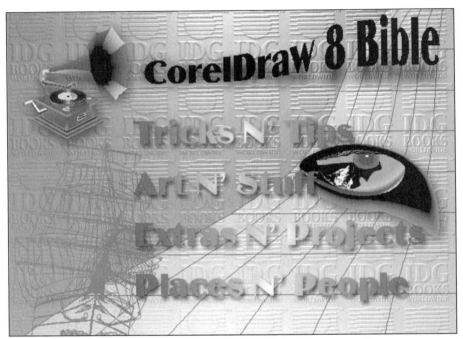

Figure 17-1: This Web page is an image map. When your pointer rolls over a mapped area, the linked URL is displayed at the bottom of the browser window. Clicking a mapped area takes you to the associated URL.

Designing HTML documents

Draw creates Web documents using a table layout by default. A table is a flexible grid of rows and columns. Tables let you place objects anywhere on the drawing page. The invisible HTML table behind the scenes adjusts to fit the layout automatically (see Figure 17-2). You can incorporate both text and graphic hyperlinks in your document. Additionally, you can add Internet objects, such as buttons and other interactive elements, to your document (be sure to check with your ISP about CGI scripts).

When creating graphics for your HTML document, you can apply special effects, such as extrusions and blends. Because all graphics are displayed at a maximum resolution of 96 dpi (dots per inch), preview any document that contains fountain fills, blends, lens effects, or extrusions to be sure that the objects don't band when displayed as low-resolution bitmaps. For best results, avoid the use of spot colors in Web documents. These colors tend to translate unpredictably from one system to the next.

Note   Because Draw supports animated gif files, you can add animation to your Draw Web documents.

> ## *Before you enter, please read!*
>
> The Dementia Web Design Art Gallery is a VRML environment. In order to view this area of our site, you must have Cosmo Player or any other 3D content viewer plug-in installed to your browser. Most browsers come with a 3D plug-in and you probably already have it installed. If you do not have a 3D plug-in, follow <u>this link</u>, download and install the plug-in and then come right back!
>
>
>
> If you already have a VRML plug-in, click on the logo below and have fun! Oh, by the way, the images on the walls in the gallery are very low resolution. To get a better view of any image just click directly on the one you want to see!
>
>
>
> If you have never visited a site which contains VRML, please read further:
>
> VRML is used to create virtual reality environments for the Web. Once you enter the page, use your mouse or arrow buttons to move through the space in real time. The arrow buttons are much easier to use to control movement. You can go in any direction you like at any time while within the VRML environment. Hold the shift key down while pressing the arrow keys to move faster when walking through the rooms. Enjoy!

Figure 17-2: This Web page, by Dementia Web Design, is a standard HTML document that incorporates hypertext to provide links to other sites.

Draw lets you import a variety of bitmap elements for use in your Web documents. You can even include animated gif files. Animated gifs don't animate within Draw, but the animation is visible when you display your htm file in a browser.

To insert an animated gif into your Web document:

1. Open the document in Draw to which you want to add an animated gif file.

2. Select File ➪ Import and then select the animated gif you want to import. Enable Link Bitmap Externally.

3. Click Import. Draw imports the animated gif.

When you publish your document to the Internet and display the document in a browser, the gif animates. For best results, copy the animated gif file to the folder where your htm document is stored *prior* to importing the gif into Draw. This helps ensure that the link won't be broken when you transfer your files to the Internet because of a change in the path. Remember to include this file when you upload your Web page to the Internet.

Tip Before publishing your Web document, select and group dynamically linked objects, such as blends and extrusions, even though they are shown as a "blend group." Grouping creates a single object and prevents them from being seen, exported, and loaded as separate objects in your HTML document.

Designing image maps

Draw's single-image or image-map format, exports your document as one bitmap with hotspots that you specify. Each hotspot is linked to an associated URL. Unlike other Web documents, Draw doesn't load one element at a time; instead, Draw loads the document in its entirety, making file size a critical factor. Factors such as page size and color depth determine the file size and, ultimately, the amount of time it takes for viewers to download your image to their computer. Image maps create two files: an htm file that contains the HTML code for the image and a jpg or gif file that contains the image.

Note   Although you can include image maps as an element in other types of HTML documents, you can't include other types of elements, such as animation, Java applets, or Internet objects, in image maps.

Defining hotspots

Specifying the hotspots (hyperlinks) on an image map or in an HTML document is basic to creating a Web document. Draw makes it easy to specify links that connect viewers to another URL. The first step toward specifying links is to display your image in the drawing window. Have a URL list ready of the linked addresses that you want to include. Draw lets you specify a link in two ways: You can either specify that the link maps to the object itself or that it links to the object's bounding box. If you have objects close together on the page, you may want to have the link map to the object. When the viewer looks at your page on the Web, the cursor changes to a hand with a pointing finger when it passes over a link hotspot.

To specify a hotspot:

1. Select Tools ➪ Options, select Customize, check Internet Objects in the Toolbars window, and then click OK to display the Internet toolbar in the drawing window. Like all toolbars, you can place this anywhere in the drawing window, or dock it on a side of the window. Draw's Internet toolbar contains everything you need to specify a hotspot and its associated URL (see Figure 17-3).

Figure 17-3: The Internet toolbar lets you specify the URL of an assigned hotspot.

2. In the drawing window, use the Pick tool to select the object for which you want to create a link. The object can be a single object, an object group, text, or any other object.

3. In the Location (URL) box, enter the address to which you want to add a link. Typically these are either www or ftp (file transfer protocol) addresses. For example, if you wanted to place a link to IDG books, you'd enter the URL `http://www.idgbooks.com` in the Location box. Note that most addresses are all lowercase and have no spaces.

4. You can also specify a bookmark by entering the information in the Bookmark box (see "Working with Bookmarks" later in this chapter).

5. Click either the Use Object Shape to Define Hotspot or Use Bounding Box to Define Hotspot button. This designates where the viewer needs to click to go to the specified URL.

6. For editing purposes, you can view which items are designated as hotspots. Click the Show Internet Objects button to view link objects (see Figure 17-4). If you want to choose a foreground and background color to aid your editing, click the color chips beside the Show Internet Objects button and select a color. These colors don't affect the colors in your image; they just make it easier to spot hotspots for editing purposes.

7. Save your file in cdr format for archive purposes. If you need to edit a hotspot or the image later, you will be able to easily retrieve the file.

Figure 17-4: Show Internet Objects makes it easier to identify hotspots in your image.

Creating an Internet page setup

Creating the page setup is one of the most important tasks involved in creating a Web page in Draw. It's a good idea to specify basic page settings before you start creating a Web page in Draw. Unlike HTML editors, the page size doesn't expand and contract to fit the quantity of information contained on the page. Although you can change the page size at any time during the creation process, remember that any elements that extend beyond the page are truncated and won't appear when you display your document in a browser.

When you specify page settings, you can save them so that they are available for future Draw sessions. Draw offers a workspace designed for creating Internet documents in the Options dialog box. You can use this preset workspace, design one of your own, or change options as needed for use with the active document. If you create Internet documents frequently, I recommend that you either use the preset workspace or create a workspace that meets your needs. Workspaces let you specify ruler, text, image, and other settings that pertain specifically to Internet documents.

Specifying ruler settings

The very nature of the WWW is one of displaying graphics. In other words, documents are created for display on monitors, rather than as printed media. Pixels are the standard unit of measure when you create Internet documents. For best results, specify that your rulers use pixels as the unit of measure.

To specify ruler settings:

1. Select Tools ⇨ Options and expand the Document category. Click Rulers to display the Rulers page.

2. In the Units section, click the down arrow next to Horizontal and choose pixels from the drop-down list.

3. Enable Same Units for Horizontal and Vertical Rulers.

4. Click OK to return to the drawing window.

Note   When you specify the horizontal unit of measurement, it also becomes the default unit. This means that other dialog boxes, roll-ups, and dockers will use the same unit of measurement, making it easier for you to size and work with elements of your document.

Specifying a page size

The page size you specify needs to be determined by the type of document you're creating and the amount of information on the page. If you are creating an image map, your requirements are going to be different than if you are creating a normal HTML document. Even though the display is in pixels, as a general rule of thumb, if you are creating an HTML document, you can specify a letter-sized page and use a portrait orientation. When creating Internet documents in either of these two formats your largest concern is the length of the page instead of the width. Image maps have different requirements because they are a single image.

When creating an image map for Web use, it's best to set your page size for 640 × 480, in the Options dialog box. Even though you may be able to display 1280 × 1024, 32-bit graphics on your computer, it's a mistake to think that everyone uses such a high-end display. The Web graphics concept is to use the least common denominator. That means you should create your page for a small display and resolution, to guarantee that everyone can see your page.

Tip

Selecting a 640 × 480 page size means it won't cover the display area from edge to edge on many monitors. This may pose a problem if you are creating an image map with a patterned background, as shown earlier in Figure 17-1. To solve this problem, specify a solid colored background and center your image map in your Web editor.

To specify a page size:

1. Select Tools ➪ Options, and expand the Document and Page categories. Click Size to display the Size page (see Figure 17-5).

2. Click the down arrow for the unit of measurement and select pixels from the drop-down list.

3. Click the down arrow next to Paper and choose a size from the list. Alternatively, you can enter a custom size in the Width and Height boxes.

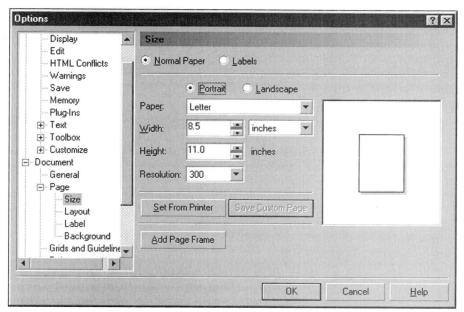

Figure 17-5: The Size page lets you specify the page size of your document.

4. If you want to save this page size for use in future Draw sessions, click the Save Custom Page button, enter a name for your custom page, and click OK.

5. Click OK on the Size page to return to the drawing window.

 Tip   You can also specify page settings on the Property bar by first deselecting all of the objects in your document to display the Page Settings property bar.

Specifying a resolution

Draw lets you specify the export resolution of your document on the Size page. Setting the resolution won't make a difference in the size of your cdr file, but it will make a huge difference in the size of the exported image. A 300-dpi image is wasted on an Internet document. The maximum display resolution of a PC monitor is 96 dpi (Macintosh displays images at 72 dpi). Any resolution above those values is ignored, and only serves to increase the file size. You aren't going to sell very many "Who-whadjets" if the person with the 9600-baud modem has to spend 30 minutes to download your Web page. I'm notorious, as my development editor will agree, for creating monstrous images. One of my more modest images will load a print buffer with a 50MB-plus file. The Web requires economy. Your file has to download quickly, or you'll lose your audience.

To specify the resolution:

1. Select Tools ➪ Options and expand the Document and Page categories. Click Size to display the Size page.

2. In the Resolution section, click the down arrow and select 96 from the drop-down list. This is the optimum resolution for Web use.

3. Click OK to return to the drawing window.

Choosing a Palette

Once you've specified your page size and unit of measure, you can create your image as you would create any document in Draw. As you create your image, remember that it will be displayed in 8-bit color, using the palette specific to the viewer's browser. Draw provides browser-specific palettes for both Netscape and Internet Explorer. I don't recommend, however, that you choose either. You can't guarantee which browser the viewer will use, and although these palettes are similar, they are not identical. If you use Netscape's palette, for example, your Web document may not display as expected in Internet Explorer or vice versa.

For best results, I recommend creating your document as you would create any document and then converting the graphics to an 8-bit CMYK palette before publishing the document. Using this method, you can preview your Web document and adjust the color, if needed, to ensure that it displays correctly. Converting your graphics to 8-bit color also reduces the your document's file size.

Creating HTML Text

You can create HTML text by converting Paragraph text using the Make Text HTML Compatible command. One advantage of HTML text is that you can edit your published document's text directly in a Web browser or another Web editor. If you don't convert Paragraph text to HTML text before you publish your document to the Internet, the text is converted to a bitmap when published and cannot be edited in a browser. Artistic text cannot be converted to HTML text and is always treated as a bitmap. I recommend that you convert Artistic text to Paragraph text and then to HTML text, unless you need to apply special effects, such as an envelope, to the text.

Using HTML text offers both advantages and disadvantages. You can specify hyperlinks for other Internet addresses and bookmarks when you use HTML text. Because the text is still considered text, the display quality is better than that of bitmapped text. The variety of fonts, sizes, and styles are limited, however. In addition, you can apply uniform fills, but not outlines, to HTML text. HTML text can't be transformed as you would other text in Draw, nor can you apply special effects, such as Fit Text to Path, to HTML text. HTML text and graphic objects reside on separate layers.

Tip   HTML text lets the viewer highlight and copy portions of the text, as text, to other documents. This is an advantage if you want to provide viewers with an easy way of inquiring about specific portions of your information. Bitmapped text is considered a graphic, and can't be copied to other documents as text.

When you use HTML text, the default HTML font is used automatically unless you override it with another font. The browser and platform of the viewer determines the default HTML font. Even if you choose to override it, the default font is used if visitors to your site don't have the same font installed on their computers. The HTML text sizes, numbered 1 through 7, correspond to specific point sizes between 10 points and 48 points. The usual text styles, including bold, italic, and underline, are also available. You can identify hyperlink HTML text in your Web browser by specifying link properties, such as underlining and color.

Caution   You can also export your text using TrueDoc font technology. TrueDoc font technology requires Netscape Communicator, however. Other browsers may not support or display the text correctly.

Specifying link properties

To specify the link properties:

1. Select Tools ⇨ Options and expand the Document and Publish to Internet categories. Click Links to display the Links page.

2. Select the options and colors to use. This guide describes the Link properties:

   • **Underline:** If you select this option, hypertext links appear underlined in your document, which assists the viewer in quickly identifying links.

- **Normal Link:** If this option is enabled, hyperlink text appears in this color within your document, allowing for easy identification.

- **Active Link:** If this option is enabled, hyperlink text turns this color when the viewer clicks the text.

- **Visited Link:** If this option is enabled, hyperlink text turns this color once the viewer has visited this link. (This color is durable only within a single browser session. The viewer will see the normal link color in future browser sessions.)

3. Click OK to return to the drawing window.

Caution

> HTML text resides on the Internet layer above all other graphic elements. You can't superimpose HTML text over other Internet objects. HTML text also can't extend beyond the boundaries of the drawing page. If the text either overlaps another Internet object or extends beyond the drawing page, it will be converted to a bitmap and lose its Internet properties.

Converting Paragraph text to HTML text

To create HTML-compatible text in your document, you must first ensure that all of the text that you wish to convert is Paragraph text. Artistic text can't be converted to HTML-compatible text unless you convert it to Paragraph text first. It is viewed as a graphics object and converted to a bitmap when you publish your document to the Internet. You can convert Paragraph text one text frame at a time, or you can select all the text on a page and perform a batch conversion. Once you've converted the text to HTML-compatible text, you are limited to specific fonts and font sizes. Although you can apply a uniform fill to HTML text, you can't apply other fills, such as fountain fills or pattern fills.

The Property bar displays both the Draw font size and the HTML font size of your text. The font determines the actual physical size of any given HTML font size. One font may appear larger or smaller than another font. Regardless of what font you choose, it will default to a font that can be displayed on the viewer's computer if they don't have the font you specify. This can cause unpredictable results when your Web page is displayed. To avoid this situation, consider using a standard font such as Times Roman.

To convert your Paragraph text to HTML-compatible text:

1. Using the Pick tool, select the text to convert. Alternatively, you can select Edit ➪ Select All ➪ Text Objects to select all the text objects on the page (this will select Artistic text objects as well).

2. Select Text ➪ Make Text HTML Compatible. Draw converts the selected Paragraph text to HTML-compatible text.

If you inadvertently selected Artistic text, don't be concerned. Draw will ignore that selection.

Note
If you have Paragraph text that hasn't been converted to be HTML compatible, the HTML Conflict Analyzer will notify you of the conflict when you try to publish your document on the Internet. You can either repair the conflict at that time, or choose to publish the document anyway. If you choose the latter, the text is converted to a bitmap and can't be edited in your htm document.

Formatting HTML text

Once you've converted your Paragraph text to HTML-compatible text, you can apply formatting commands to the text if needed. Some Paragraph text formatting features, such as bullets and drop caps, aren't available for HTML text. To format your HTML text, select Text ➪ Format Text to display the Format Text dialog box. Select the formatting options to use and click OK to return to the drawing window.

Working with Internet Objects

Draw lets you insert Internet objects into HTML documents. Internet objects are user interface (UI) controls that let you specify user interaction and perform tasks such as searches and data collection. Internet objects include buttons, checkboxes, menus, text-edit boxes, and Java applets. Draw comes with a library of these items already preconfigured for your use. You can use these objects as is, or you can customize them to meet your needs. To insert a preconfigured Internet object, select Edit ➪ Insert Internet Object, and choose the object to insert from the flyout menu.

Internet objects can be configured and customized in the Object Properties docker or by using the Property bar. Once you've customized an Internet object, you can save it for future use by dragging it to the Scrapbook.

To customize an Internet Object:

1. Using the Pick tool, right-click the Internet object to customize and select Properties to display the Object Properties docker (see Figure 17-6). Alternatively, select the object and make the modifications you want on the Property bar.

2. Click the tab associated with the object that you want to customize (each Internet object in your document has its own tab).

3. Modify the parameters to customize the object.

4. Click Apply All to return to the drawing window.

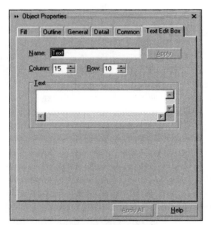

Figure 17-6: The Object Properties docker lets you customize Internet objects.

The type of Internet object that you want to customize determines the types of parameters you can specify. For example, the controls for a Text Edit Box appear in Figure 17-6. You can specify the number of columns and rows. In addition, you can enter the text you want to appear in the text box. If you want to save the customized Internet object for future use, I recommend renaming the object in the Name box before dragging it to the Scrapbook to prevent overwriting the parameters for an existing Internet object.

Note   Generally, Internet objects require CGI scripting to enable their functionality. CGI scripts are normally server-side (your ISP) rather client-side (your computer) scripts, and as such are stored on the server at your ISP. CGI scripts require programming abilities, and, for security reasons, are commonly provided by your ISP. Consult your Internet provider before inserting Internet objects into your Web documents.

Troubleshooting in Advance

There are ins and outs to any program or set of program features, and Draw is no exception. Before creating a Web document, I recommend reviewing the troubleshooting tips in this section. They can save you time and a great deal of aggravation, if you keep them in mind while designing your Web document.

✦ Do *not* put copyrighted materials on your Web page without the express (and preferably written) permission of the copyright holder. Never presume that an image, sound, or other element is in the public domain. If you have any doubts, don't use it on your Web page! It's also a matter of Web courtesy to obtain permission prior to putting a link on your Web page to another address.

✦ Always create all of the elements in your Web document *before* converting any text elements to make them HTML compliant and *before* specifying graphic objects as hotspots. Once these objects have been made "Web-ready" you can't copy them between layers and pages.

✦ Save the original Web document pages prior to making elements Web-ready, then save the Web-ready version using a different filename. This ensures that you will have a non-HTML-compliant version of your document if you need to make modifications.

✦ Be sure that all of the elements that you want to publish are within the boundaries of the drawing page. Adjust the page size, if necessary, to ensure that they fall well within the page.

✦ Make sure that Internet objects *never* overlap. If they do, they will be treated as plain bitmaps and their Internet functions won't work.

✦ Apply uniform fills to text *prior* to making the text HTML compatible. Once the text is HTML compliant, you can't change the fill in Draw.

✦ Be sure to make bitmap page background tiles smaller than 200 pixels on any side. Larger bitmap tiles may display seams or gaps between the rows and columns when displayed in a browser.

✦ Larger, multi-line form Internet objects may not display correctly in some browsers. They may cause distortion or fragmenting in superimposed graphic objects. Consider using smaller forms, another format for viewer feedback, or creating the form in a third-party Web editor.

✦ When you create an HTML document, Draw creates a subfolder that it calls Images by default. Be sure to upload this entire folder with your HTML documents when you publish the Web documents. If you don't, your document will be without images, and broken link errors will occur in browsers. In addition, this folder contains more files than you have objects in your drawing. *Do not* delete these "extra" files. They are placeholders that specify the positioning of the objects on your page.

Working with Bookmarks

Bookmarks function as addresses that let viewers navigate within a document or access a specific portion of a document from another document. For a bookmark to work properly, it must have a unique name within your document. It serves as a shorthand hyperlink to a location you specify.

Specifying bookmarks

Draw lets you specify bookmarks on the Internet Objects toolbar, on the Object Properties docker, or from the object's right mouse button menu. To assign a bookmark, use one of these methods:

✦ **On the Internet Objects toolbar:** Using the Pick tool or Text tool, select the object to which you want to assign the bookmark. You can choose a graphic or text. On the Internet Objects toolbar, enter a name in the Bookmark box and press Enter.

Note

When you use the Internet Links method of assigning a bookmark, you can't create a new bookmark. You can only choose from the existing locations or addresses. By default, Draw lists the top of each page of a multipage document as a possible bookmark.

✦ **On the Object Properties docker:** Using the Pick tool, right-click the object to which you want to assign a bookmark, and choose Properties from the right mouse button menu. Click the Internet tab and enter a name in the Bookmark box. Click Apply All to create the bookmark and to return to the drawing window.

✦ **On the right mouse button menu:** Using the Pick tool, right-click the object to which you want to assign a bookmark, and select Internet Links. From the flyout menu, select either a location or an address from the list. Click More to view addresses that may not be listed.

Caution

Avoid assigning a bookmark to a location or address that's already been assigned. Assigned bookmarks appear with a bullet beside their name. If you assign a bookmark that has been previously assigned, you overwrite the existing bookmark.

Creating bookmark hyperlinks

Once you've assigned a bookmark, you can link it to the desired location or object.

To create a hyperlink to a bookmark:

1. Select View ➪ Dockers and choose the Internet Bookmark Manager.

2. In your document, use the Pick tool or Text tool to select the object or text to which you want to create a hyperlink.

3. Click the Link button in the Internet Bookmark Manager.

Note

You can't hyperlink a bookmark to itself.

Using the Bookmark Manager

After you create a bookmark and select its hyperlink object, you can navigate to the object by clicking the name or page in the Bookmark Manager and then clicking the Select button. Using the Bookmark Manager, you can also remove a bookmark by selecting the bookmark and clicking the Remove button. If you want to rename a bookmark, click the name and enter a new name.

Publishing a Web Document

Draw provides two methods for publishing your document to the Internet. You can use the Publish To Internet dialog box or you can use the Internet Publishing Wizard. If you are new to publishing Web documents in Draw, I recommend using the Wizard until you become acquainted with the publishing process. Although both methods perform the same actions, the Internet Publishing Wizard guides you through the process.

Draw approaches Web documents differently than most HTML editors. Some layout methods for creating Web documents are browser specific. For example, Netscape 4 and later support layers, but Internet Explorer 4 and later do not. Both browsers support styles. You can choose the way Draw creates Web documents in the Options dialog box, either before you publish your document or from the Publish To Internet dialog box.

To publish your document to the Internet using the Publish To Internet dialog box:

1. Select File ⇨ Publish to Internet to display the Publish to the Internet Wizard, and click the Internet Dialog button.

2. Choose the layout you want to use in the Export to section (see Figure 17-7).

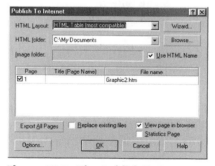

Figure 17-7: The Publish To Internet dialog box lets you specify the format and location to store your file.

3. If you haven't specified the publishing options you want to use, click the Options button to display the Image page (see Figure 17-8).

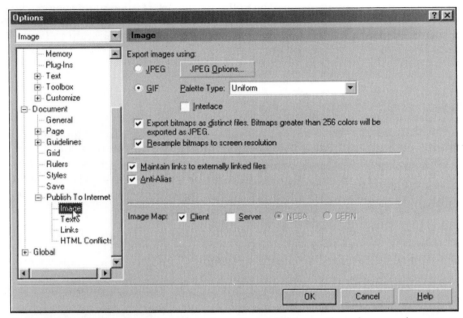

Figure 17-8: The Image page lets you specify publishing options for your document.

4. Select the options to use and click OK to return to the Publish To Internet dialog box (see "Exporting Objects for the Web" later in this chapter).

5. Select a folder in which to store your file. When creating Web documents, this step is critical. For the best results, all of your Web files that are related to any single Web site should be stored in the same folder.

6. Enter a name for your image and click OK.

Note   All layout formats are saved as .htm format files. This file contains the coding and formatting instructions for your Web page. The actual images are stored as bitmaps in the associated images folder.

Draw analyzes your document for conflicts and publishes the page or pages. If Draw finds an HTML conflict in your document, it gives you an opportunity to repair the conflict (see Figure 17-9). If you choose to repair the conflict, Draw halts the publishing process and opens the HTML Conflict Analyzer. If you click No, Draw proceeds to publish the document without repairing the conflicts.

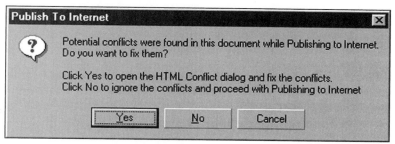

Figure 17-9: If Draw finds HTML conflicts in your document, it gives you an opportunity to repair the conflicts.

Resolving HTML Conflicts

Trying to manually find the reason why a Web page fails can take hours and become a real nightmare, especially if a Web document is large and contains many elements. The HTML Conflict Analyzer reduces that problem by automatically scanning for the common HTML errors that you specified in the Options dialog box.

Checking for conflicts

Draw lets you scan individual pages or entire documents. Once you repair individual conflicts, you can rescan the page to ensure that the conflict no longer exists.

To scan your document for conflicts:

1. Select Windows ⇨ Dockers ⇨ HTML Object Conflict. The HTML Conflict Manager appears in the drawing window. By default, it appears docked at the right side of the drawing window.

2. Click either the Rescan the Current Page button or the Rescan the Entire Document button. Draw scans your selection for HTML conflicts.

Once conflicts are identified, you can choose to repair or ignore them, and rescan as needed until you are satisfied with the results (see Figure 17-10).

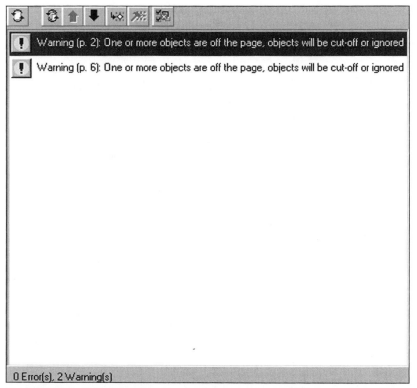

Figure 17-10: The HTML Conflict Analyzer scans your document for HTML conflicts and displays conflicts it finds in the HTML Conflict Manager.

Repairing conflicts

After the HTML Conflict Analyzer identifies the conflicts in your document, it displays them in the HTML Conflict Manager. You can select an error to address by clicking the error, or you can use the Move to Previous or Move to Next buttons to navigate through the conflicts. Some errors, such as HTML text compatibility errors, can be repaired automatically. Other errors, such as overlapping Internet Object conflicts, must be repaired manually in the drawing window. You may choose to ignore some errors entirely. For example, if your document contains Paragraph text that you want converted to a bitmap, you can safely ignore any related error messages.

To automatically repair displayed errors:

1. Click the Select Object from the Current Error button to select the conflicting object in the drawing window.

2. If you want to repair the error, click the Fix the Current Error button. Draw repairs the error, if it can be repaired automatically. If it can't be repaired automatically, you are prompted to repair the error manually.

3. Rescan your document or the current page to verify that the error has been corrected.

Specifying HTML Conflict Analyzer properties

You can specify which conflicts the HTML Conflict Analyzer considers when scanning your document for errors.

To specify the conflicts for which the HTML Conflict Analyzer searches:

1. In the HTML Conflict Manager, click the Analyzer Options button or select Tools ⇨ Options, expand the Document category, and expand the Publish To Internet subcategory. Click HTML Conflicts to display the HTML Conflicts page (see Figure 17-11).

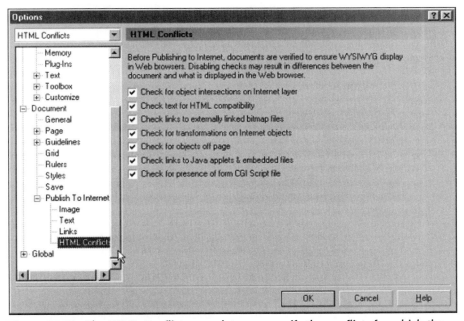

Figure 17-11: The HTML Conflicts page lets you specify the conflicts for which the HTML Conflict Analyzer scans.

2. Using this list as a guide, enable those conflicts for which you want your document scanned.

- **Check for object intersections on Internet layer:** Checks for overlapping or superimposed Internet objects.

- **Check text for HTML compatibility:** Checks Paragraph text for HTML compatibility.

- **Check links to externally linked bitmap files:** Checks that the path statements for linked bitmap files are correct.

- **Check for transformations on Internet objects:** Checks for Internet objects that have been rotated, skewed, or nondynamically scaled.

- **Check for objects off page:** Checks that all of the elements in your document are on the drawing page.

- **Check links to Java applets & embedded files:** Checks that the path statements for Java applets and embedded files are correct.

- **Check for presence of form CGI Script file:** Checks that a CGI script is present for Internet objects that require CGI scripting.

3. Click OK to return to the drawing window.

Exporting Objects for the Web

Individual elements created in Draw can be placed in Web documents by using a Web editor. The following sections deal with the issues that arise when exporting Draw documents to Web pages.

File format issues

Individual elements should be saved in gif or jpg format. All formats are saved at 96 dpi, by default, to match monitor resolution. Here's a quick overview of how the formats work:

Tip

I don't recommend changing the default 96 dpi value. Specifying a higher value creates a larger file and is a waste, because 96 dpi is the maximum resolution for monitor display.

✦ **Graphics Interchange Format (gif)** — Supports up to 8-bit (256 colors) color graphics, and provides lossless compression. This format works well cross-platform, and lets you choose transparent background and interlacing. Interlacing means that the image appears as it's loading, although it's indistinct and blurred. The image gradually becomes clearer as the file information loads. This file format is a good choice if your graphic has an irregular shape and needs a transparent background. It's also a good choice for vector graphics that contain small text or outlined graphics. The drawbacks to gif format images are that fountain fills tend to band and the image appears grainy.

✦ **Joint Photographic Experts Group (jpg or jpeg) format** — Supports up to 24-bit (16 million) color graphics and supports variable compression. This format is ideal for displaying photographic images and graphics that have a broad range of colors. Jpg images are lossy. You can control the amount of loss by specifying the compression amount. As the compression increases, the file size decreases but the image loses more information. Lower compression rates still create reasonably small files, but suffer less degradation of quality. Lossy means that unnecessary color information is removed from the image when you save it.

JPG Tips and Tricks

Jpg images degrade almost geometrically each time they are resaved in an image-editing program. This happens because the compression scheme used to create the image format is reapplied each time you save the image. You can avoid this situation, as well as deal with jpg images that require transparent backgrounds, by using these tips and tricks:

✦ To keep from degrading your jpg files, it's best to link them rather than embed them. When you link image files, only the pointer to the image is saved with the document; the image itself is reloaded as it's needed.

✦ If your Web editor doesn't support linked files, place a copy of the file in the document while you are working with the document, then swap out the image the last time it's saved to minimize the impact of resaving the image.

✦ Draw doesn't support transparent backgrounds for jpg images. If you have a jpg image that needs a transparent background, process the file through an image editor, such as Ulead's GIF/JPEG SmartSaver.

Color issues

Files that use a 24-bit color palette aren't generally recommended for Web use. Eight-bit or 256-color images are preferred because their file sizes are much smaller. If your image requires 24-bit color to display properly, however, you can reduce the file size by increasing the compression amount and, therefore, the lossiness of the image. Finding the right format and compression amount varies from one image to another. I recommend experimenting with both to find a balance that meets your needs.

Saving an image for Web use

To save an image for Web use:

1. If you are saving a single object, as opposed to the entire image, use the Pick tool to select the object to save. Even if there are no other elements on the page, you should select the object or object group if it's to be treated as a single element. This lets you create the smallest boundary, and therefore file, possible for that object.

2. Select File ➪ Export and choose the file format to use in the Save as Type box (see Figure 17-12). If you are saving a single object, choose either gif or jpg format. If you are using gif format, I recommend enabling dithering to prevent banding of fountain fills.

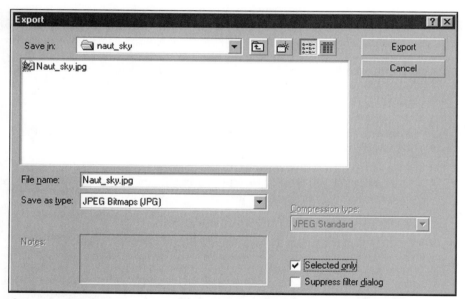

Figure 17-12: The Export dialog box lets you specify the format and location in which to store your file.

3. Select a folder in which to store your file. When creating Web documents, this step is critical. For the best results, store all of your Web files that are related to any single Web site in the same folder.

4. Enter a name for your image and click Export.

5. If you chose the gif file format, the Gif89a options dialog box appears, which lets you specify a transparency color (see Figure 17-13). Normally, this would be the color of your background. If you want the graphic to appear in the browser window quickly, but at a low image quality that steadily improves as the image loads, enable Interlace.

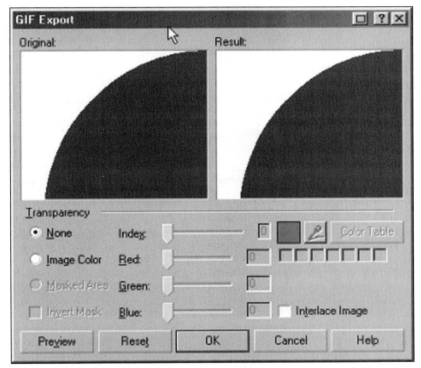

Figure 17-13: Choose the transparency option you want to use in the GIF Export dialog box.

Caution   Images that contain fountain fills tend to band when they are saved in gif format. To prevent this, enable the dithered feature when you save the image.

6. If you chose the jpg file format, the JPEG Export dialog box appears, which lets you specify the amount of compression you want (see Figure 17-14). High compression levels work well with solid colored objects. Extremely detailed photographic images should be set with low compression levels. Enabling progressive lets your image be displayed progressively when viewed.

7. Click OK to export your image.

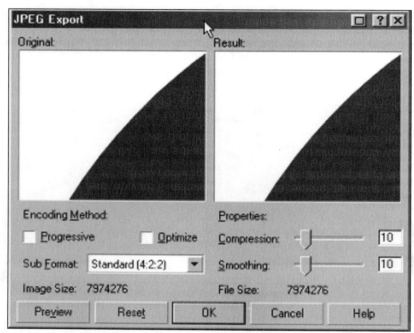

Figure 17-14: The JPEG Export dialog box lets you specify the amount of compression to use.

Specifying layout settings

You can specify the layout method Draw uses when HTML documents are published in the Options dialog box. If your document has multiple pages, the settings you specify on the Publish To Internet page apply to every page of your document.

To specify layout settings:

1. Select Tools ⇨ Options and expand the Document category. Click Publish To Internet to display the Publish To Internet page (see Figure 17-15).

2. Specify the settings you want. Use this list as a guide to specifying layout settings:

   • **HTML Tables:** Publishes Web documents using tables to position objects on the page. This is the default layout method.

   • **Layers:** Uses layers to position objects on the page. This option creates a smaller file, but is only supported by Netscape 4 and later.

   • **Styles:** Uses style sheets to position objects on the page. This option creates a smaller file, but is only supported by Netscape 4 and later and Internet Explorer 4 and later.

- **Style Options:** Selects the method of applying Cascading Style Sheets (CSS).

- **Position tolerance:** Lets you specify the amount of space text can be moved to prevent creating columns or rows of less than 2 pixels. The space cannot contain any graphics.

- **Image white space:** Lets you specify the amount of space possible in a cell before it's merged with the adjacent cell to prevent splitting graphics that span adjacent cells. Settings for this option only apply to the table layout method.

- **Position white space:** Lets you specify the amount of white space a graphic can contain within its bounding box.

- **Single Image with Image Map:** Exports the page as one gif or jpg graphic file and its accompanying HTML file.

3. Click OK to apply the settings and to return to the drawing window.

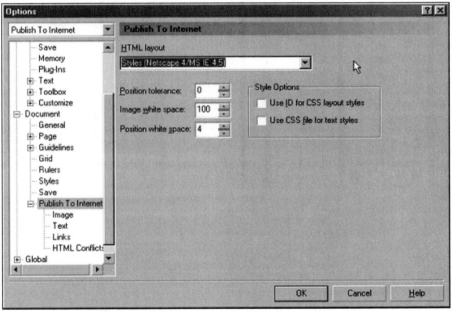

Figure 17-15: You can specify the layout method Draw uses on the Publish To Internet page.

Using the Scrapbook's FTP sites

You can now access most FTP sites from within Draw. This new feature lets you quickly download files from your favorite sites directly into Draw. Although most FTP sites let you connect anonymously, you can also access sites that require a user name and password. Once you've connected to an FTP site, you can save a shortcut as a favorite, which allows you quick access in the future. Draw provides a beginning shortcut to its site at `ftp.corel.com`. You can access a site for which you have a shortcut by double-clicking the folder, or by right-clicking the folder and selecting Open.

To access a new FTP site:

Note You can download files from your favorite FTP sites from within Draw.

1. Select Window ⇨ Dockers ⇨ Scrapbook ⇨ FTP Sites to display the FTP Sites page of the Scrapbook docker.

Caution You can't upload or delete files using the FTP Sites page. You also can't modify the structure of the site to which you are connected, even if you have the password to do so. You also can't delete folders in the FTP Sites page once you create them. To delete a folder, use the Windows Explorer or My Computer. The folders are stored in the corel\graphics8\draw\net_fav\links folder.

2. Right-click in the white space of the docker and select Go to Site from the right mouse button menu to display the Enter FTP Site Name dialog box.

3. Enter the name of the site to which you want to connect. If you want to connect anonymously, enable the Perform an Anonymous Login option and click OK. If you are connected to a secure site that doesn't allow anonymous logins, you will be prompted to enter a user name and password.

4. Draw connects you to the site, and a list of directories appears in the Scrapbook docker. You can open the folders as you would any folder, by double-clicking it. If you want to move up one level in the hierarchy of folders, click the Up One Level button.

5. To save a file to your hard disk, right-click the file to save and select Get File. The Save As dialog box appears, which allows you to choose a location and enter a name for the file. Click Save.

6. To import a file into your Draw document, do one of the following:

   • Double-click the file.

   • Right-click the file and select Import from the right mouse button menu.

   • Click and drag the file into the drawing window.

7. Right-click and drag the file into the drawing window. When you release the mouse button, select Drop CorelDRAW Internet File Data. Click Cancel if you don't want to use the file.

8. If you want to save the site as a shortcut, right-click the white area while you are connected to the site and select Save Site from the right mouse button menu.

Tip If you save a shortcut as a favorite site, Draw doesn't save the user name and password with the shortcut. This maintains the security of the site, in case someone accesses your computer.

Creating the LACC Web Page

Looking at a blank page in Draw can be daunting, if you don't have a plan of action before starting. One of the most important factors in creating a Web site that has multiple Web pages is to create a consistent theme that ties all the pages together. The elements that identify the theme don't have to be complex to be effective. LACC uses an eagle, buttons, and a common background to create the theme that ties the pages together. In the following sections, you create the foundation for the entire Web site. All of the elements are imported, but you won't be specifying the background until later. Placing the background prematurely slows the creation process due to the basic nature of bitmap images. Placement of the remaining elements is critical. HTML-linked objects cannot overlap. Each object must occupy its own space.

On the CD-ROM Several files have been provided for use in completing the exercises in this chapter. They are located on your companion CD-ROM in the tutorial\ch17 folder.

Placing theme elements

To place the theme elements:

1. Start Draw if it's not already running. If the Property bar isn't visible in the drawing window, select Window ➪ Toolbars, select the Property bar in the Toolbar window, and click OK.

2. On the Property bar, choose Letter Size and specify a Portrait Orientation. You'll need to change the page size later to accommodate the length of the text, but a letter size is a good place to start.

3. Click the Scrapbook docker icon on the toolbar to open the Scrapbook docker. Change the drive and folder to display the contents of the tutorial\ch17 folder. Press Ctrl and select eagle.cdr and buttons.cdr. Drag them to the drawing page. When you release the mouse button, the elements appear on the drawing page.

4. Using the Pick tool, select the eagle, and then select Arrange ➪ Transformation to display the Transformation docker. Click the Position button, and set the anchor to the upper-left corner. Specify 0.5 inches as the horizontal setting and 1 inch as the vertical setting. Click Apply to move the eagle into the correct position (see Figure 17-16).

5. Using the Pick tool, select the button group and set the anchor in the Position sheet of the Transformation docker to the upper-left corner. Specify 0.5 inches

as the horizontal setting and 6.25 inches as the vertical setting. Click Apply to move the buttons into the correct position.

Tip   You can also use the Import dialog box to import the elements of the Web page into Draw, but the Scrapbook lets you work faster and more efficiently.

Figure 17-16: Use the Transformation docker to position the eagle and buttons on the drawing page.

The buttons are a group of 12 objects: 6 text objects and 6 rectangles. For handling ease, leave these objects grouped. The buttons and the eagle appear on each page of the document.

This chapter includes a list of "do's and don'ts" related to creating Web pages with Draw. One bears repeating, however. When creating a document for printed media, such as a magazine ad, it makes sense to place the eagle and buttons on a master layer, rather than reproducing them on each page of the document. Draw treats HTML documents differently, however. HTML-compatible text is placed on a special layer called the Internet layer. You cannot move this layer in the hierarchy of layers, nor can you place a master drawing layer beneath it in the hierarchy. The result is that the text on the buttons may disappear beneath the buttons. Additionally, although you can publish an HTML document that contains a master drawing layer, you may not be able to reopen the cdr document in Draw if you want to modify it later. Trying to open a cdr file that contains HTML objects *and* a master drawing layer can cause an error and the program to crash. The best policy is to *never* create a master drawing layer when using Draw to create a Web document.

Placing the text

In this exercise, you place the text that completes the index page for LACC. Like the elements in the previous exercise, the text has been provided as a .cdr file.

To place the text in the document:

1. Click and drag indextxt.cdr from the Scrapbook docker to the drawing page.

2. With the text group selected, open and expand the Position Roll-Up. Set the anchor for the center right side (see Figure 17-17).

3. Specify 8 inches as the horizontal position setting, and 5.5 inches as the vertical position setting. Click Apply. Draw positions the text group 0.5 inches from the right border of the drawing page and centers it vertically on the drawing page (see Figure 17-18).

4. Select Layout ➪ Rename Page to display the Rename Page dialog box. Enter the name **index** and click OK to return to the drawing window.

5. Save your document to your hard disk as **lacc1.cdr.**

The index page for the LACC Web site is complete, except for the HTML links that you add later in "Specifying the Hypertext Links."

Although it's not absolutely necessary to name the pages of your Draw document, it's a good idea. Draw uses the names you enter as the names for the HTML pages it publishes. Entering the names of the pages as you create them saves time later, and lets you avoid confusion as you move through larger documents.

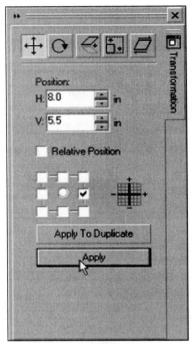

Figure 17-17: Set the anchor for the center right side.

Adding pages to your document

Once you've established the base page for your document, you are ready to create additional pages and to place the theme elements that give the Web site a consistent feel. Because each page is unique, you also need to import and place those elements, as well as adjust the page layout to suit the contents of the Web site.

Determining the page size

Draw approaches Web documents differently than do other HTML editors. The page size is flexible in most HTML editors. They allow the page size to expand and contract according to the amount of information that is placed on the page. In Draw, the pages have a finite size that you specify. Any information that falls beyond the boundaries of the drawing page, minus 0.5-inch top and bottom margins, is truncated and won't appear in the browser when you publish the HTML document. To ensure that all of your information is visible, you need to adjust the page size according to your information. The page size becomes especially critical if you are creating a multipage document in Draw. Draw lets you specify a single

La Aquila Coffee Company

HOME

COFFEES

BREWERS

ACCESSORIES

CONTACT

ORDER

Welcome!

La Aquila Coffee Co. is dedicated to providing you, the coffee lover, with the finest coffee, coffee products and accessories from around the world. We buy our coffee straight from the grower, not from an importer or wholesaler. Our worldwide team of buyers and agents scour the world for the best coffee beans, brewing equipment, and accessories.. Everything to make your coffee experience the most enjoyable possible.

We will never compromise on our standards of quality. Never! While that may mean that the coffee and coffee products we carry might cost a little more, you can be guaranteed that our products are the very best available.

Figure 17-18: Draw centers the text group on the drawing page and moves it to a position 0.5 inches from the right-hand border of the page.

page size for multipage documents. The amount of information contained on any given page can vary from that of another page, which leaves you with three basic choices that ultimately affect the design. You can

✦ **Expand the page size to accommodate the page with the most information.** This is a good choice if the pages of your document contain a large quantity of information. Expanding the page size can cause problems, however, if there's a large difference between the page containing the most information and the page containing the least information. While the larger page will look fine when the document appears in a browser, the smallest page will have too much blank space to be attractive.

✦ **Publish pages of vastly different sizes separately.** You can create separate cdr files of pages that are much larger than the rest of the pages on the Web site. This may be your only choice if the information contained on a single page can't be split into multiple pages, and if the size difference leaves too much blank space on smaller pages. The problem with creating multiple cdr files for a single Web site is one of file management.

✦ **Reorganize and edit your information to allow for a consistent page size.** If you look carefully at your document, you may be able to split one large page into two or more pages to maintain a more consistent page size. For example, in the following exercises you place the text for the balance of the Web pages on the LACC site. The text groups on pages 6 to 9 were originally all on a single page. To obtain a consistent page size, the text was split into four Web pages, with links back to the main order page.

Adding and naming the pages

In this exercise, you add and name the balance of the pages to the LACC Web document. When naming Web pages, it's a good idea to *always* use lowercase letters. Most ISPs use UNIX or LINUX as their operating system. Both of these operating systems are case sensitive, and more than one Web site has suffered *lost* files as a result of having a file named with uppercase letters while the associated HTML code specified the filename in lowercase letters.

To add and name the additional pages:

1. Select Layout ➪ Insert Page to display the Insert Page dialog box.

2. Enable After and enter **8** in the Insert box.

3. Click OK to add the pages and return to the drawing window. Draw adds eight blank pages to your document after page 1.

4. Select View ➪ Dockers ➪ Object Manager to display the Object Manager docker in the drawing window. The blank pages you added appear in the Object Manager.

5. Using the Pick tool, click the name Page 2. Click the name again to create an insertion point to rename the page. Enter the name **coffees** and press Enter to rename the page.

6. In the Object Manager, rename the balance of the pages as follows:

- Rename Page 3 to **equipt**.
- Rename Page 4 to **access**.
- Rename Page 5 to **comments**.
- Rename Page 6 to **order**.
- Rename Page 7 to **phone**.
- Rename Page 8 to **fax**.
- Rename Page 9 to **mail**.

7. Save the document.

 Tip
You can also use the Rename dialog box to name the pages of your documents. When you have many pages to rename, however, it's faster and easier to rename the pages in the Object Manager.

Placing the repeating theme elements

Once you've added and renamed the pages of the document, you can place the repeating theme elements on each page.

To copy the theme elements to the remaining pages of the document:

1. Using the page flippers at the bottom of the drawing window, click the left barstop to return to the index page.

2. Using the Pick tool, marquee-select the eagle and the button group. Press Ctrl+C to copy the objects to the Windows clipboard.

3. Change to the coffees page and press Ctrl+V to paste the elements on the page.

Underneath It All

If you are creating a simple HTML document, HTML restricts the placement of elements in a Web document. If you are familiar with creating Web pages in HTML editors, you'll notice that Draw doesn't restrict the placement and alignment of the elements of your Web page as do HTML editors. Draw gets around this restriction by using a table format.

Opening your Draw Web document in another HTML editor would show you the table underneath the elements in your document. As you add objects to your Web document, Draw adds columns and rows to the table, custom-fitting them to the size of the objects. The table method lets you place objects anywhere on the page with only a single restriction: HTML-linked objects cannot overlap one another. If you superimpose two hyperlink objects, the address you assign to the top object is used for both objects.

4. Repeat step 3 to place the eagle and the buttons on the balance of the pages. The eagle and buttons now appear on every page of the document.

5. Save the document.

Placing the remaining text elements

The rest of the text elements for the pages needs to be placed in the document. Additionally, you need to adjust the page size to accommodate the largest of the pages, creating a consistent page size. When you change the page size of a document by increasing the length of the page, Draw adds or subtracts an equal amount to both the top and bottom of the page. This results in the repositioning of the objects on the page relative to the new page size. For the purpose of creating the LACC Web site, you need to reposition the eagle and buttons on the page.

To place the rest of the text elements and change the page size of the document:

1. Open lacc1.cdr, if it's not already open, and display the Scrapbook docker in the drawing window.

2. Use the page flippers to change to the coffees page of the document.

3. Locate pg2txt.cdr in the Scrapbook. Click and drag the file to the drawing page.

4. In the Position sheet of the Transformation docker, set the anchor point for the center right side. Specify 8 inches for the horizontal position, and 5.5 inches for the vertical position. Click Apply. Draw places the text on the page 0.5 inches from the right page border and centered vertically on the page. The text also extends beyond the top and bottom of the drawing page (see Figure 17-19).

5. Repeat step 4 to place the rest of the text elements on their associated pages. Use pg3txt.cdr, pg4txt.cdr, pg5txt.cdr, pg6txt.cdr, pg7txt.cdr, pg8txt.cdr, and pg9txt.cdr, respectively. A review of the pages will show that the coffees page contains the largest quantity of text.

6. Using the page flippers, return to the coffees page to check the vertical measurement of all the elements on the page. The range of the elements on the page measures slightly less than 13 inches.

7. Press Esc to ensure that all of the objects on the page are deselected, and click the Paper Type/Size button on the property bar. Choose Legal from the list. The new page size appears in the drawing window.

La Aquila
Coffee Company

Coffees

Coffee is the heart and soul of La Aquila Coffee Co. Our buying agents travel the world visiting individual plantations searching for the finest coffee beans available.

These are just some of the wonderful coffees that we are pleased to offer.

La Aquila Breakfast Blend

This hearty robust blend of fine coffee beans are specially selected and roasted to produce a hearty, robust and full flavored coffee. A perfect start to your day!
$6.99/lb.

Kona

A light and mellow coffee. Perfect for late night coffee drinking or for when a milder cup of coffee is desired. *This is not a blend but beans obtained directly from the Kona Plantation in Hawaii!*
$9.99/lb

Columbia Supremo

These beans are the mainstay of most serious coffee drinkers. Roasted to perfection, this coffee is robust and full-flavored. This is an ideal coffee for anytime.
$6.99/lb

HOME

COFFEES

BREWERS

ACCESSORIES

CONTACT

ORDER

Figure 17-19: The text for the coffees page extends beyond the top and bottom border of the drawing page.

8. Reposition the elements on each page so that the eagle is approximately 0.5 inches from the top of the page and the text elements appear centered vertically on the page (see Figure 17-20).

9. Save the document.

Preparing your document for the Web

All of the elements required to create the LACC Web site are in place. The next step is to prepare the elements for publishing on the Web by ensuring that all the text is HTML compatible and then specifying the hyperlinks. As mentioned earlier in this chapter, all text must be HTML compatible or converted to curves in order to publish your document on the Internet. Draw doesn't see grouped text and won't let you convert grouped text to HTML-compatible text. Before converting the text, ensure that none of the text is part of a group.

Converting to HTML-compatible text

To convert the text to HTML-compatible text:

1. Using the page flippers, move to the index page of the document and select Edit ⇨ Select All ⇨ Objects. To ensure that none of the text is part of a group, click the Ungroup All button on the property bar. Repeat this step for each of the nine pages, and then return to the index page.

2. Select Edit ⇨ Select All ⇨ Text to select all of the text objects on the index page.

3. Select Text ⇨ Make Text HTML Compatible. Draw converts all the text on the page to HTML-compatible text.

4. Repeat steps 2 and 3 to convert the text on the rest of the pages to HTML-compatible text.

5. Save the document.

Note

Only Paragraph text can be converted to HTML-compatible text. Artistic text must first be converted to Paragraph text to apply the Make Text HTML Compatible command.

Regardless of what layer the text is on before converting it to HTML-compatible text, Draw moves the text to the Internet layer. This layer is reserved for Internet objects such as HTML text and java objects.

La Aquila Coffee Company

Coffees

Coffee is the heart and soul of La Aquila Coffee Co. Our buying agents travel the world, visiting individual plantations searching for the finest coffee beans available.

These are just some of the wonderful coffees that we are pleased to offer.

La Aquila Breakfast Blend

This hearty robust blend of fine coffee beans are specially selected and roasted to produce a heavy, robust and full flavored coffee. A perfect start to your day!
$6.99/lb

Kona

A light and mellow coffee. Perfect for late night coffee drinking or for when a milder cup of coffee is desired. *This is not a blend but beans obtained directly from the Kona Plantation in Hawaii!*
$9.99/lb

Columbia Supremo

These beans are the mainstay of most serious coffee drinkers. Roasted to perfection, this coffee is robust and full-flavored. This is an ideal coffee for anytime.
$6.99/lb

Figure 17-20: Reposition the elements on the enlarged page so that they appear balanced and the text appears centered vertically on the page.

Specifying the button addresses

Once your text resides on the Internet layer, you can specify hypertext links to addresses on the Internet or to other pages on your Web site. In this exercise, you specify the hyperlinks that link the pages of the LACC Web site. Each of the rectangles represents a button that is linked to an associated page on the Web site. To specify the Internet addresses for the LACC buttons:

1. Open lacc1.cdr if it's not already open in Draw.

2. Select Window ⇨ Toolbars and select the Internet Objects in the Toolbar window. Click OK to display the toolbar in the drawing window.

3. Starting on the index page, select the top rectangle and enter **index.htm** in the Internet address box on the Internet Objects toolbar.

4. On the Internet Objects toolbar, click the Show Internet Objects and the Use Object Shape to Define Hotspot buttons. Draw displays the button with crosshatched markings in the drawing window, identifying the button as a hyperlink object (see Figure 17-21).

5. Repeat steps 3 and 4 to identify the Internet address for the remaining buttons, from top to bottom, using this guide:

   • Second button: **coffees.htm**

   • Third button: **equipt.htm**

   • Fourth button: **access.htm**

   • Fifth button: **contact.htm**

   • Sixth button: **order.htm**

6. Repeat steps 4 and 5 to name the buttons on the remaining pages of the document. You don't have to retype the addresses. You can click the down arrow on the Internet address box, and select the correct Internet address from the list.

7. Save the document.

Figure 17-21: Draw displays hyperlink objects with crosshatched markings.

Specifying the hypertext links

The LACC Web site employs a few hypertext links to specify feedback addresses and to navigate the branched order pages.

To specify the hypertext links:

1. Using the page flippers, move to the Comments page.

2. Using the Text tool, click and drag to highlight the word Webmaster.

3. On the Internet Objects toolbar, enter **mailto:webmaster@lacc.com**.

Note   There are no spaces in an Internet address.

4. Using the Text tool, click and drag to highlight the address comments@lacc.com.

5. On the Internet Objects toolbar, enter **mailto:comments@lacc.com**.

6. Using the Text tool, click and drag to highlight the address info@lacc.com.

7. On the Internet Objects toolbar, enter **mailto:info@lacc.com**.

8. Using the page flippers, move to the Order page.

9. Using the Text tool, click and drag to highlight Order by phone about halfway down the page.

10. On the Internet Objects toolbar, enter **phone.htm**.

11. Using the Text tool, click and drag to highlight Order by FAX.

12. On the Internet Objects toolbar, enter **fax.htm**.

13. Using the Text tool, click and drag to highlight Order by Mail.

14. On the Internet Objects toolbar, enter **mail.htm**.

15. Using the page flippers, move to the Phone page, and highlight the text Back to main Order page.

16. On the Internet Objects toolbar, click the down arrow next to the Internet address box and select order.htm from the list.

17. Repeat steps 15 and 16 to link the Fax and Mail pages back to the Order page.

18. Save the document.

Caution   Specifying hypertext links can be tedious. Be careful to check the spelling of the addresses you enter in the Internet address box. Misspelled addresses, spaces, and mixed cases can cause errors when you try to access the links in a browser.

Adding finishing touches

The LACC Web site is nearly complete and ready to publish. You need to add a couple of finishing touches, however, as well as specify bitmap options, before you publish the Web pages.

Specifying a background

The final theme element is the background. A faded bitmap of coffee beans was created for use as the background. The bitmap is small, and tiles to fill the background behind the rest of the elements. The advantage of tiling a background is that it ensures that your page will have a consistent background without white space regardless of the viewer's screen resolution. This means that your background will look the same whether it's displayed at 640 × 480 or 1,280 × 1,024.

To specify a background:

1. Select Tools ➪ Options to display the Options dialog box. Expand the Document and Page categories, and then click Background to display the background options.

2. Enable Bitmap and click Browse. In the Import dialog box, locate coffee.jpg and select it. Click Open to display the path in the Source section.

3. Enable Embedded to embed the graphic in the document.

4. Click Custom Size in the Bitmap Size section. The size shown in the horizontal and vertical boxes is the actual size of coffee.jpg.

5. Click Print and Export Background to ensure that the background is published with the page. If you leave this option disabled, Draw assumes that you want to use it for representation purposes in the drawing window only.

6. Click OK to apply the Options and to return to the drawing window. Draw displays the pages of the Web site using the coffee bean bitmap as a background (see Figure 17-22).

When specifying a background, Draw lets you choose to link or embed the background. If your background is a large graphic, it's a good idea to link the graphic rather than embed it. Linking the graphic causes it to load separately from the rest of the page and speeds the loading process in a browser. If your background graphic is small, like the one for LACC, embedding the graphic lets it load at the same time as the rest of the Web page.

Specifying the bitmap options

The eagle contains a fountain fill that represents the colors found on the flag of Mexico. If you tell Draw to export bitmaps as gif files, the color white becomes transparent by default. To prevent part of the eagle from disappearing, you need to specify jpg as the export format for Internet bitmaps.

Figure 17-22: Draw displays the Web pages using the bitmap of the coffee beans as the background.

To specify the bitmap options:

1. Select Tools ⇨ Options to display the Options dialog box. Expand the Document and Publish To Internet categories, and then click Image to display the bitmap options.

2. Enable JPEG.

3. Click OK to return to the drawing window.

4. Save your document.

The LACC Web site is now complete, and you are ready to publish the document to the Internet.

Publishing the LACC Web site

Publishing a Web document is really anticlimactic after all the planning and work that goes into its preparation. Draw takes the work out of ensuring that all of the critical files are stored in a single location, reducing the possibility of losing a file related to your Web site.

To publish the LACC Web site:

1. Select File ⇨ Publish To Internet to display the Publish To Internet dialog box (see Figure 17-23).

2. Enable Export All Pages option.

3. Enter locations for your HTML and Images folders. By default, Draw stores the images in a subdirectory of the folder that contains your htm documents. I recommend accepting this default to ensure that your files don't accidentally get deleted or lost.

4. Click OK. Draw exports all of the files necessary to publish the LACC Web site to the Internet, and stores them in the folders you specified. This process might take a couple of minutes.

Note   Draw displays the page names as the names of the htm documents. Check these names for accuracy to ensure that they match the names of the hyperlinks in your document.

Generally, once you've exported all of the documents required for a Web document, putting them up on the WWW is a matter of uploading the htm documents and the Images folder to an ftp site on your Internet provider's site. Contact your Internet provider for specific instructions on uploading your Web pages. You can test the LACC site by opening index.htm in your Web browser. Check all the links to make sure that they work before you upload a Web document to your Internet provider.

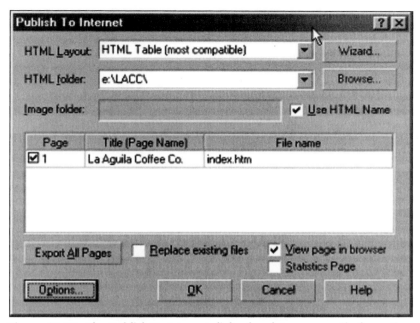

Figure 17-23: The Publish To Internet dialog box lets you specify the options to use when publishing your Web document.

Caution In the process of exporting the files necessary for publishing a Web document, Draw creates several gif images and stores them in the Images folder *even if you specify jpg bitmap output.* These gif images are important. *Do not delete them!* They are placeholders for the blank spaces in the Web pages. If you delete them, your Web document will not load accurately.

Summary

This chapter explored the process of creating and saving Web-ready graphics in Draw. You can also create Internet objects that act as hyperlink navigation tools for your HTML documents. Creating hyperlinks can connect you to any object in your document that is assigned a bookmark or to any document published on the Internet by using that document's Uniform Resource Locator (URL). The most important things to remember when creating any Web document is to plan ahead and to check the links of your pages *prior* to uploading your document to your Internet provider. In this chapter, you learned to

✦ Create a multipage Web document in Draw

✦ Specify background and bitmap options

✦ Design Web documents for HTML, Barista, and image maps

✦ Define hyperlinks and hotspots

✦ Specify resolution and page settings

✦ Create HTML-compatible text

✦ Work with Internet objects

✦ Troubleshoot your Web document

✦ Create bookmarks

✦ Select an output format

✦ Connect to FTP sites from within Draw

✦　　✦　　✦

Shortcuts

You probably already use shortcut keystrokes, such as Ctrl+S, to save your files, but keyboard shortcuts can also save time and reduce the need to continually move your mouse up to the menu and back down to the drawing window. Before using Draw's keyboard shortcuts, however, it's important to understand their types:

◆ **Main shortcuts:** These are shortcuts that impact selected objects. Main shortcuts may work from the drawing window or from within a dialog box.

◆ **Text-editing shortcuts:** This type of shortcut works when you are editing text and affects only the text or the position of your cursor in the document. Text-editing shortcuts are only available when the Text tool is selected or when you are working with a text-related dialog box, such as the Text Edit dialog box.

All shortcuts, regardless of type, can be grouped by related functions. The shortcuts in this guide are grouped in that fashion. Draw has more than 150 preset shortcuts — learning them all could take a while!

Main Shortcuts

Main shortcuts open dialog boxes and roll-ups. They also enable you to specify parameters in dialog boxes, such as the Align and Distribute dialog box. In addition to main shortcuts, you can access menus and commands by pressing Alt plus the underscored letter of any menu. For example, if you wanted to open a new drawing, you could press Alt+F and then press N. The following tables list the main shortcuts along with a brief description of each.

Toolbox Shortcuts

Shortcut	Name	Description
Spacebar	Pick	Toggles from the current tool to the Pick tool (except from the Text tool)
Ctrl+Spacebar	Pick	Toggles from any tool, including the Text tool, to the Pick tool
F5	Curve tool	Selects the last used curve tool
F10	Shape tool	Selects the Shape tool
F8	Text tool	Selects the Text tool
F7	Ellipse tool	Selects the Ellipse tool
F6	Rectangle tool	Selects the Rectangle tool
Y	Polygon tool	Selects the Polygon tool

File Management Shortcuts

Shortcut	Name	Description
Ctrl+N	New	Starts a new document
Ctrl+O	Open	Opens an existing document
Ctrl+I	Import	Imports files into Draw
Ctrl+E	Export	Exports files from Draw
Ctrl+S	Save	Saves the active document, in the current version, using the existing name (if you haven't specified a filename, Draw prompts you to name your document)
Ctrl+P	Print	Prints the active document or selection
Ctrl+J	Options	Accesses the Options dialog box, letting you specify default settings

Display Shortcuts

Shortcut	Name	Description
Ctrl+W	Refresh	Refreshes the view in the drawing window
Clicking a scroll thumb	Refresh	Refreshes the view in the drawing window
F9	Full-screen Preview	Toggles full-screen preview
Shift+F9	View	Toggles between the last two view qualities (for example, Enhanced and Wireframe)
Ctrl+Enter	Property bar	Toggles the display of the Property bar, letting you tab through the functions
PgDn	Page navigation	Displays the next page in a multipage document or inserts a new page in a document
PgUp	Page navigation	Displays the previous page in a multipage document

Zoom/Pan Shortcuts

Shortcut	Name	Description
Ctrl+F2	Zoom/Pan	Opens the View Manager
F2	Zoom In	Selects the Zoom tool — click to zoom 100 percent at the selected point, or click and drag to zoom to an area of the document
Shift+F2	Zoom to Selection	Changes the view to display the selected objects at the maximum size displayable in the window
F3	Zoom Out	Reverts to the previous zoom level view
F4	Zoom to All Objects	Changes the view to display all of the objects in the drawing window at the maximum size displayable in the window
H	Pan tool	Selects the Pan tool
Shift+F4	Zoom to page	Changes the view to display the printable page
Alt+Dn Arrow	Pan Down	Pans the document downward
Alt+Up Arrow	Pan Up	Pans the document upward
Alt+Right Arrow	Pan Right	Pans the document to the right
Alt+Left Arrow	Pan Left	Pans the document to the left

Editing Shortcuts

Shortcut	Name	Description
Ctrl+C	Copy	Copies the selection to the Clipboard
Ctrl+Insert	Copy	Copies the selection to the Clipboard
Ctrl+X	Cut	Removes the selection from the drawing and places it on the Clipboard
Shift+Delete	Cut	Removes the selection from the drawing and places it on the Clipboard
Ctrl+V	Paste	Pastes the contents of the Clipboard in your document
Shift+Insert	Paste	Pastes the contents of the Clipboard in your document
Delete	Delete	Removes the selected object from your document
Ctrl+Z	Undo	Reverses the last operation
Alt+Backspace	Undo	Reverses the last operation
Ctrl +Shift +Z	Redo	Reverses the last Undo operation
Ctrl+R	Repeat	Repeats the last action
Ctrl+Shift+A	Copy Properties From	Copies the specified properties from one object to another
Ctrl+D	Duplicate	Duplicates the selection and positions it as specified in the Options dialog box
Plus (+)	Duplicate	Duplicates the selection and superimposes it directly over the original object

Object Management Shortcuts

Shortcut	Name	Description
Ctrl+F5	Styles	Opens the Styles docker Window
Alt+Enter	Properties	Displays the properties of the active tool or object
Ctrl+Q	Convert to Curves	Converts the selected object to curves
Ctrl+L	Combine	Combines the selected objects into a single object that assumes one set of attributes
Ctrl+K	Break Apart	Breaks the selected multipath object into its individual objects

Shortcut	Name	Description
Ctrl+G	Group	Groups the selected objects
Ctrl+U	Ungroup	Ungroups the selected group
Ctrl+Y	Snap to Grid	Enables Snap to Grid feature
Ctrl+Shift+Q	Convert Outline	Converts an outline to an object
Ctrl+A	Select All Objects	Selects all objects in the drawing

Order/Position Shortcuts

Shortcut	Name	Description
Ctrl+PgDn	Back One	Moves the object back one position in the object hierarchy
Ctrl+PgUp	Forward One	Moves the object forward one position in the object hierarchy
Shift+PgDn	To Back	Moves the object to the back of the layer on which it resides
Shift+PgUp	To Front	Moves the object to the front of the layer on which it resides
Down Arrow (fl)	Nudge	Nudges the selection down by the nudge value specified in the Options dialog box
Up Arrow (>)	Nudge	Nudges the selection up by the nudge value specified in the Options dialog box
Right Arrow (fi)	Nudge	Nudges the selection to the right by the nudge value specified in the Options dialog box
Left Arrow (<)	Nudge	Nudges the selection to the left by the nudge value specified in the Options dialog box
Shift+Down Arrow (fl)	Super Nudge	Nudges the selection down by the super-nudge value specified in the Options dialog box
Shift+Up Arrow (>)	Super Nudge	Nudges the selection up by the super-nudge value specified in the Options dialog box
Shift+Right Arrow (fi)	Super Nudge	Nudges the selection to the right by the super-nudge value specified in the Options dialog box
Shift+Left Arrow (<)	Super Nudge	Nudges the selection to the left by the super-nudge value specified in the Options dialog box

Align/Distribute Shortcuts

Shortcut	Name	Description
B	Align Bottom	Aligns the selection to the bottom
C	Align Vertical Center	Aligns the selection to the vertical center
T	Align Top	Aligns the selection to the top
R	Align Right	Aligns the selection to the right
E	Align Horizontal Center	Aligns the selection to the horizontal center
L	Align Left	Aligns the selection to the left
P	Align to Center of Page	Aligns the selection to the center of the page

These shortcuts are available within the dialog box.

Fill/Outline Shortcuts

Shortcut	Name	Description
F11	Fountain Fill	Accesses the Fountain Fill dialog box
Shift+F11	Uniform Fill	Accesses the Uniform Fill dialog box
F12	Outline Pen	Accesses the Outline Pen dialog box
Shift+F12	Outline Pen Color	Accesses the Outline Pen Color dialog box

Transform Shortcuts

Shortcut	Name	Description
Alt+F7	Position	Opens the Position docker Window
Alt+F8	Rotate	Opens the Rotate docker Window
Alt+F9	Scale and Mirror	Opens the Scale and Mirror docker Window
Alt+F10	Size	Opens the Size docker Window

Effects Shortcuts

Shortcut	Name	Description
Alt+F3	Lens	Displays the Lens docker Window

Miscellaneous Shortcuts

Shortcut	Name	Description
Ctrl+F11	Symbols	Displays the Symbols docker Window
Alt+F2	Linear Dimensions	Displays the Linear Dimensions docker Window
Shift+F1	Help: What's This?	Displays context-sensitive help for the selected element
Alt+F11	VBA Editor	Runs the Visual Basic for Applications Editor

Text-Editing Shortcuts

When you are in text-editing mode, you can use shortcuts to navigate through the text, as well as apply font and formatting attributes. To use any of these shortcuts, the Text tool must be the active tool or you must be working with the Edit Text dialog box.

Global Shortcuts

Shortcut	Name	Description
Shift+F3	Case change	Changes the case of the selected text
Ctrl+F5	Styles Manager	Displays the Graphic and Text Styles docker Window
Ctrl+Shift+C	Show Nonprinting	Toggles the display of nonprinting characters when the Paragraph text is selected and the Text tool is active

Text Navigation Shortcuts

Shortcut	Name	Description
Ctrl+End	To End	Moves the text cursor to the end of the paragraph text frame
End	To End	Moves the text cursor to the end of the line
Ctrl+Home	To Beginning	Moves the text cursor to the beginning of the paragraph text frame
Home	To Beginning	Moves the text cursor to the beginning of the line
PgDn	Down	Moves the text cursor to the next paragraph text frame
PgUp	Up	Moves the text cursor to the previous text frame
Ctrl+PgDn	Down	Moves the text cursor to the end of the text
Ctrl+PgUp	Up	Moves the text cursor to the beginning of the text
Ctrl+Down Arrow (fl)	Down	Moves the text cursor to the next paragraph
Ctrl+Up Arrow (>)	Up	Moves the text cursor to the previous paragraph
Down Arrow (fl)	Down	Moves the text cursor down one line
Up Arrow (>)	Up	Moves the text cursor up one line
Right Arrow (fi)	Right	Moves the text cursor right one character
Left Arrow (<)	Left	Moves the text cursor left one character
Ctrl+Right Arrow (fi)	Right	Moves the text cursor right one word
Ctrl+Left Arrow (<)	Left	Moves the text cursor left one word

Text Selection Shortcuts

Shortcut	Name	Description
Ctrl+Shift+End	End	Selects the text to the end of the frame
Shift+End	End	Selects the text to the end of the line
Ctrl+Shift+Home	Beginning	Selects the text to the beginning of the frame
Shift+Home	Beginning	Selects the text to the beginning of the line
Ctrl+Shift+PgUp	Beginning	Selects all the text to the beginning

Shortcut	Name	Description
Ctrl+Shift+PgDn	End	Selects all the text to the end
Shift+PgUp	Beginning	Selects the text upward by one frame
Shift+PgDn	End	Selects the text downward by one frame
Ctrl+Shift+Up Arrow (>)	Up	Selects the text upward one paragraph
Ctrl+Shift+Down Arrow (fl)	Down	Selects the text downward one paragraph
Shift+Up Arrow (>)	Up	Selects the text upward one line
Shift+Down Arrow (fl)	Down	Selects the text downward one line
Ctrl+Shift+Right Arrow (fi)	Right	Selects the word to the right
Ctrl+Shift+Left Arrow (<)	Left	Selects the word to the left
Shift+Right Arrow (fi)	Right	Selects the character to the right
Shift+Left Arrow (<)	Left	Selects the character to the left
Delete	Delete	Removes the character to the right
Backspace	Delete	Removes the character to the left
Ctrl+Delete	Delete	Removes the word to the right
Ctrl+Backspace	Delete	Removes the word to the left

Text-Formatting Shortcuts

Shortcut	Name	Description
Ctrl+T	Format	Opens the Format Text dialog box
Ctrl+Shift+T	Edit text	Opens the Text Edit dialog box
Alt+F12	Align text	Aligns the selected text to the baseline
Ctrl+F8	Convert text	Converts Artistic text to Paragraph text and vice versa
Ctrl+Numpad 4	Font size	Reduces the font size to the next smaller size available from the font size list
Ctrl+Numpad 2	Font size	Reduces the font size 1 point
Ctrl+Numpad 6	Font size	Increases the font size to the next larger size available from the font size list
Ctrl+Numpad 8	Font size	Increases the font size 1 point
Ctrl+M	Bullet Text	Adds/removes bullets from the text object

Formatting Shortcuts

Shortcut	Name	Description
Ctrl+N	Justification	Changes the alignment to no justification
Ctrl+H	Justification	Changes the alignment to forced justification
Ctrl+J	Justification	Changes the alignment to full justification
Ctrl+L	Justification	Changes the alignment to left justification
Ctrl+R	Justification	Changes the alignment to right justification

Font Shortcuts

Shortcut	Name	Description
Ctrl+Numpad 4	Font size	Decreases the font size to the next smaller size available from the font size list
Ctrl+Numpad 2	Font size	Decreases the font size 1 point
Ctrl+Numpad 6	Font size	Increases the font size to the next larger size available from the font size list
Ctrl+Numpad 8	Font size	Increases the font size 1 point

✦   ✦   ✦

Resources

Agreat deal happens behind the scenes when anyone
undertakes a project such as this book. The success of
this type of venture depends on the generosity and support of
a broad assortment of people, such as those included in the
resources here.

Software Developers

Corel Corporation one more time created a great product —
the best ever, in fact! Macromedia, Inc., whose software makes
my images come alive, provided the technology for
assembling the front end of the CD-ROM. Metacreations, Inc.
provided me with demos of a sampling of their wonderful
image-enhancement products for use on the CD-ROM that
accompanies this book. Nico Mak Computing, Inc. is the
producer of Winzip, which is included on the CD-ROM.
Without Winzip, efficient file storage and transportation is
seriously limited. Ulead Systems has been creating the finest
imaging software and is a cornerstone of my graphics toolkit.

These software developers, and some other valuable
resources, can be contacted as follows:

✦ **Adobe Systems Incorporated**
345 Park Avenue
San Jose, CA 95110-2704
(408) 536-6000
Fax: (408) 537-6000
http://www.adobe.com

✦ **Corel Corp.**
Corel Building
1600 Carling Avenue
Ottawa, Ontario, K1Z 8R7
CANADA
(800) 772-6735
Fax: (613) 761-9176
http://www.corel.com

✦ **Macromedia, Incorporated**
600 Townsend Street
San Francisco, CA 94103
(415) 252-2000
Fax: (415) 626-0554
http://www.macromedia.com

✦ **Metacreations, Inc.**
6303 Carpinteria Avenue
Carpinteria, CA 93013
(805) 566-6200
http://www.hsc.com

✦ **Microsoft Corporation**
One Microsoft Way
Redmond, WA 98052
(206) 882-8080
Fax: (206) 936-7329
http://home.microsoft.com

✦ **Nico Mak Computing, Inc.**
P.O. Box 919
Bristol, CT 06011
http://www.winzip.com

✦ **Ulead Systems, Inc.**
970 West 190th Street, Suite 520
Torrance, CA 90502
(310) 523-9393
Fax: (310) 523-9399
http://www.ulead.com

Hardware Manufacturers

Seiko Instruments, USA provided the printer technology for creating color proofs of images used in this book. Here's how to contact them:

✦ **Seiko Instruments, USA**
1130 Ringwood Court
San Jose, CA 95131
(800) 553-5312
http://www.cgg.seiko.com

Corporate Resources

Dementia Web Design is constantly exploring new horizons in Web creation that feature Corel and Macromedia products. Esper Systems is one of the best Internet providers I've ever had. They understood when my file transfers exceeded normal expectations. McLean Public Relations is dedicated to keeping me abreast of graphics software development. The following is a list of those resources and the publisher of this book:

✦ **Dementia Web Design**
   stuffyroom@usa.net

✦ **Esper Systems**
   (423) 281-8066
   http://www.esper.com

✦ **IDG Books Worldwide, Inc.**
   919 E. Hillsdale Blvd., Suite 400
   Foster City, CA 94404
   (415) 655-3000
   http://www.idgbooks.com

✦ **McLean Public Relations**
   231 Second Avenue
   San Mateo, CA 94401
   (415) 513-8810

What's on the CD-ROM

The CD-ROM that accompanies CorelDRAW 9 Bible contains all the files that you need to work on the exercises in the book. In addition, there are numerous clip art samples, all the art for the color insert bound into this book, and a goodies folder that contains the elements described in the essential shareware utilities section of this appendix.

Please see the CD-ROM Installation Instructions page at the back of the book for information about installing the programs on the CD-ROM.

The files and programs on the CD-ROM are described in the following sections.

Tutorial Files

The starter files included on this CD-ROM are designed to help you quickly learn some of the basics in Draw, without having to create art from scratch. You might find it more convenient to copy these files to a folder on your hard disk, although they are ready to use directly from the CD-ROM.

If you copy them to your hard disk, substitute your folder information in the tutorials where I've directed you to open files located on your companion CD-ROM.

✦ **Quick start:** The file in this folder contains the art for completing the tutorial in this introductory exercise in Draw. The file can be found in the \tutorial\quickstart folder.

　　start.cdr

✦ **Chapter 2:** This file is used in the tutorial for transforming objects in Draw. The file may be found in the \tutorial\ch02 folder.

　　Transform1.cdr

✦ **Chapter 3:** The files in this folder are used in the tutorials on editing and manipulating objects in Draw. The files can be found in the \tutorial\ch03 folder.

    boat1.cdr

    face1.cdr

    pierce1.cdr

✦ **Chapter 4:** This file is used in the tutorial on formatting text. The file can be found in the \tutorial\ch04 folder.

    dragtxt1.cdr

✦ **Chapter 7:** The files in this folder are used in the tutorials on cloning, using the Object Manager, and working with color styles. The files will be found in the \tutorial\ch07 folder.

    card1.cdr

    city1.cdr

    par_chld.cdr

✦ **Chapter 12:** The files in this folder are used in the tutorials on creating effects with fills. These files are in the \tutorial\ch12 folder.

    duck1.cdr

    hshoe.cdr

✦ **Chapter 15:** The files in this folder are used in the tutorials for working with Draw in the office. The files are in the \tutorial\ch15 folder.

    basket1.cdr

    candy1.psd

    candy2.psd

    cookie.psd

    ellipse.cdr

    htext.cdr

    logo1.cdr

    lorem1.txt

    mirror1.cdr

    mirror2.cdr

    pots1.cdr

    room1.jpg

    shtext.cdr

    sweet.doc

✦ **Chapter 17:** The files in this folder are used in the tutorial on creating a Web presence using Draw. You will find the files in the \tutorial\ch17 folder.

> buttons.cdr
>
> eagle.cdr
>
> indextxt.cdr
>
> pg2txt.cdr
>
> pg3txt.cdr
>
> pg4txt.cdr
>
> pg5txt.cdr
>
> pg6txt.cdr
>
> pg7txt.cdr
>
> pg8txt.cdr
>
> pg9txt.cdr

Clip Art Samples

All art from the color insert in this book, as well as other free-to-use graphics, are on the CD-ROM. You will find the files for the art from the color insert in the \colorinsert folder. A selection of bitmaps and fills will be found in the \bitmaps and \fills folders. Additional CorelDRAW graphic files have been included in the \xtra-cdrs folder and the \chess folder.

Essential Shareware Utilities

Shareware has become a catchall term for a genre of software that is freely distributed, usually by private individuals or small start-up companies, often as a means of getting their programs noticed. Users are often encouraged by the makers of the shareware programs to give them to friends and other users. The user's rights and obligations often vary from one program to another. Your precise rights and obligations, as well as any registration fee, are usually spelled out in the program's user license and in the program's Help menu.

Note   The usual restriction for almost all shareware programs is that the user does not use it for professional or business purposes without paying a nominal licensing fee and does not charge a fee to redistribute the program.

Adobe Acrobat Reader

Adobe Acrobat Reader lets you read platform and media-independent documents created in the Adobe Acrobat (.pdf) file format. The Adobe Acrobat Reader can be used to read or print .pdf files online, as a browser plug-in, or offline. This is a free program from Adobe Systems. The installation file for the Acrobat Reader can be found in the \Utilities folder.

Go!Zilla

Because of the increasing program file sizes that are available for download from the World Wide Web, being interrupted in the middle of a download has become a frequent problem. Until now, an interrupted download has meant that you had to restart the download from the very beginning. Go!Zilla searches several known archives around the world to find possible alternative download sites, identifies if the server allows for download to be resumed, and tests the network response time between your location and the server. If more than one server is found with the file available for download, Go!Zilla allows for switching between servers to find the server that will give you the fastest download. It will also automatically switch between servers if one server stops responding. This is a sponsorware program. Advertisers whose banners are displayed while the program is on the screen are supporting the makers of the program. You can find the installation file in the \Utilities folder.

IrfanView

Ever gone searching through your hard drive for a particular graphic, sound, or video file only to be confused by the sometimes less-than-clear filenames? The only way you could view or hear the file was to open a resource intensive application. IrfanView is a small, non-resource intensive graphics and multimedia file viewer. It supports just about all of the available bitmap graphic, audio, and video file formats. This is a freeware program for private, non-commercial use. You can register the program, if you wish, by sending the author of the program a small registration fee. Registration details can be found under About ⇨ Info. The file, and the installation instructions, can be in the \Utilities folder.

WinZip

WinZip, from Nico Mak Computing, Inc., is an indispensable utility that lets you compress your files, making them easier to distribute on floppy disks, CD-ROM, or the Internet. This is a 21-day evaluation program. While the program is not disabled in any manner after the 21-day evaluation, the maker of the program strongly urges you to pay the one-time registration fee and register the program. Once registered, your registration number is good for all subsequent versions. You will find this indispensable program in the \Utilities folder.

Glossary

16-bit: A color depth comprised of 64K colors.

1-bit: A monochrome color depth comprised of two colors: black and white.

24-bit: A color depth comprised of 16.7 million colors.

2-bit: A color depth comprised of four colors: black, white, and two grays.

32-bit: A color depth comprised of 6.8 billion colors.

3DMF/VRML: 3D file format.

4-bit: A color depth comprised of 16 colors.

8-bit: A color depth comprised of 256 colors or shades of gray.

AI: Adobe Illustrator file format.

align: Placing objects in relationship to one another. Left alignment, for example, would align all the objects evenly on the left. *See also* distribute.

anchor point: A stationary point around which objects are rotated or skewed.

ANSI: Plain text file format.

anti-aliasing: A method of smoothing the edges of objects by blending adjacent colored pixels to create an intermediate color.

arc: A smooth curve, described as an open section of a geometric object such as a circle, measured by degrees.

Artistic text: One of two text types in DRAW. You can add a variety of effects to artistic text, or convert the text into word art. *See also* Paragraph text.

ascender: That portion of a character that extends above the main body of the character. *See also* descender.

aspect ratio: The relationship between the height and width of an object. You can maintain the ratio of width and height when resizing an object.

Auto-Close: Automatically closes an open curve by adding a line segment. *See also:* Shape tool.

Auto-Join: Automatically closes an open path, creating a closed curve object by joining the end nodes of the path.

Auto-Reduce: Reduces the number of nodes in an object by an amount determined by settings in the Options dialog box.

Auto-Trace: Traces the edges of pixels in a bitmap to create vector objects. The effectiveness of this method of tracing is determined by the contrast in the image.

autotrace tracking: Specifies how closely objects follow the bitmap when you trace a bitmap in Draw.

banding: An undesirable printing defect in which there is a sharp division between the colors of a fountain fill when they should form a smooth gradient.

bevel: A method of mitering the edges of objects.

Bézier curve: A path defined by four control points that extend beyond two nodes in a path. The amount of deviation from the path is determined by the angle of the control points.

Bézier tool: Tool used to create Bézier curves, lines, and irregular objects.

binary: A method of representing numbers in which only the digits 0 and 1 are used. Successive units are powers of 2.

bit depth: The color depth of an image. The color depth can be 1-, 2-, 4-, 8-, 16-, 24-, or 32-bit color.

bitmap: An image whose shape, size, and color is defined by pixels.

blend: To morph between two objects using intermediate transitional steps.

blur: To create the illusion of fuzziness or of being out of focus by blending the colors of adjacent pixels in a bitmap image.

BMP: Windows or OS/2 bitmap format.

Bounding box: An invisible box that describes the exterior dimensions of a selected object or objects.

Break Apart: Separates combined objects, leaving objects with their original shapes.

brighten: To alter the lightness of a bitmap.

CAL: Monochrome compressed file format.

calligraphy: A type of variable-width line drawing.

callout: A method of labeling objects in an image, generally using a connecting line, leading to a text description.

CDR: CorelDRAW native file format.

CDT: CorelDRAW template file.

CDX: A Corel metafile format which uses an internal proprietary compression algorithm to reduce file size.

center alignment: To align a body of text so that each line is centered between the margins of the text frame. *See also* justify, left alignment, right alignment.

CGM: Computer Graphics Metafile file format.

character attributes: Characteristics that identify a text character, including size, font, and style.

child color: An object whose color is linked to the style of the parent color. If the parent color is changed, the child color is updated to reflect the change.

child object: An individual object in a group of objects, or a sub-set of a group of objects. *See also* group, control object.

chunk: An amount of data, usually 64K.

cicero: A unit of measurement equal to 12 didots. 5.63 ciceros equal an inch. *See also* didot.

circle: A type of ellipse created by depressing the Ctrl key while clicking and dragging the mouse. *See also* ellipse.

client: An application capable of receiving OLE objects. *See also* server, OLE.

clipboard: Refers to the Windows clipboard, which allows you to transfer data between files and applications. The clipboard can also be used to create and hold a copy of an object for future use within a single document. *See also* cut, copy, paste.

clone: A dynamically linked duplicate object or effect. Changes made to the master object are reflected in the clone object. *See also* duplicate.

CMX: Corel Metafile Exchange format. Saves drawings as vector graphics for use with Corel applications.

CMYK: Cyan, Magenta, Yellow, Black. A process subtractive color.

Color Calibration bar: Prints a bar of six colors: red, green, blue, cyan, yellow, and black.

color correction: To modify the viewable color to match that of the selected output device, enabling you to more closely select colors.

color mask: A technique for hiding or revealing portions of a bitmap-based image.

color model: A palette that meets the standards for color within a given industry or usage.

Color Override: Displays the selected layer's contents as colored outlines.

color palette: A collection of colors within a specific range or color model.

color profile: A collection of settings specific to your computer system that allows you to view and match colors when printing.

Combine: Command that merges objects into a single object. Overlapping areas are cut out and transparent.

compound blend: A blend with three or more control objects, where one of the control objects is both the starting and ending object.

compression: A storage method that reduces the file size of your document.

connector line: A dynamically linked line between two objects. These lines assist you in creating flow charts and other similar applications.

constrain: To force a selection to stay within specified parameters when it's tranformed.

container object: In a PowerClip, the object into which other objects are placed.

contents object: In a PowerClip, the object that is placed into a container object.

Contour: An effect that generates concentric symmetrical shapes. The intermediate steps create a color transition between the start and end object.

control handle: This handle extends beyond a node, allowing you to adjust the related curve of an object.

control object: A parent object in a dynamically linked group, such as a blend. When you modify the control object, the linked group updates to reflect the change. *See also:* group, child object.

control points: Handles that extend beyond the nodes to help define the associated curve. *See also* node.

Convert Text: A command that converts Artistic text to Paragraph text and vice versa.

Convert to Curves: Command that converts geometric elements and text to curve objects.

Copy: To place a copy of the selection on the Windows clipboard. *See also:* Cut, Paste.

corner threshold: Sets the limit determining whether a node has cusp or smooth attributes. Lower values produce cusped nodes.

CPT: Corel PhotoPaint format.

CPX: Corel Presentation Exchange format. A metafile format which utilizes an internal proprietary compression algorithm to reduce file size.

CUR: Windows 3.*x*/NT cursor resource.

curve object: Object can be any shape. Curve objects are characterized by having nodes and control points that determine the shape of the curve object.

cusp nodes: Nodes that identify a radical change in direction between two line segments. *See also* smooth nodes, symmetrical.

Cut: Removes the selection from the document and places it on the Windows clipboard. *See also* Copy, Paste.

CYMK: Cyan, Yellow, Magenta, Black. This is the most popular process color model, commonly used in printing.

Delete: Removes the selection from a drawing.

densitometer scale: Prints a range of grayscale colors that can be measured with precision.

descender: That portion of a text character that is below the main body of the character. *See also* ascender.

desktop: Not to be confused with the Windows desktop, the DRAW desktop is the white space around the drawing page in the drawing window. This area is useful for holding objects being transferred from one page to another of a multi-page document.

destination color: The end color in a fountain fill.

device dependent: Color palettes that are dependent on the output device to reproduce color values. *See also* device independent.

device independent: Color palettes that are consistent regardless of the output. *See also* device dependent.

dialog box: An options box that allows you to specify settings for a command.

didot: A unit of measurement. 1 didot = 1.07 points; 67.567 didots = 1 inch.

dimension line: A dynamically linked line that measures the distance between two points on an object.

Distribute: A feature that allows you to arrange and space objects evenly within a range of a selection or on a page. *See also* align.

DOC: Microsoft Word format.

dockable: A type of roll-up or toolbar that can be snapped to an edge of the drawing window.

docker: A roll-up or manager that docks to the side of the drawing window.

DPI: Dots Per Inch. This unit of measurement is commonly associated with resolution.

drawing page: The virtual paper upon which you draw your image.

drop cap: A paragraph formatting feature that places a beginning capital letter, set in a size larger than the body copy, so that it descends below other characters in the text string as the lead character of a paragraph or sentence.

DRW: Micrografx file format.

DSF: Micrografx file format.

duplexing: Printing on both sides of a sheet of paper.

Duplicate: Command that makes a replica of the selected object and places it in your document. *See also* clone.

DWG: AutoCad drawing format.

DXF: Autocad file format.

dynamic linking: The linking relationship between two objects, such as an object and a dimension line. Changes in the control object affect the linked objects.

Edge pad: A fountain fill option that allows you to specify the distribution of color in the fill. Edge padding extends the range of the originating color, so that the color appears solid at the outer edge of the object. *See also* fountain fill.

Elastic mode: A node editing mode that allows adjacent nodes to behave in an elastic fashion, smoothing the associated curves.

ellipse: An ovoid geometric object. Circles can be made by depressing the Ctrl key while clicking and dragging the mouse in the drawing window. *See also* circle.

Ellipse tool: Tool used to draw ellipses, circles, arcs, and wedges.

EMF: Enhanced Windows Metafile.

Emulsion down: Flips the image horizontally when printing so that text and graphics appear mirrored or backwards.

Envelope: A feature that allows you to distort objects and Artistic text.

EPS: Encapsulated PostScript file format.

error diffusion: Produces a black-and-white bitmap with screen dithering applied.

EXE: Windows 3.x/NT bitmap resource.

Export: Saves a file for use in another application.

Extract: A command that extracts the selected text for editing in a word processing program. *See also* Merge Back.

extrude: A feature that gives 2D objects a 3D feel by adding additional planes to create a top, sides, and bottom for the associated control object.

facet: The distance between colors in an extrusion.

field: An entry category in a database.

film negative: Creates a photo negative of the image when it's printed by inverting the colors.

fit text to path: To flow text along the path of another object.

flyout menu: A sub-menu that appears to the side of another menu or command.

FMV: Frame Vector Metafile.

FOCOLTONE: A spot color model based upon process colors.

font: A single style, weight, and size of a typeface.

format: To apply layout styles to a block of text.

fountain fill: One of four gradient fill types: linear, radial, conical, or square.

FPO: For Position Only. A low-resolution image that's used strictly for placement in a document. At print time, this file is replaced by a higher resolution version of the object.

FPX: Kodak FlashPix file format.

Freehand Tool: A tool used to create freeform lines and objects.

freehand tracking: Specifies how closely a curve follows the movement of your mouse.

full-access: Password protects a drawing, preventing others from accessing or changing your documents. *See also* write reservation.

gamma: The mid-range tones of a bitmap image.

gamut: The range of printable colors on any given output device.

Gaussian blur: A blurring effect that uses a bell-shaped curve to determine the distribution of pixels.

GEM: A vector file format common to Delrina products, and Ventura prior to Version 4.2.

geometric object: One of a series of shapes based upon three basic shapes: an ellipse, rectangle, or polygon.

ghosting: An undesirable condition caused by anti-aliasing, where a bitmap object appears to have a white border when placed over other objects.

GIF: Compuserve bitmap file format. This file format supports lossless compression.

Graph Paper tool: Tool used to create grids.

greeking: A replacement for text that is too small to be represented on the screen. Greeking is designed to increase screen refresh speed.

grid: A non-printable element of a drawing that allows you to place objects with precision. *See also* guides.

group: A collection of objects. This command locks the spacial relationship of a selection of objects. *See also* child object, control object.

guideline: Non-printing lines used as an aid to align objects.

guides layer: A non-printing layer of your drawing containing alignment aids.

gutter: The space between columns of paragraph text.

halftone: An image that's been converted from continuous tone to dots in order to represent tonal differences when printing.

HLS: Hue – Lightness – Saturation. HLS is a color model based upon its three components: Hue, Lightness, and Saturation.

hot zone: The distance from the margin you specify for adding hyphenation.

hotspot: An area of an image map that provides a link to another URL.

HPGL: Hewlett Packard Graphics Language file format. This is a common output format for plotters.

HSB: Hue, Saturation, Brightness. A color model based upon its three components: hue, saturation, and brightness.

HTML: Hypertext Markup Language. A scripting language that allows for the display of a document on the Internet.

ICO: Windows 3.*x*/NT icon resource.

image map: An image where specified locations or objects are used as links to other URLs.

IMG: Gem Paint file.

import: To open a graphic or text in DRAW. Generally, you import files that are not native to DRAW.

imposition: A method of ordering the pages of a document for printing.

Interactive Blend tool: A tool that allows you to visually and interactively apply and adjust a blend.

Interactive Fill tool: A tool that allows you to visually and interactively apply and adjust a fountain fill.

Interactive Transparency tool: A tool that allows you to visually and interactively apply and adjust the transparency of a fountain fill.

Internet Explorer: A WWW browser.

intersect: An effect that creates additional objects whose shapes are based upon the overlapping area between objects.

ISO 9066: CD-ROM recording standard.

jaggies: An undesirable condition that causes a stair-stepped effect on the edge of objects. Anti-aliasing is designed to prevent this problem.

JPG: Joint Photographic Experts Group file format.

justify: To align a body of text so that the right and left margins are equal. *See also* left alignment, center alignment, right alignment, and forced alignment.

kerning: The space between pairs of characters. *See also* leading.

keyword: A word or words you can add to a document when saving to help identify your file.

Knife tool: A tool that is used to intersect the paths of vector objects.

layer: One of a series of transparent planes in an image upon which objects are placed.

leader: A character, usually a period (.), that precedes a text entry.

leading: The space between lines of text. *See also* kerning.

left alignment: To align a body of text so that the left margin is flush. *See also* justify, center alignment, right alignment.

lens: A series of effects applied to an object that either alter the color or distort objects that reside below the lens.

line segment: The line or curve between two control points. *See also* node.

lossy: A degradation of the quality of a bitmap due to resizing the bitmap or because of the format in which the file is saved, such as jpg.

LPI: Line Per Inch. LPI is a unit of measurement used in the commercial printing industry.

MAC: MacPaint bitmap format.

marquee select: To select an object or objects by clicking and dragging a bounding box around an area you specify.

Master layer: A layer that contains information you want to appear on every page of a multi-page document.

Merge Back: A command that re-merges extracted text into a Draw. *See also* Extract.

MET: IBM Presentation file format.

mirror: To flip an object horizontally, vertically, or both.

moíre: An undesirable wave pattern that occurs as a result of setting the wrong screen angles for printing.

monochrome: 1-bit graphic.

NAP: NAP Metafile. Vector image file format.

Natural pen: A tool for creating line objects, such as calligraphic lines.

navigator: Onscreen tool that provides the controls to add pages and move from one page to another.

Netscape: A WWW browser.

node: Control points that describe the shape of an object. *See also* line segment.

nudge: To move an object or node a small amount using the cursor. The amount of the move is determined by settings in the Options dialog box. *See also* super nudge.

Object Manager: A feature of Draw that allows you to view the hierarchy of the drawing.

offset: The amount of space between objects.

OLE: Object Linking and Embedding. OLE is a method of exchanging information between OLE compliant software packages.

order: The arrangement of hierarchy of objects that determines which objects reside above or below other objects.

orientation: The direction a page or objects on the page are displayed. A page can have either a portrait or landscape orientation.

originating color: The beginning color in a fountain fill.

overline: A text effect used for emphasis, where a line is placed over a portion of a text string. *See also* underline.

palette: A range of colors from which you can choose a color to apply as a fill or outline color.

pan: To move the view of the drawing window.

Panning tool: Tool used to pan or scroll through the drawing window.

PANTONE: A precision color-matching system.

Paragraph text: One of DRAW's two text types. Paragraph text allows for full formatting features.

Paragraph text frame: The invisible frame that contains Paragraph text.

parent color: A color style that links colors together in a parent-child relationship. When a parent color is modified, all objects containing a child color are modified as well.

paste: To place the contents of the Windows clipboard into your drawing.

Paste Special: A command that allows you to insert OLE objects into your drawing. *See also* OLE.

path: The physical outline of the select object that defines its shape. *See also* sub-path.

pattern fill: Two-color, full-color, or bitmap fills that can be applied as tiles to an object.

PCD: Kodak Photo-CD Image.

PCT: Macintosh PICT format.

PCX: Paintbrush bitmap file format.

PDF: Adobe Portable document format.

perspective: A effect that allows you to give objects a feeling of depth. You can apply 2-point or 3-point perspective to objects.

PF: IBM PIF file format.

PIC: Lotus Pic file format.

pica: A unit of measurement. There are 6 picas to the inch. *See also* points.

Pick tool: One of DRAW's primary tools used for the selection and interactive transformation of objects.

PICT: A Macintosh picture format.

pie wedge: A closed shape based upon a circle.

pixel: A variable unit of measurement based upon a single dot on your monitor.

PLT: HPGL plotter file.

PNG: Portable Network Graphics file format.

point: A unit of measurement used to measure type size. 72 points = 1 inch or 12 points = 1 pica. *See also* pica.

polygon: A multisided geometric object.

Polygon tool: A tool for creating symmetrical multisided polygons and stars.

PostScript: A page description language designed to send printing instructions to output devices.

PostScript fill: A halftone fill.

PowerClip: An effect where you can place objects inside other objects. Any portion of the contents object that is larger or overlaps the edge of the container object is cropped.

PP4: Picture Publisher bitmap file format.

PP5: Picture Publisher bitmap file format.

presets: A series of effects created by macros or scripts comprised of recorded steps to create the effect.

print range: The range of pages you want to print.

printable area: That portion of the drawing page that can be printed. This area of space is defined by the properties associated with the output device.

PRN: PostScript printer file.

Property bar: An interactive command bar that changes depending upon which tool or feature is active.

PS: PostScript Interpreted file format.

PSD: Adobe Photoshop file format.

ramp: A range of colors in a palette.

rectangle: A geometric object that has four sides, each pair of which are parallel. *See also* square.

Rectangle tool: A tool that allows you to create rectangles and squares.

Redo: To repeat an action or actions after Undo has been applied.

registration marks: Marks on film or paper that allow for separations to be aligned for printing.

relative center: The center point of a selection.

Repeat: To repeat the last action.

Resample: To change the size and resolution of a bitmap.

resolution: The number of dots per inch in an image.

Reverse Order: Reverses the order or hierarchy of objects, and effects such as blend effects.

Revert: A command that re-opens the last saved version of a document.

RGB: Red, Green, Blue. A color model that uses the three values to determine the hue of the color. RGB is the native display color model for color monitors.

right alignment: To align a body of text so that the right margins are flush. *See also* justify, left alignment, center alignment.

roll-ups: A floating dialog box that allows you to apply commands or features to selected objects.

rotate: To change the orientation of an object by moving it around its center of rotation.

RTF: Rich Text Format. RTF is a preferred text format because, unlike plain text, it retains all of its formatting when imported into other documents.

SAM: Ami Professional graphics file format.

scale: To resize an object.

SCODL: File format common to SCODL devices such as ink-jet printers, thermal printers, and film recorders.

SCT: Scitex CT bitmap.

Separate: A command that separates a control object from an effect.

server: An application capable of creating OLE objects. *See also* OLE, client.

Shape tool: A tool for reshaping objects by moving or reorienting the nodes and control points of the object. The shape tool is also used to crop bitmap objects.

shortcut: A two- or three-key combination that applies a command or feature to an object, or accesses controls for a feature.

size: To change the dimensions of an object.

skew: To slant an object or portion of an object.

smooth nodes: Nodes that create flowing transitions between two line segments. *See also* cusp nodes, symmetrical.

snap points: The points of an object that behave like a magnet, snapping to other objects, a grid, or a guideline, when Snap-To features are enabled.

spiral (logarithmic): A spiral in which the distance between revolutions increases to the outer edge of the spiral.

spiral (symmetrical): A spiral in which the distance between revolutions is constant.

Spiral tool: Used to create spirals in the drawing window.

spot color: A solid ink color that is printed separately from process colors.

square: A rectangle where all four sides are of equal length. *See also:* rectangle.

Status bar: An onscreen display that lists information about your drawing or the selected object.

straight line threshold: Specifies how closely the cursor movement is followed.

stretch: To size an object horizontally, vertically, or both.

strikethrough: A text effect where a line is placed through the main body of text characters.

style: A set of attributes that describes an object, text, or layout. *See also* template.

sub-path: A single path of an object that contains multiple paths. *See also* path.

subscript: A character format in which the size of the character is reduced and the character is placed at the bottom of adjacent characters. *See also* superscript.

subtractive color: A color model that is based upon relective light.

Super Nudge: To move an object by a factor of the amount specified for nudging an object. *See also* nudge.

superscript: A character format in which the font size is reduced and the character is placed at the top of adjacent characters.

swipe: To highlight text for editing by clicking and dragging over the text.

symmetrical nodes: Nodes that connect two line segments while maintaining the same curvature on both sides of the node. *See also* cusp nodes, smooth nodes.

template: A collection of styles that describes the layout of a document as well as objects within the document.

Text tool: A tool used to insert text into your document.

texture fill: A fill type, based upon fractal imaging, that simulates textures.

TGA: Targa bitmap.

thumbnail: A small bitmap image designed to allow you to preview an image or object.

TIF: Tagged Image File Format. This is a bitmap format that allows for cross-platform use.

tiling: A method of filling a large surface with smaller squares of a pattern or image.

tint: A shade of a particular hue or color.

Title bar: The Title bar contains the name of the active document.

transform: To change an object's size or orientation without changing its basic shape.

trap: A technique where objects overlap slightly to prevent white space between them when they are printed.

trim: Removes the area where objects overlap from one of the superimposed objects.

TRUMATCH: A process color-matching model.

TTF: TrueType Font.

TXT: ASCII or ANSI text file format.

Type 1: Adobe Type 1 PostScript font format.

underline: A text effect where a line is placed under the text for emphasis. *See also* overline.

undo: To revert to the last action (or series of actions). *See also* redo.

uniform fill: A solid-colored fill.

URL: Uniform Resource Locator. The Internet address for a Web site.

vanishing point: In a perspective or extrusion, the point where the lines would intersect if they were extended.

vector: A type of object that is described as curves and lines.

View Manager: Provides an alternate view of your document.

wedge: A close geometric object created from an ellipse. *See also* arc, ellipse.

weld: An effect that merges objects together into a single object, removing any interior lines.

WI: Wavelet Compressed bitmap.

Wireframe: A viewing mode in which objects appear as an outline.

WMF: Windows Metafile file format.

WMF: Windows metafile.

WP4: WordPerfect document format.

WP5: WordPerfect document format.

WP8: WordPerfect document format.

WPG: WordPerfect Graphic file format.

write reservation: Allows others to open a protected document as read-only. *See also* password protect.

WS1-2: WordStar for Windows text format.

WSD: WordStar 2000.

WWW: World Wide Web.

XYWrite: XYWrite for Windows text format.

YIQ: Color model used primarily for broadcast televisions.

zoom: To enlarge or reduce the active view of a document in the drawing window.

Zoom tool: Tool used to magnify or reduce portions of a drawing.

Index

M

IDG Books Worldwide, Inc.
End-User License Agreement

READ THIS. You should carefully read these terms and conditions before opening the software packet(s) included with this book ("Book"). This is a license agreement ("Agreement") between you and IDG Books Worldwide, Inc. ("IDGB"). By opening the accompanying software packet(s), you acknowledge that you have read and accept the following terms and conditions. If you do not agree and do not want to be bound by such terms and conditions, promptly return the Book and the unopened software packet(s) to the place you obtained them for a full refund.

1. **License Grant.** IDGB grants to you (either an individual or entity) a nonexclusive license to use one copy of the enclosed software program(s) (collectively, the "Software") solely for your own personal or business purposes on a single computer (whether a standard computer or a workstation component of a multiuser network). The Software is in use on a computer when it is loaded into temporary memory (RAM) or installed into permanent memory (hard disk, CD-ROM, or other storage device). IDGB reserves all rights not expressly granted herein.

2. **Ownership.** IDGB is the owner of all right, title, and interest, including copyright, in and to the compilation of the Software recorded on the disk(s) or CD-ROM ("Software Media"). Copyright to the individual programs recorded on the Software Media is owned by the author or other authorized copyright owner of each program. Ownership of the Software and all proprietary rights relating thereto remain with IDGB and its licensers.

3. **Restrictions On Use and Transfer.**

    (a) You may only (i) make one copy of the Software for backup or archival purposes, or (ii) transfer the Software to a single hard disk, provided that you keep the original for backup or archival purposes. You may not (i) rent or lease the Software, (ii) copy or reproduce the Software through a LAN or other network system or through any computer subscriber system or bulletin-board system, or (iii) modify, adapt, or create derivative works based on the Software.

    (b) You may not reverse engineer, decompile, or disassemble the Software. You may transfer the Software and user documentation on a permanent basis, provided that the transferee agrees to accept the terms and conditions of this Agreement and you retain no copies. If the Software is an update or has been updated, any transfer must include the most recent update and all prior versions.

4. **Restrictions on Use of Individual Programs.** You must follow the individual requirements and restrictions detailed for each individual program in Appendix C of this Book. These limitations are also contained in the individual license agreements recorded on the Software Media. These limitations may include a requirement that after using the program for a specified period of time, the user must pay a registration fee or discontinue use. By opening the

Software packet(s), you will be agreeing to abide by the licenses and restrictions for these individual programs that are detailed in Appendix C and on the Software Media. None of the material on this Software Media or listed in this Book may ever be redistributed, in original or modified form, for commercial purposes.

5. Limited Warranty.

(a) IDGB warrants that the Software and Software Media are free from defects in materials and workmanship under normal use for a period of sixty (60) days from the date of purchase of this Book. If IDGB receives notification within the warranty period of defects in materials or workmanship, IDGB will replace the defective Software Media.

(b) IDGB AND THE AUTHOR OF THE BOOK DISCLAIM ALL OTHER WARRANTIES, EXPRESS OR IMPLIED, INCLUDING WITHOUT LIMITATION IMPLIED WARRANTIES OF MERCHANTABILITY AND FITNESS FOR A PARTICULAR PURPOSE, WITH RESPECT TO THE SOFTWARE, THE PROGRAMS, THE SOURCE CODE CONTAINED THEREIN, AND/OR THE TECHNIQUES DESCRIBED IN THIS BOOK. IDGB DOES NOT WARRANT THAT THE FUNCTIONS CONTAINED IN THE SOFTWARE WILL MEET YOUR REQUIREMENTS OR THAT THE OPERATION OF THE SOFTWARE WILL BE ERROR FREE.

(c) This limited warranty gives you specific legal rights, and you may have other rights that vary from jurisdiction to jurisdiction.

6. Remedies.

(a) IDGB's entire liability and your exclusive remedy for defects in materials and workmanship shall be limited to replacement of the Software Media, which may be returned to IDGB with a copy of your receipt at the following address: Software Media Fulfillment Department, Attn.: *CorelDRAW 9 Bible*, IDG Books Worldwide, Inc., 7260 Shadeland Station, Ste. 100, Indianapolis, IN 46256, or call 1-800-762-2974. Please allow three to four weeks for delivery. This Limited Warranty is void if failure of the Software Media has resulted from accident, abuse, or misapplication. Any replacement Software Media will be warranted for the remainder of the original warranty period or thirty (30) days, whichever is longer.

(b) In no event shall IDGB or the author be liable for any damages whatsoever (including without limitation damages for loss of business profits, business interruption, loss of business information, or any other pecuniary loss) arising from the use of or inability to use the Book or the Software, even if IDGB has been advised of the possibility of such damages.

(c) Because some jurisdictions do not allow the exclusion or limitation of liability for consequential or incidental damages, the above limitation or exclusion may not apply to you.

7. **U.S. Government Restricted Rights.** Use, duplication, or disclosure of the Software by the U.S. Government is subject to restrictions stated in paragraph (c)(1)(ii) of the Rights in Technical Data and Computer Software clause of DFARS 252.227-7013, and in subparagraphs (a) through (d) of the Commercial Computer — Restricted Rights clause at FAR 52.227-19, and in similar clauses in the NASA FAR supplement, when applicable.

8. **General.** This Agreement constitutes the entire understanding of the parties and revokes and supersedes all prior agreements, oral or written, between them and may not be modified or amended except in a writing signed by both parties hereto that specifically refers to this Agreement. This Agreement shall take precedence over any other documents that may be in conflict herewith. If any one or more provisions contained in this Agreement are held by any court or tribunal to be invalid, illegal, or otherwise unenforceable, each and every other provision shall remain in full force and effect.

my2cents.idgbooks.com

Register This Book — And Win!

Visit **http://my2cents.idgbooks.com** to register this book and we'll automatically enter you in our fantastic monthly prize giveaway. It's also your opportunity to give us feedback: let us know what you thought of this book and how you would like to see other topics covered.

Discover IDG Books Online!

The IDG Books Online Web site is your online resource for tackling technology — at home and at the office. Frequently updated, the IDG Books Online Web site features exclusive software, insider information, online books, and live events!

10 Productive & Career-Enhancing Things You Can Do at www.idgbooks.com

- Nab source code for your own programming projects.

- Download software.

- Read Web exclusives: special articles and book excerpts by IDG Books Worldwide authors.

- Take advantage of resources to help you advance your career as a Novell or Microsoft professional.

- Buy IDG Books Worldwide titles or find a convenient bookstore that carries them.

- Register your book and win a prize.

- Chat live online with authors.

- Sign up for regular e-mail updates about our latest books.

- Suggest a book you'd like to read or write.

- Give us your 2¢ about our books and about our Web site.

You say you're not on the Web yet? It's easy to get started with IDG Books' *Discover the Internet,* available at local retailers everywhere.

CD-ROM Installation Instructions

The files and programs on the CD-ROM for *CorelDRAW 9 Bible* are arranged in a series of folders. To access the folders on the CD-ROM, you need to:

1. With the CD-ROM in your CD-ROM drive, double-click the My Computer icon on your desktop.
2. Double-click the icon for your CD-ROM drive.

Alternatively, you can use Windows Explorer to access the folders. To access the folders using Windows Explorer:

1. Click the Start button on the taskbar.
2. Click Programs ⇨ Windows Explorer.
3. Click the plus sign in front of the drive letter for your CD-ROM drive to expand the directory tree.

Each program on the CD-ROM needs to be installed individually. To use each item, please refer to the following table:

Cross-Reference For more information about the files and programs on the CD-ROM, please see Appendix C.

Content Installation Instructions		
Item	*Folder on CD-ROM*	*To install*
Tutorials	tutorial	Double-click the chapter folder and file required.
Bitmaps	bitmaps	Double-click the file to open it.
Chessmen	chess	Double-click each file to open it.
Color Insert Art	colorinsert	Double-click each file to open it.
Extra Art	xtra-cdrs	Double-click each file to open it.

Continued

Item	Folder on CD-ROM	To install
Fills	fills	Double-click each file to open it.
Adobe Acrobat Reader	Utilities	Double-click ar40eng.exe.
Go!Zilla	Utilities	Double-click gozilla.exe.
IrfanView	Utilities	Double-click iview300.zip and extract files, then double-click i_view32.exe.
WinZip	Utilities	Double-click winzip70.exe.